Dynamic Web Application Development using
XML and Java

Dynamic Web Application Development using
XML and Java

David Parsons

COURSE TECHNOLOGY
CENGAGE Learning™

Australia • Brazil • Japan • Korea • Mexico • Singapore • Spain • United Kingdom • United States

COURSE TECHNOLOGY
CENGAGE Learning

**Dynamic Web Application Development
using XML and Java**
David Parsons

Publishing Director: John Yates

Publisher: Gaynor Redvers-Mutton

Development Editor: Matthew Lane

Content Project Editor: Lucy Mills

Manufacturing Manager: Helen Mason

Production Controller: Maeve Healy

Marketing Manager: Angela Lewis

Typesetter: Newgen Imaging Systems (P) Ltd,
India

Cover design: Adam Renvoize

Text design: Design Deluxe Ltd, Bath, UK

For product information and technology assistance, contact
emea.info@cengage.com

For permission to use material from this text or product,
and for permission queries, email
clsuk.permissions@cengage.com

British Library Cataloguing-in-Publication Data
A catalogue record for this book is available from
the British Library

ISBN 13: 978-1-84480-541-9

Cengage Learning EMEA
High Holborn House, 50–51 Bedford Row
London WC1R 4LR

Cengage Learning products are represented in Canada by
Nelson Education Ltd.

For your lifelong learning solutions, visit **www.cengage.co.uk**
and **www.course.cengage.com**

Printed by Seng Lee Press, Singapore
1 2 3 4 5 6 7 8 9 10 – 10 09 08

To Jenny, my first born, and Lynne, who loved me first, last and longest.

David Parsons

CONTENTS

Preface   *xiii*
Acknowledgments   *xix*

1 Introduction to Web Applications   1

Learning Objectives   1
Introduction   1
1.1 What a Web Application Does   1
1.2 E-everything – the Internet and the World Wide Web   4
1.3 Important Internet Technologies   5
1.4 Important World Wide Web Technologies   7
1.5 Special Types of Web Application   10
1.6 Web Application Architectures   11
1.7 The Web 2.0 and Ajax   13
1.8 So You Want to Be a Web Application Developer?   14
Exercises   15
Summary   15
References and Further Reading   17

2 Web Application Requirements Analysis and Design   19

Learning Objectives   19
Introduction   19
2.1 What's Different About Web Application Requirements?   19
2.2 Software Development Lifecycles   20
2.3 The Unified Modeling Language and the Unified Process   22
2.4 A Web Application Inception Phase   26
2.5 Modeling Requirements   26
2.6 Analysis Tools – Domain Models, Use Cases and Storyboards   30
2.7 Building Further Use Cases   38
2.8 From Analysis to Design   41
2.9 Webflow Design   42
2.10 Design Patterns for Web Page Structures   45
Exercises   51
Summary   51
References and Further Reading   52

3 Structure and Content in the Presentation Layer: the HyperText Markup Language (HTML) 53

	Learning Objectives	53
	Introduction	53
3.1	Where It All Begins – SGML	53
3.2	HTML – a Language for Web Pages	56
3.3	HTML Document Structural Elements	57
3.4	HTML Document Type	61
3.5	Structuring Text	63
3.6	Lists	66
3.7	Attributes in HTML	69
3.8	Tables	74
3.9	Forms	78
	Exercises	87
	Summary	87
	References and Further Reading	89

4 Styling in the Presentation Layer: Cascading Style Sheets (CSS) 91

	Learning Objectives	91
	Introduction	91
4.1	Separating out Presentation	91
4.2	CSS Syntax	93
4.3	Style Sheets	96
4.4	Applying Styles with 'Class' and 'Id' Attributes	105
4.5	Block and Inline Elements	108
4.6	Applying Styles to Lists and Tables	111
4.7	Style Sheet Cascades	114
4.8	Using CSS for Page Layout	116
	Exercises	121
	Summary	121
	References and Further Reading	123

5 Content, Structure and Validation: XML, DTD, XHTML and XML Schema 125

	Learning Objectives	125
	Introduction	125
5.1	The Limitations of HTML	125
5.2	Semi-Structured Data	127
5.3	What Is XML?	129
5.4	Components of XML	131

5.5	Validating XML Documents	139
5.6	XHTML	151
5.7	XML Schema	155
5.8	XML Schema Tags	158
5.9	Applying an XML Schema to a Document	164
5.10	DTD or XML Schema?	165
	Exercises	166
	Summary	168
	References and Further Reading	168

6 Transforming XML: XPath and XSLT   169

	Learning Objectives	169
	Introduction	169
6.1	XPath: Querying XML	169
6.2	XSLT	176
6.3	XML Special Characters	197
6.4	Transforming from XML to XML	199
6.5	Transformations Using Template Matching	199
	Exercises	206
	Summary	207

7 Introduction to JavaScript   209

	Learning Objectives	209
	Introduction	209
7.1	JavaScript – What and Why?	209
7.2	The Document Object Model (DOM)	210
7.3	Characteristics of JavaScript	211
7.4	JavaScript Objects	212
7.5	Debugging JavaScript	217
7.6	JavaScript Types and Variables	218
7.7	Using and Creating Objects	222
7.8	Control Structures	227
7.9	Writing Functions	232
	Exercises	236
	Summary	239
	References and Further Reading	239

8 Interactive JavaScript: Dynamic HTML, Client-Side Validation and Ajax   241

	Learning Objectives	241
	Introduction	241

8.1	Dynamic HTML (DHTML)	242
8.2	JavaScript Events	245
8.3	Dynamic Style Sheets	252
8.4	Client-Side Form Validation	255
8.5	The Emergence of Ajax	264
	Exercises	276
	Summary	278
	References and Further Reading	278

9 Web Applications and Application Servers — 279

	Learning Objectives	279
	Introduction	279
9.1	Application Servers	279
9.2	Using Apache Tomcat Web Application Server	280
9.3	Web Application Structure and Deployment	283
9.4	Deploying to Tomcat	288
9.5	JBoss Application Server	294
9.6	Enterprise Application Deployment	294
9.7	Running Web Applications on the Default HTTP Port	296
9.8	Automating Build and Deploy with Ant	297
9.9	The Tomcat Web Application Manager	301
	Exercises	307
	Summary	308
	References and Further Reading	308

10 Using Java for Dynamic Content — 309

	Learning Objectives	309
	Introduction	309
10.1	Java on the Server	310
10.2	Model–View–Controller (MVC) Architecture	311
10.3	JSP Model 1 Architecture	313
10.4	Writing a JavaServer Page	319
10.5	Processing HTTP Request Data – Parameters and Forms	322
10.6	Using JavaBeans in JSPs	329
10.7	Refactoring	335
10.8	JSP Model 2 Architecture	335
10.9	Managing a Webflow	338
10.10	Session Management – Conversational State in a Web Application	340
10.11	Process Beans and the Underlying Model	353
10.12	The JSP Standard Tag Library	360

10.13 XML JavaServer Pages   367

10.14 Integrating the Three-Region Layout   371

Exercises   374

Summary   374

References and Further Reading   376

11 Using Java and XML Together   377

Learning Objectives   377

Introduction   377

11.1 XML Parsers   378

11.2 Generating XML from JavaBeans   386

11.3 Java Architecture for XML Binding   396

11.4 XML Processing with the JSP Standard Tag Library   404

11.5 Using Beans that Generate XML in JSPs   410

Exercises   419

Summary   421

References and Further Reading   422

12 Web Applications and Databases   423

Learning Objectives   423

Introduction   423

12.1 Object-Relational Mapping   424

12.2 The Example Database   425

12.3 Java and the Database   427

12.4 Integrating Persistence into a Web Application   435

12.5 Building a Persistence Layer Using Data Access Objects   440

12.6 Integrating Persistent Objects   449

12.7 The Object-Relational Impedance Mismatch   462

12.8 Technologies for Object-Relational Mapping   464

Exercises   466

Summary   467

References and Further Reading   468

13 Mobile Web Applications   469

Learning Objectives   469

Introduction   469

13.1 Evolution of Mobile Mark-Up Languages   470

13.2 The WURFL/WALL Java Framework for Device Adaptivity   475

13.3 Integrating WALL with a Web Application   481

13.4 Alternative Approaches to Adaptivity   491

Exercises   493
Summary   493
References and Further Reading   496

14 XML Messaging: Web Services and Server-Side Ajax   **497**

Learning Objectives   497
Introduction   497
14.1 Web Services   498
14.2 Web Service Technologies   498
14.3 Implementing Web Services   501
14.4 Creating a Web Service with Java 6.0   503
14.5 Integrating Web Services with Web Applications   505
14.6 Developing a Web Service Client   513
14.7 Integrating the Web Service into the WebHomeCover Application   516
14.8 Server-Side Ajax   520
Exercises   531
Summary   533

15 Apache Struts Web Application Framework   **535**

Learning Objectives   535
Introduction   535
15.1   Struts Command and Control Patterns   536
15.2   Struts Components   538
15.3   Configuring Struts   539
15.4   Managing the Webflow   541
15.5   Action Objects   545
15.6   Struts Tag Libraries   550
15.7   Validation with Message Resources   558
15.8   Using the Struts Bean Tag Library   562
15.9   Internationalization   565
15.10 The Struts Validator   569
Exercises   576
Summary   576
References and Further Reading   578

Appendix A Relational Databases, SQL and MySQL   579

Appendix B Using XMLSpy   597

Appendix C Web Application Security   607

Index   615

Introduction

Welcome to *Dynamic Web Application Development using XML and Java*. The motivation for writing this book began in the late 1990s, when I first started working with Enterprise Java for the UK office of The Object People. Later, I developed the first version of the home insurance case study when working for BEA Internal Education, followed by further Enterprise Java work with Valtech in the City of London. After I moved to Massey University in New Zealand in 2003, I had the opportunity to see web application development more from an XML perspective, while still working with professional developers through Software Education Associates. It became clear to me over this time that developing web applications is not about one technology or even one design approach; rather, it requires a broad set of skills that integrate a wide range of technologies and design issues. This book therefore grew from several years of experiences that led me to want to draw everything together in one text. It turned out to be a much greater challenge than the programming books I had written before. At the beginning of *Adolf Hitler: My Part in his Downfall*, Spike Milligan wrote, 'After Puckoon I swore I would never write another novel. This is it.' I know exactly how he felt. Nevertheless I hope it succeeds in providing a comprehensive, practical approach to developing dynamic web applications in XML and Java.

What is in the book?

This book covers the basic knowledge required for you to implement dynamic web applications using XML and Java technologies together. In order to do this, it covers a number of different, but related, topics. It begins by providing some background to web applications in order for you to put the technologies introduced later into context, and provide an overview of some of the key analysis and design activities that are used by web application developers. The next part of the book focuses on client-side technologies that can be used within web browsers, such as, Internet Explorer, Mozilla Firefox and Opera. We begin with the HyperText Markup Language (HTML), which was developed in order to write web pages, and Cascading Style Sheets, which can be used to format and present those pages. We also introduce the eXtensible Markup Language (XML) and see how HTML and XML have been brought together in XHTML. We also explain how XML documents can be validated, processed and transformed using technologies such as Document Type Definitions (DTDs), XML Schemas, XPath and eXtensible Stylesheet Language Transformations (XSLT). Moving on from mark-up languages, we introduce the JavaScript client-side scripting language which enables you to develop more interactive and powerful web applications. We also introduce and describe Ajax, a more recent mechanism for providing advanced dynamic web applications. Ajax combines a number of technologies that use asynchronous server connections and partial page updates to create web applications that look and feel more like desktop applications.

The second part of the book concentrates on the server side of web applications, looking at Java technologies that can be used to generate dynamic content for on-line applications.

We introduce the open source Tomcat web application server, both in stand-alone mode and as part of the JBoss Java Enterprise Edition application server. We introduce a number of Java Enterprise Edition programming components including servlets, JavaServer Pages and the JSP Standard Tag Library, and explore Java tools for XML processing, connecting to databases and generating web-based interfaces for mobile devices. We also look at how XML documents can be used to communicate between client and server, both within web services and as a part of Ajax systems. We conclude the book by looking at Struts, a popular open source Java framework for developing web applications.

In the remainder of this preface, we explain how we have structured this text and how we think you should use it for the greatest effect. We describe the application software you will need to use in order to make use of the different technologies described above. We describe how to install the software and where you can find more information about it. We clarify some terminology which we will introduce later in the book and also describe what additional material is available for download on the book's web site. Let us begin by describing who we wrote this text for.

Who is this book for?

The intended audience for this text is deliberately quite broad, however it is essentially for those individuals who wish to learn more about how to create professional dynamic web applications. We realize that individuals' knowledge, background and web development experience will differ considerably and what knowledge and skills you may want out of a book on the subject of dynamic web development may be very different from someone else. You may have some well-practiced web development skills already, which is good as we will move quickly onto more interesting and in-depth subjects. You may have some previous programming experience, in which case you are likely to find the chapters concerning programming and scripting quite familiar to you. What we have tried to do is create a text which encompasses all of the different technologies with which you will need to get to grips and illustrates how these can be combined in order for you to have the basic underpinnings to begin to create more sophisticated web applications. This is not a text designed for those with many years of web development experience nor is it a reference text. Furthermore, given the limitations of space, the coverage of individual subjects and technologies is necessarily introductory. For each one of the chapters in this book, you could quite easily find a book the size of a house brick dedicated to just that single technology. Therefore you are encouraged to seek further resources if you have a particular interest in any of the topics introduced in this book.

Book structure and features

This book is essentially divided into three sections, the first of which comprises Chapters 1 and 2, which give a general background and discuss analysis and design. The second section comprises Chapters 3 to 8. These chapters cover the essential aspects of mark-up languages and browser-based processing. Topics examined include HTML, cascading style sheets (CSS), XML, XSLT and Ajax. The third section of the book, Chapters 9 to 15, covers enterprise Java and illustrates how it can be used to control the generation of (X)HTML and other forms of mark-up to produce very sophisticated dynamic applications.

This section also covers converting between Java Objects and XML, object relational mapping to the database from Java objects (we use MySQL as the example database), mobile web applications, Web Services, Ajax and the Struts framework.

We have designed the book so that, depending on your background and experience and what it is that you wish to learn, you can jump directly to that chapter and begin learning from that point. So, for example, if you are already an experienced (X)HTML and CSS developer but wish to brush up on some JavaScript then you can turn directly to Chapter 6. If, on the other hand, all you want to know about is Ajax and you know (X)HTML and JavaScript then you can turn directly to Chapter 7. If you already know the basic technologies of Java web applications, such as servlets and JSPs then you can jump to Chapters 11 to 15, which cover more advanced Java topics such as XML integration, mobile web applications, web services and Struts.

Each chapter begins by outlining the key learning objectives that the chapter is designed to meet. In other words, we tell you right at the start of the chapter what it is that you will learn within the chapter. After a brief introduction to the topics covered, the main sections of the chapter begin. Each chapter is designed to be read from start to finish. We have included many figures and screen shots to complement the text and to ensure that each topic is explained as clearly as possible. In the chapters that concentrate on different languages, such as (X)HTML, CSS and Java, there are many small complete examples which you can either type in and run yourself, copy from the CD or download from the book's web site. Mark-up and source code examples are shown like this:

```
This is how source code
is shown within a chapter
```

Within the text, if there are any key points which need to be highlighted, these are drawn to your attention with the use of a note, like this one:

NOTE	Important facts are highlighted like this!

Towards the end of each chapter there are some exercises for you to check your level of understanding of the chapter contents. The answers to these exercises are available for download from the book's web site. The chapters conclude with a summary of what has been described and following this are usually some references or lists of where you can go to do some further reading on the subjects covered.

Hardware requirements

The examples in this text have all been tried and tested on a PC running Microsoft Windows XP. However, because the technologies we introduce, such as (X)HTML, Ajax, JavaScript and Java are all, in the main, platform independent, all our examples should work with computers running UNIX (or one of its many open source variants) or Apple's

OS X operating systems. The only examples which may not work as intended are those which interact with the operating system's file system, such as those that read XML documents into a program.

Furthermore, when you have developed your own web applications you may wish to host them so that anyone using the internet can see and access them. In order to do this, most people require a 'service provider' who will host your applications on their web server.

How exactly you upload your scripts and configure your database on your service provider's computer system differs considerably from one provider to the next and we couldn't possibly explain how to do this for all of them. However, in the most part, service providers have excellent help and support to guide you through the process of transferring your scripts and applications from your local PC onto their web server.

What software do you need?

As mentioned above we have tested the scripts and examples within this book on a Windows-based PC and we will assume that this is the platform which you will be using when trying out the examples and exercises within this book. However, regardless of what computer platform you are using you will need the following software to successfully implement all of the examples within this text:

- A web browser which supports (X)HTML, CSS, XSLT and JavaScript.
- An XML editor.
- A Java application server and associated tools.
- A relational database.
- A text editor.

If you are using Windows XP or Windows Vista then the great news is that it is quite easy to get all of this software and it is all free. Our recommendations for each of these different software components follows.

Web browser

The web browser is used to display page mark-up in HTML, XML or XHTML. For the examples in this book it also needs to be able to perform XSL Transformations and run JavaScript. Our examples have been tested using Microsoft Internet Explorer 7, Mozilla Firefox 2 and Opera 9. Windows Vista comes with Internet Explorer 7 pre-installed but if you are using an earlier version of the operating system you can get it from:

http://www.microsoft.com/windows/downloads/ie/getitnow.mspx

The latest version of Firefox is available from:

http://www.mozilla.com/en-US/firefox/

Opera can be downloaded from:

http://www.opera.com/download/

XML editor

To learn about XML, validation, XPath and XSLT, you need an XML editing tool that is able to support various aspects of these technologies. In this book we use Altova XMLSpy, which provides an extensive set of tools for editing and processing a wide range of XML-related document types. XMLSpy Enterprise Edition is supplied as an evaluation version with a time-limited license. However academic institutions wishing to install the software for classroom use may apply to become Altova partners and qualify for educational site licenses.

Java application server and associated tools

A Java Enterprise Edition application server hosts Java Web applications and serves dynamic content to clients. In this book we cover the open source Tomcat Java web application server and the JBoss application server, which includes Tomcat but provides some other Java Enterprise Edition services that go beyond the web application components introduced in this book. The versions used to test the examples, and which are included on the CD, are Tomcat 6.0 and JBoss 4.2.1GA.

The CD accompanying this book includes a number of open source Java tools and libraries. Several of these are freely distributed under the conditions of the Apache 2.0 license. This license applies to the following software that is provided with this book, as well as a number of other Apache or Jakarta projects that are included in some of these products:

- Apache Tomcat 6.0
- Apache Ant 1.7.0
- Apache Struts 1.3.8
- Apache Jakarta Standard Taglibs version 1.1.2

JBoss Application Server 4.2.1.GA, which includes Tomcat and is also provided on the CD, is licensed under the LGPL (GNU Lesser General Public License). Details of this license may be found at http://www.gnu.org/licenses/lgpl.html.

The NetBeans 5.5 Integrated Development Environment is included under the Common Development and Distribution License (CDDL). The full terms of this license may be found at http://www.netbeans.org/cddl.html.

The WURFL and WALL tools for generating adaptive mobile mark-up are included with the permission of Luca Passani, an expert on the mobile Internet. While revolutionary, Luca's very practical approach to the challenges posed by device fragmentation has been the most successful to date. His work with WURFL, WALL and GAP has enabled developers to create content that works across a myriad of mobile devices, without waiting for standards to keep a promise they may be unable to fulfill.

Relational database

The MySQL Community Server is used as the example relational database management system in the latter chapters of this book. MySQL software is dual licensed. Users can choose to use the MySQL software as an Open Source product under the terms of the GNU General Public License. This is the version included on the CD. Also included is the MySQL Connector/J 5.0 JDBC driver, which is covered by the same license.

A copy of all of these software components is included on the CD accompanying this text as the total download size approaches 500 MB. However, the applications bundled together in this package are regularly updated and so you may wish to visit the various web sites to check you have the latest versions.

Text editor

You will need a text editor to create and edit your mark-up and Java source code. One of the simplest editors you can use is Notepad, which comes with Windows, but it is not one we would recommend. There are many much more sophisticated script editors which have been designed to provide far more support to the developer than a simple text editor like Notepad ever could or was designed to do. One flexible option is TextPad, which can be found at http://www.textpad.com/download/index.html.

It is available in a trial version that you can download for free and is relatively inexpensive to buy. For more sophisticated editing of Java applications, there are a number of open source IDEs that can be downloaded for free, including Eclipse and NetBeans (which is included on the CD).

Most of the software used with this book requires no installation. All that is required is for the archive files to be unzipped into suitable folders in your file system. Java-based tools such as Ant, JBoss and Tomcat are platform independent, but require the Java Software Development Kit (standard edition) to be installed on the system. The version used in the book is version 6.0. Note that not all of the examples will work with earlier versions.

MySQL 5.0 and Netbeans 5.5 are provided as installation files for the Windows operating system. Versions for other operating systems may be downloaded from the following web sites:

- MySQL downloads: http://dev.mysql.com/downloads/mysql/5.0.html
- NetBeans downloads: http://www.netbeans.info/downloads/index.php

Further resources available on-line

In addition to what is included in the book and accompanying CD, we have made a number of other resources available to the reader or instructor using this textbook as their primary teaching aid:

- PowerPoint slides to accompany each chapter.
- Complete source code for the examples.
- Model solutions to the examples at the end of each chapter.
- Multiple-choice test questions.
- Bonus materials, including an integrated home insurance web application that is developed from the examples and scenarios used in the book, and additional appendices.

Summary

In this preface, we have introduced this book and described who it is targeted at and what knowledge and skills it covers. We have explained the structure of the book and how best to use it in order to get the best learning experience. We have introduced the software that we will be using and explained how to install it correctly. You are now ready to begin the first chapter of the book which introduces the concept of web applications.

Acknowledgments

I have learned a huge amount over the years from working with colleagues, customers and students, and had some very good times along the way. However I would particularly like to thank Sheila Barton for our shared experience of the Unified Process and croquet; Martin Jones, who gave me the opportunity to be possibly the only Enterprise Java trainer in New Zealand; Gaynor Redvers-Mutton, my commissioning editor, who patiently endured a series of unsuccessful book proposals before finally bringing this particular volume to print; the (anonymous) reviewers of the drafts of this book whose valuable suggestions have improved the final book enormously; Judy Le Heron for the writer's retreat in Rotoiti; Neil Young for the sound track; and Lynne Pawley, whose faith in my abilities was unflagging, despite all evidence to the contrary.

CHAPTER 1

Introduction to web applications

LEARNING OBJECTIVES

- **To understand the main features and services of web applications**

- **To understand some of the basic technological building blocks of web applications**

- **To understand how the World Wide Web has evolved from the Internet**

- **To understand some of the key aspects of the Web 2.0**

INTRODUCTION

The World Wide Web has had a profound impact on our lives since the 1990s. Some of the most successful companies that based their business on web technologies, such as Amazon, Yahoo and Google, have become as well known as the most famous global manufacturing and service companies of previous eras. We now expect all the major organizations with which we have contact to have a web presence. Not only that, we also expect that presence to include web-based applications that let us perform tasks such as managing our money, booking travel and purchasing goods and services without having to step away from the computer. Just having a web *site* is no longer enough; that *site* must support web *applications*.

In this chapter, we see what a web application does, and how it does it, by looking at the fundamental technologies that make web applications work and how they fit together. We also consider some important features of web application architecture. We conclude the chapter by looking at *Web 2.0*, a set of ideas that have had an important influence on how modern web applications are built.

1.1 What a web application does

What makes any kind of programming hard is largely a question of scale. Things that are easy to program inside a single computer become much more difficult when we want to distribute those things over space (to many users) and time (to exist beyond the run time of a single program). For example, let us assume that you are working as a software developer and, like many developers, you have a text document stored on your computer that you use as a log of things that you find helpful to keep track of, such as references to useful resources or solutions to problems you have discovered. You can use text editors or word processors installed on your own computer to access and edit that document. Now, what if you want to be able to make that document available to others, because you feel that this information may be helpful to, for example, other developers in your team? You could, of course, distribute print or email copies, but that would get very tedious if you had to keep doing this every time you made a new document entry and, after a while, there would be lots of different versions of your document floating around. What you need to do, of course, is to make the document available on a *web server* so that others can read it over the *World Wide Web*. Hey presto, your document is now a *blog* (short for *web log*). This leads us to the first thing that a web application can do:

A web application enables us to distribute documents over the World Wide Web.

Before going further we should perhaps make one thing clear, which is that we are introducing things that a web application can do, but in fact we are really talking about what a web application *server* can do. A web application server is the software that hosts your web applications and provides all of the services that we introduce in this section.

Now, maybe you are such a great writer, doing such interesting stuff, that you become a very popular blogger. Many thousands of people all over the world start reading your blog. Now, there can be many people all wanting to access your blog at the same time. Luckily, your server is able to cope with these multiple concurrent requests for your document without any problem. This brings us to another thing that web applications can do:

A web application manages concurrency, enabling access to a single web-based resource by multiple users.

After a while, you find that people reading your blog keep sending you emails for suggestions about what you should include in it. Eventually you get so fed up with this that you change your blog so that others can contribute their own entries to the on-line document. Hey presto, you have a *wiki*! (A wiki is a web site that is open to editing by anyone.) To make this work, your server has to be able to let users not only download your document, but upload their own content as well. It then has to be able to dynamically recreate the updated document for subsequent readers. This brings us to an essential role of web applications:

A web application can generate dynamic content, building web pages on the fly from sources of data that may include data supplied by users.

Eventually you find that your blog or wiki is becoming too difficult to manage because too many people are able to make changes to it and they keep messing up your pages. You decide that only people who register with you will be able to access and modify your site. This is another important service that web applications can provide:

A web application can include declarative, role-based security, which enables you to allow or deny access to specific resources to users based on their user role.

Over time, your original single document has become a large quantity of data, a kind of *Wikipedia* (www.wikipedia.org) of knowledge related to your own areas of interest, partly created by you but also created in large part by others. Instead of a single, simple piece of data, your wiki now consists of many related pieces of data. Since there is now too much information to be kept in a few pages, the underlying data that has been contributed to your system requires some kind of managed data storage so that you can keep it for a long time, re-use the same content in different contexts across different parts of the overall system, and ensure that it has some kind of existence outside of your web application. To do this, you need some kind of *persistence*, some way of storing your web application content in a database or some other form of secondary storage, and you need some way of connecting your web application to the database. Fortunately, web applications can help us to do that as well:

A web application provides facilities to connect to a database so that its content can be kept in permanent storage, to be retrieved when required.

If the content of a web application is stored in a database, then we need to make sure that any changes made to parts of it by others are handled correctly so that, for example, changes made by one client do not clash with changes made simultaneously by another. This means we have to be able to support *transactions*. Transactions make sure that any changes made to persistent data are made in a managed and consistent way, so that if two users try to change the same thing, either access is only allowed to one user at a time (pessimistic locking) or both users can try to make changes at the same time, but only the first to submit their changes (to *commit*) will be successful (optimistic locking):

A web application utilises the transactional services of a database so that updates to its content are reliable and consistent.

After all this we might also consider performance and reliability. How long might someone have to wait before getting access to the web application if many others want to do the same thing, and what happens if the machine that the application is running on fails for some reason? It may be that we need to provide more than one copy of the application so that multiple clients can access it at the same time and so that, if one machine fails, we are still able to provide the necessary services to our clients. In particular, we may find that over time we need to support more and more clients without breaking the system we already have, so we need some way of scaling our system to maintain performance and reliability:

A web application leverages the services of its underlying hardware and software infrastructure to run the same application across multiple machines, enabling scalability.

Figure 1.1 summarizes some of the web application features we have introduced in this section.

FIGURE 1.1   Some web application features

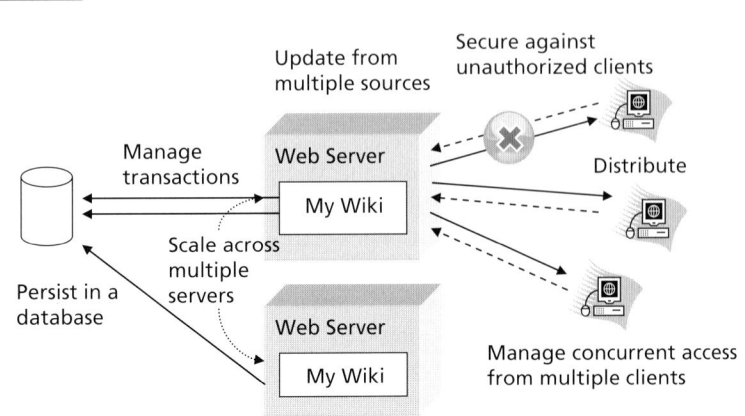

All of the issues we have touched on in this section are common to web applications, and all are difficult, tedious and expensive to program from scratch. Therefore it is very useful if we can reuse an existing set of tools to provide all of these services, leaving us free to write the code that addresses our particular business problem. The role of web application development languages and their supporting tools is to provide just such a framework for all of these services. However web applications cannot work in isolation because they rely on the fundamental technologies of the Internet and the World Wide Web. In the next section, we explain some of the most important features of these technologies.

1.2 E-everything – the Internet and the World Wide Web

Web applications rely on both the Internet and the World Wide Web to work, and one important point to bear in mind is that the Internet and the World Wide Web are not the same thing, since the first version of the Internet pre-dated the World Wide Web by more than 10 years. The Internet is a network of networks that was developed from the *ARPAnet*, a project that began in the 1970s. Its name comes from its sponsor, the US government Advanced Research Projects Agency (ARPA). It originally linked a small number of research sites together but used the same core technologies that now support the much bigger Internet. In contrast, the World Wide Web (the web, or W3, for short) is a hypertext-based collection of multimedia information accessible via the Internet that dates from the 1990s (hypertext means that the content on the web is linked together so that we can easily navigate between web pages that can be physically located anywhere in the world). We might say, perhaps, that the Internet is the information superhighway and the World Wide Web is the traffic that travels on it.

What has now become the World Wide Web was first developed by Tim Berners-Lee at CERN (originally the acronym for the French *Conseil Européen pour la Recherche Nucléair*, more generally known in English as the European Organization for Nuclear Research) in 1990. It was originally a distributed hypertext system for managing information at CERN (based on previous hypertext research), but quickly developed into something much bigger. From an academic tool that was intended to assist researchers, it evolved into both an important platform for leisure applications and a key element in business, not only for the exclusively web-based *dot coms* but also as part of the IT strategy of major corporations, governments and other organizations.

From an internal research tool, the web quickly began to evolve into something much bigger and more important. Between 1991 and 1993, web servers began to come on-line outside of CERN, using the underlying technology of the Internet. CERN made the web technology free so it was easy for others to build on these systems. Originally, communication over the web was text-based and therefore not very user friendly. The first graphical *web browser* (an application able to display content from the Web) had been written by Tim Berners-Lee in 1991, but this was internal to CERN. However, other graphical browsers were soon developed and, in 1993, the NCSA (National Center for Supercomputing Applications) made their Mosaic graphical browser publicly available. This was soon followed by the first versions of the commercial browsers, Netscape Navigator and Microsoft Internet Explorer, to be joined in subsequent years by many other increasingly sophisticated browsers including Opera, Mozilla Firefox and Safari.

Graphical browsers, being able to display images and a range of text fonts, made access to the World Wide Web easy and attractive and expanded its potential user base from just technical specialists to the general public. The web began to get press coverage and reach a wider audience, and in 1994 the World Wide Web Consortium (W3C) was formed to create web standards and ensure that the proliferation of web technologies did not lead to incompatibility between different systems. In 1993, the first tools for writing dynamic web pages on the server were created using the Common Gateway Interface (CGI) developed by the NCSA. These made it possible for web pages to be generated on the fly on the server. Instead of simply providing static content to users, where everyone sees the same pages, CGI made it possible to generate pages for individual users, so they could see their own search results, bank account details, flight bookings, shopping carts etc. Other server-side technologies followed, including PHP (originally Personal Home Page Tools but later renamed PHP: Hypertext Preprocessor), Java and Microsoft's .NET, making it possible to develop industrial-strength applications that ran over the web. In 1995, HotJava, the first Java-aware browser, was launched by Sun Microsystems and Netscape introduced the first version of JavaScript, bringing the potential for applications that could run inside a browser. As both browser and server technologies continued to develop, terms such as 'web surfing', 'going on-line' and 'e-business' entered common speech and things have never been quite the same since.

1.3 Important Internet technologies

The World Wide Web depends on some important Internet technologies in order to work. These include:

- TCP/IP (Transmission Control Protocol/Internet Protocol)
- IP addresses
- Domain names

TCP/IP (Transmission Control Protocol/Internet Protocol)

TCP/IP is actually a whole set of related protocols and tools that help computers to communicate with each other. Some that are used on the Internet include SMTP (Simple Mail Transfer Protocol) for sending email messages and FTP (File Transfer Protocol), which allows files to be easily copied to and from remote sites.

IP addresses

Computers on the Internet are initially connected to some kind of local network, either within an organization or as part of the services of an Internet service provider (ISP). To build all these separate systems into one, hardware devices known as *routers* are used to glue all the different networks together. For this to work, every machine on the Internet has to have a unique IP (Internet Protocol) address so that communications can be routed to the correct computer. An IP address is a 32-bit binary number giving billions of possible combinations, though the most recent format, known as IPv6 (IP version 6 – the previous version is actually version 4, IPv4), provides for many more by using a 128-bit binary number.

IP addresses are expressed as four sets of dotted decimal numbers using the format *nnn.nnn.nnn.nnn*. Each of these numbers falls in the range 0–255, for example, 127.0.0.1.

	NOTE	IPv6 addresses are written as eight 4-digit, hexadecimal numbers separated by colons.

Given an IP address, one machine can connect to another as if they were on the same physical network. Some machines have fixed IP addresses, while others are temporarily allocated an IP address from a pool when they connect, a technique known as DHCP (Dynamic Host Configuration Protocol). This pooling of IP addresses is more efficient in terms of being able to reuse the same address for different machines at different times. It also reduces the administration required to ensure that each machine has an appropriate address, particularly for systems that have to give Internet access to very large numbers of computers, such as commercial ISPs.

Domain names

Most computers that host web sites use *domain names* rather than actual IP addresses. This means that users can, for example, visit www.w3.org rather than use the actual IP address of the World Wide Web Consortium site. The *Domain Name System* (DNS) enables a domain name to be converted into a valid IP address. *Resolver* programs query name servers for IP addresses and enable clients to be routed to the actual host machine. The DNS consists of a number of dedicated servers (a distributed database) that maintain naming information for different *zones*. A zone is a set of related domain names, '.com', '.org', etc. that appear at the same level of the DNS, which has a tree structure (see Figure 1.2).

Specific domains appear in a particular zone, for example the W3C domain is within the 'org' zone (w3.org). The highest level zone is known as the 'root domain' and under this comes the zone that encompasses all the top-level domains, including the country code domains. For each country, there is a zone that contains the various types of domain within that country, using zones such as 'co' for companies and 'ac' for academic institutions. Because of this tree structure, with layers of zones each managed separately, several different name servers may be involved in resolving a single domain name request. Domain names are controlled by the Internet Assigned Numbers Authority (IANA), which is administered by the Internet Corporation for Assigned Names and Numbers (ICANN). The number of domain types made available by these organizations has increased steadily

FIGURE 1.2   The DNS tree structure with some of the Internet zones and domains

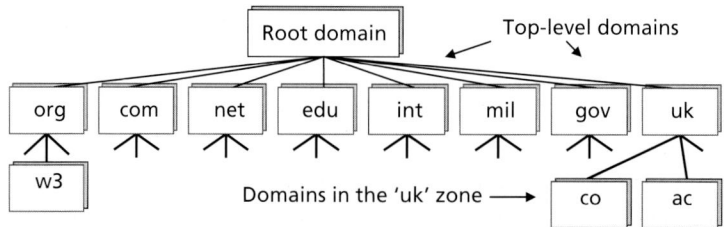

over the years as new types of web site have been developed, including the '.tv' domain for television services and '.mobi' for mobile services.

Using domain names is better than just using IP addresses because domain names are easier to remember and the names usually reflect the identity of the owner (for example, 'ibm.com', 'w3.org', 'harvard.edu'). It is also more flexible to use DNS names rather than IP numbers, since the mapping between a domain name and an IP address can change, so the same name can migrate between different host systems. Domain names are also important for email, since they are used in email addresses (for example, web-human@w3.org).

1.4 Important World Wide Web technologies

On its own, the Internet provides the possibility for different computers across the world to connect to each other and transfer data. However the World Wide Web adds some very important technologies to the underlying platform of the Internet. These include:

- HyperText Transfer Protocol (HTTP)
- HTML
- URLs, URIs and URNs

HyperText Transfer Protocol (HTTP)

The World Wide Web uses the *HyperText Transfer Protocol* (HTTP) to send information. When using this protocol, the domain name (or IP address) is preceded by 'http://' (for example, http://www.webhomecover.com). Web browsers usually have 'http://' as their default protocol so this prefix is frequently left off web site names. HTTP is a *request–response* protocol. Clients (usually browser software) send a request to a web server, which is software that is able to host web-based content and serve it to clients on request. The server handles the incoming request and provides a response, usually in the form of a page written in the HyperText Markup Language (HTML), which browsers can interpret. HTTP requests are handled by default on port 80 of the server. A server port is a number used to identify a particular process on the server that another system can connect to. Many common services, including HTTP, are allocated standard port numbers to simplify communication.

HTTP requests are always of a specific type; GET, POST, HEAD, PUT, DELETE, CONNECT, OPTIONS or TRACE. All of these request types have their uses but, in most web applications, the requests are usually limited to being either GET or POST. In most cases, either of these can be used to achieve the same result. A GET request is intended to retrieve information from the server and it often contains a search query or other parameter data. A POST request is intended to send data to the server, in most cases from an HTML form. A form is a part of a web page that lets a user provide data using components such as text fields, select lists and radio buttons. Forms have an 'action' which contains the web address of an application running on a server that knows how to process the contents of the form. This is where the data is sent when the user presses the 'submit' button on the web page.

What comes back from the server, following an HTTP request, is an HTTP response, which in many cases will be a web page, but can be some kind of code number to

FIGURE 1.3 The HTTP request–response cycle

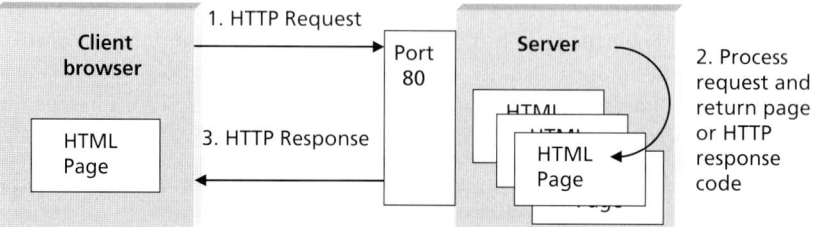

indicate errors, problems, or actions that the browser should take such as redirecting to another web site. Some examples of HTTP response codes are '200 OK' (the code that is used with a web page), '401 Unauthorized' (where security is being used) and '404 Not Found' (when the requested page cannot be found). Figure 1.3 shows the basic HTTP request–response cycle.

Normal HTTP traffic is not encrypted in any way, so is not secured against being read by a third party. In most cases this does not matter, but sometimes we need to send or receive information over the Web that we do not want others to be able to read. Therefore HTTP also comes in a secure form that allows us to transfer sensitive data, such as credit card numbers, safely across the Internet. This version of HTTP is known as HTTPS and uses a number of technologies including *Public Key Infrastructure* (PKI), encryption and *digital certificates*. The 'S' in 'HTTPS' comes from the *Secure Sockets Layer* (SSL), a secure communication protocol originally developed by Netscape. HTTPS connections use a special server port (443) to separate secure traffic from normal HTTP connections. As well as HTTPS being necessary for securing user data, many web-based systems need to authenticate users (find out who they are, generally by asking for a user name and password) and then authorize them to have access to appropriate resources. HTTPS is also used to enable this kind of secure login by ensuring that the username and password are encrypted.

HTML

As we saw in the previous section, web clients use browser software to request, download and display information from web servers. That information is mainly in the form of HTML pages. HTML pages are text documents that contain special *tags* telling the browser what type of information they contain. These tags are surrounded by angle brackets and indicate the *mark-up* of the web page, to control the structure and presentation of the content. This, for example, is how a typical HTML page begins, specifying the text to appear in the browser's title bar:

```
<html>
  <head>
    <title>My Page</title>
  </head>
<body> . . .
```

 NOTE This is a somewhat simplified view of HTML, but is perfectly acceptable to most web browsers.

Tags do not specify exactly how a page will appear. It is up to the browser to format the page and manage its content, so the same page can look different in different browsers. Users can customise their browser to make pages appear in the way that they want; they can, for example, change the size or style of the standard text font. As well as text, these pages can contain images, sound, animations and other downloadable programs.

Using a web browser as the client for a web application is great for supporting large numbers of casual users (such as those using an on-line store or downloading music to their mobile phones) because it would not be realistic to expect all users to install separate special client programs just to use a particular service. However, browsers do support 'plugins', which are programs that can be installed into the browser to provide additional functionality. Common examples of plugins include Flash, Real Player and Adobe Acrobat. Browsers can also support programming languages such as JavaScript and Java applets, enabling simple programs to be downloaded and run within the browser window.

URLs, URIs and URNs

Uniform Resource Locators (URLs) are the complete specifications of the locations of Internet resources. A URL comprises a number of elements:

- The protocol of the request (the browser's default is usually http://)
- The IP address or domain of the server
- The port number (port 80 for HTTP and 443 for HTTPS)
- The subdirectory path from the 'document root' (if applicable)
- The name of the resource (though there is often a default page which is loaded if no name is specified)

For example, the following URL includes all of these elements.

```
http://www.webhomecover.com:80/help/callcentres.htm
```

Since the http protocol is usually the browser's default and the port number is the default on the server, in most cases we can exclude them, so our previous example is more likely to be written as:

```
www.webhomecover.com/help/callcentres.htm
```

If we use only the domain name, many web sites are configured with a default resource, which is loaded when no specific file is requested. If the example domain has a default resource, then the following URL should result in a page being served to the browser:

```
www.webhomecover.com
```

A URL is a specific kind of *Uniform Resource Identifier* (URI) which identifies a resource that can be downloaded from the web. Another specific type of URI is the *Uniform Resource Name* (URN). Although these have similar formats to URLs, they do not necessarily specify a downloadable resource. The purpose of a URN is simply to provide a globally unique name for something, not necessarily to provide a name that points to a web-based resource. The term URL is very widely used, but URI is the more general (and correct) term.

1.5 Special types of web application

The web is full of public web sites that provide information using web pages to anyone who can connect to the World Wide Web using a browser. There is also a very large number of Business to Customer (B2C) web sites that make products and services available to anyone who has an Internet connection and a web browser. However there are some special-purpose web applications that have particular characteristics. Three important examples of these are intranets, extranets and portals.

Intranets

As well as having a public presence on the Internet, many organizations maintain a private *intranet* behind a security firewall. An intranet consists of web pages and other resources that are only available inside the organization. Intranets have a low cost of ownership because they use the standard technologies of the Internet. They increase internal communication while using less paper for things like internal phone books, software and procedure manuals, forms etc. They get information out of central databases in a form everyone can use from the desktop. Intranets have proved valuable for all kinds of organizations, for example, credit-card companies work with many banks and an intranet can be used as a central repository for information about all those banks, while pharmaceuticals companies have used intranets to draw information from many sources worldwide on drug trials and new drug submission regulations for all countries.

Extranets

An *extranet* falls somewhere between the Internet and an organization's intranet. Only selected outsiders, such as customers, suppliers or other trading partners, are allowed access an extranet. Extranets can range from highly secure Business to Business (B2B) systems to self-registration systems such as those frequently used for downloading evaluation software. Extranets can be used, for example, to allow web shopper customers to log in to check the status of their orders over a secure connection, or users of courier companies to check where their delivery is at any point in time.

Portals

A *portal* is a special kind of web application. Its role is to act as a gateway (the meaning of 'portal') into a number of other applications. The structure of a portal is typically to present a number of *portlets*, which are window-based links into other applications. They also commonly provide facilities for personalization, so that users can customize which portlets they are presented with and also change the layout and look and feel of the portal. Portals are often used by public sites that encourage user registration, such as Yahoo. They are also often used by organizations as a route into the various applications provided on the company intranet. In the mobile context, portals are a popular way for mobile service providers to enable easy access to the mobile Internet. Mobile portals such as Vodafone Live! provide links to various applications within the 'walled garden' of services provided by the mobile network carrier, as well as more general access to the mobile Internet.

1.6 Web application architectures

To understand how a web application provides services to clients across the web, it is necessary to have some understanding of the architectures of distributed computer systems. In this section, we introduce the concepts of layers and tiers.

Layers

The concept of a layered architecture is one where we regard different parts of a software system as having different and separate roles. This is a conceptual, rather than necessarily a physical, layering of system components. The basic three layers are the presentation layer (which deals with the user interface), the business logic layer (which handles the business processes and concepts used in the application) and the data management layer (which deals with managing and persisting the underlying data in the system).

If you think about how this model relates to, for example, the type of word processor that runs 'standalone' on a desktop computer (see Figure 1.4), you can see that there are certain parts of a word-processing program that deal with presentation, that is, how we see the document on the screen. This may be quite complex and allow multiple different views of the same document, for example an editing view and a print preview. Behind this layer is the business logic layer that contains all the processes that we need to perform when creating and editing documents, such as spell checking, formatting, paginating, editing, etc. This layer also contains the main concepts that we deal with in the application, such as documents, paragraphs, words, letters, diagrams, etc. Finally, beneath this layer, is the data management layer. The job of this layer is to enable our documents to be saved and reloaded, probably in simple flat (sequential) files so that they can persist between different runs of the word-processing program.

FIGURE 1.4   The conceptual layers of a word-processing system

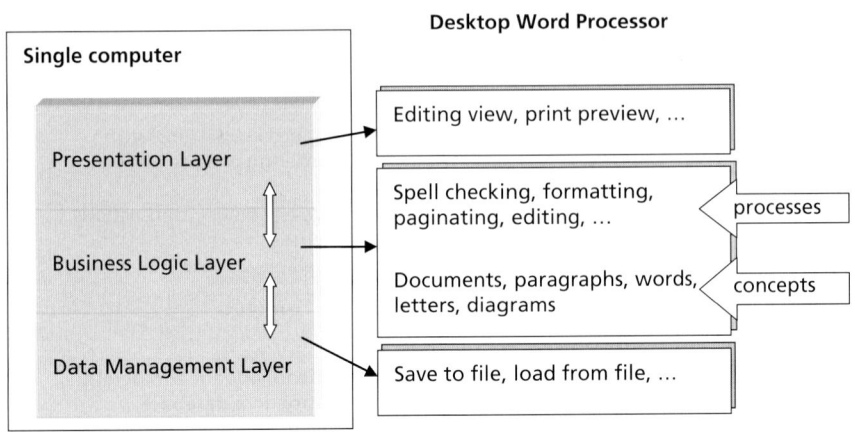

The important feature to note about our layered word-processing example is that we assume that all three layers would be implemented in a single program running on one computer. In other words the layers are conceptual, not physical.

Tiers and distributed systems

When we talk about *tiers*, we are also talking about layers. However the difference is that the term 'tiers' is generally used to mean physically separate devices. A multi tier system is therefore one that is deployed on multiple different nodes (computers). Using multiple tiers is necessary when we want to make our applications distributed and scaleable. For example, in a web-based banking system, the presentation layer, which would be a web browser, would be distributed across all the users' computers, but the application layer would be running on a central computer, or multiple computers, somewhere at the bank. This tier would manage the business processes such as checking accounts, transferring funds, ordering cheque books, etc. Also in this layer would be the business objects such as accounts, customers, transactions and statements. To cope with large numbers of users and to assist in security, the data management layer would also be run on a separate machine (probably several). For complex, large-scale data storage like this, instead of simple flat files, we would use a database management system for the four basic operations on data, namely *create*, *read*, *update* and *delete* (CRUD for short). Once we start using large numbers of computers running different parts of the system across multiple tiers, we have an *n-tier architecture* (see Figure 1.5). N-tier architectures are a fundamental part of web applications because the presentation layer (running in web browsers) is always widely distributed and the large number of users of some of these systems means that the business logic and data management layers may also have to be distributed across multiple machines.

FIGURE 1.5 The tiers of an n-tier web-based banking system

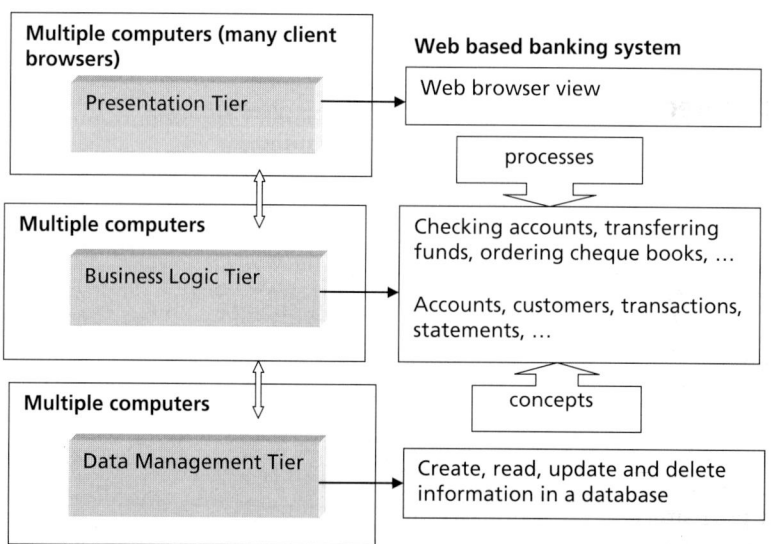

1.7 The Web 2.0 and Ajax

Since the mid 2000s, it has been hard to discuss the World Wide Web without mentioning the Web 2.0 and Ajax. Web 2.0 is a term that has become widely used since the first Web 2.0 Conference in 2004. Although it might be categorized as an umbrella marketing term rather than a specific technology or architecture, some authors, notably (O'Reilly 2005), have given it some concrete specifications through a set of published principles, practices and patterns. Many publications that discuss the Web 2.0 focus on rich user interfaces, in particular the use of asynchronous JavaScript and XML (Ajax), but the ideas of the Web 2.0 go beyond Ajax to include a wide range of ideas about how modern web applications should be developed. The key ideas underlying the Web 2.0 may perhaps be summarized as:

- The web as a software platform
- Service-oriented architectures
- User and contributor communities

In this section, we briefly explore some of these ideas, which will re-emerge at various points throughout this book. Above all, the role of the *eXtensible Markup Language* (XML), which underlies service-oriented architectures, can be seen as an important component of many of aspects of the Web 2.0.

The web as a software platform

In the past, the software platform that applications were built on was a particular computer operating system, for example Microsoft Windows or Linux. In contrast Web applications are able to span multiple operating systems because web browsers can render the same content regardless of the system from which the page was downloaded. The server may run on one operating system and its clients on many others. One key Web 2.0 pattern is *software above the level of a single device*, which is about the way that applications can span different types of device, from web servers to desktop PCs to mobile phones to portable media players. For example, to download music we might use a PC to connect to a web server and also connect a mobile device to the PC, all using a single application. In this type of situation, the platform that the overall application is running on is the web, not just a single device.

Service-oriented architectures

In the early days of the web, the focus was on the applications that were being used. For example, the 'browser wars', primarily between Netscape and Microsoft in the mid 1990s, were about which application would be used to access the web. More recently, the focus has been more on the underlying content available via the web, rather than the specific applications that are used. This content is made available using various forms of *web service*. Web services are data sources made available over the web using the eXtensible Markup Language (XML). Systems that are built by combining together multiple web services are known as *Service-Oriented Architectures* (SOA). Examples of content that can be accessed through web services include news, weather, map data, and book information. Some authors use the term *the programmable web* to describe the ability to build applications that utilise content from multiple web-based resources, using freely available application programming interfaces (APIs) to create *mashups*. A mashup, in web terms, is an application that mixes together content from different sources. Some mashups combine content from a number of different services to produce an overall application, while others use a single service but reorganize the content to suit their requirements.

One simple example of a web service is RSS (an abbreviation that has multiple roots: Really Simple Syndication, Rich Site Summary and RDF Site Summary), which uses XML to supply feeds of frequently updated information such as news and weather.

User and contributor communities

Traditional software construction is about building self-contained applications for a particular purpose, for example to process a company payroll or manage company accounts. This type of application is generally intended for 'in house' use, though it may expose certain features to customers. For example, software used by banks is primarily used internally, but may expose some web based services enabling customers to perform certain transactions on their accounts. In many Web 2.0 applications, instead of this type of central control, applications are about a community of users who participate in the application itself. A good example of this is Wikipedia, an on-line encyclopaedia where anyone can create or edit entries. Other applications may consist largely of content provided by a single organization but allow users to make some contribution. An example of this would be music download sites that enable users to post their own reviews. Of course, opening up a web application to contributions from the user community is not appropriate for every system, but certain aspects of the approach to software development can be incorporated into many different types of web application.

Ajax

Asynchronous JavaScript and XML (Ajax) is a term coined by Garrett (2005) in an article about current trends in Web development. JavaScript is a programming language that can be run inside a browser, making it possible to run programs that connect to the server while a page is being viewed. We cover Ajax in more detail later in this book, but its relationship to the Web 2.0 is primarily in the area of providing a rich user experience in the browser environment. At its simplest, Ajax makes it possible to update parts of a web page with data read from a server without having to refresh the whole page, making the user experience more like using a traditional desktop application rather than surfing a web site. There are many tools for developing Ajax applications, some very sophisticated. However it is possible to include some simple Ajax inside your web applications using a few lines of JavaScript code.

1.8 So you want to be a web application developer?

There are many challenges for developers in building web applications. There are choices about technology that have to be made, choices about architecture, choices about design, and choices about implementation. In making decisions about how to build web applications, there are always compromises and trade-offs, and we have to be aware of the reasons for making certain choices and the consequences of them. Fortunately, there are also many tools, techniques and reusable designs (*design patterns*) that can help us to meet these challenges. The purpose of this book is to explore some important issues in the development of modern web applications and provide some examples of how we might approach a solution, avoiding as best we can the hype of this week's technology while taking full advantage of the lessons we can learn from others, and getting the best from the available technologies.

Exercises

1.1 In Figure 1.2, we saw some of the top-level domains in the Domain Name System. Look up some of these domains by using a web search and find out what types of organization use, for example, the 'int' domain. Find some other top-level domains that are not included in the diagram. For your web searches, you will find the ICANN and IANA web sites useful (http://www.icann.org and http://www.iana.org).

1.2 In our example of a layered architecture we referred to a word processor running on a single machine. We compared this with a layered and tiered architecture, using the example of a web-based banking system. However, web-based word processors are becoming more popular. Do an Internet search and find some examples of word processors that work on the web. From their descriptions, how do you think the layers in the word processing example would be applied to tiers in the context of a web-based word processor? You may find it helpful in answering this question to spend some time using one of these web-based word processors.

1.3 Look at the Wikipedia web site (http://www.wikipedia.org.).What are the processes that you have to follow in order to add or modify an entry in this on-line encyclopaedia? There have been a few controversial problems with some entries made on Wikipedia in the past. See if you can find some reference to these by doing a web search, and see what policy changes were necessary in managing the web site.

1.4 Find a popular blog on the web. Describe the author and content of the blog. Why do you think this blog is popular?

1.5 One of the common features of portals is that they can be personalized. Find a web-based portal that you can personalize (for example, http://www.yahoo.com). Make a list of the things that you are able to personalize on this site.

1.6 A simple example of how Ajax can update the current page with data from the server is Google Suggest. Go to the Google Suggest home page (you can find this with a Web search) and start typing a search term. The system suggests possible searches as you type.

SUMMARY

In this chapter we introduced the principal features, technologies and uses of web applications. These covered aspects of both the Internet and the World Wide Web, the distributed architectures that web applications use and some special types of web application. Table 1.1 summarizes the various acronyms and shorthand terms that were introduced, along with their definitions.

TABLE 1.1	Terms introduced in this chapter

Acronym/ term	Meaning
Ajax	Asynchronous JavaScript and XML
API	Application Programming Interface
ARPA	Advanced Research Projects Agency (originator of the ARPANet)
B2B	Business to Business
blog	Web log; a web-based diary intended for public access
CERN	*Conseil Européen pour la Recherche Nucléair*, more generally known in English as the European Organisation for Nuclear Research
CGI	Common Gateway Interface
CRUD	Create, Read, Update, Delete
DHCP	Dynamic Host Configuration Protocol
DNS	Domain Name System
FTP	File Transfer Protocol
HTML	HyperText Markup Language
HTTP	HyperText Transfer Protocol
IANA	Internet Assigned Numbers Authority
ICANN	Internet Corporation for Assigned Names and Numbers
IPv4	Internet Protocol version 4
IPv6	Internet Protocol version 6
ISP	Internet Service Provider
NCSA	National Center for Supercomputing Applications
PHP	Originally Personal Home Page Tools, later renamed PHP: Hypertext Preprocessor
PKI	Public Key Infrastructure
RSS	Really Simple Syndication, Rich Site Summary or RDF Site Summary
SMTP	Simple Mail Transfer Protocol
SOA	Service-Oriented Architecture
SSL	Secure Sockets Layer
TCP/IP	Transmission Control Protocol/Internet Protocol
URI	Uniform Resource Identifier
URL	Uniform Resource Locator
URN	Uniform Resource Name
W3C	World Wide Web Consortium
Wiki	WikiWikiWeb; a web site that is open to public contributions and editing
WWW or W3	World Wide Web
XML	eXtensible Markup Language

References and further reading

Garrett, J.J. (2005) *Ajax: A New Approach to Web Applications*. http://www.adaptivepath.com/publications/essays/archives/000385.php

O'Reilly, T. (2005) *What is Web 2.0: Design Patterns and Business Models for the Next Generation of Software*. O'Reilly Network, http://www.oreilly.com/pub/a/oreilly/tim/news/2005/09/30/what-is-web-20.html

1

CHAPTER 2

Web Application Requirements Analysis and Design

INTRODUCTION

In this chapter, we look at some techniques for analyzing the requirements for a web application. Some of the notation used comes from the *Unified Modeling Language* (UML) with some special extensions that were developed to meet the particular requirements of designing for the web. There are also some informal diagrams that do not come from any specific notation. The process is based on aspects of the *Unified Process* (UP), but with a lightweight 'agile' approach. We conclude the chapter with some considerations relating to system design, and describe a number of web usability patterns.

2.1 What's different about web application requirements?

The development of a web application is similar in many ways to that of any other software system. We have to find out what the users require, choose an appropriate software architecture, design and build the overall framework and create all the necessary components, all the while testing the evolving system against its technical and user expectations and adapting to changing requirements and circumstances. In some ways, however, web applications have their own special requirements. Perhaps the most obvious is that web applications have a special kind of user interface. Their presentation may be via many different types of device, ranging from desktop computers to mobile phones, and that presentation is based on some form of web page running in a browser. Also, unlike many software systems, a web application often caters for very large numbers of anonymous users, potentially located anywhere in the world. This means that our design has to take account of the issues of data communications and multiple access to the same resources. Its underlying communications protocol is based on the request–response model, where the application is on a system that is remote from the user, and the user's device has to make requests of the application to perform activities on its behalf. This contrasts with desktop applications, which may have a richer, more interactive and immediate interface. In building such systems, we also have to be constantly aware that parts of our application will be running on central servers while other parts will be running on many different client devices. All of these differences (and more) mean that we have to extend our understanding of analysis and design to cater for all the special concerns of web applications.

2.2 Software development lifecycles

Although we have said that web applications have some special requirements, any development method that we adopt needs to provide four services to support us during the project *lifecycle* (the processes and events that take place between the project's beginning and its end):

- It needs to guide us through the various activities.
- It needs to specify the artefacts (such as documents, diagrams and software components) that should be created during the development of the system.
- It should direct the tasks of the individuals and teams working on the project.
- It should provide appropriate criteria for measuring and monitoring progress and production.

To achieve these objectives, it needs to help the system developers to know their roles, activities and workflows, and the final software products that they need to create. The way that these features are defined does not have to be excessively prescriptive, particularly for a small project. Many software development methods used from the 1990s onwards stress *agility*, which in many cases means producing the simplest possible artefacts by performing activities in the simplest possible workflows. Regardless, most current methods of software development use the concept of *iteration* which has gradually replaced older methods based on the *waterfall model*.

The waterfall model

Early approaches to developing software systems tended to follow a traditional engineering approach, whereby a system had to have all of its requirements gathered before it could be analyzed, be completely analyzed before it could be designed, fully designed before it could be implemented and only then could it be tested. This is known as the waterfall model because the development process can be seen as a sequence of separate stages that occur in a fixed order (see Figure 2.1). There is the notion of some feedback between adjacent stages, so that we might revisit certain aspects of the design in the light of implementation, for example, or rewrite code if it fails a test, but there is no concept of being able to cope with evolving requirements or starting to test early in the project lifecycle.

This type of approach may work well in many engineering contexts but does not work so well for most software projects. This is because the requirements for software tend to be more fluid and dynamic, changing over time to respond to changing application environments. To address this more flexible design process, *iterative* methods have been developed.

Iterative methods

An iterative approach is like a series of mini waterfalls, where we gather requirements, analyze, design, build and test part of a system, reflect on it, adapt our plans in the light of experience, and then repeat the process a number of times until the project is complete (see Figure 2.2). Thus the feedback loop, which at any given point in the waterfall model

FIGURE 2.1   The waterfall model

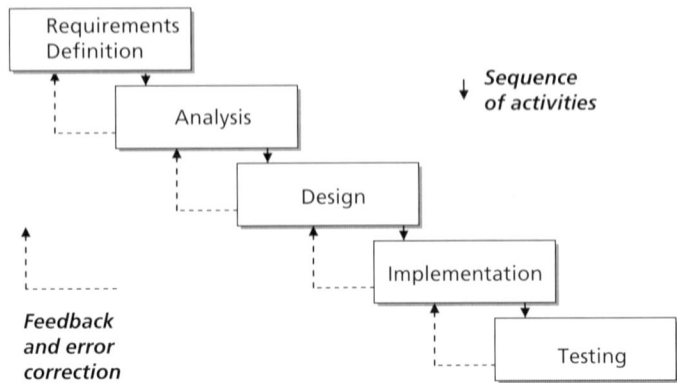

FIGURE 2.2   The iterative model

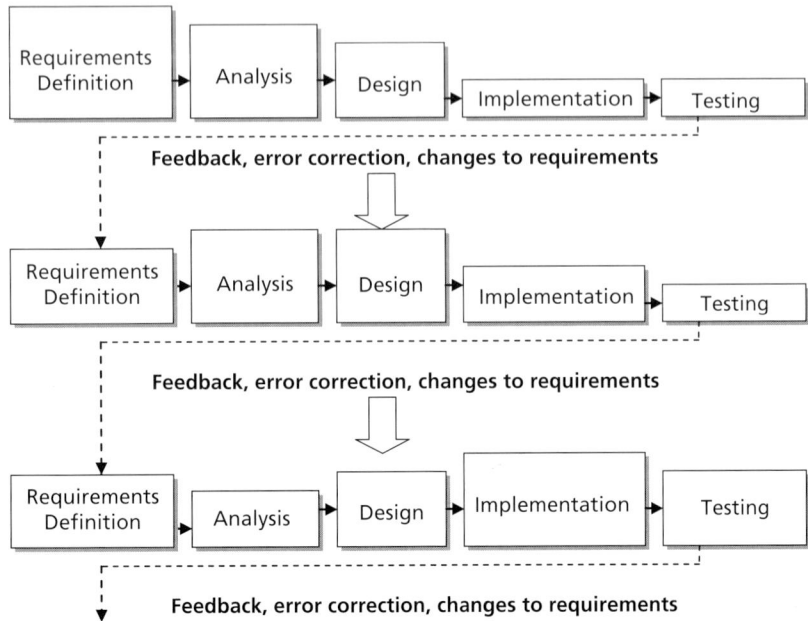

only includes the previous stage, covers all of the activities of analysis, design, implementation and testing. As we progress through the iterations, the emphasis of our activities changes. Initially, we focus mostly on requirements and analysis; later, we focus more on implementation and testing. The relative sizes of the boxes in Figure 2.2 are meant to suggest this gradual evolution through the iterations.

When using an iterative approach we still have an overall vision and plan for developing the system but we are more able to respond to new or changing requirements because we do not assume that we can identify all the requirements up front. Many iterative methods stress that each iteration should result in something concrete that provides a milestone for the project. In other words an iteration does not end just because a time period has expired but also because the required deliverable has been created. Iterative methods are also flexible in that their expected deliverables can be changed by trading off, in a managed way, new expectations against the original ones. In other words, if additional expectations are added to an iteration then an equivalent amount of effort has to be moved out of that iteration to enable the schedule to remain realistic.

2.3 The Unified Modeling Language and the Unified Process

In the 1990s, there were many notations and processes proposed for the development of object-oriented systems. So many, in fact, that the competition between the various approaches during this period became known as the 'method wars'. However, after a while it became evident that three methods in particular were gaining more traction than most of the others. These were the Object Modeling Technique (OMT) developed by a group led by James Rumbaugh at General Electric, the Booch method developed by Grady Booch at Rational Corporation, and Objectory developed by Ivar Jacobson at Eriksson. Largely at the instigation of Grady Booch, these three methods were fused with input from other methods when both Rumbaugh and Jacobson joined Booch at Rational. The first result of this collaboration was the Unified Modeling Language (the UML) which was a standard analysis and design notation for object-oriented systems. This standard language was published by the Object Management Group, a non-profit industry standards organization, with the first version being finalized in 1999. Later, a design process (the Unified Process, UP) was also published as a series of books, while a related set of tools and materials to support this process (the Rational Unified Process, RUP) was developed by Rational, a company since acquired by IBM. Although in book form the UP is not product related, it is not currently supported by an open standards organization.

The Unified Modeling Language (UML)

The UML is a very rich modeling language with many different types of diagram (18 in version 2), some of which serve very similar purposes. For example, sequence diagrams and communication diagrams can be used to represent the same information, and state diagrams and activity diagrams also have much in common. Therefore it is not necessary to use all the available diagrams of the UML, but rather to select those that are most useful for a particular type of project. State diagrams, for example, can be particularly helpful in designing hardware control systems, whilst deployment diagrams are appropriate when a system will be distributed across many different machines. Some methods that have evolved since the publication of the UML choose a specific subset of diagrams. Iconix, for example, uses only four types of diagram: the use case model, the sequence diagram, the class diagram and the (otherwise little used) robustness diagram (Rosenberg *et al.* 2005). We adopt a similar approach in this book, selecting a small number of useful diagrams from the UML along with some extensions developed specifically for designing web applications.

The Unified Process (UP)

The Unified Process is, like the UML, a rich specification with many possible activities and artefacts. Once again, we can tailor our use of the process to the practices most appropriate for our application type. As Jacobson himself has written about the RUP, it 'has grown and become too complex', so it's OK to simplify it (Jacobson 2004). Perhaps the most important aspect of the UP is that as well as using an iterative approach it describes both phases and disciplines. A phase is a group of iterations that fall within a specific time period within the overall project life cycle, while the disciplines are the various types of activity that take place during each iteration. The overall approach of the UP is neatly summed up by a commonly used 'whale diagram' that shows the relationship between iterations, phases and disciplines (see Figure 2.3). The 'whales' are the curves that show the level of activity in each discipline at various stages of the development process. Although the image is just an example of how the various activities in a project might move in and out of focus over time, it gives a clear idea of how an iterative process changes its emphasis as it moves through the various phases. This equates to the iterative model in Figure 2.2. To make sense of the rest of the diagram, we look at the four phases of the UP, which appear across the top of the diagram, and the iterations that occur within them.

FIGURE 2.3   The Unified Process 'whale' diagram

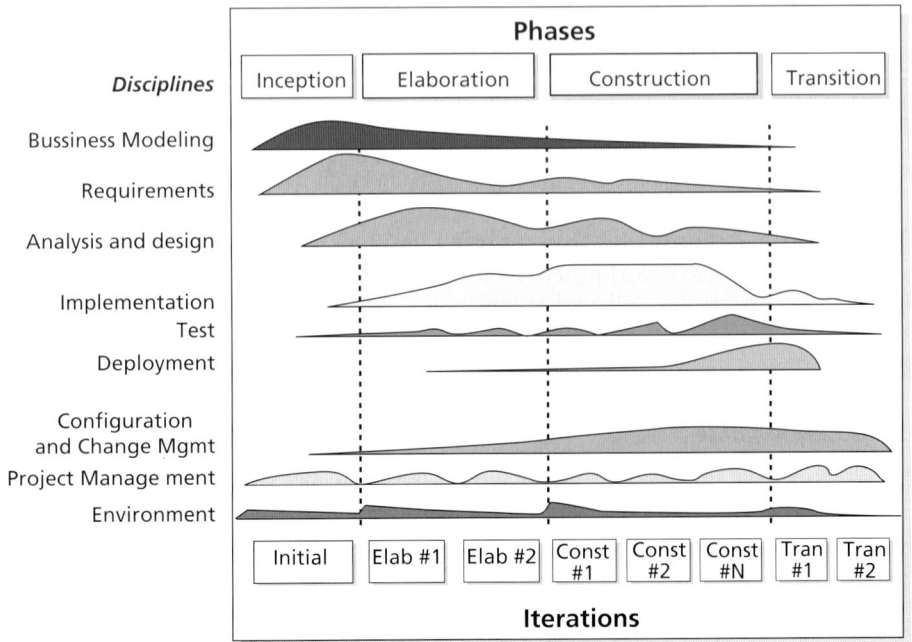

The inception phase

During the inception phase, we explore a project to a sufficient stage to understand if it is viable. This means gathering the initial requirements, investigating relevant technical issues and building software prototypes where necessary to act as proofs of concept. During this phase, new technologies and frameworks may be investigated to evaluate whether or not they would be good choices for the project in hand. At the end of the inception phase, we should have enough information to know whether the project as a whole has a realistic chance of success, and we should also have a draft plan for the entire project, including a total budget and an overall time frame. The disciplines of the UP show that during this phase we also have to establish the development environment and processes to manage software configuration and change. For a simple project, or one that is treading familiar ground, a single iteration may be sufficient for this phase. For large projects or those that involve substantially new technology and tools, more iterations will be required. At the end of each iteration, a specific milestone should be met and a meaningful deliverable should result. For example, an iteration in the inception phase might be required to deliver a working proof of concept using a particular code framework, application server and database, along with a project plan and a budget. Experimental proof of concept prototypes are sometimes known as *spikes* (Cockburn 2005).

The elaboration phase

In many ways, this is the most important phase as it demonstrates the viability (or not) of the chosen software architecture. The most important deliverable from the elaboration phase is an *executable architecture*, which we can think of as being similar to the foundations and load bearing structure (framework) of a building. Although it may take fewer people and less time for a building's foundations to be laid and its steel skeleton to be built, when compared to the time and labor required to complete all the cladding, internal walls and fittings, it is a more crucial phase. The foundations and framework need to be able to support all the subsequent work or the building will collapse, like many a software project has in the past. In a software project, the executable architecture must provide a suitable foundation and framework for all the subsequent development, so it must meet all the most important requirements of the project and have addressed its key risk factors. For example, if a project has specific requirements in terms of performance, such as the number of concurrent users that it should be able to support, then the executable architecture should have demonstrated that it can deliver this requirement. Therefore practices such as load testing are important in the elaboration phase. Although the executable architecture can be regarded as being based on a prototype, it is an architectural prototype, which means that it is intended to be refined until it is put into production. This is different from the proof of concept prototypes that are often developed during the inception phase and discarded once they have performed their roles of demonstrating or testing alternative approaches. Rather than a spike, the executable architecture is a *walking skeleton*, the beginning of the framework that will endure throughout the rest of the system lifetime (Cockburn 2005). Due to the importance of this phase, there may be several iterations.

The construction phase

In this phase, all the necessary components are added to the existing executable architecture. This is like adding the cladding, internal walls and fittings to a building. During this phase, there may be some minor changes to the executable architecture due to new or changing requirements, but its core functionality should be stable. However we should be able to be very flexible in terms of the components that we are developing within the framework. At the end of the construction phase we should have a complete software product that is ready for alpha testing. Unless the project is small, there will be many iterations in the construction phase.

The transition phase

In this final phase, the system moves from the development environment into its deployment environment; at the end of the phase, it should be in use. Activities from this phase can include alpha, beta and acceptance testing, installation, manufacture (in the case of shrink-wrapped software), parallel running and user training. We might regard this phase as being similar to the handover of a new building to its owners. The number of iterations will depend on the type of project and its means of construction. For example, an open-source project that will deploy on the web could easily have a transition phase with a single iteration, while a large custom-built system for a client with many sites running mission-critical systems would require more iterations. Figure 2.4 matches the building metaphor to the phases of the UP.

How long is an iteration?

In our discussion of phases, we made no mention of how long an iteration should be. The general practice is to make all iterations a similar length, so that the project gets its own rhythm. How long each iteration should be is open to debate, but something around four weeks is common and anything from two to six weeks is reasonable. Anything less than two weeks is unlikely to be long enough to produce a meaningful milestone, while iterations longer than six weeks may lead to a lack of project rhythm and not provide the project as a whole with enough milestones to keep it on track. Within an iteration there will also be 'time-boxed' activities that have their own internal deadlines based on estimations of effort and duration. The difference between effort (how much consistent effort it would take in an ideal world to produce a required artefact) and duration (how long it actually takes) is due to the realities of distractions such as meetings, holiday, illness, fire alarms and a whole host of other time-consuming events and activities. Various techniques can be used to estimate the actual time required for each task, but the best way is just to learn by experience how long a particular task will take. Definition of tasks may be done by use cases, or user stories, and with experience these can be written with a given scope in mind. Of course the number of iterations multiplied by the length of an iteration gives how long you plan the whole project to take.

FIGURE 2.4　The phases of the Unified Process applied to a building metaphor

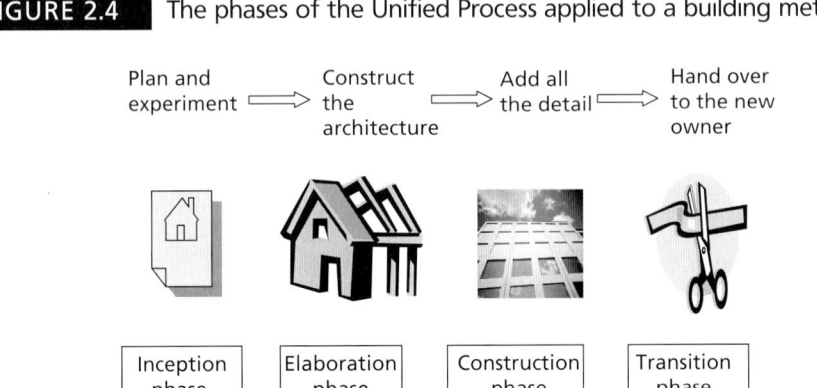

| Plan and experiment | Construct the architecture | Add all the detail | Hand over to the new owner |

| Inception phase | Elaboration phase | Construction phase | Transition phase |

2.4 A web application inception phase

In the rest of this chapter we will look at some activities that might be appropriate during the inception phase. Taking the diagram in Figure 2.3 as a rough guide (while acknowledging that this is not meant to indicate anything other than a general impression of the process), we can see that we might expect this phase to include some initial analysis and design, as well as business modeling and requirements gathering. In fact, we might regard most of this book as describing activities that are appropriate to the inception phase, in the sense that we will be exploring technologies that may be new to you and demonstrating some simple proof of concept code. As Figure 2.3 suggests, we will be doing some coding, some testing and quite a bit of exploration of a software environment. None of the application code in this book is quite sophisticated enough to be regarded as an industrial-strength architectural prototype; in fact, it could be regarded as a series of spikes. However it should provide enough material to enable a more extensible framework to be built. Taken together, it builds into something that could be regarded as a walking skeleton for further development.

The intention of the examples that we work through in the rest of this chapter is to give some flavor of how the initial business modeling and analysis process is one of investigation and discovery, where we continually revise our initial assumptions in the light of experience and experiment. Therefore you will see that we do not present something that is seen as initially perfect; rather, we present a starting point that we refine as we further explore the requirements and utilize the various analysis tools and techniques. Software development is essentially a team effort where individual skills and relationships are crucial, something that is hard to replicate in book form. Therefore you should regard the following examples as artefacts that would evolve through a process of negotiation and discussion, rather than there being one 'right answer'. Every software problem has a number of potential solutions, each with their own advantages and disadvantages. One other thing is for sure, every real-world software project is far more complex than it may at first appear!

2.5 Modeling requirements

The first step in developing any web application must be to establish the business objectives (part of the business modeling discipline of the UP). There was a time in the 'dot com' boom of the 1990s when web-based systems were developed with little realistic idea of the business objectives apart from the fact that everyone else already had a web site so 'we need one too'. Times have changed, so now there is more focus on aspects such as *return on investment* (ROI). A good focus for discussing the business objectives is to agree on a mission statement for the application, which neatly summarizes the point of the exercise.

In this book, we use a simplified case study based on a home insurance web application. This is a fictional scenario within which we will analyze and design our system:

> *Web Home Cover is a new enterprise set up to provide home insurance over the web. The business case is based on providing a service that is entirely on-line and therefore highly efficient in terms of the initial capital investment required by the insurance company. Since the company will only operate via the web, it must have a web application that meets the needs of all its customers and staff. It must also be written to ensure that it will work for as many web clients as possible, from desktop computers to mobile devices.*

This is a possible mission statement for the project:

To bring home insurance services to every corner of the web

This is the essence of the business case for our home insurance web application. It is short and to the point. Long 'buzzword bingo' phrases are best left out of the mission statement.

Web application requirements gathering

The first step we must take on the road to actually building a web-based solution is to identify the high-level requirements (or business objectives) of the proposed system. This is rather difficult in many cases, since we may not know who our actual users will be. If the web application is intended for a company intranet (an application that is used only internally within the organization), then it will be quite easy to find out who the potential users of the system are. If, however, we are launching an e-commerce web site then we are aiming our application at a largely unknown mass of users in cyberspace. How, then, can we work out what their requirements might be? There are a number of approaches we can take. One common approach is to use focus groups, where a small number of people who are representative of our possible user base are brought together to answer questions and offer opinions in a structured and controlled context, using sample materials. Another approach is to use marketing staff to take on the role of possible users and represent their requirements, presumably on the basis that their job is to tell people what they want. In either case, we need to develop a set of user profiles that will give us an idea about whose needs we are trying to meet. These user profiles can be simple demographic summaries (e.g. the age range, sex, interests, average income, etc. of our expected users) or rather more sophisticated 'personas' where fictional biographies are developed of our supposed typical users. Whoever we use to represent our actual users, at some point we need to gather a suitable set of stakeholders (those who have an interest in the system, either directly or indirectly) into a room and get them to write down an initial set of requirements in an activity known as a *joint requirements workshop*. This does not require sophisticated tools, the usual ones being flip-chart pads or whiteboards and pens. Instead of the usual brainstorming approach, card storming might be used to encourage full participation. Whereas with brainstorming the participants take turns to call out their contributions, which can be frustrating for some and intimidating for others, in a card-storming approach everyone simultaneously writes each of their contributions on a separate card. The cards are all pooled and then explored together by the group. Experience suggests that the 'magic' number of core requirements likely to emerge from such sessions is 12 (more or less), though it depends on the level of detail that you want to aim for.

We now imagine a requirements workshop for the Web Home Cover project. Who might our stakeholders be? For our purposes, we might imagine a group comprising the lead software developer, the project manager, the database administrator, the marketing person who ran the focus groups (armed with a set of user profiles), the sales manager, a claims assessor and one of the insurance underwriters. By the time all the doughnuts have gone, the flip-chart pads on the wall have a list of requirements that looks something like this:

1. New users should be able to get an instant quote for buildings insurance.
2. New users should be able to get an instant quote for contents insurance.
3. New users should have the option to apply for both, or either, type of home insurance cover.

4. Policy holders should be able to check their current policies and request changes using a secure login.
5. New users should be able to check the status of their application using a secure login.
6. Call-centre staff should be able to view and query all policy details using a secure login.
7. Underwriters should be able to access all applications waiting for processing using a secure login.
8. New users should be able to retrieve previous quotations immediately, even if they have not yet applied for a policy.
9. The web site should provide enough information for users to contact the company by email, telephone or in writing.
10. Users should be able to access the system from both desktop and mobile devices.
11. Policy holders should be able to make claims against their policies.
12. The system should be available 24/7/365 and be able to cope with 10,000 concurrent users.
13. The system should have a telepathic user interface.

There are some things to note about this set of requirements. First, while most of them are functional requirements (what the system should do), some are non-functional (the way that the system should do what it does). For example, a functional requirement is that 'new users should be able to get an instant quote for buildings insurance'. This is something the system must do for its users. Examples of non-functional requirements are the ability to access the system from multiple devices or being available all the time. These are not things that the system does but characteristics of how it delivers those things. Some requirements need further exploration, for example the last two are somewhat extreme but are meant to indicate some important considerations. While it may be desirable for a system to be available all the time, we must consider how much it costs to do this versus the real need. Likewise, the requirement includes an optimistic prediction of the possible number of concurrent users. We have all heard of a few web sites that were so popular that they quickly imploded under the strain of serving all their users. However the history of the dot com era had rather more examples of systems that anticipated huge numbers of users but ended up with a trickle. Performance, availability and security requirements, should always be looked at carefully by applying a cost-benefit analysis. For each requirement, we have to ask how much it would cost for the 'perfect' solution as opposed to an acceptable solution. The 'telepathic user interface' requirement comes from a Dilbert cartoon, but again has a serious point, which is that requirements often use arbitrary requests such as 'the interface must be user friendly' which are, in fact, meaningless. Requirements must be both realistic and measurable. Proposing a system that must pass certain usability or learnability metrics (measures) would be more useful.

Prioritizing requirements

Once we have a set of initial requirements, we need to prioritize them. This is important in an iterative development approach because we have to schedule the requirements over different iterations. Therefore if requirements will be delivered at different points in the development lifecycle then we should address the more important requirements first, particularly since new requirements may appear during the process. If any requirements get pushed to the back of the queue by this process then they should be those with a lower priority. It is not necessary to put all the requirements in order. In many cases, four levels of priority are considered acceptable, sometimes classified as:

- Must have
- Should have
- Could have
- Want to have

This prioritization method is sometimes referred to using the acronym *MoSCoW*.

One useful approach to the prioritization exercise is to have the participants vote for their requirements in two rounds from different perspectives, possibly using some multiple voting mechanism (such as the participants having four votes each). For example, round 1 could prioritize requirements from a customer viewpoint and round 2 could prioritize the requirements from the viewpoint of the staff.

Since it is difficult to cast a vote while in the context of a text book, we will have to assume that we have performed this exercise and come to some conclusions. Bearing in mind our mission statement, it would appear that the following requirements are 'must haves'.

1. New users should be able to get an instant quote for buildings insurance.
2. New users should be able to get an instant quote for contents insurance.
3. New users should have the option to apply for both, or either, type of home insurance cover.
7. Underwriters should be able to access all applications waiting for processing using a secure login.
10. Users should be able to access the system from both desktop and mobile devices.
11. Policy holders should be able to make claims against their policies.

With these requirements in place we can sell insurance over the web and reach as many people as possible

What are the 'should haves'? These are still pretty much core functions. Perhaps the following requirements fall under this category:

4. Policy holders should be able to check their current policies and request changes using a secure login.
6. Call-centre staff should be able to view and query all policy details using a secure login.
9. The web site should provide enough information for users to contact the company by email, telephone or in writing.

With these requirements we can help retain and support our existing customers and provide maximum opportunity to attract new business.

The following requirements are probably best categorized as 'could haves':

5. New users should be able to check the status of their application using a secure login.
8. New users should be able to retrieve previous quotations immediately, even if they have not yet applied for a policy.

We can live without these, but they could provide some benefit to our users. They might be regarded as 'sugar' (handy but non-essential).

These are our final two requirements:

12. The system should be available 24/7/365 and be able to cope with 10,000 concurrent users.
13. The system should have a telepathic user interface.

These will have to be put into the 'would like to have' category, at least for the moment. They certainly need some further work before being taken seriously as priority requirements.

What is the point of this exercise? It enables us to schedule the important requirements first when developing the system. Agile approaches would use 'story cards' for requirements, with each card representing a user story about what the system should do. By prioritizing these cards, we can put them into various iterations, with the most important in the early iterations.

2.6 Analysis tools – domain models, use cases and storyboards

In this section, we introduce some basic UML notations that can help us to visualize key features of the application. Even if a development project takes an agile approach that does not worry about extensive formal documentation, using standard notations for descriptive sketches can be very useful as a common communication medium between developers and users.

The domain model

A useful model to build before getting into details about the system use cases is a domain model that captures the key concepts of the business domain. The domain model helps us to begin to understand how various important concepts of the domain interact in a structural way. Again, we should develop the domain model in a workshop environment. Some analysis methods suggest that the domain model should grow piecemeal out of the use case analysis, but the advantage of developing the domain model early is that it provides a common vocabulary within which the following stages of the analysis can take place. This ensures that, for example, different threads of the analysis do not end up using two different names for the same concept because everyone can work from, and enhance, the same domain model. The model itself captures a few simple ideas:

- What are the key concepts in the domain?
- Which concepts interact with each other?
- How can we describe these interaction relationships?
- What is the *cardinality* of these interactions? (In other words, which relationships are one to one, which are one to many and which are many to many?)

We can begin to identify the core concepts in our domain by identifying nouns in our core requirements. From our set of objectives, we can find 27 nouns (plural nouns have been made singular) that can be our candidate list of concepts for the domain model. We might imagine them brainstormed onto a whiteboard or card-stormed onto sticky notes and then stuck on the wall (see Figure 2.5).

From this list, we can exclude anything clearly outside the system boundary (desktop, telephone, writing), the boundary itself (user interface) or nouns that refer to the system as a whole (web site, system). We should also get rid of synonyms ('user' and 'concurrent user' are general words for more specific types of user; 'quote' and 'quotation' are the same thing) and properties of other concepts (policy detail is a property of policy), though properties can be added to their matching concept if they look useful. 'Detail' is a very vague property of a policy but 'status' might be a useful property of an application so we might choose to include it in the diagram. In the revised list (see Figure 2.6), we have struck out twelve of the candidate concepts, leaving fifteen (including the 'status' property).

From these, we draw an initial domain model (Figure 2.7). This consists of rectangles for each concept, labelled with the concept name. Any properties that are immediately evident can also be added, separated from the concept name by a horizontal line. Concepts that have some kind of relationship with one another are linked by 'association' lines, which are labelled with text that describes the association. Arrow heads by the text can be used to show the direction in which the label should be read (for example, we are saying that a policy holder *lives at* an address, not that an address *lives at* a policy holder). By default, an association line implies that the cardinality of the relationship is 'one to one', for example there is one policy holder to one address. To show a 'one to many' relationship, we use the asterisk (*); for example, one policy can have many claims made against it. If the asterisk

FIGURE 2.5   Candidate list of concepts for the domain model

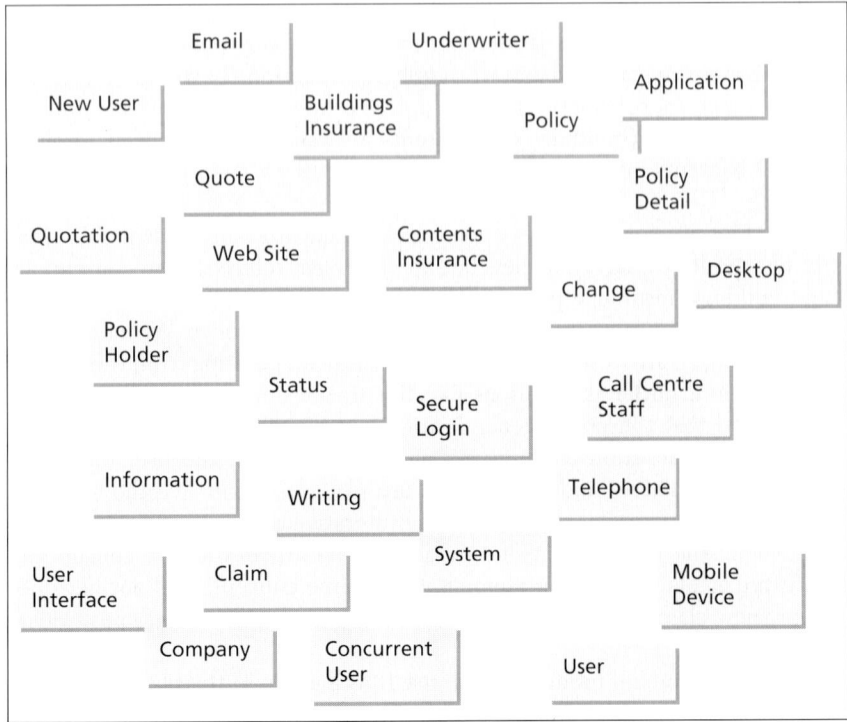

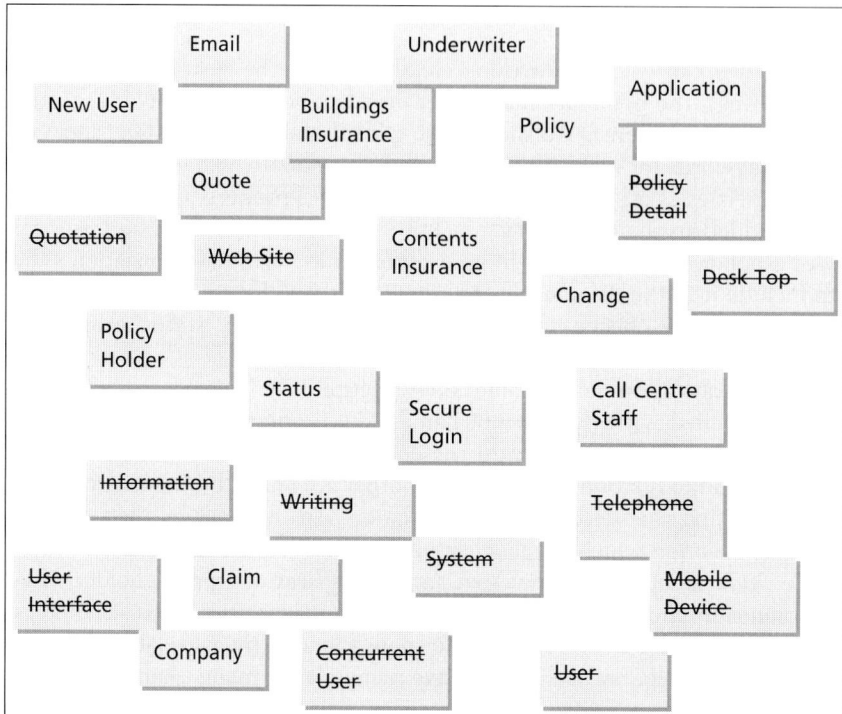

FIGURE 2.6 Modified list of candidate concepts

appears at both ends of an association then this means a 'many to many' association. In our domain model, one call-centre staff member may query many policies, and a single policy may be queried by many call-centre staff members. Occasionally we can define a cardinality number or range more exactly. For example we know that a policy holder will have either exactly one policy (buildings OR contents insurance) or exactly two policies (both buildings AND contents insurance).

Sometimes we identify concepts that appear to be specializations or generalizations of one another. In our model we have policies, but we also have references to contents insurance policies and buildings insurance polices. The concept of a policy here could be seen as a generalization of the two more specific (specialized) types of policy. We indicate this in the domain model using an arrow with an open triangular head pointing from the specializations to the generalization. Initial assumptions like this in the domain model may be modified later. We may find that the policy generalization is not useful. Alternatively, we may find that we need a generalization of new user and policy holder, the user concept that we previously discarded. These kinds of decision are made as we evolve the analysis domain model into a design class model, as the process of iterative analysis and design gives us more information about the concepts in our model. A class model shows concepts that will become software artefacts in the implementation. Some concepts will not become classes, whereas many new classes will be introduced as the need for them becomes evident.

Now that we have a domain model, we can use it as a guide in the use cases. For example there should be no ambiguities about whether we should use the concept name 'quote' or

FIGURE 2.7 A domain model for the home insurance system

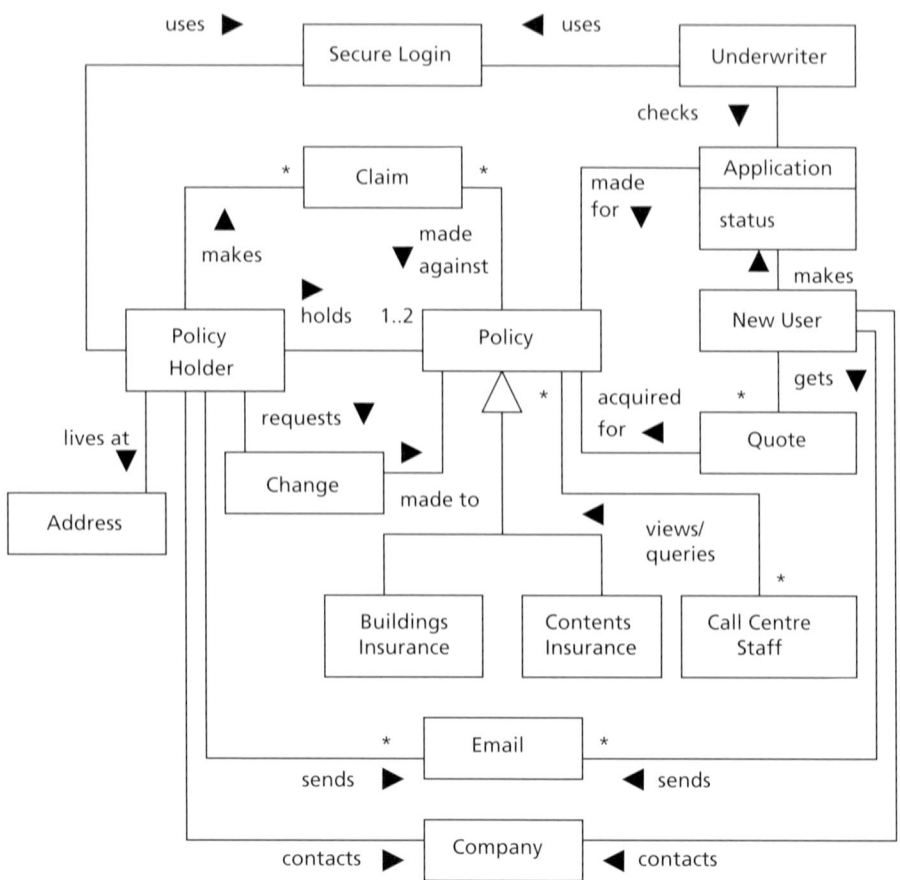

'quotation' in the use cases: we check the domain model and use 'quote'. At this stage, it is useful also to start building a glossary for the system (on a web page, of course) to define our interpretation of what these concept names mean.

Use case diagrams

Use case diagrams are very simple. They help us to show the different types of users and the goals they have in using a system. Because they are an analysis tool they do not anticipate any specific type of technology or how the system will actually deliver its requirements. All they do is specify what those requirements are (in a very broad way). Figure 2.8 shows the notation for the main component types in a use case diagram.

As you can see, there are only three: the actor, the use case and the system boundary. Use cases are inside the system boundary and actors are outside. Arrows are used to indicate which actors use which use cases. It is important to note that actors do not represent individual people, rather they represent different roles that people can take when using the system. In some cases, the same person might take on different roles at different times.

FIGURE 2.8   Use case diagram notation

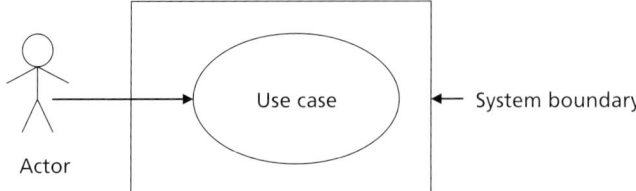

In our system, for example, a person my be a member of the call-centre staff but may also apply for insurance as a new user. Similarly, new users change into policy holders if their policy applications are approved. In addition, actors are not always roles taken by people. They can equally be representative of other systems or manual processes. For this reason, we sometimes see the arrows going out from a use case to an actor representing an external system.

Actors and use cases describe *roles* and *goals*. Each actor should be named using a noun that describes a user role, as opposed to an individual, for example 'policy holder'. Each use case should describe a user's goal in using the system, so they should be named using verb phrases (e.g. 'Apply for policy'). Although in some cases there may be a one-to-one correspondence between a use case and a requirement, a single use case may also meet more than one requirement. You will see an example of this in Section 2.7.

Figure 2.9 shows a use case diagram taken from the functional requirements we listed in our workshop. Note that we have five actors taken from our requirements: new user, policy holder, call centre staff members, claims assessor and insurance underwriter. There are eleven use cases. Note how some actors have associations with more than one use case.

Use case realization

Once we have decided on what our use cases should be, we have to find some way of showing what happens inside them. This is known as a *use case realization*. There are a number of different notations that we can use to do this, ranging from simple text descriptions to various diagrams. Here, we introduce some sequence diagram notation from the UML along with some informal storyboarding. Since we are designing a web application, the realization is specific to an environment where the actors interact with page-based presentations. Sequence diagrams capture user interaction with the system, while storyboards are useful for modeling page-based systems because they provide a simple way of describing the page flow and alternate paths that are typical of web applications. They can also be used to informally describe the layout and content of web pages. To link web pages and our UML diagrams we can use the web application extensions (WAE) to the UML for designing web-based systems (Conallen 1999). These are a special set of icons that can be used in UML models to represent components that are specific to web applications, such as web pages.

Use case descriptions

Before embarking on drawing diagrams, however, we begin by writing a textual description of each use case that summarises the sequence of interactions that the actor has with the system. It will also capture any selections or iterations that take place. The nature of these textual descriptions varies from project to project, and some suggested formats and

FIGURE 2.9 A use case diagram for the home insurance web application

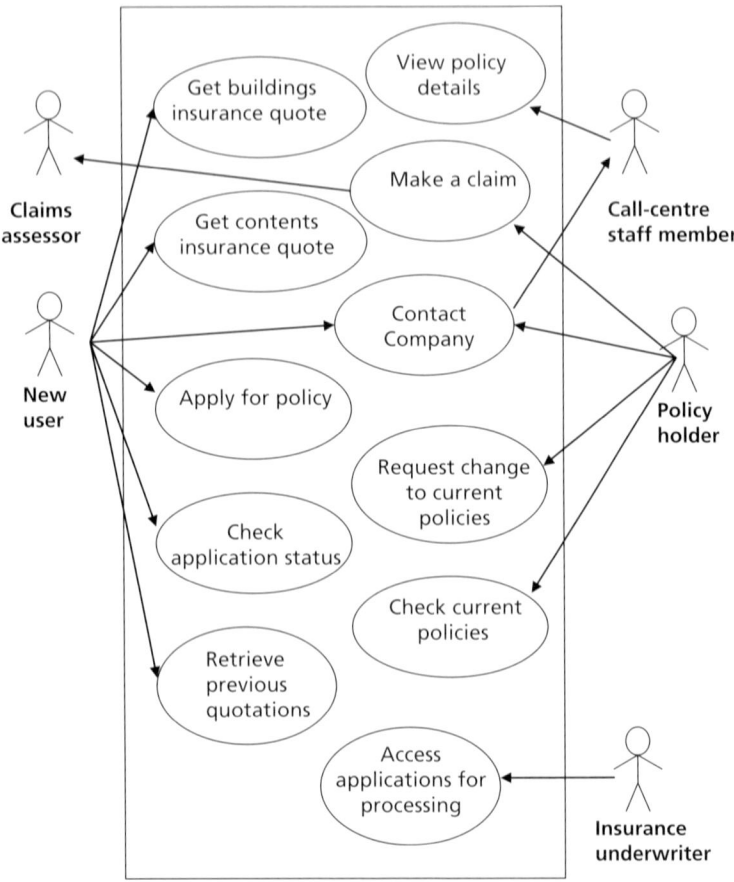

contents are much stricter and more complex than others. The approach we suggest here is to keep things simple but to number each interaction. This makes it easier to 'plug in' alterative sequences of events. The style of a use case description is conversational, that is, it describes a series of actor requests and system responses, in pairs.

As an example, we begin with the 'Get buildings insurance quote' use case. In the text description, we capture some important information:

- The name of the use case
- The actor(s) that use it
- The start page (this is specific to a web application)
- A brief description of what happens in the use case.

Use Case Name: Get buildings insurance quote

Actors: New user

Start Page: Home page

Use Case Description:

1. The actor chooses to get an insurance quote.
2. The system requests the actor's personal details.
2. The actor enters his/her personal details.
4. The system displays a choice of available insurance quotes.
5. The actor chooses to get a buildings insurance quote.
6. The system requests information about the building to be insured.
7. The actor enters data about the building.
8. The system displays the buildings insurance quote.

System sequence diagrams

Now that we have a textual description of the use case, we can draw a system sequence diagram. This shows the interactions between the actor and the system in a notation from the UML.

The components of a system sequence diagram are the actor for the use case, the component(s) that they interact with, labelled arrows showing the messages that pass between the actor and the other components and a vertical time axis. In fact, it is possible to draw sequence diagrams with a horizontal time axis but this is not usually supported by software tools. The component type that an actor interacts with is known as a boundary object, because it exists on the boundary between the system and the actors. A boundary object is usually some kind of graphical interface component. In a web application, this will be displayed on a web page. The UML notation for a boundary object is shown in Figure 2.10.

Our system sequence diagram is shown in Figure 2.11.

Designing pages and webflow with storyboards

If you have seen system sequence diagrams before, you may notice that the one in Figure 2.11 is a bit different from the norm in that it indicates the forms and pages displayed by the system interface boundary object. In a web application, the interaction is via series of pages, so the view of the system from the actor perspective is based on pages. By using the style of sequence diagram in Figure 2.11, we can begin to explore the pages and their sequences that will be used in the storyboards. The sequences of pages that appear in a use case are sometimes known as a *webflow*, which is simply a use case workflow that uses a series of web pages to achieve its goal.

FIGURE 2.10　UML notation for a boundary object

FIGURE 2.11 A system sequence diagram

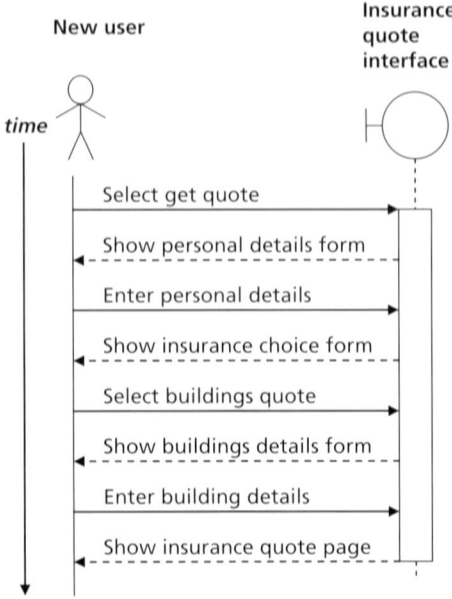

Since our interactions are with a web application, via web pages, we will utilise the web page icon from the UML web application extensions in our sequence diagram (see Figure 2.12a). Web pages are 'architecturally significant components' that exist both in the analysis and design models and the coded system (Conallen 1999). The pages may be coded in mark-up (e.g. HTML) or a programming language (e.g. Java). Using the formal symbols can be useful in documentation and artefacts created in software packages. However, when informally working through the analysis on paper or whiteboards, it is often easier just to use *stereotype* labels to indicate components such as web pages (see Figure 2.12b). Whether you use symbols or stereotypes is up to you, and the symbols do not have to be exact. Indeed, Conallen himself uses different versions of the symbols in different published sources (see (Conallen 1999) and (Conallen 2001)).

Having outlined the user interaction in the system sequence diagram, we might usefully draw a first cut of a storyboard, representing the pages that are accessed during the use case (see Figure 2.13). For this initial storyboard, we describe only the page names, the navigation routes and the events that trigger the transitions between pages.

Because storyboarding is an informal design tool, there is little consensus on notation, style or even when it should be done. Some developers suggest that you can create an entire web-site storyboard in one step. Whilst this can work for simple sites that are mostly static content, more dynamic and complex web applications require a more incremental approach. Therefore we suggest the approach of developing a storyboard for each use case. Eventually, all the storyboards can be collected together to summarise the navigation paths of the entire web application.

One option for a storyboard is to define the types of page using the UML extension symbols for client pages and forms (see Figure 2.14) rather than using the generic web page icon from Figure 2.12.

FIGURE 2.12   The UML extension symbol for a) a web page and b) its stereotype equivalent

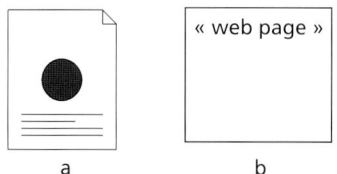

FIGURE 2.13   A simple storyboard

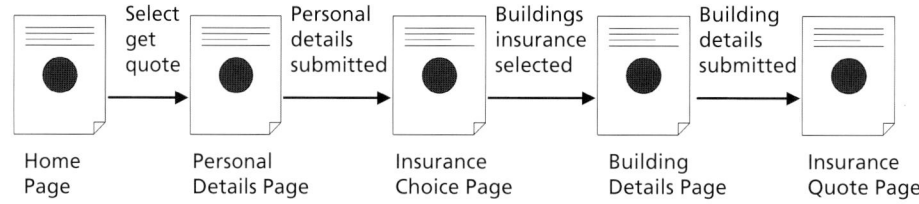

FIGURE 2.14   UML extension symbols for (a) a client page and (b) a form

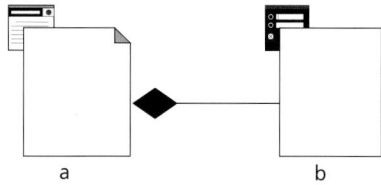

Note that in this notation, we normally use the form icon as a composition component of a client page (the black diamond indicates that the page is partly composed of the form). However if we follow the *one-form-per-page* usability pattern (Graham 2002), also known as *button gravity* because it puts the emphasis on a single 'Submit' button on each page, then we can dispense with the separate page icon and use the form icon to represent a complete form page.

Looking at each page in turn, we might define the home page and buildings quote page using the 'client page' icon, whereas the others use the 'form' icon. There is no requirement to use these symbols, but they can help to visualize a typical webflow, which will frequently start from a client page, then move through one or more form pages, gathering data in a 'wizard' style, and finally arrive at a summary page that shows the user the result of the webflow (Figure 2.15).

2.7 Building further use cases

So far, so good. We have written a use case realization for the 'Get buildings insurance quote' use case and we have a simple storyboard. As we are performing analysis activities we have made no attempt to consider data types, page layout, component types or any

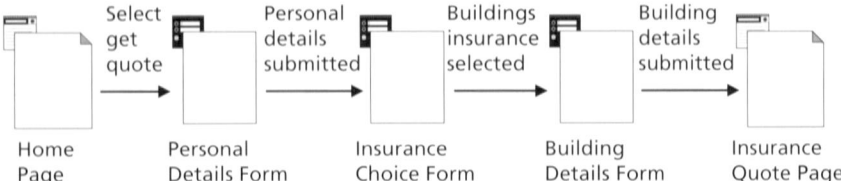

other aspect that would be considered a design activity. Now we move on to the 'Get contents insurance quote' use case. We could, of course, start writing a separate use case description, but it would soon become obvious that we start off in exactly the same way, by gathering the user's personal details and offering a choice of insurance quotes. How do we progress? We might consider adding a use case to gather the user's personal details, which we then progress from to create the two use cases for different types of insurance. However, this implies that getting the two types of insurance quote are exclusive acts. Do we want a user to have to go through two separate use cases if they want both contents and buildings insurance? Once we begin to think about this, it becomes clear that we don't really want two separate use cases for the two types of insurance. In fact we want one use case ('Get insurance quote') that is flexible enough for the user to be able to get a buildings insurance quote, a contents insurance quote, or both. In other words, we have one use case that meets two requirements. With this in mind, let's revisit our existing use case and consider the need for *alternate flows*.

An alternate flow occurs when the activities in a single use case may take different paths depending on some condition. In this example, the condition is the user's choice of insurance. Here is a modified use case description for the renamed 'Get insurance quote' use case.

Use Case Name: Get insurance quote

Actors: New user

Start page: Home page

Use Case Description:

1. The actor chooses to get an insurance quote.
2. The system requests the actor's personal details.
2. The actor enters his/her personal details.
4. The system displays a choice of available insurance quotes.
5. The actor chooses to get a buildings insurance quote.
6. The system requests information about the building to be insured.
7. The actor enters data about the building.
8. The system displays the buildings insurance quote.

Alternate flow – contents insurance only

5a. The actor chooses to get a contents insurance quote.
6a. The system requests information about the contents to be insured.

7a. The actor enters data about the contents.

8a. The system displays the contents insurance quote.

Alternate flow – both types of insurance

5a. The actor chooses to get both a buildings insurance quote and a contents insurance quote.

6, 7, 6a, 7a

8b. The system displays a contents insurance quote, a buildings insurance quote and a total.

With a modified use case, we need a modified system sequence diagram. This can be seen in Figure 2.16. There is an important addition to the notation in this diagram to show selection between alternate flows. There has historically been a degree of confusion and lack of clarity about this in the UML, but we usually show conditional statements by using square brackets, for example, [Select buildings quote OR select both quotes]. In our diagram, we then use a larger square bracket to indicate the set of operations that are part of that conditional block. There are some more complex notations but they do not add much value over this simple version.

As well as an updated system sequence diagram, we have a modified storyboard that shows the alternate flows. In this version, we also use the two icons for client pages and forms to emphasize the 'wizard' style webflow of a series of forms for user input (Figure 2.17).

FIGURE 2.16   The modified system sequence diagram

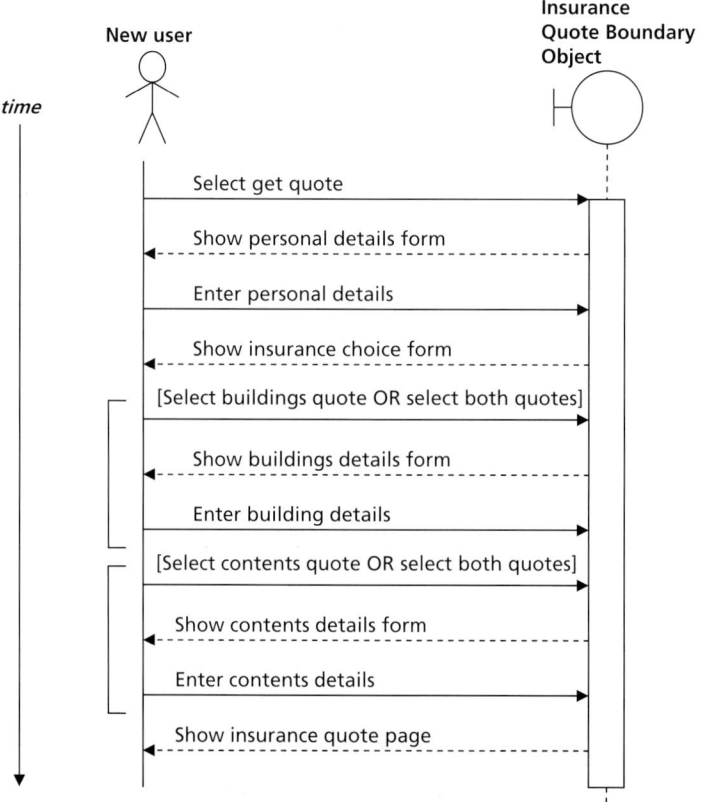

FIGURE 2.17 Updated storyboard with client page and form icons

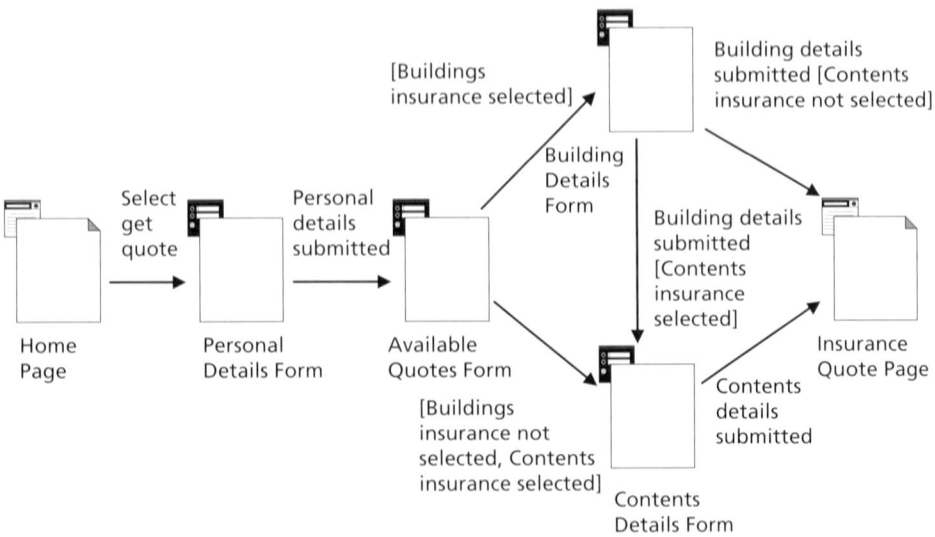

Building details
submitted [Contents
insurance not selected]

[Buildings
insurance selected]

Building
Details
Form

Select
get
quote

Personal
details
submitted

Building details
submitted
[Contents
insurance
selected]

Home
Page

Personal
Details Form

Available
Quotes Form

[Buildings
insurance not
selected, Contents
insurance selected]

Contents
details
submitted

Insurance
Quote Page

Contents
Details Form

2.8 From analysis to design

So far we have touched on the key stages of the requirements gathering and analysis processes for developing a web application by exploring some aspects of a single use case. In the last part of this chapter, we introduce some concepts related to moving from analysis to design.

In an iterative process, the transfer from analysis to design can be seamless, simply a matter of continually adding more detail. However the level of documentation that we use in the analysis discipline has the important characteristic of being largely non-technical and understandable by non-developers. As such, analysis documents such as use case diagrams and storyboards can be directly used in discussions with customers and potential users. As we move into design, we begin to move away from diagrams that are readily understood by those outside the development team and move either into more detailed diagrams that clearly reflect the chosen tools and techniques of implementation or, if using an agile approach, simply embody the emergent design in the code itself.

Design is technology-aware

Requirements analysis is about defining the problem domain and specifying how we anticipate that the system will be used from the user perspective. From this viewpoint, it is technology-agnostic, meaning that we do not have to know about the technology used to solve the problem, only the characteristics of the solution that we want. In contrast, design is about how we plan the solution, so it is technology-aware. This means that we cannot design a solution until we know something about the way that we will build it. If you were asked, for example, to design a can opener, you would probably be able to come up with a reasonable design, because you probably already have some idea about the way that can openers work. If, however, you were asked to design a time machine, you would probably struggle, being unfamiliar with time machine technology. You can contrast this with analysing the requirements for a time machine, which would be perfectly possible in the absence of knowing about the design. Although our analogy suggests that there is large gulf between analysis and design, the transition from analysis to design is a gentle one in an iterative process. Unlike going over a waterfall, our design starts off at a high level, not too far removed from our analysis, and becomes more detailed.

Architectural design

If, to successfully design in detail, you need to understand the technology of the solution, it would be premature to talk about detailed design in the early part of this book. As we work though the chapters and the case study, you will learn a number of technologies and, once you know these, you will be able to design systems that use them in detail. However, at this stage, our approach to design will be at a higher level, often known as *architectural design*. The over-all architectures of web applications reveal some common themes regardless of the actual domain of the application. These common themes can be encapsulated into design patterns, which enable us to reuse design features between different systems. The concepts of design patterns in software first became popular in the 1990s, in particular with the publication of (Gamma *et al.* 1995). This introduced the software community to the idea that common components of software design, developed over multiple applications, could be reused by other applications. These patterns can be expressed in a number of ways, but typically they include some sort of diagram, which may be written using the UML or something more informal.

Static and dynamic content

An important consideration in our design will be the balance between static and dynamic content, and how we represent that content. Our design has to take into account how much of the application will be represented by pages that are static (are the same for every client) and how much will have to be dynamically generated content. In most web applications, there will be a proportion of the site that consists of static content such as HTML, Portable Document Format (PDF), images, video or other types of content that are served to every client. On the other hand, any useful web application will almost certainly have to include dynamic content generated on the fly for specific clients, using some type of server-page technology. This is why distinguishing between different types of page is useful in design diagrams.

2.9 Webflow design

Earlier in this chapter, we introduced some analysis-level diagrams that used web application extension symbols to show how the dependencies between a series of form pages and a final client page might describe the structure of a user webflow. While this client-centric view of a webflow is helpful at the analysis stage, because it helps us to visualize how the client interacts with the web application, at the design stage we have to consider both the client and the server. In this section, we introduce a design model for webflow that describes the structural relationships between client and server that can support the generation of dynamic content. In these diagrams, we introduce another WAE icon, representing a server page (Figure 2.18).

We begin with a simple model of a single HTTP request–response interaction, where an HTML form within a static web page submits its content to the server and a client page is dynamically built and sent back to the client. In this first model (Figure 2.19), we assume

FIGURE 2.18　The WAE server page icon

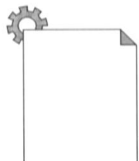

FIGURE 2.19　A form on a static web page, submitted to a server page that builds a client page

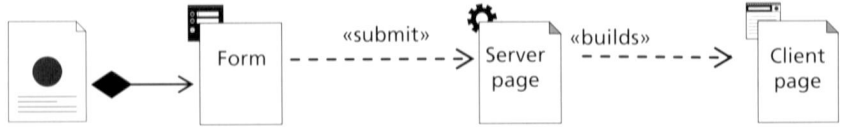

that the server page both manages any necessary business logic and generates the HTML response.

This model is similar to the ones we introduced at the analysis stage, but includes the server page, which builds the client page dynamically. Although this model of dependencies works within the context of a single request–response cycle, it has some drawbacks. The main problem is that we started with an assumption that the form was part of a static web page. This mix of static and dynamic pages does not work particularly well. For example, if the form is not dynamically generated then it cannot be repopulated with error messages and previous entries if the user makes a mistake when entering data in the form. This means that the user would have to start again from scratch if the data entered was for some reason invalid. Another serious problem is that it may not be possible to maintain a user's 'session' over a series of interactions. HTTP is a stateless protocol, which means that it does not maintain connections between a client and a server. Instead, each request–response cycle may use a new connection to the server. Because of this, the server cannot 'remember' the client using the HTTP connection, so instead we have to manage a server-side session component, which keeps track of a particular user. Each session on the server has a unique identifier for the client, and that identifier must also be available to the client. When the client sends a request, the session ID can be sent along with the request and the server can locate the client session with the matching ID. The problem with this is that the preferred way to store the session ID on the client is in a browser *cookie* (a small piece of text-based data that a browser can extract from an HTTP response and store in a file) but the user may have chosen to disable cookies in their browser. If this is the case, the server must use another way of storing the session ID on the client and this requires the use of dynamically generated web pages, because the session ID has to be written into the pages themselves.

Dynamic client pages

Given the problem with mixing static and dynamic content described above, our next design model uses only dynamically generated client pages (Figure 2.20). This makes

FIGURE 2.20 Page structure that includes dynamic form generation

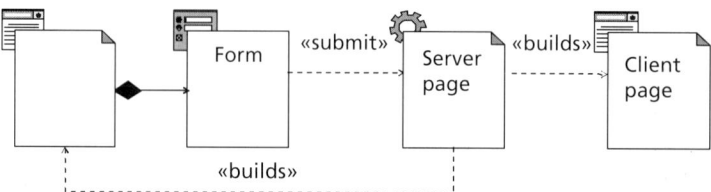

FIGURE 2.21 Including an action object and specialized server pages

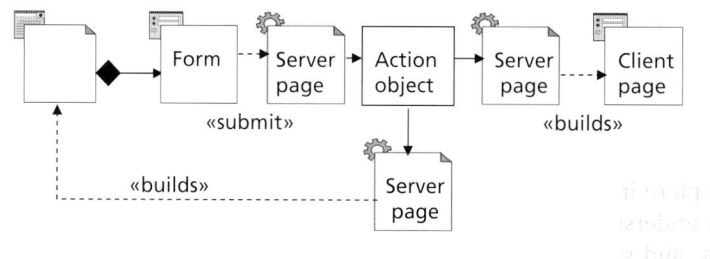

it possible for the server to guarantee that it can handle the client's session, and it is also possible for the server page to build, and rebuild, the form page so that, if the user makes a mistake when filling in the form, a new form page can be provided that contains the data they have already entered along with the necessary error messages, to help them to correct their entries.

Now, the server page dynamically generates a client page with a form, which submits back to the same server page until the next client page can be generated. Although this is a somewhat simple model, it provides the basic static structure that can provide the foundation for a dynamic webflow. There is a problem, however in that the server page is now tasked with making decisions about the webflow and generating one of two possible pages, either an updated form or the next client page. To provide a better separation of concerns a common architectural approach is to include an *action object* that takes responsibility for webflow decisions. The action object can then delegate to further server pages to either regenerate the form page or build the next client page (Figure 2.21).

Modeling dynamic webflow

The diagrams we have used so far are static diagrams showing the relationships between different web components. In order to visualize the dynamic webflow that these components contribute to, it can be useful to sketch some sequence diagrams. The sequence diagram in Figure 2.22 includes some of the participating components from the static model in Figure 2.21, identifying the messages that pass between them over time. In this case, we are only modeling the situation where the original form does not have to be regenerated, but this can easily be added to the diagram using a condition, as we did in Figure 2.16.

The diagram in Figure 2.22 represents the typical interactions in one request–response cycle for a web application. However, before digging any deeper into our own designs we

FIGURE 2.22 Modeling the dynamic webflow with a sequence diagram

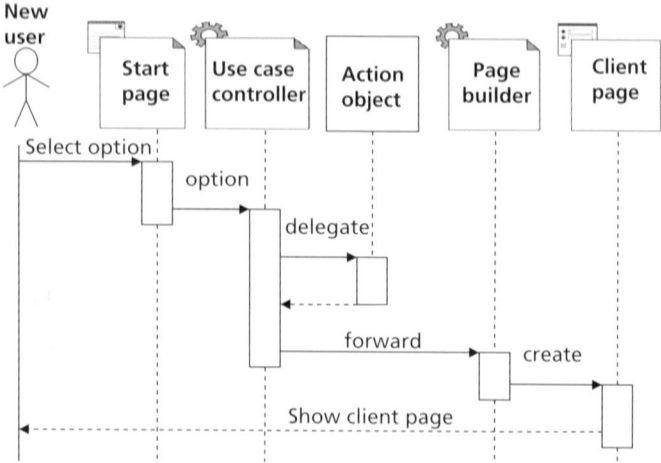

must first explore in more detail what we mean by a *server page* and an *action object*. We also need to understand what we mean by 'forward', how a server page 'delegates' to an action object, and so on. We also need to see how we can represent the contents of our domain concepts on web pages. In the chapters that follow, we explore all of these concepts and the necessary technologies to implement them. We can build a complete design once we understand how all the various components can work together.

2.10 Design patterns for web page structures

The design patterns we have looked at so far address the higher-level architecture of the system in terms of server-side components. In the final part of this chapter, we look at some page-design patterns that are relevant to the client. Like the patterns described previously, these patterns are reusable across many different web applications. We look at the following patterns:

- Site logo at top left
- Navigation bar
- Breadcrumbs
- Three-region layout
- Home page
- Site map
- Store content in the database

The main focus of these patterns is usability, making it easy for the user to navigate our web applications. These patterns all come from (Graham 2002).

Site logo at top left

The site logo at top left pattern is a very simple one, but one that you will see commonly used across the web. The site logo, as well as appearing at the top left of the page (as the name of the pattern suggests) should also always act as a hyperlink back to the site's home page (Figure 2.23). The point of this pattern is that it enables the user at any time to have a quick and easy route back to the home page. Once you are aware of this pattern, it is very irritating to visit sites that do not use it!

Navigation bar

Earlier, we introduced use cases as a way of specifying our actors' high-level goals for the web application. These main use cases will be starting points for user navigation. Within these high-level use cases, there may be a number of more detailed use cases that relate to specific tasks. The navigation bar pattern is a way of providing the user with a simple way of navigating a web site based on this combination of general tasks and related sub-tasks. The pattern suggests that the main use cases will appear in a navigation bar across the top of the page, making it easy for users to perform the most important functions easily. The left-hand side can be used for service navigation (i.e. what is inside the current use case). This would enable someone to access a high-level use case such as 'Contact Us', and the service navigation bar might include use case options inside that high-level use case, such as 'office locations', 'email addresses', 'departments' etc. Figure 2.24 shows the general layout of a page using the navigation bar pattern.

The navigation bar will include the 'site logo at top left' pattern which, as we have seen, already acts as a home page link. It also typically includes links to information about the organization or company that owns the web site, such as their privacy policy and contact information. More specific links will depend on the nature of the web application. For example, e-commerce sites would include registration and login, checkout, shopping cart and account information. There are a whole range of other possibilities, depending on the type of application. These may include downloadable items, a site map, communities, frequently asked questions, news and press releases, jobs, etc.

In the WebHomeCover application, the high-level use cases for the navigation bar would include those we have already seen, for example 'change policy details'. For this use case,

FIGURE 2.23 The 'site logo at top left' pattern

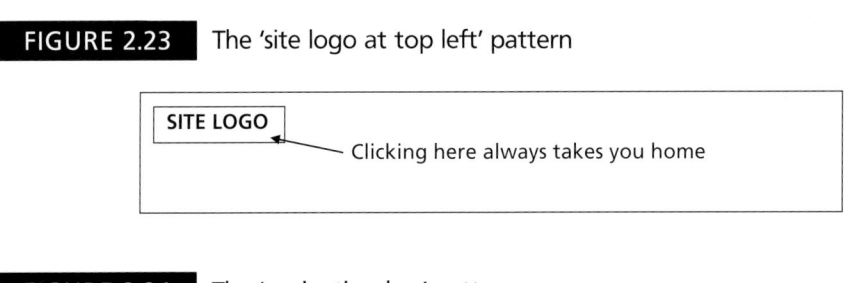

FIGURE 2.24 The 'navigation bar' pattern

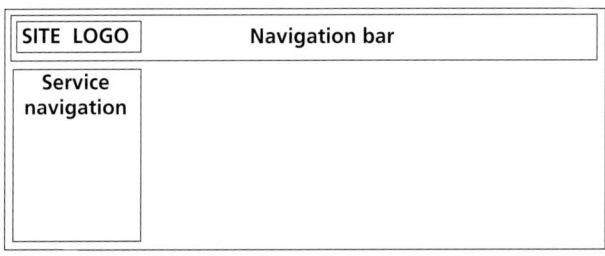

the service navigation bar might include detailed use case options such as 'change address', 'change level of cover', 'add cover', etc.

Breadcrumbs

The idea of breadcrumbs comes from fairy stories where the characters leave a trail of breadcrumbs through the woods in order to find their way home again. In stories, these are usually eaten by birds, leading to disaster, but this is unlikely to happen on web sites. The role of breadcrumbs is to tell the user where they are relative to the home page. Each time the user moves to a new page, another breadcrumb is added to the list, so it is easy for the user to see the path they have taken through the site. In addition, the components of the breadcrumb list should be hyperlinked, so clicking on any breadcrumb will take you to that page. Breadcrumbs are often a secondary part of the navigation bar and may be used in conjunction with a search box (Figure 2.25).

Three-region layout

The three-region layout pattern is actually based largely on the patterns we have already introduced (site logo at top left, the navigation bar and breadcrumbs). If we use these patterns, two regions (the top and side navigation bars) are already used, and we are left with a main page area, which will contain the current content (Figure 2.26). This pattern is very common in web applications, and can be implemented using tables, frames or style sheets. We favour style sheets over tables and tables over frames, since one rule we should be aware of is 'no frames on public sites'. The main reason for not using frames is that browser support is not very reliable for frames, in particular when presenting pages on the mobile Internet. However we may consider not using the three-region layout at all when supporting mobile clients, and favour simpler approaches that separate out the navigation

FIGURE 2.25 The 'breadcrumbs' pattern

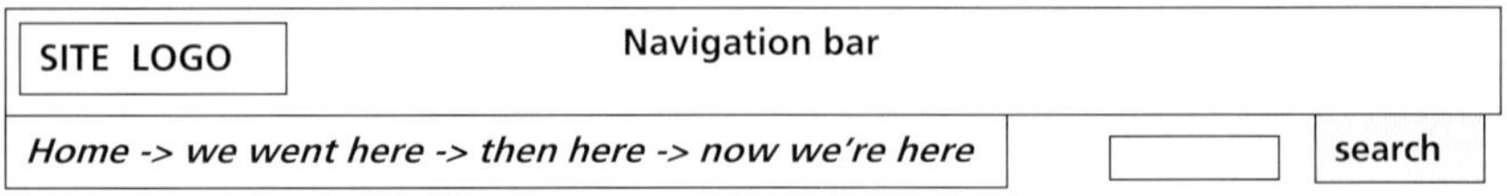

SITE LOGO	Navigation bar		
Home -> we went here -> then here -> now we're here		[ ]	search

FIGURE 2.26 The 'three-region layout' pattern

SITE LOGO	Brand and structure navigation
Service navigation	Content

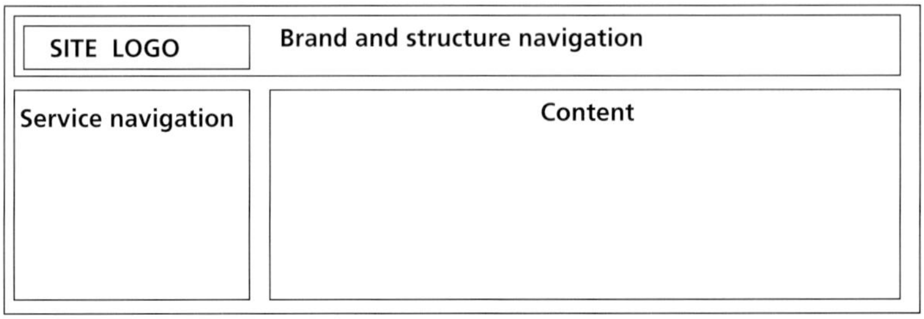

from the content. We address these issues when we look at adaptive web applications for mobile clients in chapter 14. Although many sites still use tables for structure, increasing browser support for sophisticated style sheets makes them the more favoured approach.

Home page

The three-region layout is recommended as a consistent layout for all the pages on a web site. The home page, however, can be an exception to the three-region layout rule, since it has a special role as the starting point for users, and can therefore have some special characteristics. It should not, however, be just a splash screen, which users may find frustrating as it may take a long time to load and run (if, for example, it includes an animation or movie, as some web sites favour). Rather, it needs to include navigation to the main use cases to enable the user to quickly and easily get started on their goals. Figure 2.27 shows a suggested outline for the home page pattern. It gives the site logo more prominence than does the three-region layout pattern, placing it in the centre of the screen. Beneath the logo there is some brief information that should convey the main message of the web site. Beneath this message, prominent links, perhaps using buttons or images, provide quick access to all the most important use cases in the system. Finally, some more information about the main features of the site may appear. Overall the intention of the home page pattern is to have a high level of impact while enabling the user to get started on their goals as quickly as possible.

Site map

One of the suggested links for the navigation bar is the site map. Like the home page, the site map has a special role in a web application, because it provides a bird's eye view of the whole application to the user, allowing direct access to any part of the site (or at least those parts that would sensibly allow direct access) without needing to know how to navigate through other pages. Many site maps are just lists of text. However a more interesting and useful site map would provide a workflow overview, showing not just a list of links but a visual map of the routes through the web application. Exactly how the site map might appear depends on the application, but Figure 2.28 indicates some of the features that might be included: visual components that represent hyperlinks to web pages but also some indication of the links that already exist between these pages. There are many ways of laying out a graphical site map. A web search for 'graphical site map' should give you plenty of links to sites with different styles that can be used.

FIGURE 2.27   The 'home page' pattern

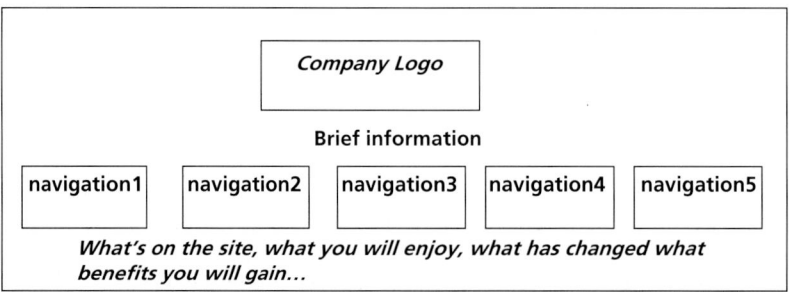

FIGURE 2.28 The 'site map' pattern

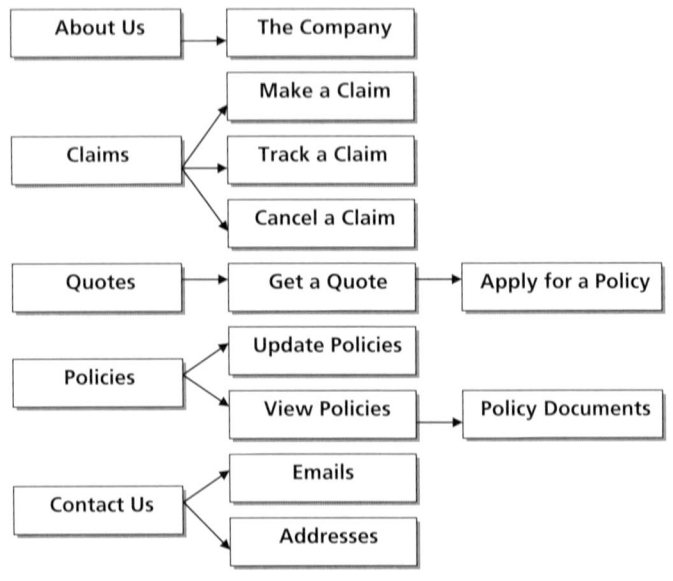

FIGURE 2.29 Reusing content across multiple pages

Store content in the database

Web applications often have to provide the same content across many different pages of a web site. Figure 2.29 shows a very simple example of this type of requirement. Here, we may want to add a simple footer ('© WebHomeCover.com 2000–2008') to the bottom of every page. The last thing we would want to have to do would be to add this to every single page and have to maintain each instance of this data separately. If, for example, we had 154 pages in our web application, and we wanted to update the footer to '© Web HomeCover.com 2000–2009', we would have to do this 154 times. It should be noted that the footer example has a number of simple solutions, because it is consistent across every page, but it illustrates a concept that is very common in web applications, which is that the same underlying data may need to appear in different ways across different parts of a web site. As a more complex example, consider a site where the user logs in. In applications like this, the user's login name, or perhaps some alias, often appears somewhere on the pages that they visit after the point where they have logged in.

The most important pattern that we have in dynamic web applications is simply to store content in a database. Maintaining a web application can get very complex, and we do not want to have to copy and paste large amounts of content for every update to the application. Therefore we need to store content in one place, in the database, and construct pages dynamically. To take our simple 'footer' example, the string of text used for the page footer could be stored in one place, in the database, and read from that database each time it is required in a page. If the footer needs to be updated, it only needs to be updated in one place – the database.

General design guidelines

There are many sources for general design guidelines for web applications. These examples are taken from (Sparks 2004).

- Design around existing content, not future content

A web application should be based around what you already have, not what you might have later. This is a basic principle of agile development – we get the simplest thing possible working early and then develop it over time. An over-complex application structure designed to cater for things that might come along later is unnecessary.

- Avoid unnecessary images

Images take time to load and every image download is a separate HTTP connection. There are many contexts (e.g. on a mobile device) where this is a major overhead. Don't use images where text will suffice.

- Exploit hyperlinks

Use hyperlinks as much as possible. This is really only directly relevant to static rather than dynamic content, since in a lot of dynamic content scenarios we have to guide the user through a restricted set of pathways. However we should make sure that the navigation around our site is well supported by hyperlinks.

- Use cascading style sheets

As well as being difficult to build and maintain, HTML that includes its own presentation specification can get very large. Using cascading style sheets (covered in Chapter 4) reduces the size of HTML page downloads.

- Make navigation flow

This is an important aspect of web applications, because the user workflow has to make sense. We need to take care to provide the right number of user pathways from particular points in time. One important aspect is making sure that the user can backtrack correctly from any point in a web application, for example being able to get out of the checkout in an on-line purchasing situation in a controlled way.

- Visit your own site regularly

You are more likely to spot problems in your web applications by approaching them as a user from the outside in, rather than just looking at them from the developer perspective, from the inside out.

Exercises

2.1 Using the example of a customer login, where the user enters a user name and password into a form on a client page, draw a sequence diagram showing the various interactions. Consider the web flow for both a successful and an unsuccessful login.

2.2 Create the following artefacts for the 'View policy details' use case:

- A use case description with at least one alternate flow
- A system sequence diagram
- A storyboard

Are there any updates that you feel are necessary to the domain model?

2.3 This exercise is best done in groups, so you can try out the idea of a requirements workshop. You need to identify some high-level requirements, a domain model and a use case diagram for this project:

Project description: Many research studies rely on questionnaires to gather their data. Doing this on-line can help to improve the number of returns, so your team has been asked to develop a web application to support the creation of web-based research questionnaires. The system needs to be able to gather questionnaire data, store it, allow it to be retrieved and generate simple statistical reports.

In your requirements workshop, adopt some roles that you think would be appropriate to this scenario and consider the requirements of the stakeholders in those roles.

2.4 Design a home page for the WebHomeCover application, selecting the most important use cases and messages from the analysis.

2.5 Design the web page structure for any of the high-level use cases described in this chapter. Use the three-region layout, with all the high-level use cases in the top-level navigation bar and service-level navigation on the left-hand side.

2.6 Take the basic designs of your home page and three-region layout from Exercises 2.4 and 2.5 and apply them to the questionnaire application from Exercise 2.3.

2.7 Consider how the webflow might work for a simple questionnaire that has five questions, each appearing on a separate page. What might the breadcrumb trail look like after you had answered the final question?

SUMMARY

This chapter began by looking at how requirements might be gathered and analysed in order to develop a web-based application, introducing some practices such as joint development workshops and use case analysis. We applied some notation from the UML, including some special extensions for web applications, to help us describe components and workflows within a web-based system. We also saw how the iterative approach and phases of the Unified Process can help us to organize a web development project. In the latter part of the chapter, we focussed on architectural approaches to web application design, introducing important aspects of server-side components and webflow. We introduced some common design patterns for web pages, intended to assist in the usability of a web application. Table 2.1 summarises the terms that were introduced in this chapter. In the chapters that follow, we apply the architectural and usability patterns as we begin to build the components and interactions of a working web application.

TABLE 2.1   Terms introduced in this chapter

Acronym	Meaning
CSS	Cascading Style Sheets
MoSCoW	Must have, Should have, Could have, Want to have
PDF	Portable Document Format
ROI	Return on Investment
UML	Unified Modeling Language
UP	Unified Process
WAE	Web Application Extensions

References and further reading

Cockburn, A. (2005) *Crystal Clear: A human-powered methodology for small teams*. Boston: Addison-Wesley.

Conallen, J. (1999) *Building Web Applications with UML*. Reading, MA: Addison-Wesley.

Conallen, J. (2001) 'Modeling Web-Tier Components'. *Dr. Dobbs Journal*. http://www.ddj.com/dept/architect/184414696

Fowler, M. (2002) *Patterns of Enterprise Application Architecture*. Addison-Wesley.

Gamma, E., Helm, R., Johnson, R. and Vlissides, J. (1995) *Design Patterns: Elements of reusable object-oriented software*. Addison-Wesley.

Graham, I. (2002) *A Pattern Language for Web Usability*. London: Addison-Wesley.

Jacobson, I. (2004) *What I don't like in RUP*. http://www.jaczone.com/postcards/.

Rosenberg, D., Stephens, M. and Collins-Cope, M. (2005) *Agile Development with Iconix Process: People, process and pragmatism*. New York: Apress.

Sparks, M. (2004) *Extreme Website Design*. Exoftware Agile Solutions, http://www.exoftware.com/whitepapers

Structure and Content in the Presentation Layer: the HyperText Markup Language (HTML)

LEARNING OBJECTIVES

- **To understand the origins of HTML**

- **To understand the importance of separating content, structure and presentation in web applications**

- **To be able to create HTML pages using mark-up**

INTRODUCTION

In this chapter, and the ones that follow, we trace the development of the mark-up languages that have been used to structure and present the pages on the web: HTML, CSS, XML and XHTML. HTML is covered in detail in this chapter and CSS in Chapter 4, followed later by various aspects of XML that relate to web applications. We begin by looking at some of the key features of the common root of these mark-up languages, SGML, which will introduce us to some of their main features. We move on to see how HTML can be used to build web page structure and content, including lists and tables. We conclude the chapter by seeing how HTML forms can be used to submit data from a browser to a server using an HTTP request.

3.1 Where it all begins – SGML

In this book we use a number of different, but similar, types of mark-up syntax. Mark-up is information that comes over and above the content of a document to give us guidance about its structure or presentation. These mark-up indicators are generally known as 'tags'. Mark-up is a type of *metadata*, in that it enables us to provide *data about data*, for example by specifying how some data should be organized on a web page. Most of the mark-up syntax we look at has a common origin in Standard Generalized Mark-up Language (SGML). Although this language had many roots, a major thread in the story was earlier work at IBM, where Charles Goldfarb, Ed Mosher and Ray Lorie developed a mark-up language in 1969 that was named after the initial letters of their surnames: GML. This was published publicly (i.e. outside of IBM) in 1973. The basic principles of this language, as expressed at that time, were that it should be possible to design a generalized mark-up language so that the mark-up would be useful for more than one application or computer system. The mark-up would be defined by tags that meant information that was marked up by a particular type of tag would be processed in exactly the same way, regardless of where the tag appeared or however many times it was used. The actual processing, however, would not be defined in the mark-up, since this would depend on the context in which the document was being processed. As GML was further developed, one of the important features that was added was the possibility of *validation*, meaning that a document that used GML mark-up could be checked to ensure that it used that mark-up in an appropriate way. This meant that it was necessary to have some way of expressing the correct ways that a particular set of mark-up tags could be used (Goldfarb 1996).

Later, SGML was developed from the foundations of GML and various other similar research efforts. In 1978, the American National Standards Institute (ANSI), with Goldfarb strongly involved, established the Computer Languages for the Processing of Text committee, and published the first draft of SGML in 1980. Unlike GML, SGML is not named after anyone, but stands for Standard Generalized Markup Language. It also differs from GML in the way that it expresses mark-up, so although it is similar in principle it is different in syntax. In 1986, with the participation of the International Standards Organisation (ISO), the first international standard for SGML was published.

Before we look at the specific mark-up languages of interest in this chapter, in particular HTML and XML, we introduce some very basic concepts that both of these languages (and others) take from SGML. These concepts are tags, elements, attributes and 'well-formedness'.

Tags

Although there is some flexibility about the way that tags can be expressed in SGML, the 'reference' syntax uses angle brackets to indicate a tag. The name of the tag appears between the angle brackets, like this:

```
<tag_name>
```

This is in fact a start tag, which means that it indicates the start of the content that is to be marked up using this tag. At the end of the marked up content, there is an end tag, which is similar to the start tag, except that the tag name is preceded by a forward slash, i.e.

```
</tag_name>
```

Elements

A pair of start and end tags, and the marked-up content in between, is known as an *element*. The general format for an element is therefore:

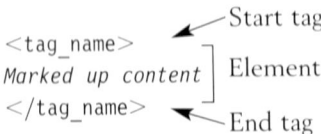

The characteristics defined by the tag are applied to the content of the element. Elements can have other elements nested inside them, to any level of nesting. A nested element is known as a 'child' element, and begins and ends inside its 'parent' element.

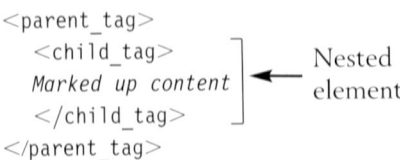

Attributes in tags

Some elements have *attributes*, which configure the element in some way. Attributes appear inside the opening tag and consist of one or more name–value pairs, using the format:

```
attribute_name="attribute_value"
```

For example, if we had an element called 'document', it might have an attribute called 'language' with a value that used a standard language code, such as French (fr):

```
<document language="fr">
```

Single quotes can be used around attribute values instead of double quotes, i.e.

```
<document language='fr'>
```

It is important to make sure that the double and single quotes you use are the vertical type (Unicode character numbers 22 and 27 respectively) known as the *quotation mark* and the *apostrophe*. Be careful if you edit your XML documents in a word processor, because it will probably use the left and right quotation marks (numbered 91–94 in Unicode), which will cause errors in your documents. Rather than a word processor, it is therefore better to use a dedicated editor for mark-up (such as XMLSpy) or a text editor to create and edit your files.

Attributes are used in a different way from elements because they are about providing metadata to an element. In other words, they are used to provide extra information about an element or apply some additional configuration to it. The language in which a document is written is information about the document, not part of its content, so specifying the language as an attribute makes more sense than using an element.

An element may have more than one attribute, in which case they all appear inside the opening tag. The 'document' element, as well as having a language attribute, may also have a 'type' element to indicate what type of document it is. For example, the document might be an instruction manual:

```
<document language="fr" type="manual">
```

Where an opening tag contains more than one attribute, their order is unimportant. Therefore this opening tag has exactly the same meaning as the previous one:

```
<document type="manual" language="fr">
```

Well-formed documents

Although things can become complex in SGML, the main rules for what constitutes a well-formed document are quite simple. Here, we lay out the four most important:

- In a well-formed document, all tags must be balanced so that an element has both an opening and a closing tag:

```
<tag>...</tag>
```

- Tags must be correctly nested so that a child tag must be closed before its parent tag is closed:

```
<parent_tag>
  <child_tag>
    . . .
  </child_tag>
</parent_tag>
```

- A document must have a root element that surrounds the whole document, so that its start tag is the first tag in the document and its end tag is the last.
- All attribute values must be written in quotes. Both single and double quotes are valid, but they must be matched correctly (i.e. you cannot mix single and double quotes around the same attribute value).

```
<tag name="value">  or  <tag name='value'>
```

These basic ideas from SGML apply to both the HyperText Markup Language (HTML) and the eXtensible Markup Language (XML), both of which are implementations of SGML. However, SGML has many complex rules about what syntax is valid, including a number of features that enable parts of the syntax to be minimized or omitted. This complexity helps to explain how HTML ended up as a seemingly rather inconsistent syntax and why browsers are very tolerant of variations in the use of HTML tags.

3.2 HTML– a language for web pages

In this section, we introduce the HyperText Markup Language (HTML), which is a specific implementation of SGML for marking up web pages and for years was the mainstay of the web. However, HTML is rather a blunt instrument for creating web application presentation, and it has evolved into XHTML, which we look at later.

Nevertheless, studying HTML is a good place to start if we are to understand the way that mark-up of web pages has evolved since the beginnings of the World Wide Web, and it also helps us to understand why other technologies have begun to complement or replace HTML in web applications.

HTML began with the advent of the World Wide Web in 1991, when Tim Berners-Lee at CERN (the European Organization for Nuclear Research) added the first web protocols and tools to the Internet. One of his contributions was the first version of HTML. Berners-Lee's original version contained a small number of tags, many of which survive into XHTML today. The main idea behind HTML was that it would enable documents to be *hypertext-linked* to one another, so that clicking on something in one document would take you to another, related, document. In principle, these *hyperlinks* were to be bidirectional, but HTML does not automatically do this, so hyperlinks in HTML pages work in one direction only. As the popularity of the web increased over subsequent years, and graphical browsers became more common, HTML evolved largely by an ad hoc process, with various features being added to different browsers and gradually becoming common practice. By 1995, with the proliferation of browsers and the increasing popularity of the World Wide Web, it was necessary to try to apply some more rigorous standards to the evolving language, so HTML version 2.0, which included the definition of HTML as the 'text/html' Internet media type, was defined by the Internet Engineering Task Force (IETF). The standard was simply a way of formalizing what was already in use, so HTML 2.0 'roughly corresponds to the capabilities of HTML in common use prior to June 1994' (Connolly 1995).

The next version of HTML was version 3.2, in 1996. This version was recommended as a specification by the World Wide Web Consortium (W3C), and was again a formalization of common practice. Some features added in version 3.2 included tables, Java applets and text flow around images.

Version 4.0 dates from 1998 and included new multimedia options, scripting languages, style sheets, better printing facilities, accessibility features for the disabled and internationalization support. Version 4.01 brought along some minor changes in 1999. Between 2000 and 2002, the W3C developed the specification for XHTML 1.0. This is the migration path from HTML, so future versions of HTML will in fact be XHTML specifications.

In this chapter, we introduce HTML before introducing XHTML in Chapter 5. This is partly because we need to look at XML in detail before we can fully understand XHTML. It is also so we can explore some of the issues that have come to the fore with web applications that have used HTML in the past, perhaps most significantly the tendency to mix content, structure and presentation in a single document. To address this problem the use of style sheets, covered in Chapter 4, has gradually become the required approach to HTML presentation, and this has assisted the transition from HTML to XHTML.

3.3 HTML document structural elements

HTML documents are plain text files with tags that mark up the content of the page. They become web pages when they are made available over the Internet using a web server and are rendered on the client machine using a web browser. HTML tags are enclosed in angle brackets, the same as the SGML reference syntax. Elements using HTML tags can be used to specify both the structure and the style of the information shown in a web page. The browser uses these tags to organize the text between them, applying the specified mark-up to anything between the opening and closing tags. For example the paragraph element, defined by the <P> tag, is used for organising text into paragraphs.

```
<P>some text in paragraph one ...</P>
<P>some text in paragraph two ...</P>
```

The use of upper case for element names (and lower case for attribute names) is recommended by the most recent HTML specification, version 4.01, though in fact HTML is not case-sensitive so this is just a convention rather than a requirement:

> Element names are written in uppercase letters. ... Attribute names are written in lowercase letters. ... Recall that in HTML, element and attribute names are case-insensitive; the convention is meant to encourage readability (Raggett *et al.* 1999).

We will see in Chapter 4 that XML and XHTML use lower case letters for element names. Therefore it will be immediately obvious to you as you see mark-up in this book that if the element names are upper case then the example is in HTML 4.01, and if they are in lower case then the mark-up is XML or XHTML.

Paragraphs, and other similar elements, can be regarded as *structural* elements because they organize the content in some semantic way. In other words, they help us to under-stand its meaning. A paragraph usually groups together some sentences that refer to the same topic. Similarly, a tag such as <H1>, for main heading elements, can be seen as structural. Organizing text into headings, subheadings, paragraphs, etc. is about providing structure in terms of how different blocks of text relate to one another. It does not, how-ever, specify how those headings, subheadings etc. should look. In contrast, HTML also contains many tags that are to do with the presentational styles of a document, to change the font, color or other aspects of style. A simple example of this type of tag is the *bold* (<B>) tag:

```
<B>this text will be presented in bold face</B>
```

A tag like this is specifically used to define how part of the document looks when displayed and has nothing to do with the structure or semantics of the text. We will not be covering presentational mark-up in this chapter. The preferred way of handling the presentation of a page is to use cascading style sheets (CSS), which we cover in Chapter 4.

Creating an HTML document

The simplest possible HTML document contains a small set of structural and content elements. These are HTML, HEAD, TITLE and BODY. The first and the last thing in an HTML document should always be the tags that surround the root (HTML) element, i.e. <HTML> ... </HTML>. Inside the HTML element, there is a nested HEAD element, <HEAD> ... </HEAD> that contains the document header information, including the title of the document. The TITLE element is nested inside the HEAD element, using <TITLE> and </TITLE> tags. The content of the TITLE element appears at the top of the browser's title bar, in the history list and in your bookmark file if you create a bookmark to the page. The BODY element comes after the HEAD element.

The BODY element represents the page content that is shown in a browser window. Here is an HTML document with this minimal set of elements:

```
<HTML>
   <HEAD>
      <TITLE> The title of the web page </TITLE>
   </HEAD>
   <BODY> body content of the web page </BODY>
</HTML>
```

Content types

Within the document body, the content is frequently organized into blocks of textual information, such as headings, paragraphs, lists and tables. There may also be other *media types* in the body, such as images, sound clips and movies. A media type is some kind of Multipurpose Internet Mail Extension (MIME) type that defines a particular type of file that can be used on the Internet. Since HTML 4, the preferred term is *content type*, since *media type* is more properly applied to types of output device. Regardless, the type of an HTML document is 'text/html', but such documents may contain references to content that is of a different type. HTML provides a large number of tags for organizing the structure of a document's content, including all the other content types that may be included inside it. In this chapter we look at the main organizing elements: headings, paragraphs, lists, tables and forms.

Text elements

Much of the content of web pages is based on the management of text. The structure of the text can be organized using headings, subheadings and paragraphs. Some other types of content can usefully be structured in terms of lists (which may be ordered in some way) or tables. There are also certain semantic aspects of text that can be included in mark-up, to provide emphasis or indicate quotations, for example. In this section, we look at some of the basic structural elements that assist in organising content in HTML pages.

A very common way of organizing text-based content is to use headings, subheadings and paragraphs. The H1, H2, H3, H4, H5 and H6 elements can be used for various levels of heading and subheading. H1 is the largest heading and H6 the smallest. Because a heading is generally larger than the text that follows, it may not be sensible to use more than the first two or three levels of heading. In many browsers, the smallest heading types are smaller than standard paragraph text.

As we have already seen, the HTML syntax for a paragraph element is <P>. You should also add the closing </P> tag at the end of each paragraph to make the element 'well formed', though most browsers will still display the page correctly without the closing tag. This is an aspect of *minimization*, a feature of SGML, which means that not all elements need to have closing tags, if the end of an element can be inferred from other parts of the document structure, such as the beginning of another paragraph inferring the end of the previous one. Browsers generally leave a blank line before a paragraph element. In the example below, we use an H1 element for a main heading and H2 elements as subheadings, with the main body of the text in paragraphs, surrounded by <P> . . . </P> tags.

This example also includes the comment syntax in HTML, which looks like this:

```
<!-- this is a comment -->
```

We will use this comment syntax throughout the book to indicate the source file that is being referred to in each example.

```
<HTML>
  <HEAD>
    <TITLE>Versions of HTML</TITLE>
  </HEAD>
  <BODY>
    <!-- File: example3-1.htm -->
    <H1>Versions of HTML</H1>
    <H2>HTML 1.0</H2>
    <P>
The first version of HTML dates from 1991, and was developed by Tim Berners-Lee.
It was very different from the HTML we know today...
    </P>
    <H2>HTML 2.0</H2>
    <P>
The second version of HTML, in 1996, was an attempt to standardise the language,
which was being widely implemented by different vendors' web browsers...
    </P>
  </BODY>
</HTML>
```

Figure 3.1 shows what the page looks like in Internet Explorer 7. Note the different sizes of text for headings, subheadings and paragraphs.

FIGURE 3.1   Headings, subheadings and paragraphs

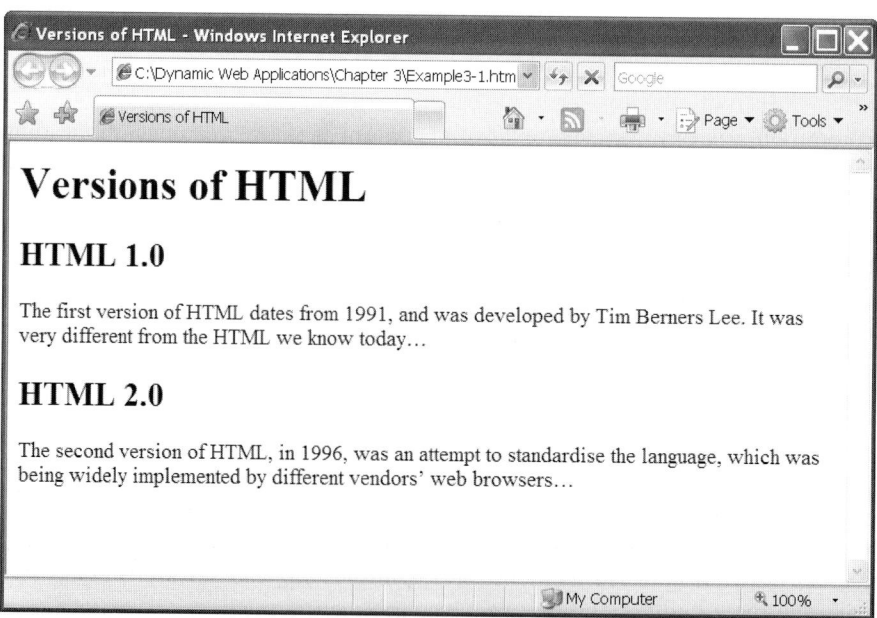

3.4 HTML document type

Browsers generally cope with poorly formed HTML syntax. However it is good practice not only to write well–formed HTML but also specify a *type definition* for the document. This helps browsers to render documents by matching their structure to a particular definition of how HTML elements and attributes should be organized.

Since HTML 4, public document type definitions (DTDs) have been available for specifying the types of HTML documents (Ragget *et al.* 1999). There are three of these DTDs: 'strict', 'transitional' and 'frameset'. The 'transitional' and 'frameset' versions allow a wider range of elements and more flexible structure than the 'strict' version and allow extensive mixing of presentation with content and structure. We look more closely at DTDs and how they can be used to validate the structure of documents in a later chapter but, in the meantime, we declare that our HTML mark-up uses the 'strict' type definition. To do this, we need to add the following line to the top of our HTML documents:

```
<!DOCTYPE HTML PUBLIC "-//W3C//DTD HTML 4.01//EN"
"http://www.w3.org/TR/html4/strict.dtd">
```

This states that the document should follow the strict rules for the structure of HTML 4.01. The 'DOCTYPE' refers to a DTD that is publicly available for specifying HTML document types. Here is our first example with the necessary definition added:

```
<!DOCTYPE HTML PUBLIC "-//W3C//DTD HTML 4.01//EN"
"http://www.w3.org/TR/html4/strict.dtd">
<HTML>
   <HEAD>
     <TITLE>Versions of HTML</TITLE>
   </HEAD>
   <BODY>
     <H1>Versions of HTML</H1>
     <H2>HTML 1.0</H2>
     <P>
The first version of HTML dates from 1991, and was developed by Tim Berners-Lee.
It was very different from the HTML we know today...
     </P>
     <H2>HTML 2.0</H2>
     <P>
The second version of HTML, in 1996, was an attempt to standardise the language,
which was being widely implemented by different vendors' web browsers...
     </P>
   </BODY>
</HTML>
```

How can we use this definition to see if our HTML is, in fact correctly structured? One option is to test our document against a web-based validator, such as the one made available by the W3C Markup Validation Service at http://validator.w3.org/. Alternatively, many web development tools that support HTML editing, such as DreamWeaver or FrontPage, have their own inbuilt validation support.

Figure 3.2 shows the main page of the web-based W3C validator, which contains three tabbed options for file validation; 'Validate by URI', 'Validate by File Upload' and 'Validate by Direct Input'.

The first method of validation is by simply entering the URL of the document you wish to validate, for example: www.webhomecover.com/welcome.htm. Documents that you wish to validate by URL have to be available on-line to web users so it is not possible to validate local documents this way.

Validating by direct input means you can copy and paste your pages into a text area on the web page. This is easy for small documents. However it may be better to validate larger documents by uploading them. In this case, you can browse for the location of a local file on your computer which you wish to validate. If you copy and paste HTML mark-up into the direct input page, then the mark-up is processed using a character encoding known as 'UTF-8' (character encoding will be covered in more detail in Chapter 5). However, if you upload a page for validation, then you may get a warning that the page can only be 'tentatively' validated, unless you specify the character encoding. To avoid this warning, you can add the following META tag to the HEAD element of your HTML documents:

```
<META http-equiv="Content-Type" content="text/html; charset=UTF-8">
```

The META element provides metadata about the page to the browser. Its 'http-equiv' attribute allows extra information to be added to the normal HTTP header sent with a web page. In this example, the additional data (in the 'content' attribute) says that the page is in HTML using the UTF-8 character set. Multiple META elements can be added to the HEAD element of a page (further examples will be seen in Chapter 4).

Figure 3.3 shows the W3C validation page in action, with the page that is displayed as a result of pressing the 'Check' button with Example3–2.htm copied into the text area of the 'Direct Input' tab. This confirms that the document is valid HTML 4.01 strict.

FIGURE 3.2   The main page of the web-based W3C validator

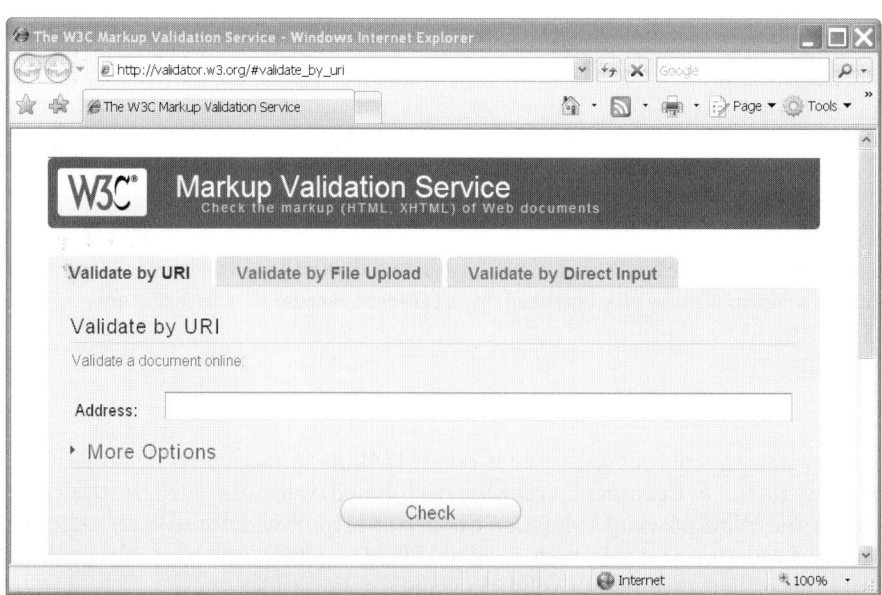

FIGURE 3.3 An HTML document being validated using the web-based W3C Markup Validation Service

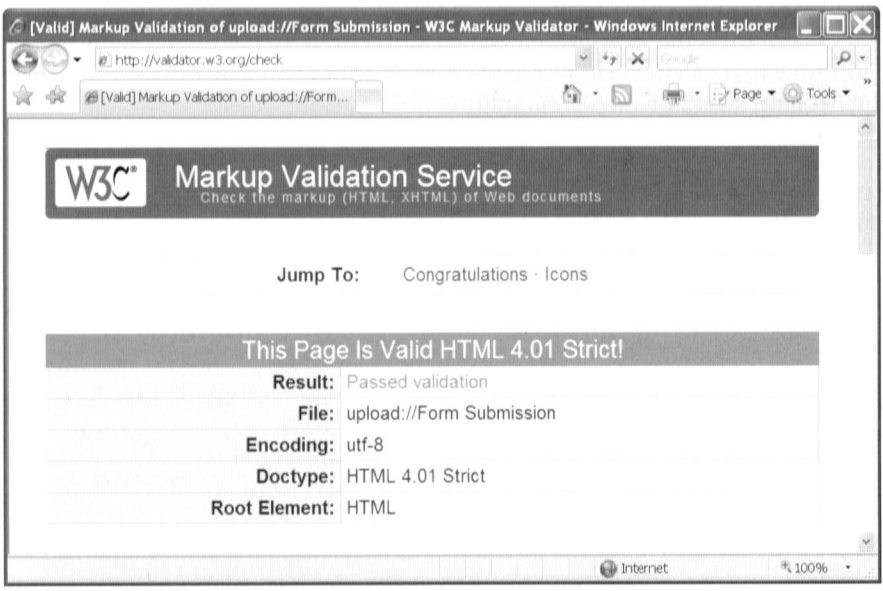

3.5 Structuring text

As well as structuring our pages into headings and paragraphs, there are a number of other structural elements that we can apply to HTML documents. In this section, we look at some of the elements that help us to structure text.

Line breaks and horizontal rules

Line breaks (BR) and horizontal rules (HR) are examples of *empty elements*. An empty element in HTML is one that, instead of having separate start and end tags, consists of a single tag, with no closing tag either required or implied. One example of an empty element in HTML is the line break, which first appeared in the HTML 2.0 specification:

```
<BR>
```

This element does not have start and end tags, but consists of a single tag that forces a line break in the document. Unlike the paragraph element, which starts a new line and leaves a space before the paragraph, a BR element starts a new line but does not force a blank line to be inserted.

The horizontal rule is another example of an empty element that dates from HTML 2.0. The tag looks like this:

```
<HR>
```

A browser usually displays the horizontal rule as a graphical line. Of course one might question whether the HR element is structural or just presentational. Its definition in the various HTML specifications has evolved from 'a divider between sections of text' via 'used to indicate a change in topic' to 'a horizontal rule to be rendered by visual user agents', so one could make a case for either interpretation (Korpela 2002).

Citations and block quotes

There are many structural elements in HTML, some more commonly used than others. Although CITE and BLOCKQUOTE are not often required, they are useful examples of elements that have some semantics attached to them; they convey something about the meaning of the text and its relationship to other parts of the document around them rather than hierarchical structure or presentation.

It is common in documents for longer quotations and citations to be structured differently from the main body of the text. HTML includes the <BLOCKQUOTE> element for long quotations and the <CITE> element for citations. The next example is similar to the last one, but is modified to include <CITE> and <BLOCKQUOTE> elements. You should note that BLOCKQUOTE elements should not directly contain text. Rather, they should contain structural elements such as paragraphs or headings, with the text inside those. Here, we use a paragraph element.

```
<!DOCTYPE HTML PUBLIC "-//W3C//DTD HTML 4.01//EN"
"http://www.w3.org/TR/html4/strict.dtd">
<HTML>
  <HEAD>
    <TITLE>Versions of HTML</TITLE>
  </HEAD>
  <BODY>
    <!-- File: example3-2.htm -->
    <H1>Versions of HTML</H1>
    <H2>HTML 1.0</H2>
    <P>The first version of HTML dates from 1991, and was developed by Tim
Berners-Lee. It was very different from the HTML we know today.
    <CITE>Tim Berners-Lee</CITE> is quoted as saying</P>
    <BLOCKQUOTE>
    <P>
If you use the original World Wide Web program, you never see a URL or have to
deal with HTML. That was a surprise to me...that people were prepared to
painstakingly write HTML.
    </P>
    </BLOCKQUOTE>
    <H2>HTML 2.0</H2>
    <P>
The second version of HTML, in 1996, was an attempt to standardise the language,
which was being widely implemented by different vendors' web browsers...
    </P>
  </BODY>
</HTML>
```

Figure 3.4 shows how the complete page looks in Internet Explorer 7.

In this browser, the citation appears in italics and the block quote is separated from the previous text and indented. It is important to note however that we are not using elements here for the purposes of indenting paragraphs or applying an italic text style. The CITE and BLOCKQUOTE elements are about the structure and meaning of the text, not controlling its appearance. We are letting the browser decide how a citation or a block quote should actually appear, so the fact that the quote is indented and the citation text is italic is not something explicitly defined.

FIGURE 3.4 Using the CITE and BLOCKQUOTE elements

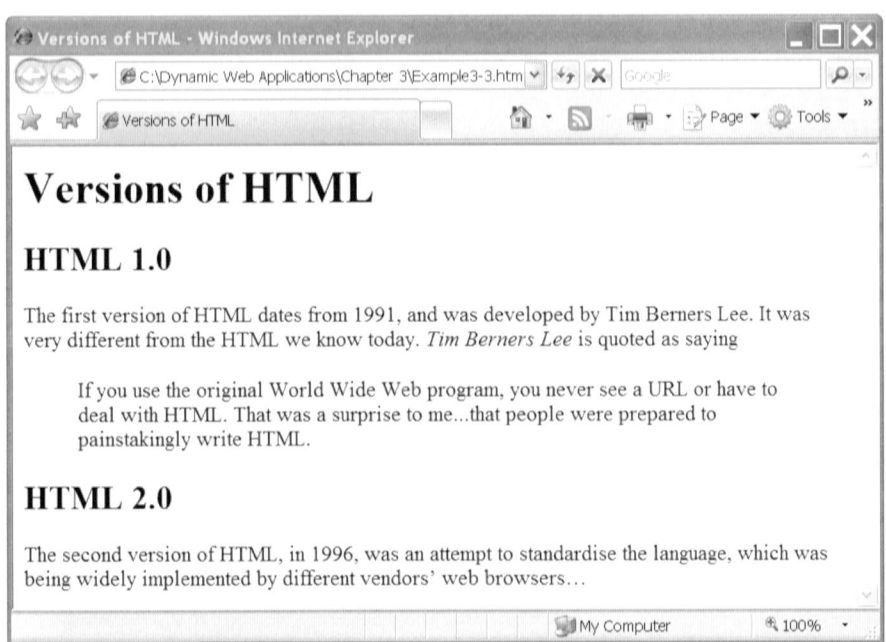

This is an important point, since we should be aware of the difference between structural and presentational tags and how to use them. The use of BLOCKQUOTE simply to indent a paragraph is *deprecated*, which means that although the tag may be displayed that way in a particular browser it should not be used simply to get that presentational effect. The BLOCK-QUOTE element is an indication that the body of the element should be given some special handling to recognize that it is a long quotation. It should not be used as a convenient way of achieving a specific format, regardless of the actual content of the element. Perhaps even more obviously, using the CITE element should not be seen simply as a way of making text italic.

Idiomatic (phrase) elements

CITE is one of the *idiomatic* or *phrase* elements. These elements relate to common types of usage in terms of how we express ourselves in writing. For example, we look for ways to emphasize specific parts of text. To support these idioms, HTML includes elements such as EM for emphasis and STRONG for stronger emphasis. Browsers usually render EM text in italics and STRONG text in bold face but, as with the CITE element, the actual way that the browser chooses to render these elements is independent of our use of the tags. We use them to indicate a type of expression, not to select a particular appearance for the text.

Subscripts and superscripts

The SUB (subscript) element uses a small font aligned towards the bottom of the regular character height; the SUP (superscript) element uses a small font aligned towards the top of the regular character height. These elements might appear to occupy a grey area between the structural and the presentational. However there are important accepted uses for these aspects of content, for example in scientific notation or in rendering some languages. Superscript is commonly used to indicate references, footnotes or trademarks,

TABLE 3.1   HTML character references

HTML character reference	Equivalent character	Meaning
&lt;	<	Less than
&gt;	>	Greater than
&quot;	"	Quotation mark
&amp;	&	Ampersand
	(a space)	Non-breaking space
&reg;	®	Registered trademark
&copy;	©	Copyright

and in mathematical formulae, while subscript is used in chemical formulae. The HTML 4 specification includes these two useful examples of superscript and subscript:

H₂0   to represent H_2O (the chemical symbol for water)

E = mc²   to represent $E = mc^2$ (Einstein's formula for relativity)

Because of these specific applications, the use of the <SUB> and <SUP> elements can be seen as structural, as long as they are applied in these generally accepted contexts rather than just for effect.

Special characters

Because HTML pages use a markup syntax, there are certain symbols, in particular < and > that have special meaning to the applications (such as browsers) that process them. HTML character references are numeric or symbolic names that can be used instead of literal characters in an HTML document. They are useful for referring to special characters outside the normal number and letter ranges in character sets, or those that have other meanings in the mark-up language and could therefore cause processing problems for browsers. All of the HTML character references begin with an & sign and end with a semicolon. Some examples of HTML character references are shown in Table 3.1.

3.6 Lists

Lists can be appropriate ways of structuring certain types of content in an HTML document. A list can present short, related items of information in an easy-to-read layout, and may be nested (i.e. a list inside a list) to produce structures such as tables of contents, indexes or document outlines. There are three types of list in HTML:

- Unordered lists
- Ordered lists
- Definition lists

Unordered lists

An unordered list is one that is given a list structure but there is no numbering or lettering to suggest a meaningful sequence. In other contexts, this type of list is known as a *bulleted list*. The browser will probably display each item in the list with a bullet symbol prefix. The tag name for an unordered list element is UL and it can contain any number of nested LI (list item) elements:

```
<UL>
   <LI> a list item </LI>
   <LI> another list item </LI>
   . . .
</UL>
```

Ordered lists

In an ordered list, the list items are numbered or lettered. This is useful for lists that have a meaningful order, such as instructions, chapters, recipes or league tables. The tag name for an ordered list is OL, with LI again used for nested list item elements:

```
<OL>
   <LI> the first list item </LI>
   <LI> the second list item </LI>
   . . .
</OL>
```

Nesting ordered and unordered lists

Lists can be nested and combined together as appropriate for the content. However there is an important thing to bear in mind when doing this, which is that any list that is nested inside another one must be in its own list item (LI) element, using this kind of structure:

```
<UL>
   <LI> an item in the main list</LI>
   <LI> Here comes a nested list. . .
     <OL>
        <LI> an item in the nested list</LI>
        <LI> another item in the nested list</LI>
        . . .
     </OL>
   </LI>
   <LI> another item in the main list</LI>
   . . .
</UL>
```

In this example from the home insurance system domain, we use both ordered and unordered lists:

```
<!DOCTYPE HTML PUBLIC "-//W3C//DTD HTML 4.01//EN"
"http://www.w3.org/TR/html4/strict.dtd">
<HTML>
   <HEAD>
     <TITLE> Making a Claim</TITLE>
   </HEAD>
   <BODY>
```

```
<!-- File: example3-3.htm -->
<H1>Useful Tips</H1>
<UL>
   <LI> Making a Claim
   <OL>
      <LI>Find as much documentation as you can (photos, receipts, etc.)
      </LI>
      <LI> Fill in the on-line claim form</LI>
      <LI> Don't do anything until an assessor has contacted you</LI>
   </OL>
   </LI>
   <LI>Changing your policy
      <OL>
         <LI> Log in to your user account </LI>
         <LI> Select 'update policy details' from the list of options </LI>
         <LI> Follow the on-screen instructions to make the required changes
         </LI>
      </OL>
   </LI>
</UL>
</BODY>
</HTML>
```

Figure 3.5 shows how the page looks in Opera 9. You will notice that the main unordered list has round bullets and the nested ordered lists are labelled with Arabic numbers. This is the behavior of the browser, not specified by our list elements.

Definition lists

Definition lists are a bit different from the other types of list because they are structured as a glossary of terms. The outer element of a definition list uses the <DL> ... </DL>

FIGURE 3.5 How nested ordered and unordered lists appear in a browser

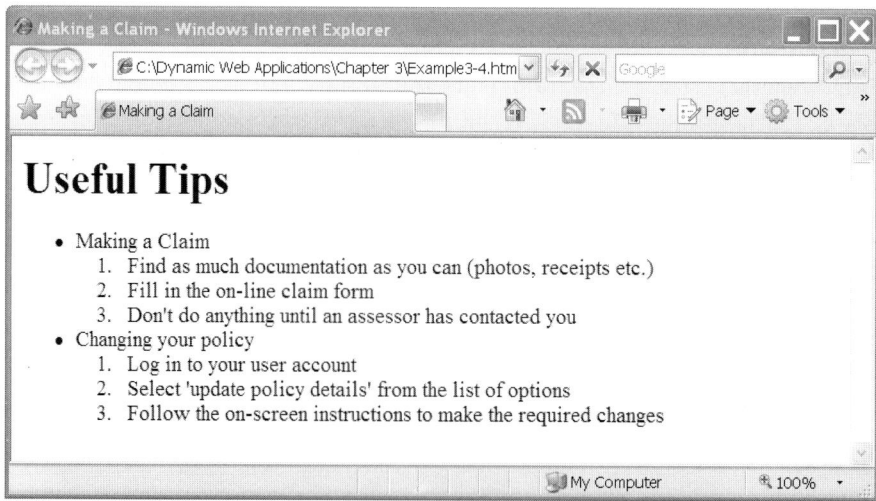

(definition list) tags. Inside this element appear one or more pairs of terms and definitions. In each pair, the term is defined by a DT (definition term) element and the definition appears in a DD (definition list definition) element. Here is an example of an HTML document containing a definition list:

```
<!DOCTYPE HTML PUBLIC "-//W3C//DTD HTML 4.01//EN"
"http://www.w3.org/TR/html4/strict.dtd">
<HTML>
    <HEAD>
        <TITLE>Markup Languages</TITLE>
    </HEAD>
        <!-- File: example3-4.htm -->
    <BODY>
        <DL>
            <DT> SGML </DT>
            <DD> Standard Generalised Markup Language </DD>
            <DT> HTML </DT>
            <DD> HyperText Markup Language </DD>
            <DT> XML</DT>
            <DD> eXtensible Markup Language </DD>
        </DL>
    </BODY>
</HTML>
```

Figure 3.6 shows how the definition list looks in Internet Explorer 7. In this browser, there is no difference in the font size or style between the definitions and the terms, only the layout is affected. We could, however, add EM or STRONG tags to provide some further semantic differentiation between definitions and terms.

3.7 Attributes in HTML

So far we have seen a number of HTML elements but none of these have included attributes. Nevertheless many HTML tags can have attributes. Many of these attributes could

FIGURE 3.6   Definition lists

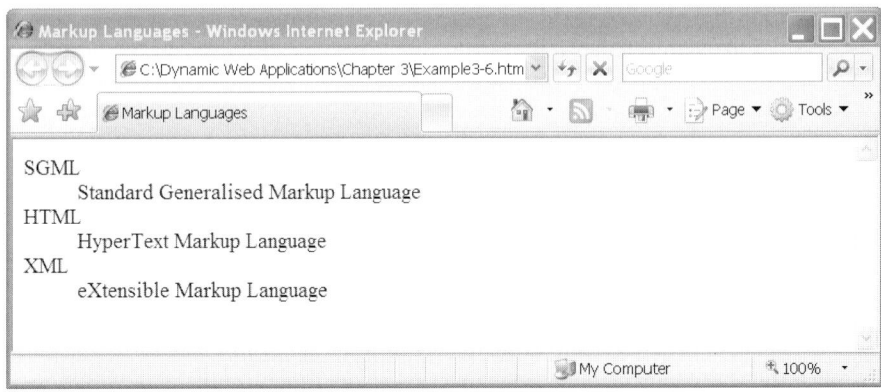

be categorized as presentational, and in fact the use of attributes for presentation in HTML gives us a good indication of how the usage of elements and attributes differs. Elements are intended for the content of a document, whereas attributes tend to provide additional configuration of these elements. If we regard presentation of an element as part of its metadata, then we can see that attributes are a good way of applying metadata to HTML elements. However attributes are not confined solely to defining presentation. They can also be used for some structural aspects, as we will see in the coming examples.

Images

Having said that we are currently dealing with content and structure rather than presentation, it may at first glance seem a little strange to be introducing images. However, an image in a web page is an instance of a *content type*, which means that it is part of the content of the page, not its presentation. It just happens to be content that has visual characteristics. Images can be added to a web page using the IMG empty element, but unlike the empty elements (BR and HR) we have seen, IMG elements cannot be used without attributes. The essential attribute is 'src', which indicates the URI of the image file to be included in the page. The most common image file types used on the web are GIF (Graphics Interchange Format), JPEG (Joint Photographic Experts Group) and PNG (Portable Network Graphics), since these have relatively small file sizes and can therefore be downloaded reasonably quickly. GIF and PNG files are typically used for drawings, while JPEGs are used for photographs as they can manage more colors than GIFs and have a more flexible compression algorithm than PNGs. The PNG format was developed when Unisys held a patent on the GIF compression algorithm, but it is also better than GIF files for rendering more than 256 colors, though the equivalent files tend to be larger than GIFs.

As well as defining the source for the image, we must also provide an alternative text value using the 'alt' attribute. This is useful both for providing a text alternative if the image cannot be loaded (for example if the user has disabled image loading in the browser for speed) and for providing text to be read out for those users who are unable to see images. Here is an IMG element that uses a GIF file as its source:

```
<IMG src="logo.gif" alt="WebHomeCover Logo">
```

The other attributes that can be used with images are 'height' and 'width', which can be used to scale the image on the page from its original size, but are more often used to specify the actual dimensions of the image (in pixels) to enable the browser to load the page faster, since it is able to anticipate the display space required before downloading the file:

```
<IMG src="logo.gif" alt="WebHomeCover Logo" height="115" width="102">
```

Links

One of the most important aspects of the World Wide Web is the *link*, also known as a *hyperlink* or a *web link*, which enables us to go from one web-based resource to another, regardless of where on the web the other resource may be. A link has two ends known as *anchors*, with the source anchor being in the current document and the destination anchor being the web resource (document, image, sound file, etc.) that is being linked to. Clicking on a link in a web page lets us retrieve the linked web resource. The full detail of links in HTML is quite complex, so we cover only the basics here.

The element name used for anchors in HTML documents is A, and the most important attribute is 'href' (hypertext reference), which contains the URI of the linked resource. Here, for example is an anchor that links to the URI of the WebHomeCover site:

```
Click <A href="http://www.webhomecover.com">here</A> for a great
insurance deal. . .
```

The text in the body of the anchor element ('here') is the actual hyperlink that appears in the browser.

Not all URIs in anchor elements need to include a full web address. Many anchors used in web applications link to other pages in the same application, so the URI can be a filename using a local path. Here, for example, the anchor refers to a file in the local directory:

```
<A href="aboutus.htm">About Us</A>
```

Relative paths can also be used. Here, we assume that there is an image file stored in an 'images' folder beneath the current folder (indicated by the '.'):

```
<A href="./images/map.gif">Find Us</A>
```

As well as linking to other files, anchors in an HTML page can link to specific parts of a document. If the target anchor is not a complete URI but within a document, then the anchor element can be used at the destination end of the link. For example, we might want to link to a part of a document that contains some terms and conditions about our insurance policies. To link to part of the same document, the URI used in the source anchor is the name of the destination anchor, preceded by a hash, for example:

```
<A href="#terms">terms and conditions</A>
```

In this example we assume that there is a destination anchor in the same document called 'terms'. This will be defined somewhere else in the document using the 'id' attribute of the anchor element, for example:

```
<A id="terms">Terms and Conditions</A>
```

Clicking on the hyperlink of the source anchor takes the user to the part of the document containing the destination anchor. The following mark-up shows how the source and destination anchors might appear in the same document:

```
Our insurance is offered according to our standard <A href="#terms">terms and
conditions</A> which you should read carefully before making a claim. . .

blah blah blah. . .

<H2><A id="terms">Terms and Conditions</A></H2>
WebHomeCover reserve the right to. . .
```

The same approach can be used when the destination anchor is in part of another document. The only difference is that the anchor name is preceded by the URI of the containing page, for example:

```
<A href="legal.htm#terms">terms and conditions</A>
```

In this case we assume that the 'terms' anchor is in another document called 'legal.html'. A full address can also be used:

```
<A href="http://www.webhomecover.com/legal.htm#terms">
  terms and conditions
</A>
```

Images, as well as text, can be used as link anchors by nesting IMG elements inside anchor elements, for example:

```
<A href="home.html">
  <IMG src="logo.gif" alt="WebHomeCover Logo">
</A>
```

This is a useful technique for implementing the 'sitelogo at top left' pattern we saw in Chapter 2, where clicking on the company logo always takes you to the home page.

If your pages pass validation by the W3C validator, you can add the following image link to them, which uses the various elements and attributes that we have introduced in this section:

```
<P>
<A href="http://validator.w3.org/check?uri=referer">
<IMG src="http://www.w3.org/Icons/valid-html401"
  alt="Valid HTML 4.01 Strict" height="31" width="88">
</A>
</P>
```

Clicking on the image invokes the validator on the W3C web site, though if your server does not send the 'referer' header in its HTTP request (for example, because a firewall has removed it), then the automatic validation cannot work.

Email links

Anchors can also be used for email links. To do this you simply use a 'mailto' value in the 'href' attribute, which takes this format:

```
<A href="mailto:help@webhomecover.com">Email the help desk</A>
```

When 'Email the help desk' is clicked, the web browser *may* open your email client to compose a message, though this does depend on the browser configuration so its behavior cannot be guaranteed.

The following example shows an HTML page that includes both links and images:

```
<!DOCTYPE HTML PUBLIC "-//W3C//DTD HTML 4.01//EN"
"http://www.w3.org/TR/html4/strict.dtd">
<HTML>
```

```
<HEAD>
  <TITLE>Our Insurance</TITLE>
</HEAD>
<BODY>
  <! - File: Example3-5.htm - >
  <P>
  <A href="home.htm">
  <IMG src="logo.gif" alt="WebHomeCover Logo" height="67" width = "294">
  </A>
  </P>
  <H1>Our Insurance</H1>
  <P>
    Our insurance is offered according to our standard
    <A href="#terms">terms and conditions</A>
    which you should read carefully before making a claim … blah blah
blah …
  </P>
  <P>
  If you have any enquiries, please <A
href = "mailto:help@webhomecover.com">
Email the help desk</A>
<H2><A id = "terms">Terms and Conditions</A></H2>
  <P>
  WebHomeCover reserve the right to … blah blah blah …
  </P>
</BODY>
</HTML>
```

Figure 3.7 shows the page displayed in Internet Explorer 7. To see the effect of the internal link, you need to resize the window so that the Terms and Conditions section is not visible before clicking the 'terms and conditions' link.

FIGURE 3.7   Links and images displayed in Internet Explorer 7

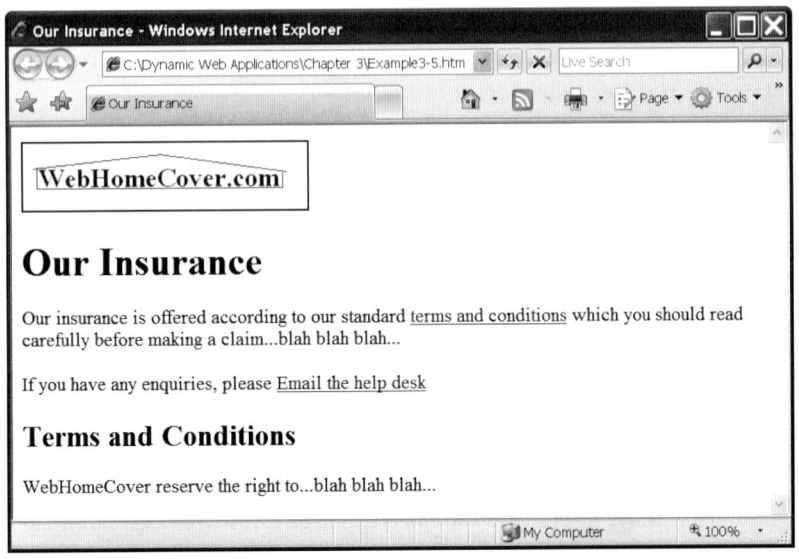

3.8 Tables

Tables can be a useful structural element in a web page. Information can often be displayed effectively using a table-based format, particularly if the data being presented has been read from a relational database, since these databases store data in tables. A table consists of rows and columns, with optional column headings and a caption. Each part of table (where a row and column meet) is known as a cell (Figure 3.8).

Table tags

In HTML 4, the table is quite a complex element, with a number of nested elements used to represent the table model which is the underlying table structure. This can be divided into the header, body and footer, and columns can be grouped together. However in this overview we cover only the basics of tables.

Table elements and rows

A table element in HTML is defined by <TABLE>...</TABLE> tags. The table element contains all the other table-related tags that specify, for example, captions, headings and data cells. The CAPTION element is optional, but it can be used to describe the table, for example:

```
<CAPTION>Our Call Centres</CAPTION>
```

Each row in the table is defined by a table row (TR) element:

```
<TR>...</TR>
```

Table cells

There are two types of table cell, those that contain column headings and those that contain data. The <TH>...</TH> (table heading) tags can optionally be used to define heading elements that are used in the top row of the table columns. Other cells are defined using the <TD>...</TD> (table data) tags.

Table example

As we work through the various aspects of HTML tables, we develop a simple example of a table that shows the locations and contact numbers of call centres. For the purposes of this example we assume that WebHomeCover has call centres in various territories, and this information will be presented on a web page in the form of a table. The following document includes TABLE element for the basic table. There is a caption ('Our Call Centres') and four columns, each with a heading cell: 'Territory', 'Location', 'Phone' and 'Fax'. There are four rows, one for each call centre.

FIGURE 3.8 The components of a table

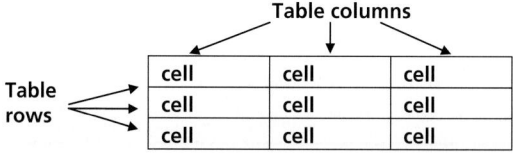

```
<!DOCTYPE HTML PUBLIC "-//W3C//DTD HTML 4.01//EN"
"http://www.w3.org/TR/html4/strict.dtd">
<HTML>
   <HEAD>
      <TITLE>Our Call Centres</TITLE>
   </HEAD>
   <BODY>
      <!-- File: example3-6.htm -->
      <TABLE>
         <CAPTION>Our Call Centres</CAPTION>
         <TR>
            <TH>Territory</TH> <TH>Location</TH> <TH>Phone</TH> <TH>Fax</TH>
         </TR>
         <TR>
            <TD>Americas</TD> <TD>New York</TD>
            <TD>0800 1425364</TD> <TD>0800 1122334</TD>
         </TR>
         <TR>
            <TD>EMEA</TD> <TD>London</TD>
            <TD>0800 1324536</TD> <TD>0800 8444463</TD>
         </TR>
         <TR>
            <TD>EMEA</TD> <TD>Cape Town</TD>
            <TD>0800 9009586</TD> <TD>0800 9944474</TD>
         </TR>
         <TR>
            <TD>APAC</TD> <TD>Sydney</TD>
            <TD>0800 1114445</TD> <TD>0800 1114445</TD>
         </TR>
      </TABLE>
   </BODY>
</HTML>
```

Figure 3.9 shows what the table looks like displayed in a browser. Note that, in this browser at least (Internet Explorer 7), the table headings are displayed in bold face to differentiate them from the table data cells.

FIGURE 3.9   A table displayed in Internet Explorer 7

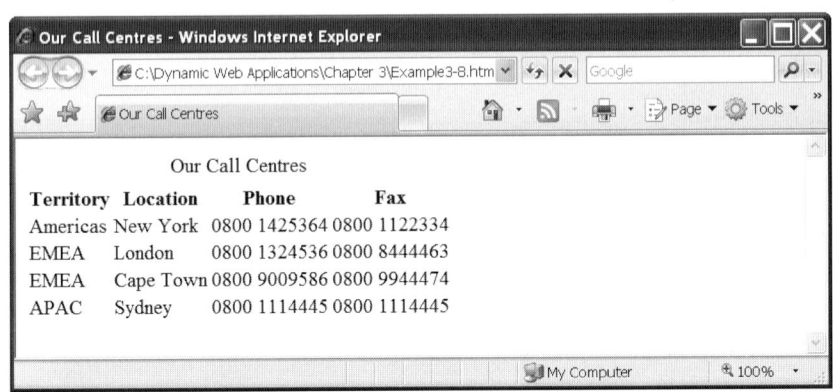

Table organization

The organization of a table can be flexible in the sense that we can choose to leave cells blank if there is no data available for them and we can also span multiple cells or columns. To leave cells blank, we can simply remove data from between the TH or TD tags. Just for the sake of this example, we might assume that the Cape Town office does not have a fax number. To leave this cell blank we just remove the data from that cell and replace it with a non-breaking space character ( ):

```
<!-- File: example3-7.htm -->
<TR>
    <TD>EMEA</TD> <TD>Cape Town</TD>
    <TD>0800 9009586</TD> <TD> </TD>
</TR>
```

Now the table displays as in Figure 3.10.

Spanning with attributes

Tables include a useful example of how attributes can be used to change the configuration of an element in HTML. As well as leaving data out of cells we can also make data span more than one cell. This is done using the 'rowspan' or 'colspan' attributes that can be applied to the TD or TH tags. For example colspan="2" means span two columns and rowspan="3" means span three rows. Figure 3.11 shows how these attributes affect the structure of the table.

In our example, there are a couple of places where the same data appears in adjacent cells. EMEA appears twice in the Territory column and the phone and fax numbers for the APAC office are the same. We might choose to restructure the table so that the same data can span across multiple cells to avoid repeating the data unnecessarily. In this version of the table, we use rowspan in the Territory column and colspan in the APAC row:

```
<!DOCTYPE HTML PUBLIC "-//W3C//DTD HTML 4.01//EN"
"http://www.w3.org/TR/html4/strict.dtd">
```

FIGURE 3.10   Leaving a blank cell in a table

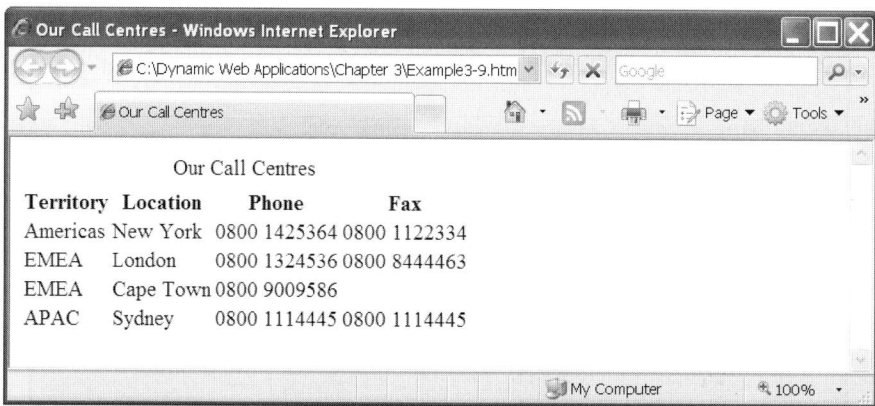

FIGURE 3.11 The effect of rowspan and colspan attributes on table cells

\<TD\>...\</TD\>	\<TD\>...\</TD\>	**\<TD rowspan="3"\>...\</TD\>**
\<TD colspan="2"\>...\</TD\>		
\<TD\>...\</TD\>	\<TD\>...\</TD\>	

```
<HTML>
  <HEAD>
    <TITLE>Our Call Centres</TITLE>
  </HEAD>
  <BODY>
    <!-- File: example3-8.htm -->
    <TABLE>
    <CAPTION>Our Call Centres</CAPTION>
      <TR>
        <TH>Territory</TH> <TH>Location</TH> <TH>Phone</TH> <TH>Fax</TH>
      </TR>
      <TR>
        <TD>Americas</TD> <TD>New York</TD>
        <TD>0800 1425364</TD> <TD>0800 1122334</TD>
      </TR>
      <TR>
        <TD rowspan="2">EMEA</TD> <TD>London</TD>
        <TD>0800 1324536</TD> <TD>0800 8444463</TD>
      </TR>
      <TR>
        <TD>Cape Town</TD> <TD>0800 9009586</TD> <TD> </TD>
      </TR>
      <TR>
        <TD>APAC</TD> <TD>Sydney</TD> <TD colspan="2">0800 1114445</TD>
      </TR>
    </TABLE>
  </BODY>
</HTML>
```

Figure 3.12 shows the table displayed in the browser. The spanned rows are easy to see because 'EMEA' has been centred between the rows. The spanned columns are not so obvious because the Sydney number is still aligned to the left. As in many other examples we have seen, presentational decisions like this are being made by the browser.

Table borders

Changing the border style of a table is presentational, not structural. However at this point it is useful to introduce a table border so we can see the effect of the spanning attributes used in the previous example. The width of the table and cell borders can be controlled using the 'border' attribute of the TABLE tag. The value of this attribute defines the width in pixels of the table and cell borders. By implication, it also sets the frame to have a border around it and displays both vertical and horizontal rules around individual cells. The

FIGURE 3.12   The effect of spanning cells in a table

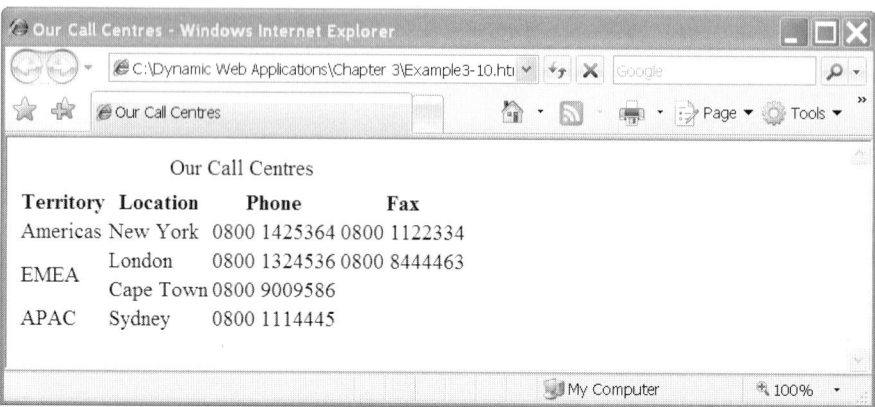

FIGURE 3.13   The table with visible cell frames

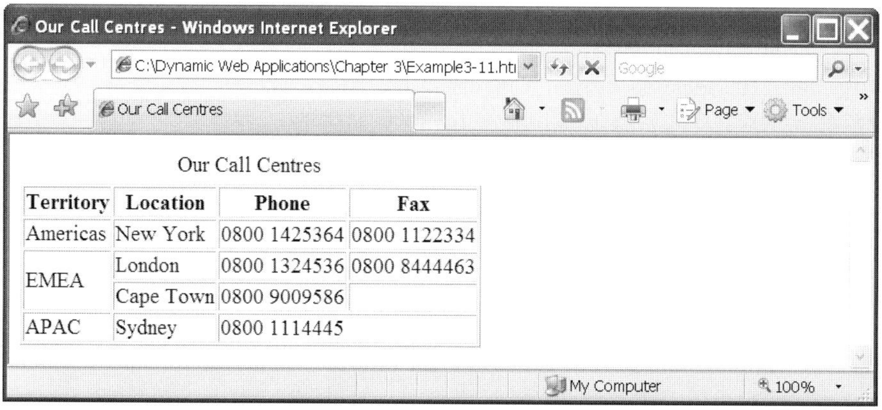

default value of 'border' is '0', meaning that no borders are visible, making it difficult to see the effect of the horizontal spanning in our table. Here, we set the border value to '1', which means that each cell has a visible frame:

```
<TABLE border="1">
```

Making this single change to our previous example changes the browser display as shown in Figure 3.13 (and the modified source file is 'example3–9.htm').

Now we can see that the Sydney phone number spans two cells, whereas the Cape Town number does not. Using the presentational 'frame' attribute is not the best approach, however. We will see how to manage table presentation using style sheets in the next chapter.

3.9 Forms

Forms are a very important part of any web application, because they allow the user to send information to an application running on the server. Much of the user interaction on the web is based on HTTP 'GET' requests, which enable a client to request data from a server. In contrast, forms enable an HTTP 'POST' request to be made, which sends data from a client to a server. As we saw in Chapter 2, a form is part of an HTML page, which submits its data to a server page (Figure 3.14).

Form elements

Forms are defined in HTML using the FORM element. Form attributes include the 'method' attribute, which defines the type of HTTP request that is to be used (usually 'post' for a form) and the 'action' attribute, which specifies a URI to identify which server-side component is to receive the data from the form. In this example, we assume that the server-side process is called 'insuranceQuote'. Programs that run on the server to process forms may be written using any of a number of server side technologies, including Java servlets or JavaServer Pages (JSPs), Active Server Pages (ASPs), Perl or PHP, among others. Of course in this book, we will be implementing these processes in Java.

3

Here is a FORM element with an action and a method:

```
<FORM action="insuranceQuote" method="post" >
   ...components of the form
</FORM>
```

As with links, the URI used in the form does not have to be a complete URI if the page containing the form is from the same web application as the component that is receiving the form data.

The 'method' attribute of the form element specifies how the browser transfers HTML form data to a server program. The most common methods used with forms are 'post' and 'get', but 'post' is preferable. 'get' requests are the default type of HTTP request, but are mainly intended for getting data from the server, for example requesting an HTML page to be downloaded. Therefore although a 'get' request can involve sending some data to the server (e.g. the identity of the request page or the parameters for a search query), only a small amount of data needs to be sent to the server. Because of this, only a limited amount of data can be transferred to the server using this request type (240 characters on some web servers). There are also some security issues associated with 'get' requests, since all parameter data is attached to the URL. Consequently it is visible in the browser address bar, so the URL, including the parameter data, can be 'bookmarked' and used again.

In contrast, when using the 'post' method, an unlimited amount of data can be transferred, URLs cannot be 'bookmarked' and form data is hidden from the user.

FIGURE 3.14   Forms are part of client pages and submit their content to server pages

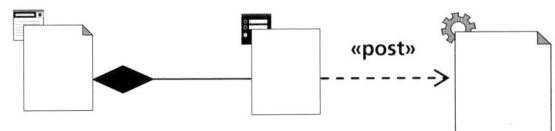

 NOTE	Although there is no specific limit on the size of the data that can be sent with a post request, servers may be configured to limit the actual amount of data that can be posted. This may be necessary to prevent *denial of service* attacks, where large amounts of data could be posted to a server to overwhelm its resources.

In addition to the 'get' and 'post' methods, there are several other lesser-used methods (mostly used by web browser software to obtain document information from the web server). These are 'head', 'delete', 'put', 'trace' and 'options'. These can occasionally be useful but are often not implemented by web applications, so attempting to use these methods may return HTTP response error number 501, the 'not implemented' error.

Input types

Inside the FORM element we define the components of the form. These components enable the user to input data, so include things such as text fields, radio buttons, check boxes and select lists. Components that enable input are known as *controls*. Many of these controls are specified using the empty INPUT element, with the specific type of component defined by the 'type' attribute. Another essential attribute is 'name', which is used to identify the source of the data entered by the user when it is sent to the server. For example, we might have a text field in a form that is used to enter a person's email address. The type of the input element would be 'text' and the name of the element might be 'email' (or something similar). This name can be used by the server-side application to retrieve whatever the user typed into that text field. This is how the element might be written:

```
<INPUT type="text" name="email">
```

There are other attributes that may also be used in the INPUT element. For example, there is a 'value' attribute that can be used to give a default value to an input type:

```
<INPUT type="text" name="email" value="email@address">
```

Another simple input type is 'password'. This is similar to a text field, but when characters are typed into the field they appear on the screen as some other character, such as an asterisk:

```
<INPUT type="password" name="pword">
```

Each control can have a text label associated with it, using the LABEL element. A label must be associated with a control, or group of controls, using the 'for' attribute, which must match the 'id' attribute of a control on the form. Therefore if we want to use the LABEL tag with a form control then the control will need an 'id' attribute as well as a name. Here, for example, is a label for the password input type with the id 'pword':

```
<LABEL for="pword">Password:</LABEL>
```

This would mean the element for the password input would need to include this id:

```
<INPUT type="password" name="pword" id="pword">
```

Associating a label with a control does not affect its position in the form; you have to organize that manually. However, it does have the effect that if you click on the label in the browser, the associated control immediately gets focus.

One essential component of any HTML form is an INPUT element of type 'submit'. This adds a button to the form that enables the form data to be sent in an HTTP request to the server. When the submit button is pressed, the 'action' attribute of the form is used to direct the HTTP request to the appropriate server-side resource. A form must have a 'submit' button in order to invoke its action, unless the HTTP request is managed by a client-side scripting language such as JavaScript, in which case the script may submit the form data.

Forms may also have a reset button, defined by an INPUT element with a type of 'reset'. Pressing the reset button returns the components in the form to their default values, though it is debatable whether reset buttons provide any real benefit from the users' perspective. In general, a reset button should only be used on a form if it has a useful and valid set of default values. For both submit and reset input types, the 'value' attribute can be used to provide a text label for the button.

Here is a very simple page with a login form that uses labels, text and password input types, and submit and reset buttons. Here we assume that there is a server-side component called 'login' to which the form submits its data. The form includes a table to help to organize the components into a neat layout.

```
<!DOCTYPE HTML PUBLIC "-//W3C//DTD HTML 4.01//EN"
"http://www.w3.org/TR/html4/strict.dtd">
<HTML>
   <HEAD>
      <TITLE>Customer Login</TITLE>
   </HEAD>
   <BODY>
      <!-- File: example3-10.htm -->
      <FORM action="login" method="post">
         <TABLE>
           <TR>
              <TD><LABEL for="loginid">Login Name:</LABEL></TD>
              <TD><INPUT type="text" name="loginid" id="loginid"></TD>
           </TR>
           <TR>
              <TD><LABEL for="pword">Password:</LABEL></TD>
              <TD><INPUT type="password" name="pword" id="pword"></TD>
           </TR>
           <TR>
              <TD></TD>
              <TD>
                 <INPUT type="submit" value="Login">
                 <INPUT type="reset" value="Clear form">
              </TD>
           </TR>
         </TABLE>
      </FORM>
   </BODY>
</HTML>
```

FIGURE 3.15   A form displayed in Internet Explorer 7

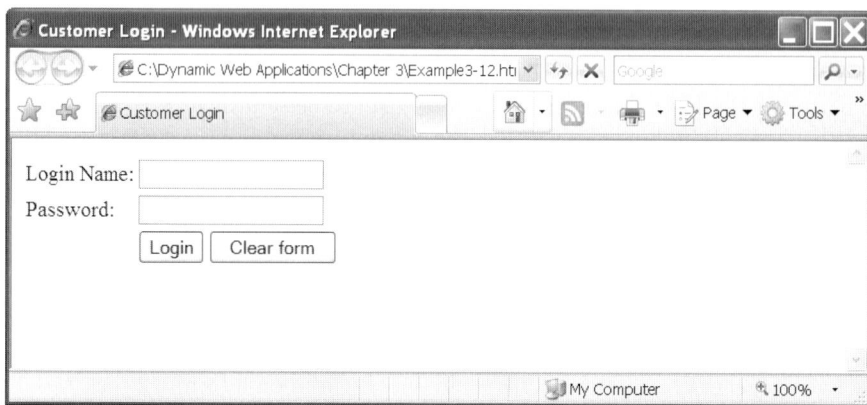

Figure 3.15 shows how the form appears in Internet Explorer 7. Of course, pressing the 'Login' button simply gives an HTTP '404 not found' error, since we are not yet running anything on the server.

There are several other input types used in HTML forms. Two related types are checkboxes and radio buttons. The only difference between these is that checkboxes are always independent of any other component, whereas radio buttons can be grouped together so that only one radio button in a given group can be selected at any one time. A checkbox is defined by setting the INPUT element's 'type' attribute to 'checkbox'. Here we use a checkbox to indicate whether a user wishes to be added to a mailing list. A checkbox effectively represents a Boolean value; it is either checked (true) or not (false).

```
<INPUT type="checkbox" name="mailinglist">
```

A check box is unchecked by default. However we can change this by setting the value of the 'checked' attribute to 'checked'.

```
<INPUT type="checkbox" name="mailinglist" checked="checked">
```

Radio buttons are similar to checkboxes, in the sense that they may either be selected or not, but can be grouped together by having a common value for the 'name' attribute. In the next example, we use radio buttons to ask the user if they want to use our web site as a guest, set up a new account or log in using an existing account. Because the name for all three radio buttons is 'status', they will be treated as a group so that only one of these buttons can be selected at any one time. The 'value' attribute defines the value that will be sent to the server if that particular radio button is selected when the form is submitted. By default, the 'login' radio button is selected because its 'checked' attribute has been set to 'checked'. Here are the INPUT and LABEL elements used for the three radio buttons:

```
<INPUT TYPE="radio" name="status" id="guest" value="guest">
<LABEL for="guest">Access the site as a guest</LABEL>
<INPUT TYPE="radio" name="status" id="new" value="new">
<LABEL for="new">Set up a new user account</LABEL>
<INPUT TYPE="radio" name="status" id="login" value="login"
```

```
checked="checked">
<LABEL for="login">Login using an existing account</LABEL>
```

 NOTE Since the 'id' attribute for a radio button must have a unique value in a page it cannot have the same value as the 'name' attribute. The approach used here is to give the 'id' and 'value' attributes the same values.

Here is a page that includes our example of radio buttons and a check box. Both the submit and reset buttons have default values for their 'value' attributes, which not surprisingly are 'Submit' and 'Reset'. In this example, we have omitted the 'value' attribute for the reset button, so its label will be the default ('Reset').

```
<!DOCTYPE HTML PUBLIC "-//W3C//DTD HTML 4.01//EN"
"http://www.w3.org/TR/html4/strict.dtd">
<HTML>
  <HEAD>
    <TITLE>Site Access</TITLE>
  </HEAD>
  <BODY>
    <!-- File: example3-11.htm -->
    <FORM action="siteaccess" method="post">
      <TABLE>
        <TR>
          <TD colspan="2">
            Welcome to our site. How would you like to continue?
          </TD>
        </TR>
        <TR>
          <TD>
            <INPUT TYPE="radio" name="status" id="guest" value="guest">
          </TD>
          <TD><LABEL for="guest">Access the site as a guest</LABEL></TD>
        </TR>
        <TR>
          <TD><INPUT TYPE="radio" name="status" id="new"
          value="new"></TD>
          <TD><LABEL for="new">Set up a new user account</LABEL></TD>
        </TR>
        <TR>
          <TD>
            <INPUT TYPE="radio" name="status" id="login" value="login"
            checked="checked">
          </TD>
          <TD>
            <LABEL for="login">Login using an existing account</LABEL>
          </TD>
        </TR>
```

```
              <TR>
                <TD colspan="2">
                  <LABEL for="mailinglist">Please check this box if you would
                  like to be added to our mailing list</LABEL>
                </TD>
                <TD>
                  <INPUT type="checkbox" name="mailinglist"
                  id="mailinglist" checked="checked">
                </TD>
              </TR>
              <TR>
                <TD></TD>
                <TD>
                  <INPUT type="submit" value="Continue">
                  <INPUT type="reset">
                </TD>
              </TR>
            </TABLE>
          </FORM>
        </BODY>
      </HTML>
```

Figure 3.16 shows the page with radio buttons and a checkbox displayed in Opera 9.

Text areas

Text areas, which allow the input of multiple lines of text, do not use the INPUT element but are defined by a TEXTAREA element. This element includes optional attributes to set the number of rows and columns of text (the 'rows' and 'cols' attributes). The text typed into a TEXTAREA automatically wraps at the end of a line. If any text is added to the body of the element, then it appears inside the text area, as in this example (see Example 3-12.htm):

```
<TEXTAREA name="description" rows="2" cols="30">
   Describe your insurance claim here
</TEXTAREA>
```

FIGURE 3.16   A form with radio buttons and a checkbox

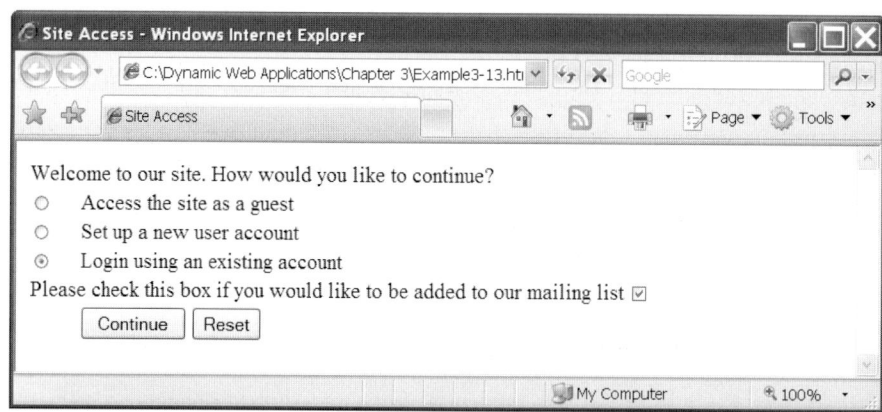

FIGURE 3.17   A TEXTAREA component with some default text

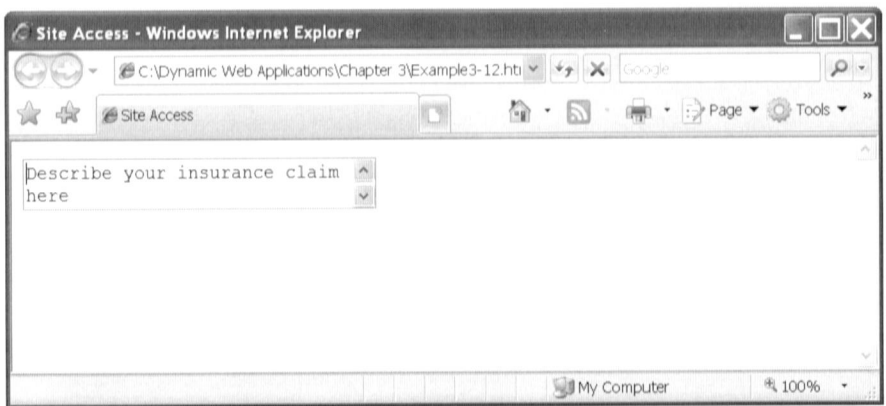

3

Figure 3.17 shows the TEXTAREA with its default text being displayed.

Select lists

Select lists can be used to choose one or more options from a list. The list can be drop down, scrollable or just a list of items, and can optionally enable multiple items to be selected. A select list comprises a SELECT element and one or more nested OPTION elements. Each OPTION has a 'value' attribute that specifies which value is sent to the server if that option is selected when the form is submitted. The body of the OPTION element contains the text that is used when displaying that option in the list. In this example, a select list is used to choose an amount of insurance cover. The default format for this will be a drop-down list (see Example 3-13.htm).

```
<SELECT name="cover">
<OPTION value="10000">10,000</OPTION>
<OPTION value="20000">20,000</OPTION>
<OPTION value="30000">30,000</OPTION>
<OPTION value="50000">50,000</OPTION>
<OPTION value="100000">100,000</OPTION>
</SELECT>
```

To create a scrolling or complete list rather than a drop-down, we can use the 'size' attribute of the SELECT element. If we set the size to '1', this is the default and creates a drop-down list. Anything larger will create a list with a scroll bar (if the size is less than the total number of options) or a simple list, if the size is greater than or equal to the number of options. In our example, this opening tag would create a list with a scroll bar:

```
<SELECT name="cover" size="3">
```

And this would create a non-scrolling list because there are five options:

```
<SELECT name="cover" size="5">
```

Figure 3.18 shows how the select list would appear using the three size settings.

FIGURE 3.18   A SELECT component controlled by the value of the 'size' attribute

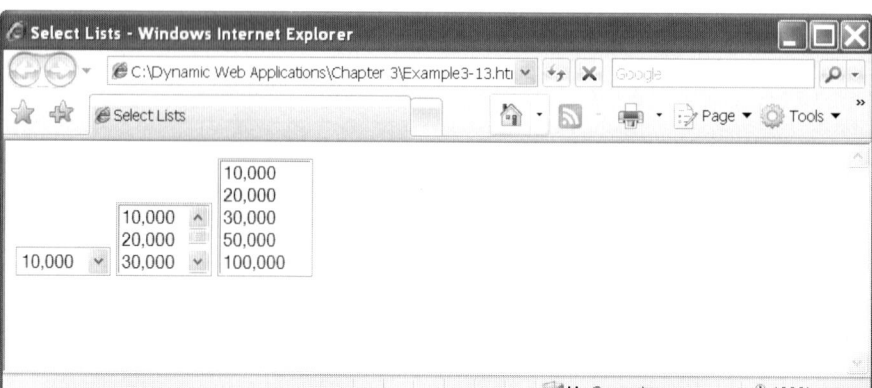

Exercises

In this series of exercises, we develop some pages for the home insurance web site. At this stage, we are only looking at static pages that might be used to introduce and explain the site, not the web application processes making claims or buying insurance.

3.1 Using HTML, implement the content and structure of the home page from the design you created at the end of Chapter 2.

3.2 Using HTML, implement an 'about us' page for the web site that uses the three-region layout you designed at the end of Chapter 2. Use a table to implement this layout (we will see how to do this layout with a style sheet in Chapter 4). You will need a reasonable amount of content on this page, which should include different types of information such as 'our history', 'our mission', 'our people, etc.

3.3 Create a company logo using a suitable software package and use it in your three-region layout (you may also wish to include images from other sources).

3.4 Figure 3.17 shows an HTML form from the home insurance application, to gather data about contents insurance. Write an HTML page that creates a form similar to this one.

3

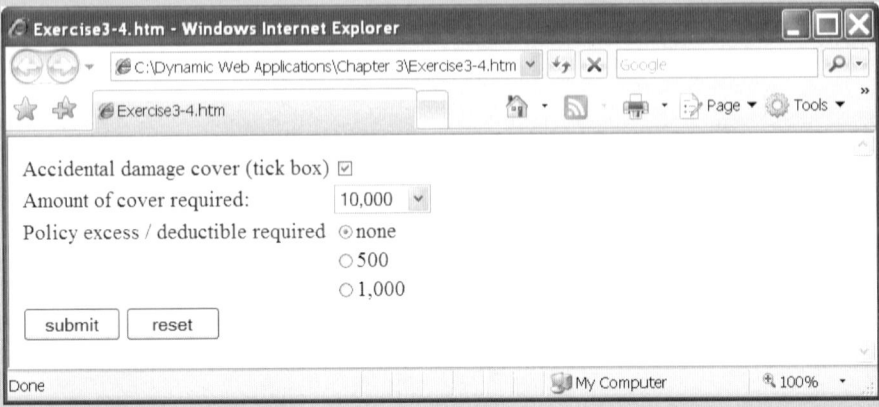

FIGURE 3.19 An HTML form organized using a table

SUMMARY

We began this chapter by introducing SGML, the mark-up language from which HTML and many other mark-up languages have evolved. We followed the evolution of HTML through to version 4, and then looked at some of the most important elements used for structuring HTML documents, including headings, lists, tables and forms. Table 3.2 provides a summary of the HTML elements introduced in this chapter, while Table 3.3 summarizes the new terms that were also introduced.

TABLE 3.2	HTML elements introduced in this chapter
Element	**Meaning**
HTML	The root element that surrounds the whole document
HEAD	Document header information
TITLE	The text that appears in the browser's title bar
BODY	The body content of the page displayed in the browser
P	Paragraph
HI, H2 H3, H4, H5 and H6	Levels of heading
BR	Line break
HR	Horizontal rule
CITE	Citation
BLOCKQUOTE	Block quotation
EM	Emphasis
STRONG	Strong emphasis
SUB	Subscript
SUP	Superscript
UL	Unordered list
LI	List item
OL	Ordered list
DL	Definition list
DT	Definition list term
DD	Definition list definition
IMG	Image
A	Anchor
TABLE	Table
CAPTION	Table caption
TR	Table row
TH	Table heading
TD	Table data
FORM	Form
INPUT	Form component for inputting data
LABEL	Text label for a form component
TEXTAREA	Multi-line text entry box
SELECT	Select list
OPTION	An option in a select list
& ;	Character reference (start and end characters)
<!-- -->	Comment text (start and end characters)

TABLE 3.3	Terms introduced in this chapter
Acronym term	**Meaning**
ANSI	American National Standard Institute
GML	Goldfarb, Mosher, Lorie
ISO	International Standards Organisation
MIME	Multipurpose Internet Mail Extension
SGML	Standard Generalized Markup Language

References and further reading

Connolly, D. (1995). *HTML 2.0 Materials*. W3C. http://www.w3.org/MarkUp/html-spec/

Goldfarb, C. (1996). *The Roots of SGML – A personal recollection*. http://www. sgmlsource.com/history/roots.htm

Korpela, J. (2002). *Empty Elements in SGML, HTML, XML, and XHTML*. http://www.cs.tut.fi/~jkorpela/html/empty.html

Raggett, D., Le Hors, A. and Jacobs, I. (1999). *HTML 4.01 specification*. http://www.w3.org/TR/html401/

3

CHAPTER 4

Styling in the presentation layer: Cascading Style Sheets (CSS)

LEARNING OBJECTIVES

- **To be able to apply in-line styles to HTML elements**
- **To be able style individual HTML pages using cascading style sheets (CSS) in the document head**
- **To be able to create external CSS files and link them to multiple HTML pages**
- **To be able to apply style sheet cascades to individual documents**
- **To be able to use CSS to control the layout of a web page**

INTRODUCTION

In Chapter 3 we concentrated on looking at some of the important structural elements in HTML. HTML also provides a range of elements and attributes that support the presentation of a document, including text styles and fonts, foreground and background colors, content alignment, and list and table formatting. Using this type of mark-up, however, mixes presentation with structure and content, making it hard to separately develop and maintain the presentation layer of a web application. A much better approach is to use cascading style sheets (CSS) to apply presentational formatting independent of the HTML mark-up. In this chapter, we explore the syntax and use of cascading style sheets and see how they can be applied to HTML pages.

4.1 Separating out presentation

HTML 4.0 was the first version of HTML that explicitly attempted to separate out structure from presentation. Although the LINK element, used for attaching a separate style sheet to an HTML document, had been available since early versions of HTML, it was rarely used. In this section, we see how HTML developed into a mark-up language that included presentational tags, explore the development of separate style sheets and see how CSS can be used to separate out the presentation of an HTML document from its content and structure.

In Chapter 3 we looked at HTML syntax and saw how HTML is used to specify the content and structure of a web page. Structural elements of HTML pages include elements such as paragraphs, headings and tables. Although HTML also has presentational elements and attributes, it is preferable that any specification of style (colors, font sizes, etc.) is done separately by using a style sheet language. Why, then, does HTML have presentational tags if we are not supposed to use them? This is in fact a consequence of the way that web technologies have evolved, through a combination of influential individuals, browser vendors and standards bodies. These various influences meant that the separation of structure and content for presentation using style sheets was an approach that developed rather erratically. In the early days of HTML, there was some debate about how HTML should be styled, and whether it should be based on browser configuration or some other mechanism. Although it was always recognized that it would be good practice to separate the content of a page from the specification of its presentation, there was no common agreement on how this should be done. There was also some debate as to who should have control over the appearance of a document, the author, the viewer, or a combination of both. Various early browsers had their own ways of applying style sheets to manage the appearance of HTML documents, but this was from the perspective of controlling the way that documents were configured in a given browser. It did not enable the author of an HTML page to specify how it should be presented. To address this issue, HTML tags that related to presentational aspects began to be supported by browsers. For example, the first version of Netscape Navigator in 1994 supported the CENTER element. Since the early HTML specifications were simply a drawing together of syntax that was already being used by the leading browsers, the introduction of such tags led to their subsequent inclusion in the standard HTML specification. However, around the same time that Netscape Navigator was introducing the first presentational HTML tags, Häkon Lie at CERN published the first proposal for what he called 'cascading HTML style sheets' (Lie and Bos 1999). The concept of the cascade was that an HTML document could be presented using an ordered list of style sheets, so that there might be a number of different style sheets applied one after the other to a given HTML document, each providing more specialized formatting. Lie's proposal contained the idea of the LINK element in an HTML document that provides the URL of a separate style sheet. The original version of this proposal looked like this:

```
<LINK REL="style" HREF="http://NYT.com/style">
```

As the idea of style sheets was debated by the web technology community it became clear that they need be applicable not only to HTML but to other types of document as well. The reference to HTML was dropped and they were renamed simply Cascading Style Sheets (CSS). Although there were alternative proposals for style sheet technologies made around that time, CSS became the clear leader after the formation of the World Wide Web Consortium in 1995, which held an international workshop on CSS. This was followed in 1996 by the first W3C recommendation, CSS level 1, with support from the leading browsers of the time, Microsoft Internet Explorer and Netscape Navigator, though the implementations in both at that stage were limited, neither of them fully implementing the level 1 specification. The next version, CSS level 2, was published in 1998 and CSS level 3 is an ongoing recommendation.

We have talked about the need to separate structure and content from presentation, but why is this so important? Specifying the appearance of the pages in a web site is not only an issue for graphic designers, but is also a management problem. It is important to maintain a uniform appearance across the pages of a web site, while indicating the differences between the various concerns of the site in an organized way. For example, different color schemes might be used in different parts of a web site. An associated issue is that it should be possible to change the appearance of a web site consistently across all pages without having to undertake a major maintenance exercise.

How, then, does CSS help us to manage the presentation of a web application in a way that enables us to apply a consistent look and feel, with customisation for different parts of our web site, and make it easy to change? CSS does this by providing the ability to specify style information in-line, internal to a document or externally. This means that styles can be applied at different levels of granularity: across the whole web site, to a specific page, or to a specific element. CSS also provides the ability to cascade a series of style sheets to apply to a single document, enabling a combination of styles to be blended together.

4.2 CSS syntax

CSS syntax can vary slightly, depending on where it is being used. In-line styles, internal style sheets and external style sheets each involve a particular type of syntax, though all are similar.

The simplest way to use CSS is with inline styles, which is where styles are added directly to HTML elements using the 'style' attribute. The value of this attribute consists of two parts separated by a colon. The first part is the style property that is being applied, the second the actual value of that property. For example, one of the style properties is 'color' (the foreground, text, color) and one of the possible values for that property is 'blue'. Here, we set the style of an H1 element to be the color 'blue'.

```
<H1 style="color: blue">Heading</H1>
```

 NOTE — The space after the colon is used here to aid readability, it is not required.

The color value 'blue' is one of the 16 color names specified in the W3C HTML 4.0 standard: aqua, black, blue, fuchsia, gray, green, lime, maroon, navy, olive, purple, red, silver, teal, white, yellow.

A large number of other color names are also recognized by many browsers and, in addition to the named colors, you can 'mix' your own using red, green, blue (RGB) values in this property format:

```
color: rgb(r, g, b)
```

In this format, each of the three color values is specified by an integer in the range 0 to 255, each of which represents the intensity of the red, green, or blue component of the desired color. Using the maximum values for all three, 'color: rgb(255,255,255)' gives white, while zero values for all three, 'color: rgb(0,0,0)' gives black.

Style sheets can also be used to set the background color, using the 'background-color' property. In this example we set the text color to white and the background color to black. If we are applying multiple styles to a single element, the styles are separated by semi-colons, as we can see here:

```
<H2 style="color: white; background-color: black">Sub heading</H2>
```

If we use in-line styles in an HTML document, we should indicate to the browser which stylesheet language we are using. Although the default is CSS, the specification states that 'Documents that include elements that set the style attribute but which don't define a default style sheet language are incorrect.' (Raggett *et al.* 1999)

Therefore we should add the following META element to the HEAD element, declaring 'text/css' as the style type:

```
<META http-equiv="Content-Style-Type" content="text/css">
```

 NOTE There are many possible attributes that can be used with the META element, which provides various types of information about the document that includes it. A single HEAD element can contain multiple META elements.

In this example we add the necessary META tag and apply in-line styles to an H1 element and two H2 elements. The second H2 style demonstrates the RGB color syntax to specify white text on a black background, though the effect is exactly that same as the first H2 element style, which uses the standard color names to achieve the same effect. The style elements appear in bold type:

```
<!DOCTYPE HTML PUBLIC "-//W3C//DTD HTML 4.01//EN"
"http://www.w3.org/TR/html4/strict.dtd">
<HTML>
  <HEAD>
    <META http-equiv="Content-Style-Type" content="text/css">
    <TITLE>Our Insurance Cover</TITLE>
  </HEAD>
  <BODY>
  <!-- File: example4-1.htm -->
<H1 style="color: blue">
  We provide the following types of insurance</H1>
<H2 style="color: white; background-color: black">
  Buildings Cover</H2>
    <P>You may think you're "safe as houses" but you'd be surprised how many
things can damage the building you live in. Fires, earthquakes, subsidence, runaway
trucks, cricket balls through windows or the occasional meteor. Best to be
covered!
```

```
      </P>
  <H2 style="color: rgb(255,255,255); background-color: rgb(0,0,0)">
    Contents Cover</H2>
      <P>You may not realise just how much the stuff you have would cost to replace.
If the burglars move in while you're on holiday, could you afford to replace the
TV, the stereo, the chairs, the cupboards, the crockery, etc?
      </P>
      <P>Not only that, our contents cover means that if you have your bike stolen,
drop the vase your mother-in-law gave you as a wedding present, lose your camera,
leave your glasses on the train or have your mobile phone stolen, you'll be fully
compensated.
      </P>
    </BODY>
</HTML>
```

Figure 4.1 shows how the styled page appears in Internet Explorer 7.

 NOTE In the early days of web page design, a 216-color 'browser-safe palette' was proposed that indicated which combinations of colors would work best across multiple browsers in a world where many computers supported only 8-bit color (256 colors). The 'safe' palette eliminated the 40 colors that were most likely to vary on different displays. However in the vast majority of cases this limitation no longer applies so the safe palette is largely redundant (Weinman 2007).

FIGURE 4.1   In-line styles applied to an HTML document

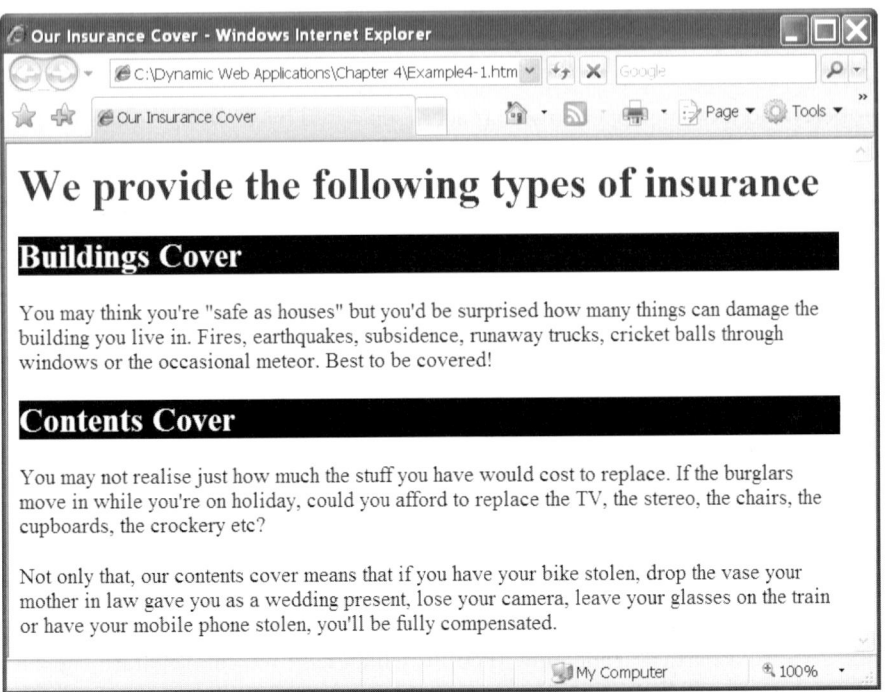

4.3 Style sheets

Using only in-line styles inside tags has no real benefit over using presentation elements and attributes from standard HTML. Although we are using a different syntax, we do not actually separate out structure and content from presentation, and do not gain any of the benefits of applying a generic style to a document. Styles only become useful when they are also applied to a whole document, so that we can, for example, apply a standard style to *all* H1 elements in a document rather than doing this on an individual basis. In this context, in-line styles are useful for fine-tuning the presentation but should not be used to style a whole document. Applying styles more generally is done using style sheets, either internal to the HTML page or as external documents, linked to the HTML page using the LINK element. First, we look at how to include a style sheet inside an HTML page.

Internal style sheets

Internal style sheets are those that are included in the HEAD element of an HTML document using the STYLE element. This type of style sheet applies only to that document. For CSS, the value of the STYLE element's 'type' attribute is set to 'text/css', as it is when using the META element for in-line styles.

```
<STYLE type="text/css">
   ...styles defined here
</STYLE>
```

The syntax for defining styles in a STYLE element is similar to the inline style, except that we must also specify to which element types we are applying styles. Each component of a style sheet is made up of three parts:

- The name of an HTML element type
- The name of a presentational property of that element
- The value of the property that is to be applied.

The property and its value appear inside braces (separated by a colon, as they are for inline styles):

```
element {property: value}
```

For example, if we want to change all of the H1 (main heading) elements so that they are styled in blue, we can add the following style element:

```
<STYLE type="text/css">
   h1 {color: blue}
</STYLE>
```

Note that we will be using lower case for element names in our CSS because we will be applying them to XHTML pages later. In XHTML, element names must be in lower case. For HTML, which is not case-sensitive, the case used in the style sheet does not matter.

The difference between our in-line example and this style is that this one will apply to all 'h1' elements in the page that is being formatted. Sometimes we will want to apply more than one style to a particular element type, in which case we can separate the different styles using semicolons. For example, if we want to make our main headings both blue and centred, we could use the following style (with 'text-align' the additional property and 'center' the chosen value):

```
<STYLE type="text/css">
   h1 {color: blue; text-align: center}
</STYLE>
```

 NOTE The other possible values for the 'text-align' property are 'left', 'right' and 'justify'.

Grouping styles

As well as applying multiple styles to a single element type, we might want to apply the same style(s) to more than one type of element. Here, for example, we use the centred, blue style for both main headings (h1) and subheadings (h2) by putting them together in a comma-separated list:

```
<STYLE type="text/css">
   h1,h2 {color: blue; text-align: center}
</STYLE>
```

Line feeds and spacing can be used to make style sheets more readable, without having an effect on their processing, as in this example:

```
<STYLE type="text/css">
h1,h2
{
   color: blue;
   text-align: center
}
</STYLE>
```

Further text formatting styles

So far we have seen styles that can be applied to text that affect the color and alignment. Other CSS text formatting styles include 'font-style', 'font-weight', 'font-size' and 'font-family'. A common value to use with the 'font-style' property is 'italic', while a common value of the 'font-weight' property is 'bold'. The value of the 'font-family' property can be one of many font names, but you are dependent on the browser having that font family available, so using unusual font families is not a good idea if you want your pages to look consistent across a wide range of browsers. There are five generic font families that should be supported by any browser: 'serif', 'sans-serif' 'cursive', 'fantasy' and 'monospace'. The browser should provide a font mapping for all of these font families, but the actual mapping is browser-specific. We can see this from Figure 4.2, which shows the same page of text using the five generic font families displayed in three browsers. The differences in appearance are because the generic font families have been mapped to different actual fonts by the different browsers.

Since using the generic font families is somewhat unpredictable in terms of the specific font being used, we may prefer to specify actual font names. Some widely supported fonts include 'Times New Roman' (a serif font), 'Arial' (a sans-serif font) and 'Courier' (a monospaced font). If the name of a font family contains spaces then it should be put inside quotes or apostrophes, for example:

```
font-family: 'Times New Roman'
```

Figure 4.3 shows some text using these three fonts in the three browsers. Note how they all look very similar.

FIGURE 4.2 The five generic font families displayed by a) Mozilla Firefox 2, b) Opera 9 and c) Internet Explorer 7

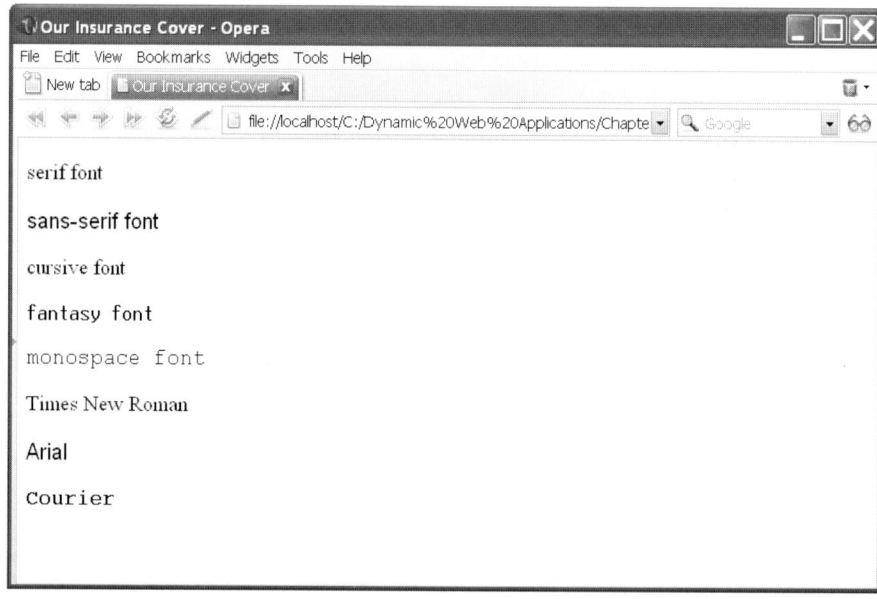

FIGURE 4.2 Continued

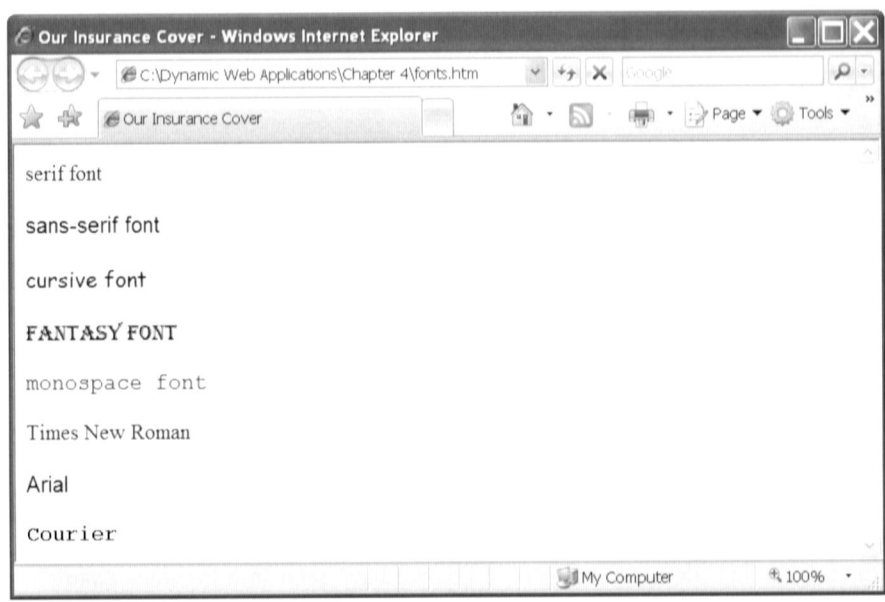

FIGURE 4.3 The Times New Roman, Arial and Courier fonts displayed by a) Mozilla Firefox 2, b) Opera 9 and c) Internet Explorer 7

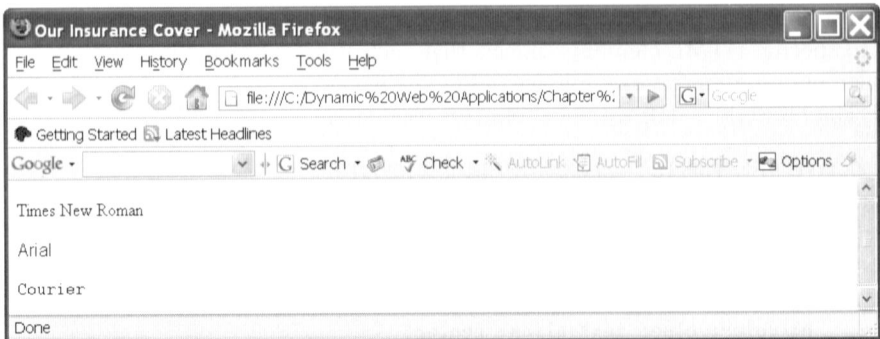

FIGURE 4.3   Continued

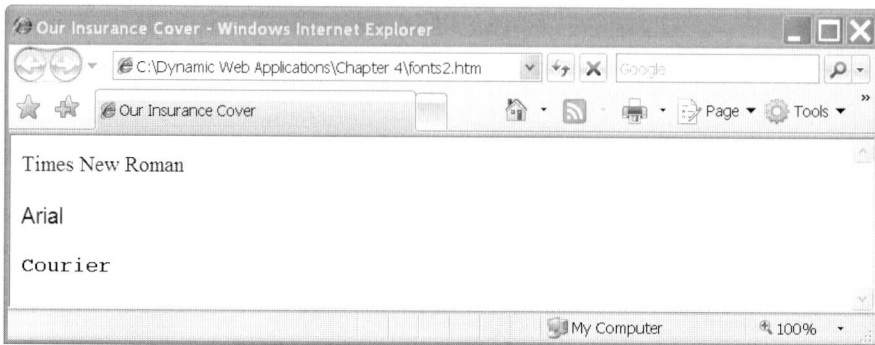

Applying multiple styles with the STYLE element

The body of the STYLE element can contain as many style entries as is required for the HTML document. In the following example, we apply different styles to all H1, H2 and P elements. The H1 element is formatted as we have seen in a previous example (blue, centered). The H2 element is formatted using the 'red' value for the 'color' property, and also uses the 'font-style' property, setting its value to 'italic'. Finally, the paragraph (P) elements are styled using the 'font-family' property and the 'sans-serif' value. Depending on the browser's built-in style, this may make the paragraphs appear in a different font from the headings.

The important point to note here is that defining the styles in one place, rather than attaching them to specific HTML elements, means that each style only has to be defined once for each element type. In this example we define the paragraph style once, but it is used three times. The H2 style is defined once, but it is used twice.

```
<!DOCTYPE HTML PUBLIC "-//W3C//DTD HTML 4.01//EN"
"http://www.w3.org/TR/html4/strict.dtd">
<HTML>
  <HEAD>
    <STYLE type="text/css">
      h1{color: blue; text-align: center}
      h2{color: red; font-style: italic}
      p{font-family: sans-serif}
    </STYLE>
    <TITLE>Our Insurance Cover</TITLE>
  </HEAD>
  <BODY>
  <!-- File: example4-2.htm -->
    <H1>We provide the following types of insurance</H1>
    <H2>Buildings Cover</H2>
    <P>You may think you're "safe as houses" but you'd be surprised how many
things can damage the building you live in. Fires, earthquakes, subsidence, runaway
trucks, cricket balls through windows or the occasional meteor. Best to be covered!
    </P>
    <H2>Contents Cover</H2>
```

```
        <P>You may not realise just how much the stuff you have would cost to replace.
If the burglars move in while you're on holiday, could you afford to replace the
TV, the stereo, the chairs, the cupboards, the crockery, etc?
        </P>
        <P>Not only that, our contents cover means that if you have your bike stolen,
drop the vase your mother-in-law gave you as a wedding present, lose your camera,
leave your glasses on the train or have your mobile phone stolen, you'll be fully
compensated.
        </P>
    </BODY>
</HTML>
```

Figure 4.4 shows how the page looks in Internet Explorer 7.

Setting the font size

The size of the font can be set using a number of different types of measurement, including absolute measures in inches, centimetres, millimetres, points or picas. However, setting sizes to specific measurements is not very flexible across different browser contexts, and should only be used in specialized applications where the target client device is known. This is not the case for most web applications, so the better approach is to use a relative method of sizing text. Even here, there is more than one option: we can use a percentage measure (%), a pixel measure (px), the 'x height' of the font (x) or 'em'

4

FIGURE 4.4   Styles applied to multiple headings and paragraphs

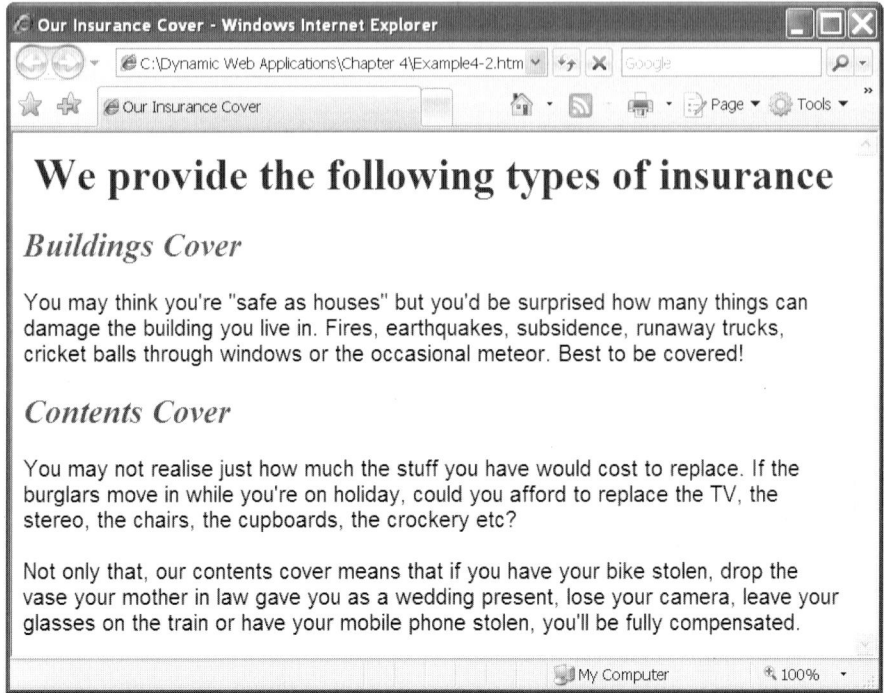

which relates to the both the width and height of the font. Apart from pixels, all of these work in a way that is relative to the context within which an element is used. If we apply a relative size to an element of a specific type (for example, a paragraph element), then the actual size is based on the one that would normally be applied. In other words, setting a paragraph's font to be 1.5em would make it half as big again as the normal font size for that paragraph:

```
<P style="font-size: 1.5em">
```

It is also possible to use more generic descriptions of text size, including 'large', 'small', 'x-large' (extra large) and 'x-small' (extra small), for example:

```
<P style="font-size: large">
```

External style sheets

Using an internal style sheet has the advantage that we only need to define a style for each type of element once, rather than every time it appears, as we would have to do if we were using in-line styles. However, the drawback of internal style sheets is that the styles we define can only be used in the current HTML document. It is likely that we would want to apply the same styles right across our web application, so that all of our pages have a consistent look and feel. If, for example we want all our major headings on all pages to be blue and center-aligned, we would have to repeat this style in an internal style sheet for every single page. Worse, if we decided to change the look and feel so that all major headings were, for example, to be made left-aligned, we would have to change the internal style sheet on every page. Fortunately, we can specify an external stylesheet in a separate document and use the LINK element (in the HTML document's HEAD element) to apply the required stylesheet. The name and location of the stylesheet is specified by the 'href' attribute, and the relationship between the HTML page and the stylesheet by the 'rel' attribute. The value of the 'rel' attribute should be set to 'stylesheet'.

 NOTE Another possible value for the 'rel' attribute is 'alternate stylesheet', where the browser may enable switching between different stylesheets, provided more than one stylesheet LINK element is include in the HEAD element. However this option is poorly supported by current browsers.

There is also a 'type' attribute that indicates the type of the linked document. As with the internal style sheet, the value of the 'type' attribute for a stylesheet is 'text/css'. There are some other attributes that may be used in the LINK element but we do not need to be concerned with them here. Taking our previous internal style sheet example, the content of the STYLE element can be extracted into a separate CSS file, which would simply list the styles (STYLE tags are not required in an external style sheet). Here is our external CSS file, which we will call 'webhomecover.css':

```
h1{color: blue; text-align: center}
h2{color: red; font-style: italic}
p{font-family: sans-serif}
```

To apply this style sheet to an HTML page, we need to add the appropriate LINK element to the page's HEAD element. This LINK example specifies the 'webhomecover. css' file:

```
<LINK href="webhomecover.css" rel="stylesheet" type="text/css">
```

This example assumes that the CSS file is in the same folder (either locally or on the web server) as the HTML file. Otherwise the value of the 'href' attribute could be written to include a directory pathway or a full URL, depending on the circumstances.

Here is our previous example HTML page but using an external style sheet instead of an internal one.

```
<!DOCTYPE HTML PUBLIC "-//W3C//DTD HTML 4.01//EN"
"http://www.w3.org/TR/html4/strict.dtd">
<HTML>
   <HEAD>
     <LINK href="webhomecover.css" rel="stylesheet" type="text/css">
     <TITLE>Our Insurance Cover</TITLE>
   </HEAD>
   <BODY>
       <!-- File: example4-3.htm -->
     <H1>We provide the following types of insurance</H1>
     <H2>Buildings Cover</H2>
     <P>You may think you're "safe as houses" but you'd be surprised how many
things can damage the building you live in. Fires, earthquakes, subsidence, runaway
trucks, cricket balls through windows or the occasional meteor. Best to be covered!
     </P>
     <H2>Contents Cover</H2>
     <P>You may not realise just how much the stuff you have would cost to replace.
If the burglars move in while you're on holiday, could you afford to replace the
TV, the stereo, the chairs, the cupboards, the crockery, etc?
     </P>
     <P>Not only that, our contents cover means that if you have your bike stolen,
drop the vase your mother-in-law gave you as a wedding present, lose your camera, leave
your glasses on the train or have your mobile phone stolen, you'll be fully compensated.
     </P>
   </BODY>
</HTML>
```

Once we have a separate style sheet, we can use it with multiple HTML pages. Here, we apply the same style sheet to a different page:

```
<!DOCTYPE HTML PUBLIC "-//W3C//DTD HTML 4.01//EN"
"http://www.w3.org/TR/html4/strict.dtd">
<HTML>
   <HEAD>
     <LINK href="webhomecover.css" rel="stylesheet" type="text/css">
     <TITLE>Our Promise to You</TITLE>
   </HEAD>
   <BODY>
```

```
<!-- File: example4-4.htm -->
  <H1>Our Promise to You</H1>
  <H2>No Unreasonable Exclusions</H2>
  <P>
Many insurance companies include many exclusions in their policies, making it
difficult to claim for events such as 'acts of God', terrorism or subsidence. We
have the smallest set of exclusions of any fictional insurance company.
  </P>
  <H2>Rapid Response</H2>
  <P>
If you make a claim, we promise to respond to you within 24 hours, either by
settling immediately or putting you in contact with one of our insurance assessors.
  </P>
  <H2>Low, Low, Rates</H2>
  <P>
We constantly monitor our prices against our competitors and guarantee that we
provide the best-value insurance that you can't actually buy.
  </P>
 </BODY>
</HTML>
```

Figure 4.5 shows that the same styles have been applied as appear in Figure 4.4.

FIGURE 4.5 Reusing the same styles in another page

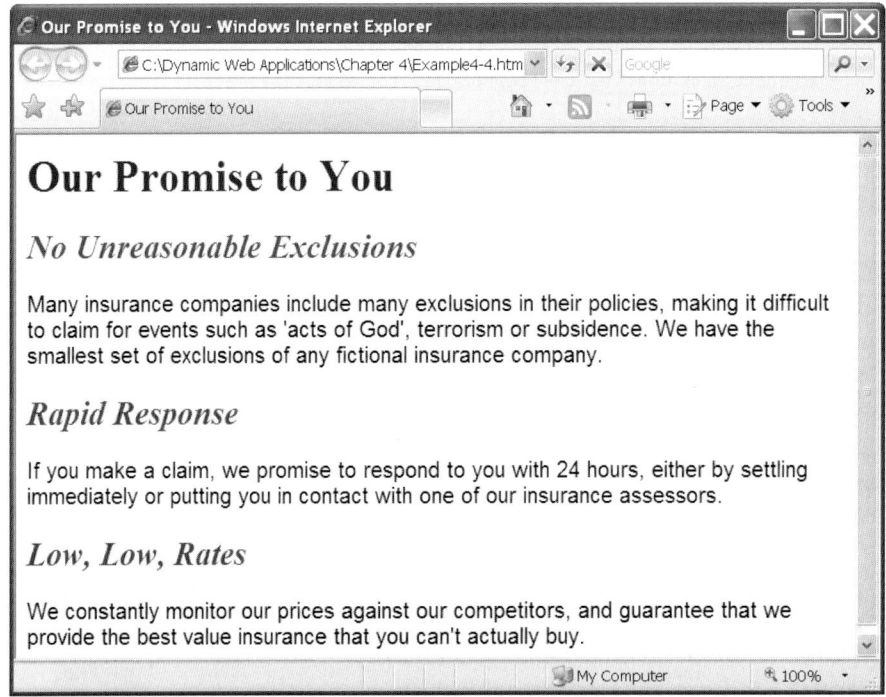

4.4 Applying styles with 'class' and 'id' attributes

So far we have looked at how to apply styles to specific HTML elements, such as H1, H2 and P. In many cases this is useful, but there are occasions when we want to:

- Apply the same style to more than one type of HTML element.
- Apply a style to some, but not all, instances of a particular HTML element.
- Apply a style to one specific instance of an element.

To do this we need some way of labelling parts of our HTML so that we can apply styles to elements that are identified by these labels. We can do this in two ways:

- We can use the 'class' attribute. This enables us to group a number of elements as belonging to a single class. Then we can apply a style to all members of the class.
- We can use the 'id' attribute. This can be used to give an element a unique id. This id can be used to apply a style that is not used anywhere else in the document.

Using the 'class' attribute

The class attribute can be applied to many elements. In addition, a given element can belong to more than one class. The class attribute is very useful as a way of applying styles across a range of different elements. For example, let us assume that we want both major headings (H1) and subheadings (H2) to be centred. We could, of course, apply the same style separately to both H1 and H2 elements in the style sheet. However a more flexible and maintainable approach is to use a class attribute. The first step is to identify both H1 and H2 elements as belonging to the same class. The name of a class is decided by the author of the page. In the next example we apply the class name 'heading' to all instances of both H1 and H2 elements.

```
<!DOCTYPE HTML PUBLIC "-//W3C//DTD HTML 4.01//EN"
"http://www.w3.org/TR/html4/strict.dtd">
<HTML>
   <HEAD>
      <LINK href="webhomecover.css" rel="stylesheet" type="text/css">
      <TITLE>Our Insurance Cover</TITLE>
   </HEAD>
   <BODY>
      <!-- File: example4-5.htm -->
      <H1 class="heading">We provide the following types of insurance</H1>
      <H2 class="heading">Buildings Cover</H2>
      <P>You may think you're "safe as houses" but you'd be surprised how many
things can damage the building you live in. Fires, earthquakes, subsidence, run-
away trucks, cricket balls through windows or the occasional meteor. Best to be
covered!
      </P>
      <H2 class="heading">Contents Cover</H2>
      <P>You may not realise just how much the stuff you have would cost to replace.
If the burglars move in while you're on holiday, could you afford to replace the
TV, the stereo, the chairs, the cupboards, the crockery, etc?
      </P>
```

```
      <P>Not only that, our contents cover means that if you have your bike stolen,
   drop the vase your mother-in-law gave you as a wedding present, lose your camera,
   leave your glasses on the train or have your mobile phone stolen, you'll be fully
   compensated.
         </P>
      </BODY>
   </HTML>
```

We also need to apply a style to 'heading' elements in the style sheet. To do this we simply precede the class name with a period and specify the style for that class. In this example, we centre all members of the 'heading' class:

```
h1{color: blue}
h2{color: red; font-style: italic}
p{font-family: sans-serif}
.heading{text-align: center}
```

Now, any elements that belong to the 'heading' class will be centre-aligned, regardless of which HTML elements the class is applied to.

Applying class styles to a subset of elements

In the previous example, we used the class attribute to apply a style to multiple different elements. Another way of using the class attribute is to apply a style to a subset of elements of a specific type. For example, we could apply a special style to some subheadings but not others. In this example, we change the style sheet so that some paragraphs are emphasized while others are not. We do this by putting a HTML element name in front of the class name, like this:

```
elementname.classname {style}
```

To change 'emphasis' paragraphs, we add 'p.emphasis' to the style sheet:

```
h1{color: blue}
h2{color: red; font-style: italic}
p{font-family: sans-serif}
.heading{text-align: center}
p.emphasis{font-weight: bold}
```

Now, all paragraphs will be in sans-serif font, but only those marked as belonging to the 'emphasis' class will be displayed in bold font:

In the following example we make two of the paragraphs belong to the 'emphasis' class:

```
<!DOCTYPE HTML PUBLIC "-//W3C//DTD HTML 4.01//EN"
"http://www.w3.org/TR/html4/strict.dtd">
<HTML>
   <HEAD>
      <LINK href="webhomecover.css" rel="stylesheet" type="text/css">
      <TITLE>Our Insurance Cover</TITLE>
   </HEAD>
   <BODY>
         <!-- File: example4-6.htm -->
```

```
<H1 class="heading">We provide the following types of insurance</H1>
<H2 class="heading">Buildings Cover</H2>
<P>You may think you're "safe as houses" but you'd be surprised how many
things can damage the building you live in. Fires, earthquakes, subsidence, runaway
trucks, cricket balls through windows or the occasional meteor.</P>
    <P class="emphasis">Best to be covered!</P>
    </P>
<H2 class="heading">Contents Cover</H2>
<P>You may not realise just how much the stuff you have would cost to replace.
If the burglars move in while you're on holiday, could you afford to replace the
TV, the stereo, the chairs, the cupboards, the crockery, etc?
    </P>
    <P class="emphasis">
Not only that, our contents cover means that if you have your bike stolen, drop
the vase your mother-in-law gave you as a wedding present, lose your camera, leave
your glasses on the train or have your mobile phone stolen, you'll be fully
compensated.
    </P>
  </BODY>
</HTML>
```

Figure 4.6 shows the page displayed in Internet Explorer. Note the second and fourth paragraphs are in bold font.

FIGURE 4.6   Applying styles to paragraphs using 'class' attributes

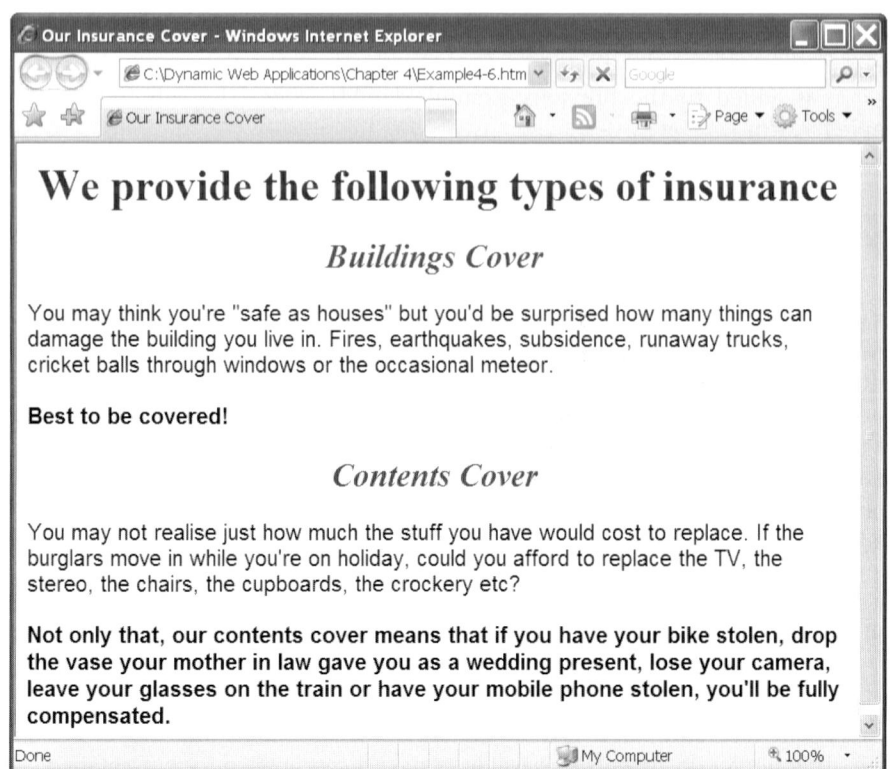

Element id attributes

Sometimes we may want to apply a style to one specific element, and no other. In this case, the element needs a unique identifier that will make it different from every other element in the document. Since the 'class' attribute can be applied to multiple elements, it cannot be used to uniquely identify a specific element. Instead, we use the 'id' attribute to identify a unique instance of an element within the document, such as a particular paragraph or heading. Here, we apply a unique 'id' to a single paragraph:

```
<P id="footer"> &copy;WebHomeCover.com 2008 </P>
```

Only this element on the page can have the id of 'footer'. To style 'id' elements in a style sheet we use the following syntax:

```
#idvalue{style}
```

Here, we apply some special styles to the 'footer' paragraph

```
#footer
{
    font-weight: bold;
    font-style: italic;
    color: white;
    background-color: black;
    text-align: center
}
```

Figure 4.7 shows how the footer appears in the browser using our special footer style, if it is added to the previous example HTML page (the full source file is in 'Example4-7.htm').

4.5 Block and inline elements

So far we have been applying styles to some of the HTML elements that we introduced in the previous chapter. One issue with many HTML elements is that they already have some presentational implications, for example the relative size of headings or the way that STRONG elements are rendered, even before style sheets are applied. Sometimes it is useful to be able to apply styles to elements that specify only the very basics of structure, with no presentational implications. In general terms, HTML elements can be either *block-level* or *inline*. A block-level element implies a block of content that is separated in some way from other blocks of content, usually by beginning on a new line, while inline content is part of a block and not separated from it in any way. Blocks can appear inside other blocks, and inline elements can appear inside other inline elements. Figure 4.8 shows the general relationships between block and in-line elements.

Block level elements in HTML are indicated by the DIV (division) element, while inline elements are indicated by the SPAN element. Their main value is in being able to provide a generic structure for documents that will have style sheets applied for presentation. The 'id'

FIGURE 4.7   Applying styles to an element using an 'id' attribute

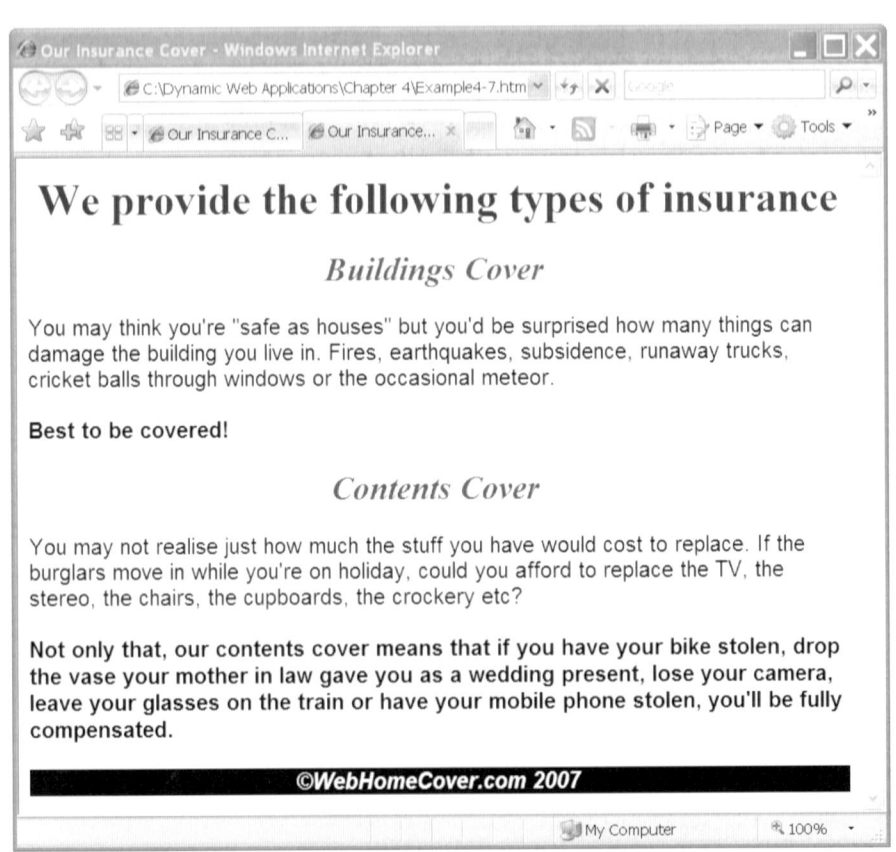

FIGURE 4.8   Block and inline elements

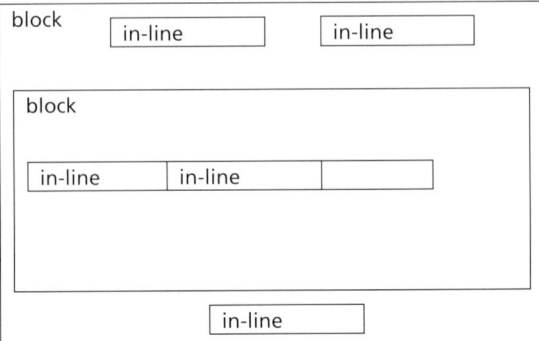

and 'class' attributes can be used with these elements to indicate where styles can be applied to add presentational features.

The next example shows how the DIV and SPAN elements can be used to structure the block and inline components of an HTML document. Within these elements, we can apply more specific HTML structures, such as paragraphs. In this example, paragraph elements have been used within the blocks. It is important to note that a paragraph element should not be a parent of a DIV element, but should be nested inside it. This makes sense, since DIV and SPAN are the generic organizational elements, within which the more detailed structures and presentation can be managed.

Because these tags are generic, we are unlikely to apply styles directly to them, since the number of styles would be limited to two. Instead, we use attributes to specify ids or classes for DIV and SPAN elements so that we can apply styles to them later. In this example we apply 'heading', 'bigger' and 'text' class attributes to various elements, and 'id' attributes called 'risk' and 'items'.

 NOTE This example also shows how more than one class can be applied to a single element, by using multiple class names separated by spaces, e.g. class="heading bigger".

```
<!DOCTYPE HTML PUBLIC "-//W3C//DTD HTML 4.01//EN"
"http://www.w3.org/TR/html4/strict.dtd">
<HTML>
   <HEAD>
      <LINK href="divspanstyles.css" rel="stylesheet" type="text/css">
      <TITLE> Making a Claim</TITLE>
   </HEAD>
   <BODY>
      <!-- File: example4-8.htm -->
      <DIV class="heading bigger">Buildings Insurance</DIV>
      <DIV class="text">
      <P>
      You need this type of insurance to cover you in case of
      <SPAN id="risk">severe damage to your home</SPAN>
      (for example fire, flood, vehicle or tree crashing into it)
      as well as more everyday risks like accidentally breaking a window
      </P>
      </DIV>
      <DIV class="heading bigger">Contents Insurance</DIV>
      <DIV class="text">
      <P>
      You need this type of insurance to cover the
      <SPAN id="items">things in your house</SPAN>,
      such as furniture, electrical goods, carpets and curtains, against risks such
      as fire, theft, water damage (due to burst pipes, etc) or accidental breakage
      </P>
      </DIV>
   </BODY>
</HTML>
```

On their own, the only effect of these elements is that DIV forces a new line. To overlay presentational styles on top of a document written using these tags the 'class' and 'id' attributes

FIGURE 4.9   Styles applied using DIV and SPAN

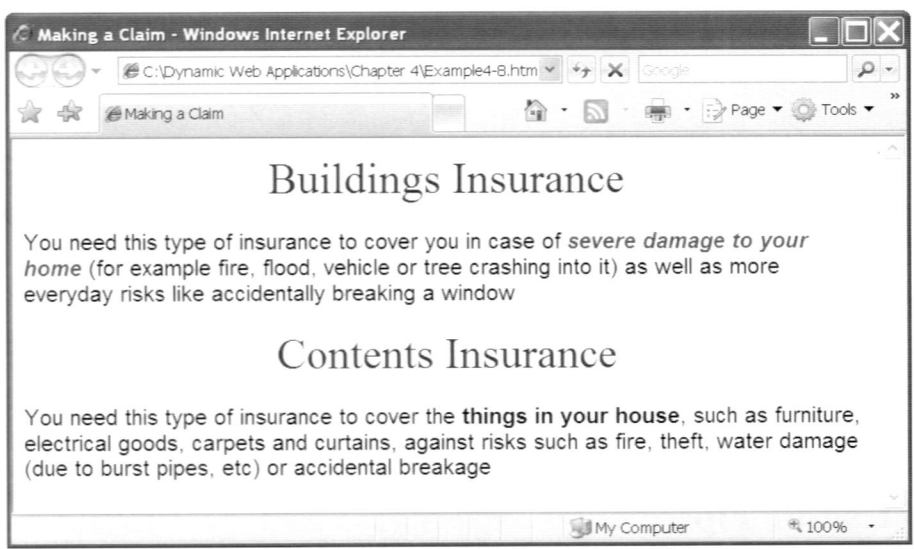

can be linked to a cascading style sheet. The following style sheet ('divspanstyles.css') applies styles to the classes and ids used in the example above. Note that there are no styles applied here to HTML tags, only to the classes and ids that we have defined ourselves.

```
.heading{text-align: center; color: blue}
.text{text-align: left; font-family: Arial}
.bigger{font-size: 2em}
#items{font-weight: bold}
#risk{font-weight: bold; font-style: italic; color: red}
```

Figure 4.9 shows the HTML page displayed in a browser, with all styles applied using only DIV and SPAN elements.

4.6 Applying styles to lists and tables

There are some styles that can be applied to lists. For example, the symbol used can be specified using the 'list-style-type' property. Unordered list bullets can be styled as 'disc', 'circle' or 'square'. These can be used to override the browser's default use of bullet symbols. The number format of an ordered list can also be specified using the 'type' attribute to select a number (Arabic or Roman) or letter format (Table 4.1). Alternatively we can set the value to 'none' to remove any symbols or numbers.

Figure 4.10 shows a modified version of the page from 'Example3-5.htm', which includes nested ordered and unordered lists, displayed in Internet Explorer 7. The only change to the page is the inclusion of the necessary LINK element to apply the stylesheet (the modified HTML is in the file 'Example4-9.htm'). Two lines are added to the stylesheet to

TABLE 4.1 Styles that can be applied to ordered lists

list-style-type attribute	Numbering style
decimal	(1,2,3, …) – the default
upper-alpha	(A,B,C …)
lower-alpha	(a,b,c …)
upper-roman	(I,II,III,IV …)
lower-roman	(i,ii,iii,iv …)

FIGURE 4.10 Formatting lists using styles

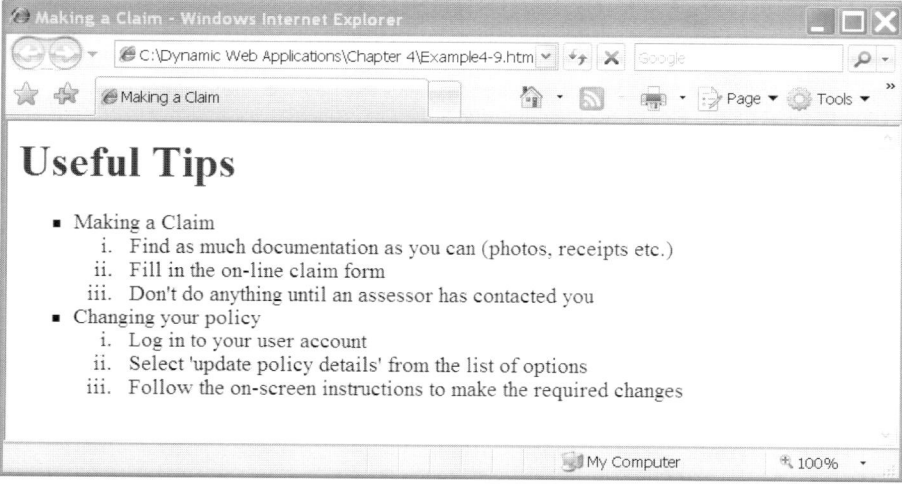

format lists, changing the unordered list bullets to the 'square' style and using lower case Roman numerals for the ordered list:

```
ul{list-style-type: square}
ol{list-style-type: lower-roman}
```

There are many ways that we can change the presentation of a table. These include:

- Adding spacing inside cells
- Adding padding between cells
- Setting the colors of the table
- Adding borders
- Aligning the table and its contents
- Setting the width of the table

Some of these will be applied to the whole table, some to parts of the table (e.g. a table row) and others could be applied using class or id attributes. To keep the following example simple, we will focus on styles that may be applied to HTML table elements. For example, the following style sets the 'width' property of the table to be 50% of the current window, while the external 'border' property of the table will be set to 3 pixels wide, drawn solid black:

```
table{width: 50%; border: 3px black solid}
```

 **NOTE** As well as 'solid', other styles for borders include 'dotted', 'dashed', 'double' and 'groove'. Styles can, of course, also be applied to rows or cells.

There is no specific table style for aligning the table on the page. However we can use the generic 'margin' property, which sets all four margins round an element. If we set the value of this property to 'auto', the table will automatically be centred.

```
table{width: 50%; border: 3px black solid; margin: auto}
```

As well as applying styles to the main TABLE element, we can apply them to any of the other elements that appear inside tables. Here, we apply some styles to the table header cells, setting the text color to white on a black background.

```
th{color: white; background-color: black}
```

Here, a solid border of 1 pixel is added around each cell:

```
td{border: 1px black solid}
```

Figure 4.11 shows the effect of these styles on the presentation of the table from 'Example3.8.htm'. The only change to the HTML page is the inclusion of the LINK element that applies the style sheet (the modified HTML is in the file 'Example4-10.htm').

If you do not like the separation of the cell borders, then you can collapse them together using the 'border-collapse' property:

```
table{width: 50%; border: 3px black solid; border-collapse: collapse}
```

The effect is shown in Figure 4.12.

The styles we have applied to our table are just a brief introduction to what is possible. We have glossed over much of the underlying HTML table model and the complex ways that style sheets can be used with it. If you wish to explore this further, the 'Tables' chapter of the CSS specification provides much more detail (Bos *et al.* 1998).

FIGURE 4.11 The effect of setting styles for elements within a table

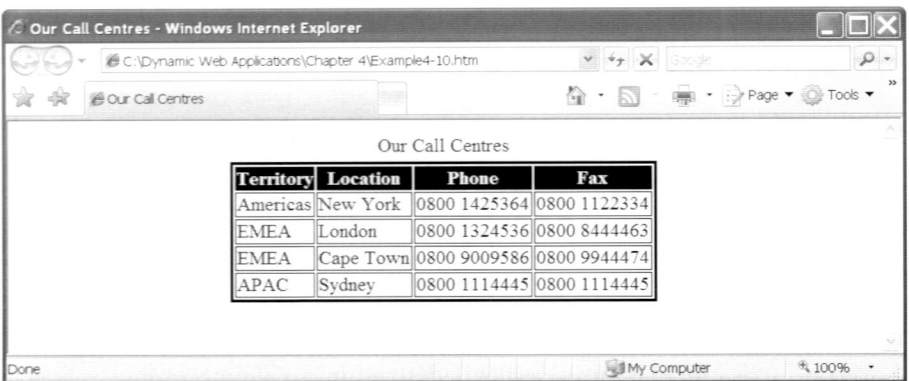

FIGURE 4.12   The effect of collapsing table borders

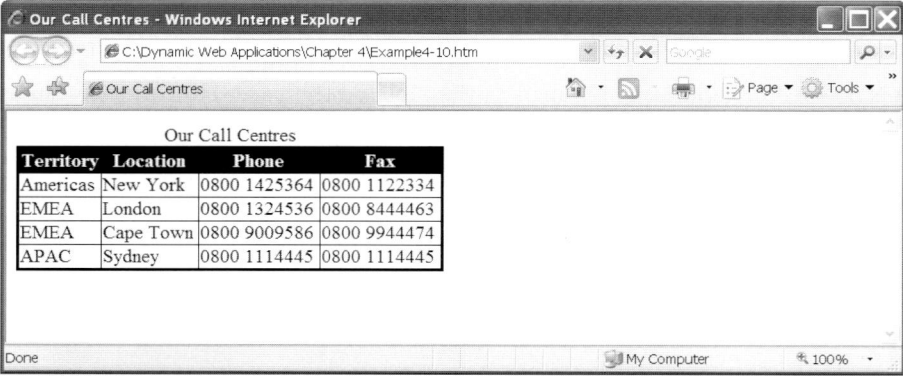

4.7 Style sheet cascades

At the beginning of this chapter we said that cascading style sheets provide for an ordered list of style sheets to be 'cascaded' in the same document, each one adding more specific styles. In this way, style information from several sources can be combined together. The following example uses two external style sheets and one internal style sheet:

```
<LINK href="webhomecover.css" rel="stylesheet" type="text/css">
<LINK href="informationpage.css" rel="stylesheet" type="text/css">
<STYLE type="text/css">
p.important{color: red; font-size: large}
</STYLE>
```

For the purposes of this example, 'informationpage.css' contains the following styles, left-aligning members of the 'heading' class and applying the 'courier' font to second-level headings:

```
.heading{text-align: left}
h2{font-family: courier}
```

When we have a series of cascading styles applied to the same document, styles are aggregated together so that the final style is a combination of multiple style sheets. In case of conflicts, where different styles are applied to the same types of element, styles defined more locally will always override those defined more globally. For example, styles defined using internal style sheets (with the 'style' element) will override any styles defined in external style sheets. In addition, if more than one style sheet of the same type (e.g. two external style sheets) are listed in a page, styles that appear later will override those that appear earlier. In our example, any styles defined in 'informationpage.css' would override styles for the same elements defined in 'webhomecover.css'. Specifically, the 'heading' style in 'informationpage.css' would override the 'center' alignment of members of the 'heading' class defined in 'webhomecover.css'. Other styles defined in 'webhomecover.css' would continue to be applied.

Any styles defined in a 'style' element in the header will override external styles, though in our example the only style applied (to 'important' paragraphs) is a new style so does not override anything in the external stylesheets. Any in-line styles will override all the rest, as in our example where we apply the 'normal' font style to both second-level headings:

```
style = "font-style: normal"
```

This overrides the italic style applied by 'webhomecover.css'. Here is the complete HTML page:

```
<!DOCTYPE HTML PUBLIC "-//W3C//DTD HTML 4.01//EN"
"http://www.w3.org/TR/html4/strict.dtd">
<HTML>
  <HEAD>
    <LINK href="webhomecover.css" rel="stylesheet" type="text/css">
    <LINK href="informationpage.css" rel="stylesheet" type="text/css">
    <STYLE type="text/css">
      p.important {color: red; font-size: 1.2em}
    </STYLE>
    <TITLE>Information About Our Insurance Cover</TITLE>
  </HEAD>
  <BODY>
  <!-- File: example4.11.htm -->
    <H1 class="heading">Important Information</H1>
    <H2 class="heading" style="font-style: normal">Buildings Cover</H2>
    <P>Buildings cover is subject to an inspection by a structural engineer prior
to insurance being approved should WebHomeCover require this inspection.
    </P>
    <H2 class="heading" style="font-style: normal">Contents Cover</H2>
    <P>You will be required to provide documentary and/or photographic evidence
of items to be covered on your policy where an individual item may be classified
as a valuable antique.
    </P>
    <P class="important">
    Failure to meet these terms and conditions may invalidate your insurance cover.
    </P>
    <HR>
    <P id="footer"> &copy;WebHomeCover.com 2007 </P>
  </BODY>
</HTML>
```

Figure 4.13 shows the effect of the cascading style sheets on the page in Internet Explorer. Note the change in style of all the headings from the second external style sheet, the large font of the 'important' paragraph style from the internal style sheet, and the non-italic second-level headings, specified by in-line styles. Other styles, such as those applied to the footer, are unaffected.

FIGURE 4.13 The effect of cascading multiple style sheets

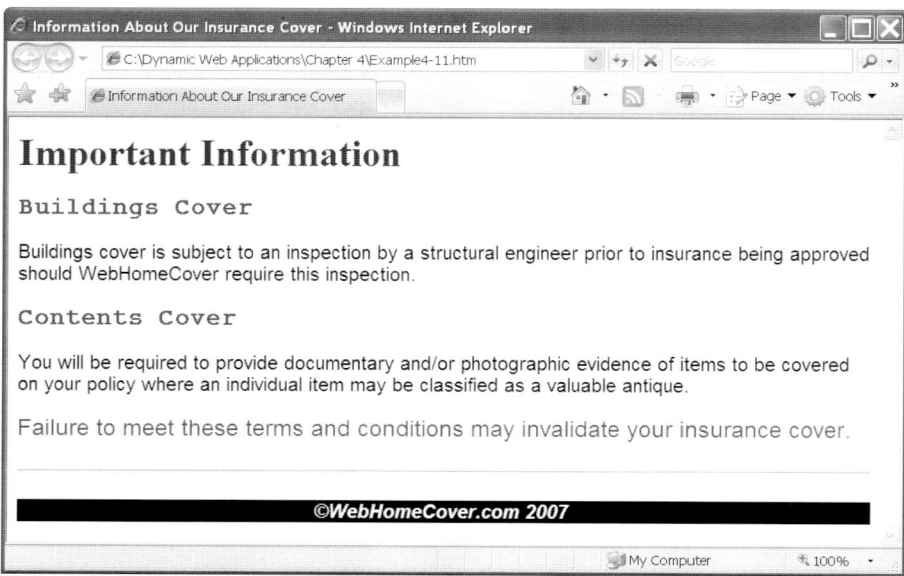

4.8 Using CSS for page layout

So far we have been looking at ways of changing the appearance of parts of a document using CSS. However we can also use it to manage the layout of a document. This is quite a complex topic, and not one we can do justice to here, but this section serves as an introduction to the general concept of page layout with CSS.

We previously introduced some design patterns related to generic page layout, such as the navigation bar, a site logo in the top left corner and the three-region layout. In the final example in this chapter, we see how CSS can be used to implement a three-region layout.

In a previous exercise, you were asked to implement a three-region layout using a table, but many authors claim that it is better to use style sheets for this type of layout. There are many ways to approach this problem, but here we will introduce a very simple solution using the 'float' and 'clear' style properties. We can set the value of the 'float' property to 'left' or 'right' to make the associated element appear on the right or left of the page, with other elements wrapped around it. This can be useful for setting up the left hand navigation bar of the three-region layout. To set up other elements that do not wrap around floating elements we can use the 'clear' property. The values of this property can be 'left' (do not wrap around floating elements on the left), 'right' (do not wrap around floating elements on the right) or 'both' (do not wrap around any floating elements). Figure 4.14 shows the general layout of a page with a three-region layout and a page footer. Note that the side navigation bar uses the 'float' property to float to the left hand side of the page and allow the main content to wrap to the right. To maintain the column layout where the content area may be longer than the side navigation bar we set the width of the navigation bar and also the left margin of the content to the same value. This stops the content from wrapping underneath the navigation bar. We don't use 'clear' because we want the content to appear next to the side navigation bar, not above or below it. However, to keep the top navigation bar above the side navigation bar and the page footer below it, we use the 'clear' property on both.

Using CSS with anchors

In our three-region layout we are going to have links along both the top and side navigation bars. To style anchors with CSS we have to use a slightly different approach from styling simple text, because an anchor can be in one of four possible states, and each one can have a different style applied to it. The four states are:

- **link**: a link that has not been clicked on and the mouse pointer is not hovering over it
- **visited**: a link that has previously been visited and the mouse pointer is not hovering over it
- **hover**: a link with the mouse pointer hovering over it
- **active**: a link that is being clicked on by the mouse

To apply styles to these states we use a CSS *pseudo-class*, which appears after the element name, separated from it by a colon. For example, to set the color of an anchor that has not been clicked on using the 'link' pseudo-class, we would use the following style:

```
a:link{color: black}
```

When applying styles to these pseudo classes they must appear in the correct order in the style sheet (the order used in the list above). Here are some styles we might apply to these four anchor states:

```
a:link{color: black}
a:visited{color: blue}
a:hover{font-weight: bold}
a:active{font-style: italic}
```

Applying the layout styles

Here are the styles that would be added to the style sheet to enable the three-region layout. So that the layout can be applied separately from other style information, we will save it in a separate file ('threeregion.css'). In addition to the layout styles, we also apply some styles to the hyperlink anchors that appear in the two navigation bars. Notice too the reference to 'margin-left'. In the table example, we introduced the 'margin' property, which applied the same value to all four margins of an element; left, right, top and bottom. To control the margins individually, there are 'margin-left', 'margin-right', 'margin-top' and 'margin-bottom' properties. Here, we use the 'margin-left' property.

```
a:link{color: white}
a:visited{color: red}
a:hover{font-weight: bold}
a:active{font-style: italic}
#navigationbar {color: white; background-color: rgb(0,0,150)}
#sidenavigation {float: left; height: 400px; color: white; background-color:
rgb(0,0,150)}
#content {margin-left: 10em}
#pagefooter {clear: left}
.topnavigationlink {clear: left; margin-left: 1em; font-size: 1.1em}
.sidenavigationlink {font-size: 1em}
```

Here is a simple page that uses the three-region style. The content here is just mocked up, with some fictional names of hyperlinked pages.

```
<!DOCTYPE HTML PUBLIC "-//W3C//DTD HTML 4.01//EN"
"http://www.w3.org/TR/html4/strict.dtd">
<HTML>
  <HEAD>
    <LINK href="webhomecover.css" rel="stylesheet" type="text/css">
    <LINK href="threeregion.css" rel="stylesheet" type="text/css">
    <TITLE>WebHomeCover.com</TITLE>
  </HEAD>
  <BODY>
    <!-- File: example4.12.htm -->
    <DIV id="navigationbar">
      <A href="home.htm">
        <IMG src="webhomecoverlogo.gif" alt="WebHomeCover logo">
      </A>
      <SPAN class="topnavigationlink">
        <A href="quote.htm">Get a quote</A>
      </SPAN>
      <SPAN class="topnavigationlink">
        <A href="claim.htm">Make a claim</A>
      </SPAN>
      <SPAN class="topnavigationlink">
        <A href="policies.htm">See my policies</A>
      </SPAN>
    </DIV>
    <DIV id="sidenavigation">
```

```
        <DIV class="sidenavigationlink">
          <A href="build.htm">buildings cover</A>
        </DIV>
        <DIV class="sidenavigationlink">
          <A href="content.htm">contents cover</A>
        </DIV>
        <DIV class="sidenavigationlink">
          <A href="deal.htm">special deals</A>
        </DIV>
        <DIV class="sidenavigationlink">
          <A href="more.htm">more info</A></DIV>
        </DIV>
        <DIV id="content">
        <H1 class="heading">We provide the following types of insurance</H1>
          <H2 class="heading">Buildings Cover</H2>
          <P>You may think you're "safe as houses" but you'd be surprised how many
things can damage the building you live in. Fires, earthquakes, subsidence, runaway
trucks, cricket balls through windows or the occasional meteor. Best to be covered!
          </P>
          <H2 class = "heading">Contents Cover</H2>
          <P>You may not realise just how much the stuff you have would cost to
replace. If the burglars move in while you're on holiday, could you afford to
replace the TV, the stereo, the chairs, the cupboards, the crockery, etc?
          </P>
          <P>Not only that, our contents cover means that if you have your
bike stolen, drop the vase your mother-in-law gave you as a wedding present, lose
your camera, leave your glasses on the train or have your mobile phone stolen,
you'll be fully compensated.
          </P>
        </DIV>
        <DIV id="pagefooter">
          <HR>
          <P id="footer"> &copy;WebHomeCover.com 2007 </P>
        </DIV>
    </BODY>
</HTML>
```

Figure 4.15 shows how the page looks in the Opera 9 browser.

FIGURE 4.15   The three-region layout using style sheets, as displayed in the Opera 9 browser

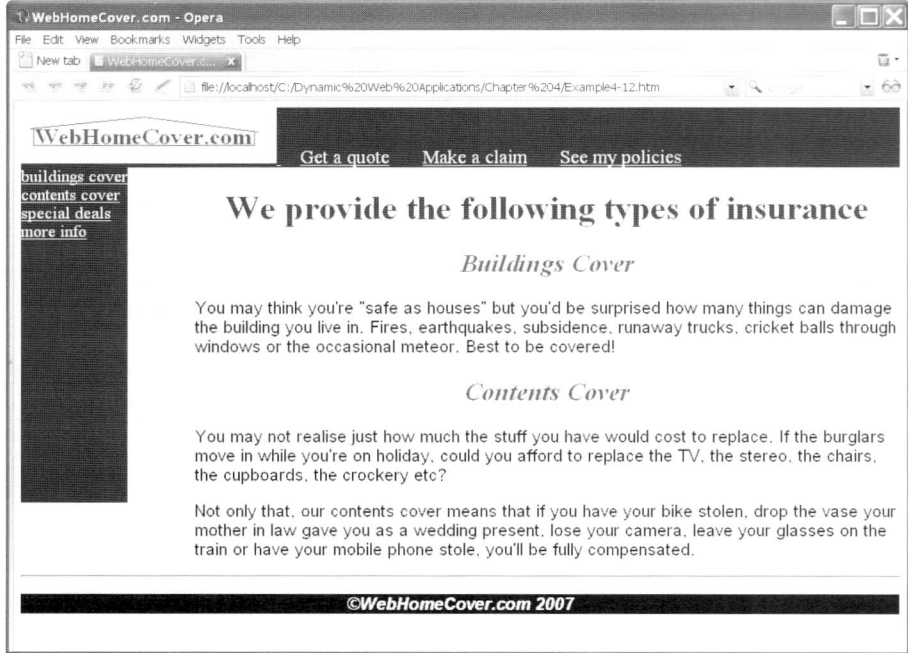

Exercises

4.1 Create a simple web page with some text. Using a style sheet and the RGB color syntax, color the text blue.

  • What do you get if you mix red and green without blue?
  • What do you get if you mix green and blue without red?

4.2 Add some images of houses (provided on the CD) to the bottom of the left-hand region of the three-region layout example for the home insurance system.

4.3 Create a CSS file called 'basic.css' that will provide the presentation for the pages of the research questionnaire web site. At this stage, we are only looking at static pages that might be used to introduce and explain the site, not the questionnaires themselves. In the first version, provide formats only for HTML elements.

4.4 Look at your 'About Us' page to identify parts of the content that might be usefully categorized using the 'class' attribute. Having identified one or more classes of content, modify your CSS to apply styles as appropriate.

4.5 Create a CSS file called 'infopage.css'. Add at least one style that is not in 'basic.css' that can be applied to your 'About Us' page.

4.6 Use CSS to manage the layout of your pages, applying the three-region layout.

4.7 Experiment with using CSS to manage the layout of your home page.

SUMMARY

In this chapter we saw how CSS can be used to provide the presentation for HTML files. We began by applying in-line styles, added to elements using the 'style' attribute. We then saw how to include style sheets in the document header using a STYLE element, so that styles could be reused for elements of the same type. The next stage covered how to write and link external style sheets that could be used across multiple web pages. We concluded the chapter by using CSS to manage the layout of a page. There are many aspects to CSS, far too many to cover in this chapter. Table 4.2 summarizes the CSS properties and some of their possible values that we have introduced in this chapter. This is of course just a small subset of the full CSS syntax, but there are many books and on-line resources available, if you want to explore stylesheets further.

TABLE 4.2	CSS properties introduced in this chapter		
Property	Meaning	Possible values	Examples
color	Foreground (text) color	Any of the 16 color names defined in HTML 4.0: aqua, black, blue, fuchsia, gray, green, lime, maroon, navy, olive, purple, red, silver, teal, white, yellow. RGB color values: color: rgb (R,G,B)	color: blue color: rgb (255, 255, 255) color: rgb (0, 0, 0)
background-color	Background color	Same values as color	background-color: black
text-align	Text alignment	left, right, center, justify	text-align: center
font-style	Font style	normal, italic, oblique	font-style: italic
font-weight	Font weight	normal, lighter, bold, bolder	font-weight: bold
font-size	Font size	A measurement in pixels, em, a percentage or name: large, small, x-small, x-large	font-size: 110% font-size: .8em font-size: 20px font-size: x-large
font-family	Font family	serif, sans-serif, cursive, fantasy, monospace, Arial, Courier, 'Times New Roman'	font-family: sans-serif font-family: 'Times New Roman'
list-style-type	Styles for list numbers or bullets	decimal, upper-alpha, lower-alpha. upper-roman. lower-roman	list-style-type: square list-style-type: lower-roman
width	Width of element (e.g. table width)	Percentage of page width	width: 50%
border	Table border	Number of pixels and line style: solid, dotted, dashed, double, groove	border: 3px solid
margin	All element margins	auto	margin: auto
margin-left	Left element margin	A measurement in em	margin-left: 1em
margin-right	Right element margin	A measurement in em	margin-right: 3em
margin-top	Top element margin	A measurement in em	margin-top: 5em
margin-bottom	Bottom element margin	A measurement in em	margin-bottom: 2em
border-collapse	Table border style	collapse	border-collapse: collapse
link visited hover active	Pseudo-classes for anchor elements	a: link a: visited a: hover a: active	a: link{color: black}
float	Relative alignment within the page	left, right	float: left;
clear	Stop content wrapping around elements on the right or left	left, right, both	clear: both

References and further reading

Bos, B., Lie, H., Lilley, C. and Jacobs, I. (1998) *Cascading Style Sheets*, level 2 CSS2 Specification, W3C Recommendation 12-May-1998, Chapter 17, http://www.w3.org/TR/REC-CSS2/tables.html

Lie, H. and Bos, B. (1999) *Cascading Style Sheets, designing for the Web*, 2nd edition. Chapter 20, 'The CSS saga'. Addison Wesley.

Raggett, D., Le Hors, A. and Jacobs, I. (1999) *HTML 4.01 Specification*, Section 14, 'Style Sheets'. http://www.w3.org/TR/html4/present/styles.html

Weinman, L. (2007) *The Browser-Safe Web Palette*. http://www.lynda.com/hex.asp

4

CHAPTER 5

Content, Structure and Validation: XML, DTD, XHTML and XML Schema

LEARNING OBJECTIVES

- To understand the concepts of semi-structured data
- To be able to construct well-formed XML documents
- To be able to create document type definitions
- To be able to validate XML documents against document type definitions
- To be able to validate XML documents against XML Schemas
- To be able to create well-formed and valid XHTML documents

INTRODUCTION

In this chapter, we begin by looking at some of the limitations of HTML, then explore how XML and XHTML can be used to provide a more flexible approach to both representing data and building web pages. Along the way, we see how some of these markup languages can be validated by document type definitions (DTDs) and XML Schemas. We also see what tools may be used to test the well-formedness and validity of XML and XHTML documents, using these DTDs and Schemas.

5.1 The limitations of HTML

HTML has been very successful in providing a relatively simple way of presenting data on the web. It enables the rapid creation of web pages that can contain a number of different content types (text, images, videos, sounds, etc), and these pages can be presented to the user by commonly available browsers such as Internet Explorer and Mozilla Firefox. However, as web applications have become more sophisticated and addressed more complex needs, the limitations of using HTML as the main way of managing the content of a web application have become apparent. One of the main problems is that 'traditional'

HTML combines content, structure and presentation, which works against the idea of separation of concerns. As an example, take this very short piece of HTML source that uses the FONT element (this was not covered in our HTML chapter because we did not look at presentational elements):

```
<FONT color="red"><P>Hello...</P></FONT>
```

In this markup, we can see some content ('Hello . . . '), a structural element (the paragraph tags) and a presentation element (the FONT element, used here to set the font color to red). If we were to build the pages of our web application using this type of mark-up, then it would be very difficult to separate out the different concerns of content, structure and presentation both for original development and for making changes to pages. Therefore using just HTML makes our web applications difficult both to build and to maintain. Of course, one part of the solution is to use cascading style sheets (CSS) for presentational mark-up, as we saw in the previous chapter. However, the mix of presentation with content and structure is not the only issue. Another serious problem with HTML is that it does not have to be well-formed. Take the following example, which most browsers would be able to deal with, as they are usually tolerant of poorly formed HTML:

```
<DIV CLASS=intro><p><STRONG><EM>Hello...</STRONG></EM></DIV>
```

Here, there are four aspects where the mark-up is not well formed. First, there is an attribute value ('intro') that is not surrounded by either speech marks or apostrophes. Secondly, there is an element that has a start tag but no end tag (<p>). Then, there is improper nesting: the terminating </STRONG> tag appears before the terminating </EM> tag, but should appear after it. Finally, there are inconsistent and incorrect uses of case (the tags are all in upper case except the <p> tag and the attribute name, 'CLASS', is in upper case).

The effects of poorly formed documents

Why does this lacked of well-formedness matter? There are several reasons why this can be a problem. Perhaps the most important is that a document that is not well-formed cannot be validated. This is significant because validation, which checks a document to ensure that the correct elements and attributes appear in the right order and number, is the first step in successfully processing the content of a document. Since the exact structure of documents created using a mark-up language cannot be known in advance, a program that processes documents like this needs to know that they will meet certain structural rules. One example of a software application that needs to process mark-up is a web browser. On the whole, browsers have had to be very tolerant of poorly formed HTML and do their best to render an HTML page however badly formed it is. However there are limits to how flexible a browser can be. Browser processing can arbitrarily fail if an HTML document is particularly poorly formed, in some cases resulting in the user seeing a blank page. This can happen because a browser often ignores those parts that cannot be properly processed, and sometimes most or all of the page is ignored. In this sense, browsers are a victim of their own success, having been historically able to manage poorly formed documents, there is perhaps an expectation that poorly formed documents are acceptable.

In a 'smart client' application that supports some client-side processing over and above the normal page rendering of the browser, such as one that uses the document object model (DOM), there can be problems with the program scripts that are running within

5

the browser. The DOM is a standard interface to the content, structure and style of a document, enabling applications to access and update that document. The programming language that is often used to interact with the DOM in a web browser is JavaScript (for example, in Ajax applications) and JavaScript errors are common in web applications. The problem is that the DOM represents the structure of the HTML document within the browser and JavaScript programs often need to navigate through the DOM to process various parts of the page. If the DOM is not well constructed due to poorly formed HTML, the JavaScript may be unable to find what it is looking for.

Why HTML alone is not enough

The problem of poorly formed documents can be resolved by validating an HTML page against a DTD. However there is a further important issue with HTML, which is that HTML cannot be used to represent anything other than web page mark-up. This means that the content that we represent in web pages has no structure applied to it other than the specific structure of an individual web page. However the data that underlies a web application may need to be used in different pages, and in different ways, across many parts of the application, or even between different applications. Ideally we would like to be able to have a separate method of representing the underlying structure of our content regardless of the ways that it might be organized and presented in web pages.

In summary, HTML has many strengths as a simple, flexible language for creating web pages that combine content, structure and presentation. However, it does not have enough intrinsic structural and syntactic rules to enable applications other than browsers (which are only concerned with presentation) to process them effectively. Further, the syntax of HTML is fixed to a set of tags that are intended only for the rendering of web pages. It cannot be used to represent more general types of content. If we want to use mark-up to present content in a more rigorous and useful way, then we need some language other than HTML. That language is the *eXtensible Markup Language* (XML).

5

5.2 Semi-structured data

In this section, we look at the relationship between the eXtensible Markup Language (XML) and the concept of semi-structured data. We see how semi-structured data can be represented in an XML document using both elements and attributes, and explain how to choose between elements or attributes when structuring XML documents.

Semi-structured data contains no type information, is self-describing and can have variations in its structure. Semi-structured data is self-describing because it contains labels; each piece of data contains some metadata that tells us about that data element. This means that a document of semi-structured data can support interoperability between systems, because when it is serialized (sent as a stream of data) between different applications it carries its own labels with it, helping the receiving system to process its content. This is the basis upon which XML web services work.

Perhaps the best way to explain semi-structured data is to start with an example of some structured data:

```
02 03 1959 15 08 1977 08 04 1994
```

If you look at this data you can see that it follows a repeating and consistent structure. There are three groups of numbers, and in each group there are two numbers of two digits followed by a third number of four digits. The different numbers are separated by spaces. The important feature of structured data is that it follows a consistent and predictable format. In this case, you can probably see that the data represents a series of dates, though there is nothing in the data to tell you that, other than the knowledge you already have about dates (that they have a day number, a month number and, particularly since the 'millennium bug' panic, a four-digit year). If you look a bit more closely you might assume that the day number comes before the month number in each group, because '15' could not be a month number. However with just the structured data to go on this is just supposition. The data may not represent dates at all. Maybe it is a single part number from a catalogue, or some sports results. Without a bit of metadata to help us we do not really know.

Assuming that the data is, in fact, a series of dates, any application that processes this data needs to know that each data item is separated from its neighbours by spaces and that it occurs in groups of three, each group representing the day, month and year of the date in that order. That information is not carried with the data itself, so we have to 'just know' it. In contrast, semi-structured data is human-readable and self-describing. This example shows the same data in semi-structured format (this is not a 'real' syntax, just one used as an example).

```
[dates
  [date [day: 03] [month: 02] [year: 1959] ]
  [date [day: 15] [month: 08] [year: 1977] ]
  [date [day: 08] [month: 04] [year: 1994] ]
]
```

In this version, the data is both human-readable and self-describing because the data describes itself using recognisable names. Thanks to the labels, we can clearly see that the data represents a series of dates, and that each date consists of the day, the month and the year.

Variations in structure

One of the key features of semi-structured data is that it allows for variations in the structure of the data so that the order and number of elements can be varied. In this version of the data, we add a 'day-name' element to the first date but not to the other dates.

```
[dates
  [date [day-name: Tuesday] [day: 03] [month: 02] [year: 1959] ]
  [date [day: 15] [month: 08] [year: 1977] ]
  [date [day: 08] [month: 04] [year: 1994] ]
]
```

This type of structure would be very difficult, if not impossible, to process without the metadata provided by the labels. An application would have to check for the type of data at the beginning of every date to see if it was text (the day name) or a number (the day). Imagine, however, if we made the structure more complex, with many optional parts to the data. Eventually, it would be impossible to process this information without the identifying labels. The point about semi-structured data is that the self-descriptiveness makes it possible for the data to vary in structure, because it provides the context for

FIGURE 5.1 A tree of nodes and edges

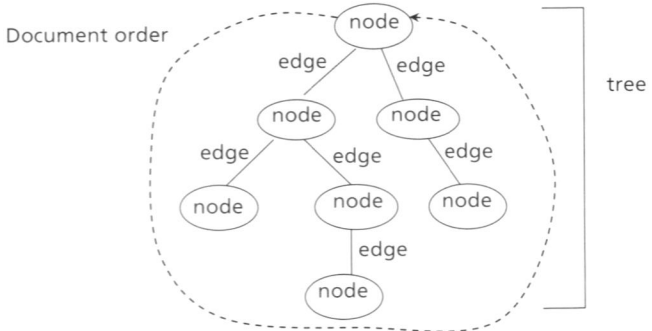

applications to identify the nature of a piece of data by the label that is attached to it. As a side effect, making these labels human-readable can be very useful as well.

Semi-structured data as a tree

Semi-structured data is generally grouped into related types using a nested structure and can be visualized as a tree. We can think of a tree as being composed of nodes and edges, with edges providing the links between the nodes (Figure 5.1). When we look later at the elements in an XML document we can think of them as being like the nodes in this kind of tree structure. What this means is that an XML document is fundamentally a tree that can therefore be traversed in a specific order (known as the *document order*). Because of the flexible nature of semi-structured data, the trees that represent different documents can vary widely.

5.3 What is XML?

XML is not so much a language as a *metalanguage*. The term 'meta' means 'about', so a metalanguage can provide information about a specific language. In the case of XML, it is a metalanguage used to describe other specific mark-up languages, specifying the syntax of the language being defined. XML is designed to be semi-structured, enabling exact, yet flexible, rules to be applied about how data can be organized. Importantly, it is also designed to be extensible in the sense that many different XML-based languages can be built from it, which is what makes it a metalanguage. XML has no predefined tags so you can define your own terms and markup. In contrast, HTML is not a metalanguage because it consists of a set of predefined tags that can be used in a document. You cannot invent new tags for HTML because they are already specified as part of its syntax.

XML is an official recommendation of the W3C that aims to accomplish what HTML cannot and to be simpler to use and implement than SGML. Unlike HTML, it has no presentational components, though CSS can be used to present XML in a similar way to HTML. Many other specifications are based upon XML, including XHTML, which we introduce in Section 5.6. In addition, there are many other special- purpose XML-based specifications that are beyond the scope of this book.

The design goals for XML (Bray *et al.* 2006) were that it should:

- Be simple to use over the Internet.
- Support a wide variety of applications.
- Be compatible with SGML.
- Make it easy to write programs that process XML documents.
- Have the minimum possible number of optional features (ideally zero).
- Be human-legible and reasonably clear.
- Have its design prepared quickly.
- Have a formal and concise design.
- Make documents easy to create.
- Not consider terseness important.

Among other many other uses, XML can be used as an alternative to HTML in creating web pages, but with a separation of content and presentation. Rather than combining, as HTML does, content, structure and presentation into a single language, XML is purely a data description (mark-up) language that manages content. It provides a definition of data structures and syntax, but not semantics (it does not specify what the data actually means). It performs a number of roles that go beyond the capabilities of HTML, for example the exchange of data between different applications (e.g. web services). Using XML as a communication mechanism between different systems avoids having to use many different file formats. Various industries have standardized on special XML-based languages, enabling them to exchange data using a common format. Examples of this type of format include the B2B (business to business) XML document specifications defined by the RosettaNet organization, principally for the electronic component industry and HL7 (Health Level 7) for clinical and administrative data in health care. XML can be (and has been) used to represent a huge range of different types of information. The following example is a fragment of a much larger document from the universal protein knowledge-base (UniProt 2005), that describes the DNA of tuberculosis. Here, XML is being used to represent non-textual data.

```
<?xml version="1.0" encoding="UTF-8"?>
  <organism key="2">
    <name type="scientific">Mycobacterium tuberculosis</name>
    <dbReference type="NCBI Taxonomy" id="1773" key="3"/>
  </organism>

  <sequence length="325" mass="34581" checksum="B993B5442FD5557D"
modified="1993-07-01" version="1">
MTDVSRKIRAWGRRLMIGTAAAVVLPGLVGLAGGAATAGAFSRPGLPVEY
LQVPSPSMGRDIKVQFQSGGNNSPAVYLLDGLRAQDDYNGWDINTPAFEW
YYQSGLSIVMPVGGQSSFYSDWYSPACGKAGCQTYKWETFLTSELPQWLS
ANRAVKPTGSAAIGLSMAGSSAMILAAYHPQQFIYAGSLSALLDPSQGMG
PSLIGLAMGDAGGYKAADMWGPSSDPAWERNDPTQQIPKLVANNTRLWVY
CGNGTPNELGGANIPAEFLENFVRSSNLKFQDAYNAAGGHNAVFNFPPNG
THSWEYWGAQLNAMKGDLQSSLGAG
  </sequence>
</entry>
<copyright>
Copyrighted by the UniProt Consortium, see http://www.uniprot.org/terms
```

```
Distributed under the Creative Commons Attribution-NoDerivs License
</copyright>
</uniprot>
```

The next example also uses XML, but is very different. This is again a tiny fragment of a much larger XML document, but this time it contains TV listings, in XMLTV format (Eden 2005), from the UK Radio Times (BBC 2005). Here, the content is primarily text-based.

```
<?xml version="1.0" encoding="ISO-8859-1"?>
<!DOCTYPE tv SYSTEM "xmltv.dtd">
<tv source-info-name="Radio Times"
   generator-info-name="XMLTV"
   generator-info-url="http://membled.com/work/apps/xmltv/">
   <channel id="channel4.com">
      <display-name>Channel 4</display-name>
      <display-name>4</display-name>
   </channel>
   <programme start="20050102010500 UTC" stop="20050102024000 UTC"
channel="channel4.com">
   <title>The Rachel Papers</title>
   <desc lang="en">A 19-year-old studying to go to Oxford enters all the infor-
mation about his love life into his computer in a determined effort to find the
perfect seduction technique. But his system collapses when he meets and falls in
love with the beautiful Rachel, an American living in London. The couple spend a
passionate weekend together, but then the dream begins to fall apart.</desc>
<credits>
   <director>Damian Harris</director>
   <actor>Dexter Fletcher</actor>
   <actor>Ione Skye</actor>
   <actor>Jonathan Pryce</actor>
   <actor>James Spader</actor>
   <actor>Bill Paterson</actor>
   <actor>Shirley Anne Field</actor>
</credits>
<date>1989</date>
<category lang="en">film</category>
<category lang="en">Film</category>
<video>
   <aspect>15:9</aspect>
</video>
<subtitles type="teletext" />
</programme>
</tv>
```

5.4 Components of XML

Like an HTML document, an XML document consists of a series of tags surrounded by angle brackets and start tags may include attributes. There are, however, one or two additional aspects to XML, including what is known as the *prolog*. There are a number of possible parts to the prolog, but here we introduce two of them, the *XML declaration* and the *processing instructions*.

The XML declaration

An XML document should begin with the XML declaration. This identifies it as an XML document and also declares its version number. Note the question marks that come inside the angle brackets.

```
<?xml version="1.0"?>
```

 NOTE The 'xml' should be in lower case, though XML processors recognize all the different possible case combinations of these three letters, so using upper case would not actually result in an error.

The most commonly used version of XML is version 1.0. There is a version 1.1 specification (Bray *et al.* 2004) but this is largely to enable wider character sets in names than are specified by XML version 1.0, to be able to adapt to the continued development of the Unicode character set.

 NOTE The XML version 1.1 specification states that any XML document that does not explicitly have an XML declaration with a version value of 1.1 will be assumed to be using version 1.0.

The character encoding used in the document may also be specified, though it will default to utf-8 (Unicode Transformation Format 8). This is an encoding scheme that is backward-compatible with ASCII (American Standard Code for Information Interchange, an older standard, 8-bit character encoding) and uses from 1 to 4 bytes to represent each character. You can choose to explicitly specify utf-8 as the encoding, like this:

```
<?xml version="1.0" encoding="utf-8"?>
```

Other common encodings that you may see used include ISO-8859-1, which is for the Latin character set on the Internet, and utf-16, which uses at least two bytes per character (i.e. is at least 16 bits). Either of these, or indeed any of a number of other character encodings, can appear in the 'encoding' attribute for example:

```
<?xml version="1.0" encoding="ISO-8859-1"?>
```

or

```
<?xml version="1.0" encoding="utf-16"?>
```

The implication of these differences in encoding is that you should make sure that whatever editor you may be using to create and edit XML documents is saving those documents in the same encoding that you have specified. If not, software tools, including browsers, will not be able to process the XML properly.

Processing instructions

The XML declaration can be followed by *processing instructions* that are intended to provide information to applications that need to process the document, such as software that transforms the XML into another type of document. Browsers and other tools can understand this type of processing instruction and handle the XML document accordingly. A processing instruction is identified by special tags that include question marks, similar to the XML declaration.

```
<? processing instruction ?>
```

An example of a processing instruction is one that applies a CSS stylesheet to an XML document. Such an instruction looks something like this:

```
<?xml version="1.0"?>
<?xml-stylesheet href="styles.css" type="text/css"?>
```

Elements and parsed character data

Regardless of the content of the prolog, at a minimum, an XML document must contain a root element, which may be the only element in the document, for example:

```
<weather-forecast>rain</weather-forecast>
```

In XML version 1.0, everything except the declaration of the root element can be omitted. Nevertheless we will be including the XML declaration at the top of all our XML files from now on (the XML version 1.0 specification states that XML documents 'should' begin with this declaration, even though it is not compulsory).

The content in the body of an XML element ('rain', in our example) is *parsed character data*. This means that it is data that will be parsed (processed) by any program that handles the XML document. Parsed character data has no type defined by XML, it is just characters.

An XML document will generally consist of the root element, parsed character data and sub-elements (elements nested inside other elements). For example, we might extend our 'weather-forecast' example to include nested elements to describe the weather forecast for today and tomorrow:

```
<?xml version="1.0"?>
<!-- File: Example5-1.xml -->
<weather-forecast>
  <today>
    rain
  </today>
  <tomorrow>
```

```
      showers
   </tomorrow>
   <long-range>
      unsettled
   </long-range>
</weather-forecast>
```

 NOTE You will see from these XML examples that the comment syntax is the same as HTML: <!-- a comment -->

Although our example so far only nests elements to a depth of one, elements can be nested to any depth. XML itself allows any combination of elements to be used, but we should group related elements together to give them some meaningful structure. For example, we might provide some temperature information that relates to either today or tomorrow, and group this information into nested elements, as in the next example. Note how this XML document has now acquired a more flexible structure (i.e. it is evidently semi-structured). The 'today' and 'tomorrow' elements now have different structures from the 'long-range' element.

```
<?xml version="1.0"?>
<!-- File: Example5-2.xml -->
<weather-forecast>
   <today>
      <general>Rain</general>
      <temperature>
         <maximum>15</maximum>
         <minimum>11</minimum>
      </temperature>
   </today>
   <tomorrow>
      <general>Showers</general>
      <temperature>
         <maximum>20</maximum>
         <minimum>15</minimum>
      </temperature>
   </tomorrow>
   <long-range>Unsettled</long-range>
</weather-forecast>
```

It is perhaps worth emphasising at this point that an XML document says nothing about the presentation of data, it is primarily about the representation of data. The weather forecast document is only about the underlying structure of its data content, not about how it might, for example, be presented on a web page. It is also not comprized of predefined elements, as an HTML document would be. The elements 'weather-forecast', 'today', 'temperature' etc. have been created specifically as mark-up for this document.

FIGURE 5.2   An XML document displayed in the Mozilla Firefox 2 browser

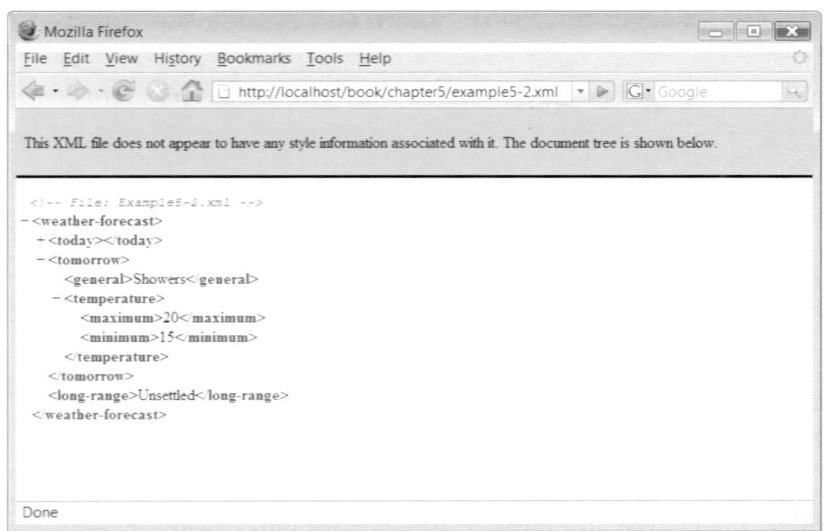

Viewing XML pages

So far we have seen a couple of XML documents, but what can we do with them? Later we will be using the XML-based language XHTML to create web pages, but in the meantime we can view XML documents directly in a browser. Providing you are using a browser that can understand XML, an XML document can be opened directly as a local file, just like an HTML document. Figure 5.2 shows how our weather forecast XML document appears in the Mozilla Firefox 2 browser. The behavior of this browser (though not all) is to show an XML document as a tree structure, and enable elements to be expanded or collapsed. As you can see from this figure, the first 'temperature' element has been collapsed, and is preceded by a '+' symbol to indicate this, but the second 'temperature' element is expanded (all expanded elements are preceded by a '-' symbol). Clicking on these symbols will expand or contract the element they are associated with.

Well-formed XML

Unlike an HTML document, which may be well-formed but does not have to be, an XML document *must* be well-formed. The rules for well-formed XML are similar to those for well-formed HTML, but you will note that there are one or two important differences:

- Empty tags must be expressed properly, with the trailing forward slash before the closing angle bracket, i.e.

  $<tag/>$

  This is different from HTML where empty tags such as <BR> do not require a trailing slash.

- Unlike HTML, text in XML is case-sensitive. Also, unlike in the HTML 4.0 specification, you should always use lower case for XML element names, as well as for attribute names.

- Element and attribute names must start with a letter but may also include numbers, underscores, hyphens, periods or colons. In HTML, of course, these names are predefined by the HTML syntax.

One useful feature of being able to load an XML document into a browser is that the browser will check if it is well-formed. The following XML document is not well-formed because the 'average-winter-temperature' element is missing its closing tag:

```
<?xml version="1.0"?>
<!-- File: Example5-3.xml -->
<climate>
   <average-winter-temperature>
      10
   <average-summer-temperature>
      20
   </average-summer-temperature>
</climate>
```

Attempting to open this document as a local file into Mozilla Firefox 2 results in the error message shown in Figure 5.3. The browser complains that the closing tag is missing.

Attributes versus elements in XML

As in HTML, XML opening tags may contain attributes to define properties that are related directly to this element rather than being defined by other elements. When you use

FIGURE 5.3 The error message in Mozilla Firefox 2 when attempting to load a poorly formed XML document

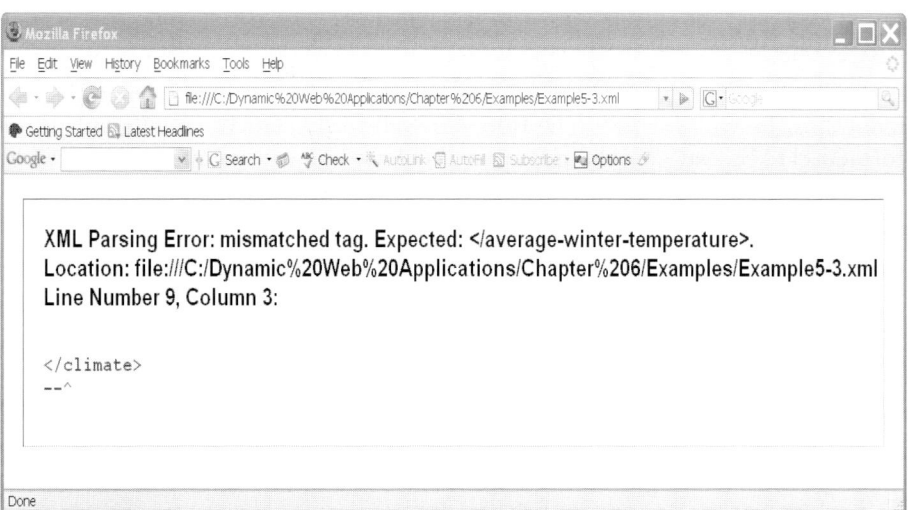

attributes in HTML, you are constrained by HTML syntax. In contrast, if you are creating an XML document structure then you will have to decide what data should be represented by elements and what should be represented by attributes. Being more tightly coupled to their host element than nested tags, attributes are less flexible but have some special properties. How do you decide, then, whether a particular piece of data should be modelled as an element or an attribute? The general rule of thumb is that you should use elements unless you have a particular need to use attributes. This is because there are many advantages to using elements:

- You cannot have multiple attributes of the same name in a single element, but you can have multiple nested elements that have the same name.
- Attributes are less flexible if you want to change the structure of a document later.
- Attributes cannot be used to describe hierarchical structures, but elements can be nested into these hierarchies.
- Attributes are more difficult to manipulate by software programs that process XML.
- You cannot specify a meaningful order of attributes, but a series of elements at the same level of nesting do have a meaningful order (they are part of the document order).

 NOTE Apart from the metadata attributes, the aspects of attributes listed here are related to the use of DTDs (covered later). XML Schemas (also covered later) additionally enable elements to have some of these features.

The overall message is that if you use attributes simply as a way of holding the data in your XML document, then you end up with documents that are difficult to read and maintain. Why, then, would we ever want to use attributes instead of elements? In fact attributes are very useful in special circumstances. These include:

- Representing metadata. Elements should be used to contain data, but attributes are good for providing further information about that data, for example the language in which it is presented, or perhaps the version number of the content if it relates to some product documentation.
- Providing unique IDs for elements that can be used to cross reference data. There are special types of attribute to do this, and these enable an XML tree to also act like a graph (i.e. elements that are not nested inside each other can still be associated).
- Specifying a set of possible values for some piece of data. For example, you want to say that a traffic light can be only red or green and no other color. This is known as an enumerated type. Attributes can be used for enumerated types but elements cannot.
- Specifying a fixed value (a constant). You can do this with an attribute but not with an element.
- Specifying default values. You can do this with an attribute but not with an element.
- Referencing external entities (such as other files) in your XML document. Attributes have special types that do this.

A more specialized requirement, but one that may be useful to know, is that attributes are often better where processing speed is important. The way that some programs process XML means that you can get better performance from these programs using attributes (Eckstein 2002).

The following example shows an XML document that includes attributes. In this case, we have some 'date' elements with 'calendar' attributes. We could, of course, use an element to contain the information about the type of calendar being used, (the Gregorian calendar, in this example), but this could reasonably be regarded as metadata, and therefore may be better represented as an attribute.

```
<?xml version="1.0"?>
<!-- File: Example5-4.xml -->
<dates>
   <date calendar="gregorian">
      <day>1</day>
      <month>3</month>
      <year>2005</year>
   </date>
   <date calendar="gregorian">
      <day>2</day>
      <month>3</month>
      <year>2005</year>
   </date>
</dates>
```

What about the other uses of attributes? As we will see, they only start to be usable when we combine XML documents with validating documents such as document type definitions (DTDs), so we will revisit this in Section 5.5.

CDATA sections

Some characters (such as < and >) can disrupt the correct parsing of an XML document by a program, and make it appear to be not well-formed. One example of this might be some kind of relational expression from a programming language using the '>' and '<' symbols:

```
<relational-expression>
   if(a > b && c < d)
</relational-expression>
```

In cases like this we can make the XML parser ignore the whole sequence by using a CDATA section. CDATA stands for 'character data' (as opposed to PCDATA, which is 'parsed character data'). A CDATA section looks like this:

```
<![CDATA[content]]>
```

It may look unnecessarily complex, but bear in mind that it is essential that such sections should be easily recognized by an XML parser and not be confused with other types of mark-up that may be present in the document. Using this complex format guarantees that a parser will be able to recognize a CDATA section. Here is our example using CDATA:

```
<relational-expression>
   <![CDATA[if(a > b && c < d)]]>
</relational-expression>
```

5.5 Validating XML documents

It is possible to use an XML document for a variety of purposes as long as it is well-formed. The problem is that a well-formed XML document can still be totally unpredictable. Since XML-based languages are extensible, we can create new elements and attributes using names that we decide to use, and we can put any number of elements in an arbitrary order and nest them to any depth that we choose. The consequence of this is that XML documents do not, on their own, help us to know what would be an acceptable structure for a given type of document. Ideally, we need some way of specifying:

- Which element names can be used in an XML document, how many times they might occur and in what order
- Which attribute names can be used, which elements they can be used with, and whether they are compulsory or optional
- Any default or allowed values that an attribute may have.

Rules like this help to describe how an XML document of a particular type should be structured so that others can create valid documents according to these rules. Checking an XML document against one of these rule sets is called *validation*. For example, an XML document might be used to contain the content for a magazine article. The article might contain a title, section headings and subheadings, paragraphs of text, footnotes, sidebars and references. We would expect these different types of content to have certain relationships to one another, for example, we might assume that a subheading must appear in the context of a heading, and precede a paragraph of text, that the references appear at the end, the title at the beginning, and so on. We might also expect there to be one title and one set of references, but perhaps many headings, subheadings and paragraphs. XML on its own cannot enforce any of these rules, making it difficult to process documents that do not follow them. Perhaps articles need to be submitted to a magazine's editorial department in XML format, but they must follow the type of agreed structure we have described here. To enforce this type of structure we need to validate the XML document against some other definition of the rules for how such a document can be organized. These definitions can be expressed either as document type definitions (DTDs) or XML Schemas (there have been other approaches but DTDs and XML Schemas are the most common). Either type of validation may be used but for a specific validation process we would choose one or the other (Figure 5.4).

DTDs have been around for a long time, because they are a part of SGML, whereas XML Schemas are a more recent type of validation that has been strongly supported by Microsoft. We begin by introducing DTDs and then cover XML Schemas. As well as defining the acceptable structure of an XML document's elements, validating documents, such as DTDs and XML Schemas, can provide default values, enumerated types and other useful 'sanity checks' for an XML document.

Document type definitions (DTDs)

We can use DTDs to validate XML documents, but what exactly is a DTD? It is basically a special type of mark-up that contains a definition of the permitted structure of a particular

FIGURE 5.4

A well-formed XML document may be validated either by a DTD or by an XML schema

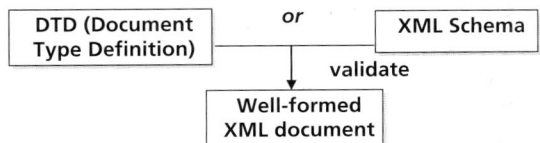

type of document. A DTD describes, among other things:

- What names can be used for element types
- How many times a given element may, or must, be used
- In what order elements at the same level of nesting may occur
- How elements can be nested
- The attributes that may, or must, be used with a specific element

An XML document can be linked to a DTD either by including the DTD mark-up inside the XML document itself or by referring to it externally using a URI.

Defining elements in a DTD

For our first example DTD we will describe a simplified 'weather-forecast' XML document type. In this DTD, there are no attributes, we are simply describing elements. You will see from this example that DTD syntax is not the same as XML syntax. It does use angle brackets, but is otherwise quite different:

```
<!ELEMENT weather-forecast (today, tomorrow, long-range)>
<!ELEMENT today (#PCDATA)>
<!ELEMENT tomorrow (#PCDATA)>
<!ELEMENT long-range (#PCDATA)>
```

The first line of the DTD indicates that the first element (weather-forecast) is the root. The other elements (today, tomorrow and long-range) are sub-elements of the root (i.e., they are nested inside it) and are defined in the order in which they must appear in a valid XML document. The remaining three lines indicate that each of these three nested elements contains parsed character data (#PCDATA). This means that the element will contain character data that an XML processor will parse as it reads through the document. Our first XML example (shown again here) would be valid against this DTD. We have the necessary root element, with the three nested elements in the correct order:

```
<?xml version="1.0"?>
<!-- File: Example5-1.xml -->
<weather-forecast>
  <today>
    rain
  </today>
  <tomorrow>
    showers
  </tomorrow>
```

```
    <long-range>
        unsettled
    </long-range>
</weather-forecast>
```

In contrast, the following document is well formed, but is not valid according to our DTD:

```
<?xml version="1.0"?>
<weather-forecast>
    <today>
        Rain
    </today>
    <tomorrow>
        Showers
    </tomorrow>
</weather-forecast>
```

'long-range' element missing here

It is invalid because the 'long-range' element is missing, yet the DTD says that it should appear. Similarly, the following document is also invalid. Here, all the necessary elements are present, but they appear in the wrong order – 'tomorrow' should appear before 'long-range':

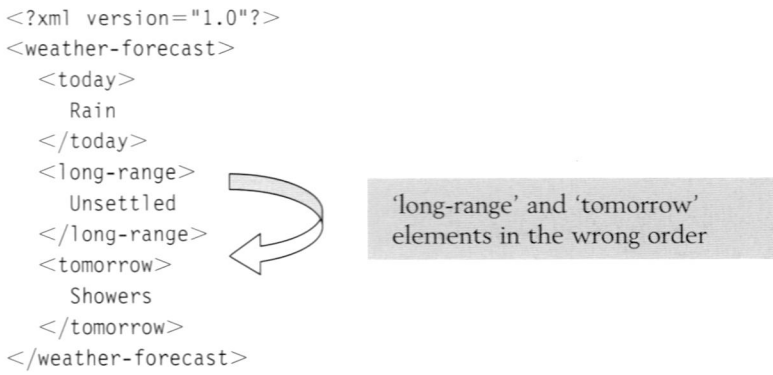

```
<?xml version="1.0"?>
<weather-forecast>
    <today>
        Rain
    </today>
    <long-range>
        Unsettled
    </long-range>
    <tomorrow>
        Showers
    </tomorrow>
</weather-forecast>
```

'long-range' and 'tomorrow' elements in the wrong order

Adding the DTD to the prolog

The DTD appears as part of the prolog of an XML document. It is possible to put the XML and its complete DTD definition in the same document. To do this we put the DTD inside a DOCTYPE declaration, which contains the name of the root element:

```
<!DOCTYPE rootelement [. . .DTD here. . .]>
```

The name of the root element in the XML must be the same as the name used in the DTD. In contrast, if the document is just XML that is not validated against a DTD then the name of the root element can be chosen arbitrarily. In our example, the root element is 'weather-forecast'. Using this approach means that the name of the root element appears three times, once in the DOCTYPE, once as an element declaration in the DTD and once again in the XML document. When an XML document includes a DTD, we can also use the 'standalone' attribute of the XML declaration to indicate this, by setting its value to 'yes'

(i.e. this document does not depend on any external documents.)

```
<?xml version="1.0" standalone="yes"?>
<!-- File: Example5-5.xml -->
<!DOCTYPE weather-forecast[
   <!ELEMENT weather-forecast (today, tomorrow, long-range)>
   <!ELEMENT today (#PCDATA)>
   <!ELEMENT tomorrow (#PCDATA)>
   <!ELEMENT long-range (#PCDATA)>
]>
<weather-forecast>
   <today>
     Rain
   </today>
   <tomorrow>
     Showers
   </tomorrow>
   <long-range>
     Unsettled
   </long-range>
</weather-forecast>
```

If you open this document in a standard browser, you will see that the browser does not use the DTD for validation. Instead, it simply displays the XML file as it did before. Figure 5.5 shows the document loaded into Internet Explorer, which acknowledges the presence of the DTD but does not validate the XML.

NOTE	Although browsers may not use DTDs to validate XML, they may check that the DTD is well-formed and display an error message if it is not.

FIGURE 5.5   Standard browsers do not validate XML documents, so a DTD used with an XML file is ignored

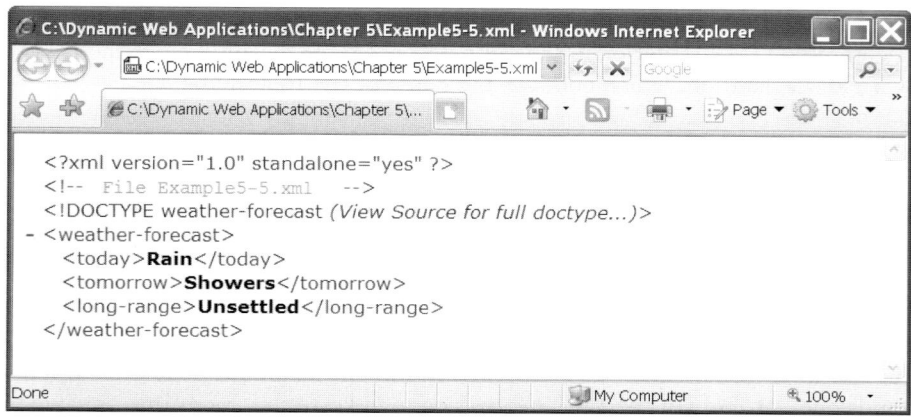

Validating XML with XMLSpy

In the previous example, we saw that web browsers do not validate XML documents, even if a DTD is provided. Although there are a number of add-ons that can be used with browsers for XML validation, none of them are particularly easy to use and they often have limitations. Therefore it can be helpful to use some other tool to test if our XML documents are valid. One such tool is XMLSpy, which can be used for many different XML-based processes. Appendix B contains a brief introduction to XMLSpy and how to use it to validate XML documents.

Separating the DTD from the XML document

Including the DTD in the same document as the XML is all very well, but we cannot then reuse the DTD with multiple documents. Looking again at our example should make it clear that this is not very helpful. Let us have a look at another weather forecast document.

```
<?xml version='1.0'?>
<!-- File: Example5-6.xml -->
<weather-forecast>
    <today>
        Sunshine
    </today>
    <tomorrow>
        Sunshine
    </tomorrow>
    <long-range>
        Thunder storms
    </long-range>
</weather-forecast>
```

This document has different content from the first, but still needs to be validated against the DTD because it is of the same document type. In fact, we would expect there to be a new weather forecast document every day, each of which would need to be validated against the DTD. Rather than continually repeating the DTD inside each XML document, we can reuse the same DTD by storing it as a separate document. Since this kind of flexibility is frequently required, DTDs are normally written in a separate file, referenced by a URL or local filename. Figure 5.6 shows how a single DTD, 'forecast.dtd', might be used to validate a number of separate XML files, for example one weather forecast file for each day of the week.

System or public doctype?

When a DTD is stored separately from the XML in an external file, it can be referred to within the DOCTYPE as either a *system* or a *public* DTD. A system doctype is from your own local system, either a URI or a file path. For any DTDs developed internally for your own applications, 'system' would be the appropriate type. In contrast, a public doctype is one that has some kind of globally known identifier because it is used by many different applications. A good example of this is the set of common DTDs that can be used to validate HTML or XHTML documents. Since many people use the same DTD to write valid web pages, public doctypes are used. The format of a public doctype identifier is not

FIGURE 5.6 Validating multiple XML documents with a single DTD

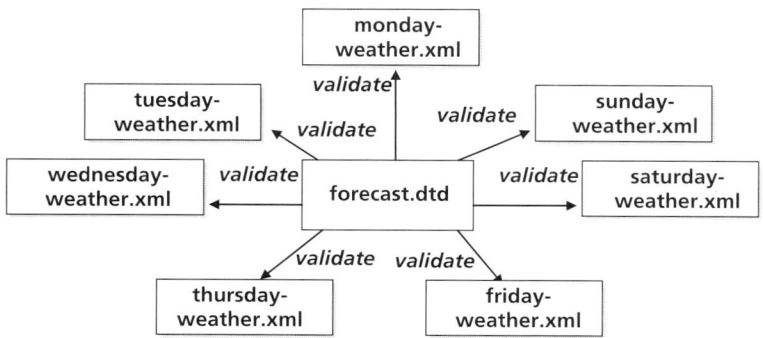

a URL but a *Formal Public Identifier* (FPI). FPIs have the following structure:

```
-//owner//keyword description//language
```

We can see this structure in the public doctype for HTML 4.01 documents:

```
-//W3C//DTD HTML 4.01//EN
```

The owner is the 'W3C', the keyword (followed by a space) is 'DTD', the description is 'HTML 4.01' and the language is English ('EN'). The language relates to the DTD, not the language that the document is written in.

The software that is processing the document (e.g. a browser) should be able to recognize these standard doctype names and locate the necessary DTD. However, because it would not be wise to rely on this mechanism in every application, any reference to a public doctype must also be followed by another reference to a system doctype. If the public doctype cannot be found, the XML processor uses the system doctype instead. Since this is a requirement, only the public doctype needs to be specifically labelled. The system doctype follows the public, but without a label. The HTML 4.01 doctype shows this clearly:

```
<!DOCTYPE HTML PUBLIC "-//W3C//DTD HTML 4.01//EN"
"http://www.w3.org/TR/html4/strict.dtd">
```

In this example, '-//W3C//DTD HTML 4.01//EN' is the public doctype and 'http://www.w3.org/TR/html4/strict.dtd' is the system doctype. The value of the system doctype can be changed from the standard URL to a local file name if required.

The next example shows our weather forecast XML document referring to a separate system DTD in the local file system. Here is the content of the DTD file ('forecast.dtd'):

```
<!ELEMENT weather-forecast (today, tomorrow, long-range)>
<!ELEMENT today (#PCDATA)>
<!ELEMENT tomorrow (#PCDATA)>
<!ELEMENT long-range (#PCDATA)>
```

This contains the DTD definition, as it appeared in our earlier example. The system DOCTYPE entry remains in the XML document and references the DTD filename. If the

DTD is separate from the XML file, then the value of the 'standalone' attribute should be 'no' instead of 'yes', as it was in the previous example. Since the default value for this attribute is 'no', it is not actually essential here.

```
<?xml version="1.0" standalone="no"?>
<!-- File: Example5-7.xml -->
<!DOCTYPE weather-forecast SYSTEM "forecast.dtd">
<weather-forecast>
   <today>
      Rain
   </today>
   <tomorrow>
      Showers
   </tomorrow>
   <long-range>
      Unsettled
   </long-range>
</weather-forecast>
```

In this document, the DTD for the weather forecast ('forecast.dtd') is assumed to be stored in the same folder of local file system as the XML file.

Element declarations in DTDs

As we have seen from our first DTD example, the general form of an element declaration is

```
<!ELEMENT element-name (regular-expression)>
```

The 'regular-expression' describes the way the element can be used. A list of comma-separated element names defines the order in which those elements may occur, as we saw with the nested tags inside the weather forecast:

```
<!ELEMENT weather-forecast (today, tomorrow, long-range)>
```

In contrast, an element that is defined as #PCDATA will not contain any nested elements:

```
<!ELEMENT today (#PCDATA)>
```

So far we have looked at a simple example where just a sequence of elements was defined by the DTD. However, as we discussed in the context of XML, semi-structured data does not necessarily need to have such a predictable structure, but we would still like to be able to validate XML documents that exhibit semi-structured characteristics, such as optional elements, elements appearing in different orders and elements appearing many times in the same document. To explore validation of these types of document we will use a slightly more complex example. Let us assume that WebHomeCover wants to manage information about job applicants in some kind of candidate management system. This information would contain data about candidates' qualifications, skills, experience etc, but this information is likely to vary widely between different candidates. They may have different types and numbers of qualifications, have held varying numbers of previous jobs and have a wide variation in their skill sets. To store such data in XML we have to be able to take advantage of its semi-structured properties to cater for these variations in data structure.

We will begin with a simple but not very flexible DTD that deals simply with qualifications. This DTD is very similar to our weather forecast DTD:

```
<!ELEMENT qualification (certificate, diploma, degree)>
<!ELEMENT certificate (#PCDATA)>
<!ELEMENT diploma (#PCDATA)>
<!ELEMENT degree (#PCDATA)>
```

The problem here is that qualifications are not as predictable as the structure of the weather forecast (though perhaps more predictable than the weather itself!). The DTD as it stands assumes that each candidate will have a certificate, a diploma and a degree. This is no good for representing candidates who do not have all three. Fortunately, DTD syntax includes a number of operator symbols that provide the kind of flexibility that we need in order to specify our actual requirements.

DTD operator symbols

One way we might address the current limitation of requiring all three qualifications is by using the vertical bar operator (|), which in DTD syntax means 'or'. In this version of the first line of the DTD, a candidate might have any one of these elements appear in their XML document (a certificate, a diploma or a degree).

```
<!ELEMENT qualification (certificate | diploma | degree) >
```

This is some improvement, but on the other hand each candidate can now only have any one of these qualifications, but not more than one. We can solve this problem by nesting the qualification element inside another element ('qualifications') that may occur more than once. The asterisk operator (*) is used to specify that an element may occur zero or more times, as in this example, where the 'qualifications' element consists of zero of more 'qualification' elements:

```
<!ELEMENT qualifications (qualification*)>
```

This is much better. Now we can have as many qualifications as we want. However, this still may not be ideal, since the qualification element may occur zero times, meaning the candidate has no qualifications at all. To ensure that there is at least one qualification included in the document we can use the '+' operator, which means 'one or more', instead of the '*' operator. In this version, there must be one or more qualifications.

```
<!ELEMENT qualifications (qualification+)>
```

Another useful specification is to make an element optional, so that it may appear zero or one times (but no more than one.) The operator used to indicate an optional element is the question mark. Perhaps we are interested in whether a candidate has some kind of higher qualification as well, but do not need to know if they have more than one. We might add a 'higher qualification' element, but make it optional:

```
<!ELEMENT qualifications (qualification+, higher-qualification?)>
```

From these examples we can see that we need to design the DTD specification carefully to match our requirements. Table 5.1 summarizes the various operator symbols that we have introduced for specifying element characteristics in a DTD.

Operator Symbol	Meaning
|	Or
*	Zero or more
+	One or more
?	Optional (zero or one)

TABLE 5.1 The operator symbols used in DTDs

Empty elements

We might choose to make an element specifically empty, which means that a valid XML document cannot include a body for tags of this type. Tags that have a body of content are, as we have seen, specified using the #PCDATA type. In contrast, empty elements are defined using EMPTY. For example, the 'higher-qualification' element might be declared to be empty:

```
<!ELEMENT higher-qualification EMPTY>
```

Although it is possible to have an empty element that also has no attributes, perhaps to be used as some kind of 'switch' in a document to indicate simply if something is there or not, most empty tags do include attributes. For example, the 'higher-qualification' element might contain an attribute that contains the type of the qualification. We will see how to include attributes in a DTD a little later.

The following example ('qualifications.dtd') is a DTD consisting purely of element declarations (no attributes) that includes examples of the syntax that we have introduced so far. There are some additional elements (year, institution and name) added to our previous examples.

```
<!ELEMENT qualifications (qualification+, higher-qualification?,
institution+)>
<!ELEMENT qualification (year, (certificate | diploma | degree) ) >
<!ELEMENT higher-qualification EMPTY>
<!ELEMENT year (#PCDATA)>
<!ELEMENT certificate (#PCDATA)>
<!ELEMENT diploma (#PCDATA)>
<!ELEMENT degree (#PCDATA)>
<!ELEMENT institution (name)>
<!ELEMENT name (#PCDATA)>
```

In the example DTD, the first line says that a 'qualifications' (root) element contains one or more elements of type 'qualification', an optional 'higher-qualification' and one or more 'institution' elements, in that order.

The second line says that each 'qualification' element contains first a 'year' element, then either a 'certificate', 'diploma' or 'degree' element. 'certificate', 'diploma' and 'degree' elements contain just character data. An 'institution' element contains a 'name' element.

The more complex a DTD, the more flexibly-structured its valid XML documents can be. With a DTD that has optional elements and elements that can occur more than once, there can be many variations in structure for valid XML. The next example is a valid XML document for this DTD. This document contains two 'qualification' elements and two 'institution' elements, as well as an (empty) 'higher-qualification' element.

```
<?xml version='1.0'?>
<!-- File: Example5-8.xml -->
<!DOCTYPE qualifications SYSTEM "qualifications.dtd">
<qualifications>
  <qualification>
    <year>2001</year>
    <diploma>Electronic Engineering</diploma>
  </qualification>
  <qualification>
    <year>2005</year>
    <degree>Computer Science</degree>
  </qualification>
  <higher-qualification/>
  <institution>
    <name>Oxford University</name>
  </institution>
  <institution>
    <name>MIT</name>
  </institution>
</qualifications>
```

The next XML document is also valid against 'qualifications.dtd'. Note that it is much shorter, including only one 'qualification' and one 'institution', and no 'higher-qualification'.

```
<?xml version='1.0'?>
<!-- File: Example5-9.xml -->
<!DOCTYPE qualifications SYSTEM "qualifications.dtd">
<qualifications>
  <qualification>
    <year>1999</year>
    <certificate>Baking</certificate>
  </qualification>
  <institution>
    <name>Springfield College</name>
  </institution>
</qualifications>
```

Attribute declarations in DTDs

So far, our validated XML examples have only used elements, but sometimes attributes can be used to do things that elements cannot. This becomes very clear once we start to validate our XML against DTDs, because DTDs can provide some very useful data and metadata about attributes. Attributes can be used in conjunction with DTDs to:

- Define a default value
- Define a set of valid values

- Define fixed values (constants)
- Create references between elements.

None of these features can be described with XML alone, only by using a DTD.

To start validating XML documents with attributes we need to look at the DTD syntax for describing attributes. The attributes of an element are declared in a single list using ATTLIST:

```
<!ATTLIST element-name attribute-specification...attribute-specification>
```

The element must be defined in the same DTD. More than one attribute can be specified in a single ATTLIST element.

Each attribute specification will have the form *name type value*. 'name' is an arbitrarily chosen name for the attribute; each name may only appear once in the attribute declaration, but the same attribute name can be used in different elements. In other words the name of an attribute, unlike the name of an element, does not have to be unique in a DTD.

The CDATA attribute type

There are many attribute types, but the most common is CDATA, which means 'character data', This is not quite the same as the #PCDATA type used with elements, because the attribute values are not parsed by XML processors in the same way as the data in the body of an element.

Attribute keywords

Attribute keywords specify whether an attribute is required (compulsory), implied (optional) or fixed (constant). In this example the 'type' attribute of the 'higher-qualification' element is shown as #REQUIRED, which makes it compulsory:

```
<!ATTLIST higher-qualification type CDATA #REQUIRED>
```

In contrast, the 'internationally-recognised' attribute of the 'qualification' element is optional, as indicated by the #IMPLIED keyword:

```
<!ATTLIST qualification internationally-recognised CDATA #IMPLIED>
```

An attribute with a fixed value (a constant) can be indicated by the #FIXED keyword, like this 'name' attribute of the 'company' element:

```
<!ATTLIST company name CDATA #FIXED "WebHomeCover.com">
```

The partial DTD in the next example includes a compulsory attribute declaration; the 'institution' element includes a compulsory 'is-university' attribute. This means that any XML document that is valid according to this DTD must include an 'is-university' attribute in any 'institution' elements.

```
<!ELEMENT institution (name, location)>
<!ATTLIST institution is-university CDATA #REQUIRED>
<!ELEMENT name (#PCDATA)>
```

Other attribute types

Not all attributes are simple character data (CDATA). Attributes that are not declared as CDATA can include those with default values, enumerated types and those of type NMTOKEN.

Default values are declared in quotes after the attribute name. In this example of a default value, a 'qualification' element has a 'years-of-study' attribute with a default value of '3':

```
<!ATTLIST qualification years-of-study "3">
```

When using an enumerated type, the attribute must have one of a set of specified values when it is used in an XML document. The possible values are separated by vertical bars (i.e. the 'or' character):

```
(value1|value2|..)
```

In this example of an enumerated type, the 'is-university' attribute can only be 'true' or 'false'. A default of 'false' is used here, though providing a default is not essential.

```
<!ATTLIST institution is-university (true | false) "false">
```

Defining REQUIRED or IMPLIED is not relevant when a default value is provided, but is otherwise. Any number of possible values can be provided for an enumerated type. Here, the names of the days of the week are used for a 'day-name' attribute:

```
<!ATTLIST calendar day-name (Monday | Tuesday | Wednesday | Thursday |
Friday | Saturday | Sunday) #REQUIRED>
```

Since no default value is provided, the attribute has been marked as required.

The NMTOKEN attribute type means 'name token'. If you use this type instead of CDATA, it restricts the set of characters that the attribute can contain to letters, numbers, periods, dashes, underscores and colons:

The following DTD ('qualifications2.dtd') is based on the one we looked at earlier, describing qualifications and institutions, but has had several attributes added to it:

```
<!ELEMENT qualifications (qualification+, higher-qualification?, institution+)*>
<!ELEMENT qualification (year, (certificate | diploma | degree) ) >
<!ATTLIST qualification level CDATA #REQUIRED
     internationally-recognised CDATA #IMPLIED
  years-of-study CDATA "3">
<!ELEMENT higher-qualification EMPTY>
<!ATTLIST higher-qualification type CDATA #REQUIRED>
<!ELEMENT year (#PCDATA)>
<!ELEMENT certificate (#PCDATA)>
<!ELEMENT diploma (#PCDATA)>
<!ELEMENT degree (#PCDATA)>
<!ATTLIST degree type CDATA #REQUIRED>
<!ELEMENT institution (name)>
<!ATTLIST institution is-university (true | false) "false">
<!ELEMENT name (#PCDATA)>
```

5

Here is an XML document that is valid against this DTD.

```
<?xml version="1.0"?>
<!DOCTYPE qualifications SYSTEM "qualifications2.dtd">
<! -- File: Example5-10.xml -->
<qualifications>
  <qualification level="3" internationally-recognised="no">
    <year>1999</year>
    <certificate>Baking</certificate>
  </qualification >
  <higher-qualification type="Master of Baking" />
  <institution is-university="false">
    <name> The McBaking Institute of Culinary Technology</name>
  </institution>
</qualifications>
```

Entities

ENTITY declarations can be used to define references to values that are either internal or external to the DTD. Here for example, we declare an entity called 'whc' to refer to the internal value 'WebHomeCover.com'

```
<!ENTITY whc "WebHomeCover.com">
```

The entity reference can be used in an XML document to refer to this value. An entity reference has the same format as a special character in HTML: it is preceded by an ampersand and followed by a semicolon, for example:

```
<company-name>&whc;</company-name>
```

When the XML document is processed by a browser or other tool, the original value is substituted for the entity reference.

5.6 XHTML

In this section, we introduce the eXtensible HyperText Markup Language (XHTML). XHTML provides a way to write HTML documents using well-formed and valid XML syntax, and is the W3C replacement for version 4 of HTML.

In early versions of HTML, there was no requirement that it should necessarily be well-formed. Although DTDs have been available for validating HTML documents since version 2.0, they were not widely used in the early years. Further, only since HTML 4.01 have we had a 'strict' document type that enforces the separation of content and structure from presentation. XHTML is a fully XML-compliant development of HTML 4.01. Like any XML document, an XHTML document must be well-formed and should be valid against the appropriate DTD. The first version of XHTML (version 1.0) included three different DOCTYPES that were similar in intent to those available for HTML 4. These were the 'transitional', 'frameset' and 'strict' doctypes. The frameset and transitional doctypes allowed many 'deprecated' elements to be used for backward compatibility (a deprecated element is one that should no longer be used). Only the strict doctype provided a rigorous validity check that separated content and structure from presentation. We will be using the XHTML 1.1 DTD, which is the most recent version at the time of writing and does not have transitional or frameset options. However, this version is to be superseded by XHTML 2.0, 'a general purpose markup language without presentation elements . . . designed for representing documents for a wide range of purposes across the web' (Pemberton 2007).

Here is the XHTML 1.1 DOCTYPE:

```
<!DOCTYPE html PUBLIC "-//W3C//DTD XHTML 1.1//EN"
"http://www.w3.org/TR/xhtml11/DTD/xhtml11.dtd">
```

The XHTML 1.1 specification also says that in addition to defining the document type, the root element of the document should also designate the XHTML *namespace* using the 'xmlns' attribute of the 'html' element, like this:

```
<html xmlns="http://www.w3.org/1999/xhtml">
```

The namespace is a way of uniquely identifying the origin of a particular tag and is based on a URN.

Further, we should also use the 'xml:lang' attribute to declare the language of the page (English in this case):

```
<html xmlns="http://www.w3.org/1999/xhtml" xml:lang="en">
```

 NOTE The 'xml:lang' attribute replaces the 'lang' attribute that was used in HTML and was allowed in XHTML version 1.0.

As well as being well-formed, an XHTML document that is valid against the document type must follow a number of other rules, which we will outline in this section. Perhaps the most obvious is that XHTML tags must be written in lower case, whereas in HTML 4, either case may be used but upper case is the normal convention.

XHTML, like strict HTML 4.01, explicitly forbids presentational mark-up, assuming the use of CSS. Further, we should also avoid using the bold <b> or italic <i> tags, which are still legal in XHTML version 1.1, but are likely to be invalid elements in future versions.

In general terms, XHTML is a little more demanding than HTML 4.01 in terms of being well-formed. For example, whereas you can omit the closing BODY tag in a valid HTML 4.01 document, because browsers are able to automatically complete some unfinished elements, you cannot do so in a valid XHTML document.

Empty elements

One of the main differences between strict HTML 4.01 and XHTML is the way that empty elements are expressed. In HTML, there are a number of empty elements.

These include LINK, IMG, BR and HR. In HTML they are normally written as if they were opening tags, such as this line break element:

```
<BR>
```

In contrast, we should express an empty element like this in XML syntax:

```
<br/>
```

In order to ensure backward compatibility with older browsers, the W3C recommendation is that all empty elements in XHTML should also have a space before the final '/>' characters. Here are some empty elements as they should be expressed in XHTML:

```
<link href="webhomecover.css" rel="stylesheet" type="text/css" />
<img src="webhomecoverlogo.gif" alt="the WebHomeCover company logo" />
<br />
<hr />
```

No minimized attributes

XHTML attributes cannot be 'minimized'. In HTML there are some examples where attribute values are expressed in a shorthand form, usually where the attribute name and its allowed value are the same. An example of this is the OPTION element in a select list, where we can define a default selection for the list of items by adding 'selected' to one of the options. Here, the 'house' option is the default selection.

```
<SELECT name="property-type">
  <OPTION value="house" selected>house</option>
  <OPTION value="apartment">apartment</option>
  <OPTION value="shack">shack</option>
  </SELECT >
```

In XHTML, this type of minimization is invalid, so every attribute must have both a name and a value. In XHTML, the select list would have to be rewritten like this:

```
<select name="property-type">
  <option value="house" selected="selected">house</option>
  <option value="apartment">apartment</option>
  <option value="shack">shack</option>
  </select>
```

Validating XHTML

It is easy to check if your XHTML documents are valid using the same web–based validator that we used in Chapter 3 to validate HTML.

This document, for example, would be valid HTML 4.01, but applying the XHTML 1.1 DTD (as we do here) would mean that it fails validation.

```
<!DOCTYPE html PUBLIC "-//W3C//DTD XHTML 1.1//EN"
  "http://www.w3.org/TR/xhtml11/DTD/xhtml11.dtd">
```

```
<html>
  <head>
    <title>HTML document</title>
  </head>
  <body>
  <!-- File: Example5-11.htm -->
    <p>
      <img src="image.gif" alt="image file image.gif">
    </p>
  </body>
</html>
```

It is not valid XHTML 1.1 because the opening 'html' tag does not contain a namespace attribute, and the 'img' element should be expressed as an empty element with a terminating '/>'.

Figure 5.7 shows the response from the W3C validator, including the first of a series of validation errors (the number of reported errors is somewhat exaggerated because an error in one element causes errors to be reported about any nested elements as well.)

Here is a modified version of the document, with valid 'html' and 'img' elements:

```
<!DOCTYPE html PUBLIC
  "-//W3C//DTD XHTML 1.1//EN"
```

FIGURE 5.7 The output from the W3C XHTML Validator

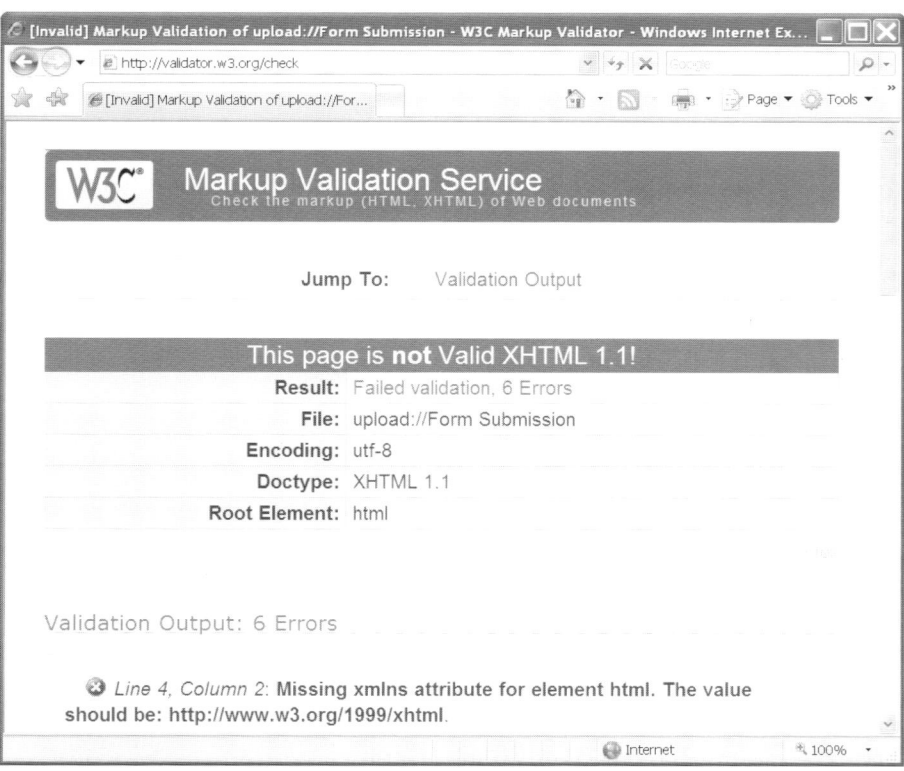

```
        "http://www.w3.org/TR/xhtml11/DTD/xhtml11.dtd">
<html xmlns="http://www.w3.org/1999/xhtml" xml:lang="en">
  <head>
    <title>XHTML document</title>
  </head>
  <body>
  <!-- File: Example5-12.htm -->
    <p>
       <img src="image.gif" alt="image file image.gif" />
    </p>
  </body>
</html>
```

Figure 5.8 shows that we now have an XHTML document that passes on-line validation.

5.7 XML Schema

DTDs provide a mechanism for validating XML documents based principally on their element and attribute structure. This provides a useful way of specifying how a particular type of XML or XHTML document should be organized, but there are a number of areas

FIGURE 5.8   The result of successful on-line validation

where DTDs do not provide all the features that we might like. One issue is that the syntax of DTDs, though superficially similar in some respects to XML, is not in fact well-formed XML syntax. It would be helpful if we could express a document's type definition in XML, rather than using a separate syntax. This would mean that we could handle these definitions using standard XML editing and processing tools and they could even be validated.

Perhaps even more importantly, DTDs do not have much to say about the data types that are used in an XML document. Most of the data definition in a DTD simply says that the content of an element is PCDATA (parsed character data). Although there are one or two other types, such as ID for some attributes, there is nothing that helps us to check the data type of an element. This means that although we can validate the structure of an XML document using a DTD, we cannot do much about validating its content. For example, we cannot check that an element that should contain a numeric value actually has a number inside it, and we cannot check that an element that should contain a date has suitably formatted information in it.

Data-typing problems with DTDs

The following XML document relates to our home insurance domain. It shows a single 'policy' element (inside a 'policies' root element) that contains data of different types. The 'policy-type' is character data, the 'start-date' represents a date, the 'annual-premium' is a decimal number, the 'number-of-claims' is an integer and a Boolean value (true or false) is used to indicate whether the policy is 'paid-up' (i.e. that there are no payments outstanding).

```
<?xml version="1.0"?>
<!-- File: Example5-13.xml -->
<!DOCTYPE policies SYSTEM "policies.dtd">
<policies>
   <policy policy-number="14235465">
      <policy-type>contents</policy-type>
      <start-date>2007-12-12</start-date>
      <annual-premium>127.85</annual-premium>
      <number-of-claims>1</number-of-claims>
      <paid-up>true</paid-up>
   </policy>
</policies>
```

The following example shows a DTD that could be used to validate the previous XML document. As we indicated before, DTDs are not XML documents. For example, although they use angle brackets they are not used in the same way as angle brackets in XML elements, since there are no start and end tags, and the way the content inside the angle brackets is expressed is nothing like XML elements and attributes.

```
<!ELEMENT policies (policy*)>
<!ELEMENT policy (policy-type, start-date, annual-premium, number-of-claims, paid-up)>
<!ATTLIST policy policy-number CDATA #REQUIRED>
<!ELEMENT policy-type (#PCDATA)>
<!ELEMENT start-date (#PCDATA)>
<!ELEMENT annual-premium (#PCDATA)>
<!ELEMENT number-of-claims (#PCDATA)>
<!ELEMENT paid-up (#PCDATA)>
```

Using this DTD, our example XML document would be valid XML, which is fine, but only the structure is validated by the DTD. The problem is that the following XML document would also be valid according to the DTD.

```
<?xml version="1.0"?>
<!DOCTYPE policies SYSTEM "policies.dtd">
<policies>
   <policy policy-number="abc">
      <policy-type>contents</policy-type>
      <start-date>1.2.3</start-date>
      <annual-premium>none</annual-premium>
      <number-of-claims>true</number-of-claims>
      <paid-up>not</paid-up>
   </policy>
</policies>
```

Here, the content is clearly garbage, but the DTD does not help us to check this. It cannot help us to ensure, for example, that the 'annual-premium' element actually contains a numeric value, or that the 'paid-up' element, which should be a Boolean value, only contains either 'true' or 'false'. To overcome this type of problem, XML Schemas have been developed. (Some argue that the plural of 'schema' is 'schemata', but the W3C (and others) use 'schemas'.) XML Schemas enable us to specify the data types in an XML document. One of the major advantages of this is that it becomes easier to map data between XML documents and components developed in programming languages that also use strict data typing. The first W3C XML Schema recommendation was published in 2001 and version 1.1 is the most recent. A specific instance of an XML Schema is known as an *XML Schema Definition*, in the same that way a DTD is a Document Type Definition. Therefore the usual file extension for an XML Schema Definition is 'xsd'.

XML namespaces

Before we can begin looking at how to write and apply an XML Schema, we first need to understand something of XML namespaces, because they are used both in XML Schemas and in XML documents that are validated by schemas. A namespace is a way of avoiding name conflicts between XML elements or attributes where the same name may be defined in different places.

To specify a namespace, we use an attribute that starts with 'xmlns:' (XML namespace) and is followed by a namespace prefix associated with a URI. The prefix is used in the XML document as a namespace identifier to link elements and attributes with this particular namespace. The namespace URI is just a string of characters with some guarantee of uniqueness. It does not actually have to refer to a real web-based resource, since the role of the URI is just to be an identifying string (i.e. it is a URN rather than a URL). URIs are a useful way of doing this since Internet domains are globally unique. Although a URI used as a schema namespace does not actually need to work as a web address, a resource is often placed at that URI for reference. For example, the URI http://www.w3.org/2001/ XMLSchema, which is used for XML Schemas, contains some reference material.

When we create an XML Schema, we use the standard schema URI and apply a suitable prefix to the XML Schema elements. Commonly used prefixes include 'xs' and 'xsd'. In our examples, we use the 'xs' prefix, so our schema definition begins like this:

```
<xs:schema xmlns:xs="http://www.w3.org/2001/XMLSchema">
   . . .
</xs:schema>
```

The 'xs' prefix is, therefore, the namespace identifier for an XML Schema definition. The actual definition of the schema comes within the opening and closing tags of the 'xs:schema' element. This definition uses special schema tags that define element and attribute types and other aspects of a valid document structure.

5.8 XML Schema tags

XML Schemas are composed of XML elements that are defined in the XML Schema definition. In the following section, we look at some simple examples of XML Schemas and some XML documents that may be validated by them. Much of what we do with an XML Schema is, of course, the same as what we do with a DTD, such as specifying element and attribute names.

Complex types and elements

A complex type is an element that has nested elements. This is the same as listing child elements in a DTD, but is more explicit. The 'fullname' element in the following simple XML document would be a complex type because it has other elements ('firstname' and 'lastname') nested inside it:

```
<?xml version="1.0"?>
<!-- File: Example5-15.xml -->
<fullname>
   <firstname>Richard</firstname>
   <lastname>Lionheart</lastname>
</fullname>
```

In an XML Schema, we declare a complex type using two elements. The 'xs:complexType' element is nested inside the 'xs:element' element. The 'xs:element' start tag contains a 'name' attribute that defines the name of the element.

```
<xs:element name="fullname">
   <xs:complexType>
 . . .
   </xs:complexType>
</xs:element>
```

Declaring a sequence

A sequence of elements is defined within a complex type using the 'xs:sequence' element. A sequence can contain any number of elements, declared in their document order.

```
<xs:complexType>
  <xs:sequence>
    . . .
  </xs:sequence>
</xs:complexType>
```

Data types

An element that is not a complex type is one of the 40 or so specified simple data types. These include commonly used types such as 'string', 'boolean', 'decimal', 'time' and 'date'. The specification makes a distinction between primitive and derived types (for example, 'integer' is derived from 'decimal') but this need not concern us particularly. In this example, the 'firstname' and 'lastname' elements are not complex types but simply 'string' data types. As well as the 'name' attribute, an element that is not a complex type also has a 'type' attribute, in this example setting the data types of both elements to 'xs:string'.

```
<xs:element name="firstname" type="xs:string"/>
<xs:element name="lastname" type="xs:string"/>
```

Here is the complete XML Schema:

```
<?xml version="1.0"?>
<xs:schema xmlns:xs="http://www.w3.org/2001/XMLSchema">
  <xs:element name="fullname">
    <xs:complexType>
      <xs:sequence>
        <xs:element name="firstname" type="xs:string"/>
        <xs:element name="lastname" type="xs:string"/>
      </xs:sequence>
    </xs:complexType>
  </xs:element>
</xs:schema>
```

One of the most useful features of XML Schemas is that we can explicitly define the data types of elements and attributes and use these types in validation. This is important, since if we only use 'string' as our data type then pretty much any character data is acceptable so we end up with something very similar to the #PCDATA of a DTD.

Returning to the elements that appeared in the example XML file from the insurance company domain, we could use an XML Schema to specify the required types: 'string', 'date', 'decimal', 'integer' and 'boolean':

```
<xs:element name="policy-type" type="xs:string"/>
<xs:element name="start-date" type="xs:date"/>
<xs:element name="annual-premium" type="xs:decimal"/>
<xs:element name="number-of-claims" type="xs:integer"/>
<xs:element name="paid-up" type="xs:boolean"/>
```

Attributes

Attributes are declared in XML Schemas using the 'attribute' element, which defines the name and data type of the attribute, similar to an element declaration. Here is an example declaration for a 'policy-number' attribute of type 'integer':

```
<xs:attribute name="policy-number" type="xs:integer" />
```

The 'xs:attribute' element appears after any nested sequences of elements. In the following schema we add the 'policy-number' attribute to the 'policy' element.

```
<xs:element name="policy">
  <xs:complexType>
    <xs:sequence>
      <xs:element name="policy-type" type="xs:string"/>
      <xs:element name="start-date" type="xs:date"/>
      <xs:element name="annual-premium" type="xs:decimal"/>
      <xs:element name="number-of-claims" type="xs:integer"/>
      <xs:element name="paid-up" type="xs:boolean"/>
    </xs:sequence>
    <xs:attribute name="policy-number" type="xs:integer"/>
  </xs:complexType>
</xs:element>
```

By default, attributes are optional. This means that the 'policy-number' attribute is optional, because we have not specified otherwise. To make an attribute compulsory we need to set the value of its 'use' attribute to 'required' in the XML Schema:

```
<xs:attribute name="policy-number" type="xs:integer" use="required"/>
```

The default value of 'use' is 'optional'; it can also be set to 'prohibited'.

Specifying default values for attributes is equally simple. All we have to do is add a 'default' attribute value to the XML Schema. Here, for example, we set the default value of an 'approved' attribute to 'true':

```
<xs:attribute name="approved" type="xs:boolean" default="true"/>
```

In fact the same attribute can be used with elements, making it possible to provide default element values with an XML Schema, something that is not possible with a DTD. For example, we could set the default value of the 'paid-up' attribute to be 'false':

```
<xs:element name="paid-up" type="xs:boolean" default="false"/>
```

Element multiplicity

Element multiplicity is defined using the 'minOccurs' and 'maxOccurs' attributes (note the unusual use of embedded upper case letters in XML attribute names). The default values for these attributes is '1', meaning that the element is compulsory and can only occur once. Possible values for both attributes are any positive integer, though it is important to ensure that the value of 'minOccurs' for any element is no higher than the value for 'maxOccurs'. In addition, 'minOccurs' can have the value '0' (zero) to specify that an element is optional. 'maxOccurs' may have the value 'unbounded' if there is no upper limit on how many times an element may occur. The next example shows a slightly different version of our schema with some multiplicity added. Note how the 'policy' element must occur at least once but can occur many times. Because there is no other multiplicity defined, the multiplicity for all the other elements will be 1 (the default).

```
<xs:element name="policy" minOccurs="1" maxOccurs="unbounded">
  <xs:complexType>
    <xs:sequence>
      <xs:element name="policy-type" type="xs:string"/>
      <xs:element name="start-date" type="xs:date"/>
      <xs:element name="annual-premium" type="xs:decimal"/>
      <xs:element name="number-of-claims" type="xs:integer"/>
      <xs:element name="paid-up" type="xs:boolean"/>
    </xs:sequence>
  <xs:attribute name="policy-number" type="xs:integer"
   use="required"/>
  </xs:complexType>
</xs:element>
```

Here is the complete schema, including the 'policies' root element:

```
<?xml version="1.0"?>
<xs:schema xmlns:xs="http://www.w3.org/2001/XMLSchema">
  <xs:element name="policies">
    <xs:complexType>
      <xs:sequence>
        <xs:element name="policy" minOccurs="1" maxOccurs="unbounded">
          <xs:complexType>
            <xs:sequence>
              <xs:element name="policy-type" type="xs:string"/>
              <xs:element name="start-date" type="xs:date"/>
              <xs:element name="annual-premium" type="xs:decimal"/>
              <xs:element name="number-of-claims" type="xs:integer"/>
              <xs:element name="paid-up" type="xs:boolean"/>
            </xs:sequence>
            <xs:attribute name="policy-number" type="xs:integer"
             use="required"/>
          </xs:complexType>
        </xs:element>
      </xs:sequence>
    </xs:complexType>
  </xs:element>
</xs:schema>
```

Enumerated types and restrictions

We have already seen that DTDs can be used to define attributes as enumerated types, but in an XML Schema we can define enumerated types for both attributes and elements.

We do this by defining special data types, using the 'simpleType' element. Inside this element (which has a 'name' attribute for the type we are creating) there is a 'restriction' element (which restricts the data type of the set of possible values of this type). Within this element, we specify the possible values for the enumerated type using 'enumeration' elements. In this example, we create a special type called 'scaleType' to represent two temperature scales, 'Centigrade' and 'Fahrenheit' (both of type 'string').

```
<xs:simpleType name="scaleType">
  <xs:restriction base="xs:string">
    <xs:enumeration value="Centigrade"/>
    <xs:enumeration value="Fahrenheit"/>
  </xs:restriction>
</xs:simpleType>
```

Once a simple type has been declared, it can be used elsewhere in the XML Schema. Here for example, we use the 'scaleType' as part of the specification of a compulsory 'scale' attribute. This means that the only valid values for this attribute are 'Centigrade' or 'Fahrenheit'.

```
<xs:attribute name="scale" type="scaleType" use="required"/>
```

XML Schema types can be used with elements, as well as attributes. Here is an enumerated type that specifies two valid values for types of insurance policy, 'Contents' and 'Buildings':

```
<xs:simpleType name="policyType">
  <xs:restriction base="xs:string">
    <xs:enumeration value="Contents"/>
    <xs:enumeration value="Buildings"/>
  </xs:restriction>
</xs:simpleType>
```

We can apply this type to the 'policy-type' element declaration in our XML Schema, rather than using the 'string' type:

```
<xs:element name="policy-type" type="policyType"/>
```

Unlike the string type, which allows any set of characters, we now ensure that any valid XML document provides a valid string to represent the policy type.

As well as being used to specify special data types in an XML Schema, restrictions can be used to give us fine-grained control over the contents of an element or attribute.

For example, we can restrict a string data type to allow only a certain set of characters to be valid, and specify a minimum and maximum number of characters. In this example, we create a 'phoneNumber' type that is between 7 and 20 characters, uses only the numeric characters 0 to 9 or white space, and preserves the white space in the character string. Note the 'pattern' attribute, which specifies the allowed characters in square brackets. The '-' specifies a range of characters (here between 0 and 9) and the '\s' is the XML Schema 'escape' character for white space. The parentheses and '*' are used to specify 'many' of these characters may be used (otherwise we would only be able to use a single character from the allowed set).

```
<xs:simpleType name="phoneNumber">
  <xs:restriction base="xs:string">
```

```
        <xs:pattern value="([0–9\s])*"/>
        <xs:minLength value="7"/>
        <xs:maxLength value="20"/>
        <xs:whiteSpace value="preserve"/>
    </xs:restriction>
  </xs:simpleType>
```

An example from the insurance policy schema might be that policy numbers must fall in the range 100,000 to 999,999 inclusive. We can specify this is a restriction element by using the 'minInclusive' and 'maxInclusive' elements.

```
<xs:simpleType name="policyNumber">
  <xs:restriction base="xs:integer">
    <xs:minInclusive value="100000" />
    <xs:maxInclusive value="999999" />
  </xs:restriction>
</xs:simpleType>
```

Here is the final version of our 'policies.xsd' XML Schema, including all the features we have introduced in this section:

```
<?xml version="1.0"?>
<xs:schema xmlns:xs="http://www.w3.org/2001/XMLSchema">
  <xs:simpleType name="policyType">
    <xs:restriction base="xs:string">
      <xs:enumeration value="Contents"/>
      <xs:enumeration value="Buildings"/>
    </xs:restriction>
  </xs:simpleType>
  <xs:simpleType name="policyNumber">
    <xs:restriction base="xs:integer">
      <xs:minInclusive value="100000" />
      <xs:maxInclusive value="999999" />
    </xs:restriction>
  </xs:simpleType>
  <xs:element name="policies">
    <xs:complexType>
      <xs:sequence>
        <xs:element name="policy" maxOccurs="unbounded">
          <xs:complexType>
            <xs:sequence>
              <xs:element name="policy-type" type="policyType"/>
              <xs:element name="start-date" type="xs:date"/>
              <xs:element name="annual-premium" type="xs:decimal"/>
              <xs:element name="number-of-claims" type="xs:integer"/>
              <xs:element name="paid-up" type="xs:boolean"
                default="false"/>
            </xs:sequence>
            <xs:attribute name="policy-number" type="policyNumber"
              use="required"/>
          </xs:complexType>
```

```
            </xs:element>
          </xs:sequence>
        </xs:complexType>
      </xs:element>
    </xs:schema>
```

5.9 Applying an XML Schema to a document

Previously, we have used DTDs to validate our XML documents by adding a DOCTYPE entry to the top of the document. Using an XML Schema is a little different, not least because we have to specify that we are creating an instance of an XML Schema Definition by including the appropriate namespace. The URI of the XML Schema instance namespace is http://www.w3.org/2001/XMLSchema-instance. Since this is an instance of a schema definition, the 'xsi' prefix is often used, which is an abbreviation of 'XML Schema Instance'.

```
xmlns:xsi="http://www.w3.org/2001/XMLSchema-instance"
```

We must also provide the URI of the XML Schema file we are using to do the validation. Although we have to use namespaces to create an XML Schema, we do not necessarily have to use namespaces in the XML documents that we want to validate, which is probably just as well because the syntax can get quite complex. The alternative is to use the 'noNamespaceSchemaLocation' attribute of the root element. This must have the same prefix as the reference to the XML Schema definition URI, and its value is the URI of the XML schema we want to use to validate this XML document, e.g.:

```
xsi:noNamespaceSchemaLocation="fullname.xsd"
```

This example shows a modified version of 'fullname.xml' that now includes a reference to the XML Schema URI and the name of the file ('fullname.xsd') that contains the Schema definition to be used for validation.

```
<?xml version="1.0"?>
<!-- File: Example5-16.xml -->
<fullname xmlns:xsi="http://www.w3.org/2001/XMLSchema-instance"
    xsi:noNamespaceSchemaLocation="fullname.xsd">
    <firstname>Richard</firstname>
    <lastname>Lionheart</lastname>
</fullname>
```

One of our example schema definitions can be used to validate the data types in XML documents representing insurance policies. Earlier, we saw two examples of XML documents that would be valid against a DTD, even though the data types in the second document were inappropriate. The next example shows a document that can be validated by this schema. In this example there is only one policy, but of course the schema allows for an unbounded number of policy elements. The main aspect to note is that the elements each contain valid data for their declared data type.

```
<?xml version="1.0"?>
<!-- File: Example 5-17.xml -->
<policies xmlns:xsi="http://www.w3.org/2001/XMLSchema-instance"
```

```
        xsi:noNamespaceSchemaLocation="policies.xsd">
    <policy policy-number="885342">
        <policy-type>Contents</policy-type>
        <start-date>2007-12-12</start-date>
        <annual-premium>45.6</annual-premium>
        <number-of-claims>5</number-of-claims>
        <paid-up>true</paid-up>
    </policy>
</policies>
```

The most important thing about using our schema instead of a DTD is that the following XML document, which we saw earlier would be valid according to the DTD, will fail validation against the XML Schema, because the data types or values in the elements are incorrect.

```
<?xml version="1.0"?>
<!-- File: Example5-18.xml -->
<policies xmlns:xsi="http://www.w3.org/2001/XMLSchema-instance" xsi:noNamespace
  SchemaLocation="policies.xsd">
    <policy policy-number="123456789">
        <policy-type>contents</policy-type>
        <start-date>1.2.3</start-date>
        <annual-premium>none</annual-premium>
        <number-of-claims>true</number-of-claims>
        <paid-up>not</paid-up>
    </policy>
</policies>
```

5.10 DTD or XML Schema?

We have covered both DTDs and XML Schemas in this chapter, as different ways of validating XML documents. Which, then, should be used? The simple answer is that, given the choice, you should use XML Schemas, since they give you control over data types as well as structures. In some contexts, you may find that you need to create documents, such as HTML pages, for which DTDs are the only available form of validation. You may also find yourself working with third-party Java libraries that still validate their configuration files with DTDs rather than XML Schemas. Increasingly, however, XML Schemas have begun to replace DTDs, and there are some situations where DTDs simply cannot be used, for example when using tools that convert between XML documents and components built with strongly typed programming languages. In other cases, such as the XML configuration files used with Enterprise Java deployments, you will find that newer versions of the specifications use only XML Schemas, as the DTDs used with earlier versions are no longer provided.

Exercises

5.1 Here is the XML document, from Section 5.4, that is not well formed:

```
<?xml version="1.0"?>
<climate>
   <average-winter-temperature>
      10
   <average-summer-temperature>
      20
   </average-summer-temperature>
</climate>
```

As we saw from the example, if you load this into a browser, an error message complains that the closing 'average-winter-temperature' tag is missing when it gets to the closing 'climate' tag. Why doesn't it fail as soon as it gets to the opening 'average-summer-temperature' tag?

5.2 Here is a simple DTD:

```
<!ELEMENT building (address, value, construction)>
<!ELEMENT address (#PCDATA)>
<!ELEMENT value (#PCDATA)>
<!ELEMENT construction (#PCDATA)>
<!ATTLIST building rental (true|false) #REQUIRED>
```

Write an XML document that is valid against this DTD that describes an insured building, at 100 Seaview Road, worth $400,000, of timber construction and used as a rental.

5.3 Earlier in this chapter, we saw the following XML document:

```
<?xml version="1.0"?>
<!-- File: Example5-2.xml -->
<weather-forecast>
   <today>
      <general>Rain</general>
      <temperature>
         <maximum>15</maximum>
         <minimum>11</minimum>
      </temperature>
   </today>
   <tomorrow>
      <general>Showers</general>
      <temperature>
         <maximum>20</maximum>
         <minimum>15</minimum>
      </temperature>
   </tomorrow>
   <long-range>Unsettled</long-range>
</weather-forecast>
```

Write a DTD against which this document would be valid.

5.4 Write a DTD against which this XML document would be valid

```xml
<?xml version="1.0"?>
<policy-list>
  <description>Policies taken out in January</description>
  <policy type="contents">
    <policy-number>1234557</policy-number>
  <policy-holder>A. Liu</policy-holder>
  </policy>
  <policy type="buildings">
    <policy-number>1234558</policy-number>
    <policy-holder>C. Jones</policy-holder>
  </policy>
  <report-date>01/01/2008</report-date>
</policy-list>
```

Assume there can be zero or more 'policy' elements, and that the 'type' attribute is compulsory.

5.5 Write a DTD that encompasses these rules for elements and attributes

Elements:

- A 'policy-report' root element consists of an optional 'description' element, one or more 'policy' elements and a 'report-dates' element.
- 'report-dates' is an empty element.
- 'policy' elements consist of a 'policy-number' element, followed by either a 'personal-customer' element or a 'corporate-customer' element.
- 'description', 'policy-number', 'personal-customer' and 'corporate-customer' are parsed character data.

Attributes:

- 'policy' elements have a compulsory type attribute that can only have the value 'buildings' or 'contents'.
- 'report-dates' has two attributes, a compulsory 'start' attribute and an optional 'end' attribute.

5.6 Now write an XML document that is valid against the DTD that you created for Exercise 5.5.

5.7 Take the HTML document from Example 4.12.htm, which demonstrates the three region layout, and convert it to valid XHTML. You will need to:

- Change the DOCTYPE
- Add the namespace and language to the opening HTML tag
- Change all the element names to lower case
- Make sure the empty elements are correctly terminated.

SUMMARY

We began this chapter by describing the limitations of HTML in its role as a mark-up language that combines page content, structure and presentation. We introduced the concept of semi-structured data and saw how XML follows its principles. We looked at how XML is a metalanguage, able to be used to define any number of specific mark-up languages due to its extensible nature. We explored the concept of validation, both for XML and HTML, and finally XHTML, which is the evolutionary path that has seen the joining together of HTML and XML. Along the way we saw how document validation may be performed using DTDs or XML Schemas, to ensure that our documents are structured correctly.

References and further reading

BBC (2005) *Radio Times*. http://www.radiotimes.com/

Bray, T., Paoli, J., Sperberg-McQueen, C., Maler, E. and Yergeau, F. (2004) *Extensible Markup Language (XML) 1.1*. W3C. http://www.w3.org/TR/2004/REC-xml11–20040204/

Bray, T., Paoli, J., Sperberg-McQueen, C., Maler, E. and Yergeau, F. (2006) *Extensible Markup Language (XML) 1.0 (Fourth Edition)*. W3C http://www.w3.org/TR/REC-xml/#sec-origin-goals

Eckstein, R. (2002) *Java Enterprise Best Practices*. Farnham: O'Reilly.

Eden, R. (2005) *XMLTV wiki*. http://xmltv.org/

Pemberton, S. (2007) *XHTML2 Working Group Home Page*. http://www.w3.org/MarkUp/

Uniprot (2005) *The Universal Protein Resource*. http://www.ebi.uniprot.org/index.shtml

5

CHAPTER 6

Transforming XML: XPath and XSLT

LEARNING OBJECTIVES

- **To understand the syntax of XPath expressions**
- **To understand and be able to navigate the tree structure of XML documents**
- **To be able to construct XPath expressions that will extract nodes from an XML document**
- **To be able to write XSL Transformations that generate output documents in XML or XHTML**
- **To understand the use of different character encodings when generating XML documents**
- **To understand the difference between output-driven and input-driven transformations**

INTRODUCTION

This chapter provides the link between XML for representing the data in a web application and XHTML for presenting that data in web pages. We begin by looking at how XPath can be used to write expressions that can select certain parts of an XML document. We then look at how eXtensible Stylesheet Language Transformations (XSLT), which utilize XPath, can be used to query and transform XML documents into (X)HTML pages or other XML documents.

6.1 XPath: Querying XML

XML Path (XPath) provides a language for accessing parts of an XML document. It is used by both eXtensible Stylesheet Language Transformations (XSLT), which we look at later in this chapter, and the XML Pointer Language (XPointer). XPointer is not covered in this book, but it provides a way of identifying parts of XML documents that are partly identified by a URI. XPath on its own does not do very much, but it is an essential part of querying and transforming XML documents in XSLT. In order to try out XPath without using it as part of either XSLT or XPointer, it is necessary to use a tool that is able to evaluate XPath expressions. XMLSpy includes an evaluation tool for XPath expressions that displays the selected nodes.

The main role of XPath is to provide an expression syntax appropriate for selecting one or more nodes from an XML document. To extend this role it also provides some facilities for manipulating strings, numbers and Booleans. In the context of XSLT, it is used for pattern matching, which is the aspect we will focus on in this chapter.

XPath and XML trees

To understand the way that the XPath data model works, we need to visualize an XML document as a tree of nodes, as we did in the previous chapter (Figure 5.1). There are seven types of node, all of which you should at least recognize from our previous exploration of XML, though we have not looked at all of them in detail:

- Root nodes
- Element nodes
- Text nodes
- Attribute nodes
- Namespace nodes
- Processing instruction nodes
- Comment nodes

However the main nodes that we process in XPath expressions are element and attribute nodes.

For most of the examples in this section we look at XML documents that are valid against the following XML Schema from the home insurance domain, representing claims made against policies. The root 'policy-claims' element contains one or more 'policy' elements, each of which has a 'type' attribute, a 'policy-holder' element (a string) and may contain a 'claims' element. If present, the 'claims' element will contain one or more 'claim' elements, and each of these will contain a 'year' (using the gYear type, which is a year in the Gregorian calendar) and 'details' (a string):

```
<?xml version="1.0"?>
<xs:schema xmlns:xs="http://www.w3.org/2001/XMLSchema">
  <xs:element name="policy-claims">
    <xs:complexType>
      <xs:sequence>
        <xs:element name="policy" minOccurs="1" maxOccurs="unbounded">
          <xs:complexType>
            <xs:sequence>
              <xs:element name="policy-holder" type="xs:string"/>
              <xs:element name="claims" minOccurs="0" maxOccurs="1">
                <xs:complexType>
                  <xs:sequence>
```

```
                      <xs:element name="claim" minOccurs="1" maxOccurs=
                      "unbounded">
                        <xs:complexType>
                          <xs:sequence>
                            <xs:element name="year" type="xs:gYear"/>
                            <xs:element name="details" type="xs:string"/>
                          </xs:sequence>
                        </xs:complexType>
                      </xs:element>
                    </xs:sequence>
                  </xs:complexType>
                </xs:element>
              </xs:sequence>
              <xs:attribute name="type" type="xs:string"/>
            </xs:complexType>
          </xs:element>
        </xs:sequence>
      </xs:complexType>
    </xs:element>
  </xs:schema>
```

We might visualize these 'policy-claims' documents as a tree, where the root (denoted by the '/' character) contains the document element (the main branch of the tree) and the nested elements branch from it, something like Figure 6.1. This represents one instance of an XML document that conforms to the schema. Each instance may have different numbers of branches since there may be many 'policy' nodes, and the optional 'claims' node may contain many 'claim' nodes. Text nodes (elements that contain PCDATA) are shown on the diagram as circles at the end, looking something like leaves. Attributes (here, the 'type' attributes of the policy elements) are shown as ovals.

FIGURE 6.1 Mapping the XML nodes to the document tree structure

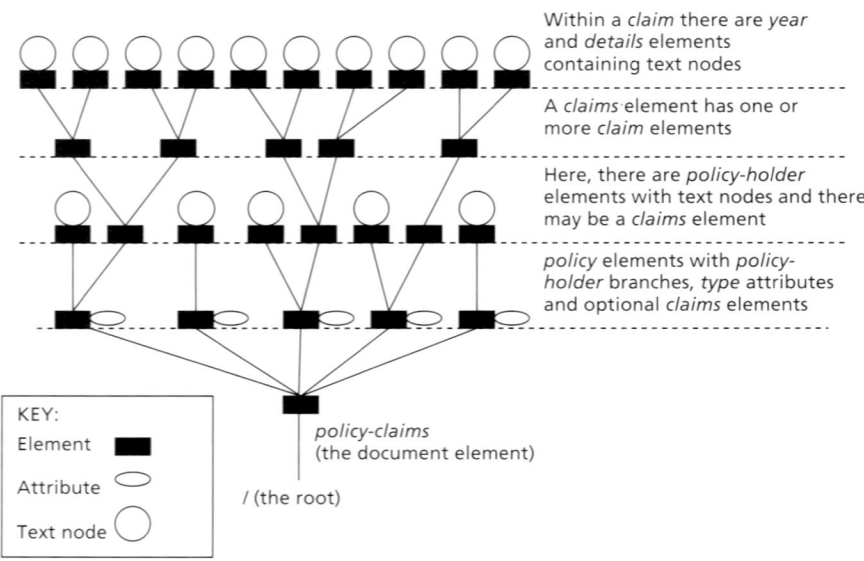

Within a *claim* there are *year* and *details* elements containing text nodes

A *claims* element has one or more *claim* elements

Here, there are *policy-holder* elements with text nodes and there may be a *claims* element

policy elements with *policy-holder* branches, *type* attributes and optional *claims* elements

KEY:
Element ▮
Attribute ⬭
Text node ◯

policy-claims
(the document element)

/ (the root)

6

'Family tree' vocabulary

Much of the syntax in XPath is based on the relationships between nodes, expressed as if the tree was in fact a family tree. Therefore we refer to 'parent', 'child', 'ancestor' and 'descendant' nodes. In our example tree in Figure 6.1, for example, 'policy-holder' is a child node of 'policy'. From the other perspective, 'policy' is therefore the parent of 'policy-holder'. 'policy' is an ancestor of 'claim', because 'claim' is ultimately nested within 'policy', although it is not its direct child. Of course, this being the case, 'claim' is a descendant of 'policy'.

Document order

As a consequence of having a tree-like structure, the nodes in an XML document appear in a document order. To visualize the document order we can think of traversing the tree clockwise from the root. If we do this using the example in Figure 6.1, the 'trunk' of the tree, the 'policy-claims' element, which is at the document root, comes first in the document order. Then we come to the first 'policy' node, followed by a 'claims' node. Inside the 'claims' node is a 'claim', followed by 'year' and 'details' nodes, before traversing on to the next 'claim' node, and so on until we have traversed the whole tree and got back to the root.

XPath takes account not only of the tree structure of an XML document, but also of the document order. When several elements are returned by an XPath expression, they are returned in the same order as they are encountered in the document. Attributes however, do not have a document order, so if more than one attribute is returned the order is not fixed.

Context – the starting point of an XPath expression

XPath is primarily a way of writing expressions that return an object that may be one of the following:

- A set of nodes
- A Boolean value
- A floating-point number
- A string of Unicode characters

In order to evaluate an expression, the XPath query has to start at a particular node. The starting node used for the query is known as the *context*.

The most important part of XPath is the ability to express a *location path* to identify parts of an XML document. Much of this syntax is based on the concepts of child, ancestor and descendant nodes. For example, the expression 'child::*' selects all elements that are children of the current context node. Ancestors and descendants nodes are indicated by 'ancestor::' and 'descendant::' respectively. In addition, we can select attribute nodes by using the 'attribute::' prefix in an XPath expression. For example, 'attribute::type' would select the 'type' attribute of the 'policy' node, if that was the current context node.

Location paths can be either relative to the current node or absolute (from the root node). A relative path begins with the name of a node. The path from a parent node to a child node is indicated by the '/' character. For example, the expression:

```
child::policy/child::policy-holder
```

would be relative to the current context node, and would therefore only make sense if the current context was the 'policy-claims' node. In contrast, an absolute path begins with the root node, which is the '/' character with no preceding parent node, as in this example:

```
/child::policy-claims/child::policy/child::policy-holder
```

Here, it does not matter what the current context is because we are not using an expression that is relative to it. An absolute path is the same regardless of the current context.

Abbreviated XPath operator syntax

Before looking at any more XPath examples, we will introduce the *abbreviated syntax*, which is much simpler. The most important abbreviation is that 'child::' can be left out of the location path. In effect, 'child::' is the default, so the location path

```
/policy-claims/policy/policy-holder
```

is an abbreviation of

```
/child::policy-claims/child::policy/child::policy-holder
```

There is also an abbreviation for attributes; 'attribute::' can be abbreviated to '@'. For example, instead of referring to 'attribute::type' in a location path we could use the abbreviated form '@type'. Table 6.1 lists a few of the main abbreviated XPath operators and their meanings.

XPath examples

To explore how XPath works, we use the following policy claims XML document and see the results of applying different XPath queries to it.

```
<?xml version="1.0"?>
<policy-claims xmlns:xsi="http://www.w3.org/2001/XMLSchema-instance"
xsi:noNamespaceSchemaLocation="policy-claims.xsd">
   <policy type="contents">
      <policy-holder>A. Liu</policy-holder>
      <claims>
```

TABLE 6.1   Abbreviated XPath operators

Operator	Meaning
/	Child operator selects children of whatever is to the left of it. If there is nothing to the left, it starts at the root element. In XPath, a 'child' is an immediate child (i.e. grandchildren are not children).
//	Stands for any number of intermediate elements, to express ancestor – descendant relationships.
.	The current context (the current node).
..	The parent of the current node.
*	Wildcard matches all elements.
@	Distinguishes attributes from elements (attribute prefix).

```
        <claim>
            <year>2002</year>
            <details>Stolen TV</details>
        </claim>
    </claims>
  </policy>
  <policy type="contents">
      <policy-holder>B. Singh</policy-holder>
</policy>
<policy type="buildings">
    <policy-holder>C. Jones</policy-holder>
        <claims>
            <claim>
                <year>2004</year>
                    <details>Fire damage to Kitchen</details>
            </claim>
        </claims>
    </policy>
<policy type="contents">
<policy-holder>D. Umaga</policy-holder>
    <claims>
        <claim>
            <year>1998</year>
                <details>Stolen bike</details>
        </claim>
        <claim>
            <year>2005</year>
                <details>Dropped Ming Vase</details>
        </claim>
    </claims>
</policy>
<policy type="buildings">
        <policy-holder>E. Tolstoy</policy-holder>
    </policy>
</policy-claims>
```

To access nodes that are nested, one approach is to use a series of 'child' operators to specify the full path through the document. Starting from the document root, the following XPath expression traverses through the nodes of the XML tree to the <policy-holder> elements, returning them in their original document order.

```
/policy-claims/policy/policy-holder
```

The resulting nodes would therefore be the five policy-holder elements.

Instead of navigating through each sub-element to define the query context, we can use the // (descendant) operator to directly select an element without specifying the full path. Using the wildcard character (*) matches all the sub-elements beneath the selected nodes. This expression, which uses both the '//' operator and the wildcard, will return all the 'year' and 'details' elements because they are both children of 'claim' elements.

```
//claim/*
```

These would be the resulting nodes (note they are returned in the document order).

```
year – 2002
details – Stolen TV
year – 2004
details – Fire damage to Kitchen
year – 1998
details – Stolen bike
year – 2005
details – Dropped Ming Vase
```

Filtering

When we execute XPath expressions against an XML document, we may want to search for specific elements, attributes or values. We can do this by applying filter patterns, enclosed in square brackets, to the XPath expression. The filter pattern must evaluate to a Boolean value and is tested against each node that is selected by the main part of the expression, so that only nodes that pass the test are returned. A simple example of this is to include the name of an element in the square brackets, for example:

```
/policy-claims/policy[claims]
```

This filter pattern would match only the policy elements that contain at least one 'claims' element child. In the case of our example document, this would return three 'policy' nodes. This type of filtering may not be very useful on its own, however. It is more likely that we would want to query the text nodes in elements or the values of attributes. For example, we might want to use a filter to find all the claims from 2002. We can do this using the equality operator (=) in the filter:

```
//claim[year = 2002]
```

This would select only one of the 'claim' nodes in our document. There is also the usual set of relational operators (>, <, >=, <=) and the '!=' symbol for 'not equals', that work with numeric data. XPath expressions can also do arithmetic and express quite complex query criteria. However, for the purposes of this book, we only introduce basic aspects of XPath syntax.

Attributes in XPath queries

In the abbreviated syntax, attributes are indicated in XPath queries by preceding the name of the attribute with '@'. XPath syntax is designed so that attributes are treated as similarly as possible to elements, the only difference in the query expressions being the addition of the '@' symbol. For example, the following expression returns the attribute 'type' nodes that have the value 'contents' (three of the policy nodes in our example document):

```
/policy-claims/policy[@type = "contents"]
```

If 'type' had been an element, then the expression would be identical except that the '@' operator would not be needed. We can see this from the following expression, which combines a query on an attribute with a query on an element. Here, we use the query to select buildings policies that have claims made against them (this would select only the 'C. Jones' policy in our example document).

```
/policy-claims/policy[@type = "buildings"][claims]
```

Having introduced some very basic features of XPath, we move on to use it as part of the process of transforming XML documents into XHTML web pages using XSLT.

6.2 XSLT

In this section, we look at how XML documents can be transformed into new documents using eXtensible Stylesheet Language Transformations (XSLT). Among other things, XSLT can be used to generate web pages from XML documents. XSLT is part of the Extensible Stylesheet Language Family (XSL), which is a set of standards for XML document transformation and presentation. It consists of three parts; XSLT, XPath and XSL Formatting Objects (XSL-FO). XSL Transformations can transform XML documents into various types of document. These may be other XML documents, HTML or XHTML documents or any type of text document. For our purposes in the context of building web applications, the main focus is the generation of XHTML pages from XML documents. As we saw in the previous section, XPath is an expression language that can select certain parts of an XML document. It is used by XSLT to specify which parts of the source document are to be included in the output document. XSL-FO provides a way of formatting XML in other presentational formats; for example, it can be used to create a Portable Document Format (PDF) document from an XML document. XSL-FO can be used in web applications where we want to provide content in a variety of presentational formats, not just XHTML.

XSLT, HTML and CSS

Although XSL refers to style sheets, it does not replace CSS. In fact XSLT, HTML and CSS are complementary. The data from an XML document can be given structure appropriate to a web page by transforming it into (X)HTML with XSLT. The presentation of the resulting (X)HTML document can then be provided using a cascading style sheet. Figure 6.2 shows how XSLT uses XPath (both of which are part of XSL) to transform an XML document into (X)HTML which is presented by CSS.

Processing XSLT

An XSLT style sheet, or transform, consists of a number of aspects. An important part of XSL is XPath, because it is XPath that is used to identify content from the input document that will be included in the output document. Other parts of the transform are also meant

FIGURE 6.2 The relationships between XSL, XSLT, XPath, XML, (X)HTML and CSS

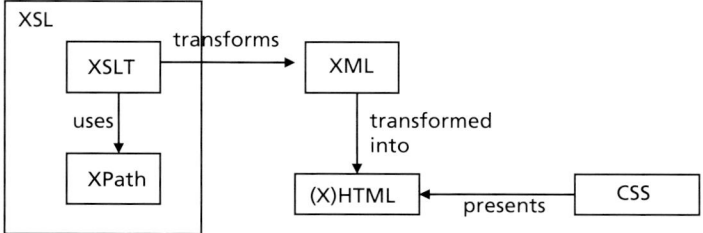

to be used directly in the output document, for example, (X)HTML tags. XSLT uses *template matching* to process different parts of the input document in different ways. When an XML document is transformed using an XSLT style sheet, a process of pattern matching takes place, where the XPath expressions used in the XSLT identify particular parts of the input document. Nodes that match the template's XPath expression are included in the output document. For most of the examples in this section we will be using the 'policy-claims.xml' document that we saw in Section 6.1.

XSL namespace

The first element of an XSL document consists of a version number (1.0 or 2.0) and a namespace reference. The usual prefix for the XSLT namespace is 'xsl':

```
<elementname version="1.0"
xmlns:xsl="http://www.w3.org/1999/XSL/Transform">
. . .
</elementname>
```

The namespace reference is a good example of a URN. It does not represent a download-able resource. However, if you put the URN into a browser, it identifies it as being the XSLT namespace (Figure 6.3).

Style sheets and transforms

The root element for an XSL transform can be <xsl:stylesheet . . . >, as in this example:

```
<xsl:stylesheet version="1.0"
xmlns:xsl="http://www.w3.org/1999/XSL/Transform" >
```

Alternatively, the root element can be <xsl:transform . . . >, as it is here:

```
<xsl:transform version="1.0"
xmlns:xsl="http://www.w3.org/1999/XSL/Transform" >
```

Both mean exactly the same thing, so which one you use depends on your personal preference. Since the two words have somewhat different meanings, one might choose to use the 'transform' root element for converting one XML document to another and the 'stylesheet' root element when converting to a presentational format such as XHTML. The 'xsl' prefix can also be replaced by something else, as with all namespace prefixes, but is the usual naming convention. In the remainder of this book, whenever we refer to XSLT element

6

FIGURE 6.3 The web page served from the address of the XSLT namespace URI, http://www.w3.org/1999/XSL/Transform

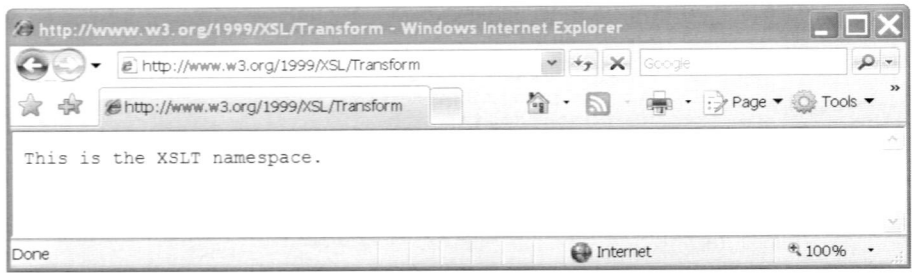

names, they will have the prefix 'xsl'. We will also use '.xsl' as the file extension for any XSL transformations.

Template matching

An XSL transform contains one or more <xsl:template . . . > elements. These elements have a 'match' attribute, the value of which is an XPath expression:

```
<xsl:template match="XPath expression">
```

This expression must match something in the XML document being processed. The basic idea is that an XSL Transformation includes one or more 'template' elements that match some part, or parts, of a source XML document, with the matching being done by XPath expressions. The body of the template element defines what is sent to the output document if that element is matched. This is likely to be a combination of data from the original XML document plus other mark-up, such as HTML, that is to be included in the output. An 'xsl:template' element therefore has this structure:

```
<xsl:template match="XPath expression">
specify what goes to the output document here
this may be mark-up and XSLT elements that
process the input XML document
</xsl:template>
```

Figure 6.4 shows how the template elements in the XSLT document contain XPath expressions to pick out parts of the input XML document and a body that defines what is written to the output document.

FIGURE 6.4 An XSL Transformation uses template matching to (a) identify parts of an XML document to be used in the output and (b) provide additional mark-up to be written to the output

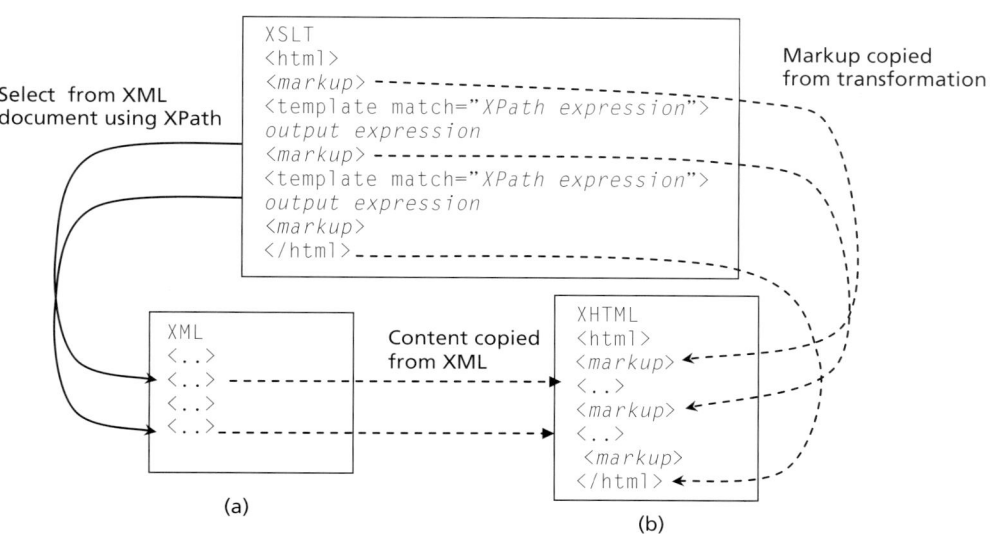

(a)   (b)

The 'match' attribute of an 'xsl:template' start tag must contain a valid XPath expression, using the syntax we introduced in the first part of this chapter. To apply a template to the root element, for example, the value of the 'match' attribute is the XPath expression for the root element, which is '/'

```
<xsl:template match="/">
. . . define the transformation for the root element here
</xsl:template>
```

Another example from the 'policy-claims.xml' document might be to match the 'policy' node, again using standard XPath:

```
<xsl:template match="/policy-claims/policy ">
. . . define the transformation for the policy element here
</xsl:template>
```

Output types

XSL Transformations can generate output using three different methods:

- xml
- html
- text

The method can be specified using the 'xsl:output' element, which has a 'method' attribute. In this example, the method is set to 'xml'.

```
<xsl:output method="xml" version="1.0"/>
```

In fact the default output method for XSLT is to generate an XML document, so the 'xsl:output' element is required (in most cases) if we want to generate HTML or a text document. Here, for example, we specify that the output document is to be HTML 4.0:

```
<xsl:output method="html" version="4.0"/>
```

There is a further aspect to the output method, which is that if the first non-XSL child node of the root element is <html>, then the output is automatically an HTML document instead of XML. A transformation that begins as follows, for example, generates an HTML output document even though the 'method' attribute has not been set to HTML.

```
<xsl:stylesheet version="1.0"
  xmlns:xsl="http://www.w3.org/1999/XSL/Transform" >
  <xsl:template match="/">
    <html>
```

To help to illustrate how this works, our first couple of examples generate HTML output documents. Later, we see how we can use XSLT to generate valid XHTML documents.

Linking an XSLT style sheet

To link XSLT to an XML document, we can add an XML style sheet processing instruction to the top of the document. You may recall that a processing instruction looks very much like the XML declaration, because it is also surrounded by the '<?' and '?>' characters. The processing instruction for an XSLT transformation is 'xml-stylesheet' with 'text/xsl' as the value of the 'type' attribute. For example, here we link to an XSLT style sheet called 'policy-claims.xsl'.

```
<?xml version="1.0"?>
<?xml-stylesheet type="text/xsl" href="policy-claims.xsl"?>
```

This processing instruction can be used by, for example, an XSLT-enabled browser (such as Internet Explorer 7) to transform the XML into the specified output document. However, not all processing applications need this instruction in the XML because some will apply the transformation to the XML externally. Other style sheet types can also be used with XML documents, for example, CSS.

Linking style sheets to an XML document like this is actually rather inflexible, because it means that we cannot dynamically apply different transformations to the same XML document. However, we will see later how Java can dynamically apply an XSLT at run time.

Testing XSL transformations in Internet Explorer

An XSLT-enabled browser, such as Internet Explorer 7, can perform XSL Transformations without additional configuration. If an XML document has a link element to an XSL style sheet, then loading that XML document into the browser will trigger the transformation. The document that results from this transformation will be shown in the browser.

There is, however, one limitation to this. When you choose the 'view source' option from the pop-up menu in the Internet Explorer window, you see the original XML document, not the generated page. If you want to see what page has been generated, you can use the 'msxmlvw' tool, which is part of the 'iexmltls.exe' application that can be downloaded from the Microsoft web site and installed into your browser. If you install this tool, then the pop-up menu includes the additional menu option 'View XSL Output'. Selecting this menu option shows you the document that the browser generated from the transformation.

An alternative to using Internet Explorer or similar browser-based tools is to use XMLSpy. One feature of XMLSpy is that an XSLT can be applied to an XML document without having to include an 'xml-stylesheet' processing instruction.

Selecting values from the XML document

In order to transform an XML document into an output document, we have to use special XSLT tags to specify how the data is to be transformed. In XSLT, the 'xsl:value-of' element is used to indicate that the transformation selects the value of an element or an attribute from the source document. This element contains a 'select' attribute which specifies the XPath expression that is used to identify the required node.

```
<xsl:value-of select="XPath expression"/>
```

The value returned from the XPath expression is inserted into the output document. A single 'xsl:value-of' element matches only a single node from the source document, the first one that it matches in the document order.

The following example shows a very simple XSL Transformation that generates an HTML output document (note the use of upper case HTML tags to indicate that this is not meant to be XHTML). In this example, there is only one 'xsl:template' element, which is used to match the root of the XML input document (we assume that it is 'policy-claims.xml'). Inside this element there are some HTML tags that will be written to the output document exactly as they appear in the XSLT. There is also a single 'value-of' element that uses an XPath expression to locate a 'policy-holder' node, using the XPath 'ancestor//descendant' syntax:

```
<xsl:value-of select="//policy-holder"/>
```

The effect of this element is that the value of the (first) policy-holder element (a descendant of the root) is selected and written to the output document.

```
<?xml version="1.0"?>
<!-- File: Example6-1.xsl -->
<xsl:stylesheet version="1.0"
xmlns:xsl="http://www.w3.org/1999/XSL/Transform">
   <xsl:template match="/">
      <HTML>
         <HEAD>
            <TITLE>Insurance Claims</TITLE>
         </HEAD>
         <BODY>
            <H1>Claimants</H1>
            <H2>
               <xsl:value-of select="//policy-holder"/>
            </H2>
         </BODY>
      </HTML>
   </xsl:template>
</xsl:stylesheet>
```

The following HTML document is the result of the transformation when processed by Internet Explorer 7. The META tag, indicating that this is an HTML document, was generated by the browser when it processed the XSL Transformation, so other tools may give a slightly different result. However the main points to note are that the document is HTML and that only the first claimant ('A. Liu') has been selected by the 'xsl:value-of' element.

```
<HTML>
   <HEAD>
      <META http-equiv="Content-Type" content="text/html; charset=UTF-16">
      <TITLE>Insurance Claims</TITLE>
   </HEAD>
   <BODY>
      <H1>Claimants</H1>
      <H2>A. Liu</H2>
   </BODY>
</HTML>
```

Figure 6.5 shows what the generated HTML looks like in Internet Explorer 7.

The 'xsl:value-of' element can be used to select either element or attribute values from the source document. The only difference is the use of the XPath syntax to select an attribute (preceding it with the '@' symbol). In the next example, there are two 'xsl:value-of' elements being used: the 'policy-holder' element is selected from the input document and then the 'type' attribute from the 'policy' element. One thing to note here is how we can reorder data in our transformations. In this example, the type appears after the policy holder, though the element to which it belongs (policy) comes before the policy holder element

FIGURE 6.5 The result of the XSL Transformation displayed in Internet
Explorer 7

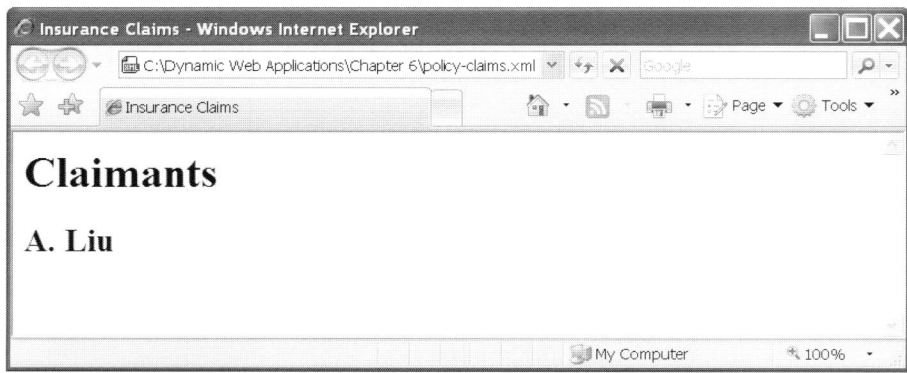

in the original document order. The full path has been used here for each element, simply
to make it clear to where in the source document the XPath expression is matching.

There is another feature of this transformation that provides some insight into the effect
of choosing an HTML method for the transformation rather than XML. Note the
(deliberate) use of an XHTML style <br /> element in the XSLT, between the two
'xsl:value-of' elements.

```
<?xml version="1.0"?>
<!-- File: Example6-2.xsl -->
<xsl:stylesheet version="1.0"
xmlns:xsl="http://www.w3.org/1999/XSL/Transform">
<xsl:template match="/">
<HTML>
   <HEAD>
      <TITLE>Insurance Claims</TITLE>
   </HEAD>
   <BODY>
      <H1>Claimants and policy types </H1>
      <H2>
         Name: <xsl:value-of select="policy-claims/policy/policy-holder"/>
      <br />
         Policy type: <xsl:value-of select="policy-claims/policy/@type"/>
      </H2>
   </BODY>
</HTML>
</xsl:template>
</xsl:stylesheet>
```

Here is the resulting HTML document:

```
<HTML>
<HEAD>
<META http-equiv="Content-Type" content="text/html; charset=UTF-16">
<TITLE>Insurance Claims</TITLE>
```

```
  </HEAD>
  <BODY>
    <H1>Claimants and policy types </H1>
    <H2>
    Name: A. Liu
    <br>
    Policy type: contents
    </H2>
  </BODY>
</HTML>
```

Notice what has happened to our <br /> element; it has been converted to the HTML version without the trailing forward slash. The point of this example is to show that creating XHTML documents from a transformation is not simply a question of putting XHTML style tags into the XSLT document, because some of them will be converted into HTML format. Transformations do this when generating HTML output to ensure that the resulting document will be handled by 'legacy' browsers that may not be able to process XHTML documents.

Figure 6.6 shows the result of the transformation displayed in Internet Explorer 7.

Generating XHTML

As we can see from the previous examples, one feature of XSL Transformations is that if the first child element of a transformation (other than 'xsl' elements) is <html>, then the output document is automatically processed as an HTML document. One effect of this is that some tags are converted from XHTML format to HTML format to ensure browser backward compatibility. If we want to generate a valid XHTML document from a transformation than we must use the 'output' element and set the value of the 'method' attribute to 'xml'. In addition to using XHTML-style tags in the output document, to generate valid XHTML we need to include the DOCTYPE entry at the top of the XSLT document so that it will appear in the output document. It is not possible to simply put a DOCTYPE reference in the source, because this would not be valid XML. Since XSLT documents are written in XML, we need another approach. To assist us here the 'output' element includes the 'doctype-public' and 'doctype-system' attributes that can be used to reference the XHTML DTD (remember that we can't have a public doctype unless we also provide a system doctype). The following example is a modified version of the previous transformation that generated HTML, but it this case it generates valid XHTML. The additional attribute

FIGURE 6.6   The HTML transformation displayed in Internet Explorer 7

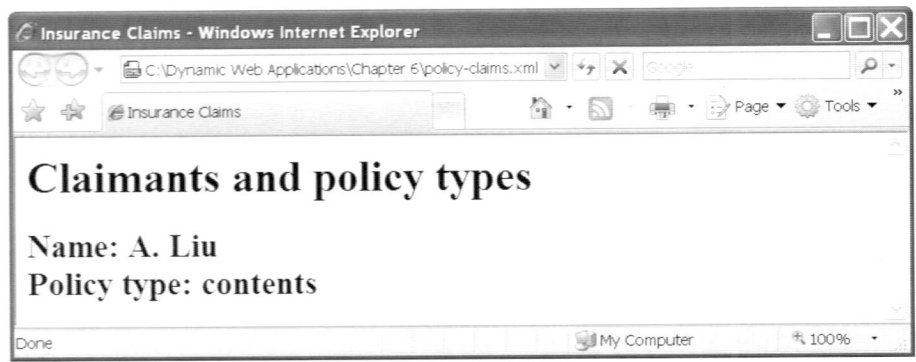

values have been added to the 'output' element and the HTML tags have been re-written in lower case to make them valid XHTML tags.

```xml
<?xml version="1.0"?>
<!-- File: Example6-3.xsl -->
<xsl:stylesheet version="1.0"
xmlns:xsl="http://www.w3.org/1999/XSL/Transform">
<xsl:output method="xml"
   doctype-public="-//W3C//DTD XHTML 1.1//EN"
   doctype-system="http://www.w3.org/TR/xhtml11/DTD/xhtml11.dtd"/>
   <xsl:template match="/">
      <html xmlns="http://www.w3.org/1999/xhtml" xml:lang="en">
        <head>
           <title>Insurance Claims</title>
        </head>
        <body>
           <h1>Claimants and policy types </h1>
           <h2>
             Name: <xsl:value-of select="policy-claims/policy/policy-holder"/>
             <br/>
             Policy type: <xsl:value-of select="policy-claims/policy/@type"/>
           </h2>
        </body>
      </html>
   </xsl:template>
</xsl:stylesheet>
```

Running the transformation (using XMLSpy) generates the following output document, where the result is a valid XHTML 1.1 document. The page appears in the browser exactly as in Figure 6.6. For the remainder of this chapter, we generate XHTML from our transformations rather than HTML.

```xml
<?xml version="1.0"?>
<!DOCTYPE html PUBLIC "-//W3C//DTD XHTML 1.1//EN"
"http://www.w3.org/TR/xhtml11/DTD/xhtml11.dtd">
<html xmlns="http://www.w3.org/1999/xhtml" xml:lang="en">
   <head>
      <title>Insurance Claims</title>
   </head>
   <body>
      <h1>Claimants and policy types </h1>
      <h2>Name: A. Liu
         <br />
         Policy type: contents
      </h2>
   </body>
</html>
```

Iterating over multiple elements

So far, we have only been getting the first match from each 'xsl:value-of' element, but in many cases we would prefer to select the values from all occurrences of a particular element. To do this, the 'xsl:for-each' element enables us to iterate over all the matching nodes in the XML document. Like 'xsl:value-of', its 'select' attribute uses an XPath expression to find all the matching nodes. The following example shows a transformation that uses an 'xsl:for-each' element to select all the 'policy' nodes.

```
<?xml version="1.0"?>
<!-- File: Example6-4.xsl -->
<xsl:stylesheet version="1.0"
xmlns:xsl="http://www.w3.org/1999/XSL/Transform">
<xsl:output method="xml"
   doctype-public="-//W3C//DTD XHTML 1.1//EN"
   doctype-system="http://www.w3.org/TR/xhtml11/DTD/xhtml11.dtd"/>
   <xsl:template match="/">
      <html xmlns="http://www.w3.org/1999/xhtml" xml:lang="en">
         <head>
            <title>Insurance Claims</title>
         </head>
         <body>
            <h1>Claimants and policy types</h1>
            <xsl:for-each select="policy-claims/policy">
               <h2>Name: <xsl:value-of select="policy-holder"/>,
                  Policy type: <xsl:value-of select="@type"/>
               </h2>
            </xsl:for-each>
         </body>
      </html>
   </xsl:template>
</xsl:stylesheet>
```

Here is the document that results from the transformation. Because of the iteration, all of the policy elements have been included in the output document.

```
<?xml version="1.0"?>
<!DOCTYPE html PUBLIC "-//W3C//DTD XHTML 1.1//EN"
"http://www.w3.org/TR/xhtml11/DTD/xhtml11.dtd">
<html xmlns="http://www.w3.org/1999/xhtml" xml:lang="en">
   <head>
      <title>Insurance Claims</title>
   </head>
   <body>
      <h1>Claimants and policy types</h1>
      <h2>Name: A. Liu, Policy type: contents</h2>
      <h2>Name: B. Singh, Policy type: contents</h2>
      <h2>Name: C. Jones, Policy type: buildings</h2>
      <h2>Name: D. Umaga, Policy type: contents</h2>
      <h2>Name: E. Tolstoy, Policy type: buildings</h2>
   </body>
</html>
```

Figure 6.7 shows the generated result of the transformation displayed in Internet Explorer 7.

Selection elements

Sometimes we might need to apply some conditional criteria to our transformations to select particular elements or attributes. We can use 'xsl:if' elements to conditionally

FIGURE 6.7 The result of an XSL Transformation that uses an iteration

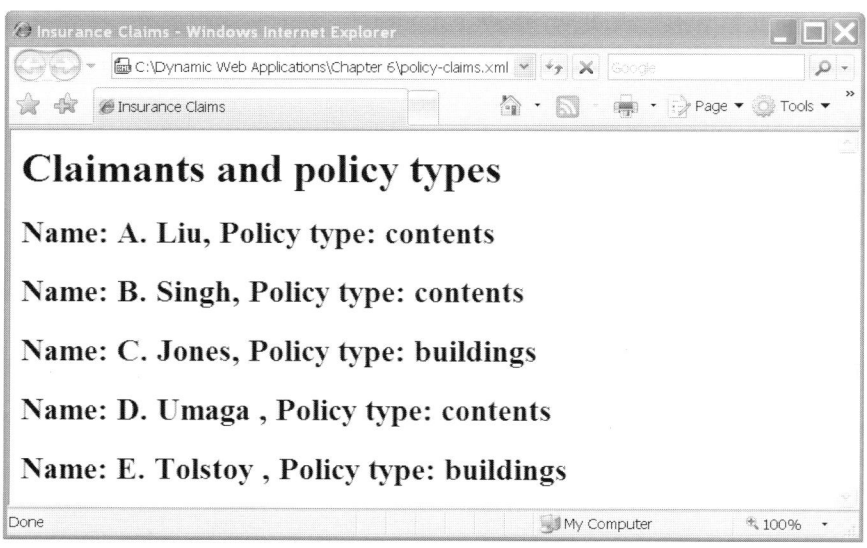

include elements or attributes in the output document. The 'test' attribute contains a conditional XPath expression:

```
<xsl:if test="XPath expression">
. . .
</xsl:if>
```

The following example shows an 'xsl:if' element being used in a transformation. In this example, there is a conditional expression in the iteration that selects policies that have claims made since 2003 (though all previous claims for that policy are included in the output document.) The 'xsl:if' appears inside an iteration defined by an 'xsl:for-each' element.

```
<?xml version="1.0"?>
<!-- File: Example6-5.xsl -->
<xsl:stylesheet version="1.0"
xmlns:xsl="http://www.w3.org/1999/XSL/Transform">
<xsl:output method="xml"
   doctype-public="-//W3C//DTD XHTML 1.1//EN"
   doctype-system="http://www.w3.org/TR/xhtml11/DTD/xhtml11.dtd"/>
   <xsl:template match="/">
<html xmlns="http://www.w3.org/1999/xhtml" xml:lang="en">
   <head>
      <title>Insurance Claims</title>
   </head>
   <body>
      <h1>Claimants since 2003</h1>
      <h2>
         <xsl:for-each select="policy-claims/policy">
            <xsl:if test="claims/claim[year >2003]">
               Name: <xsl:value-of select="policy-holder"/>,
               <br/>
```

```
        Claim dates:
          <xsl:for-each select="claims/claim">
            <xsl:value-of select="year"/>,
          </xsl:for-each>
          <hr/>
        </xsl:if>
      </xsl:for-each>
    </h2>
  </body>
</html>
</xsl:template>
</xsl:stylesheet>
```

Here is the document that results from this transformation:

```
<?xml version="1.0"?>
<!DOCTYPE html PUBLIC "-//W3C//DTD XHTML 1.1//EN"
"http://www.w3.org/TR/xhtml11/DTD/xhtml11.dtd ">
<html xmlns="http://www.w3.org/1999/xhtml" xml:lang="en">
  <head>
    <title>Insurance Claims</title>
  </head>
  <body>
    <h1>Claimants since 2003</h1>
    <h2>
    Name: C. Jones,
    <br />
    Claim dates: 2004,
    </h2>
    <hr />
    <h2>Name: D. Umaga,
    <br />
    Claim dates: 1998,2005,
    </h2>
    <hr />
  </body>
</html>
```

Figure 6.8 shows this XHTML document displayed by Internet Explorer 7.

There is no alternative action that can be specified with the 'xsl:if' element, in other words there is no 'if ... else' syntax in XSLT. To provide an alternative we must use a different set of related elements; 'xsl:choose', 'xsl:when' and 'xsl:otherwise'. The 'xsl:choose' element is the parent of the whole conditional expression. Nested within it there are 'xsl:when' and 'xsl:otherwise' elements. The 'xsl:when' element includes a 'test' attribute similar to the 'xsl:if' element. However, the 'xsl:otherwise' element has no 'test' attribute since it is the alternative path if the result of the test is false. This is the basic syntax:

```
<xsl:choose>
<xsl:when test="XPath selection expression">
Action for all selected nodes
</xsl:when>
```

FIGURE 6.8   The result of a transformation that uses selections

```
<xsl:otherwise>
Action for all other nodes
    </xsl:otherwise>
</xsl:choose>
```

The next transformation shows an 'xsl:choose' example, similar to our previous example using 'xsl:if'. Again, the expression in the 'test' attribute identifies all claims made since 2003. However, this time we also process all the elements that are not selected by this condition. We use this selection construct to generate one or other of two possible messages about the customers' claims.

```
<?xml version="1.0"?>
<!-- File: Example6-6.xsl -->
<xsl:stylesheet version="1.0"
xmlns:xsl="http://www.w3.org/1999/XSL/Transform">
<xsl:output method="xml"
   doctype-public="-//W3C//DTD XHTML 1.1//EN"
   doctype-system="http://www.w3.org/TR/xhtml11/DTD/xhtml11.dtd"/>
   <xsl:template match="/">
      <html xmlns="http://www.w3.org/1999/xhtml" xml:lang="en">
        <head>
           <title>Insurance Claims</title>
        </head>
        <body>
           <h1>Claimant History</h1>
           <h2>
              <xsl:for-each select="policy-claims/policy">
                 <xsl:choose>
                   <xsl:when test="claims/claim[year >2003]">
                     customer has recent claims
                     <br/>
                     Claim dates:
                     <xsl:for-each select="claims/claim">
                       <xsl:value-of select="year"/>,
                     </xsl:for-each>
                     <br/>
```

```
            </xsl:when>
            <xsl:otherwise>
               customer has no recent claims
               <br/>
            </xsl:otherwise>
         </xsl:choose>
         Name: <xsl:value-of select="policy-holder"/>,
         Policy type: <xsl:value-of select="@type"/>
         <hr/>
      </xsl:for-each>
   </h2>
</body>
</html>
   </xsl:template>
</xsl:stylesheet>
```

In this generated XHTML page we can see that the 'choose .. when .. otherwise' construct results in a message that indicates whether a customer has recent claims or not.

```
<?xml version="1.0"?>
<!DOCTYPE html PUBLIC "-//W3C//DTD XHTML 1.1//EN"
"http://www.w3.org/TR/xhtml11/DTD/xhtml11.dtd ">
<html xmlns="http://www.w3.org/1999/xhtml" xml:lang="en">
   <head>
      <title>Insurance Claims</title>
   </head>
   <body>
      <h1>Claimant History</h1>
      <h2>
      customer has no recent claims<br />
      Name: A. Liu, Policy type: contents</h2>
      <hr />
      <h2>
      customer has no recent claims<br />
      Name: B. Singh, Policy type: contents</h2>
      <hr />
      <h2>
      customer has recent claims<br />
      Claim dates:2004,<br />
      Name: C. Jones, Policy type: buildings</h2>
      <hr />
      <h2>
      customer has recent claims<br />
      Claim dates:1998,2005,<br />
      Name: D. Umaga, Policy type: contents</h2>
      <hr />
      <h2>
      customer has no recent claims<br />
      Name: E. Tolstoy, Policy type: buildings</h2>
      <hr />
</body>
</html>
```

Figure 6.9 shows the result of the transformation displayed in Internet Explorer. Because we have a 'when ... otherwise' construct, we can see that there are two types of information about customer claims included in the generated web page.

Sorting output

So far we have seen that the document order of the input document has been preserved in the output document. We may however wish to sort the output on some criterion. We can do this with the 'xsl:sort' element, which has several attributes:

- The 'select' attribute defines an XPath expression to identify the sort keys.
- The 'data-type' attribute states whether the sort key is 'text' or a 'number'.
- The 'order' attributes determines whether the sort order should be 'ascending' or 'descending'.
- The 'case-order' attribute determines which case is sorted first when sorting text that may include both upper and lower case letters. The value can be either 'upper-first' or 'lower-first'.

FIGURE 6.9 The result of a transformation that includes selections and alternative actions

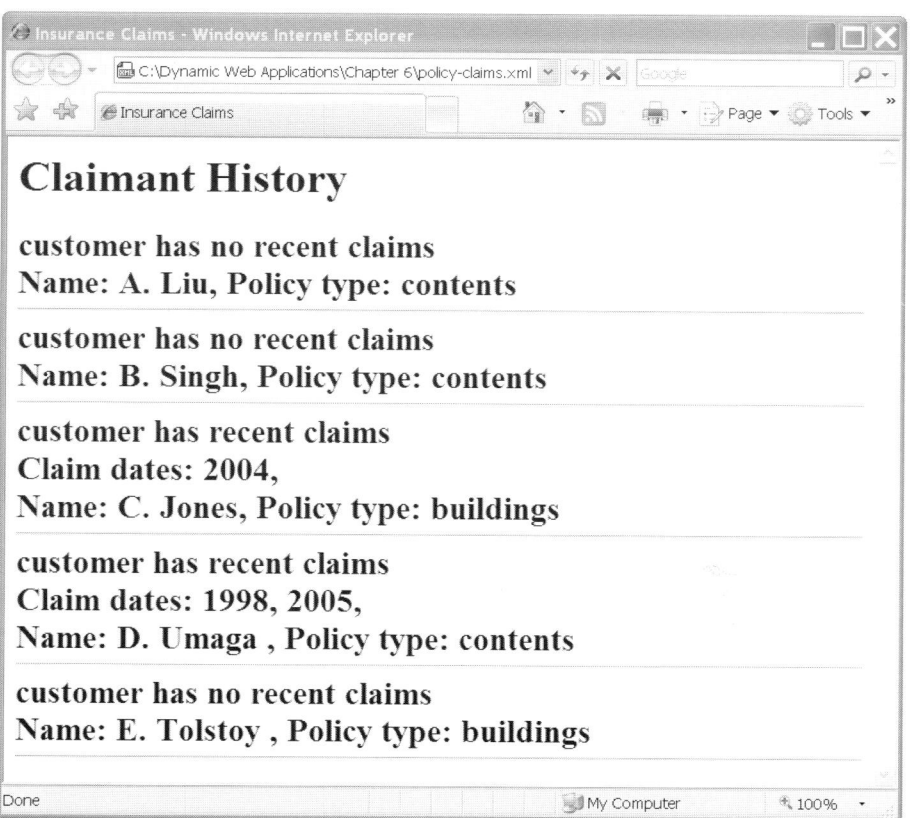

An 'xsl:sort' element can appear either as a child of an 'xsl:apply-templates' element (which we introduce in Section 6.5) or an 'xsl:for-each' element. If it is a child of an 'xsl:for-each', it must be the first child of that element. It is possible to apply more than one 'xsl:sort' element to a single node, so we can define a primary sort key using the first 'xsl:sort' element, a secondary sort key by the second 'xsl:sort' element, and so on.

In the next example, we sort the resulting nodes according to the ascending alphabetical order of their insurance 'type' attribute. Since the possible values of these attributes are either 'buildings' or 'contents', the 'buildings' policies will appear before the 'contents' policies.

```xml
<?xml version="1.0"?>
<!-- File: Example6-7.xsl -->
<xsl:stylesheet version="1.0"
xmlns:xsl="http://www.w3.org/1999/XSL/Transform">
<xsl:output method="xml"
   doctype-public="-//W3C//DTD XHTML 1.1//EN"
   doctype-system="http://www.w3.org/TR/xhtml11/DTD/xhtml11.dtd"/>
   <xsl:template match="/">
      <html xmlns="http://www.w3.org/1999/xhtml" xml:lang="en">
        <head>
          <title>Insurance Claims</title>
        </head>
        <body>
          <h1>Claimants and policy types</h1>
            <xsl:for-each select="policy-claims/policy">
              <xsl:sort select="@type" data-type="text" order="ascending"/>
              <p>
                Name: <xsl:value-of select="policy-holder"/>,
                Policy type: <xsl:value-of select="@type"/>
              </p>
            </xsl:for-each>
        </body>
      </html>
   </xsl:template>
</xsl:stylesheet>
```

Here is the output document with the policy types sorted in ascending alphabetical order

```xml
<?xml version="1.0" encoding="UTF-16"?>
<!DOCTYPE html PUBLIC "-//W3C//DTD XHTML 1.1//EN"
"http://www.w3.org/TR/xhtml11/DTD/xhtml11.dtd ">
<html xmlns="http://www.w3.org/1999/xhtml" xml:lang="en">
   <head>
     <title>Insurance Claims</title>
   </head>
   <body>
     <h1>Claimants and policy types</h1>
     <p>Name: C. Jones, Policy type: buildings</p>
     <p>Name: E. Tolstoy, Policy type: buildings</p>
     <p>Name: A. Liu, Policy type: contents</p>
     <p>Name: B. Singh, Policy type: contents</p>
     <p>Name: D. Umaga, Policy type: contents</p>
   </body>
</html>
```

FIGURE 6.10 The result of the sorting transformation (sorted by policy type)

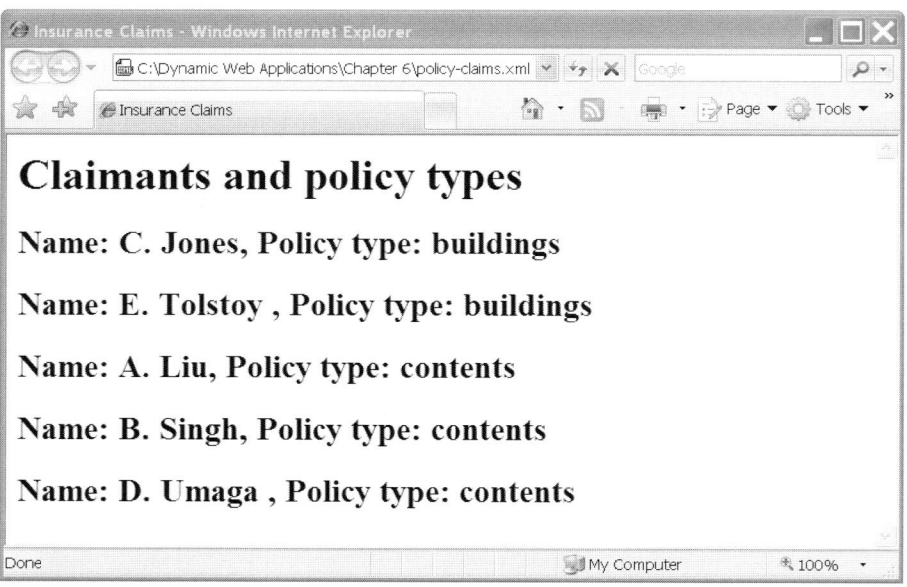

FIGURE 6.10 The result of the sorting transformation (sorted by policy type)

Figure 6.10 shows the result of the transformation displayed in Internet Explorer 7.

Writing attributes to the output document

In all the XSL Transformation examples we have seen so far, we have been selecting elements using XPath expressions in 'value-of' elements to include their contents in the output document. Writing attributes is a little more complicated, since it requires both an 'xsl:value-of' element to select the value of the attribute, and an 'xsl:attribute' element to create the attribute itself. Let us assume, for example, that we want to apply a 'class' attribute to the paragraphs in the output document. The 'xsl:attribute' element lets us apply the attribute name to the paragraphs:

```
<p><xsl:attribute name="class"> . . .
```

Now we need to be able to supply the value of that attribute. In this example, we assume that the paragraph class is based on the type of insurance. So we use an 'xsl:value-of' element to select the insurance type as the attribute value:

```
<p><xsl:attribute name="class">
    <xsl:value-of select="@type"/>
  </xsl:attribute>
```

Now when the document is transformed, the attribute will be added to each paragraph with the appropriate value. The following example shows an XSL Transformation that uses this syntax to create an output document that lists the policy-holder names in paragraphs that have been classified using the policy type.

```
<?xml version="1.0"?>
<!-- File: Example6-8.xsl -->
<xsl:stylesheet version="1.0"
xmlns:xsl="http://www.w3.org/1999/XSL/Transform">
```

```
<xsl:output method="xml"
    doctype-public="-//W3C//DTD XHTML 1.1//EN"
    doctype-system="http://www.w3.org/TR/xhtml11/DTD/xhtml11.dtd"/>
  <xsl:template match="/">
    <html xmlns="http://www.w3.org/1999/xhtml" xml:lang="en">
      <head>
        <title>Insurance Claims</title>
      </head>
      <body>
        <h1>Claimants and policy types</h1>
        <br/>
        <xsl:for-each select="policy-claims/policy">
          <p>
            <xsl:attribute name="class">
              <xsl:value-of select="@type"/>
            </xsl:attribute>
            Name: <xsl:value-of select="policy-holder"/>
          </p>
        </xsl:for-each>
      </body>
    </html>
  </xsl:template>
</xsl:stylesheet>
```

The result can be seen from this generated page, where the attribute from the XML element has been successfully transformed into an attribute of an HTML element. This could be used to apply different styles, via CSS, to the different types of policy holder.

```
<?xml version="1.0" encoding="UTF-16"?>
<!DOCTYPE html PUBLIC "-//W3C//DTD XHTML 1.1//EN"
"http://www.w3.org/TR/xhtml11/DTD/xhtml11.dtd ">
<html xmlns="http://www.w3.org/1999/xhtml" xml:lang="en">
  <head>
    <title>Insurance Claims</title>
  </head>
  <body>
    <h1>Claimants and policy types</h1>
    <br />
    <p class="contents">Name: A. Liu</p>
    <p class="contents">Name: B. Singh</p>
    <p class="buildings">Name: C. Jones</p>
    <p class="contents">Name: D. Umaga</p>
    <p class="buildings">Name: E. Tolstoy</p>
  </body>
</html>
```

Here is a simple CSS file that could be applied to the generated HTML page, using the 'class' attributes.

```
.contents{color:white; background-color:black}
.buildings{color:black; background-color:white}
```

Figure 6.11 shows the generated XHTML page with styles applied to class attributes.

Other non-presentational attributes that might come from an XML transformation include anchors and image files. To explore these attribute types, we expand our XML source document a little so that it contains elements that refer to anchor and image information. Here is part of a modified XML Schema that includes three additional elements: 'company-domain', 'contents-image' and 'buildings-image', shown here in bold. There are no other changes to the schema.

```xml
<?xml version="1.0"?>
<xs:schema xmlns:xs="http://www.w3.org/2001/XMLSchema">
    <xs:element name="policy-claims">
        <xs:complexType>
            <xs:sequence>
                <xs:element name="company-domain" type="xs:string"/>
                <xs:element name="contents-image" type="xs:string"/>
                <xs:element name="buildings-image" type="xs:string"/>
                <xs:element name="policy" minOccurs="1" maxOccurs="unbounded">
```

Here are the first few lines of an XML document that is valid against this XML Schema. The remainder of the document is the same as our previous version

```xml
<?xml version="1.0"?>
<policy-claims xmlns:xsi="http://www.w3.org/2001/XMLSchema-instance"
xsi:noNamespaceSchemaLocation="policy-claims-extra.xsd">
    <company-domain>http://www.webhomecover.com</company-domain>
    <contents-image>contents.gif</contents-image>
    <buildings-image>buildings.gif</buildings-image>
    <policy type="contents">
```

FIGURE 6.11 Applying a style sheet to the generated pages using 'class' attributes added by the transformation

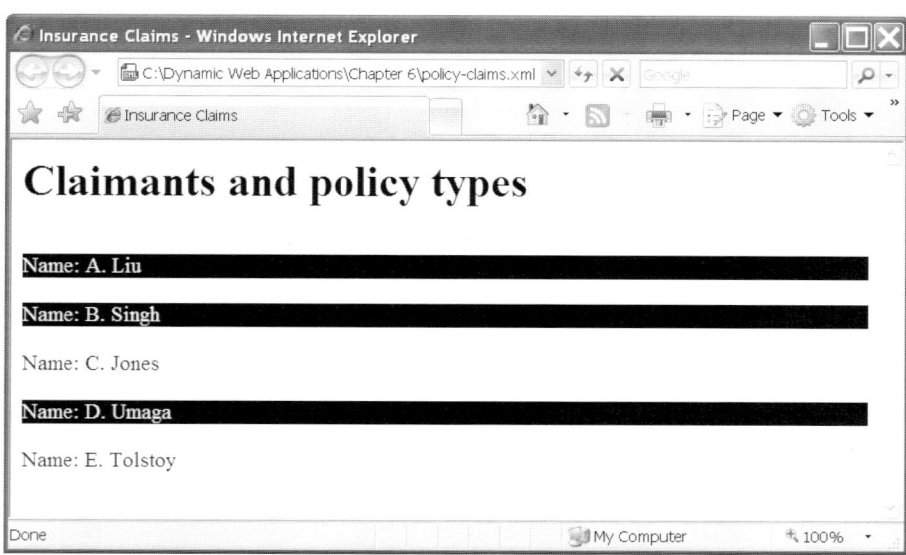

```
<policy-holder>A. Liu</policy-holder>
  <claims>
  . . . etc.
```

Our next example shows the syntax we introduced previously to enable values from the input document to be used as attribute values in the output document. Note that the XPath expressions need to start from the root in this example, because the current context at this point of the transform is 'policy', but the two image elements are children of the 'policy-claims' element. Therefore the first part of the path used in the expression is:

```
/policy-claims/. . .
```

'policy' is at the same level of nesting as the two image filename elements.

```
<?xml version="1.0"?>
<!-- File: Example6-9.xsl -->
<xsl:stylesheet version="1.0"
xmlns:xsl="http://www.w3.org/1999/XSL/Transform">
   <xsl:output method="xml"
     doctype-public="-//W3C//DTD XHTML 1.1 //EN"
     doctype-system="http://www.w3.org/TR/xhtml11/DTD/xhtml11.dtd"/>
   <xsl:template match="/">
     <html xmlns="http://www.w3.org/1999/xhtml" xml:lang="en">
       <head>
         <title>Insurance Claims</title>
       </head>
       <body>
         <h1>Claimants and policy types</h1>
         <xsl:for-each select="policy-claims/policy">
           <p>
             <xsl:attribute name="class">
               <xsl:value-of select="@type"/>
             </xsl:attribute>
             Name: <xsl:value-of select="policy-holder"/>
             <xsl:choose>
               <xsl:when test="@type='contents' ">
                 <img>
                   <xsl:attribute name="src">
                     <xsl:value-of select="/policy-claims/contents-image"/>
                   </xsl:attribute>
                   <xsl:attribute name="alt">contents</xsl:attribute>
                 </img>
               </xsl:when>
               <xsl:otherwise>
                 <img>
                   <xsl:attribute name="src">
                     <xsl:value-of select="/policy-claims/buildings-image"/>
                   </xsl:attribute>
                   <xsl:attribute name="alt">buildings</xsl:attribute>
                 </img>
               </xsl:otherwise>
             </xsl:choose>
           </p>
```

```
            </xsl:for-each>
            <div>
              <a>
                <xsl:attribute name="href">
                  <xsl:value-of select="policy-claims/company-domain"/>
                </xsl:attribute>Company home page
              </a>
            </div>
          </body>
        </html>
      </xsl:template>
    </xsl:stylesheet>
```

Here is the XHTML that results from this transformation, with the filenames and URI provided as attribute values. The data from the original document appears as <img src. . .>and <a href. . .>attributes. Note how the empty 'img' element has been rendered correctly by the transformation.

```
<?xml version="1.0" encoding="UTF-8"?>
<!DOCTYPE html PUBLIC "-//W3C//DTD XHTML 1.1//EN"
"http://www.w3.org/TR/xhtml11/DTD/xhtml11.dtd ">
<html xmlns="http://www.w3.org/1999/xhtml" xml:lang="en">
  <head>
    <title>Insurance Claims</title>
  </head>
  <body>
    <h1>Claimants and policy types</h1>
    <p class="contents">
      Name: A. Liu<img src="contents.gif" alt="contents"/>
    </p>
    <p class="contents">
      Name: B. Singh<img src="contents.gif" alt="contents"/>
    </p>
    <p class="buildings">
      Name: C. Jones
      <img src="buildings.gif" alt="buildings"/>
    </p>
    <p class="contents">
      Name: D. Umaga
      <img src="contents.gif" alt="contents"/>
    </p>
    <p class="buildings">
      Name: E. Tolstoy
      <img src="buildings.gif" alt="buildings"/>
    </p>
    <div>
      <a href="http://www.webhomecover.com">Company home page </a>
    </div>
  </body>
</html>
```

Figure 6.12 shows the generated page displayed in Internet Explorer. The images and hyperlink are visible on the page.

FIGURE 6.12 The result of a transformation that includes attributes for images and a hyperlink

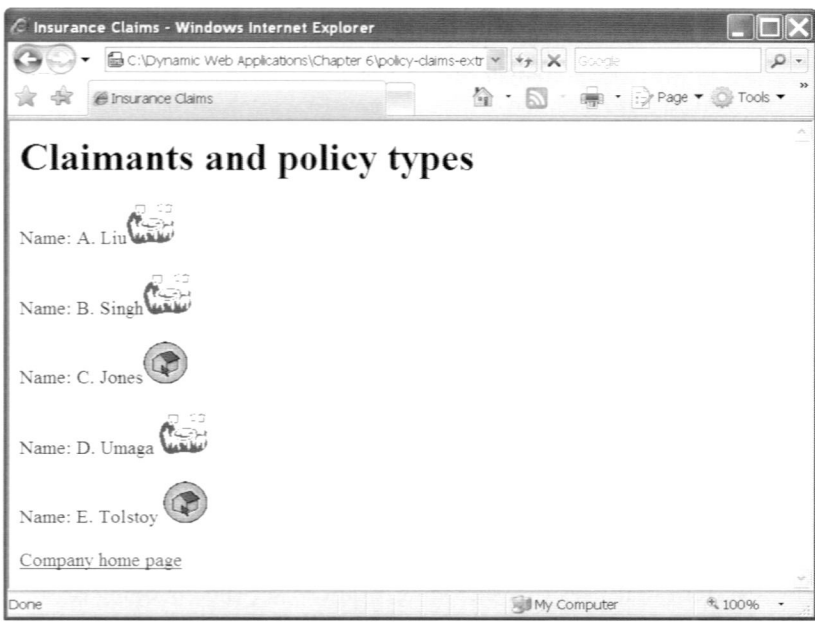

6.3 XML special characters

In HTML we can use special *entity* characters, such as   for a non-breaking space, © for a copyright symbol (©), etc. Unfortunately, these are not recognized in XML, so we cannot use them in XSL transformations. The workaround is to use the decimal Unicode values of the special characters. For example, the numeric equivalent of the non-breaking space is   and the copyright symbol is ©.

Table 6.2 shows some of the more commonly needed characters and their numeric codes.

There is, however, an associated problem when using these character codes, which is that the character numbers may be interpreted differently depending on which character encoding is being used. This can mean that an XML transformation converts the codes to the wrong characters in the generated XHTML document.

To resolve this problem, we can specify the character encoding of the generated page in the 'charset' attribute of a 'meta' element in the generated XHTML document. Since XML defaults to 'utf-8', this would be the normal encoding used by an XSL transformation.

```
<head>
  <meta http-equiv="Content-Type" content="text/html" charset="utf-8" />
</head>
```

There may be some situations where you need to generate documents from an XSL transformation that use some other character encoding, perhaps because they need to be

TABLE 6.2		Numeric codes for special characters			
Code	Symbol	Meaning	Code	Symbol	Meaning
&#33;	!	Exclamation mark	&#58;	:	Colon
&#34;	"	Quotation mark	&#59;	;	Semi-colon
&#35;	#	Number sign	&#60;	<	Less than
&#36;	$	Dollar sign	&#61;	=	Equals sign
&#37;	%	Percent sign	&#62;	>	Greater than
&#38;	&	Ampersand	&#63;	?	Question mark
&#39;	'	Apostrophe	&#64;	@	Commercial at sign
&#40;	(	Left parenthesis	&#91;	[	Left square bracket
&#41;	)	Right parenthesis	&#93;	]	Right square bracket
&#42;	*	Asterisk			Non-breaking space
&#43;	+	Plus sign	&#162;	¢	Cent sign
&#44;	,	Comma	&#163;	£	Pound sterling
&#45;	-	Hyphen	&#169;	©	Copyright
&#46;	.	Period (full stop)	&#174;	®	Registered trademark

processed by a system that uses that encoding. You can set the encoding of the generated document to something other than 'utf-8', but you must match it in the META element. For example, 'ISO-8859–1' is a 'legacy' encoding for HTML pages that is still sometimes used. To generate an XHTML page using this encoding, we would set the 'encoding' attribute of the 'xsl:output' element to 'ISO-8859–1', as in this example:

```
<?xml version="1.0" encoding="utf-8"?>
<xsl:stylesheet version="1.0" xmlns:xsl="http://www.w3.org/1999/XSL/Transform">
<xsl:output method="xml" encoding="ISO-8859–1"
doctype-public="-//W3C//DTD XHTML 1.1//EN"
doctype-system="http://www.w3.org/TR/xhtml11/DTD/xhtml11.dtd"/>
<xsl:template match="/">
<html xmlns="http://www.w3.org/1999/xhtml" xml:lang="en">
<head>
<meta http-equiv="Content-Type" content="text/html"
  charset="ISO-8859–1" />
<title> . . . </title>
</head>
```

Note that the XSL transformation in this example is written using 'utf-8', but it generates a document that uses the 'ISO-8859-1' encoding.

In general, unless there is a specific need to do otherwise, you should always generate your transformations using 'utf-8':

```
<?xml version="1.0" encoding="utf-8"?>
<xsl:stylesheet version="1.0" xmlns:xsl="http://www.w3.org/1999/XSL/Transform">
<xsl:output method="xml" encoding="utf-8"
doctype-public="-//W3C//DTD XHTML 1.1//EN"
doctype-system="http://www.w3.org/TR/xhtml11/DTD/xhtml11.dtd"/>
```

```
<xsl:template match="/">
<html xmlns="http://www.w3.org/1999/xhtml" xml:lang="en">
<head>
<meta http-equiv="Content-Type" content="text/html" charset="utf-8" />
<title> . . . </title>
</head>
```

6.4 Transforming from XML to XML

The examples we have seen so far have been from XML to (X)HTML, but we may also want to transform one XML document into another, in which case we may want to transfer whole XML elements (including their tags) from the source document to the destination document. The 'xsl:copy-of' element can be used to include parts of the source document as the original XML (rather than as the text values of elements or attributes). The following transformation shows an 'xsl:copy-of' element that uses an XPath expression to select all the policy-holder elements.

```
<?xml version="1.0"?>
<!-- File: Example6-10.xsl -->
<policy-holders xsl:version="1.0"
    xmlns:xsl="http://www.w3.org/1999/XSL/Transform">
  <xsl:copy-of select="/policies/policy/policy-holder"/>
</policy-holders>
```

Because 'xsl:copy-of' includes the entire element in the transform, the output document will include the tags as well as the element body. Here is the document that is generated by the transformation.

```
<?xml version="1.0"?>
<policy-holders>
   <policy-holder>A. Liu</policy-holder>
   <policy-holder>B. Singh</policy-holder>
   <policy-holder>C. Jones</policy-holder>
   <policy-holder>D. Umaga</policy-holder>
   <policy-holder>E. Tolstoy</policy-holder>
</policy-holders>
```

6.5 Transformations using template matching

XSLT gives us two different ways of designing a transformation: output driven (pull) and input driven (push). The examples we have seen so far are output-driven (pull) transformations, where we have structured the style sheets based on the structure of the output XHTML that we wanted to generate. A single 'xsl:template' element has been used, mapping to the root element. Starting from the root, at each step of the transformation the relevant input has been read from the source document and written to the output document using programmatic structures of sequence, selection and iteration. Although in many cases this pull approach is fine, the semi-structured nature of XML means that elements may appear in an arbitrary order in very large documents. It is therefore not always the best approach to match the root node and work though the source document in sequence. Instead, we can write an input-driven transformation that applies template rules to particular elements wherever, and however many times, they may be found in the input document. In this type of transform we define multiple rules, with each 'xsl:template' element providing a rule for how one particular type of node should be processed when it is found, enabling us to transform the nodes of an XML document without having to anticipate their order or number. Instead of managing the flow of execution, we leave the XSL processor to apply the template rules to the input document, generating the output from the structure of the input (Figure 6.13).

The following example is an XML document that would lend itself to 'push' processing. Within the 'document' element there are a series of elements that are either of type 'heading', 'subheading' or 'paragraph'. This is a good example of semi-structured data, since not only are there varying numbers of paragraphs under each heading, but there may be more than one subheading or no subheading at all. This would make this document difficult to transform using a 'pull' approach because of its unpredictable structure.

```xml
<?xml version="1.0"?>
<?xml-stylesheet type="text/xsl" href="Example6-11.xsl"?>
<document>
    <heading>My first heading</heading>
    <subheading>My first subheading</subheading>
    <paragraph>Para 1</paragraph>
    <paragraph>Para 2</paragraph>
    <heading>My second heading</heading>
    <subheading>My second subheading</subheading>       Two subheadings
    <paragraph>Para 3</paragraph>
    <subheading>My third subheading</subheading>
    <paragraph>Para 4</paragraph>
    <paragraph>Para 5</paragraph>
    <paragraph>Para 6</paragraph>
    <heading>My third heading</heading>                  No subheadings
    <paragraph>Para 7</paragraph>
    <paragraph>Para 8</paragraph>
    <heading>My fourth heading</heading>
    <subheading>My fourth subheading</subheading>
    <paragraph>Para 9</paragraph>
</document>
```

FIGURE 6.13 Output-driven (pull) and input-driven (push) transformations

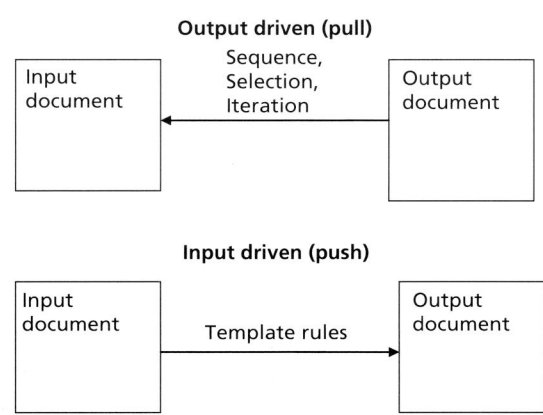

We might provide an XSL transformation for this document by template matching several different types of node, using the 'xsl:template' element. Each of the three types of document sub-element is processed differently, so we have three template rules for this document, plus the one we are familiar with that matches the root, using the following 'xsl:template' elements:

```
<xsl:template match="/">
<xsl:template match="heading">
<xsl:template match="subheading">
<xsl:template match="paragraph">
```

To trigger the process of pattern matching that will apply all of the template rules, we need to use the 'xsl:apply-templates' element. This has the effect of applying all the template rules that match any descendants of the current node. The XSLT processor then works through all the template matches beneath this level and applies the necessary templates, preserving the original document order.

The next example shows an XSL Transformation that uses an input-driven (push) approach to transforming the XML document. The template rule that matches the root includes the 'xsl:apply-templates' element, which then applies further template rules to all its descendant nodes. In this example, the other three template rules have deliberately been put into an arbitrary order to make the point that, unlike in a 'pull' XSLT where the structure of the output document drives the process, it is the structure of the original document that is important. Because 'apply-templates' matches every template rule in the document, there is no need for constructs such as 'xsl:for-each' to iterate through the input document.

```
<?xml version="1.0"?>
<!-- File: Example6-11.xsl -->
<xsl:stylesheet version="1.0"
    xmlns:xsl="http://www.w3.org/1999/XSL/Transform">
  <xsl:output method="xml"
      doctype-public="-//W3C//DTD XHTML 1.1//EN"
      doctype-system="http://www.w3.org/TR/xhtml11/DTD/xhtml11.dtd"/>
  <xsl:template match="/">
    <html xmlns="http://www.w3.org/1999/xhtml" xml:lang="en">
      <head>
        <title>Document</title>
      </head>
      <body>
        <xsl:apply-templates/>
      </body>
    </html>
  </xsl:template>
  <xsl:template match="paragraph">
    <p>
      <xsl:value-of select="."/>
    </p>
  </xsl:template>

<xsl:template match="subheading">
  <h2>
    <xsl:value-of select="."/>
  </h2>
```

```
  </xsl:template>

  <xsl:template match="heading">
    <h1>
      <xsl:value-of select="."/>
    </h1>
  </xsl:template>

</xsl:stylesheet>
```

Here is the generated XHTML document that results from the push transformation.

```
<?xml version="1.0" encoding="UTF-16"?>
<!DOCTYPE html PUBLIC "-//W3C//DTD XHTML 1.1//EN"
"http://www.w3.org/TR/xhtml11/DTD/xhtml11.dtd ">
<html xmlns="http://www.w3.org/1999/xhtml" xml:lang="en">
  <head>
    <title>Document</title>
  </head>
  <body>
    <h1>My first heading</h1>
    <h2>My first subheading</h2>
    <p>Para 1</p>
    <p>Para 2</p>
    <h1>My second heading</h1>
    <h2>My second subheading</h2>
    <p>Para 3</p>
    <h2>My third subheading</h2>
    <p>Para 4</p>
    <p>Para 5</p>
    <p>Para 6</p>
    <h1>My third heading</h1>
    <p>Para 7</p>
    <p>Para 8</p>
    <h1>My fourth heading</h1>
    <h2>My fourth subheading</h2>
    <p>Para 9</p>
  </body>
</html>
```

Figure 6.14 shows the result of the push transformation displayed in Internet Explorer 7.

For our final example, we apply an input-driven transformation to the 'claimsextended.xml' document. In this example, there are four input nodes to which we apply template rules. These are the root, the 'policy' node, the 'claims' node and the 'claim' node.

```
<xsl:template match="/">
<xsl:template match="policy">
<xsl:template match="claims">
<xsl:template match="claim">
```

Unlike our previous example which had a very flat structure, there are more nested elements in this input document so we need to organize the transform in such a way that we ensure that the transforms are correctly related to specific nodes, without necessarily

FIGURE 6.14   The result of the 'push' transformation

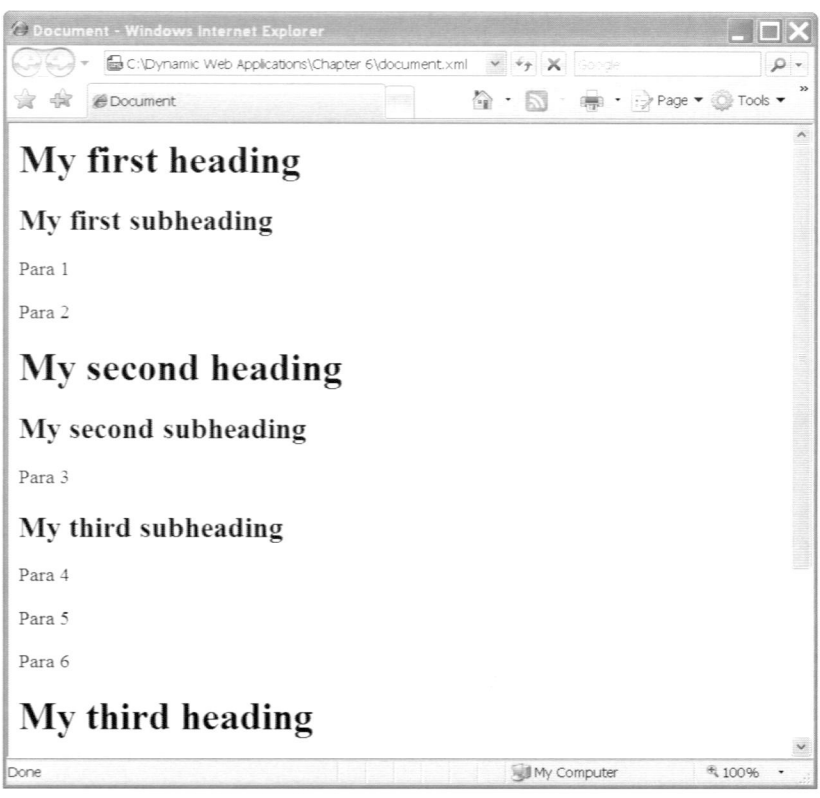

cascading down to all descendants (as 'xsl:apply-templates' will do by default). To stop all descendants of the current node having templates applied, we can specify individual nodes to be selected using the 'select' attribute, as here, where we apply a template to the 'policy' node, but not to all its descendants:

```
<xsl:apply-templates select="policy-claims/policy"/>
```

Here is the template applied to the root node. As well as providing the main tags for the XHTML output document, this template specifies that the next template rule only applies to 'policy-claims/policy'.

```
<?xml version="1.0"?>
<xsl:stylesheet version="1.0"
    xmlns:xsl="http://www.w3.org/1999/XSL/Transform">
  <xsl:output method="xml"
    doctype-public="-//W3C//DTD XHTML 1.1//EN"
    doctype-system="http://www.w3.org/TR/xhtml11/DTD/xhtml11.dtd"/>
  <xsl:template match="/">
    <html xmlns="http://www.w3.org/1999/xhtml" xml:lang="en">
    <head>
      <title>Insurance Claims</title>
    </head>
    <body>
      <h1>Claimants and policy types</h1>
```

```
<xsl:apply-templates select="policy-claims/policy"/>
<div>
<a><xsl:attribute name="href">
  <xsl:value-of select="policy-claims/company-domain"/>
 </xsl:attribute>
 Company home page </a>
</div>
</body>
</html>
</xsl:template>
```

The next template rule shows how a template is applied within the policy node. The policy holder's name is extracted from the input document, and an image tag is added with the correct image file for the type of policy. Then the next template rule is applied, specifically to the 'claims' node.

```
<xsl:template match="policy">
  <p><xsl:attribute name="class">
  <xsl:value-of select="@type"/>
  </xsl:attribute>
    Name: <xsl:value-of select="policy-holder"/>
    <xsl:choose>
      <xsl:when test="@type='contents' ">
        <img><xsl:attribute name="src">
        </xsl:value-of select="/policy-claims/contents-image"/>
        </xsl:attribute>
        <xsl:attribute name="alt">contents </xsl:attribute>
        </img>
    </xsl:when>
    <xsl:otherwise>
        <img><xsl:attribute name="src">
        <xsl:value-of select="/policy-claims/buildings-image"/>
        </xsl:attribute>
        <xsl:attribute name="alt">buildings</xsl:attribute>
        </img>
    </xsl:otherwise>
    </xsl:choose>
    </p>
  <xsl:apply-templates select="claims"/>
</xsl:template>
```

Here is the template rule applied to 'claims' nodes. In this case, the template rule is mainly concerned with setting up a table structure. Since the only child of 'claims' is 'claim', we can simply call 'apply-templates', because there are no further descendant nodes beneath 'claim'.

```
<xsl:template match="claims">
  <table>
    <caption>Claims</caption>
    <tbody>
        <tr>
          <th>Year</th>
          <th>Details</th>
        </tr>
```

```
        <xsl:apply-templates/>
      </tbody>
    </table>
  </xsl:template>
```

Finally, we process the 'claim' nodes. Since there are no further nodes to process, there is no 'apply-templates', so there is no further processing for the child nodes 'year' and 'details'.

```
<xsl:template match="claim">
  <tr>
    <td>
      <xsl:value-of select="year"/>
    </td>
    <td>
      <xsl:value-of select="details"/>
    </td>
  </tr>
</xsl:template>
```

Figure 6.15 shows the document that results from the various parts of the transformation. (the page is too long to see in one view, so this is only the first part of the page).

FIGURE 6.15 The resulting output from the push transformation of the 'claimsextended.xml' document

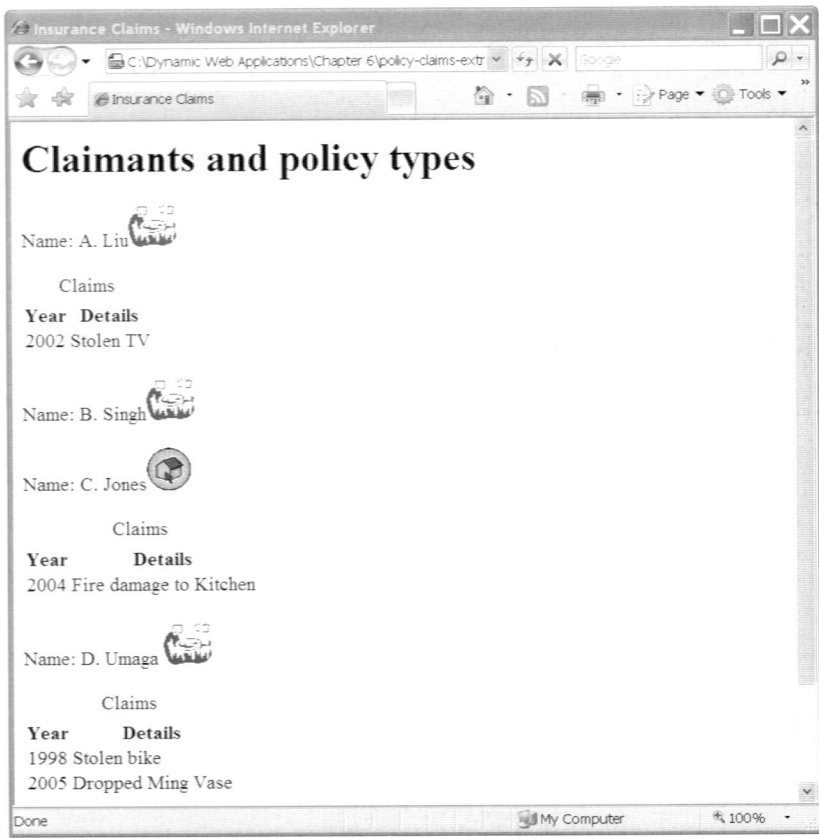

Exercises

We use the following XML document that shows some insurance policy details:

```
<?xml version="1.0"?>
<policies>
   <policy policy-number="1625344">
      <policy-type>buildings</policy-type>
      <start-date>2007-12-12</start-date>
      <annual-premium>45.6</annual-premium>
      <number-of-claims>5</number-of-claims>
      <paid-up>true</paid-up>
   </policy>
<policy policy-number="9384756">
      <policy-type>contents</policy-type>
      <start-date>2005-02-03</start-date>
      <annual-premium>84.0</annual-premium>
      <number-of-claims>0</number-of-claims>
      <paid-up>false</paid-up>
</policy>
<policy policy-number="4337362">
      <policy-type>contents</policy-type>
      <start-date>2000-10-26</start-date>
      <annual-premium>75.5</annual-premium>
      <number-of-claims>2</number-of-claims>
      <paid-up>true</paid-up>
   </policy>
<policy policy-number="9993654">
      <policy-type>buildings</policy-type>
      <start-date>1998-06-30</start-date>
      <annual-premium>59.0</annual-premium>
      <number-of-claims>1</number-of-claims>
      <paid-up>true</paid-up>
   </policy>
</policies>
```

6.1   Write an XPath expression that selects all the start dates from the XML document.

6.2   Write an XPath expression that selects all the policy numbers from the XML document.

6.3   Write an XPath expression to select all policies where the annual premium is more than 50.

6.4   Write an XPath expression to select all buildings insurance policies.

6.5   It is possible to combine conditions together using 'and', i.e.

[*condition1* and *condition2*]

Write an XPath expression to select all policies that are paid up and have had more than one claim.

6.6 For some XPath operations, such as comparing dates, we need to use the XML Schema namespace. Change the root element of the XML document to use this namespace:

```
<policies xmlns:xs="http://www.w3.org/2001/XMLSchema" >
```

Make sure you are evaluating your expressions using XPath 2.0 (XMLSpy's XPath evaluation tool has buttons to select version 1.0 or 2.0).

Write an XPath expression to find all the policies with a start date of more than five years ago. You can create a date for comparison using the following format:

```
xs:date('2007–04–01')
```

SUMMARY

We began this chapter by looking at XPath, and the basics of how XPath expressions can pick out parts of an XML document. We then looked at how XPath is used as part of XSLT to transform documents from one structure or type to another. In particular, we looked at using XSLT to transform XML documents into HTML and XHTML, with a brief mention of transforming from XML to another XML document. We concluded the chapter by exploring the differences between input-driven push transformations and output-driven pull transformations.

6

Introduction to JavaScript

INTRODUCTION

In this chapter, we introduce the JavaScript language, which can be used to write code that runs inside the browser. We apply some of the most important concepts in JavaScript, including the document object model (DOM) and the built-in JavaScript objects. Examples in this chapter show how to use the properties and methods of JavaScript objects, how to work with simple data types including numbers, strings, dates and arrays, and how to use the arithmetic operators. We explore the control structures of JavaScript programming and see how to write code in script elements, functions and external files.

7.1 JavaScript – what and why?

Scripting languages are lightweight programming languages that are usually interpreted rather than compiled and run inside a particular environment. '*a client-side* script *is a program that may accompany an HTML document or be embedded directly in it*' (Ragget *et al*. 1999).

JavaScript is the most commonly used of a number of scripting languages that can run inside web browsers. JavaScript code can be embedded in, or called from, HTML documents and these scripts can generate page content dynamically. In general, JavaScript is used for three main purposes:

- To improve the visual look and feel of the user's experience using a browser-based application. For example, JavaScript can be used to create pop up windows and interactive menus, and to enable parts of the page, such as images, to respond to *mouse events*, such as the mouse pointer passing over them. JavaScript, combined with the DOM and cascading style sheets (CSS), is the basis for Dynamic HTML (DHTML), which enables browser-based applications to become more interactive.
- To offload some of the web application processing from the server to the client. A good example of this is the ability to perform client-side form validation, checking the contents of an HTML form before it is submitted to the server for further processing. Not all validation can be done on the client, but simple things like checking that required fields are not empty can still be very useful.
- To enable Asynchronous JavaScript and XML (Ajax) implementations to provide a more seamless interaction between client and server.

JavaScript was originally developed in 1995 by Netscape and introduced into Netscape Navigator 2.0. It was originally called 'LiveScript' but later became 'JavaScript', and is therefore often confused with Java, though there are many differences between them. Although the term 'JavaScript' is widely used, strictly speaking the name only applies to the Netscape version. The version that runs in Microsoft browsers is called 'JScript', and there is also a standard version of the language known as 'ECMAScript'. ECMA is a European standards consortium that began as the European Computer Manufacturers' Association, hence the acronym.

7.2 The document object model (DOM)

The DOM is a W3C specification that enables scripting languages, like JavaScript, to access and update the content, structure and style of documents, regardless of the platform or scripting language being used. The first DOM specification (level 1) was published in 1998, the second (level 2) in 2000 and the third (level 3) in 2004. The DOM consists of a set of core interfaces that apply to any structured document, with additional interfaces that are specifically intended for use with XML or HTML documents. As HTML has grown closer to XML with the XHTML specification, this distinction between XML and HTML has become less important. The term 'DOM level 0' is sometimes used to refer to the de facto object model that was used in browsers (such as Internet Explorer 3 and Netscape Navigator 3) prior to the first formal DOM specification. Some parts of the DOM API that relate specifically to HTML were included to ensure backward compatibility with these earlier document models.

The DOM represents a document as a hierarchy of nodes, some of which can have child nodes and some that are leaf nodes. You will recognize core aspects of the DOM from our prior discussions of the structure of XML documents. For example the *document* node can only have one child of type *element* (which of course is the root element of the document). An *element* node, however, can have multiple child nodes, and these may also be elements. A *text* node is a leaf, meaning that it cannot have any child nodes. As we look at JavaScript, you will find that it has its own way of modeling the document object, some of which comes directly from the standard W3C DOM and some of which is specific to JavaScript.

7.3 Characteristics of JavaScript

The language constructs in JavaScript are similar to a number of other languages, including C, C++, C# and Java, but there are some important differences. Perhaps the most obvious difference is that JavaScript is loosely typed, meaning that when we declare a variable we only have to declare its name, not its type. We can also use the same variable to reference different types of data at different times. This is not possible in strongly typed languages like Java.

JavaScript is not a fully object-oriented language, and does not allow the creation of new object types (though more recent versions of ECMAScript have begun to move in this direction). Rather it is an object-based, or *prototype* language, where there are a number of built-in objects and object types that can be used in programs. For example the top-level object in the JavaScript DOM is the *window*, which represents the browser window (or frame).

Setting the default scripting language for a web page

Since JavaScript is only one of a number of scripting languages that may be supported by browsers (others include VBScript and Tcl), it is necessary to specify that JavaScript is the language being used in a particular page. The 'meta' element should be used inside the 'head' element to set the default scripting language, like this:

```
<meta http-equiv="Content-Script-Type" content="text/javascript" />
```

It is important to set the default scripting language for scripts that are linked to *intrinsic events*, such as mouse buttons being pressed, keys on the keyboard being pressed and HTML documents being loaded.

 NOTE 'text/javascript' is likely to be replaced by 'application/javascript' in forthcoming standards but is not yet widely supported by browsers.

Adding scripts to web pages

Scripts can be added to a web page by using <script>...</script> elements. These can be added either to the head or the body elements of the HTML, or even as a separate element outside of the page definition. Scripts can also be written as reusable functions in separate files (described in Section 7.9). Script elements that are *not* part of JavaScript functions will be run when the page is loaded, whereas functions can be invoked at other times, for example, by clicking on a button. In addition to setting the default scripting language in the document's *meta* tag, each script element should also define the scripting language being used for that particular element by setting the *type* attribute to 'text/javascript'. All script elements that use JavaScript, regardless of where they appear in the document, should therefore appear like this:

```
<script type="text/javascript">
  ... JavaScript source code goes here
</script>
```

7.4 JavaScript objects

Now we know what sort of tag to use to include JavaScript in our web pages, what type of code goes into these elements? One important aspect of JavaScript is its ability to interact with objects of various types. Some of these relate to the DOM components of the browser environment, such as *window*, *document*, *location* and *navigator*. Some relate to common data types such as *Array*, *String* and *Date*, while others, such as *Math*, provide some standard utility functions. The objects that relate to the browser environment have parent–child relationships, where one object contains another. Figure 7.1 shows the relationships between just a few of the browser-related JavaScript objects. The window object contains the document (that is loaded in the browser window) and the location and navigator objects, and the document may contain one or more forms that in turn contain various HTML controls such as text fields and buttons.

Object properties

JavaScript objects have *properties*, *methods* and *event handlers*. Properties are values that reflect the state of an object; methods are operations that an object can perform; and event handlers enable state changes or methods to be invoked when an event, such as a button being pressed, a component losing or gaining focus, or a document being loaded, occurs. An object's properties can be accessed using 'dot' notation, where the name of the object is followed by the name of the property, separated by a dot:

```
object.property
```

The value of the property can be set using the ' = ' operator. One of the properties of the document object for example is the *title*. This is the text that appears in the title bar at the top of the browser window. This example shows the title property of the document being set.

```
document.title="JavaScript document title"
```

Here is the full source of an XHTML page that sets the document title property using a script element in the body of the page. Note that the XHTML head element needs to contain a title element, even if it is empty, in order to be valid XHTML and, of course, for JavaScript to locate the element in order to populate it.

```
<?xml version="1.0"?>
<!DOCTYPE html PUBLIC "-//W3C//DTD XHTML 1.1//EN"
```

```
      "http://www.w3.org/TR/xhtml11/DTD/xhtml11.dtd">
  <html xmlns="http://www.w3.org/1999/xhtml" xml:lang="en">
    <head>
      <meta http-equiv="Content-Script-Type" content="text/javascript"/>
      <title></title>
    </head>
    <body>
      <!-- File: Example7-1.htm -->
      <script type="text/javascript">
        document.title="JavaScript document title"
      </script>
    </body>
  </html>
```

Since scripts included in the body are executed when the document is loaded, the title bar appears as shown in Figure 7.2 when the document is loaded into a browser (this example uses Internet Explorer 7).

Comments in JavaScript source code

There are two ways that comment syntax can be useful in JavaScript. First, we can use the JavaScript comment syntax simply to add comments to our code to help others to understand it, and second, we sometimes need to 'hide' JavaScript code from the browser, for reasons we explain shortly.

There are two types of comment syntax in JavaScript, for single-line or multiple-line comments. Single line comments, similar to C++ comment syntax, are preceded by two forward slashes:

```
// this is a single line comment
```

Multiple-line comments use C-style syntax, beginning with a forward slash and an asterisk, and ending with an asterisk and a forward slash:

```
/*
This is a
multiple-line comment
*/
```

FIGURE 7.2   The Internet Explorer 7 title bar set using the 'document.title' property

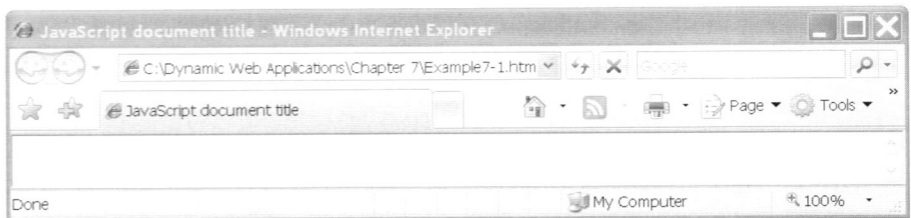

These types of comment are useful to help other JavaScript developers understand the scripts you have written. The second use of comment syntax is to wrap an HTML or XML comment, combined with a JavaScript single line comment, around the code in your script elements. There are two reasons to do this:

- If the client's browser does not support JavaScript, or if JavaScript is disabled, the code can be hidden from the browser.
- If you want the rest of your page to be valid XHTML, JavaScript syntax needs to be hidden from the validator, because some characters commonly used in JavaScript (e.g. '<' and '>') cause problems in validation.

The way that we wrap comments around our scripts is to precede them with the HTML comment opening sequence, '<!--', which JavaScript treats as if it were a single line comment. Then at the end of the script, use the HTML comment closing sequence but precede it with the JavaScript single-line comment, i.e. '// -- >' The effect of this is that JavaScript ignores the closing HTML comment character but the browser recognizes it as the end of the HTML comment. Here is a modified version of the script that changes the document's title property but with the comment syntax added. Using this approach means that your scripts will not cause problems in browsers where JavaScript is not supported and your documents can still be valid XHTML.

```
<script type="text/javascript">
<!--
document.title="JavaScript document title"
// -->
</script>
```

Objects as properties

Some properties of objects are also objects. For example the *location* property of the window is actually a 'Location' object, with its own properties and methods. We can navigate through the object hierarchy using dot notation, access the 'location' property of the 'window' object and then access its own properties. In this example, the 'protocol' property of the 'location' is accessed:

```
window.location.protocol
```

Here is an XHTML page with a script that sets the document's title property using the value of the location's protocol.

```
<?xml version="1.0"?>
<!DOCTYPE html PUBLIC "-//W3C//DTD XHTML 1.1//EN"
   "http://www.w3.org/TR/xhtml11/DTD/xhtml11.dtd">
<html xmlns="http://www.w3.org/1999/xhtml" xml:lang="en">
  <head>
    <meta http-equiv="Content-Script-Type" content="text/javascript"/>
    <title></title>
  </head>
  <body>
  <!-- File: Example7-2.htm -->
    <script type="text/javascript">
      <!--
```

```
        document.title = window.location.protocol
      // -->
    </script>
  </body>
</html>
```

Figure 7.3 shows the title bar of Mozilla Firefox 2, displaying the http: protocol when a file has been loaded into the browser. Depending on what the browser is being used to display, other possible values of the 'protocol' property would include 'http:' and 'ftp:'.

 NOTE 'Location' is not a DOM object, but a JavaScript object, based on the 'location' property of the window in the DOM hierarchy.

Object methods

Methods are things that an object can do. Simple examples of object methods are the 'write' and 'writeln' methods of the 'document' object, which allow us to write page contents to the current document. The only difference between them is that 'writeln' adds a carriage return and new line to the generated HTML after writing the contents, but this does not insert a line break element into the actual HTML document. To invoke a method, we use the same dot notation as when accessing properties.

Methods can have parameter arguments passed to them, in parentheses. In this example, a 'write' method is passed some string data (which may include mark-up) as a parameter. String data is a collection of characters enclosed by speech marks (single or double).

```
document.write("<h2>Subheading</h2>")
```

Positioning scripts in the document

In the next example we use the 'document.write' method to illustrate the difference between putting a script in the body of the document as opposed to the head. If we put a script in the document body, we can position it within the rest of the document

FIGURE 7.3 The Mozilla Firefox 2 title bar set using the 'protocol' property

in a specific place. In contrast, scripts in the head element are run before the body content is rendered. The following example shows a script element that writes out a subheading being placed between HTML tags that write out a main heading and some paragraph text.

```
<?xml version="1.0"?>
<!DOCTYPE html PUBLIC "-//W3C//DTD XHTML 1.1//EN"
   "http://www.w3.org/TR/xhtml11/DTD/xhtml11.dtd">
<html xmlns="http://www.w3.org/1999/xhtml" xml:lang="en">
  <head>
    <meta http-equiv="Content-Script-Type" content="text/javascript"/>
    <title>JavaScript</title>
  </head>
  <body>
    <!-- File: Example7-3.htm -->
    <h1>Main Heading</h1>
      <script type="text/javascript">
        <!--
        document.write("<h2>Subheading</h2>")
        // -->
      </script>
    <p>paragraph text</p>
  </body>
</html>
```

The page displayed in a browser (see Figure 7.4) shows that the script has been executed in the position where it appears in the body, between the main heading and the paragraph.

In contrast, this version of the page has the script in the 'head' element:

```
<?xml version = "1.0"?>
<!DOCTYPE html PUBLIC "-//W3C//DTD XHTML 1.1//EN"
   "http://www.w3.org/TR/xhtml11/DTD/xhtml11.dtd">
<html xmlns = "http://www.w3.org/1999/xhtml" xml:lang="en">
  <head>
    <meta http-equiv="Content-Script-Type" content="text/javascript"/>
    <title>JavaScript</title>
    <script type="text/javascript">
      <!--
      document.write("<h2>Subheading</h2>")
      // -->
    </script>
  </head>
  <body>
    <!-- File: Example7-4.htm -->
    <h1>Main Heading</h1>
    <p>paragraph text</p>
  </body>
</html>
```

Figure 7.5 shows the resulting document in the browser. Note that the script has been run before the body, meaning that the subheading now comes first.

FIGURE 7.4 The script appears in its sequence within the document body

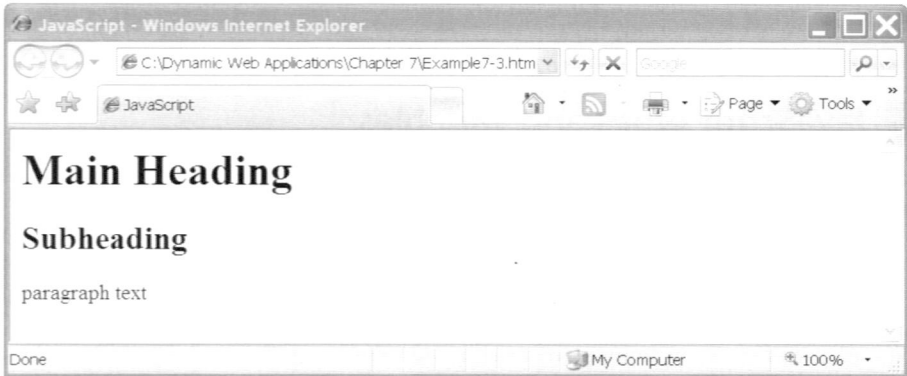

FIGURE 7.5 The head element's script output appears before the content of the document body

In summary, you should put your scripts in the body element if the order of their execution in terms of other body elements is important. Otherwise they can be put into the head element.

7.5 Debugging JavaScript

Before long, you will no doubt be having problems with errors in your JavaScript code, but how can you see what is wrong? In many cases, faulty JavaScript will mean the browser just displays a blank page. Fortunately, browsers provide various tools for debugging JavaScript. In Internet Explorer 7, select Tools, Internet Options. Select the Advanced tab and check the 'Display a notification about every script error' box. If something goes wrong with a page containing JavaScript, a yellow triangle with an exclamation mark will appear in the bottom left corner of the browser frame. If you double-click this, you will get a pop-up dialog that will show you any error messages. However, the debugging services in Internet Explorer are not always very helpful and it can be easier to debug your scripts in other browsers. Mozilla Firefox 2, for example, has a very good error console that shows a lot of information about JavaScript errors. To access this console, just select Tools, Error Console. Similarly, Opera 9 has an error console that can be accessed from its Tools menu; select Advanced and then Error console.

NOTE	In earlier versions of Firefox, the error console was called the JavaScript console, so the relevant menu item is 'JavaScript Console'.

7.6 JavaScript types and variables

In an earlier section we looked at some aspects of JavaScript objects that relate to the JavaScript DOM; the 'window' and 'document' objects and some of their properties. In this section we look at some data types in JavaScript, some of which are very simple types (numbers, strings, Booleans) and others that represent more complex types (Date, Math, Array). We also see how variables can be declared, and how their values may be manipulated, for example by using arithmetic expressions.

Declaring and using variables

In the examples we have seen so far, JavaScript objects have been used to modify the browser window or to provide values that have been written directly to the document object. Sometimes, however, we need to store a value, which may be the result of calling an object's method, in a variable. In JavaScript, a variable is just a name used to refer to a particular value. It is not declared to be of any specific type, but is simply declared using the reserved word 'var', e.g.

```
var myVariable
```

Although variables need not necessarily be declared using the 'var' reserved word, it is important to understand that declaring a variable without preceding it with 'var' will make it a *global* variable. Global variables are visible to all scripts in the current page. Therefore, unless you really need to declare a global variable, always use the 'var' keyword. There are a few simple rules for JavaScript variable names:

- The first character must be a letter (upper or lower case) or an underscore.
- The rest of the name can include upper or lower case letters, numbers and underscores.
- Names should not begin with two underscores because names in this format are used by JavaScript for internal purposes.
- Names cannot include spaces.
- Names cannot be JavaScript reserved words.
- Names are case sensitive.

Although variables do not have a specific type, the values that they refer to do have a type. These types include simple numbers, strings (of characters) and Booleans. It can be useful to name variables in such as way that their type is indicated by their name. For example we can start each variable name with a three-letter indicator of its type, e.g. 'int' for integers, 'boo' for Booleans, 'str' for strings, and so on. This fragment of JavaScript shows some literal values of these three types being assigned to three variables. In each case, the variable declaration is the same, since no data typing is used.

```
var intSomeNumber = 4
var strSomeCharacters = "characters"
```

```
var booSomeIndicator = true
```

In the example above, the three variables are declared on separate lines. Using a new line as a separator between different statements in JavaScript is acceptable, but statements should really be separated by semicolons, like this:

```
var intSomeNumber = 4;
var strSomeCharacters = "characters";
var booSomeIndicator = true;
```

This approach is more robust than just using new lines, because the semicolon will separate statements even if they appear on the same line.

Arithmetic on numeric variables

We can perform arithmetic with JavaScript numeric variables using these five operators:

add   +
subtract   −
multiply   *
divide   /
modulus   %

All arithmetic statements have the same format, namely that a variable on the left of an assignment (=) operator is made to equal the result of an arithmetic expression on the right:

```
var = expression;
```

Some examples (where the 'flt' prefix indicates a floating point number) might be:

```
var intTotalBananas = intMyBananas + intYourBananas;
var fltNetPay = fltGrossPay − fltDeductions;
var fltArea = fltHeight * fltWidth;
var fltDistanceInKm = fltDistanceInMiles / 0.62137;
var intParentsBiscuits = intNumberOfBiscuits % intNumberOfChildren;
```

Increment and decrement operators

There are also some simple operators to increment and decrement the value of a variable by. The most commonly used is probably the '++' operator, which adds 1 to a variable.

```
var intCounter = 1;
intCounter++;
```

In this example, the variable 'intCounter' would be incremented to hold the value 2. We can see that the increment operator is simply shorthand for:

```
intCounter = intCounter + 1;
```

There is also a decrement operator, which, logically enough, is '--' and subtracts 1 from the value of a variable:

```
intCounter --;
```

This would subtract 1 from the current value of 'intCounter', and is shorthand for:

```
intCounter = intCounter - 1;
```

Prefix and postfix operators

The previous examples of the increment and decrement operators both used 'postfix' nota-tion (i.e., the '++' or ' – ' appears after the variable). We may also use 'prefix' notation (the operator appears before the variable):

```
postfix notation:  intCounter++  or  intCounter--
prefix notation:  ++intCounter  or  --intCounter
```

This makes no difference if the operator is not used as part of a larger expression, but can be significant if it is. If one of these operators is used in prefix notation, then the operator will execute before the rest of an expression, but if postfix notation is used then it will be executed afterwards. For example, if the value of our 'intCounter' variable is to be assigned to another variable in the following expression:

```
var intCounter = 1;
var intCurrentCount = intCounter++;
```

The value of 'intCurrentCount' is 1, because the increment operator (which adds 1 to 'intCounter') is evaluated after the assignment of the value of 'intCounter' to 'intCurrentCount' (postfix notation). With prefix notation, where the increment takes place before the assignment, the value of 'intCurrentCount' will be 2:

```
var intCounter = 1;
var intCurrentCount = ++intCounter;
```

To avoid confusion, the increment and decrement operators will not be used as part of larger expressions in this book and the postfix notation will be adopted in all cases.

Other shorthand expressions

The increment and decrement operators are appropriate only when we need to add 1 to, or subtract 1 from, the existing value of a variable. However, we also have shorthand for changing the value of a variable by arithmetic on its existing value. As one example, we could replace the expression:

```
fltVariable = fltVariable + 5;
```

with:

```
fltVariable += 5;
```

As you can see, when we are changing the value of a variable, this shorthand form simply avoids having to write the name of the variable twice. Variables can be decremented similarly, so to subtract 4 from 'fltVariable' we could write:

```
fltVariable  -= 4;
```

Table 7.1 shows examples of shorthand expressions for all five arithmetic operators.

Order of precedence

When writing expressions that contain more than one arithmetic operator, you need to be aware of the 'order of precedence' i.e., which part of the expression will be evaluated first. There is a standard (and quite large) table for this that applies to virtually all languages, but the most important parts of it are shown in Table 7.2.

Consider this example:

```
var intVar = 4 + 2 * 3;
```

TABLE 7.1   Using the shorthand expressions for arithmetic operators

Usual expression	Shorthand expression
fltVariable = fltVariable + 5;	fltVariable +=5;
fltVariable = fltVariable – 4;	fltVariable – =4;
fltVariable = fltVariable * 2;	fltVariable *=2;
fltVariable = fltVariable / 3;	fltVariable /=3;
fltVariable = fltVariable % 4;	fltVariable %=4;

TABLE 7.2   Some important elements of the order of precedence table

Order of precedence	Symbols	Description
Higher	( )	parentheses
	++	increment and decrement operators
	—	
	*	multiply, divide and modulus operators
	/	
	%	
	+	addition and subtraction operators
	—	
	* =	shorthand assignment expressions
	/ =	
	+ =	
	- =	
Lower	% =	

7

Since the multiplication is executed before the addition, the result would be 10. If this is not what we want, we can use parentheses to change the order in which parts of an expression are evaluated. To force the addition to be executed first we can write:

```
var intVar = (4 + 2) * 3;
```

As you would expect, this gives the result of 18, since the addition is now performed before the multiplication. If two operators of the same precedence (i.e., add and subtract, or multiply, divide and remainder) appear in the same expression, then they are evaluated from left to right. For example, in the following expression, the multiplication is evaluated before the division, giving the answer 15:

```
var intVar = 10 * 3 / 2;
```

7.7 Using and creating objects

In Section 7.4, we introduced some of the JavaScript objects that relate to the DOM, such as 'document' and 'window'. There are a number of other types of object available to us in JavaScript. Some of these are single objects that can be used directly, such as the 'Math' object, while others are types that we can create on the fly, such as Strings and Dates. In this section, we introduce some of these object types and see how they can be created and used.

The Math object

The arithmetic operators are fine for simple calculations, but sometimes we need the services of something that can do more complex mathematics. In these situations, the 'Math' object provides support for a number of mathematical operations, including methods for geometry, raising a number to a power, rounding and random-number generation. The following script uses the 'random' method to generate a pseudo-random number between zero and one.

```
<!-- File: Example7-5.htm -->
<script type = "text/javascript">
  <!--
    document.write("Here is a random number between zero and one: ");
    document.write(Math.random())
  // -->
</script>
```

Figure 7.6 shows one possible output from this script. Since the number generated by the random method is always between zero and one, deriving random numbers in other ranges, or random integers, requires some further work.

Since the various methods of the Math class return the values of mathematical operations, these returned values may be assigned to variables, for example,

```
var fltRandomNumber = Math.random();
```

The Math class also has some properties representing common mathematical values. One of these is 'PI'. The following script element uses 'Math.PI', and the 'Math.pow' method,

FIGURE 7.6 A pseudo-random number generated by the Math.random() method

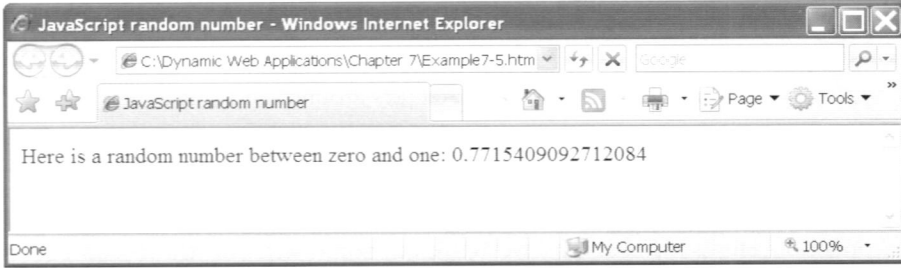

FIGURE 7.7 The area of the circle resulting from the calculation using the Math object

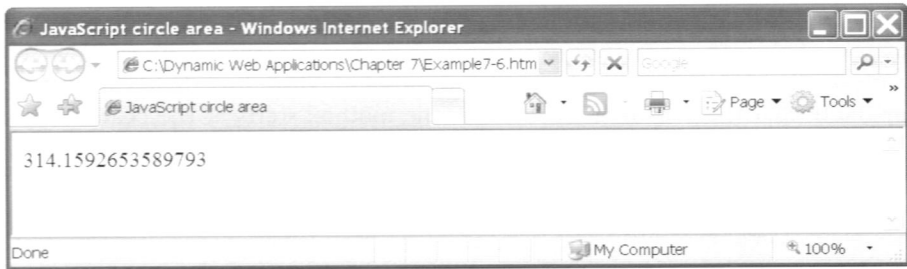

which raises the first parameter to the power of the second, to calculate the area of a circle. Though this is a simple example, it shows both properties and methods of the Math class, assigning results to variables, and using parentheses to ensure that parts of the calculation take place in the correct order (that is, we square the radius before multiplying by 'PI').

```
<!-- File: Example7-6.htm -->
<script type="text/javascript">
  <!--
    var intRadius = 10;
    var fltArea = Math.PI * (Math.pow(intRadius, 2));
    document.write(fltArea);
  // -->
</script>
```

Figure 7.7 shows the result of the calculation displayed in the browser.

Strings

A JavaScript string is simply a sequence of zero or more characters enclosed by either single or double quotes. It does not matter which of these you use, but having the choice does enable you to enclose one type of quote within another, which can be particularly useful when combining JavaScript and HTML. For example, this is a valid JavaScript string, containing HTML that includes quoted attributes:

```
'<img src = "logo.gif" alt = "logo">'
```

Or, of course, we could switch the quote characters around:

```
"<img src = 'logo.gif' alt = 'logo'>"
```

Another useful aspect of strings is that they can be concatenated (joined together) using the '+' operator. Here, for example, we write out some text and the document title by concatenating them:

```
document.write("Document title is " + document.title);
```

You can concatenate different data types together with strings and they will be treated as a single string. Strings also have a number of properties and methods. The 'length' property, for example, returns the number of characters in a string, while the 'substring' method returns part of the string between two specified character positions. The following script uses both the 'length' property and the 'substring' method to display the last character of a string. Note that the substring returned by the method starts at the character position *after* the one specified by the first parameter, but includes the character at the position specified by the second parameter:

```
<!-- File: Example7-7.htm -->
<script type = "text/javascript">
  <!--
    var strFullString = "a string";
    var intLength = strFullString.length;
    var strSubString = strFullString.substring(intLength-1, intLength);
    document.write("Last character is " + strSubString);
  // -->
</script>
```

Figure 7.8 shows the result of the script in a browser.

FIGURE 7.8   A substring displayed in a browser window

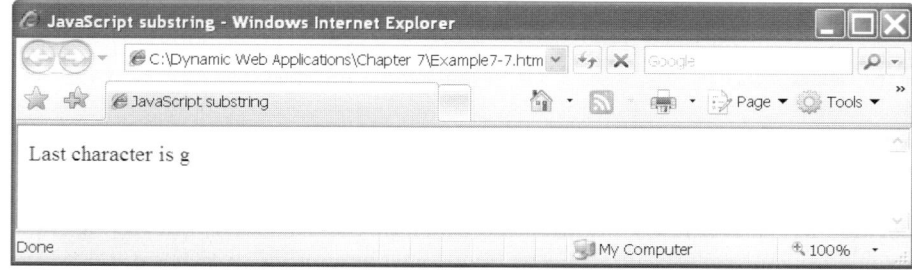

Date objects

Unlike objects that exist as part of the browser environment, and the 'Math' object which is built into JavaScript, 'Date' objects, which represent both a date and a time, need to be created when required. Being able to create 'Date' objects on the fly also means that we can create and manipulate as many of them as we like. Creating objects in JavaScript is done using the reserved word 'new' and the constructor method, which has the same name as the object type and, like other methods, is followed by parentheses. The newly created 'Date' object can be assigned to a variable:

```
var dateToday = new Date();
```

What can we do with a date? Basically we can either use the default settings, which include the date and time of its creation, or specifically set its values. If you simply write the date object to the document, you will get the current date and time of the locale being used by your machine, relative to coordinated universal time (UTC), which is based on Greenwich Mean Time. You can also display the current date and time in UTC, using the 'toUTCString' method, or display the time in the current locale with reference to UTC, using the 'toLocaleString' method. In the following script, we display the same date object in these three different ways:

```
<!-- File:Example7-8.htm -->
<script type="text/javascript">
  <!--
    var dateToday = new Date();
    document.write("The current date and time is: " + dateToday);
      document.write("<br />The date and time in Coordinated Universal Time is:
    " + dateToday.toUTCString());
      document.write("<br />The date and time using the current locale is: " +
    dateToday.toLocaleString());
  // -->
</script>
```

The way that different browsers display dates varies slightly. Figure 7.9 shows how the three versions of the date are displayed in Mozilla Firefox 2, but other browsers will give slightly different results in terms of presentation.

Table 7.3 shows some of the other methods of the Date class.

Arrays

An Array is a collection of values that have the same name but are identified by an index value, which appears in square brackets. Like Date objects, Arrays can be created on the fly, and we can have as many of them as we like, so again they are created using the reserved word 'new', for example:

```
var arrMyArray = new Array(size);
```

The 'size' parameter would be a number specifying the number of elements in the array. We can set or retrieve the values in the array using square brackets containing an index

FIGURE 7.9   The result of a script that displays a 'Date' object in Mozilla Firefox 2

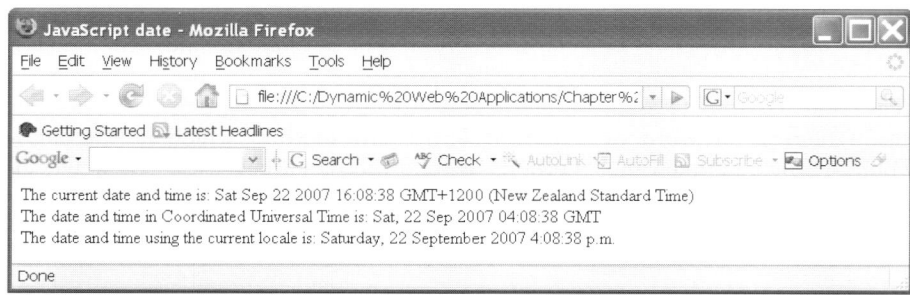

TABLE 7.3   Some methods of the Date class

Method	Purpose
getDate setDate	Returns or sets the day of the month (a number between 1 and 31)
getDay	Returns the day of the week as a number between 0 (Sunday) and 6 (Saturday)
getHours setHours	Returns or sets the hours value as an integer between 0 (midnight) and 23 (11 pm)
getMinutes setMinutes	Returns or sets the minutes value as an integer between 0 and 59
getSeconds setSeconds	Returns or sets the seconds value as an integer between 0 and 59
getFullYear setFullYear	Returns or sets the year value as a four-digit integer
getTime setTime	Returns or sets the date as the number of milliseconds since the beginning of January 1st 1970

number. The array index starts at zero, so to set a value in the first element of the array, we use zero in the brackets.

```
arrMyArray[0] = "a string";
```

Since the array has no specified type, the elements of the array can contain values of different JavaScript types. For example the next element of the array could contain a number:

```
arrMyArray[1]=10;
```

Here is a simple script that uses an array to write the name of the current day to the document. It uses a JavaScript Date object to get the number of the day of the week (using the 'getDay' method), then uses an array of strings to return the actual name of the day. Note that the 'getDay' method uses a zero to represent Sunday and then counts up from there through the days of the week, with six representing Saturday. This fits in quite neatly with an array, which also starts its index at zero.

```
<!-- File: Example7-9.htm -->
<script type="text/javascript">
<!--
  var date=new Date();
  var arrDayNames=new Array(7);
  arrDayNames[0]="Sunday";
  arrDayNames[1]="Monday";
  arrDayNames[2]="Tuesday";
  arrDayNames[3]="Wednesday";
  arrDayNames[4]="Thursday";
  arrDayNames[5]="Friday";
  arrDayNames[6]="Saturday";
  var strToday=arrDayNames[date.getDay()];
  document.write("Today is " + strToday);
// -->
</script>
```

Figure 7.10 shows the result of running this script on a Thursday.

Rather than assigning the elements of an array one at a time, an alternative approach is to use an initialization list, where instead of creating an empty array and then adding data to elements using the index numbers, we simply provide the actual data in a comma-separated list. For example we can both create and populate the 'arrDayNames' array like this:

```
var arrDayNames =
["Sunday","Monday","Tuesday","Wednesday","Thursday","Friday","Saturday"];
```

7.8 Control structures

JavaScript has control structures for looping and decision-making similar to those in many other languages. The 'if' and 'if. . .else' structures can be used to evaluate a conditional statement and respond accordingly. There are also two types of loop, the 'while' loop and the 'for' loop.

FIGURE 7.10 Using an array of day names to display the current day

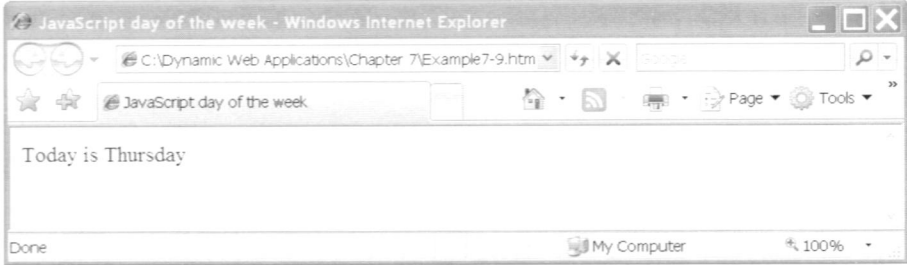

'if. . .else' statements

An 'if' statement consists of two (and only two) different courses of action and a condition. A condition in JavaScript will always return a Boolean value, and which of the two courses of action is taken depends on whether that value is true or false. One course of action may be, in fact, to do nothing. 'if' statements look like this:

```
if(condition)
{
   // do this
}
else
{
   // do this instead
}
```

The 'else' part is optional. If the condition is false and there is no 'else' part then the script will carry on executing after the 'if' statement.

Relational operators

When writing any kind of conditional statement, including 'if' statements and loops, we need to express conditions that compare variables using relational operators. The operators used in JavaScript are shown in Table 7.4.

The only operators that might cause confusion here are the 'identical to' and 'not identical to' operators. They differ from the 'equal to' and 'not equal to' operators only in that some type conversions are allowed for equality that do not apply with identity. The example shown in the table should illustrate this. If we test the expression:

```
1 == true
```

Then this will return true, because 1 can be converted to the Boolean value 'true'. However, this expression:

```
1 === true
```

will return 'false', since the identity operator does not allow type conversions when making comparisons.

| TABLE 7.4 | JavaScript relational operators |

Condition	Relational Operator	Example
equal to	==	if(intTemperature == 100)
Identical to	===	if(1 === true)
not equal to	!=	if(chrGrade != 'F')
not identical to	!==	if(1 !== false)
less than	<	if(fltSales < fltTarget)
less than or equal to	<=	if(int EngineSize <= 2000)
greater than	>	if(intHoursWorked > 40)
greater than or equal to	>=	if(intAge >= 18)

TABLE 7.5	Logical operators	
Operator	Meaning	Example
&&	AND	if(intAge > 4 && intAge < 16)
||	OR	if(intTimeElapsed > 60 || booStopped == true)
!	NOT	if(!booFormValidated)

To evaluate more complex conditions we need to use logical operators to combine the simple relational operators shown in Table 7.4. The three logical JavaScript operators are shown in Table 7.5.

All these expressions return either true or false. The 'not' operator (!) can be confusing because it returns 'true' if the expression is 'false'. For example, the expression 'if(!booFormValidated)' in the table will be true if 'booFormValidated' is false, i.e., if the form has not been validated then 'not validated' is true. We often find this operator being used to test Boolean 'flag' variables that indicate when something has happened. The 'not' operator is matched by the ability to do a test for true, for example 'if(booFormValidated)' is an equally valid expression.

Using selection: simulating throwing a coin

The next script example makes a selection using an 'if' statement. This selection is based on using a randomly generated number to simulate throwing a coin, which may land either heads or tails. In order to represent the flipping of the coin, we need to randomly generate a value, which of course we can do with the 'Math.random' method, which returns a random value between 0.0 and 1.0. According to the ECMA specification, the function may return zero but should never return one.

```
var fltRandomNumber = Math.random();
```

Having got this value from the 'random' method, the script then uses an 'if' statement to choose whether the coin is showing heads or tails. If the random number is less than 0.5 then the coin is set to heads, otherwise it is set to tails. Of course, from the point of view of the program it makes no difference whether we use 'less than' or 'greater than', since either way we get a 50/50 chance (more or less).

```
<!-- File: Example7-10.htm -->
<script type="text/javascript">
  <!--
    document.write("The coin has landed on ");
    var fltRandomNumber = Math.random();
    if(fltRandomNumber < 0.5)
    {
      document.write(" Heads!");
    }
    else
    {
      document.write(" Tails!");
    }
  // -->
</script>
```

FIGURE 7.11 One of the two possible outcomes from a script that simulates the tossing of a coin

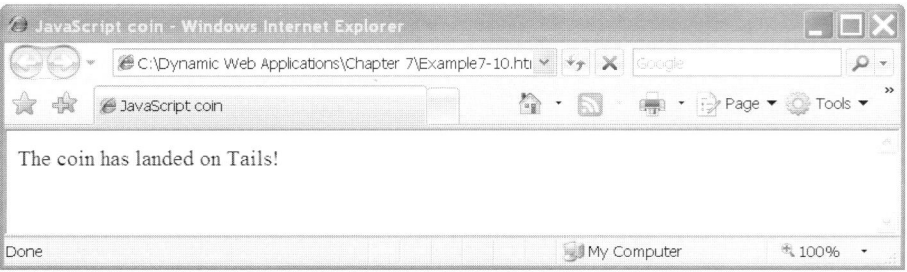

Figure 7.11 shows one of the two possible outcomes from running this script.

'while' loops

A 'while' loop can be used to write code that repeats while a given condition is true. The condition is shown in parentheses after the 'while' reserved word:

```
while(condition)
{
    // code here
}
```

In the next example a while loop is used to simulate the throwing of a dice, again using the Math.random method to generate a pseudo-random floating point number. To get a random integer in the range 1 to 6, we first multiply the result of the Math.random method by 6, which will give us a floating point number in the range 0 to 6 (but not including exactly 6). To turn that floating point number into an integer, the 'floor' method is used, which simply truncates the number by removing any values after the decimal point, giving us an integer. The predictable behavior of 'floor' gives us a more 'random' number than using 'round'. Finally, this is then incremented by 1 to give an integer number in the range 1 to 6. The 'while' loop repeats until the simulated dice 'throws' a 6.

```
<!-- File: Example7-11.htm -->
<script type="text/javascript">
  <!--
    var intDieValue=Math.floor(Math.random()*6);
    intDieValue++;
    while(intDieValue !=6)
    {
      document.write("You threw a " + intDieValue + "<br/>");
      intDieValue=Math.floor(Math.random()*6);
      intDieValue++;
    }
    document.write
      ("You threw a " + intDieValue + " - game over! <br/>");
  // -->
</script>
```

Figure 7.12 shows one possible output from running this script.

FIGURE 7.12 One example of output from a script that simulates the throwing of a die using a 'while' loop

'for' loops

A 'for' loop is very similar to a 'while' loop, because it repeats while a condition remains true. However it also has two other elements, an initialization section that can be used to set the initial value of variables used in the loop, and a section that can be used at the end of each loop to change the value of a variable:

```
for(initialize; condition; increment)
{
  // code here
}
```

A typical 'for' loop will initialize a variable at the beginning, use that variable as its conditional value, and increment (or decrement) the value of the variable at the end of each iteration.

In the next script we generate a times table. The 'for' loop is used to initialize the multiplier for the times table (at 1), provide the 'while' condition (while the multiplier is less than or equal to twelve) and the increment (incrementing the multiplier by 1). The value for the times table is generated by a random number in the range 1 to 12.

```
<!-- File: Example7-12.htm -->
<script type="text/javascript">
  <!--
  var intRandomInteger=Math.floor(Math.random()*12);
  intRandomInteger++;
  document.write(intRandomInteger + " times table <br/>");
  for(var intMultiplier=1; intMultiplier <=12; intMultiplier++)
  {
    document.writeln(intMultiplier + " x " + intRandomInteger + " = " +
    intMultiplier * intRandomInteger);
    document.writeln("<br/>");
  }
  // -->
</script>
```

FIGURE 7.13 One possible output from a script that generates times tables

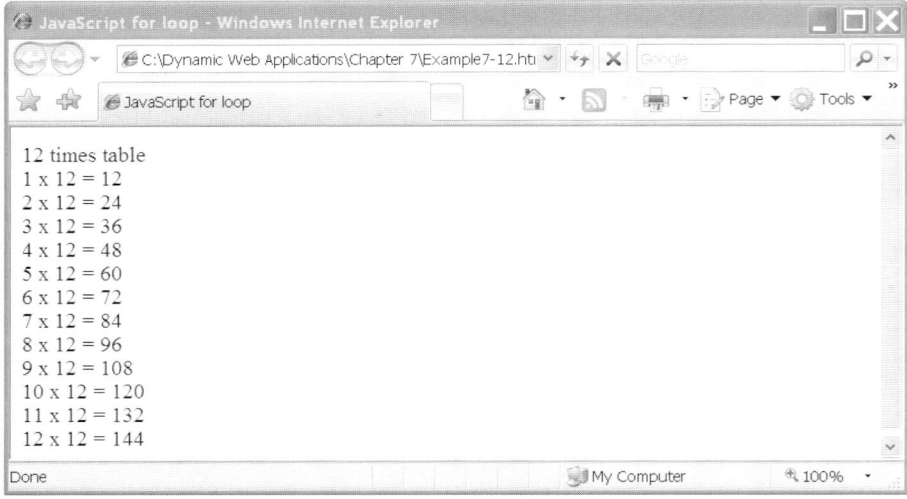

Figure 7.13 shows one of the possible outcomes from this script, generating a times table.

7.9 Writing functions

So far all our JavaScript code has been written in scripts in the body or head elements, which execute when the document is loaded. However you can also write your JavaScript code inside functions, and then call these functions from a script element somewhere else in your page. The same function can also be called from more than one place in the same page if necessary. Functions can be written inside script elements in the head or body of an HTML document, as we have already done with our previous scripts, but may also be written in a separate file. The main advantage of writing functions in separate files is that they can be re-used by scripts in different web pages. Files that contain JavaScript functions are normally given a '.js' file extension.

Regardless of where they are written, functions are not invoked automatically, even if they appear in the body of the document, so they have to be called by some other script or triggered by some kind of event.

A JavaScript function is declared simply by using the key word 'function', followed by the name of the function and any parameters, in parentheses. The body of the function is surrounded by braces:

```
<script type="text/javascript">
function functionname(parameters)
{
}
</script>
```

A function may return a value, representing the end result of the function, using the reserved word 'return' followed by the variable or value that is being returned:

```
<script type="text/javascript">
function functionname(parameters) {
. . .
   return value
}
</script>
```

If it is included, the line that returns the value is normally the last line in the function. This is because nothing after a return statement is executed; the function terminates at that point. This behavior can also be used to deliberately 'short circuit' a function in cases where we want to exit from the function before executing all the code, perhaps because of some error condition or because we already have the result we need.

The following script shows a simple function that uses the same array of day names that we saw in an earlier script example. The difference is that instead of writing the day name out to the document, the function returns the name of the day.

```
<script type="text/javascript">
   <!--
   function getDayName()
   {
      var date=new Date();
      var arrDayNames=["Sunday","Monday","Tuesday","Wednesday",
      "Thursday","Friday","Saturday"];
      return arrDayNames[date.getDay()]
   }
// -->
</script>
```

Defining functions outside the body element

So far, we have been embedding our scripts into the body of the document, which means that the JavaScript will run as soon as the page is loaded. However, once we start using functions, we can put them into the head element of the document or outside the document altogether, and invoke them from another script or an event.

In the following example, we see how a function (in this case added to the head of the document) can be invoked from a script in the body of the document. Because the script in the body is invoked when the document is loaded, the function is called at the same time. A JavaScript function is called simply by using its name and passing any required parameters. Unlike an object method, there is nothing that needs to precede the name of the function. If the function returns a value, that value can be used by the code that invokes the function. In this XHTML page, a script invokes the 'getDayName' function. There are no parameter values to be passed, but the string that is returned from the function is written out to the document.

7

```xml
<?xml version="1.0"?>
<!DOCTYPE html PUBLIC "-//W3C//DTD XHTML 1.1//EN"
    "http://www.w3.org/TR/xhtml11/DTD/xhtml11.dtd">
<html xmlns="http://www.w3.org/1999/xhtml" xml:lang="en">
  <head>
    <meta http-equiv="Content-Script-Type" content="text/javascript"/>
    <title>JavaScript day name function</title>
    <script type="text/javascript">
      <!--
        function getDayName()
        {
          var date=new Date();
          var arrDayNames=
          ["Sunday","Monday","Tuesday","Wednesday","Thursday","Friday",
          "Saturday"];
          return arrDayNames[date.getDay()]
        }
      // -->
    </script>
  </head>
  <body>
  <!-- File: Example7-13.htm -->
    <script type ="text/javascript">
      <! --
        document.write(getDayName() );
      // -->
    </script>
  </body>
</html>
```

Figure 7.14 shows the result of loading the page on a Thursday.

Using external JavaScript files

In all of the examples, we have seen so far, the JavaScript has appeared in the HTML source file. However, if we want to reuse any of our JavaScript functions then they need to be

FIGURE 7.14 A web page displaying the current day using the 'getDayName' function

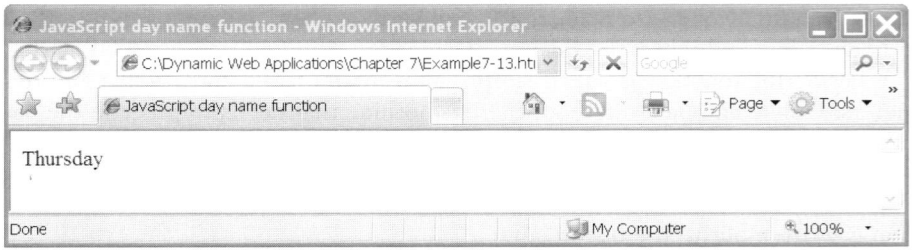

stored separately from HTML pages. In the previous example, we used a function called 'getDayName'. Simple as it is, this function might be reusable in multiple pages, so instead of putting it into the HTML document's header, we could put it into a separate file. Files that contain JavaScript code are usually given a '.js' extension, so in this example we assume a file called 'dayname.js'. Note that when JavaScript is stored separately from the XHTML source file, there is no 'script' element, just the JavaScript source code. The script element remains in the web page to specify the file that contains the JavaScript function.

```javascript
// File: dayname.js
function getDayName()
{
   var date=new Date();
   var arrDayNames=
   ["Sunday","Monday","Tuesday","Wednesday","Thursday","Friday",
   "Saturday"];
   return arrDayNames[date.getDay()];
}
```

To use functions defined in external files, the script element needs to include the 'src' attribute, which specifies the path and filename of the JavaScript source file

```html
<script type="text/javascript" src="path/filename.js"></script>
```

It is important to note that the script element is never an empty element, in other words it always has separate opening and closing tags, even though nothing appears between them. This is necessary because some browsers cannot process the script element unless it has both start and end tags.

Here is an XHTML page that uses the 'getDayName' function by referencing the external JavaScript file using the script element's 'src' attribute.

```html
<?xml version = "1.0"?>
<!DOCTYPE html PUBLIC "-//W3C//DTD XHTML 1.1//EN"
   "http://www.w3.org/TR/xhtml11/DTD/xhtml11.dtd">
<html xmlns="http://www.w3.org/1999/xhtml" xml:lang="en">
   <head>
      <meta http-equiv="Content-Script-Type" content="text/javascript"/>
      <title>JavaScript day name function</title>
      <script type="text/javascript" src="dayname.js">
      </script>
   </head>
   <body>
      <script type="text/javascript">
        <!--
           document.write(getDayName());
        // -->
      </script>
   </body>
</html>
```

Exercises

7.1 One of the browser properties that can be set is the status of the window. Add a line to 'Example7–1.htm' to set the window status text to 'status bar'. (Note that some browsers, such as Mozilla Firefox, will not let scripts change this property until you enable it in your browser preferences.)

7.2 Write a script that uses either a 'for' or a 'while' loop to create a table showing the numbers from 1 to 10 and their squares (see Figure 7.15).

You will need to put all of the code that creates the table inside the script, because if you put some of the table tags outside the script the page will not be valid XHTML. Use a style sheet to display table and cell borders.

7.3 Write a script that generates and displays a 'hand' of five cards from a potential pack of 52 (this script could be used as part of a larger card-game application). JavaScript's loose typing is quite useful here, because we can create an array that contains the names and numbers of playing cards. In your script, first create an array that contains these names and numbers:

```
'Ace','2','3','4','5','6','7','8','9','10','Jack','Queen','King'
```

Then create a second array containing the four suits:

```
'Hearts','Diamonds','Clubs','Spades'
```

Use a 'for' loop that iterates five times (for five cards). In each iteration, use the 'Math.Random()' method to get a name or number and a suit from the arrays and display the resulting card on the screen. The final output might look something like Figure 7.16.

FIGURE 7.15   A table of the numbers from 1 to 10 and their squares

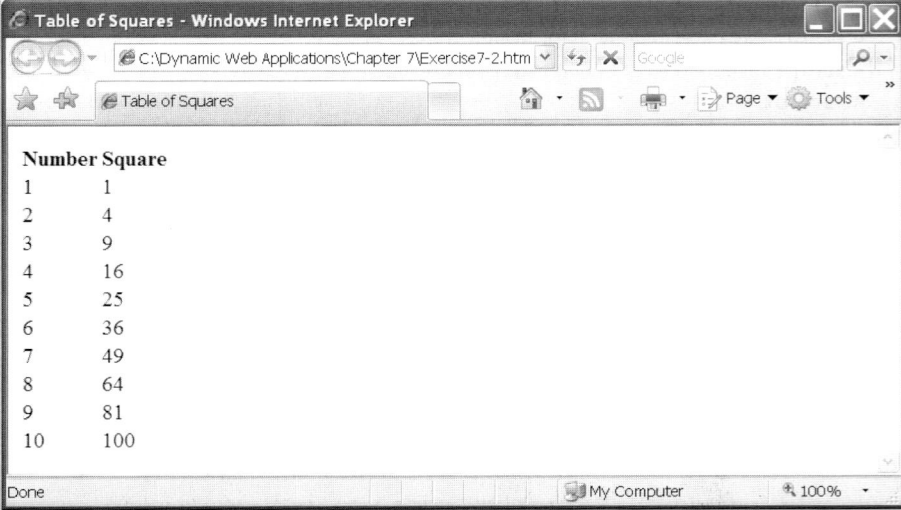

FIGURE 7.16   A possible output from the hand of cards script

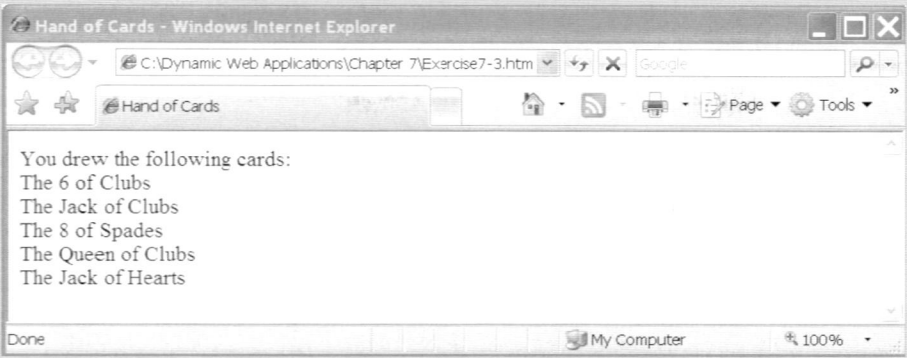

TABLE 7.6   Some time zones and their difference from UTC in hours

Time Zone	Difference from UTC in Hours
Eastern Standard	−5
Pacific standard	−8
UTC	0
Central European	+1
Baghdad	+3
Japan Standard	+9
West Australian Standard	+10
New Zealand Standard	+12

7.4   This exercise is quite complex and involves many steps, but provides practice with the arithmetic operators and should give you a deeper understanding of Date objects.

Write a script that creates a table of the current time in different parts of the world. You can do this by creating a Date object to get the current time, converting it to UTC, and then adding or subtracting the time differences for different places (we will not, however, concern ourselves with daylight saving, so the results may not be completely accurate). Table 7.6 shows some example time zones with their difference from UTC in hours. A more complete table can be found at http://setiathome.berkeley.edu/utc.php.

The names of the time zones can be stored in an array, and the current times in each zone generated by simple arithmetic on the millisecond value of the Date. Here is an XHTML page you can use to call your function. Note that the page assumes the function is called 'showTimeZones' and is in a file called 'timezones.js'.

```
<?xml version="1.0"?>
<!DOCTYPE html PUBLIC "-//W3C//DTD XHTML 1.1//EN"
   "http://www.w3.org/TR/xhtml11/DTD/xhtml11.dtd">
<html xmlns="http://www.w3.org/1999/xhtml" xml:lang="en">
```

7

```
<head>
    <meta http-equiv = "Content-Script-Type" content = "text/javascript"/>
    <title>International Time Zones</title>
    <script type = "text/javascript" src = "timezones.js">
    </script>
</head>
<body>
    <!-- File: exercise7-4.htm -->
    <script type = "text/javascript">
    showTimeZones();
    </script>
</body>
</html>
```

Here are the steps your function should go through:

1   Create an array of time zones.

2   Create an array of the time offsets of these zones.

3   Create a new Date object. This will contain the date and time in the current locale (which may not be UTC).

4   Use the 'getTime( )' method to get the current date and time as a value in milliseconds to make it easy to change by arithmetic.

5   Find out the difference between the current locale and UTC in minutes by using the 'getTimezoneOffset' method.

6   Convert the time in the current locale (in milliseconds) to UTC by adding the offset between them. There are 60,000 milliseconds in a minute, so you need to multiply the offset value by 60,000 before adding it to the millisecond value of the current time.

7   Write out the necessary tags to begin a table, something like this:

```
document.write("<table><tr><th>Time Zone</th><th>Offsets from
UTC</th><th>Current Date and Time</th></tr>");
```

8   Start a 'for' loop to go through each zone in turn (use the 'length' property of the time zone array to control the loop).

9   For each time zone, work out the difference from UTC in milliseconds. There are 3,600,000 milliseconds in each hour, so multiply that by the number of hours in the offset (stored in the array) for the current zone.

10   Work out the time for the current zone (in milliseconds) by adding the offset to the UTC time.

11   Create a new Date object using the adjusted millisecond value (you can create a new Date by passing the millisecond value as a parameter to the constructor).

12   Write the next row of the table (you need to include the HTML tags for the table row and cells.) The code might look something like this:

```
document.write("<tr><td>" + arrTimeZones[i] + "</td><td>" +
arrOffsets[i] + "<td>" + zoneDate.toLocaleString() + "</td></tr>");
```

13   Close the 'table' element.

SUMMARY

In this chapter, we introduced the main features of JavaScript syntax, including interacting with parts of the document object model (DOM); declaring variables, arrays and objects; performing arithmetic; concatenating strings; expressing conditions and controlling loops. We saw how it is possible to use the language to create client-side processes that can integrate small programs into the browser environment. We used a number of JavaScript object methods to, for example, generate random numbers and access date and time information. We looked at various ways of adding JavaScript code to a web page, including in the body or the head of a document or in a separate '.js' file, which makes it possible to reuse the same code, encapsulated in JavaScript functions, in different pages. Table 7.7 provides a summary of the JavaScript keywords, JavaScript object types and built-in objects that were introduced in this chapter. In the next chapter, we build on these foundations to see how JavaScript can be used in conjunction with the DOM, style sheets, and server-side processes to make the web client more interactive and dynamic.

TABLE 7.7   JavaScript keywords, types and objects introduced in this chapter

Keywords	Object Types	Built-In Objects
new	Date	document
var	String	window
function	Math	navigator
if		location
else		
while		
for		
return		
true		
false		

References and further reading

Raggett, D., Le Hors, A. and Jacobs, I. 1999. *HTML 4.01 specification*, Section 18, 'Scripts'.
http://www.w3.org/TR/html4/interact/scripts.html

7

Interactive JavaScript: Dynamic HTML, Client-side Validation and Ajax

LEARNING OBJECTIVES

- **To know the various components of Dynamic HTML (DHTML) and how they work together**

- **To understand how to navigate the document object model (DOM) using JavaScript**

- **To be able to use events to trigger JavaScript functions**

- **To understand the principles and practices of client-side form validation**

- **To be able to make connections to a server using Asynchronous JavaScript and XML (Ajax)**

INTRODUCTION

In Chapter 7 we saw how JavaScript could be used to write simple scripts and functions that run inside the client browser. This JavaScript code can be used to implement client-side processes such as calculating values, manipulating strings of data and interacting with objects from the document object model (DOM). In this chapter, we see how JavaScript, along with the DOM and style sheets, can be used to create Dynamic HTML (DHTML) pages that provide a more interactive experience for the user by responding to events in the browser and dynamically modifying the page or browser presentation. We will also see how JavaScript can contribute to the interaction between client and server by concentrating on two particular types of JavaScript programming. First, we will see how JavaScript can be used for simple ('surface') form validation. In this role, JavaScript can relieve the load on the server by passing the data that users have entered into forms through some basic 'sanity checking' before it is submitted to the server. Secondly, we see how JavaScript can be used to build Ajax applications that are able to communicate behind the scenes with the server and update pages asynchronously, without the need to replace or refresh the whole of the current web page.

8.1 Dynamic HTML (DHTML)

Dynamic HTML is not a specific technology but refers to using a combination of JavaScript, the DOM and cascading style sheets (CSS) to make web pages more dynamic and interactive. JavaScript code can be used to locate nodes of the DOM and interact with their contents, while styles can be used to enhance the dynamic aspects of presentation, such as showing or hiding parts of a page. The credit for 'inventing' DHTML is generally given to Scott Isaacs at Microsoft, though since DHTML is not so much a technology as a collection of techniques, perhaps 'inventing' is not the right term. DHTML relies on aspects of HTML that were introduced with version 4.0, along with elements of CSS, so it will not work on older browsers (e.g. before version 4 of Internet Explorer or Netscape Navigator).

Navigating the DOM

To write DHTML code we need to be able to navigate through the DOM. We saw some aspects of this early in Chapter 7, when we used the document object. The tree of nodes in the DOM in fact begins with the document object, from which we can navigate to other nodes, either by using unique ids (if the 'id' attribute has been used on element nodes) or by traversing parts of the document tree, using an approach similar to XPath. Two ways of doing this are to use the 'firstChild' property, which simply identifies the first child of the current node, or the 'childNodes' property, which is accessed like an array using an index number. However, attempting to use these methods of navigation through the DOM can be very problematic due to browser incompatibilities. A more reliable approach is to use 'id' attributes on the nodes that you wish to access in your JavaScript code, and navigate to them using the 'getElementById' method. There is also a 'getElementsByTagName' method that locates all the occurrences of a particular HTML tag. To explain how these methods work we will refer to the following XHTML document, which has several elements with id attributes:

```
<?xml version="1.0"?>
<!DOCTYPE html PUBLIC "-//W3C//DTD XHTML 1.1//EN"
   "http://www.w3.org/TR/xhtml11/DTD/xhtml11.dtd">
<html xmlns="http://www.w3.org/1999/xhtml" xml:lang="en">
  <head>
    <meta http-equiv="Content-Script-Type" content="text/javascript"/>
    <title>Our Insurance</title>
  </head>
  <body>
    <!-- File: example8-1.htm -->
    <div id="heading1">Buildings Insurance</div>
    <p id="para1">
    You need this type of insurance to cover you in case of
    <span id="risk">severe damage to your home</span>
    (for example fire, flood, vehicle or tree crashing into it)
    as well as more everyday risks like accidentally breaking a window
    </p>
    <div id="heading2">Contents Insurance</div>
    <p id="para2">
    You need this type of insurance to cover
    <span id="items">things in your house</span>,
```

```
        such as furniture, electrical goods, carpets and curtains, against risks such
        as fire, theft, water damage (due to burst pipes, etc) or accidental breakage
            </p>
        </body>
    </html>
```

In order to navigate to the second paragraph of this document, which has the id 'para2', we can use the following expression:

```
document.getElementById("para2");
```

Another way of achieving the same result would be to use the appropriate tag name (in this case 'p') with the getElementsByTagName method, which takes the name of an HTML tag as a parameter (the tag name parameter is not case sensitive). This is a useful alternative for elements that do not have 'id' attributes. Since the 'getElementsByTagName' method will locate all instances of the specified tag, the results are indexed like an array, starting at zero. The second paragraph therefore would have the index '1' in the collection of paragraph tags, and would be accessed like this:

```
document.getElementsByTagName("p")[1];
```

Interacting with nodes

Once we know how to navigate to a node using the DOM, we can interact with that node to access its properties. Properties of nodes include the 'nodeName' and 'nodeType'. These expressions, for example, would get the 'nodeName' and 'nodeType' of the first paragraph:

```
document.getElementById("para1").nodeName;
document.getElementById("para1").nodeType;
```

In this case, the node name would be 'p' and the type would be '1'.

 | **NOTE** | Elements are type 1, attributes are type 2 and text nodes are type 3. (Knowing this can occasionally be useful for debugging purposes – sometimes the node you are accessing is not the one you think it is!)

We can access the contents of a text node using the 'nodeValue' property. Since a paragraph is an element node and not a text node, we need to navigate to its child node to get to the text inside it. We can access the first child node of an element by using the 'firstChild' property, and then get its node value, like this:

```
document.getElementById("para1").firstChild.nodeValue;
```

This will return the text from the opening paragraph tag to the following span tag.

As well as accessing the properties of nodes we can access attributes using the 'getAttribute' method, which takes an attribute name as a parameter. To access the 'id' attribute for the first 'div' element, for example, we could use the following expression:

```
document.getElementById("heading1").getAttribute("id");
```

If you add the following script to the body of the XHTML page previously described, you can test out some of the expressions we have introduced in this section:

```
<script type="text/javascript">
  <!--
  document.write("Paragraph 1 is node name " +
     document.getElementById("para1").nodeName);
  document.write("<br />Paragraph 1 is node type " +
     document.getElementById("para1").nodeType);
  document.write("<br />The text node inside paragraph 1 is " +
     document.getElementById("para1").firstChild.nodeValue);
  document.write("<br />The attribute value of the first div is " +
     document.getElementById("heading1").getAttribute("id") );
  // -->
</script>
```

You should be aware that if you want to navigate the DOM in your script you cannot put the script in the head element, because it will execute before the body has loaded and the DOM will not yet be built! Therefore this particular script needs to be in the body.

 NOTE In fact, you should never put scripts in the header that write content to the document, unless they are in functions, because they will write their output before the document body has been loaded.

The output from the script should include the information shown in Figure 8.1.

FIGURE 8.1 Displaying node types, names and values using the DOM

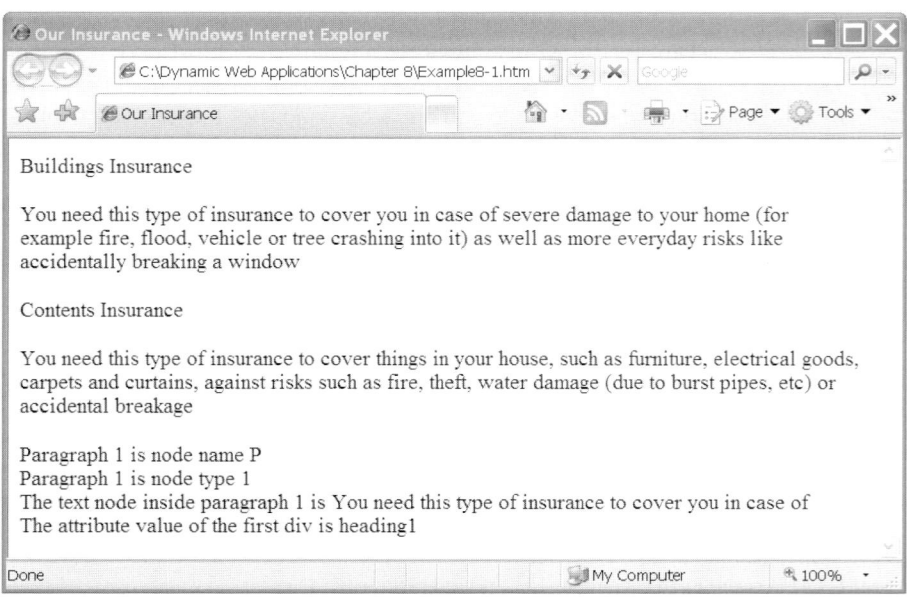

Changing values in the DOM

As well as reading node properties, JavaScript and the DOM can be used to change the content of parts of a document. In the next example, we are going to use a text field to display the time by setting its value inside a script. The text field is given a unique id of 'clock' so that we can access it easily using the 'getElementById' method. It is also set to be read only (using the 'read-only' attribute), since it is only intended for display purposes and not for user input:

```
<input type="text" size="6" id="clock" readonly="readonly"/>
```

The following JavaScript function ('showClock') uses a newly created Date object to show the time that the page was loaded. It uses 'getElementById' to locate the text field within the document, using its 'id' attribute. It then sets the 'value' property of the text field (this is from the HTML part of the DOM) to a string comprising the hours and minutes from the Date object.

```
<!-- showclock.js -->
function showClock()
{
  var date=new Date();
  document.getElementById("clock").value =
    date.getHours() + ":" + date.getMinutes();
}
```

The following XHTML page invokes the 'showClock' function using a script in the body:

```
<?xml version="1.0"?>
<!DOCTYPE html PUBLIC "-//W3C//DTD XHTML 1.1//EN"
   "http://www.w3.org/TR/xhtml11/DTD/xhtml11.dtd">
<html xmlns="http://www.w3.org/1999/xhtml" xml:lang="en">
  <head>
    <meta http-equiv="Content-Script-Type" content="text/javascript"/>
    <title>JavaScript clock</title>
    <script type="text/javascript" src="showclock.js">
    </script>
  </head>
  <body>
    <!-- File: example8-2.htm -->
    <div>
      <input type="text" size="6" id="clock" readonly="readonly"/>
    </div>
    <script type="text/javascript">
      showClock();
    </script>
  </body>
</html>
```

Figure 8.2 shows the time displayed in a text field in a browser.

8.2 JavaScript events

So far, all our JavaScript code has been run as part of the XHTML page being loaded, triggered by script elements in the document body. However we do not always want

FIGURE 8.2 The time the page was loaded displayed in a text field

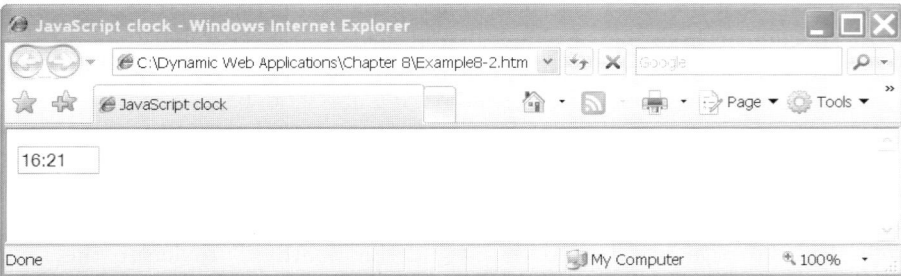

JavaScript, particularly functions, to be run only when the document loads. To give us more control over the running of our scripts, and make our browser-based applications more interactive, we can use various types of event to trigger the running of JavaScript code. These events include the document being loaded in the browser (the 'onload' event), the mouse moving over a component of the page ('onmouseover') or a button being pressed ('onclick'). Event handlers enable JavaScript objects and functions to respond to these events.

The 'onload' event

In our next example, instead of adding a script element to the body of the document, we will invoke the 'showClock' function from the 'onload' event, which is triggered when the document body is loaded.

```
<body onload="showClock()">
```

This approach means that we can have a JavaScript function run as soon as the document is loaded without using a script element in the document body.

 NOTE Note that 'onload' here is all in lower case. You will see examples from other sources of this event referred to as 'onLoad'. However, because the event appears as an attribute of the body tag, using any upper case letters will mean your pages are not valid XHTML.

This script shows an XHTML page that invokes the 'showClock' function using the 'onload' event:

```
<?xml version="1.0"?>
<!DOCTYPE html PUBLIC "-//W3C//DTD XHTML 1.1//EN"
  "http://www.w3.org/TR/xhtml11/DTD/xhtml11.dtd">
<html xmlns="http://www.w3.org/1999/xhtml" xml:lang="en">
  <head>
    <meta http-equiv="Content-Script-Type" content="text/javascript"/>
    <title>JavaScript clock</title>
    <script type="text/javascript" src="showclock.js">
    </script>
  </head>
```

```
<body onload="showClock()">
   <! -- File: example8-3.htm -- >
   <div>
   <input type="text" size="6" id="clock" readonly="readonly"/>
   </div>
</body>
</html>
```

Timer events

As we saw in the previous example, using the 'onload' event has the same effect as triggering a JavaScript function from a script in the document body. In the case of our clock, this is not really very helpful, since the time will soon (in no more than a minute) be wrong. We can, however, solve this problem using a JavaScript timer event. The 'setTimeOut' method can be used to set a timer that will call a function after a given interval, specified in milliseconds. In this modified version of the original 'showClock' function (called 'showTimer'), we add a 'setTimeOut' event to recursively call the 'showTimer' function approximately every 1000 milliseconds (every second). To see this working more easily, the seconds, as well as the minutes and hours, are written to the text field.

```
// File: showtimer.js
function showTimer()
{
   var date=new Date();
   document.getElementById("clock").value=date.getHours() + ":" +
     date.getMinutes() + ":" + date.getSeconds();
   setTimeout("showTimer()", 1000);
}
```

The page to call this function only needs to be modified in two places, first to call the new function in the header, and second to call the new function with the 'onload' event. Therefore the only changes are to the name of the '.js' file being used and the name of the function being called:

```
<?xml version = "1.0"?>
<!DOCTYPE html PUBLIC "-//W3C//DTD XHTML 1.1//EN"
   "http://www.w3.org/TR/xhtml11/DTD/xhtml11.dtd">
<html xmlns="http://www.w3.org/1999/xhtml" xml:lang="en">
   <head>
      <meta http-equiv="Content-Script-Type" content="text/javascript"/>
      <title>JavaScript clock</title>
      <script type="text/javascript"src="showtimer.js">
      </script>
   </head>
   <body onload="showTimer()">
      <!-- File: example8-4.htm -->
      <div>
         <input type="text" size="6" id="clock" readonly="readonly"/>
      </div>
   </body>
</html>
```

FIGURE 8.3 The text field showing the time in hours, minutes and seconds

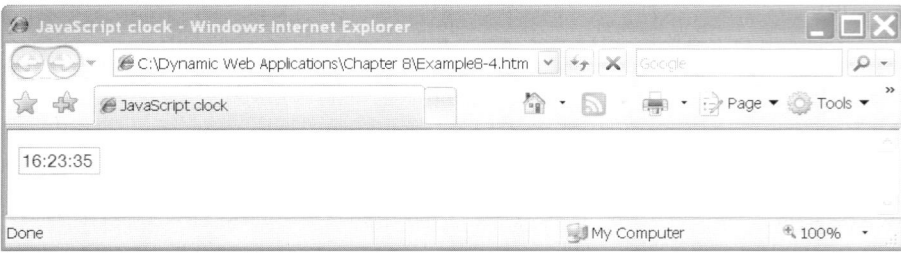

Figure 8.3 shows the modified text field, with the function showing the time in hours, minutes and seconds.

innerHTML and the DOM

In the previous examples, we used a text field to display the current time. An alternative approach to displaying content in a specific part of the browser is to write to a node of the document. One way of doing this is to use the interfaces of the DOM, but this can be quite complex and different browsers can react in different ways to the same scripts. Another way is to use the 'innerHTML' property of HTML elements. This enables us to access text nodes directly and update their contents.

The 'innerHTML' property is not part of the formal HTML DOM specification, and was introduced by Microsoft in Internet Explorer 4 in 1997. However due to its popularity it has been incorporated into other browsers, despite not being included in any public standard, and is therefore quite reliable in terms of cross-browser support. There has been much debate about whether using 'innerHTML' is wise or not. However, it is simple to use and has been used in many Ajax implementations. One of the objections to the use of 'innerHTML' is that it can be used to include structural elements (i.e. mark-up) inside the processes of client-side scripts, which is a poor separation of concerns. It is therefore preferable to restrict the use of 'innerHTML' to the manipulation of content rather than using it to dynamically generate mark-up.

In the next example, we modify the 'showTimer' function to use the 'innerHTML' property. The changes are relatively simple. First, we replace the text input field with a suitable document node, in this case a simple 'div' element that contains no text.

```
<div id="clock"></div>
```

Then all we have to do in the JavaScript function is modify the 'div' element, accessed using the 'getElementById' method, by setting the value of its 'innerHTML' property:

```
// File: showinnertimer.js
function showTimer()
{
  var date=new Date();
  document.getElementById("clock").innerHTML=date.getHours() + ":" +
  date.getMinutes() + ":" + date.getSeconds();
```

```
        setTimeout("showTimer()", 1000);
    }
```

Otherwise everything looks, and works, pretty much the same as before, except that the time appears in the browser simply as text, and not in a text field component. Here is the full XHTML page, with the 'div' element used by the function.

```
<?xml version="1.0"?>
<!DOCTYPE html PUBLIC "-//W3C//DTD XHTML 1.1//EN"
    "http://www.w3.org/TR/xhtml11/DTD/xhtml11.dtd">
<html xmlns="http://www.w3.org/1999/xhtml" xml:lang="en">
    <head>
        <meta http-equiv="Content-Script-Type" content="text/javascript"/>
        <title>JavaScript clock</title>
        <script type="text/javascript" src="showinnertimer.js">
        </script>
        </head>
        <body onload="showTimer()">
            <!-- File: example8-5.htm -->
            <div id="clock"></div>
    </body>
</html>
```

Figure 8.4 shows the output in the browser. The time is no longer in a text field but simply a text node of the document.

Responding to button events

The events we have used so far, the 'onload' event and timer events, are not related to user activity. However, if we want to make web pages more dynamic we need to be able to respond to the user's actions in the page. One way of doing this is to trigger JavaScript functions with user-instigated events such as buttons being pressed. HTML button components can be linked to JavaScript functions by using their 'onclick' event. In our next example, we use button events to call the window object's 'resizeTo' method, which sets the browser window to a specified width and height. The values for the width and height appear in parentheses after the method name, separated by a comma. This example would set the window size to 400 pixels wide and 200 pixels high:

```
window.resizeTo(400,200);
```

FIGURE 8.4   The current time displayed in a browser using the 'innerHTML' property

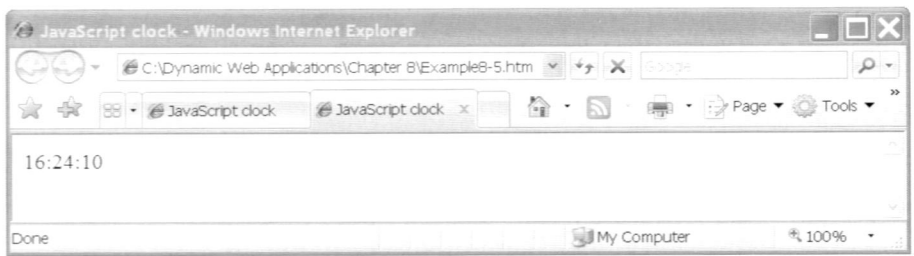

Our next script example shows button events being used to resize the window. It also shows how a JavaScript function can be called from more than one place in a script. The function we use is called 'resizeWindow', takes two parameters for the width and the height, and sets the size of the window accordingly:

```
// File: resize.js
function resizeWindow(width, height)
{
   window.resizeTo(width,height);
}
```

In the body of the document, there are two buttons, both of which use the 'onclick' event to call the 'resizeWindow' function. The first button (labelled 'shrink window') sets the window to be 400 by 300 pixels. The second uses two properties of the screen ('availWidth' and 'availHeight') to set the window size to the maximum available. The 'screen' object is a property of the window object.

```
<?xml version="1.0"?>
<!DOCTYPE html PUBLIC "-//W3C//DTD XHTML 1.1//EN"
   "http://www.w3.org/TR/xhtml11/DTD/xhtml11.dtd">
   <html xmlns="http://www.w3.org/1999/xhtml" xml:lang="en">
   <head>
      <meta http-equiv="Content-Script-Type" content="text/javascript"/>
      <title>JavaScript window resize</title>
      <script type="text/javascript" src="resize.js">
      </script>
   </head>
   <body>
      <!-- File: example8-6.htm -->
      <div>
      <input type="button" onclick="resizeWindow(400,300)"
        value="shrink window"/>
      <input type="button"
         onclick="resizeWindow(window.screen.availWidth,
         window.screen.availHeight)" value="restore window"/>
      </div>
   </body>
</html>
```

Figure 8.5 shows the window in Mozilla Firefox 2 before the 'shrink window' button has been pressed.

 NOTE Different browsers may give you slightly different behaviors using this function. For example, Opera 9 will only resize the window if it is detached, not if it is part of a tabbed window.

FIGURE 8.5 The window before resizing using a button 'onclick' event

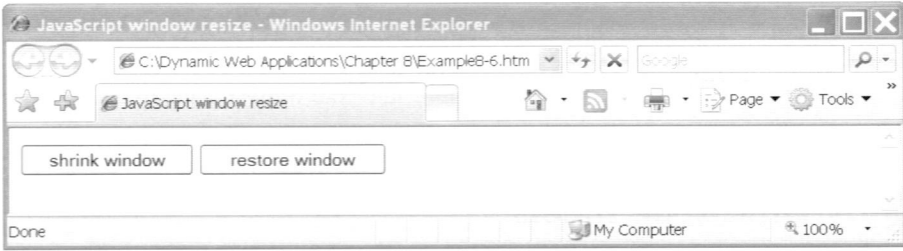

JavaScript URLs

In the previous example we saw how button events can be used to invoke JavaScript functions. Another approach to triggering JavaScript code from user actions is to use JavaScript URLs, which are preceded by a 'javascript:' prefix. This special protocol type can be used anywhere that a regular URL can be used, for example in hypertext anchors or form actions. We can follow this protocol with any JavaScript code, including function calls. This approach works well if we want to use an anchor to trigger a script or function. For example, this fragment of code shows an HTML anchor element where the URL is a JavaScript function called 'openWindow' that takes the name of an HTML page as a parameter:

```
<a href="javascript:openWindow('about.htm')">open window</a>
```

When the anchor is clicked in the browser, the 'openWindow' function is invoked. Here is the 'openWindow' function implementation, which uses the 'open' method of the window object.

```
// File: openwindow.js
function openWindow(url)
{
    window.open(url);
}
```

Here is an XHTML page that includes the JavaScript URL, which invokes the function when the user clicks on the hyperlink:

```
<?xml version="1.0"?>
<!DOCTYPE html PUBLIC "-//W3C//DTD XHTML 1.1//EN"
    "http://www.w3.org/TR/xhtml11/DTD/xhtml11.dtd">
    <html xmlns="http://www.w3.org/1999/xhtml" xml:lang="en">
        <head>
            <meta http-equiv="Content-Script-Type" content="text/javascript"/>
            <title>JavaScript open window</title>
            <script type="text/javascript" src="openwindow.js">
            </script>
        </head>
        <body>
            <!-- File: example8-7.htm -->
            <div>
            <a href="javascript:openWindow('about.htm')">open window</a>
```

```
        </div>
      </body>
   </html>
```

The effect of clicking the hyperlink in the page varies from browser to browser. In some cases, a new window is created and in others a new tab appears. Figure 8.6 shows how Internet Explorer 7 responds to the function, opening a new window.

8.3 Dynamic style sheets

As well as interacting with the DOM, another important feature of DHTML is the use of style sheets to dynamically change the presentation of the document. A commonly used example of this technique is to apply JavaScript and style sheets to show or hide parts of a page. This technique can be used, for example, to add expandable menus to web pages. To interact with styles inside our scripts, we can use the 'style' property of the elements in the DOM to dynamically apply styles to parts of the document. The CSS style property that we can use to show or hide parts of the page is 'display', which can have the value 'block' to make the content visible, or 'none' to make it invisible. The following function uses an 'if' statement to switch the display style of an element between 'none' and 'block'. In this example, 'element' is a variable that references an element node from the current document, identified by its 'id' attribute.

```
// File: changedisplay.js
function changeDisplay(id)
{
```

FIGURE 8.6   The effect of the 'openWindow' function in Internet Explorer 7, triggered by a JavaScript URL

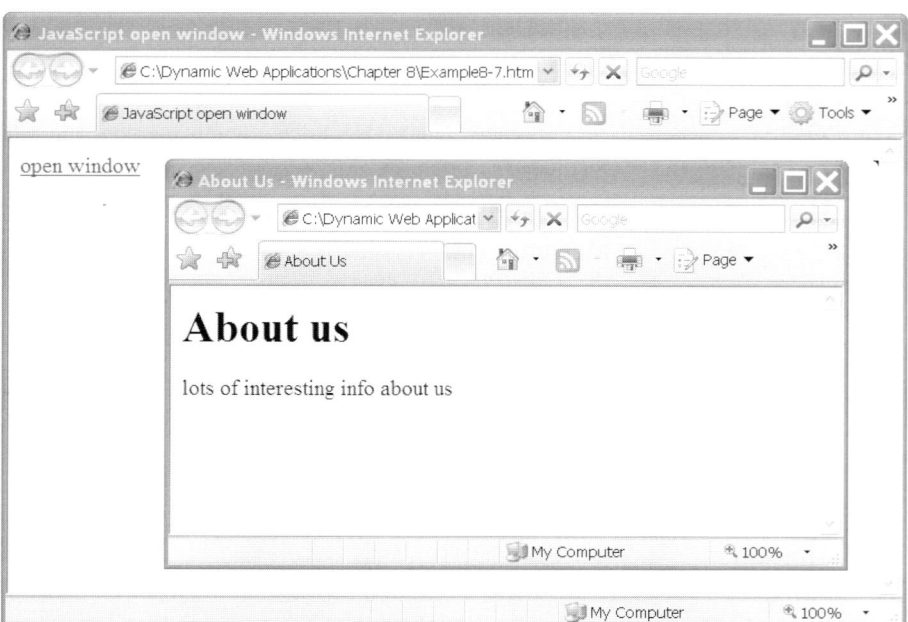

```
  var element=document.getElementById(id);
  if(element.style.display=='none')
  {
    element.style.display='block';
  }
  else
  {
    element.style.display = 'none';
  }
}
```

So far in this chapter we have looked at how we can use JavaScript to navigate to nodes in the DOM and to access the properties of these nodes, including the 'style' property. We have also looked at the use of events to trigger JavaScript functions. In the next example, we draw all of these techniques together into a DHTML page that shows and hides parts of a page when a JavaScript URL is clicked. The page consists of two sections with titles 'JavaScript' and 'DHTML (Dynamic HTML)' that are in anchors that use JavaScript URLs. When either of these titles is clicked, the detail text (enclosed in 'div' tags with unique ids) switches between shown and hidden. The ids of the 'div' elements are passed to the 'changeDisplay' function in order to switch their state.

We need to be able to invoke this function in two ways. First, we need to invoke it when the page is loaded, to set the initial state of the page, using the 'onload' event. To call more than one function from the 'onload' event or, as in this case, to call the same function more than once, the function calls can be put into a comma-separated list, like this:

```
<body onload="changeDisplay('jsdetail'), changeDisplay('dhtmldetail')">
```

Since the display state of the two 'div' elements has not been set initially, the first time it is called for a particular element, the function executes the 'else' block and sets the display state to 'none'. From that point onwards, the JavaScript URLs invoke the function when either one of them is clicked and switches the display state. Here is one example of these two URLs:

```
<a href="javascript:changeDisplay('jsdetail')">JavaScript</a>
```

Note how it passes the id of one of the 'div' elements to the function. Here is the complete XHTML page:

```
<?xml version="1.0"?>
<!DOCTYPE html PUBLIC "-//W3C//DTD XHTML 1.1//EN"
  "http://www.w3.org/TR/xhtml11/DTD/xhtml11.dtd">
<html xmlns="http://www.w3.org/1999/xhtml" xml:lang="en">
  <head>
    <meta http-equiv="Content-Script-Type" content="text/javascript"/>
    <title>DHTML show and hide</title>
    <script type="text/javascript" src="changedisplay.js">
    </script>
  </head>
  <body onload="changeDisplay('jsdetail'), changeDisplay('dhtmldetail')">
      <!-- File: example8-8.htm -->
      <div>
        <a href="javascript:changeDisplay('jsdetail')">JavaScript</a>
      </div>
      <div id="jsdetail">
```

JavaScript is a scripting language that can be run inside the browser to enable client-side processes.

```
        </div>
        <div>
            <a href="javascript:changeDisplay('dhtmldetail')">
            DHTML (Dynamic HTML)</a>
        </div>
        <div id="dhtmldetail">
DHTML is a label given to techniques that use JavaScript, CSS and the DOM to make
web pages more dynamic and interactive.
        </div>
    </body>
</html>
```

Figure 8.7 shows the page once it has been initially loaded into the browser, with both div element styles in the 'none' display state.

Figure 8.8 shows how the page looks if both the 'div' element styles are in the 'block' state (i.e. visible).

FIGURE 8.7 The 'div' elements hidden by setting the display property of the style to 'none'

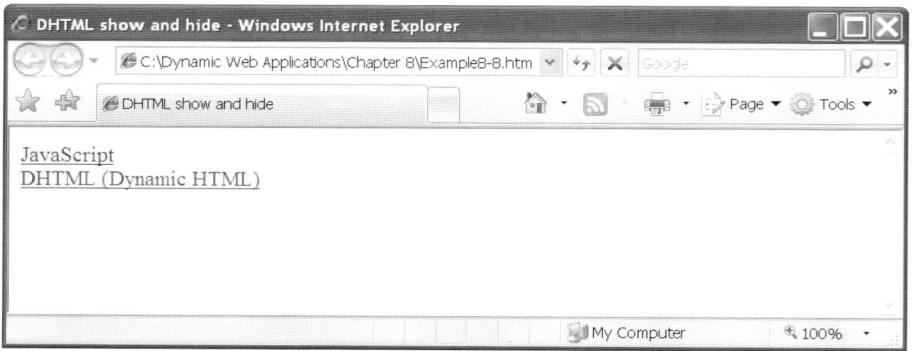

FIGURE 8.8 The 'div' elements made visible by setting the display property of the style to 'block'

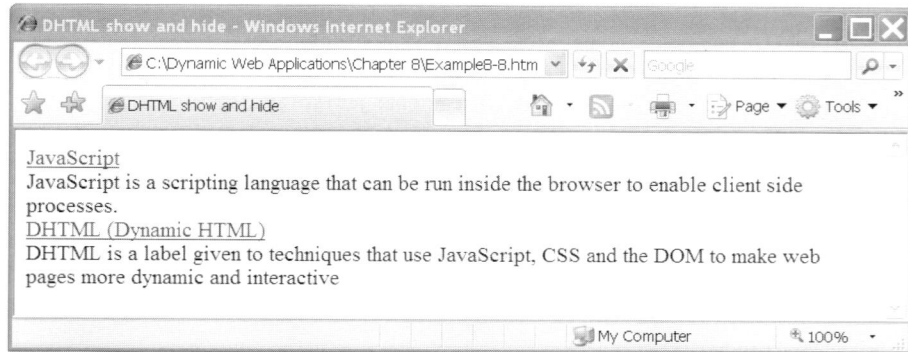

8.4 Client-side form validation

One of the most useful roles that JavaScript can perform in a web application is client-side validation of the data that users enter into web page forms. We can only provide *surface validation* on the client. For example, we can check that a credit card number matches the correct format for credit card numbers, or check that a particular type of card, such as a Visa card, starts with the correct numbers for that type, but we could not actually check the validity of the credit card itself in the browser. That would have to be done by a server-side process. Surface validation includes checking for empty fields, checking that selections have been made (for example from radio buttons or drop-down lists) rather than leaving empty defaults, checking that numeric, date, email or credit card fields contain the right types of characters, and so on.

Functions that process forms

With a normal HTML form, pressing the 'submit' button posts the HTTP request to the URI defined by the form element's 'action' attribute. For example, this simple form contains input fields for a user ID and a password and submits to a server-side application called 'customerLogin':

```
<form action="customerLogin" method="post">
  <table>
    <tr>
      <td><label for="loginid">Login Name:</label></td>
      <td><input type="text" id="loginid"/></td>
    </tr>
    <tr>
      <td><label for="pword">Password:</label></td>
      <td><input type="password" id="pword"/></td>
    </tr>
    <tr>
      <td></td>
      <td><input type="submit" value="Login"/>
      <input type="reset" value="Clear form"/></td>
    </tr>
  </table>
</form>
```

Once the form is submitted to the server, it is too late to validate any of the form data in the browser. Therefore, JavaScript provides us with a special 'onsubmit' event that lets us invoke a function when the button is pressed, rather than submitting directly to the server. We can use the function to validate the form and return either 'true' or 'false' depending on whether the contents of the form are valid or not. If it returns 'true', then the form data is submitted to the server-side application. If it returns 'false', then the submission is cancelled and we can give the user the opportunity to correct the data they have entered.

There are two ways that the JavaScript function can access the components of the form in order to check their validity:

- The function can use the DOM to access the form's components via the document object.
- The form can be passed as a parameter to the function.

As an example of the first approach, this form tag includes the 'onsubmit' event handler, invoking a JavaScript method called 'validate' that takes no parameters:

```
<form action="customerLogin" method="post" onsubmit="return validate()">
```

If a reference to the form is not passed to the function, the 'getElementById' method of the DOM can be used to locate the input fields of the form, as long as they have 'id' attributes. In this example, the function accesses the 'loginid' text field using the DOM, checking if it is an empty field (using double speech marks with nothing in between represents an empty string, which would be the contents of an empty text input field).

```
function validate()
{
   if(document.getElementById("loginid").value=="")
   . . .
```

In contrast, this version of the form element takes the second approach, passing the form to the 'validate' method as a parameter. The form is referred to using the reserved word 'this', (i.e. pass *this* form to the function):

```
<form action="customerLogin" method="post" onsubmit="return validate(this)">
```

If a reference to the form is passed as a parameter to the function, the form controls can be accessed as sub-elements of the parameter object. In this example, we navigate to the same text field ('loginid') but via the form, rather than the document object.

```
function validate(loginForm)
{
   if(loginForm.loginid.value=="")
   . . .
```

Which one of these approaches you use is up to you, but passing the form to the function seems to be more commonly used in validation routines.

Pop-up dialogs

So far in this section we have looked at some JavaScript code that checks the state of the components in a form, but what do we do if we want to indicate to the user that there is a problem? We could use the technique that we have already introduced to write to the page using the DOM, but a more common approach to indicating problems occurring in an application is to display a pop-up dialog box. JavaScript provides three types of pop-up dialog, the *alert*, *confirm* and *prompt* dialogs. These are modal dialogs, which means that you cannot do anything else in the browser until you have closed them. They are invoked by using the 'alert', 'confirm' and 'prompt' methods of the window object.

An alert is used simply to show a message to the user. The only button on an alert is an 'OK' button, which makes the dialog disappear when it is clicked. Creating an alert is very simple; we just pass the text we want to display as a parameter (in parentheses) to the alert function:

```
alert("message");
```

The confirm dialog is similar to the alert in that it will contain some type of message. However it has two buttons, 'OK' and 'Cancel'. If the user clicks 'OK', the box returns true. If the user clicks 'Cancel', the box returns false.

```
var boo Confirm=confirm("message");
```

Unlike the other two dialogs, the prompt dialog asks the user to enter a value. As well as a text entry field, it contains 'OK' and 'Cancel' buttons. If the user clicks 'OK' the box returns the input value, but if the user clicks 'Cancel' the box returns *null*. A null value in JavaScript means that the variable has no value.

```
var str ReturnValue=prompt("prompt text", "default value");
```

Here is a simple JavaScript function that creates all three of these dialog types in turn. When the function is called, the dialogs appear one after the other.

```
// File: showdialogs.js
function showDialogs()
{
   alert("This is an alert");
   confirm("This message wants confirmation");
   prompt("Please enter something in the text area", "I'm a default");
}
```

Here is an XHTML page that calls this function when it loads:

```
<?xml version="1.0"?>
<!DOCTYPE html PUBLIC "-//W3C//DTD XHTML 1.1//EN"
   "http://www.w3.org/TR/xhtml11/DTD/xhtml11.dtd">
<html xmlns="http://www.w3.org/1999/xhtml" xml:lang="en">
   <head>
      <meta http-equiv="Content-Script-Type" content="text/javascript"/>
      <title>JavaScript Dialogs</title>
      <script type="text/javascript" src="showdialogs.js">
      </script>
   </head>
   <body onload="showDialogs()">
      <!-- File: example8-9.htm -->
   </body>
</html>
```

Figure 8.9 shows how the three dialogs look when displayed by the Mozilla Firefox 2 browser. They look a little different in other browsers but the content and buttons are very much the same.

Using dialogs in validation routines

All three of these dialog types could be used in validation routines. However, perhaps the simplest approach is to use an alert to inform the user if there errors in the form data.

Here is a complete 'validate' function, using a form parameter and an alert. The function checks if either the username or password text fields in the login form are empty. In each

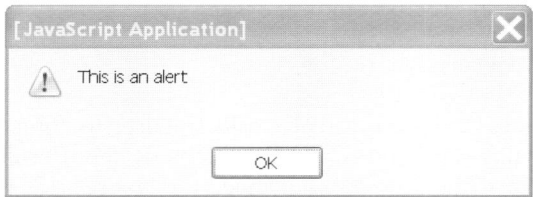

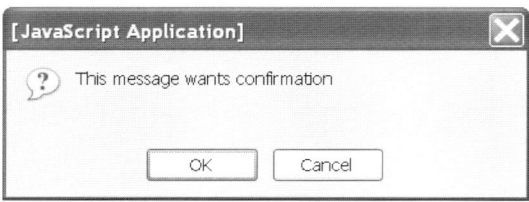

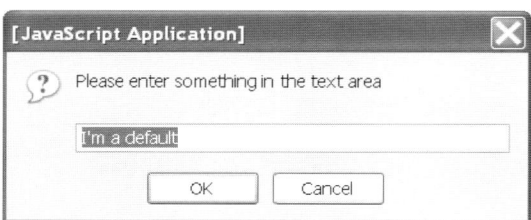

case, the value of the text field is compared to an empty string (""). If the field is empty, some error text is added to the 'strErrorMessage' variable and the value of the 'booValid' variable is set to 'false'. After both fields have been checked, if the 'booValid' variable is 'false' then an alert is displayed showing the error messages, and the form is not submitted, as the method itself returns 'false'.

```
// File: validateform.js
function validate(loginForm)
{
   var booValid=true;
   var strErrorMessage="";
   if(loginForm.loginid.value=="")
   {
      strErrorMessage +="user name field cannot be empty\n";
      booValid=false;
   }
   if(loginForm.pword.value=="")
```

```
    {
       strErrorMessage +="password field cannot be empty";
       booValid=false;
    }
    if(!booValid)
    {
       alert(strErrorMessage);
    }
    return booValid;
}
```

Here is an XHTML page that calls the 'validate' function using the 'onsubmit' event of the form:

```
<?xml version="1.0"?>
<!DOCTYPE html PUBLIC "-//W3C//DTD XHTML 1.1//EN"
   "http://www.w3.org/TR/xhtml11/DTD/xhtml11.dtd">
<html xmlns="http://www.w3.org/1999/xhtml" xml:lang="en">
  <head>
     <title>Customer Login</title>
     <script type="text/javascript" src="validateform.js">
     </script>
  </head>
  <body>
  <!-- File: example8-10.htm -->
     <form action="customerLogin" method="post"
       onsubmit="return validate(this)">
       <table>
         <tr>
         <td><label for="loginid">Login Name:</label></td>
         <td><input type="text" id="loginid"></td>
         </tr>
         <tr>
           <td><label for="pword">Password:</label></td>
           <td><input type="password" id="pword"></td>
         </tr>
         <tr>
           <td></td>
           <td><input type="submit" value="Login">
             <input type="reset" value="Clear form">
           </td>
         </tr>
       </table>
     </form>
  </body>
</html>
```

8

Figure 8.10 shows both the form and the alert that appears if both of the fields are empty. If only one field is empty, then only one message appears in the alert. If both fields have some content then the form data is submitted to the server.

FIGURE 8.10 The form and the alert that appears if both fields are left empty, running in Internet Explorer 7

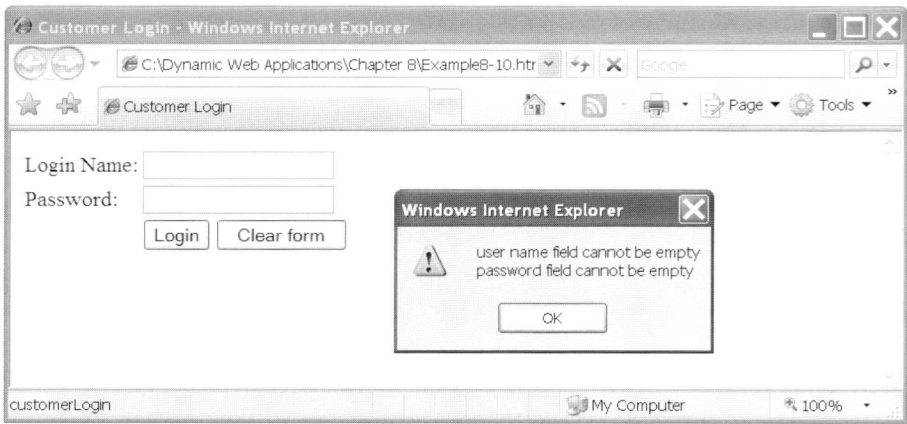

Validating other types of form component

In addition to checking if text fields contain characters, a common process for mandatory fields, we can do other types of check. For example we can see if the user has made a selection from a select list, or see if a radio button or check box has been checked.

It is useful to add an empty option to a 'select' component to confirm that the user has made a choice. If they accept the default (i.e. nothing selected) then we can flag that as an error using the JavaScript validation function. In this select, for example, the first option is empty. This means we can ensure that the user specifically chooses either 'Administrator' or 'User' from the list by validating that the zero-indexed selection (the empty one) has not been selected.

```
<select id="loginoptions" size="1">
  <option></option>
  <option>Administrator</option>
  <option>User</option>
</select>
```

In our JavaScript validation function, we can check the index of the selected option using the 'selectedIndex' property. If the index is zero then we can do some error notification.

```
if(loginForm.loginoptions.selectedIndex == 0 )
{
   strErrorMessage += "you must select your Login role\n";
   booValid=false;
}
```

In this example, we have radio buttons in the form.

```
<input type="radio" name="action" value="view"/> View settings
<input type="radio" name="action" value="update"/> Update settings
```

By not providing a default checked button, we can force the user to select one of these buttons specifically, and again check that they have done so using JavaScript validation. In this part of the 'validate' function, we see if the 'checked' property of both of the radio buttons is false. If neither button is checked, we flag an error.

```
if( (!loginForm.action[0].checked) && (!loginForm.action[1].checked) )
{
    strErrorMessage +="You must select View or Update settings\n";
    booValid=false;
}
```

Another possible form of validation is to check that different choices made within the same form are consistent with one another, for example in our login form it may be that only administrators are able to update the settings. This means that anyone attempting to log on as a user, but also selecting the 'change settings' radio button would be making an invalid choice. In this part of the 'validate' method, we combine these conditions together.

```
if( (loginForm.action[1].checked) &&
(loginForm.loginoptions.selectedIndex !=1) )
{
    strErrorMessage +=
        "You cannot update settings unless you are an administrator\n";
    booValid=false;
}
```

Here is the complete 'validate' function (in a different file to separate it from the previous version).

```
// File: validateloginform.js
function validate(loginForm)
{
    var booValid = true;
    var strErrorMessage = "";
    if(loginForm.loginid.value == "")
    {
        strErrorMessage += "user name field cannot be empty\n";
        booValid=false;
    }
    if(loginForm.pword.value == "")
    {
        strErrorMessage += "password field cannot be empty\n";
        booValid=false;
    }
    if(loginForm.loginoptions.selectedIndex == 0 )
    {
        strErrorMessage += "you must select your Login role\n";
        booValid=false;
```

8

```
      }
      if( (!loginForm.action[0].checked) && (!loginForm.action[1].checked) )
      {
         strErrorMessage += "You must select View or Update settings\n";
         booValid=false;
      }
      if( (loginForm.action[1].checked) &&
      (loginForm.loginoptions.selectedIndex != 1) )
      {
         strErrorMessage += "You cannot update settings unless you are
         an administrator\n";
         booValid=false;
      }
      if(!booValid)
      {
         alert(strErrorMessage);
      }
      return booValid;
   }
```

The following XHTML page contains the various form components that are validated by the JavaScript 'validate' function.

```
<?xml version="1.0"?>
<!DOCTYPE html PUBLIC "-//W3C//DTD XHTML 1.1//EN"
   "http://www.w3.org/TR/xhtml11/DTD/xhtml11.dtd">
<html xmlns="http://www.w3.org/1999/xhtml" xml:lang="en">
   <head>
      <title>Customer Login</title>
      <script type="text/javascript" src="validateloginform.js">
      </script>
   </head>
   <body>
<!-- File: example8-11.htm -->
      <form action="customerlogin" method="post"
      onsubmit="return validate(this)">
         <table>
            <tr>
               <td><label for="loginid">Login Name:</label></td>
               <td><input type="text" id="loginid"/></td>
            </tr>
            <tr>
               <td><label for="pword">Password:</label></td>
               <td><input type="password" id="pword"/></td>
            </tr>
            <tr>
               <td><label for="loginoptions">Select Login role:</label></td>
               <td><select id="loginoptions" size="1">
                     <option></option>
                     <option>Administrator</option>
```

```
            <option>User</option>
          </select>
        </td>
      </tr>
      <tr>
        <td>Select Action:</td>
        <td>
          <input type="radio" name="action" value="view"/> View settings
          <input type="radio" name="action" value="update"/> Update
            settings
        </td>
      </tr>
      <tr>
        <td></td>
        <td><input type = "submit" value = "Login"/>
            <input type = "reset" value = "Clear form"/>
        </td>
      </tr>
    </table>
  </form>
  </body>
</html>
```

Figure 8.11 shows what the alert looks like if a user name and password has been entered but the user has attempted to log in as a user (rather than an administrator) and selected 'update' settings.

8.5 The emergence of Ajax

One of the big talking points around web application development in 2005 was the emergence of Ajax as a way of bringing some aspects of the desktop application experience into browser-based applications. Ajax is not a particularly new concept, following on as it does from a longer tradition of client-side processing that includes JavaScript, Java applets and DHTML. However the significant difference between Ajax and previous approaches is the concept of the 'one-page web application', whereby page content is updated asynchronously from the server without the whole page being rebuilt. An early example of this approach was Google Suggest, which was able to dynamically populate a search text box with suggestions for search terms as characters were typed into it, providing, of course, that the browser was able to support it. The most important component of an Ajax application is the 'XMLHttpRequest' component, which was first introduced by Microsoft into Outlook Web Access 2000 and later into Internet Explorer 5.0. Other browsers have since followed with their own implementations of the 'XMLHttpRequest'. This component enables browser-hosted applications to send requests to the server and receive responses without replacing or fully refreshing the current web page. Instead, the response that is returned from the server, which may be an XML document or a simple stream of characters, can be handled by a client-side script and used to update parts of the page using the DOM. Figure 8.12 shows the general architecture of Ajax-based systems. The key to this architecture is that the Ajax engine mediates between the user interface and the server, processing on the client where possible (using DHTML) and, where necessary, sending asynchronous HTTP requests and receiving XML data (or indeed data in any other suitable format) that it renders in the browser via the DOM.

Equally importantly, this processing can take place asynchronously. This means that the user does not have to wait for the server to respond in order to continue interacting with the application. Instead, the application is able to continue serving the user while at the same time handling the server response as and when it arrives. Figure 8.13 shows the general idea. User activity in the browser continues even while the Ajax engine is submitting XMLHttpRequests to the server and waiting for responses. The Ajax engine is responsible for handling events associated with getting back the server response but the user does not have to wait for it. Ajax applications do not have to be asynchronous, however. In some cases it might be appropriate to wait for the server's response before continuing with the current process.

FIGURE 8.12   Ajax architecture, adapted from (Garrett 2005)

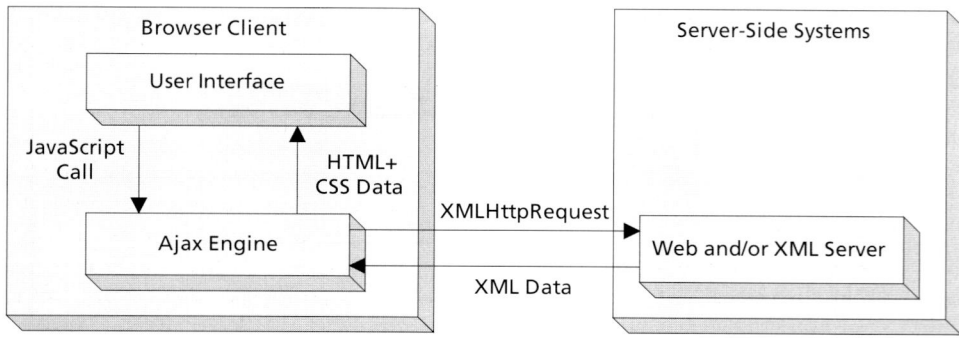

Using asynchronous communication in Ajax, adapted from (Garrett 2005)

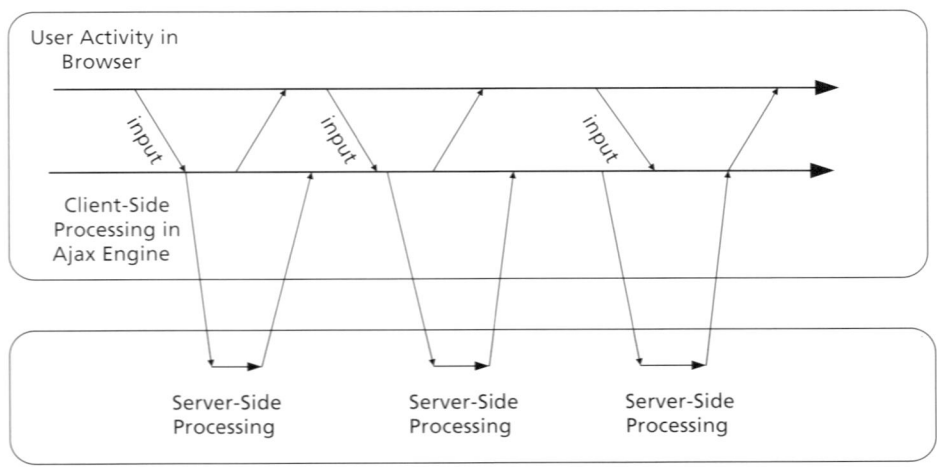

Ajax itself is not a technology but a label, applied by Garrett (2005), to a way of building web applications that uses the 'XMLHttpRequest' object within client-side scripts to seamlessly update web pages. Garrett summarized Ajax as a combination of:

- Standards-based presentation using XHTML and CSS
- Dynamic display and interaction using the document object model
- Data interchange and manipulation using XML and eXtensible Stylesheet Language Transformations (XSLT)
- Asynchronous data retrieval using the 'XMLHttpRequest'
- JavaScript binding everything together

Of course the technologies listed by Garrett are not the only way to provide one-page applications on the web; alternative technologies, such as Flash, can be used to similar effect.

Writing Ajax code with JavaScript

There are basically two approaches to writing an Ajax application. One is to build your own Ajax code using standard JavaScript. The other is to use some kind of API and/or development tool that encapsulates the underlying Ajax code, for example, the Google Ajax API (though this is just one example of many). In this chapter, we focus on using standard JavaScript to develop relatively simple Ajax applications. However, for more complex systems it may be more appropriate to look at using Ajax development tools.

If you are writing Ajax applications without using a tool or framework, one of the most important things to build is a JavaScript function that is able to acquire the appropriate type of 'XMLHttpRequest' object, depending on which browser the script is running in. The main choice to be made is between older Microsoft browsers and newer Microsoft, or non-Microsoft, browsers. This is because Microsoft has, over time, developed different implementations of the 'XMLHttpRequest' component. In earlier versions (used in

Internet Explorer 5 and 6), they used an ActiveX object to implement the 'XMLHttpRequest' as part of Microsoft XML Core Services (MSXML), and even within these Microsoft browser versions there are slightly different types of ActiveX objects. However, from Internet Explorer 7.0 onwards, the implementation is based on native scripting and works in a similar way to other browsers. Therefore in order to make sure we get the right type of 'XMLHttpRequest' object in our JavaScript, we need to write a function that tries to access these different implementations in turn until it finds a match. There are various ways of doing this, including the following simple example (Dutta 2006). It uses properties of the window object to identify which type of 'XMLHttpRequest' is available. For more recent versions of Internet Explorer and other browsers, there will be an 'XMLHttpRequest' property. If this is not present, then the browser may be an older version of Internet Explorer, in which case the window should have an 'ActiveXObject' property. Of course, if both of these tests return 'false' then the browser is not capable of supporting Ajax.

```
if(window.XMLHttpRequest)
{
   // If IE7, Mozilla, Safari, etc: Use native object
   var xmlHttp = new XMLHttpRequest();
}
else
{
   if(window.ActiveXObject)
   {
      // otherwise, use the ActiveX control for IE5.x and IE6
      var xmlHttp = new ActiveXObject("Microsoft.XMLHTTP");
   }
}
```

A slightly more detailed approach is described by (Zakas *et al.* 2006), which takes into account the several different versions of the ActiveX object that have been implemented. It also uses JavaScript exception handling as well as 'if' statements. Exception handling code uses the reserved words 'try' and 'catch'. Code that may throw an exception (i.e. an error condition) is put inside a block of code labelled with 'try', and code that can handle that exception, if it occurs, is put into a following 'catch' block. The code in the 'catch' block is only executed if an exception is thrown. Otherwise only the code in the 'try' block is executed. This is the basic structure of a 'try ... catch' block:

```
try
{
   // Attempt to execute some code here
}
catch(e)
{
   // If it throws an exception, handle it here
}
```

Here is an 'if' statement (as part of a function) that also includes a 'try ... catch' block. It attempts to create an 'XMLHttpRequest' object and return it to the caller of the function, but if this fails, an exception is thrown, which is handled by the catch block. In this case, we do not do anything other than allow the code to continue executing, because the next step is to look for the correct type of ActiveX object.

```
if(window.XMLHttpRequest)
{
   // If IE7, Mozilla, Safari, etc: Use native object
   try
   {
      xhrequest = new XMLHttpRequest();
      return xhrequest;
   }
   catch(exception)
   {
      // OK, just carry on looking
   }
}
```

There are five different versions of the ActiveX object that we may be able to identify in some versions of Internet Explorer. A useful way of checking for each of them is to put their various names into an array and then iterate through them using a 'for' loop until a match is found. The array needs to contain the names of the various objects starting with the most recent, because the more recent ActiveX components are likely to perform better than the older ones. Here is an array containing the relevant names of the various ActiveX objects:

```
var IEControls = ["MSXML2.XMLHttp.5.0", "MSXML2.XMLHttp.4.0", "MSXML2.XMLHttp.3.0",
"MSXML2.XMLHttp", "Microsoft.XMLHttp"];
```

Here is a complete function, 'getXMLHttpRequest', which uses the various techniques and methods that we have introduced:

```
function getXMLHttpRequest()
{
   var xhrequest = null;
   if(window.XMLHttpRequest)
   {
   // If IE7, Mozilla, Safari, etc: Use native object
   try
   {
      xhrequest = new XMLHttpRequest();
      return xhrequest;
   }
   catch(exception)
   {
      // OK, just carry on looking
   }
}
else if(window.ActiveXObject)
   {
   // ... otherwise, use the ActiveX control for IE5.x and IE6
      var IEControls=["MSXML2.XMLHttp.5.0", "MSXML2.XMLHttp.4.0",
         "MSXML2.XMLHttp.3.0", "MSXML2.XMLHttp", "Microsoft.XMLHttp"];
      for(var i=0; i < IEControls.length; i++)
```

```
        {
            try
            {
                xhrequest = new ActiveXObject(IEControls[i]);
                return xhrequest;
            }
            catch(exception)
            {
            // OK, just carry on looking
            }
        }
    }
    // if we got here we didn't find any matches
    throw new Error("Cannot create an XMLHttpRequest");
    }
}
```

Once we have an 'XMLHttpRequest' object, we can open a connection to a server URL with it, using the 'open' method. This takes at least three parameters (it can take more, if a username and password are required for the connection). The first is the HTTP method for the connection (usually 'GET' or 'POST'), the second is the URL of the server-side application that we want to connect to, and the third parameter is a Boolean value that specifies if we want to make an asynchronous (true) or a synchronous (false) connection. Since one of the basic concepts behind Ajax is that we make asynchronous connections, the third parameter would normally be set to 'true', unless there was a good reason for waiting for the response before continuing.

```
    xhrequest.open("GET", url, true);
```

The URL string comprises the name of the server-side program that will deal with the request. In many cases, where the request type is 'GET', it also includes request parameters from the current page.

Once the connection to the server has been made, we have to have some way of knowing when, and if, a successful response has been received from the server.

Perhaps the most important aspect therefore of the 'XMLHttpRequest' object is its 'onreadystatechange' event, which is triggered when the request changes state. We can respond to this state change by assigning the name of a function to the event, so that the function is called when there is a state change.

```
    xhrequest.onreadystatechange = nameoffunction;
```

It is important to note that the name of the function that is associated with the 'onreadystatechange' is *not* followed by parentheses in this line of code. Parentheses are only used if the function is anonymous, and declared in-line, in other words the function definition appears as part of the same statement, like this:

```
    xhrequest.onreadystatechange = function()
    {
      // body of in-line function here
    };
```

Note the use of the reserved word 'function', and the semicolon at the end of the closing brace. In our first example, we use a function that is declared separately, called 'processResponse', so the assignment of the function name looks like this:

```
xhrequest.onreadystatechange = processResponse;
```

There are five possible states that the request can be in:

0 = uninitialized
1 = loading
2 = loaded
3 = interactive
4 = complete

The 'onreadystatechange' event is triggered every time the state changes, which means that our function is called several times as it works though the various stages from 0 to 4. However we do not usually want to respond to these events until the state has reached 4 (complete), at which point we have successfully received a server response and can process it accordingly. The function associated with the 'onreadystatechange' event has to be written to check the state before it continues processing and handle any problems. Even if we got a response back, it may not be the one we were expecting, for example we may get an HTTP response code back that is something other than 200 (the 'OK' response). Therefore we also need to check that the response is OK before attempting to process it. Here is an outline of a function that checks the status of the 'XMLHttpRequest' and the HTTP status code.

```
function processResponse()
{
   if(xhrequest.readyState == 4 && xhrequest.status == 200)
   {
      // now we can do something with the response
   }
}
```

Once everything else is in place, we need to open a connection to the server using the 'open' method (as we have already described) and then send our request using the 'send' method, which may simply send the request or also send some data, perhaps as a string of data to be posted to the server (this may be necessary if we are not appending query parameters to the URL as a get request) or it may be an XML document. If we are not sending either of these data items then the parameter value can be set to null.

```
xhrequest.send(null);
```

Once the request has been sent to the server, and there is a function able to respond to the 'onreadystatechange' event, the next step is to be able to process the response. Depending on how the server-side implementation works, the data that comes back as a response could be either a simple string of data or an XML document. If the response is string data, then the appropriate property to use to handle it is 'responseText'. If the response is in the form of an XML document, then the appropriate property to use is 'responseXML'.

Tables 8.1 and 8.2 summarize the properties and methods of the 'XMLHttpRequest' object.

8

TABLE 8.1 'XMLHttpRequest' object properties

Property	Description
onreadystatechange	Event handler for an event that fires at every change in the readyState
readyState	The status of the request, which can be in the following states: 0 = uninitialized 1 = loading 2 = loaded 3 = interactive 4 = complete
responseText	Data returned from the server as a string
responseXML	Data returned from the server as an XML document
status	HTTP status code, for example 200 (OK), 404 (not found)
statusText	Message string describing the status code

TABLE 8.2 'XMLHttpRequest' object methods

Method	Description
abort()	Aborts the current request
getAllResponseHeaders()	Returns all headers (names and values) as a single string
getResponseHeader (*headerName*)	Returns the value of the specified header
open (*method, URL, asyncFlag, username, password*)	Opens a connection and retrieves a response from the specified URL. The method is usually either GET or POST; optionally, there can be a username and password for secure sites
send (*content*)	Sends the request to the server (can include data as a string or DOM object if it is a post request)
setRequestHeader(*name, value*)	Assigns the given value to the named header

Using Ajax and RSS

Later in this book, we see how to build Ajax applications where we connect from our JavaScript client to our own server-side applications. However, as a first example, we see how to create an Ajax application that connects to server-side data sources that are available from web sites in the public domain. There are many types of data on the web that we could potentially connect to using an Ajax application, but one of the simplest would be an RSS feed. RSS feeds were first introduced in 1999 and have become increasingly popular. During this time, increasing standardization has been applied to try to ensure interoperability. RSS is an acronym that has some confused roots, standing variously for

8

FIGURE 8.14 The standard RSS feed icon

Really Simple Syndication, Rich Site Summary or RDF Site Summary. However they all have much the same intent: to provide a way of aggregating frequently updated content into web applications so that content can be syndicated. Increasingly, the standard 'feed' icon is becoming used across web applications to indicate the availability of RSS content (Figure 8.14).

The format of an RSS feed is basically a simple XML document that has a root element called 'rss'. Inside this element is a single 'channel' element, which describes the content of the channel and contains a series of item elements. Here are some of the main elements in RSS version 2.0 documents.

```xml
<?xml version="1.0"?>
<rss version="2.0">
  <channel>
     <title>...</title>
     <link>...</link>
     <description>...</description>
     ...
     <item>
        <title>...</title>
        <link>...</link>
        <description>...</description>
        <pubDate>...</pubDate>
        <guid>...</guid>
     </item>
     <item>
     ...
     </item>
  </channel>
</rss>
```

Security issues with the 'XMLHttpRequest'

One of the security issues with the 'XMLHttpRequest' is that browsers guard against cross domain requests, meaning that they either warn against, or disallow, any attempt to send an 'XMLHttpRequest' to a domain other than the one that the web page came from. This means, in fact, that using the 'XMLHttpRequest' as part of an RSS reader is perhaps not an ideal solution, since we then have to start looking into issues such as signing our scripts with security certificates. When we are connecting to our own test server this is not going to cause any problems, because we either create our own RSS feeds or use our server as a proxy between the browser and the original source of the RSS feed. Unfortunately, however, the security restrictions also apply to HTML pages that are loaded as local files. In order to test the Ajax examples in this chapter as local files, we have had to use Internet Explorer 7.0, because there are some browsers (for example, Firefox and Opera) that do not allow you to access the RSS content using 'XMLHttpRequest'. Of course, once we start to deploy our own web applications, this will no longer be an issue.

Connecting to a server using an 'XMLHttpRequest'

Because there are a number of different aspects to using Ajax, our first example simply tries to make a connection to a server using an 'XMLHttpRequest' and shows an alert if the connection is successful. The following function ('processResponse') simply checks that the ready state of the request is '4' and the HTTP status code is '200' (OK). If so, an alert is shown. The 'xhrequest' variable shown here is declared elsewhere as a global variable:

```
// File: processresponse.js
function processResponse()
{
   if(xhrequest.readyState == 4 && xhrequest.status == 200)
   {
      alert("Got Response!");
   }
}
```

Here is an XHTML page that uses the 'getXMLHttpRequest' function (in 'getxml-httprequest.js') to get hold of an 'XMLHttpRequest' object. If it is successful, it uses the 'processResponse' function (in 'processresponse.js') to show the alert. The two functions are in separate files because the 'getXMLHttpRequest' function is generic and can be reused across many different pages, whereas the 'processResponse' function is specific to this example. The URL used here is for the Yahoo RSS news feed, but since we are just testing to see if we have made a connection, any valid URL can be used instead.

```
<?xml version="1.0"?>
<!DOCTYPE html PUBLIC "-//W3C//DTD XHTML 1.1//EN"
   "http://www.w3.org/TR/xhtml11/DTD/xhtml11.dtd">
<html xmlns="http://www.w3.org/1999/xhtml" xml:lang="en">
   <head>
      <title>Ajax RSS Reader</title>
      <script type="text/javascript" src="getxmlhttprequest.js">
      </script>
      <script type="text/javascript" src="processresponse.js">
      </script>
   </head>
   <body>
```

```
<!-- File: example8-12.htm -->
  <script type="text/javascript">
  // no 'var', so this is a global variable!
    xhrequest = null;
    try
    {
      xhrequest = getXMLHttpRequest();
    }
    catch(error)
    {
      document.write("Cannot run Ajax code using this browser");
    }
    if(xhrequest != null)
    {
      xhrequest.onreadystatechange = processResponse
      xhrequest.open("GET", "http://rss.news.yahoo.com/rss/topstories", true);
      xhrequest.send(null);
    }
  </script>
  </body>
</html>
```

Figure 8.15 shows the alert that appears if you make a successful connection using the 'XMLHttpRequest'.

Reading XML data using the 'XMLHttpRequest'

For our final example, we build on the code that makes an Ajax connection and retrieve some data from an RSS feed into a web page. The first thing that we need is something on

FIGURE 8.15   The alert that appears if a successful connection to the server is made using the 'XMLHttpRequest'

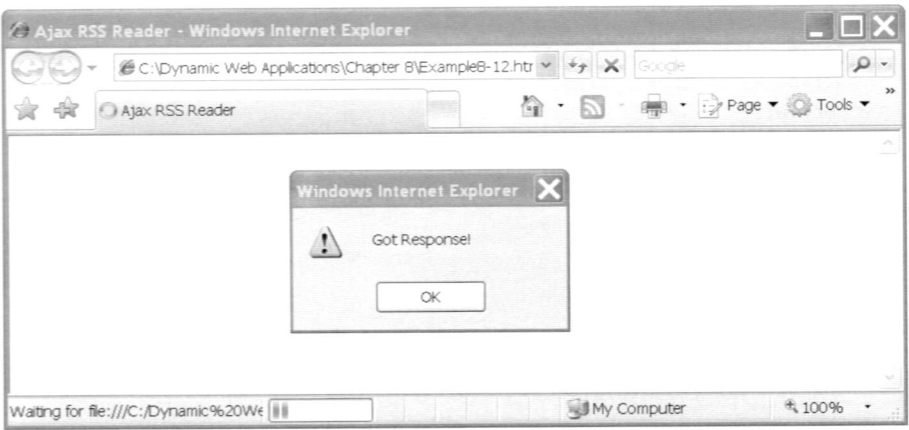

8

the page to display the content we are reading from the server. In our example, we use a 'div' with the id of 'feed':

```
<div id="feed"></div>
```

This is where we write the content to when we get the response.

The other main change that we need to make is to provide a function that does more than just show an alert when it makes a connection. We need instead to navigate the DOM of the RSS XML document. You will note from the structure of RSS documents that there is a 'description' element inside the 'channel' element, and another inside each 'item' element. In the following function we use the 'getElementsByTagName' method to get a collection of all the description elements. Then we navigate to the first of the item descriptions using the index '1' (since the first index, 0, would be the channel description). We then set the 'innerHTML' property of the 'div' to the value of the content of the element. When we connect to the Yahoo news feed, the content is a set of anchors that link to HTML content.

```
// File: processnewsfeed.js
function processYahooNewsFeed()
{
    if(xhrequest.readyState == 4 && xhrequest.status == 200)
    {
        var descriptions=xhrequest.responseXML.getElementsByTagName('description');
        var firstItemDescription=descriptions[1];
        feed.innerHTML=firstItemDescription.firstChild.nodeValue;
    }
}
```

Here is the web page that retrieves the content and displays it. It is similar to the last example, except that it includes the div tag and calls the 'processYahooNewsFeed' function.

```
<?xml version="1.0"?>
<!DOCTYPE html PUBLIC "-//W3C//DTD XHTML 1.1//EN"
    "http://www.w3.org/TR/xhtml11/DTD/xhtml11.dtd">
<html xmlns="http://www.w3.org/1999/xhtml" xml:lang="en">
    <head>
        <title>Ajax RSS Reader</title>
        <script type="text/javascript" src="getxmlhttprequest.js">
        </script>
        <script type="text/javascript" src="processnewsfeed.js">
        </script>
    </head>
    <body>
    <!-- File: example8-13.htm -->
        <h1>Yahoo News Feed</h1>
        <div id="feed"></div>
        <script type="text/javascript">
            // no 'var', so this is a global variable!
            xhrequest=null;
```

```
      try
      {
         xhrequest = getXMLHttpRequest();
      }
      catch(error)
      {
         document.write("Cannot run Ajax code using this browser");
      }
      if(xhrequest != null)
      {
         xhrequest.onreadystatechange = processYahooNewsFeed;
         xhrequest.open("GET", "http://rss.news.yahoo.com/rss/topstories", true);
         xhrequest.send(null);
      }
      </script>
   </body>
</html>
```

Figure 8.16 shows how the page looks when it has retrieved the first item from the feed. Of course the actual content changes on a daily basis.

FIGURE 8.16   Part of the Yahoo news feed included in a web page using Ajax

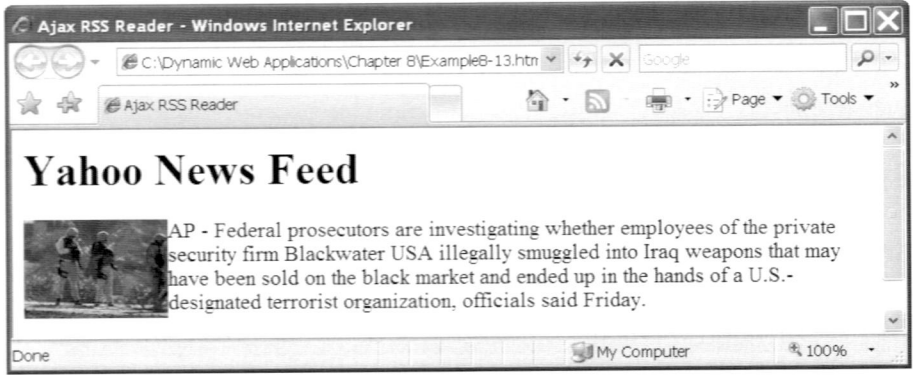

Exercises

8.1 Using the document in 'example7-1.htm', write a JavaScript function (in a separate '.js' file) that uses appropriate DOM properties and methods to locate the 'span' elements with the ids 'risk' and 'items'. Using the DOM (you can assign the values either to the 'nodeValue' property of the element's 'firstChild' or the 'innerHTML' property), replace the text in these spans with 'domestic disaster' and 'your possessions' respectively.

Invoke the function using the 'onload' event of the document body. The resulting page should appear as in Figure 8.17.

8.2 Modify the validation function in the file 'validateform.js', which currently just checks that the login id and password fields are not empty, to include these additional validations:

- Login IDs should be based on an email address, so the input must contain the '@' character.
- Passwords must be at least 5 characters long, but have no more than 10 characters.

Add an appropriate message to the alert if either of these conditions is not met.

You can use the length property of strings to check the length of the password.

To check for the '@' character (substring) in the login id, you can use the 'string.indexOf( )' function. If the function returns −1, it means the substring you are searching for is not in the string:

```
if(loginid.indexOf("@") == -1)
{
// not there!
```

8.3 There is no need to write all your own validation code since there are many JavaScript validation routines available to download on the web. Find one of these

---

FIGURE 8.17   The expected result from Question 1

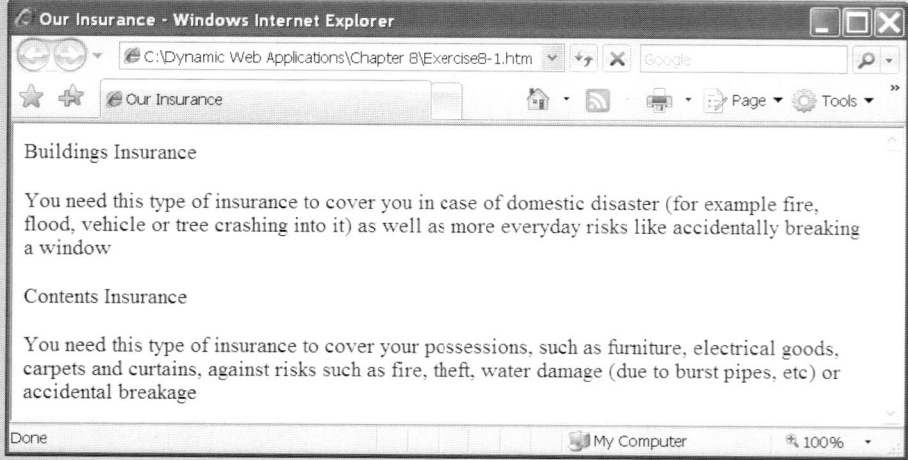

and use it to validate a form containing fields such as credit card numbers, dates and floating point numbers.

8.4 In an external file called 'mouseover.js', write two JavaScript functions to animate the WebHomeCover logo by using two different versions of the logo and switching between them when the mouse passes over the logo position. Here is an XHTML page that includes an anchor that uses the 'onmouseover' and 'onmouseout' events to trigger JavaScript functions.

```
<?xml version="1.0"?>
<!DOCTYPE html PUBLIC
  "-//W3C//DTD XHTML 1.1//EN"
  "http://www.w3.org/TR/xhtml11/DTD/xhtml11.dtd">
<html xmlns="http://www.w3.org/1999/xhtml" xml:lang="en">
  <head>
    <meta http-equiv="Content-Script-Type" content="text/javascript"/>
    <title>Mouse over logo</title>
    <script type="text/javascript" src ="mouseover.js"></script>
  </head>
  <body>
    <!-- File: Exercise8-4.htm -->
    <h2>WebHomeCover Logo</h2>
    <div>
      <a href="http://www.webhomecover.com" onmouseover="mouseOver()"
      onmouseout="mouseNotOver()">
      <img src="webhomecoverlogo.gif" alt="WebHomeCover logo"
        id="logo"/>
      </a>
    </div>
  </body>
</html>
```

You will need to implement the 'mouseOver' and 'mouseNotOver' functions. In these functions, use the getElementByID method to navigate to the 'logo' (the 'img' element) and set the name of the 'src' attribute to one of the two image file names (one in each function). The two files (supplied on the CD) are 'webhome coverlogo.gif' and 'webhomecoverlogoinverted.gif'.

8.5 Write an Ajax function called 'processWeatherFeed' that accesses the first title element and second description element of an RSS document, concatenates them together and writes their content to an element of an XHTML document. You can use the URIs of various RSS weather feeds. Yahoo, for example, provides a simple RSS URI for weather feeds where you append a 'p' request parameter that has the value of a location. For example, the following URI would get the weather in London, UK.

```
http://weather.yahooapis.com/forecastrss?p=UKXX0085
```

You can find out the code for any global weather location by navigating from the main Yahoo weather page:

```
http://weather.yahoo.com/
```

There are other weather feeds that you can also use, for example RSSWeather.com. Here is the URL for accessing the weather in London using their RSS feed

```
http://www.rssweather.com/icao/EGLC/rss.php
```

You will find other feeds on the web that you may be able to connect to, depending on how they are configured. Remember that all RSSfeeds use the same XML document structure, so you can create a generic function that is able to read data from any RSS feed, not just news or weather as we have done so far.

SUMMARY

In this chapter, we built on the basics of JavaScript syntax introduced previously to explore some aspects of DHTML, form validation and Ajax. We began the chapter by describing some features of JavaScript that let us navigate to parts of an XHTML document using the DOM and dynamically change their state. We then looked at an important aspect of JavaScript, which is client-side validation. We concluded the chapter by looking at some fundamental aspects of Ajax, which use JavaScript to communicate with the server and change the content of the current page without needing to reload it.

References and further reading

Dutta, S. (2006) *Native XMLHTTPRequest object.* http://blogs.msdn.com/ie/archive/2006/01/23/516393.aspx
Garrett, J.J. (2005) *Ajax: A New Approach to Web Applications.* http://www.adaptivepath.com/publications/essays/archives/000385.php
Zakas, N., McPeak, J. and Fawcett, J. (2006) *Professional Ajax.* Wrox/Wiley 2006

8

Web Applications and Application Servers

INTRODUCTION

A web application is, simply, an application that is distributed over the worldwide web, using HTTP as its transport mechanism. The most important aspect of a web application is that it provides dynamic, rather than static, content. A web site that consists only of prewritten HTML pages or other files that are the same for every client only delivers *static content*, because its content is fixed when it is deployed. This type of content is presented to clients using an *HTTP server*, or *Web server*, such as Apache (Apache HTTP 2007), and does not require an application server. In contrast, web applications include dynamically generated pages that can be tailored to each individual client. This *dynamic content* can be used to show a client their shopping trolley, bank account, order status, loyalty card points or any other type of information. Dynamic content is what enables e-commerce and is a core aspect of enterprise systems. It also enables a huge range of other interactive applications that range from music downloads and on-line gaming to virtual worlds and communities.

9.1 Application servers

The job of an application server is to support the delivery of dynamic content, using some kind of server-side process that does more than just serve HTML pages or other static files to clients. The way that the application server does this can vary, because there are many server-side technologies that can be used to create dynamic content. One early technology for supporting this type of content was Common Gateway Interface (CGI) scripts. CGI provides a way for server-side applications written in various programming languages such as C and C++ to be plugged into a web server using a standard interface, but these are inefficient due to the separation of the server from the CGI implementation. There are also a number of interpreted server-side scripting languages that have become popular for developing dynamic content. These include Perl, Python and PHP, and these languages are often used for relatively lightweight web applications that do not need to scale to large numbers of users or support the integration of other large-scale enterprise systems. In fact there is an acronym sometimes applied to systems that use these scripting languages in conjunction with open-source tools to provide a flexible and cheap way of developing web applications: LAMP (Kunze 1998), which stands for Linux (an open-source operating system), Apache (an open-source HTTP server), MySQL (an open-source database, which we also introduce in this book) and PHP (Hypertext Preprocessor, an open-source scripting language). Within the Windows operating-system environment, the Microsoft .NET platform contains a full set of tools and technologies for enterprise-level web application development, using languages that support the Common Language Runtime (CLR) such as VB.Net and C#. In a .NET web application, dynamic content can be generated using Active Server Pages (ASPs). However in this book we are focusing on Java web applications, so the servers we will be looking at are those that support the web application components of the Java Enterprise Edition (Java EE). Developing web applications in Java has a number of advantages over most of the other alternative technologies. It is more efficient than many of the scripting languages, and provides full integration with all the rich and varied APIs that are available in the Java Enterprise Edition. Unlike some languages, a Java web application can be scaled to handle very large numbers of clients, with a high level of security. It also has the advantage over .NET of being able to run across a wide range of operating systems.

9.2 Using Apache Tomcat web application server

Tomcat is an open source Java application server that supports the web application components of the Java EE specification (Apache Software Foundation 2007). The technologies that support Java-based web applications are primarily servlets and JavaServer Pages (JSPs), both of which we explore in detail in Chapter 10. These are deployed on a Java application server, which is typically a combination of a *servlet engine* and a *JSP compiler*. For example, the Tomcat web server comprises the *Catalina* servlet engine and the *Jasper* JSP compiler. However, in practice the distinction between these two aspects of the server is not important and is not really visible to the user. Application servers such as Tomcat can also usually serve static content through a built-in HTTP server, so it is not necessary to have a separate HTTP server to do this, though this is often done in practice to assist the scalability of the system. For testing purposes, there is no need to use a separate HTTP server for performance, so we use the one that is included with Tomcat, which is the *Coyote* HTTP server. Figure 9.1 shows the various components of the Tomcat application server.

In the example systems in this book, we see how Tomcat can be used to serve both static and dynamic content.

FIGURE 9.1   Components of the Tomcat application server

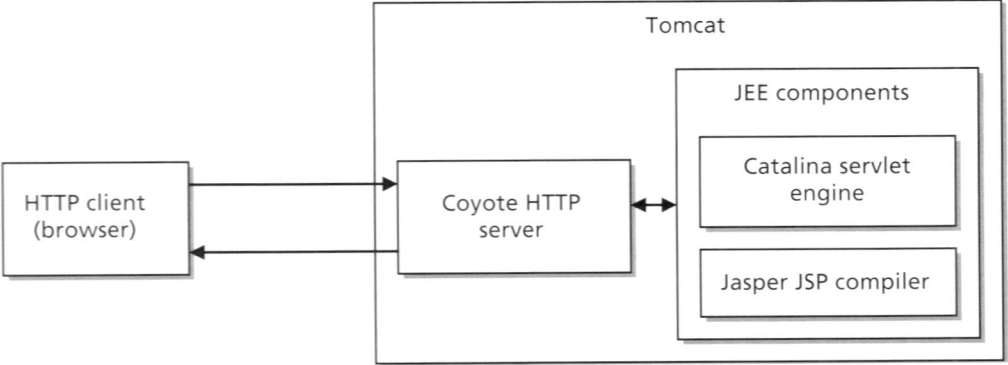

Starting Tomcat

If you are using the Windows operating system, Tomcat can be downloaded in two different forms, either as a zipped archive or a Windows installer. It is recommended that you use the zipped archive version, which is the one used in the examples in this book and works across multiple operating systems. All that is required is for you to download the archive file and unzip it to a suitable location on your computer. The version of Tomcat referred to in this book is version 6, though the examples may also work with newer versions. You may find it useful to rename the root folder of the Tomcat installation to 'Tomcat 6', since this is the folder name referred to in this book.

 NOTE   It is not recommended for you to attempt the examples and exercises in this book with versions of Tomcat prior to version 6 due to variations in their folder structures and performance.

To start Tomcat, first navigate to the 'bin' folder of the Tomcat installation directory. For example, if Tomcat has been installed into C:\Tomcat 6, the 'bin' folder will be immediately underneath this directory:

```
C:\Tomcat 6\bin
```

In the 'bin' folder, there is a batch file called 'startup' that can be used to start the server, either by running it from File Explorer or from a command prompt.

NOTE

In the installed Windows version, the 'startup' batch file is not present, so you need to start the program either by typing the name of the '.exe' file into a command prompt open in the bin folder, or by double clicking on the file in File Explorer. The name of this file will vary between versions, for example in version 6 it is called 'tomcat6.exe'.

The Windows installer starts Tomcat running as a Windows service. If you are using this version it is recommended that you disable this functionality and start Tomcat manually, as this helps debugging when you are testing web applications.

As Tomcat starts up, you should see a command window appear, with some log messages, similar to Figure 9.2. Do not close this window, as this will stop the server.

The 'localhost' URL and port number

When we run a test server on the local machine, we use the *loopback address*. This is IP address 127.0.0.1, which is also known as 'localhost' (assuming the usual default setting on your machine). The HTTP server that is included with Tomcat runs by default on port 8080. Therefore the URL that can be used to connect to the server running on the local machine is http://localhost:8080. To check that Tomcat is running correctly, open a web browser and direct it to this URL. You should see the default Tomcat server home page (Figure 9.3).

A quick (and dirty) way to stop the server is simply to close the command window in which it is running. A better approach, which enables Tomcat to shut down its threads in an orderly manner, is to use the 'shutdown' batch file in the 'bin' folder of your Tomcat installation.

FIGURE 9.2   Some startup message from the Tomcat application server

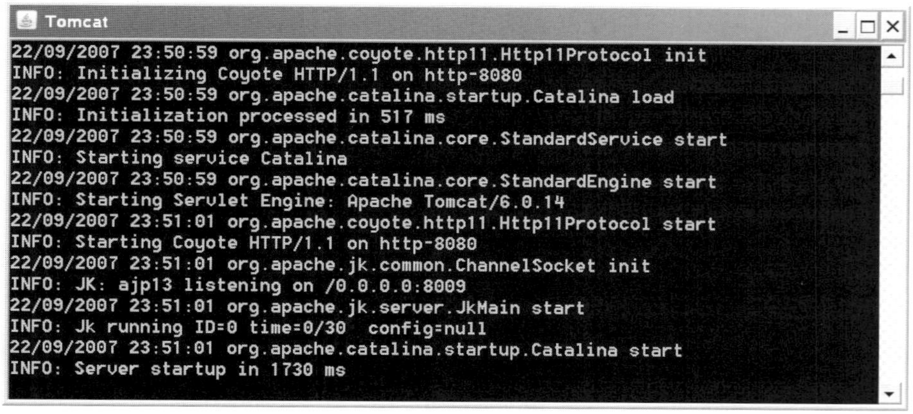

```
Tomcat                                                          _ □ ×
22/09/2007 23:50:59 org.apache.coyote.http11.Http11Protocol init
INFO: Initializing Coyote HTTP/1.1 on http-8080
22/09/2007 23:50:59 org.apache.catalina.startup.Catalina load
INFO: Initialization processed in 517 ms
22/09/2007 23:50:59 org.apache.catalina.core.StandardService start
INFO: Starting service Catalina
22/09/2007 23:50:59 org.apache.catalina.core.StandardEngine start
INFO: Starting Servlet Engine: Apache Tomcat/6.0.14
22/09/2007 23:51:01 org.apache.coyote.http11.Http11Protocol start
INFO: Starting Coyote HTTP/1.1 on http-8080
22/09/2007 23:51:01 org.apache.jk.common.ChannelSocket init
INFO: JK: ajp13 listening on /0.0.0.0:8009
22/09/2007 23:51:01 org.apache.jk.server.JkMain start
INFO: Jk running ID=0 time=0/30  config=null
22/09/2007 23:51:01 org.apache.catalina.startup.Catalina start
INFO: Server startup in 1730 ms
```

FIGURE 9.3 The Tomcat server home page

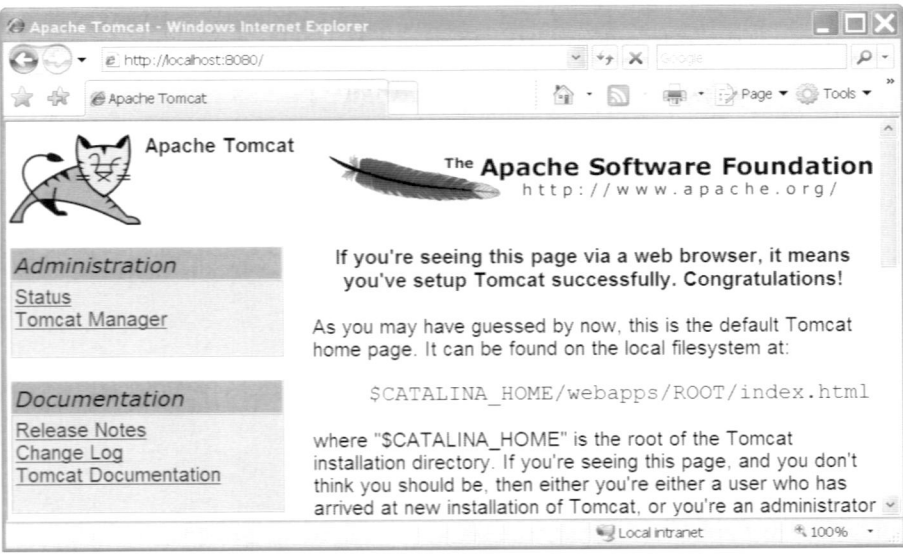

9.3 Web application structure and deployment

Web applications are part of the Java Enterprise Edition, which specifies some folders and files that must be present to successfully deploy Java web applications. In particular, a Java web application must include a *deployment descriptor*, which is an XML file used to configure how the web server deploys the resources in the web application. This file is called 'web.xml'. Deployment descriptors provide a declarative way of configuring program URLs, security, transactions, etc. when using dynamic content. As we work through the example system, we explore a number of aspects of the web application deployment descriptor, but we begin by looking at the directory structure that contains our web application resources.

A web application is a collection of related resources made available via an application server. An individual web application, deployed on a server, is called a *context* and each context may be started, stopped and deployed independently of any others on that server. The resources for a context are deployed into a folder known as the *context root*, or its subdirectories, so everything in or under a context root is part of the same web application.

Deploying static content on an HTTP server

Any static content that is part of the web application is stored in the context root or its subfolders. Static content can be HTML/XHTML files, XML linked with XSLT and CSS, images, sounds, videos, etc. In fact any type of file that can be served via an HTTP response. Figure 9.4 shows the interaction between an HTTP client and the application server when static content, such as an HTML page, is requested. In this case, the embedded HTTP server deals with the request, and static content is sent back to the client from the context root. The other components of the application server (the servlet container and the JSP engine) are not required in this interaction.

FIGURE 9.4 Serving static content from the HTTP server

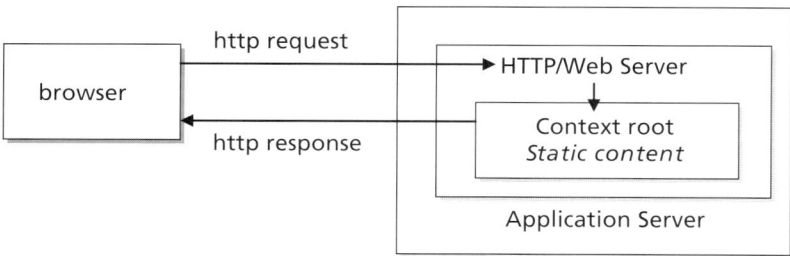

Java web application deployment

To deploy a web application to a Java server, we have to provide at least one XML deployment descriptor ('web.xml') and organize our files into a specified folder structure. Sometimes additional configuration files are also required, depending on the server that is being used or the particular requirements of the Web application. For efficient deployment we also need to package the files that make up the application into a Java archive (a 'JAR' file) and then copy the archive file to a deployment directory on the server, either directly or by using a management utility of the server.

Java EE packaging

All Java EE application components are packaged in Java archive (JAR) file formats so that they can be easily deployed. JAR files are similar to ZIP files, but the main motivation is grouping files into a single unit of deployment rather than using compression. Although all the deployment units in Java EE are JAR files, different extensions are used to identify their purpose. For example, a JAR file for a Web application archive is given a '.war' extension, but a JAR file for an enterprise application is given a '.ear' extension. This makes it easier to manage different types of deployment unit by their file extensions. Although we do not need to use them for deployment in Tomcat, the other types of archive used in Java EE deployment are:

- .jar files for Enterprise JavaBeans
- .rar files for resource adapters.

Web application folders and resources

Web applications usually contain many resources, including both static content and dynamic content generated by Java components. This content must be deployed using a standard folder structure defined by the Java EE specification, with content and configuration files located in the correct folders. The main distinction in this folder structure is between files that are directly available for a client to download (such as HTML pages) and those that are not, for example configuration files and server-side Java code. Files that are in the root directory of the web application are available to be downloaded, as are resources in most subdirectories. To separate the publicly accessible files from the non-public configuration files, a web application's context root contains a special folder called 'WEB-INF'.

The Java EE configuration file, hidden from clients in the WEB-INF folder, is the web application deployment descriptor ('web.xml'). Figure 9.5 shows the required web application folder structure.

To get started, we need to create a working folder (*not* within the Tomcat installation folders) that we will use for the incremental development of our web application. We will assume a folder called 'webhomecover' that will represent the context root of the web application. For reasons that will become clear later, the name of the context root folder will be the same as the name of the web application. The reason for using a context name that is all in lower case letters is that mixing case can cause problems later on with URIs, so it is best to stick to all lower case letters. In our first example we see one file that is available for download ('welcome.htm') in the context root and the web application deployment descriptor ('web.xml') in the 'WEB-INF' folder (Figure 9.6).

FIGURE 9.5 The required folder structure for Java EE web applications

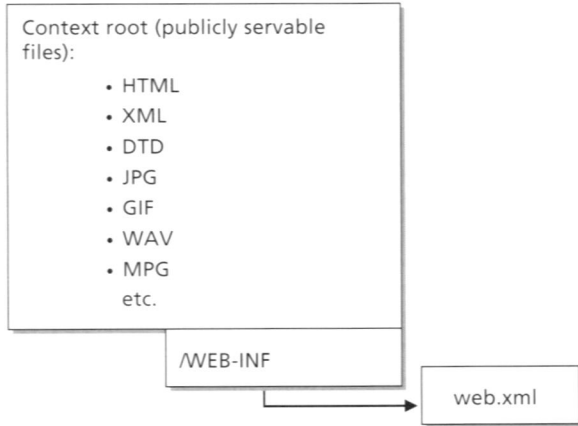

FIGURE 9.6 The folders and files of the 'webhomecover' application

Here is a very basic XHTML implementation of 'welcome.htm', containing some basic web site 'welcome' text:

```
<!DOCTYPE html PUBLIC "-//W3C//DTD XHTML 1.1//EN"
    "http://www.w3.org/TR/xhtml11/DTD/xhtml11.dtd">
<html xmlns="http://www.w3.org/1999/xhtml" xml:lang="en">
    <head>
        <title>Welcome to WebHomeCover</title>
    </head>
    <body>
        <h1><em>Welcome to</em> WebHomeCover.com</h1>
        <h2>
            Your home and possessions are important.
            <br/>
            We give you the very best insurance cover at the lowest prices.
        </h2>
    </body>
</html>
```

XML deployment descriptors

The 'web.xml' deployment descriptor must be both well formed and valid XML so that its elements can be processed by the application server. An application server usually validates any deployment descriptors when an application is deployed, and cannot load the application if any of the descriptors are not valid. Depending on the version of the web application descriptor that is being used, there may be either a DTD or an XML Schema available to validate Java EE deployment descriptors. In J2EE versions 1.2 and 1.3, DTDs were used for validation, but since J2EE 1.4, XML Schemas have been used. For a web application deployment descriptor version 2.5, which is part of Java Enterprise Edition 1.5, the following XML Schema is used:

```
<?xml version="1.0" ?>
<web-app xmlns="http://java.sun.com/xml/ns/javaee"
    xmlns:xsi="http://www.w3.org/2001/XMLSchema-instance"
    xsi:schemaLocation="http://java.sun.com/xml/ns/javaee
    http://java.sun.com/xml/ns/javaee/web-app_2_5.xsd"
    version="2.5">
    ...
</web-app>
```

If you open a web browser to the URI http://java.sun.com/xml/ns/javaee/ you can link to a number of Java EE XML Schemas, including 'web-app_2_5.xsd'. Here are a few fragments from that XML Schema, relating to some of the aspects of the 'web.xml' file that we will be introducing in this and the following chapters.

```
<xsd:element name="web-app" type="javaee:web-appType">
...
</xsd:element>

<xsd:complexType name="servlet-mappingType">
    <xsd:sequence>
```

```
        <xsd:element name="servlet-name" type="javaee:servlet-nameType" />
        <xsd:element name="url-pattern" type="javaee:url-patternType"
          minOccurs="1" maxOccurs="unbounded" />
    </xsd:sequence>
    <xsd:attribute name="id" type="xsd:ID" />
    </xsd:complexType>

  <xsd:complexType name="servletType">
    <xsd:sequence>
      <xsd:element name="servlet-name" type="javaee:servlet-nameType" />
    <xsd:element name="servlet-class"
      type="javaee:fully-qualified-classType">
    </xsd:sequence>

      <xsd:element name="servlet" type="javaee:servletType" />
      <xsd:element name="servlet-mapping"
        type="javaee:servlet-mappingType" />

    <xsd:element name="welcome-file-list"
      type="javaee:welcome-file-listType" />
        </xsd:choice>
  <xsd:complexType name="welcome-file-listType">

  <xsd:sequence>
  <xsd:element name="welcome-file" type="xsd:string"
    maxOccurs="unbounded">
    </xsd:element>
    </xsd:sequence>
    <xsd:attribute name="id" type="xsd:ID" />
    </xsd:complexType>
  </xsd:schema>
```

You can see from this schema that the root element is called 'web-app'. Inside this element are many nested elements, which must of course appear in the order specified. With the exception of the compulsory root element, all the other elements are either optional or may occur zero or more times. This means that the number of elements used in a valid 'web.xml' file can vary a great deal between applications.

The following 'web.xml' file is valid according to the 'web-app_2_5.xsd' XML Schema. It contains the necessary reference to the schema and has the compulsory root element ('web-app'). It includes only one nested element, the 'welcome-file-list'. The role of this element is to configure the default page that is served when a client connects to the URI of the web application.

```
  <?xml version="1.0" ?>
  <web-app xmlns="http://java.sun.com/xml/ns/javaee"
    xmlns:xsi="http://www.w3.org/2001/XMLSchema-instance"
    xsi:schemaLocation="http://java.sun.com/xml/ns/javaee
    http://java.sun.com/xml/ns/javaee/web-app_2_5.xsd"
    version="2.5">
    <welcome-file-list>
      <welcome-file>/welcome.htm</welcome-file>
```

```
    </welcome-file-list>
  </web-app>
```

You can see from the earlier schema extract that the 'welcome-file-list' element, if present, must contain at least one 'welcome-file' entry, which is string data representing the name of a file. This defines which default page is served to the client if they do not request a specific resource. In our example, if the client sends a request to the URI of the Web application without specifying a particular resource name, the default response will be the 'welcome.htm' page. The forward slash before the file name indicates the 'context root' of the web application, which corresponds to the root directory ('webhomecover') of our web application folder structure. The ability to provide more than one 'welcome-file' element means that we can list multiple files, and the server will respond with the first matching file that it finds. For example, if we were to add another element referring to 'index.htm', the server would first look for 'welcome.htm' in the context root and, if it was found, provide it as the response. However, if 'welcome.htm' could not be found it would look for 'index.htm' and, if it found it, serve that instead.

```
  <welcome-file-list>
    <welcome-file>/welcome.htm</welcome-file>
    <welcome-file>/index.htm</welcome-file>
  </welcome-file-list>
```

This can be useful where our preferred welcome file is generated using some dynamic content. If there is some problem serving the dynamic content and the file has been removed we could have a fall back position of serving some static content instead.

The structure and data types of the XML file are validated by the server using the XML Schema when the web application is deployed, and any error messages will appear in the server's output window (the one shown in Figure 9.2). The actual content between the tags is not, of course, specified by the schema (e.g. what constitutes a valid file name). This information is, however, also processed by the application server when it tries to deploy the application. This means that even an XML document that is valid according to the schema may have errors in its content that prevent the application from deploying properly.

9.4 Deploying to Tomcat

So far our web application consists of two files in a specific folder structure. In order to get it running on Tomcat, we have to deploy it to the 'webapps' folder of the server. There are two approaches to this deployment:

- Copy the existing directory structure to the 'webapps' (deployment) directory of the application server.
- Use the 'jar.exe' utility to create a web archive file (a '.war' file) and deploy this into the server's 'webapps' folder.

Although it works, the first option is rather inflexible, and is not an approach that can be used on many other application servers, so we will follow the other strategy of creating a web archive and deploying that to the server.

Creating a web archive

Creating a Java web archive file is quite simple, and is done using the 'jar' utility that is included in the JDK. Assuming you have the 'bin' folder of the JDK (where the 'jar.exe' program is located) on your system path, you will be able to invoke it from the command line simply by typing 'jar'. This will give you a list of options for using the command, beginning something like this:

```
Usage: jar {ctxu}[vfmOM] [jar-file] [manifest-file] [-C dir] files
. . .
Options:
       -c create new archive
       -t list table of contents for archive
       -x extract named (or all) files from archive
       -u update existing archive
       -v generate verbose output on standard output
       -f specify archive file name
```

Creating a jar file is simply a way of grouping multiple folders and files together into a single unit of deployment. The important thing about a Java archive is that its internal structure must be the same as that used in the source directories. For example, to put the files for our web application into a JAR file we must make sure that the internal structure (i.e. the 'WEB-INF' folder) is preserved inside the JAR. The easiest way to do this is to create the JAR from the root directory of the web application, in our case 'webhomecover'. Because we are creating a JAR file for a web application archive, we give it the '.war' file extension. This file extension has no effect on the file itself but it is important that we call the file 'webhomecover.war' since it identifies the intention of this archive, both to developers and to application servers. To create a new web archive, we need to use the following options when invoking the 'jar.exe' program:

- c → this option is for creating a new archive file
- f → this option enables us to specify the name of the file we are creating

Another useful option is 'v', which prints 'verbose' output when the jar utility is running, which helps us to see what is going on. To create a JAR that contains the necessary files in the correct structure, but writes the resulting archive to the directory above, we would invoke the 'jar' utility from within the document root ('webhomecover') like this:

```
path/webhomecover> jar cvf ..\webhomecover.war *
```

'*path*' represents the folder structure above the 'webhomecover' folder and '..\' is used to refer to the parent folder. '*' includes all files and folders beneath (and including) the current folder in the archive.

This creates a new file called 'webhomecover.war' that contains our web application files and folders. Writing the war file to the parent folder keeps the resulting archive separate from the content of the web application. Otherwise the archive will end up inside itself! On running the 'jar' utility you should see something similar to the following:

```
added manifest
adding: WEB-INF/(in = 0) (out = 0)(stored 0%)
```

```
adding: WEB-INF/web.xml(in = 275) (out = 182)(deflated 33%)
adding: welcome.html(in = 290) (out = 174)(deflated 40%)
```

You can check the contents of the JAR file using any archive file viewer.

Deploying a web archive

Now that we have our war file containing a web application, we can deploy it to the server. This is quite simple with Tomcat, since all we need to do is to copy it to the 'webapps' folder under the Tomcat server's installation folder. The application will be deployed using the name of the war file as the name of the web application. In this example, then, the web application will be called 'webhomecover'. This application context needs to be specified when we want to access the application as an HTTP client (i.e. via a web browser). Once the web application has been deployed and the server has been started, the web application is available to browser clients using the following URL (assuming a local test server):

```
http://localhost:8080/webhomecover
```

The context root of the URL can be followed with the name of any resource deployed in that web application. In this case, there is only one resource, namely the HTML welcome page. Because 'welcome.htm' is specified in the 'web.xml' deployment descriptor as the default welcome file, this page should appear in the browser without needing to be specifically requested. However, we could alternatively invoke it directly like this:

```
http://localhost:8080/webhomecover/welcome.htm
```

Figure 9.7 shows what the page looks like in Internet Explorer 7. Note the URI of the page in the address bar.

Any other resource names will not be found, since 'welcome.htm' is the only resource that we have deployed. If you try to load 'index.htm' for example, which does not exist in our application, then the server will return error code 404, which is the 'page not found' error.

FIGURE 9.7   The 'welcome.htm' page in Internet Explorer 7, downloaded from the local server

Adding style sheets and XML

As well as simple HTML pages, the document root may contain many other types of static file. One such file type would be the cascading style sheets used for the pages in the application. For the purpose of this example, we use the following simple style sheet ('webhomecover.css'):

```
h2 {font-style: italic; color: blue}
.companyname {color: red}
```

Here is a modified version of 'welcome.html' that links to this style sheet and includes the 'companyname' style:

```
<!DOCTYPE html PUBLIC "-//W3C//DTD XHTML 1.0 Strict//EN"
   "http://www.w3.org/TR/xhtml1/DTD/xhtml1-strict.dtd">
<html xmlns="http://www.w3.org/1999/xhtml" xml:lang="en">
  <head>
    <title>Welcome to WebHomeCover</title>
    <link href="webhomecover.css" rel="stylesheet" type="text/css" />
  </head>
  <body>
    <h1><em>Welcome to </em>
    <span class="companyname">WebHomeCover.com</span>
    </h1>
    <h2>
      Your home and possessions are important.
      <br/>
      We give you the very best insurance cover at the lowest prices.
    </h2>
  </body>
</html>
```

Since the 'href' attribute in the 'link' element simply refers to the style sheet file name ('webhomecover.css') without any URI or folder name, it must be in the same document folder as the HTML file, in this case the document root of the web application. To update the web application to use the modified HTML page and the style sheet, you need to rebuild the JAR file and replace the existing JAR file in the server's 'webapps' folder. If you replace an existing war file in the deployment folder, Tomcat will automatically *hot deploy* it, replacing the existing application with the new version without needing to restart the server.

 NOTE In order for Tomcat to hot deploy a modified web application, it must be running when the new war file is copied to the 'webapps' folder.

Figure 9.8 shows the modified page displayed in Mozilla Firefox 2, using the style sheet. Although the colors will be difficult to discern, the italic style of the second-level heading text is obvious.

FIGURE 9.8 'welcome.html' displayed in Mozilla Firefox 2, styled by 'webhomecover.css'

Instead of serving HTML or XHTML documents, we may prefer to serve static XML to the client, along with linked XSLT style sheets to convert these to XHTML. This assumes, of course that the client is a browser that is able to perform these transformations. In this example, we assume that the page content is stored not in an XHTML file but in an XML file linked to an XSL transformation:

```
<?xml version="1.0"?>
<?xml-stylesheet type="text/xsl" href="welcome.xsl"?>
  <welcomepage>
     <title>Welcome to WebHomeCover</title>
     <message>Welcome to </message>
     <company>WebHomeCover.com</company>
     <para>Your home and possessions are important</para>
     <para>
        We give you the very best insurance cover at the lowest prices.
     </para>
  </welcomepage>
```

Here is the XSL transform, in this case generating an XHTML 1.1 page:

```
<?xml version="1.0"?>
<xsl:stylesheet version="1.0"
xmlns:xsl="http://www.w3.org/1999/XSL/Transform">
  <xsl:output method="xml"
     doctype-public="-//W3C//DTD XHTML 1.1 //EN"
     doctype-system="http://www.w3.org/TR/xhtml11/DTD/xhtml11.dtd"/>
  <xsl:template match="welcomepage">
     <html xmlns="http://www.w3.org/1999/xhtml" xml:lang="en">
        <head>
           <title>
              <xsl:value-of select="title"/>
           </title>
```

```
            <link rel="stylesheet" href="webhomecover.css" type="text/css" />
        </head>
        <body>
            <h1>
                <xsl:value-of select="message"/>
                <span class="companyname">
                    <xsl:value-of select="company"/>
                </span>
            </h1>
            <h2>
                <xsl:for-each select="para">
                    <xsl:value-of select="."/>
                    <br />
                </xsl:for-each>
            </h2>
        </body>
    </html>
    </xsl:template>
</xsl:stylesheet>
```

Figure 9.9 shows the result when the XML document ('welcome.xml') is opened using Internet Explorer 7. Note the URL in the address bar:

```
http://localhost:8080/webhomecover/welcome.xml
```

The XSL Transformation is performed by the browser, generating an XHTML page. Although this is very similar to the original XHTML version, you will see that the 'Welcome to' text is not emphasized (just to make the point that this is not the same page that we used before).

FIGURE 9.9 A page generated by an XSL Transformation in Internet Explorer 7 from files served by the web application

9.5 JBoss application server

Tomcat is a Java application server that includes only the web application aspects of the Java Enterprise Edition. It does not include other components of a Java EE server such as an Enterprise JavaBeans container or resource adapters (used to connect an application server to other enterprise applications). There are a number of servers that do provide this functionality, including BEA Weblogic, IBM Websphere, Sun and JBoss Application Servers. Each of these servers includes a web application server product as well as the other aspects of a complete Java EE application server. JBoss Application Server (one of a number of JBoss products) is an open-source Java EE server that includes an embedded version of Tomcat as its web application server. Since many people use Tomcat as part of a JBoss installation, we briefly cover its use in this section. JBoss can be downloaded from the JBoss web site (JBoss 2007) as a zipped archive, just like Tomcat, so installation is equally straightforward. The version of JBoss used in this book is JBoss Application Server 4.

Deploying a web archive to JBoss is very simple. The only difference is that, instead of copying the war file to the 'webapps' folder, as we do for a standalone installation of Tomcat, we deploy our war file to the 'deploy' folder, which is in the following path under the JBoss deployment folder:

```
JBoss\server\default\deploy
```

Like Tomcat, JBoss has scripts to start and stop the server in its 'bin' folder. The script to start JBoss is called 'run' and the script to stop it is called 'shutdown'. When JBoss is running, its embedded Tomcat server runs on port 8080 by default, just like the standalone version.

9.6 Enterprise application deployment

 NOTE This section is for information only and is not necessary for understanding the following sections.

The unit of deployment to a web application server such as Tomcat is the Web archive. However, application servers that include an EJB container, for example the JBoss application server, enable the deployment of more complex enterprise applications that include a web application layer and other enterprise Java components. In this type of application, in addition to deploying one or more '.war' files, we may also need to deploy one or more JAR files that contain Enterprise JavaBeans or other Java EE components. To package these various components together, Java EE includes the concept of the enterprise application, which is packaged up into another JAR file called an Enterprise Archive. This type of JAR file always has the extension '.ear' to differentiate it from '.war' and '.jar' files.

Some Java application servers (though not JBoss) require that all Java EE deployments are done in the context of an enterprise application, so even if all you want to do is deploy a single web application WAR file, it still needs to be packaged inside an EAR file. Therefore you may find it useful to understand how to build an Enterprise Archive.

Enterprise application folder structure

Creating an enterprise application to deploy a web application is quite simple. All we need to do is provide a simple XML deployment descriptor (this time called 'application.xml') and add it, along with our existing WAR file, to an EAR file. This can then be deployed to our server. The 'application.xml' file must appear in a folder called 'META-INF', similar to the placement of 'web.xml' in the 'WEB-INF' folder of a web application. Figure 9.10 shows the structure of a simple enterprise archive, containing a single web archive and a 'META-INF' folder containing the 'application.xml' deployment descriptor.

The 'application.xml' file mainly lists the components of the enterprise archive and contains a list of modules (web applications and other Java EE modules) that are contained within it. These modules must be added to the specified directory of the enterprise archive. In our case, there is only one module, our 'webhomecover' web application, located in the root of the archive, so the deployment descriptor appears as below. Note that the module entry for a web application contains the name (the 'web-uri') of the WAR file ('webhomecover.war') and the context root for the web application, which appears as part of the complete URL ('webhomecover'):

```xml
<?xml version="1.0"?>
<application xmlns="http://java.sun.com/xml/ns/javaee"
    xmlns:xsi="http://www.w3.org/2001/XMLSchema-instance"
    xsi:schemaLocation="http://java.sun.com/xml/ns/javaee
    http://java.sun.com/xml/ns/javaee/application_5.xsd"
    version="5">

    <display-name>Insurance Application</display-name>
    <module>
      <web>
        <web-uri>webhomecover.war</web-uri>
        <context-root>/webhomecover</context-root>
      </web>
    </module>
</application>
```

FIGURE 9.10 The structure of a simple enterprise archive (EAR)

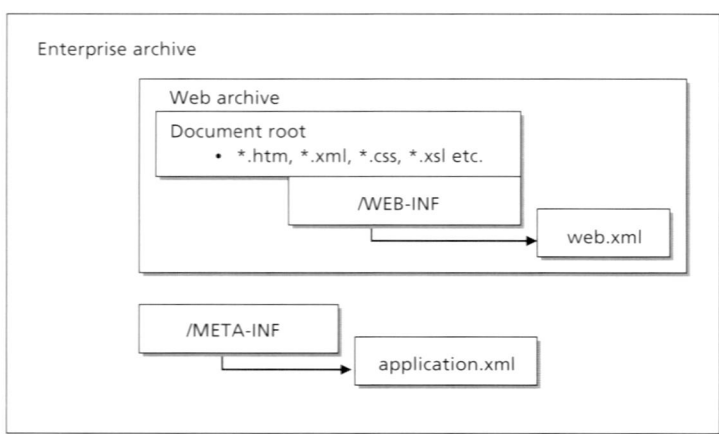

Note that this file uses a different XML Schema than 'web.xml' with a different set of tags (the XML Schema being used here is 'application_5.xsd'). Being able to specify the name of the context root in this file means that we do not have to name the application the same as the WAR file.

To build an enterprise archive to contain our web application, we need to create a new folder in our working folder (for our example this will be called 'ear'.) This folder must contain a 'META-INF' subfolder, where the 'application.xml' file should be located. The existing WAR file will have to be copied to the 'ear' folder before we create the EAR file.

Creating the enterprise archive

Assuming that the appropriate folders and files are in place, we create the EAR file using the jar utility in a similar way to creating the original WAR file. Navigate to the 'webhome-cover\ear' folder and create the enterprise archive file in the folder above:

```
path\webhomecover\ear> jar cvf ..\webhomecover.ear *
```

The '.ear' file can be copied to the JBoss deploy folder and JBoss will deploy the web application.

 NOTE Make sure you do not try to deploy the same web application to JBoss as both a '.war' file and a '.ear' file or there will be deployment problems.

9.7 Running web applications on the default HTTP port

So far, whether using Tomcat or JBoss, we are assuming the HTTP server will be running on its default HTTP port (8080). However web applications normally run on port 80. This is why we need to include the port number in our URLs, because otherwise the browser assumes the application is running on port 80 and is not able to locate it. To change the server to run on port 80, we have to make a simple modification to the 'server.xml' file, which (for standalone Tomcat installations) can be found in the 'conf' folder in the root of your Tomcat installation. If you search through this file, you should find a 'Connector' element that looks something like this, and specifies the port number as '8080':

```
<Connector port="8080" protocol="HTTP/1.1"
    connectionTimeout="20000"
    redirectPort="8443" />
```

All you need to do is to change this attribute value to '80':

```
<Connector port="80" protocol="HTTP/1.1"
    connectionTimeout="20000"
    redirectPort="8443" />
```

Changes to XML configuration files are not read dynamically by the server, so if Tomcat is already running you will need to stop it and restart it so that it reads the updated XML file. Then you should be able to connect to your web application using a URL without a port number:

```
http://localhost/webhomecover
```

If you are using Tomcat as part of JBoss, the 'server.xml' file is located at:

```
JBoss\server\default\deploy\jboss-web.deployer
```

The 'Connector' element looks a little different but again you only need to change the value of the 'port' attribute.

```
<Connector port="8080" address="${jboss.bind.address}"
maxThreads="250" maxHttpHeaderSize="8192"
emptySessionPath="true" protocol="HTTP/1.1"
enableLookups="false" redirectPort="8443" acceptCount="100"
connectionTimeout="20000" disableUploadTimeout="true" />
```

9.8 Automating build and deploy with Ant

Although so far we only have a very simple web application with some static content, it is already a bit fiddly to create the JAR file and deploy it to the server. Even more so to create an enterprise archive. To automate this process, we can use an open-source tool called Ant (an acronym for 'Another Neat Tool'), which uses a combination of Java and XML to create platform-independent build and deploy scripts (Apache Ant Project 2007).

Installing and configuring Ant

To use Ant to build and deploy an application, you have to ensure that you have Ant installed on your machine. It is easily downloaded as a zip archive from the Apache Ant project web site, and simply needs to be unzipped into a suitable directory (e.g. 'c:\ant').

Ant requires that you set up two environment variables, 'JAVA_HOME' and 'ANT_HOME'. 'JAVA_HOME' must be set to the root folder of your Java SDK installation, while 'ANT_HOME' should be set the root folder of your Ant installation. You must also add 'ANT_HOME\bin' to your system path so you can invoke Ant from the command line. Once Ant has been installed, and assuming the environment has been set up properly, it can be run from the command line simply by typing 'ant'. By default it looks for an Ant build file called 'build.xml' in the current folder, though other file or folder names can be specified.

The Ant build file

The Ant 'build.xml' file basically consists of a project which compromises a set of *tasks* that perform operations such as compiling code, building jar files and copying files to deployment folders. Tasks are put into named *targets* that we can invoke by name. It also enables us to provide *properties*: names for files and directories that we can refer to within the file.

The root element of the file is the 'project' element, which specifies the name of the project. It can also specify the default target, the one that is executed if Ant is invoked without a named target. In this example, it is a target called 'copy-war' (it will copy the WAR file to Tomcat's deployment folder). We also define the base directory ('basedir') of the files used in this build. Here, the base directory is set to the current folder (using '.'), though this is in fact the default.

```
<project name="webhomecover" default="copy-war" basedir=".">
```

Ant properties

The project element can include any number of 'property' elements that give local names to various files and directories used in the web application. For example, we might define a property called 'root' to be the current directory, and another property called 'webapp', which refers to the name of the web application.

```
<!-- source code directories -->
<property name="root" value=".\" />

<!-- web application name -->
<property name="webapp" value="webhomecover" />
```

Once a property has been declared, it can be referred to inside an Ant build file using this syntax:

```
${propertyname}
```

Here, for example, we use the 'root' and 'webapp' properties to create the 'web-root' property:

```
<!-- war file assembly directory -->
<property name="web-root" value="${root}\${webapp}" />
```

The point of doing this, of course, is to ensure that each piece of information (such as the name of the web application) only needs to appear in the build file once. After that, the property name can be used instead. This means that changes (for example to the name of the web application) only need to be made in one place in the build file.

 NOTE It is important to remember when writing an Ant build file that a property can only be referred to after it has been declared.

In the complete file you will see that we also declare a number of other properties, some that relate to folder names and another that refers to the name of the output WAR file. Not all folders are local, for example we include a reference to the Tomcat deployment folder (see the full listing at the end of this section).

The 'jar' task

To build a jar file there is a 'jar' task, which takes the names of the output file ('jarfile') and the 'base directory' ('basedir') as parameters. Again, these are expressed in this example using property names.

```
<target name="package"
  <jar jarfile="${war-file}" basedir="${web-root}" />
</target>
```

In fact there is a special 'war' task in Ant, designed to create a web archive. However, it gives a warning if the 'web.xml' file is already in the 'WEB-INF' folder when the task executes, since it expects this file to be edited somewhere else. To avoid this warning, we simply use the 'jar' task instead, which achieves the same result. The 'war' task is useful if the source files for the web application are not already organized in the correct structure for web application deployment.

Deploying the WAR file

We can also use Ant to deploy the web application by copying the '.war' file to the server's deployment folder. Here, the 'copy-war' target uses the 'copy' task to do this. Note that we do not want to copy the WAR file unless we are sure that it has been rebuilt. To do this we can use the 'depends' attribute of the 'target' element. If a target depends on another target, then Ant will execute the other target first. In this example, the 'copy-war' target depends on the 'package' target:

```
<target name="copy-war" depends="package">
  <copy file="${war-file}" todir="${tomcat-deploy}" />
</target>
```

The effect of this 'depends' attribute is that each time we run Ant with the 'build.xml' file using the default target ('copy-war'), the 'package' target is executed first, followed by the 'copy-war' target. Here is the complete build.xml file:

```
<?xml version="1.0"?>
<project name="webhomecover" default="copy-war" basedir=".">

  <!-- source code directories -->
  <property name="root" value=".\" />

  <!-- web application name -->
  <property name="webapp" value="webhomecover" />

  <!-- war file assembly directory -->
  <property name="web-root" value="${root}\${webapp}" />

  <!-- target war file -->
  <property name="war-file" value="${root}\${webapp}.war" />

  <!-- Tomcat home -->
  <property name="tomcat-home" value="d:\Tomcat 6" />
```

```
<!-- Tomcat deployment directory -->
<property name="tomcat-deploy" value="${tomcat-home}\webapps" />

<!-- build the war file -->
<target name="package">
  <jar jarfile="${war-file}"
    basedir="${web-root}" />
</target>

<!-- copy the war file to the Tomcat server -->
<target name="copy-war" depends="package">
  <copy file="${war-file}" todir="${tomcat-deploy}" />
</target>

</project>
```

 NOTE The folder separator character in an Ant build script can be either the forward slash or the backslash. Both are equally acceptable.

Because 'build.xml' is the default file name that Ant looks for in the current folder, running the Ant batch file automatically processes this file using the default target ('copy-war'). You should see output similar to this:

```
Buildfile: build.xml

package:
     [jar] Building jar: D:\webappsbook\version3ant\
webhomecover.war

deploy:
     [copy] Copying 1 file to C:\Tomcat 5.5\webapps

BUILD SUCCESSFUL
Total time: 0 seconds
```

You can see from this output that the war file is built, and then it is deployed to the server. Since this build script hot deploys to Tomcat, you should find that your web application has been rebuilt and redeployed.

To deploy to JBoss, all you would need to do is to change the server's home folder and the path to the deployment directory. Alternatively we could use the same build file to deploy to either server by adding the following tasks for JBoss:

```
<!-- JBoss home -->
<property name="jboss-home" value="c:\jboss" />

<!-- JBoss deployment directory -->
<property name="jboss-deploy"
  value="${jboss-home}\server\default\deploy" />
```

```
<!-- copy the war file to the JBoss server -->
<target name="jboss-copy-war" depends="package">
  <copy file="${war-file}" todir="${jboss-deploy}" />
</target>
```

To deploy to JBoss using these additional targets, you need to specify a non-default target, in this case 'jboss-copy-war', when invoking Ant:

```
ant jboss-copy-war
```

This will deploy the WAR file to the JBoss deployment folder.

9.9 The Tomcat Web Application Manager

 NOTE This section does not apply to JBoss deployment, since JBoss has a different set of server management tools.

The Tomcat 'manager' is a pre-built web application included in the Tomcat installation, but not automatically enabled. It provides us with the ability to manage the web applications deployed to the server, either through a browser or by running special Ant tasks. Although our deployment strategy of copying the WAR file to the 'webapps' folder is perfectly workable, it is useful to know how to use the manager application, particularly if you are going to deploy multiple web applications onto the same server.

In earlier versions of Tomcat, hot deployment did not work particularly well, and in fact the Tomcat manager was a very necessary deployment tool. Since version 6.0, hot deployment in Tomcat has become more reliable, so knowledge of the manager application is not quite so essential. However it is still useful to have some familiarity with it, and configuring it will give us a little insight into the Tomcat security realm.

Enabling the Tomcat Web Application Manager

To enable the manager application we need to add a user in the 'manager' role to the XML file that Tomcat uses by default for its security roles. This file is called 'tomcat-users.xml' and can be found in the 'conf' folder, which is in the root of your Tomcat installation. The default file should look something like the one below, with no users or roles defined.

```
<?xml version='1.0' encoding='utf-8'?>
<tomcat-users>
</tomcat-users>
```

 NOTE The Windows installer version of Tomcat adds some default roles and users to this file.

To enable the manager application, we have to set up a 'manager' security role and a user who is given that role. To include the 'manager' role, we need to add a 'role' element, and set its 'rolename' attribute to 'manager':

```
<role rolename="manager"/>
```

For our example, we assume a user with the name 'webhomecover' who will have the manager role. To keep things simple (if rather insecure) we also use 'webhomecover' as the password. The 'user' element includes 'username' and 'password' attributes, and a 'roles' attribute, which must include 'manager' (though multiple roles are not necessary here, more than one role can be included, separated by commas):

```
<user username="webhomecover" password="webhomecover"
roles="manager"/>
```

Here is the complete 'tomcat-users.xml' file with the necessary role and user added.

```
<?xml version='1.0' encoding='utf-8'?>
<tomcat-users>
  <role rolename="manager"/>
  <user username="webhomecover" password="webhomecover"
    roles="manager"/>
</tomcat-users>
```

Now it should be possible to log into the manager application using 'webhomecover' as the user ID and password.

Running the Tomcat Web Application Manager

If Tomcat is already running, you will need to stop it and restart it so that it reads the updated XML file. When the server is running, test that the manager application is now available by typing the following URI into a browser (assuming the HTTP port has been changed to '80'):

```
http://localhost/manager/list
```

Because the manager application uses role-based security, you will be required to log in as a user in the 'manager' role. Figure 9.11 shows the login dialog that will appear. Use the 'webhomecover' user to log in, with the 'webhomecover' password.

Following a successful login, a list of currently running Web applications will be displayed, for example:

```
OK - Listed applications for virtual host localhost
/:running:0:ROOT
/manager:running:1:manager
/docs:running:0:docs
/examples:running:0:examples
/host-manager:running:0:host-manager
/webhomecover:running:0:webhomecover
```

FIGURE 9.11 Logging into the Tomcat Web Application Manager as a user in the 'manager' role

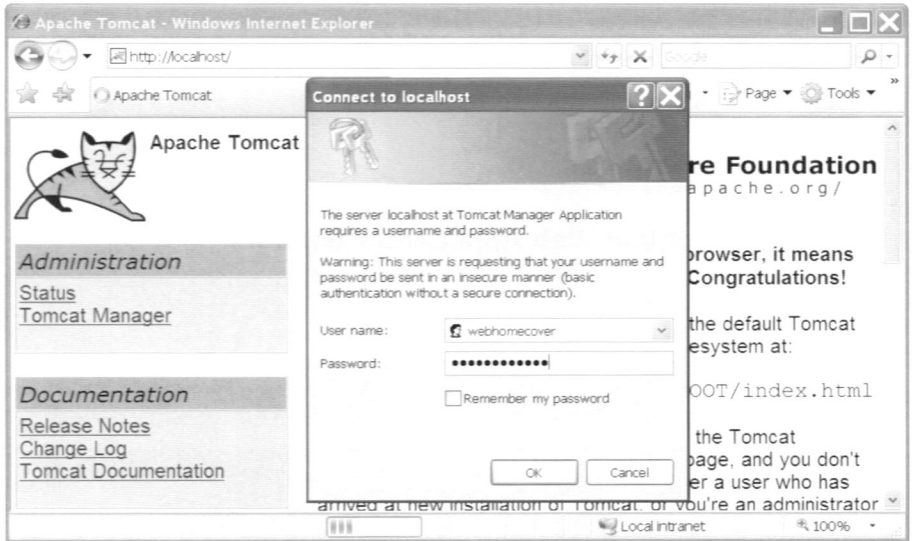

FIGURE 9.12 The link to the Tomcat Manager application on the Tomcat home page

You can also access the manager application by loading the Tomcat default web application at

```
http://localhost
```

You should see a link to the Tomcat Manager on the left of the page (Figure 9.12). Clicking on this link will take you to the 'manager' web page where you can list, deploy, start, stop, reload or undeploy your applications. Once again you will need to login (unless a previous login has not yet expired).

Figure 9.13 shows the Tomcat Web Application Manager page that is displayed following a successful login.

FIGURE 9.13   The Tomcat Web Application Manager page

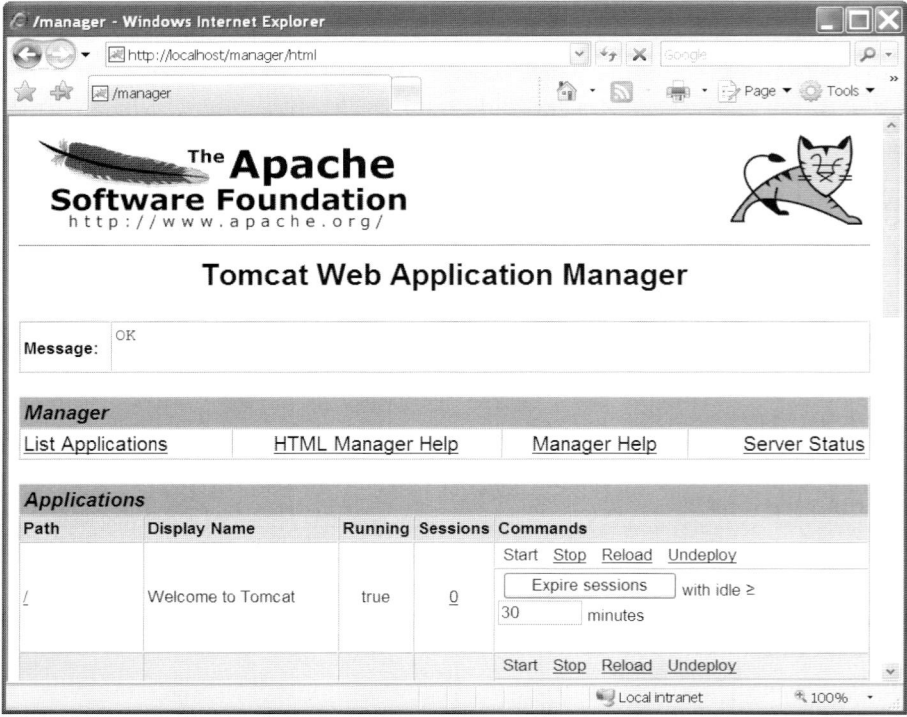

Connecting to the Tomcat Web Application Manager remotely

Once the manager application is enabled with a username given the manager role, we can use it remotely from Ant to manage web application deployment. To do this, we need to add quite a few new entries to our 'build.xml' file, but these will be useful for future management of our web applications. The first thing we need to add is a series of new properties that will be used in the new targets that will be added to the build file. These properties include the server's library folder, the server's domain ('localhost' in our example), the URL of the Tomcat manager application and the username and password of the Tomcat user with the manager role ('webhomecover' in both cases):

```
<!-- Tomcat property definitions -->
<property name="tomcat-lib" value="${tomcat-home}\lib" />
<property name="tomcat-server" value="localhost" />
<property name="tomcat-manager-url"
  value="http://${tomcat-server}/manager" />
<property name="tomcat-username" value="webhomecover" />
<property name="tomcat-password" value="webhomecover" />
```

The 'tomcat-home' property, which we already had in the previous version of build.xml, will also be useful here, as will the 'webapp' and 'war-file' properties.

Including the Tomcat Ant tasks

Once we have set up these properties they can be used in later parts of the file. The Ant tasks used to manage Tomcat are not part of the standard Ant installation but in fact are included with Tomcat. Therefore we need to ensure that the necessary Tomcat files are included in the classpath used by the build file. The following 'path' element is used to set up a classpath that includes the JAR files in both Tomcat's 'lib' folder and its 'bin' folder. The Tomcat manager uses JAR files from both of these folders.

```
<!-- set up a classpath to the server's 'jar' files -->
<path id="project-classpath">
  <fileset dir="${tomcat-lib}">
    <include name="*.jar/" />
  </fileset>
  <fileset dir="${tomcat-home}\bin">
    <include name="*.jar/" />
  </fileset>
</path>
```

Another important element in the build file is the 'taskdef' that specifies the Ant tasks that can be used with the Tomcat manager and the Java classes that implement these tasks (included in the provided classpath).

```
<!-- add the 'catalina ant' tasks using the classpath -->
<taskdef resource="org/apache/catalina/ant/catalina.tasks"
  classpathref="project-classpath" />
```

There are ten Catalina tasks listed in the 'catalina.tasks' file, of which we will be using six in our build file; 'deploy', 'list', 'reload', 'start', 'stop' and 'undeploy'. To avoid confusion, we will use the same names for our Ant targets as the Catalina tasks they invoke. You can see from the following Ant targets that they all look very similar. All require the name of the task, the URI of the manager application, along with the name and password of a user in the manager role, and the name of the web application (as used in the URI). In addition, the 'deploy' task requires the name of the WAR file that is to be deployed. The 'list' task (which we saw being used earlier via a browser) does not require an application name since it lists all current applications.

```
<!-- targets for the Tomcat manager -->

<target name="deploy" description="Install application in Tomcat">
  <deploy url="${tomcat-manager-url}"
    username="${tomcat-username}"
    password="${tomcat-password}"
    path="/${webapp}"
    war="${war-file}" />
</target>

<target name="undeploy" description="Remove application from Tomcat">
  <undeploy url="${tomcat-manager-url}"
    username="${tomcat-username}"
    password="${tomcat-password}"
```

```
          path="/${webapp}"/>
    </target>

    <target name="reload" description="Reload application in Tomcat">
      <reload url="${tomcat-manager-url}"
        username="${tomcat-username}"
        password="${tomcat-password}"
        path="/${webapp}"/>
    </target>

    <target name="start" description="Start Tomcat application">
      <start url="${tomcat-manager-url}"
        username="${tomcat-username}"
        password="${tomcat-password}"
        path="/${webapp}"/>
    </target>

    <target name="stop" description="Stop Tomcat application">
      <stop url="${tomcat-manager-url}"
        username="${tomcat-username}"
        password="${tomcat-password}"
        path="/${webapp}"/>
    </target>

    <target name="list" description="List Tomcat applications">
      <list url="${tomcat-manager-url}"
        username="${tomcat-username}"
        password="${tomcat-password}"/>
    </target>
```

All of these targets should now be available to you when you run the Ant build file.

Exercises

9.1 Deploy the example web application onto the Tomcat server and test that it is working.

```
http://localhost:8080/webhomecover
```

a) Add a new 'index.htm' page to the context root.

b) Register it as the welcome file in 'web.xml'.

c) Rebuild and redeploy the web application to the server.

d) Use a browser to connect to your application.

9.2 Try out all the new tasks from your Ant build file. Remember that the default task is still 'copy-war', so simply typing 'ant' on the command line will not invoke any of our Tomcat manager tasks. To run other Ant tasks, simply add the name after 'ant' on the command line, For example, to undeploy the application (which removes the expanded folders for the application from the 'webapps' folder) type:

```
ant undeploy
```

Then you should be able to deploy the application successfully. Try out the other tasks: start, stop, reload and list.

You will find that some tasks may fail depending on the current state of the application. For example, if you try to run the 'deploy' task when the application has already been deployed then you will get an error message. Another potential source of error is that the manager tasks can only work if Tomcat is running. If Tomcat is stopped then all of these tasks will return error messages because they cannot connect to the manager application on the server.

9.3 Add the following 'redeploy' target to your Ant build file. It uses the 'antcall' element, which is able to invoke other Ant targets. In this case it first calls 'undeploy' and then calls 'deploy' If you use this task when you update anything in your application it will ensure that the war file is rebuilt and redeployed without error. Note that it depends on the 'package' task, so that it will always deploy a rebuilt war file.

```
<target name="redeploy" description="Redeploy application"
depends="package">
   <antcall target="undeploy" />
   <antcall target="deploy" />
</target>
```

9.4 When running on Windows, Ant can be used to start or stop Tomcat using the following targets, which use the Windows 'cmd.exe' program to run the 'startup' and 'shutdown' batch files. The 'spawn' attribute is necessary to run the batch file in another process, because otherwise the Ant script will freeze once the server has started. To make this work, you will also need to set the 'CATALINA_HOME' environment variable to point to the Tomcat installation folder. This is because when the 'startup.bat' script is run, Tomcat guesses that 'CATALINA_HOME' is the current folder. This is fine as long as we run the script from the 'bin' folder of Tomcat, but when we run it from somewhere else, like this, we have to specify a value for 'CATALINA_HOME'.

```
<target name="starttc">
  <exec executable="cmd" spawn="true">
    <arg value="/c"/>
    <arg value="${tomcat-home}\bin\startup.bat"/>
  </exec>
</target>

<target name="stoptc">
  <exec executable="cmd" spawn="true">
    <arg value="/c"/>
    <arg value="${tomcat-home}\bin\shutdown.bat"/>
  </exec>
</target>
```

Add these two targets to your Ant build script, and test that they start and stop Tomcat correctly.

SUMMARY

In this chapter, we introduced the Tomcat Java web application server, both as a standalone application and as part of the JBoss application server. We saw how a Java web application has to be structured in order to include both public content and configuration files, and how a web application in a 'war' archive can be deployed to a server. We also explored how an enterprise archive can be used to deploy web applications to servers, such as JBoss, that support the full Java EE specification. We introduced the Ant build tool as a way of automating the build and deploy process of a web application, and also introduced the Tomcat Web Application Manager, which can help us to manage web applications running in a standalone instance of Tomcat. At the end of the chapter, we integrated Ant and the Tomcat Web Application Manager by using some special Ant tasks that are provided with Tomcat.

References and further reading

Apache Ant Project (2007) *Ant*. http://ant.apache.org/
Apache HTTP (2007) *Apache HTTP Server Project*. http://httpd.apache.org/
Apache Software Foundation (2007) *Apache Tomcat*. http://tomcat.apache.org/
JBoss (2007) *JBoss Application Server*. http://www.jboss.org/products/jbossas
Kunze, M. (1998) Let There be Light – LAMP: Freeware Web Publishing System with Database Support. *c't Magazine*, December 1998, p. 230, http://www.heise.de/ct/english/98/12/230/

CHAPTER 10

Using Java for Dynamic Content

LEARNING OBJECTIVES

- **To understand JSP Model 1 and Model 2 architectures**

- **To create dynamic content using servlets and JavaServer Pages (JSPs)**

- **To use JavaBeans within the view and controller layers of a web application**

- **To manage the routing of a webflow**

- **To maintain user sessions**

- **To use tags from the JSP Standard Tag Library (JSTL)**

- **To create XML JSP (JSPX) pages**

INTRODUCTION

So far in this book, we have seen how to use static pages to provide web-based content to client browsers. We have seen some aspects of how dynamic content might be provided when XSLT transformations have been used to provide different views of an XML document. However, the underlying XML document has been static content stored in a file, and we have not seen a way of dynamically applying the XSL Transformation to an XML document outside a tool such as XML Spy, since using the 'link' element in an XHTML page only provides a fixed reference to a single transformation. JavaScript enables us to provide some dynamic behavior within the browser, but only in the context of manipulating the DOM of static pages. In order to provide true dynamic content in a web application, we have to use some kind of programming language on the server that is able to generate web pages on the fly by building XHTML pages and applying XSL transformations to XML documents at run time. In this book, our language of choice is Java, and in this chapter we explore some aspects of the design of Java web applications using the 'Model 1' and 'Model 2' architectures. We also see how to encapsulate our underlying model in JavaBeans, plug these JavaBeans into our JSP pages and manage user sessions over multiple request–response cycles.

10.1 Java on the server

There are many languages that can be used to build distributed systems, but few have the range of facilities offered by Java. It provides services for many types of distribution, using several different communications protocols, and includes Application Programming Interfaces (APIs) for developing code in any layer of an n-tier architecture. Java began as an object-oriented programming language with some supporting tools, such as the *javac* compiler and the *javadoc* documentation generator. Associated with these was a set of APIs for specific types of programming, for example, Java Database Connectivity (JDBC) for database access. As Java developed, there was a proliferation of ever more specialized APIs, so that with the arrival of the Java 2 platform in 1999, Java was divided into three editions: Standard, Micro and Enterprise. For some years these were known as the Java 2 Standard Edition (J2SE), Java 2 Micro Edition (J2ME) and Java 2 Enterprise Edition (J2EE). When Java Platform 5.0 was released in 2004, however, the '2' was dropped from these titles and they have since been referred to as Java SE, Java ME and Java EE.

Java Standard Edition (Java SE)

Many Java programs are not distributed at all, and consist of a single local application running on one machine. We may also want to build a Java-based two-tier system, with a Java application accessing a database. These types of application are possible with the Java Standard Edition, also known as the Java Development Kit (JDK) or more accurately the Java Software Development Kit (Java SDK). This comprises the core Java functionality with all the libraries (APIs) and tools necessary for developing stand-alone desktop applications. The standard APIs cover fundamental aspects of programming such as mathematical functions, string (text) manipulation, calendar and date manipulation, formatting of numbers, currencies and dates, stream input and output (e.g. flat files) and graphical user interfaces (GUIs). In addition, with each new version of the Java SDK, new APIs are added.

Java Micro Edition (Java ME)

This comprises the necessary core libraries and tools for writing Java for embedded systems and other small footprint platforms, along with some specialized libraries for specific types of device such as mobile phones.

Java Enterprise Edition (Java EE)

This is the focus of this chapter, and comprises the core parts of the standard edition plus many additional APIs that enable us to write enterprise-level software. This edition addresses all aspects of developing enterprise-level systems, including distribution, security, transactions and persistence. In this book we look in detail at what Java EE has to offer the web application developer. Java EE is an application development platform designed to provide services that work across the Internet and the worldwide web. It consists of many standard APIs that are implemented by both commercial vendors and open-source projects. The core components of Java EE systems are servlets, JavaServer Pages (JSPs) and Enterprise JavaBeans (EJB), though there are many other aspects to the enterprise software architectures supported by this edition.

Java EE web components

In this book, we explore those aspects of Java EE that relate to the development of web applications. At the client-facing presentation layer, we primarily have servlets and JSPs to service web-based clients. This chapter mostly focuses on JSPs, but provides a brief introduction to servlets and also discusses the relationship between servlets and JSPs. In this layer, we also have JavaBeans that can be used to provide a link with the underlying model that contains the application functionality of our systems. These components in the model are supported by other Java APIs such as extensions to JDBC for enterprise-level database access. To look up supporting resources, such as the databases that our web application connects to, a naming system is required to manage the lookup between names and resources. Java EE systems use the Java Naming and Directory Interface (JNDI) to do this (Figure 10.1).

10.2 Model–view–controller (MVC) architecture

Model–view–controller (MVC) is a well-known design pattern that was first formalized as part of the Smalltalk programming language. The original idea was that a single data model (for example, information about the state of a virtual airplane in a flight simulator) can be simultaneously viewed in different ways in different concurrent windows (e.g. a cockpit view, a view from above the plane and a radar view). In addition, the user's control of the system (for example, using the flight controls in the cockpit) will update the underlying model, changes which should then be seen automatically in the other views. For example, if the flight controls in the cockpit view are used to turn the aircraft to the left, then not only will the cockpit view change but so will the other views (Figure 10.2).

The MVC architecture explicitly separates the roles of the model (the underlying data), the view (what is presented to the user) and the controller (the handling component that manages user interaction and triggers appropriate updates to the model). In the context of a web application, we have a slightly different perspective on what is meant by multiple

FIGURE 10.1   The core components of Java EE web applications

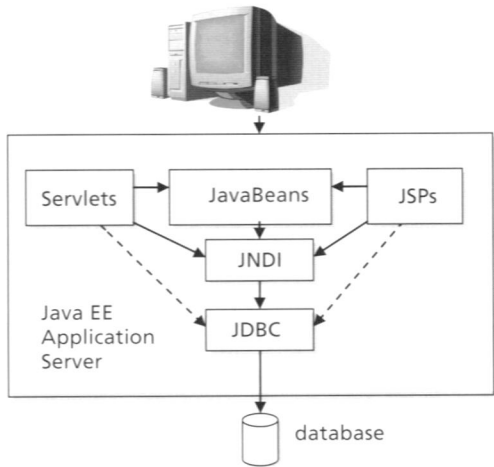

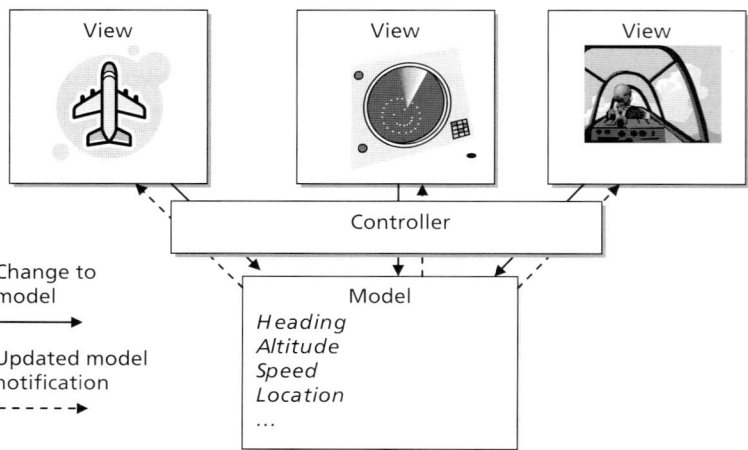

FIGURE 10.2 Model–view–controller (MVC) interactions in a flight simulator

views, because instead of having multiple views on a single screen, the multiple views are different clients with separate browsers looking at the same application in different ways. For example, if there are many people shopping on-line, each one may be looking at a different part of the catalog, but the underlying model (the catalog itself) is the same for all of these views. Updates to the model (e.g. a shopper buying an item) need to be reflected in all the views, so that what the users see in terms of product availability is always as up to date as possible. In the following sections, we look at two architectures for web applications, *Model 1* and *Model 2*, and see how they relate to the MVC pattern.

Much of the server-side development introduced in this chapter uses JavaServer Pages (JSPs) to generate dynamic content. In the original JSP specification (version 0.92), Model 1 and Model 2 architectures were introduced as two different approaches to building the view and controller layers of web applications.

Simply put, in a Model 1 architecture, a single server-side component processes both the HTTP request and the HTTP response. In contrast, in a Model 2 architecture, one server-side component processes the request and another processes the response. This separation of concerns makes the Model 2 approach more scalable and flexible, but Model 1 is suitable for simple applications. Version 1.1 of the JSP specification chose to describe a slightly different view of these approaches, describing the two components of the Model 2 architecture as the 'front component' and the 'presentation component'.

Although this type of design discussion was removed from JSP specification documents after version 1.1, the important architectural aspects have been taken up in other publications, notably by Seshadri (1999) and Mahmoud (2003). It is important to note that one reason for this separation is that these models are not restricted to JSP technologies, but in fact have more general application in terms of designing web applications. Even within Java implementations, there are variations in how these architectures might be built, for example the 'front component' in a Model 2 architecture can be either a JSP or a servlet. The Model 2 architecture has been applied across many web applications and frameworks, including the 'Struts' framework (Chapter 15) where the front component is a servlet, not a JSP. Figure 10.3 summarizes the main differences between the Model 1 and Model 2 approaches to web application design.

FIGURE 10.3   Model 1 and Model 2 compared

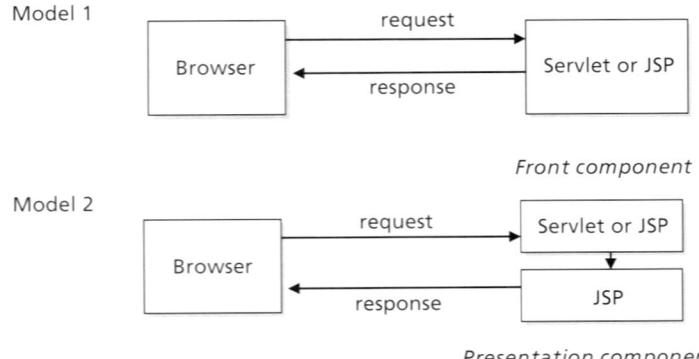

Model 1

Model 2

Front component

Presentation component

10.3 JSP Model 1 architecture

We begin the examples in this chapter by looking at an implementation of a Model 1 architecture using a servlet. Servlets were the first web application components to be specified by Java standards, with the first servlet specification being published in 1996. A servlet is a server-side Java program that is managed by a *servlet container*. A servlet container (sometimes called a *servlet engine*) manages the lifecycle of the servlets and handles all the client threads that access them. The basic role of a servlet is to receive a request from a remote client, process it and return a response. In a web-based system, we would expect to receive an HTTP request and to send back an HTTP response. In most server configurations, for purposes of efficiency, there is a single instance of each servlet class in the system, with that single instance servicing multiple client threads. This means that servlets cannot have client-specific attributes, since all clients share the same servlet.

The Java Enterprise Edition provides two servlet-related packages, 'javax.servlet' and 'javax.servlet.http'. Servlets are intended to provide a generic mechanism for request–response style programming over the Internet, using any protocol. The generic interfaces and classes that support this style of programming are in the 'javax.servlet' package. However, the vast majority of servlet implementations use HTTP as their communications protocol, so a number of special servlet interfaces and classes for HTTP are provided in the 'javax.servlet.http' package.

Writing a servlet that can respond to HTTP requests is simple, since Java EE includes an HttpServlet class (in the 'javax.servlet.http' package) that does much of the work for us. All we need to do is to write a subclass of HttpServlet and provide implementations of any methods that we want to override. The HttpServlet class includes a method called 'service' that is always the first method that is called when a request is made on a servlet. Although it is possible to override this method so that all types of request get exactly the same response, it is usual to retain its default behavior. The 'service' method's default implementation is to forward the request to another method that matches the type of HTTP request. These methods have to be implemented by the servlet developer, and have names that match the type of HTTP request that they process, preceded by 'do'. For example the method that handles 'get' requests is called 'doGet', while the method that handles 'post' requests is called 'doPost'. The developer is not required to implement all (or indeed any) of these methods. If there is no matching method implemented for a particular request type then the 'service' method will return HTTP error 405 (method not supported).

Creating a servlet

In our first servlet, we implement a 'doGet' method to respond to HTTP 'get' requests. The 'doGet' method has the following signature (this will look a bit tidier if we import various classes first):

```
public void doGet
    (javax.servlet.http.HttpServletRequest request,
    javax.servlet.http.HttpServletResponse response)
    throws javax.servlet.ServletException, java.io.IOException
```

In this method, we can gather information about the client's HTTP request from the HttpServletRequest parameter and send a response back to the same client using the HttpServletResponse parameter. This enables us to create dynamic content, since we can use Java to programmatically build an HTML page that contains data generated on the fly, which may include client-specific information.

In the example that follows, we create an HTTP servlet that responds to a 'get' request by dynamically sending an HTML page back to the client. This page will display the details of the client's browser type, using information that is available in the 'User-Agent' field of the HTTP request header.

Servlet classes have a typical set of imports, shown below. Generic servlet classes (such as ServletException) are in the 'javax.servlet' package, while classes specific to writing HTTP servlets are in 'javax.servlet.http'. In addition, the 'java.io' package includes the IOException and PrintWriter classes (a PrintWriter is used to write the page content to the HTTP response).

```
import javax.servlet.ServletException;
import javax.servlet.http.HttpServlet;
import javax.servlet.http.HttpServletRequest;
import javax.servlet.http.HttpServletResponse;
import java.io.IOException;
import java.io.PrintWriter;
```

The servlet itself should be a subclass of 'HttpServlet', enabling it to inherit the necessary set of methods. In this example, the servlet is called 'UserAgentServlet':

```
public class UserAgentServlet extends HttpServlet
```

The first thing we should do in the body of the 'doGet' method is to set the content type of the response we are sending back to the browser, in this case to 'text/html'. The HttpServletResponse has a 'setContentType' method to do this:

```
response.setContentType("text/html");
```

We then use the 'getWriter' method of the HttpServletResponse to get an instance of a PrintWriter:

```
PrintWriter out = response.getWriter();
```

Now we can write HTML content to the response. This is a rather tedious way of constructing a page (for example writing out the XHTML doctype requires several uses of the \" escape character to embed speech marks into the output), but serves as a useful example of how servlets can generate dynamic content. Note how the HTML markup is written using 'out.print' or 'out.println', just like using 'System.out' for standard output.

```
out.println("<!DOCTYPE html PUBLIC \"-//W3C//DTD XHTML 1.1//EN\"");
out.println(" \"http://www.w3.org/TR/xhtml11/DTD/xhtml11.dtd\">");
out.println("<html>");
```

Using 'println' does not force a line feed in the resulting HTML page; you have to use HTML elements to do this. However the advantage of using 'println' over 'print' is that it makes the resulting HTML page source easier to read and therefore easier to debug.

The most important aspect of this servlet example is that it shows how HTML and Java can be combined to produce dynamic content. Here, we use the 'getHeader' method of the HttpServletRequest object (passed to the 'doGet' method as a parameter). This method returns the value of the named header field as a String. This line of code stores the value of the header's 'User-Agent' field in a string called 'userAgent':

```
String userAgent = request.getHeader("User-Agent");
```

This string can then be combined with HTML to produced dynamic content:

```
out.println("Your browser sent the following header: <strong>" +
userAgent + "</strong>");
```

Note how we combine HTML text and tags with a Java variable to send the content to the response. This is the complete UserAgentServlet class:

```
package com.webhomecover.servlet;
import javax.servlet.ServletException;
import javax.servlet.http.HttpServlet;
import javax.servlet.http.HttpServletRequest;
import javax.servlet.http.HttpServletResponse;
import java.io.IOException;
import java.io.PrintWriter;

public class UserAgentServlet extends HttpServlet
{

public void doGet(HttpServletRequest request,
                  HttpServletResponse response)
   throws ServletException, IOException
{
// set the content type of the response
   response.setContentType("text/html");
// get a PrintWriter from the response object
   PrintWriter out = response.getWriter();
//get the user agent header from the request
   String userAgent = request.getHeader("User-Agent");
// write out the HTML page
   out.println("<!DOCTYPE html PUBLIC \"-//W3C//DTD XHTML 1.1//EN\"");
```

```
    out.println("  \"http://www.w3.org/TR/xhtml11/DTD/xhtml11.dtd\">");
    out.println("<html>");
    out.println("<head><title>User Agent Servlet</title></head>");
    out.println("<body><div>");
// this line includes the dynamic content
    out.println("Your browser sent the following header: <strong>"
       + userAgent + "</strong>");
    out.println("</div></body>");
    out.println("</html>");
// close the output stream
    out.close();
  }
}
```

Deploying a servlet

To deploy a servlet within a web application, we must provide a URL that clients can use to invoke the servlet. We do this in the 'web.xml' deployment descriptor, using the following tags, which appear immediately after the opening 'web-app' tag:

```
<servlet>
   <servlet-name>UserAgentServlet</servlet-name>
   <servlet-class>
    com.webhomecover.servlet.UserAgentServlet
   </servlet-class>
</servlet>

<servlet-mapping>
   <servlet-name>UserAgentServlet</servlet-name>
   <url-pattern>/useragent</url-pattern>
</servlet-mapping>
```

The 'servlet-name' element serves as a cross-reference between the 'servlet' and 'servlet-mapping' elements. This is necessary since a single web application can contain many servlets, and we need to provide each one with a unique name. The 'servlet' tag maps this servlet's name to the fully qualified class name of the compiled servlet, but this is not used directly by clients. They must invoke the servlet using a URL pattern, which in this example is '/useragent'. Clients can invoke the servlet by using this pattern as the resource name, e.g.

```
http://localhost/webhomecover/useragent
```

 NOTE If there are multiple servlets in a Web application, all the 'servlet' elements appear first in 'web.xml', followed by all the 'servlet-mapping' elements.

Including the Java compiler in an Ant script

Having added a Java servlet to our web application, we need to modify the Ant script we introduced in Chapter 9 to include a task that compiles the servlet and puts it into the correct folder for deployment within the web application. The first thing we have to add is a property that refers to the name of the folder containing the source code. In the following examples, we assume that all Java source code is in a folder called 'java', located under the root of our current build folder. We also need to specify the destination folder for the compiled byte code. In Java web applications this must be a special folder called 'classes' that needs to be located within the 'WEB-INF' folder. (You will need to manually create this folder before running the modified Ant script.) Here are property entries for the two folders, with the name 'java-source' pointing to the 'java' folder, and the name 'java-build' pointing to the 'WEB-INF\classes' folder:

```
<!-- source folder for Java code -->
<property name="java-source" value="${root}\java" />

<!-- destination folder for compiled Java bytecode -->
<property name="java-build" value="${web-root}\WEB-INF\classes" />
```

The task that compiles Java code in Ant is called, unsurprisingly, 'javac', and requires the source and destination directories to be provided as attributes. An additional element can be used to specify the classpath. The various Java EE servlet classes required for compilation can be found in JAR files in the server's 'lib' folder. Fortunately, we have already created a 'path' element for use with the Tomcat manager application, which includes all the JAR files in this folder. Therefore we can use the same classpath ('project-classpath') to compile our servlets (make sure that the 'compile' task appears after the 'path' element in the 'build.xml' file).

```
<!-- Compile the java code from source to build folders -->
<target name="compile">
  <javac srcdir="${java-source}" destdir="${java-build}">
    <classpath refid="project-classpath"/>
  </javac>
</target>
```

When the 'compile' target runs, it automatically builds the necessary folders for the package structure beneath the destination directory ('WEB-INF\classes'). Note that the source and destination directories are expressed in this target using the property names we have already defined. Since we do not want to build the WAR file unless we are sure that the Java class files are up to date, we need to add a 'depends' attribute to the 'package' target, so that the 'compile' target always precedes it:

```
<target name="package" depends="compile">
  <jar jarfile="${war-file}" basedir="${web-root}" />
</target>
```

The rest of the 'build.xml' file remains unchanged. When running the build file, you should see output similar to this:

```
C:\Example 10-1 Servlet>ant
Buildfile: build.xml

compile:
[javac] Compiling 1 source file to C:\Example 10-1 Servlet\
webhomecover\WEB-INF\classes
```

```
package:
[jar] Building jar: C:\Example 10-1 Servlet\webhomecover.war

copy-war:
[copy] Copying 1 file to C:\Tomcat 6\webapps

BUILD SUCCESSFUL
Total time: 3 seconds
```

You can see from this output that the servlet is compiled first, then the war file is built, and finally the war file is deployed to the server. Figure 10.4 shows the result of connecting to the servlet when using Internet Explorer 7, Mozilla Firefox 2 and Opera 9. We can see that a dynamic page is generated that is specific to the client browser.

Servlets are very useful components of web applications, but they are more suited to being 'front components' (i.e. processing the request) than they are at being 'presentation

FIGURE 10.4 The UserAgentServlet generating content for a) Internet Explorer 7, b) Mozilla Firefox 2 and c) Opera 9

(a)
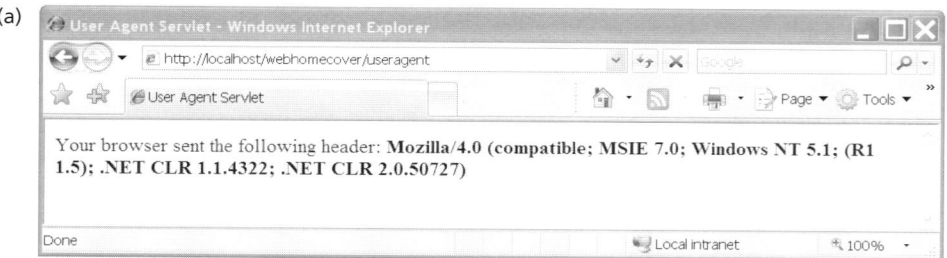

(b)
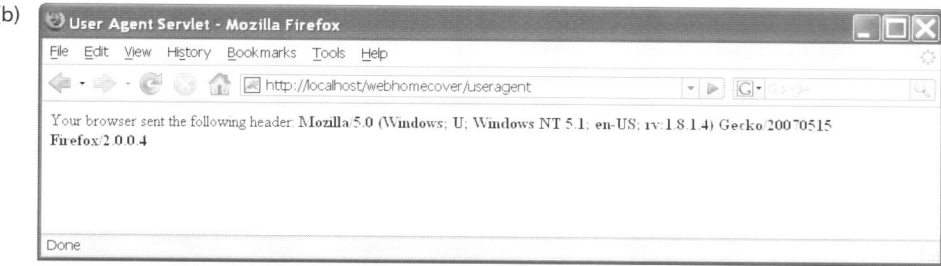

(c)
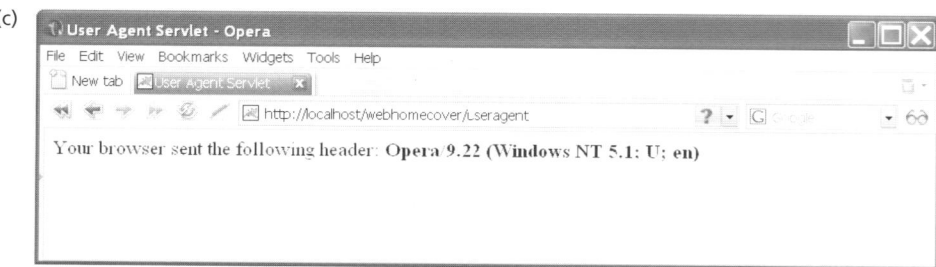

components' (i.e. generating the response). Manually writing out HTML tags, as we did in our servlet example, is very tedious, error-prone and hard to maintain. Because of this, JavaServer Pages (JSPs) were first introduced in 1999 as a way of overcoming the difficulty of generating mark-up using servlets. Whereas servlets are Java programs that can contain some code that generate mark-up, a JSP is a page of mark-up that can contain some Java programming elements. This makes them more suited to being presentation components than servlets, but they can also be used as front components. JSPs are converted into servlets by the application server's JSP engine, so in fact writing a JSP is just another way of writing a servlet, but in many ways JSPs are easier to write and maintain than servlets. In the next section, we introduce JSPs and implement a simple Model 1 architecture using a JSP.

10.4 Writing a JavaServer Page

A JavaServer Page is usually an (X)HTML page with some dynamic Java content embedded inside it, using special tags that are understood by a JSP compiler. The ways that Java content can be embedded using these tags are quite varied, so we look at a number of different techniques in this chapter. In addition, the JSP specification has evolved so that many of the JSP tags that enable dynamic content now come in two forms, the original syntax (similar to that used in Microsoft Active Server Pages) and one that is XML compliant. This is so that JSP pages can be treated as XML documents to make them compatible with other technologies such as XSLT.

In the main body of this chapter, we introduce the original syntax, which is still commonly used, while the XML syntax is introduced towards the end of the chapter. We could begin by writing a JSP from scratch, but it is quite informative to see how easy it is to take an existing static page and convert it into a JSP. Our starting point will be to take the current 'welcome.htm' page from the simple web application we developed in Chapter 9, and make it a JSP. We will then introduce some new pages to the web application to demonstrate dynamic content, using a number of different *JSP tags*. The first step is easily accomplished by simply changing the file extension, renaming the file from 'welcome.htm' to 'welcome.jsp'. The file does not even need to be moved from the document root of the web application. If you rebuild and deploy your application after renaming the file then you will find that the welcome page no longer loads automatically, because the 'welcome-file-list' entry in web.xml still refers to 'welcome.htm', which no longer exists. To make your JSP page appear, you will have to add the name of the page to the URI in the browser's address bar, i.e.

```
http://localhost/webhomecover/welcome.jsp
```

You will not notice any difference in the way the page appears, though you may find that it takes a while to load. This is because the server handles JSPs in a very different way from how it handles static content. Static pages are served directly from the web server (Coyote, if you are using Tomcat). In contrast, a JSP page is first converted into a Java servlet source file by the server's JSP engine (Jasper, in Tomcat), then the generated servlet is automatically compiled and run. As it runs, the generated servlet writes the XHTML content to the response (servlets are handled by Tomcat's servlet engine, Catalina). Because of this rather complex set of steps, the first time a JSP page is requested by a client it can take a while to load. After the first time, however, the compiled servlet is used directly so the page is sent to the response much more quickly.

We might well wonder at this stage what we have achieved, since the resulting page in the browser is the same as it was when it was provided by static XHTML. However, the reason for using JSPs is that are they are Java components, making it possible to insert dynamic Java content into the page when the JSP is transformed into a servlet. The JSP compiler is able to translate the content of special JSP tags in the page to the appropriate Java implementation, merging it with the code that generates the XHTML elements of the page.

Because a JSP is converted into a servlet in the server's JSP engine, it is the generated servlet that is actually used to generate the response. If you are using Tomcat, you can see the generated servlet source code in the following folder:

```
Tomcat_home\work\Catalina\localhost\webhomecover\org\apache\jsp
```

If you are using JBoss, the folder is:

```
jboss_home\server\default\work\jboss.web\localhost\webhomecover\
org\apache\jsp
```

These servlets do not contain code designed for readability, since they are only for processing by the server, but you should be able to see some similarities with our own servlet example in terms of the way that the page is generated.

Making the JSP the welcome file

Having renamed 'welcome.htm' to 'welcome.jsp', the web server can no longer find the default welcome page. To fix this problem, we can edit the 'web.xml' deployment descriptor so that it lists 'welcome.jsp' as the default welcome file, like this

```
<welcome-file-list>
   <welcome-file>welcome.jsp</welcome-file>
</welcome-file-list>
```

If you make these changes, then rebuild and redeploy your web application, you should find that the welcome page behaves as it did before, and is loaded automatically when we browse to the web application URL:

```
http://localhost/webhomecover
```

Writing JSP expressions

The next step is to take advantage of having a JSP instead of a static page by adding some dynamic content, so we can see some reward for making the change from static XHTML. There are many different ways to add dynamic content to a JSP, but we will begin by using an example of a *JSP expression*. An expression contains some Java code to provide a value that can be written to the HTTP response. This value can come from anything that can be converted to a String in Java, which includes all primitives and objects. In fact the only thing that cannot be put into an expression is a call to a method that has a *void* return value, and therefore does not provide a value to be converted to a String. The other thing to be careful about is that although all objects in Java can be converted into Strings, only those that provide useful implementations of the 'toString' method will give helpful information on a JSP page. Those that use the default Object version of 'toString' will only display their class name and hash code.

The 'java.util.Date' class has a 'toString' method that displays some useful data about the date and time of its creation, so we will start by using that in an expression. JSP expressions have the following syntax:

```
<%=value %>
```

You will see from this example and the others that follow that several JSP tags are surrounded by angle brackets and percentage characters.

Inside the tag we must provide a Java value or a method call that returns a value. For example, we can create a new 'java.util.Date' object, which the expression will convert to a String for display on the page:

```
<%=new java.util.Date() %>
```

Although this is a fragment of Java code, when used in a JSP expression it does not finish with a semicolon, as it would if it were part of a normal Java source file. Here is a complete JSP page that generates valid XHTML and includes the JSP expression to display the date and time.

```
<?xml version="1.0"?>
<!DOCTYPE html PUBLIC
   "-//W3C//DTD XHTML 1.1//EN"
   "http://www.w3.org/TR/xhtml11/DTD/xhtml11.dtd">
<html xmlns="http://www.w3.org/1999/xhtml" xml:lang="en">
   <head>
      <title>Current Date and Time</title>
   </head>
   <body>
   <!-- File: datetime.jsp -->
      <p>
      Today's date is
      <%=new java.util.Date() %>
      </p>
   </body>
</html>
```

To deploy this JSP to the server, simply place the JSP file in the document root of your web application and rebuild and redeploy the application with Ant. You can access the page by adding its name to the URI of the Web application, as we did for the 'welcome.jsp' page, i.e.

```
http://localhost/webhomecover/datetime.jsp
```

Figure 10.5 shows the JSP page in Internet Explorer 7.

You can see that the date being displayed is dynamic, because every time you refresh the page in the browser, the time changes. Because the page is regenerated on the server each time it is requested, the expression creates a new 'Date' object and the time of creation gets updated.

JSP directives

In the previous example, we referred to the 'java.util.Date' class using its full name, including the package name. In Java code, we frequently use import statements to enable us to refer

FIGURE 10.5 The JSP page displayed in Internet Explorer 7

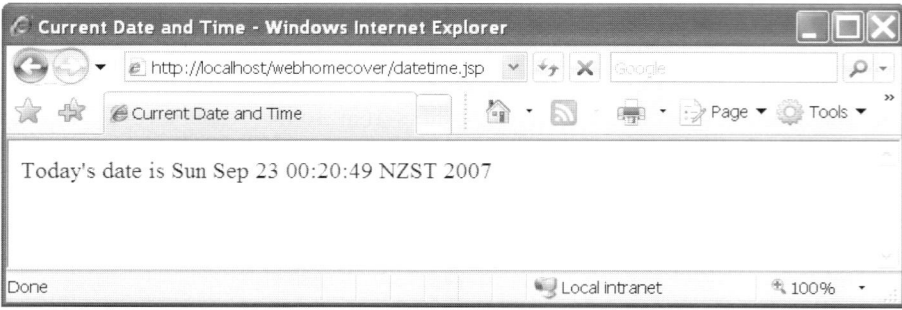

to classes without their full package names. JSPs too have an import syntax, which takes the form of a JSP *directive*. There are three different types of directive, and to import a Java class or package we use what is known as a *page directive*. This is the page import directive for the 'java.util.Date' class (directives appear at the top of a JSP):

```
<%@page import="java.util.Date" %>
```

With the import in place, our JSP expression need only refer to the class name:

```
<%= new Date() %>
```

The full source for the modified page can be found in the file 'datetime2.jsp'.

10.5 Processing HTTP request data – parameters and forms

Our first JSP examples simply wrote some HTML output to the HTTP response. The next step in developing our Model 1 JSP web application is to write a JSP that can do something with the client's HTTP request as well as writing the response. One of the most useful aspects of the HTTP request is that it can pass parameter data from the client to the server. When using a GET request, this data is appended to the URL by the browser. The data itself frequently comes from XHTML forms that are filled in by the user and sent to the server when a 'submit' button is pressed.

For this example, we create a simple XHTML form from one of our insurance system use cases, a customer lodging an insurance claim. We will need a form that asks the user for their policy number, what type of claim they are making (buildings or contents policy), an approximate amount for the claim and a general description of the claim. Here is an XHTML page ('claimform.htm') containing the necessary 'form' element. The most important lines, which refer to the input components of the form and its action, are highlighted in bold type.

```
<?xml version="1.0"?>
<!DOCTYPE html PUBLIC "-//W3C//DTD XHTML 1.1//EN"
    "http://www.w3.org/TR/xhtml11/DTD/xhtml11.dtd">
<html xmlns="http://www.w3.org/1999/xhtml" xml:lang="en">
  <head>
    <title>Insurance Claim Form</title>
```

```
    </head>
    <body>
    <!-- File: claimform.htm -->
      <form action="claimserverpage.jsp" method="get">
        <table>
          <tr>
            <td><label for="policynumber">Policy Number:</label></td>
            <td>
            <input type="text" id="policynumber" name="policyNumber" />
            </td>
          </tr>
          <tr>
          <td><label for="claim">Amount Claimed:</label></td>
          <td><input type="text" id="claim" name="claim" /></td>
          </tr>
          <tr>
          <td></td><td>
        <input type="radio" name="type" id="buildings" value="buildings" />
            <label for="buildings">Make a buildings insurance claim</label>
          </td>
          </tr>
          <tr>
          <td></td><td>
        <input type="radio" name="type" id="contents" value="contents" />
            <label for="contents">Make a contents insurance claim</label>
      </td>
      </tr>
          <tr>
            <td><label for="description">Description of claim:</label></td>
            <td>
              <textarea id="description" name="description"
               rows="5" cols="30">
              </textarea>
            </td>
          </tr>
          <tr>
            <td></td>
            <td>
             <input type="submit" value="Submit" />
            </td>
          </tr>
        </table>
      </form>
    </body>
  </html>
```

The key part of this page is the form and its 'action' attribute, which defines where its data
will be sent when the 'submit' button is pressed. The 'method' attribute sets the type of
HTTP request, which is normally 'post' but for this example we will use 'get', which can
be useful in understanding how form parameters are attached to a request.

```
<form action="claimserverpage.jsp" method="get">
```

The action destination will be a JSP. Note that if the relative URL string is not preceded by a forward slash ('/'), then the resource is assumed to be in the same web application. If we precede it with a forward slash then we must also define the name of the web application, e.g.

```
<form action="/webhomecover/claimserverpage.jsp" method="get">
```

The 'name' attributes of the components on the form are very important because they are used to identify the data when it is sent to the server as part of the HTTP request. For example, the chosen value from the radio buttons will be called 'type' (case is significant here).

 NOTE For most HTML elements, the 'id' attribute has replaced the 'name' attribute, which was used in early versions of HTML. Form components are, however, an exception, and can have both 'id' and 'name' attributes.

You can add as many buttons to a form as you like, but it must have a 'submit' button to trigger its 'action' and send the form data to the server.

```
<input type="submit" value="Submit" />
```

You may recall that only the 'type' attribute has to have the value 'submit'. The 'value' attribute is simply the text that will appear on the button.

Sending HTTP request parameters

If you add the XHTML form page to the document root of your web application, then rebuild and redeploy it, you should be able to load the page from the server using the following URL:

```
http://localhost/webhomecover/claimform.htm
```

If you fill in the form and press the 'submit' button, you should be able to see how parameters are appended to a 'get' request. Figure 10.6 shows an example of some data entered into the claim form.

Here is what the URL looks like when the data is appended to it for submission to the server. You should be able to see this in the browser's address bar after you press the 'submit' button.

```
http://localhost/webhomecover/claimserverpage.jsp?policyNumber=123456&claim=150.00
&type=buildings&description=Broke+the+kitchen+window+with+a+football
```

This shows the names of the parameters being passed to the JSP, along with their values.

Assuming that we have this XHTML form page, we now need to write a JSP that can process the contents of the form. To do this we use a special built-in JSP object called 'request', an instance of the class 'HttpServletRequest', which has a 'getParameter' method.

FIGURE 10.6 Some data entered into the form in 'claimform.htm'

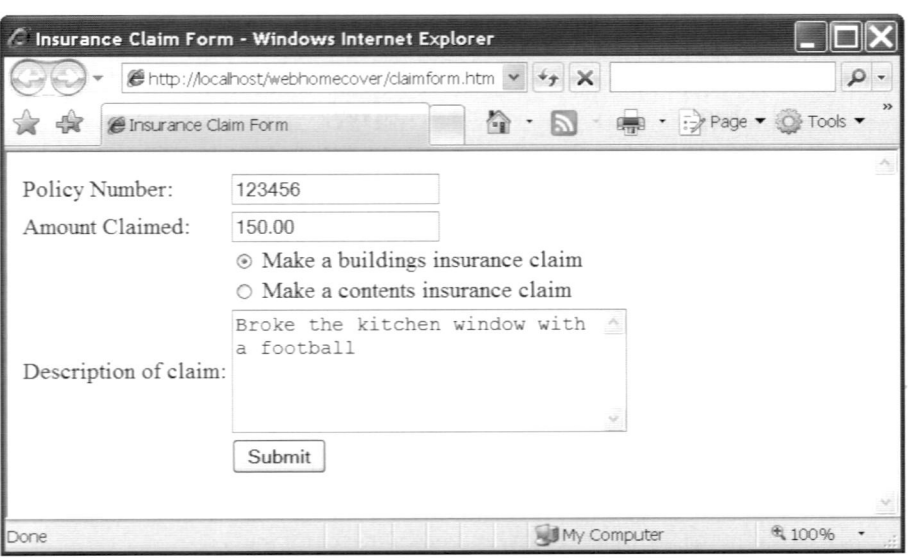

This method takes a String parameter, representing the name (the value of a 'name' attribute) of one of the components on the XHTML form, and returns the value of that form component (e.g. the text entered into a text field) as a String. If the parameter name is not matched by anything in the request, then the method returns 'null'. For example, to get the value of the policy number from our HTML form using Java code, we would write something like:

```
String policyNumber=request.getParameter("policyNumber");
```

Case is important here, since the name of the parameter must exactly match the name used in the HTML form. In the example we have used 'camel case', where the first letter of the parameter is in lower case, but the first letter of any subsequent words are in upper case. The main reason for doing this is to be compatible with JavaBean properties, which we introduce later in this chapter.

The question is, how can we write multiple lines of Java code inside a JSP to retrieve and process all the parameter values? The answer is that we can use *scriptlet* elements.

JSP scriptlets

As well as using single Java expressions, JSP pages allow us to include arbitrary sections of Java code as 'scriptlets'. In fact, a JSP could potentially contain nothing but Java code in a single scriptlet. The scriptlet tags looks like this:

```
<% Java code %>
```

Unlike expressions, which can contain only a single Java expression, scriptlets can contain multiple lines of Java code. As well as declaring their own variables and objects, they can also use a number of 'built-in' objects, such as the 'request' object we have already introduced, that are provided by the JSP engine. These objects are created as part of the generated servlet and are visible within the scope of any scriptlet. The built-in objects include the following:

- out – a JSPWriter object for writing content to the response
- request – an HttpServletRequest object that gives us access to the HTTP request
- response – an HttpServletResponse object that gives us access to the HTTP response
- session – an HttpSession object that represents an individual user's session

We will be using these objects in various examples throughout this chapter.

Here is a scriptlet that retrieves the values of the four components of the XHTML form from the request and stores them in String variables (we treat the two radio buttons as a single component because they share the same name). It uses the built-in JSP 'request' object and its 'getParameter' method:

```
<%
   String policyNumber = request.getParameter("policyNumber");
   String claimValue = request.getParameter("claim");
   String claimType = request.getParameter("type");
   String description = request.getParameter("description");
%>
```

Processing form data in the controller layer

Once we have retrieved the parameter values from the request, the next step will depend very much on the context of the page within the web application. In most cases, data submitted by a user via a form page will need to be sent on from the controller layer to the underlying model for processing. However there are one or two processes that may take place in the controller layer, such as data conversion and validation. Here, we look at a simple example of data conversion.

Since all the parameters are returned from the 'request' object as Strings, we sometimes need to perform conversion processes to change these Strings into more suitable data types. For example, the value of the insurance claim is a number, but it arrives as a String, so if we want to perform any calculations with that value we need to convert it to a floating point number, commonly represented in Java using the 'double' data type. The conversion from a String to a double is simple, using the static 'parseDouble' method of the 'java.lang.Double' class. Of course String conversions like this can potentially throw a 'NumberFormatException', because the user may not have correctly entered numeric characters into the text field on the form, so we should put a 'try . . . catch' block around this conversion. In this example, if such an exception occurs we just print error messages to standard output (i.e. the server log) and the value of 'valueOfClaim' remains at 0.0 (a real system would have to do proper error handling here, an issue we will address later in this book). The following code can be added to our existing scriptlet:

```
//convert claimValue attribute to a double
double valueOfClaim = 0.0;
try
{
   valueOfClaim = Double.parseDouble(claimValue);
}
```

```
catch(NumberFormatException e)
{
    e.printStackTrace();
}
```

Presenting client data in the view layer

In a Model 1 architecture, the same server page acts as both controller and view, so there are some data formatting processes that can usefully reside in this layer of the system, for example to format dates, numbers and currencies. In our example JSP, we do not yet have a model layer to pass our client data on to, so we simply present the data that has been entered back to the user, but as an example of data formatting we will format the value of the insurance claim using a currency formatter. Java provides us with the NumberFormat class in the 'java.text' package, enabling currency formatting using the static 'getCurrencyInstance' method. This (factory) method returns a NumberFormat object that supports a 'format' method to create a currency String from a number.

 NOTE A 'factory' method is one that creates an object for us without us needing to use a constructor method. It is a static method called directly on the class, returning a subclass or the implementation of an interface.

This scriptlet shows how we can format the 'valueOfClaim' variable that is declared in the existing scriptlet (it also assumes a directive has been used to import the java.text.NumberFormat class):

```
<%
    NumberFormat currencyFormat = NumberFormat.getCurrencyInstance();
    String valueOfClaimFormatted = currencyFormat.format(valueOfClaim);
%>
```

To write values to the client page, JSPs have a built-in object called 'out' (an instance of the JSPWriter class) that writes content to the HTTP response. Here is the complete JSP, which simply writes the values from the form to the generated client page using the 'out' object:

```
<?xml version="1.0"?>
<!-- File: claimserverpage.jsp -->
<%@ page import="java.text.NumberFormat"%>
<%
    String policyNumber = request.getParameter("policyNumber");
    String claimValue = request.getParameter("claim");
    String claimType = request.getParameter("type");
    String description = request.getParameter("description");
    //convert claimValue attribute to a double
    double valueOfClaim = 0.0;
```

```
   try
   {
      valueOfClaim = Double.parseDouble(claimValue);
   }
   catch(NumberFormatException e)
   {
      e.printStackTrace();
      System.out.println(claimValue + " is not a valid number");
   }
%>

<!DOCTYPE html PUBLIC
   "-//W3C//DTD XHTML 1.1//EN"
   "http://www.w3.org/TR/xhtml11/DTD/xhtml11.dtd">
<html xmlns="http://www.w3.org/1999/xhtml" xml:lang="en">
   <head><title>Insurance Claim Details</title></head>
   <body>
      <p>Thank you for making your insurance claim</p>
      <p>Here are the details you entered</p>
      <p>Policy number: <%= policyNumber %>
         <%
            NumberFormat currencyFormat = NumberFormat.getCurrencyInstance();
            String valueOfClaimFormatted =
               currencyFormat.format(valueOfClaim);
         %>
         <br /> Value of claim: <%= valueOfClaimFormatted %>
         <br /> Type of insurance policy: <%= claimType %>
         <br /> Description of claim: <%= description %>
      </p>
   </body>
</html>
```

Figure 10.7 shows the generated XHTML page that is produced by the JSP if the data shown in Figure 10.6 has been entered into the form.

Posting data from an HTML form

In our example so far, we have been using the HTTP 'get' method to send the request to the server. As we have discussed previously, this is not the ideal choice for form data, since sending data in a form usually means changing the state of something on the server. Forms usually contain information that is stored on the server or used by other processes that lead to changes in state. For example, submitting an order form to an e-commerce web site implies that some kind of business transaction will take place. Sending the same information twice could lead to two orders being made instead of one. In contrast, 'get' requests are meant to be repeatable and have no effect on the server's state. In addition, a 'get' request appends its parameters to the URL, meaning that these parameters are visible in the browser. Although this can be a useful technique when testing or debugging, it can be a security risk if used in production, since the request URL can be revisited or bookmarked. This could be a potential problem if a form contained sensitive personal data. Finally, 'get' requests are limited in size, meaning that a large set of form data might be too

FIGURE 10.7 The XHTML page generated by 'claimserverpage.jsp' in response to the input data shown in Figure 10.6

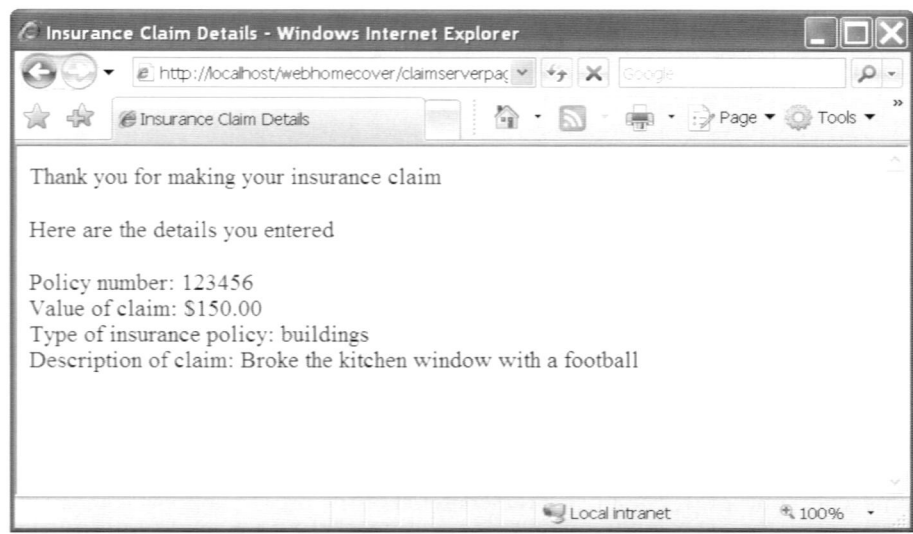

long to append to the URL. For all of these reasons, we should use the 'post' method to send form data to the server. This means that we should modify our HTML form page to use 'post' instead of 'get', i.e.

```
<form action="claim" method="post">
```

If you make this change and redeploy the application, you should find that when you press the 'submit' button in the claim form, the URL no longer has visible parameter data appended to it.

10.6 Using JavaBeans in JSPs

In the JSP we have developed so far, we are beginning to see a quite complex mix of XHTML content and Java code, embedded in scriptlets. Continuing with this approach is not going to give us a very good separation of concerns between different parts of the model, view and controller layers. To provide a better organization of components with different roles in the system, JSP Model 1 includes JavaBean components that act as intermediaries between the view and controller layers and the underlying model (Figure 10.8). The important aspect here, in terms of separating out the different parts of the architecture, is the role of the JavaBean, representing the interaction between the view and controller layers of a web application and the underlying data source. Figure 10.8 is a general view of the components in the system rather than a specific example. In practice, a server page may interact with more than one JavaBean.

A JavaBean is a Java programming component that represents either a *Data Transfer Object* (DTO), which is used to encapsulate related sets of data for transfer between different web application components, or a process or concept from the business logic layer.

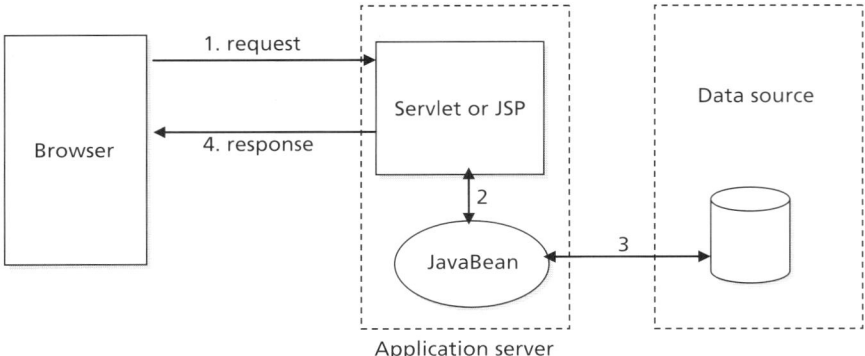

FIGURE 10.8 Model 1 architecture, adapted from (Seshadri 1999)

For example, a JavaBean might represent a user's shopping cart, or be responsible for a business process such as validation, which may of course require interacting with a database or other persistent data store. For example, if the request contained data sent from a form on a 'checkout' page, comprising the contents of the user's shopping cart, a JavaBean would have to interact with the data store containing the part of the system that can process the contents of the shopping cart. Introducing a JavaBean to our interaction model enables us to separate the model from the web interaction layer, so the server page can delegate any business logic processes to the JavaBean. However from an MVC perspective, the single JSP acts as both controller and view, a role that is sometimes known as a 'view–controller pair'.

A JavaBean (as opposed to an Enterprise JavaBean, which is a different type of component) is an ordinary Java object that follows the JavaBeans specification, or at least some of the core aspects of it. This specification (first released in 1996) was intended to define a component architecture for Java objects that would enable them to be manipulated by application-building tools such as visual programming environments. Although the full specification is quite complex, we only need to understand certain key elements of it to use JavaBeans within a web application environment. One of the main features of a JavaBean is that it supports 'properties', and it is this aspect that we will explore here. The property-related rules are:

- JavaBeans have properties that are defined by methods.
- A property is readable if it has a matching 'get*Propertyname*' method. For example if a JavaBean has a method called 'getDescription' then it has a readable property called 'description'.
- A property is writeable if it has a matching 'set*Propertyname*' method. For example if a JavaBean has a method called 'setDescription' then it has a writeable property called 'description'.
- A property is not necessarily an attribute.

As you can see from the examples above, the standard way of writing accessor method names for JavaBeans is to precede the name of a property by 'get' or 'set' in the method name, where the first letter of the property is in upper case. This is a very simple and basic rule, but one that makes it easy for JavaBeans to be handled by tools such as JSP engines. Here are examples of how we might write the 'getDescription' and 'setDescription' methods using standard Java. In this example, we assume that the class has a private field called 'claimDescription':

```
public String getDescription()
{
   return claimDescription;
}

public void setDescription (String description)
{
   claimDescription = description;
}
```

In this case, there is an attribute that contains the value of the property, though it is clear that the name of the attribute and the name of the property need not be the same. Furthermore, some properties do not relate directly to attributes. Here, for example, is a method called 'getYear' that returns the current year when called (using a 'java.util.Calendar'):

```
public int getYear()
{
   Calendar cal = Calendar.getInstance();
   int year = cal.get(Calendar.YEAR);
   return year;
}
```

In this method, the 'year' is not an attribute of the class but is generated within the body of the method. However it is still a 'readable' property of the class.

In the next example, we write a JavaBean called 'ClaimBean' in the 'com. webhomecover.beans' package. It is essential that JavaBeans that are used by JSPs are defined within named packages, rather than the (unnamed) default package, or the JSP engine will not be able to process them correctly. The 'ClaimBean' includes properties that match the data that is being submitted from our 'claimform' page: 'policyNumber', 'claim', 'type' and 'description'. Note that although property names always begin with a lower case letter, where property names consist of more than one word the subsequent words begin with an upper case letter, which is the case for 'policyNumber' here. It should be noted that this is merely a convention, and does not make any difference to the Java compiler. However it is very important to adopt a consistent convention if we are matching JavaBean properties to the names of components on a form, since both the spelling and the case must match exactly. Figure 10.9 shows a UML diagram of the 'ClaimBean' class, with its attributes and methods. Three of the properties are handled very simply, just storing and returning a String value. However you will note that the bean is also taking responsibility for the validation and formatting processes that we currently have in scriptlets within the JSP. Note also that the 'claim' property is of type 'String', to work with the HTTP request and response, but the internal attribute that stores this value ('claimValue') is of type 'double'.

Note also that one requirement of JavaBeans is that they should have a zero-argument constructor. Since this matches the normal default constructor in Java, we do not need to code this explicitly. However it is important to note that should we add any parameterized constructors we also need to explicitly add a zero-argument constructor. To ensure that we always have a zero-argument constructor available within the bean, even if other constructors are added later, we include the implementation of a zero-argument constructor here, even

FIGURE 10.9 A UML class diagram of the 'ClaimBean'

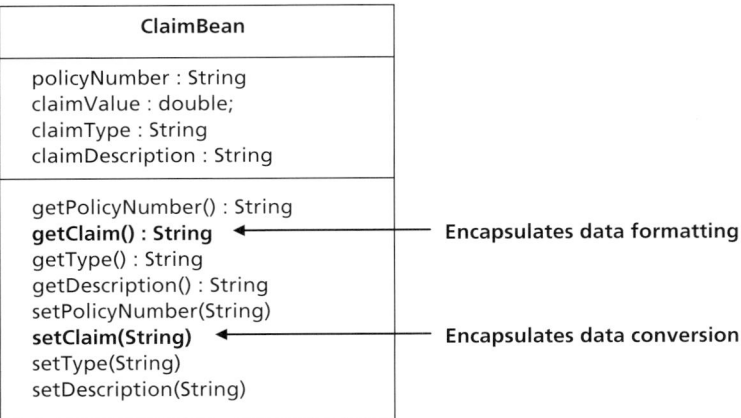

though its behavior is the same as the one that will be available by default. Finally, JavaBeans should also implement the 'java.io.Serializable' interface, so that they can be written to file storage or streamed between the various layers (and possibly tiers) of a web application.

```java
package com.webhomecover.beans;

import java.text.NumberFormat;
import java.io.Serializable;
public class ClaimBean implements Serializable
{
   private String policyNumber;
   private double claimValue;
   private String claimType;
   private String claimDescription;

public ClaimBean() { super(); }

public String getPolicyNumber() { return policyNumber; }

public String getClaim()
{
   NumberFormat currencyFormat = NumberFormat.getCurrencyInstance();
   String valueOfClaimFormatted = currencyFormat.format(claimValue);
   return valueOfClaimFormatted;
}

public String getType() { return claimType; }

public String getDescription() { return claimDescription; }

public void setPolicyNumber(String policynumber)
{ policyNumber = policynumber; }

public void setClaim(String claim)
{
   try
   {
```

```
      claimValue = Double.parseDouble(claim);
    }
    catch(NumberFormatException e)
    {
      e.printStackTrace();
      System.out.println(claimValue + " is not a valid number");
    }
  }

  public void setType(String type) { claimType = type; }

  public void setDescription(String description)
  { claimDescription = description; }
}
```

With what we know so far, along with some standard Java code, we could use the JavaBean in a scriptlet. However, a better approach is to use the special JSP tags, known as *standard JSP actions*, which can be applied to JavaBeans. This reduces the amount of Java code in our JSP pages, replacing it with XML-compliant tags.

JSP Tags for JavaBeans

JavaBeans can be used in JSPs using special tags that make it very easy to get and set their properties, and even automatically populate them from the HTTP request. In the next example, we replace the existing scriptlet code with JavaBean tags. These tags (JSP actions) are very simple and enable us to create a new instance of a JavaBean or access one that has already been created within the web application. We can also use JSP tags to set the properties of a JavaBean or write its properties to the response as part of a dynamic page. The tag that either creates or accesses a Java bean is 'useBean', which has a number of possible attributes. Here we introduce the 'id' and 'class' attributes. Unlike the JSP tags we have introduced previously, the action tags follow the XML element format, and you can see that 'useBean' here is an empty element, with a 'jsp' prefix that specifies its namespace.

```
<jsp:useBean id="claimBean" class="com.webhomecover.beans.ClaimBean" />
```

This tag uses the 'id' attribute to try to locate the bean in a particular *scope*, if it already exists. The default scope is 'page' which means it will look for an existing bean of that name and class in the scope of the current JavaServer Page. If the object already exists in the page, it will simply use it. Otherwise it will create a new instance of 'com.webhomecover. beans.ClaimBean' (the fully qualified class name specified in the 'class' attribute) and put that into the page scope using the identifier specified.

Having created or accessed the JavaBean, there are additional tags that allow us to set its properties, or write them out to the response. The 'setProperty' tag (which, of course, we use to set the properties of a JavaBean) comes in a number of forms, but perhaps the most elegant is one that automatically sets matching properties of the bean from the request parameters:

```
<jsp:setProperty name="claimBean" property="*" />
```

 NOTE The 'name' attribute in a 'jsp:setProperty' element must match the 'id' attribute of a previous 'jsp:useBean' element.

If we use the tag in this way, with the '*' wildcard for the property name, then any property of the bean that matches the name of a request parameter is automatically set using the parameter value. However, if there are any differences in spelling or case then the automatic population of properties will not work. For example, if the bean property that was intended to store the 'claim' parameter was called 'claimValue' (i.e. the bean had 'getClaimValue' and 'setClaimValue' methods), then the automatic setting of the property would not work because the parameter and property names would not match. In cases like this, we can use the 'param' attribute of the 'setProperty' tag that explicitly sets a named property from a named parameter, e.g.

```
<jsp:setProperty name="claimBean" property="claimValue" param="claim" />
```

This means we do not have to have bean property names that match the names of HTML components, but of course each property would have to be set separately. If the value of a property needs to be set using a value that does not come from a request parameter, then we use the 'value' attribute. We might use this to set a property to a literal value in the JSP, as in this example:

```
<jsp:setProperty name="claimBean" property="description" value=
"No Description" />
```

Writing bean properties to the response

We can write bean properties out to the response using the 'getProperty' tag. This, for example, would write the value of the 'type' property to the response:

```
<jsp:getProperty name="claimBean" property="type" />
```

Here is a revised version of our previous JSP, but this time using the JavaBean to retrieve the parameter data from the request, validate and format the value of the claim, and write the parameter values back to the response. Note that using the JavaBean means that we no longer need the scriptlets or the page directive that imported the 'NumberFormat' class, and we have a much simpler, cleaner, JSP without any Java code.

```
<jsp:useBean id="claimBean" class="com.webhomecover.beans.ClaimBean" />
<jsp:setProperty name="claimBean" property="*" />

<!DOCTYPE html PUBLIC
"-//W3C//DTD XHTML 1.1//EN"
"http://www.w3.org/TR/xhtml11/DTD/xhtml11.dtd">
<html xmlns="http://www.w3.org/1999/xhtml" xml:lang="en">
<head><title>Insurance Claim Details</title></head>
<body>

<p>Thank you for making your insurance claim</p>
<p>Here are the details you entered</p>
Policy number:
<jsp:getProperty name="claimBean" property="policyNumber"/>
<br /> Value of claim:
<jsp:getProperty name="claimBean" property="claim"/>
<br /> Type of insurance policy:
<jsp:getProperty name="claimBean" property="type"/>
<br /> Description of claim:
<jsp:getProperty name="claimBean" property="description"/>
```

```
</body>
</html>
```

Note that to invoke this JSP you should modify the action in your 'claimform.htm' file to submit to this server page:

```
<form action="claimbeanserverpage.jsp" method="post">
```

10.7 Refactoring

Of course the actual behavior of the application is unchanged. We have improved the architecture but have not affected the way the application works. This is an example of *refactoring*: improving the design of existing code without changing its behavior (Fowler 1999). Refactoring is important because it means we can replace a complex or confusing architecture with a better, simpler one that makes it easier to progress with subsequent enhancements and new requirements. As we move into the next section, which introduces Model 2 architecture, you will find that we are continuing to refactor the same web application. Although the behavior remains the same, we are making an important series of improvements to the software architecture of the application. Refactoring should normally be done in conjunction with a testing framework that makes sure that changes do not have any adverse effects on the functionality of the system. However for the tiny example we are working with here, it is sufficient to manually test the code by filling in the form and making sure everything still works each time we modify the application.

10.8 JSP Model 2 architecture

The interaction model that we have been using, based on the Model 1 architecture, is perfectly workable but is not ideal. The main problem is that our server page has multiple responsibilities. We have a single component that is both receiving the HTTP request and sending the HTTP response, mixing the responsibilities of both the controller and the view. To improve this design, we need more than one component where the 'server page' appears in the Model 1 architecture, in order to separate receiving the request from building the response. To address this problem we can apply the JSP Model 2 architecture (Figure 10.10).

In this architecture, instead of having a single server page to both process the request and generate the response, we have two server pages, one to process the request and the other to handle the response. This enables us to easily separate out those parts of the logic that process the (single) request, from those that process the response, which may be one out of many possible pages. Figure 10.11 shows how we might represent the static model of our page structure following the JSP Model 2 architecture. Separating out the roles of the server pages between the request and the response means that the server page that receives the request can delegate to other pages to, for example, either rebuild a form page if the data entered was invalid, or build the next client page if the data was valid.

What we are now beginning to see in our design is a web-based Model–View–Controller pattern. The JavaBeans represent the model, the server page that receives the request is the controller and the server pages that build the response are the view.

FIGURE 10.10 JSP Model 2 architecture, adapted from (Seshadri 1999)

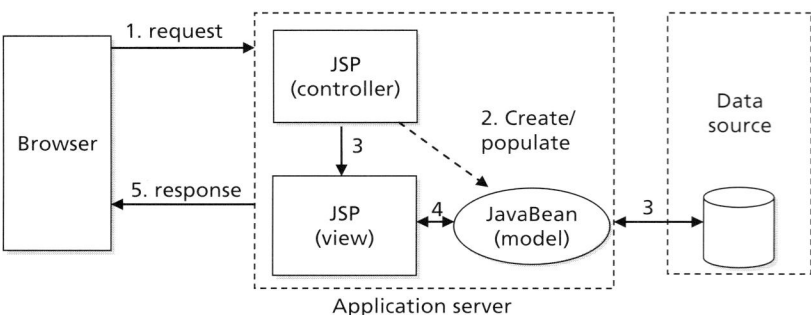

FIGURE 10.11 Page structure following JSP Model 2 architecture

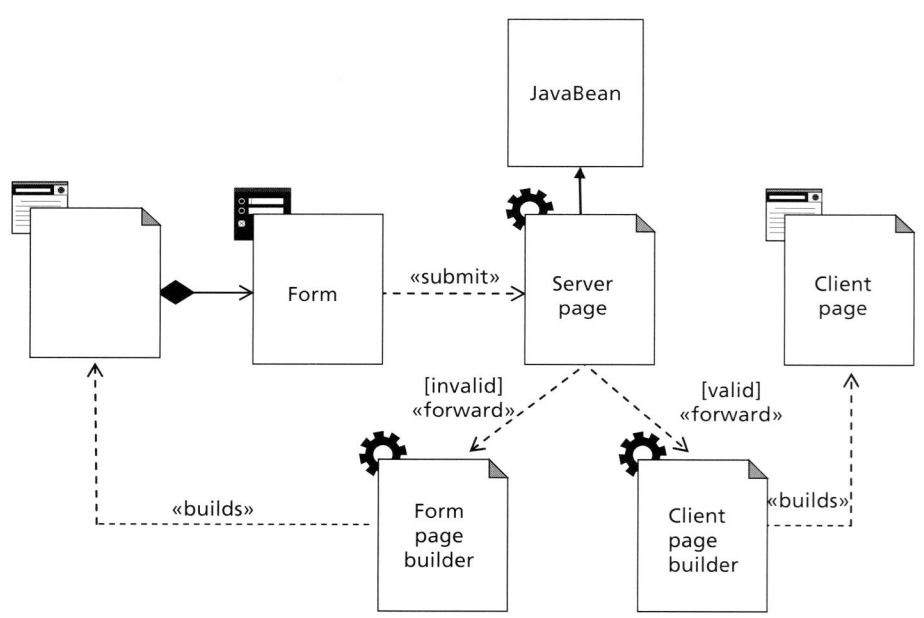

To modify our existing JSP to use the Model 2 architecture, we need to split the page into two separate JSPs. We then need to be able to *forward* from one page to the other. We do this using the 'jsp:forward' tag, which is one of the standard action tags. It simply specifies the name of the page to which we are forwarding on the server. In our example, this is called 'claimresponseserverpage.jsp'.

```
<jsp:forward page="claimresponseserverpage.jsp" />
```

We should always ensure that after forwarding we do not have any more processing in the JSP, since a forward should be the last thing that happens in a page (after all, we don't expect to be coming back).

When we apply the Model 2 architecture we have two server pages, but both use the same JavaBean. The first page creates and populates the bean, and the second retrieves the bean and displays its contents. Remember, however, that the default scope of a JavaBean is 'page' scope which means it is local to the JSP within which it is created. This does not work when we have more than one JSP using the same bean. To solve this problem we put the bean in 'request' scope, which means it is available for the lifetime of the current request (the request remains available on the server until the response has been sent back to the client). We can do this using the 'scope' attribute, which we set to the value 'request':

```
<jsp:useBean id="claimBean" class="com.webhomecover.beans.ClaimBean"
scope="request"/>
```

Figure 10.12 shows how when the 'claimrequestserverpage' JSP forwards to the 'claim-responseserverpage' JSP, the 'claimBean' object is put into the request by the first JSP and retrieved from it by the second.

In the first JSP, using this scope both creates the bean and adds it to the scope of the current HTTP request. Since this request is also visible to the second JSP, we are able to retrieve the bean from it. In the second 'jsp:useBean' tag, because the bean has already been created in the specified scope, the existing bean is used rather than a new one being created.

Here is the (rather short) first JSP, 'claimrequestserverpage.jsp'. This creates the bean, sets its properties and then forwards to the second JSP on the server using the 'forward' action.

```
<!-- File: claimrequestserverpage.jsp -->
<jsp:useBean id="claimBean" class="com.webhomecover.beans.ClaimBean"
scope="request"/>
<jsp:setProperty name="claimBean" property="*" />
<jsp:forward page="claimresponseserverpage.jsp" />
```

FIGURE 10.12 Using request scope to pass a JavaBean from one JSP to another

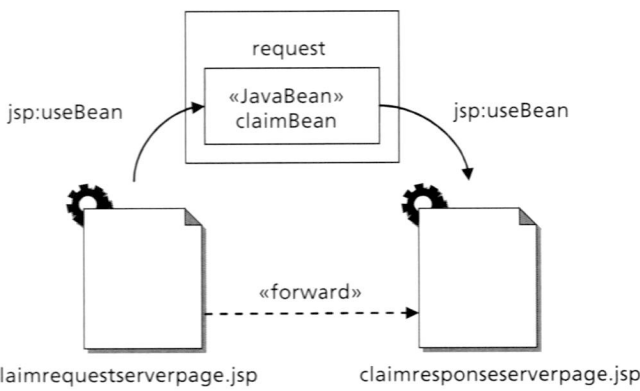

Here is the second JSP page, 'claimresponseserverpage.jsp'. Note how we get the 'claimBean' from the request scope. The 'jsp:useBean' tag here does not create a new bean but uses the existing one that it finds in the scope of the HTTP request.

```
<?xml version="1.0"?>
<!-- File: claimresponseserverpage.jsp -->
<jsp:useBean id="claimBean" class="com.webhomecover.beans.ClaimBean"
scope="request"/>

<!DOCTYPE html PUBLIC
    "-//W3C//DTD XHTML 1.1//EN"
    "http://www.w3.org/TR/xhtml11/DTD/xhtml11.dtd">
<html xmlns="http://www.w3.org/1999/xhtml" xml:lang="en">
<head><title>Insurance Claim Details</title></head>
<body>

<p>Thank you for making your insurance claim</p>
<p>Here are the details you entered</p>
Policy number: <jsp:getProperty name="claimBean"
property="policyNumber"/>
<br /> Value of claim: <jsp:getProperty name="claimBean"
property="claim"/>
<br /> Type of insurance policy: <jsp:getProperty name="claimBean"
property="type"/>
<br /> Description of claim: <jsp:getProperty name="claimBean"
property="description"/>
</body>
</html>
```

Once again, to test this version of the application you modify the 'action' of the claim form, this time to invoke 'claimrequestserverpage.jsp':

```
<form action="claimrequestserverpage.jsp" method="post">
```

Having refactored, through a series of steps, our single JSP Model 1 architecture into a Model 2 architecture using JavaBeans, we now move on to managing a series of JSPs in a webflow.

10.9 Managing a webflow

So far our examples have covered a single HTTP request–response cycle. However, when a web client is interacting with a web site, there will be many different request–response cycles that together make up the workflow of the web application, the *webflow*, and they may take different paths through the application depending on the choices they make. In the next example, we take one of the scenarios from our insurance policy application that was described in Chapter 2, where a user has the option to get a quote for contents insurance, buildings insurance, or both. In this situation, we have to manage the webflow according to the user's choices. To make this work, we not only need to route the user between JSPs on the server, but we also need to maintain user *sessions* over multiple request–response cycles. In addition, we will be using multiple JavaBeans for different steps of the webflow. Figure 10.13 shows the various dependencies between the form pages, server pages, Java Beans and final client page that are included in the webflow.

FIGURE 10.13 The webflow design for the 'get insurance quote' use case

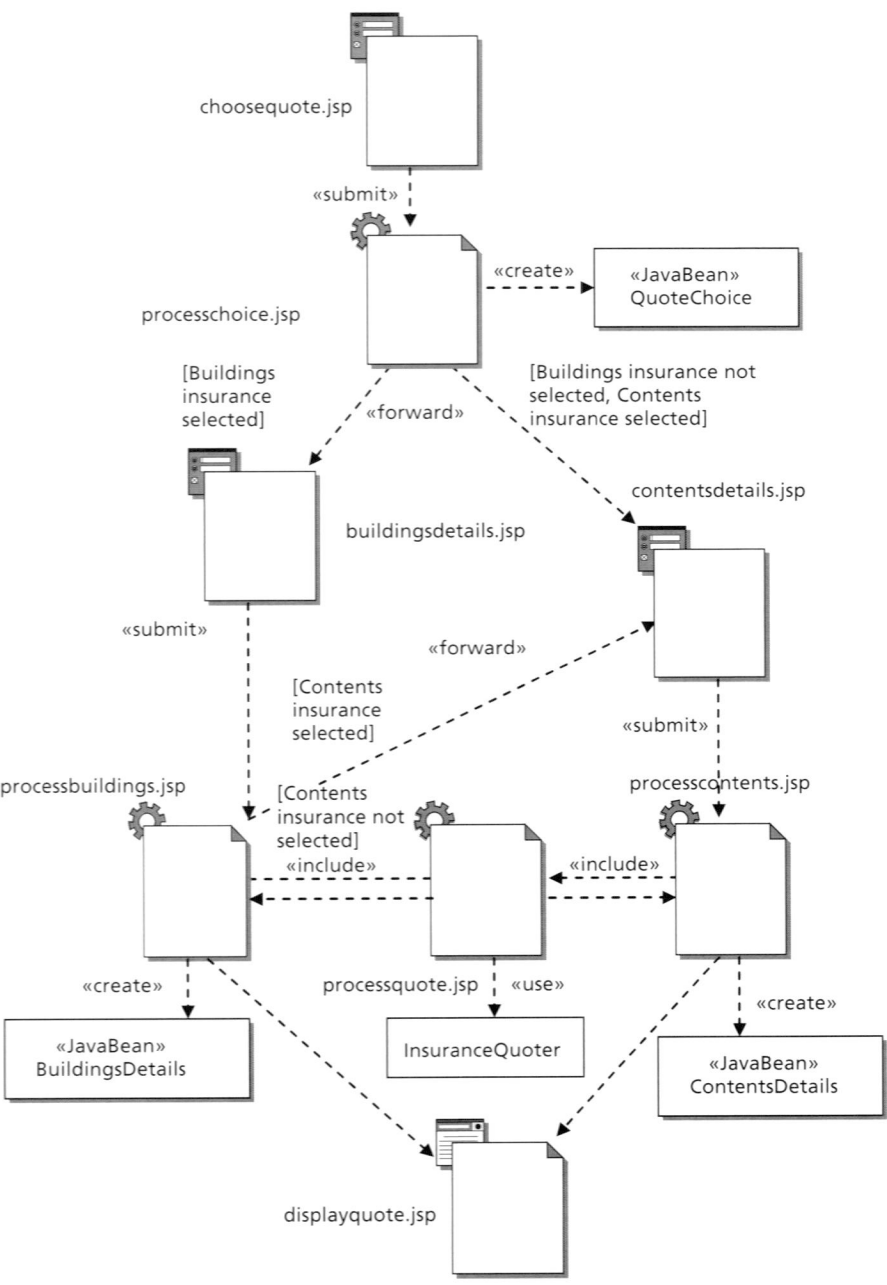

To simplify the example a little, the first step in the use case (getting customer details) has been omitted, so we start at the point of asking the customer which types of insurance they require. Although all of the pages are actually implemented as JSPs, the diagram shows only the JSPs that process the request as server pages. JSPs that represent the response are shown as form or client pages. This makes it easier to see the Model 2 architecture in action.

It is also perhaps useful in terms of highlighting that JSPs that represent the view need to generate valid XHTML, whereas JSPs that act as controllers do not generate XHTML but are responsible for page routing and other server-side processes. Note, in particular, the role of 'processquote.jsp' in the webflow. This server page is used to provide server-side processes that are common to both 'processbuildings.jsp' and 'processcontents.jsp'. Rather than duplicating this in both pages, they 'share' this implementation by both *including* the same JSP. They then forward on to 'displayquote.jsp'. There is an important difference between one JSP including another, and one that forwards to another, because after a JSP has been included, control passes back to the first JSP, which then continues with the webflow. The tag for an 'include' action is similar to the one for the 'forward' action:

```
<jsp:include page="processquote.jsp" />
```

The role of this JSP is basically that of a *command object*, which we introduced briefly in our design discussions in Chapter 2. Controller pages manage the routing of the application, but command objects perform interactions with the model.

To successfully route a web client between pages we need to be able to move between server-side resources depending on the state of the user within a webflow without unnecessarily returning to the client. For example, we sometimes need to move from one server page to another without committing the response or losing the contents of the request. As soon as we send a response back to the client, neither the original request nor the response is available to us. In the webflow described in Figure 10.13, we need to make decisions about page routing at several points, and at several stages we forward between, or include, server-side resources, enabling us to pass on the request and response object to another JSP. Note that each time a JSP submits to the server, a new HTTP request object is created.

10.10 Session management – conversational state in a web application

Having looked at the syntax for forwarding between server pages within a web application, we now need to look at how we can maintain client information on the server as we move through a webflow. So far we have presented the client with one HTML form and processed it with two JSPs and a JavaBean. However, the data that we enter each time is lost as soon as the second JSP sends the response back to the client. In web applications that gather client data, we need a solution that can reliably store client data on the server over several pages so that, for example, a client using an on-line store can start shopping, browse through a catalog, add items to their shopping cart and eventually purchase all the items in the cart. For this to work, we need to maintain state on the server because HTTP is a *stateless protocol*, which is not designed to keep long-term connections open between the client and the server. This means that something other than the HTTP connection has to be used to keep information on behalf of the client. We cannot store state on the client if the client is a browser, so we must keep it on the server, along with some way of identifying the client so that everyone has access to their own shopping cart, claim details, bank account, etc. (and no-one else's). In a web application, we can maintain this type of information in an 'HttpSession' object, an instance of which can be created for each client that is using the web application. This object represents a client session, which is effectively a conversation between a client and a server that includes multiple request–response cycles. A session could be a shopping process at an on-line store, a series of interactions with a share-trading system, or any other application where the client needs to maintain some state (shopping cart, logon information, etc.) over a series of different web pages.

The built-in JSP 'session' object is an instance of 'HttpSession' and can be used within JSPs to store client data. When a JSP that uses sessions is loaded, if a session object for the current client already exists then it is used, but if it does not already exist then a new session is created. Either way, we have a session object available.

An 'HttpSession' is basically like a HashTable or HashMap, in that it can contain a collection of key–value pairs, where the keys are Strings and the values are Objects. We can add objects to a session using the 'setAttribute' method, e.g.

```
session.setAttribute("firstName", fname);
```

assuming in this example that we have an object in scope called 'fname'. Note that since the second parameter to 'setAttribute' is always an Object, we cannot directly store primitives. To store these we must use the Java wrapper classes. For example, we can use the Integer class to wrap an int called 'yearOfBirth':

```
session.setAttribute("yearOfBirth", new Integer(yearOfBirth) );
```

| NOTE | Since Java 5.0, it is unnecessary to wrap primitives explicitly, since Java now supports 'autoboxing' of primitives, where the wrapping with an object is done automatically. This means that a primitive value (such as 'yearOfBirth', which is an int) can be added directly to a session object or, indeed, any type of Java collection class. The wrapper class is still being used, but transparently–we do not have to code it. See Flanagan (2005, page 88) for further information. |

We can get a reference to an object in a session using the 'getAttribute' method. The return type of this method is 'Object', so we have to cast the returned value to the appropriate type. If we assume that, in our first example, 'fname' is a String, we could write the following:

```
String fname = (String)session.getAttribute("firstName");
```

Typically, we put data into a session in one JSP and retrieve it in another. 'getAttribute' returns a reference to an object but leaves it in the session. To remove an object from the session (if a client chooses to remove something from a web site shopping trolley, for example), we use the 'removeAttribute' method, passing in the necessary key value:

```
session.removeAttribute("itemKey");
```

There are some other useful methods associated with sessions that enable us to successfully manage client state. One important aspect of session management is freeing up resources that are no longer required. When we purchase the items in a shopping cart, for example, then the shopping cart is no longer needed. If the cart is represented by an 'HttpSession' then we should dispose of the session at the end of the webflow, since as long as it exists it is taking up storage space and having to be managed by the server. To get rid of a session that has served its purpose we can use the 'invalidate' method to dispose of the session and any objects within it:

```
session.invalidate();
```

At the beginning of a webflow we may want to check if the session that we have acquired from the request is in fact a new one, or whether the client has restarted their activity with an existing session. To do this we can use the 'isNew' method, which returns 'true' if the session has just been created and 'false' if it already existed. At this point we may choose to invalidate an existing session and start a new one. Similarly, we may find ourselves in a JSP where the session should already exist but, for some reason, does not. If the session turns out to be new we can send the client back to start the webflow from the beginning. We could do this by forwarding or redirecting. A redirect sends a response to the browser that causes it to be redirected to another page, as opposed to forwarding directly to another server-side resource. This means of course that the current request object is discarded. This example illustrates the basic idea:

```
<%
   if(session.isNew()
   {
%>
<jsp:redirect page="choosequote.jsp"/>
<%
   }
%>
```

JavaBeans and sessions

So far we have seen that the default scope of a JavaBean is the 'page', but that we can change that using the 'scope' attribute of the 'jsp:useBean' tag. In a previous example, we added the 'claimBean' to the request using 'request' scope. To put a JavaBean into the session, we do not need to write any code to add it to the session object. Instead, we simply set the value of the 'scope' attribute to 'session', as in this example using 'claimBean':

```
<jsp:useBean id="claimBean" class="com.webhomecover.beans.ClaimBean"
scope="session"/>
```

If we use this attribute value, the JSP looks for the bean in the session rather than the page or request, and adds it to the session when it creates it. Note that when we are using JavaBeans and tags, session management is largely transparent to us. There is no need to manually add our beans to the session or retrieve them from it: that work is done by the implementation of the tag. However, we occasionally have to interact directly with the session object to manage the state of the webflow.

NOTE	So far we have introduced three scopes: 'page', 'request' and 'session'. Objects can be stored in all three of these scopes. There is also a fourth scope, 'application', which is accessible to all the components in the web application. Objects that need global visibility across the application can be stored in this scope.

Creating JSPs and JavaBeans for the webflow

Having discussed the need for session management, we now work our way through each stage of the webflow. First, there is a JSP form page that asks the user which types of insurance they would like a quote for. Here is the page ('choosequote.jsp'). Initially, both the check boxes are 'checked', so the default selection is for both contents and buildings insurance:

```xml
<?xml version="1.0"?>
<!DOCTYPE html PUBLIC "-//W3C//DTD XHTML 1.1//EN"
   "http://www.w3.org/TR/xhtml11/DTD/xhtml11.dtd">
<html xmlns="http://www.w3.org/1999/xhtml" xml:lang="en">
  <head>
    <link href="webhomecover.css" rel="stylesheet" type="text/css" />
    <title>WebHomeCover - Insurance Quote Request</title>
  </head>
  <body>
  <!-- File: choosequote.jsp -->
    <h1>Choose your quote!</h1>
    <h2>Please choose buildings insurance, contents insurance, or both,
        by checking the boxes below</h2>
    <form action="processchoice.jsp" method="post">
      <table>
        <tr>
          <td>
             What kind of quote do you require?
          </td>
        </tr>
        <tr>
        <td>
          <label for="buildings">Buildings insurance quote</label>
          <input type="checkbox" name="buildings" id="buildings"
            checked="checked" />
        </td>
        </tr>
        <tr>
          <td>
            <label for="contents">Contents insurance quote</label>
            <input type="checkbox" name="contents" id="contents"
              checked="checked" />
          </td>
        </tr>
        <tr>
          <td>
            <input type="submit" value="Submit" />
          </td>
        </tr>
      </table>
    </form>
  </body>
</html>
```

Figure 10.14 shows what this page looks like in Internet Explorer 7.

FIGURE 10.14 The 'choosequote.jsp' page

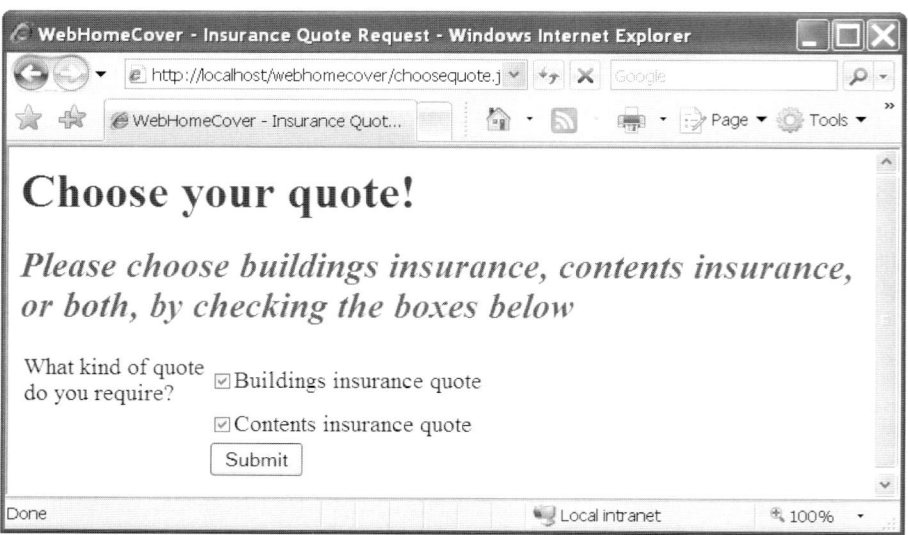

From a programming point of view, the important aspects are the names of the two check boxes: 'contents' and 'buildings'. These need to match properties in the JavaBean ('QuoteChoice') that will store this information on the server, inside the session object. Here is the JavaBean source code. The bean only has two Boolean properties, 'contents' and 'buildings'.

```java
package com.webhomecover.beans;
import java.io.Serializable;

public class QuoteChoice implements Serializable
{
    private boolean contents;
    private boolean buildings;

    public QuoteChoice()
    { super(); }

    public boolean getBuildings()
    { return buildings; }

    public boolean getContents()
    { return contents; }

    public void setContents(boolean contents)
    { this.contents = contents; }

    public void setBuildings(boolean buildings)
    { this.buildings = buildings; }
}
```

When data is sent from check boxes in an HTTP request, it is represented as String data, containing either the name of the checked box, or 'null' if it is unchecked. However, when we use the 'jsp:setProperty' tag in a JSP, the conversion from the required parameter to the Boolean property is done automatically by the underlying implementation of the tag, so there is no need for us to include any code to convert from HTML parameter values to Boolean values. The properties are set automatically.

The server page to which the form page submits is called 'processchoice.jsp'. This server page has two responsibilities:

- To create and populate an instance of the 'QuoteChoice' JavaBean
- To direct the user to the next form page, depending on the choices they have made.

The following code is the source of 'processchoice.jsp'. Note that the scope of the 'choice' bean is set to 'session' to ensure that the bean remains in the session over multiple request–response cycles. Scriptlets are used to choose whether to forward to 'buildings.jsp' or 'contents.jsp' as the next form page. You may wonder why we also set the 'buildings' and 'contents' properties to 'false' in this JSP. This is because we may have returned to the page with the bean still in the session, remembering previous state. If a check box is unchecked it sends a 'null' value, which won't overwrite a previously set 'true' value in the bean.

```jsp
<jsp:useBean id="choice" class="com.webhomecover.beans.QuoteChoice"
scope="session" />
<jsp:setProperty name="choice" property="buildings" value="false" />
<jsp:setProperty name="choice" property="contents" value="false" />
<jsp:setProperty name="choice" property="*" />
<%
// select which page to go to depending on the check box selected

if(choice.getBuildings())
{
%>
<jsp:forward page="buildings.jsp"/>
<%
}
else
{
   if(choice.getContents())
   {
%>
<jsp:forward page="contents.jsp"/>
<%
   }
}
%>
```

NOTE The mix of JSP tags and Java code in scriptlets here is a little ugly. In Section 10.12, we look at a way of replacing the scriptlets with tags from the JSP Standard Tag Library (JSTL).

If the user has chosen to get a buildings insurance quote, then the application forwards to the 'buildings.jsp' form page, which looks like this:

```xml
<?xml version="1.0"?>
<!DOCTYPE html PUBLIC "-//W3C//DTD XHTML 1.1//EN"
  "http://www.w3.org/TR/xhtml11/DTD/xhtml11.dtd">
<html xmlns="http://www.w3.org/1999/xhtml" xml:lang="en">
  <head>
    <link href="webhomecover.css" rel="stylesheet" type="text/css" />
    <title>WebHomeCover - Building Details</title>
  </head>
  <body>
  <!-- File: buildings.jsp -->
    <h1>Buildings Policy Details</h1>
    <h2>Please provide information about where you live in the form
        below, then click submit</h2>
    <form action="processbuildings.jsp" method="post">
      <table>
        <tr>
          <td><label for="propertyType">Type of building:</label></td>
          <td>
            <select name="propertyType" id="propertyType" size="1">
             <option value="apartment">Flat / Apartment</option>
             <option value="terraced">Terraced</option>
             <option value="semi">Semi-Detached</option>
             <option value="detached">Detached</option>
            </select>
          </td>
        </tr>
        <tr>
          <td><label for="bedroomCount">Number of bedrooms:</label></td>
          <td>
            <select name="bedroomCount" id="bedroomCount" size="1">
             <option value="1">1</option>
             <option value="2">2</option>
             <option value="3">3</option>
             <option value="4">4</option>
             <option value="5">5</option>
             <option value="6">More than 5</option>
            </select>
          </td>
        </tr>
        <tr>
          <td><label for="constructionDate">
            Date of construction:</label></td>
          <td>
            <select name="constructionDate" id="constructionDate" size="1">
             <option value="1900-01-01">pre 1900</option>
             <option value="1901-01-01">1901 - 1950</option>
             <option value="1951-01-01">1951 - 1970</option>
             <option value="1971-01-01">1971 - 1990</option>
```

```
        <option value="1991-01-01">after 1990</option>
       </select>
      </td>
    </tr>
    <tr>
      <td>Type of construction</td>
      <td>
       <input type="radio" name="constructionType" id="timber"
        value="timber" checked="checked" />
       <label for="timber">Timber</label>
      </td>
    </tr>
    <tr>
      <td>
      </td>
      <td>
       <input type="radio" name="constructionType" id="masonry"
        value="masonry" />
       <label for="masonry">Masonry</label>
      </td>
    </tr>
    <tr>
      <td>Estimated market value:</td>
      <td>
       <select name="marketValue" size="1">
        <option value="30000">up to 30,000</option>
        <option value="60000">30,000 - 60,000</option>
        <option value="100000">60,000 - 100,000</option>
        <option value="200000">100,000 - 200,000</option>
        <option value="500000">200,000 - 500,000</option>
        <option value="1000000">above 500,000</option>
       </select>
      </td>
    </tr>
    <tr>
      <td> </td>
      <td>
       <input type="submit" value="Submit" />
      </td>
    </tr>
  </table>
 </form>
 </body>
</html>
```

Figure 10.15 shows what this page looks like in Internet Explorer 7, with the default data selected in the form components.

The information gathered from the user on this page includes the type of building ('propertyType'), the number of bedrooms ('bedroomCount'), the approximate date of

FIGURE 10.15   The 'buildings.jsp' page

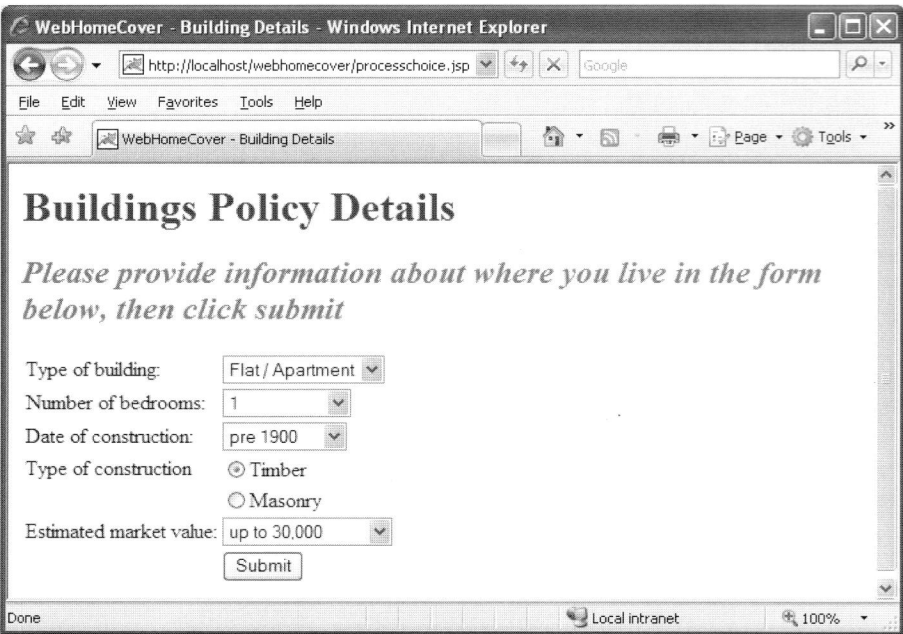

construction ('constructionDate'), the type of construction ('constructionType') and the approximate market value of the property ('marketValue'). All of these form components are mirrored in the 'BuildingsDetails' JavaBean. The bean also includes a field to store the insurance quote once it has been calculated, associated 'get' and 'set' methods and a method to return the quote as a formatted currency String:

```java
package com.webhomecover.beans;

import java.text.NumberFormat;
import java.io.Serializable;

public class BuildingsDetails implements Serializable
{
   private String propertyType;
   private int bedroomCount;
   private String constructionDate;
   private String constructionType;
   private int marketValue;
   private double insuranceQuote;

   public BuildingsDetails()
   { super(); }

   public int getBedroomCount()
   { return bedroomCount; }
```

```java
   public String getConstructionDate()
   { return constructionDate; }

   public String getConstructionType()
   { return constructionType; }

   public int getMarketValue()
   { return marketValue; }

   public String getPropertyType()
   { return propertyType; }

   public double getInsuranceQuote()
   { return insuranceQuote; }

   public String getFormattedInsuranceQuote()
   {
      NumberFormat currencyFormat = NumberFormat.getCurrencyInstance();
      return currencyFormat.format(getInsuranceQuote() );
   }

   public void setInsuranceQuote(double quote)
   { insuranceQuote = quote; }

   public void setBedroomCount(int newBedroomCount)
   { bedroomCount = newBedroomCount; }

   public void setConstructionDate(String newConstructionDate)
   { constructionDate = newConstructionDate; }

   public void setConstructionType(String newConstructionType)
   { constructionType = newConstructionType; }

   public void setMarketValue(int newMarketValue)
   { marketValue = newMarketValue; }

   public void setPropertyType(String newPropertyType)
   { propertyType = newPropertyType; }
}
```

When 'processbuildings.jsp' receives the HTTP request from the form page, it creates an instance of the 'BuildingsDetails' bean and populates its properties from the request. It also needs to retrieve the 'QuoteChoice' bean from the session to find out where to forward to next. If the user has also chosen a contents quote, the next page will be 'contents.jsp'. If not, we need to calculate the insurance quote. This task is performed by another server page called 'processquote.jsp'. In other words the 'processbuildings.jsp' page is responsible only for managing the page routing in the webflow. In contrast, 'processquote.jsp' is responsible for managing the interaction with the underlying model to get an insurance quote:

```jsp
<jsp:useBean id="choice" class="com.webhomecover.beans.QuoteChoice"
scope="session" />
```

```
<jsp:useBean id="buildings"
class="com.webhomecover.beans.BuildingsDetails" scope="session" />
<jsp:setProperty name="buildings" property="*" />


<%
// select which page to go to depending on whether contents insurance is also
required
if(choice.getContents())
{
%>
<jsp:forward page="contents.jsp" />
<%
}
else
{
%>
<jsp:include page="processquote.jsp" />
<jsp:forward page="displayquote.jsp" />
<%
}
%>
```

Here is the 'contents.jsp' page that gathers information from the user about their contents insurance requirements, if the user has chosen to ask for a contents insurance quote:

```
<?xml version="1.0"?>
<!DOCTYPE html PUBLIC "-//W3C//DTD XHTML 1.1//EN"
   "http://www.w3.org/TR/xhtml11/DTD/xhtml11.dtd">
<html xmlns="http://www.w3.org/1999/xhtml" xml:lang="en">
   <head>
      <link href="webhomecover.css" rel="stylesheet" type="text/css" />
      <title>WebHomeCover - Contents Details</title>
   </head>
   <body>
   <!-- File: contents.jsp -->
      <h1>Contents Policy Details</h1>
      <h2>Please provide information about the contents cover you require in the
form below, then click submit</h2>
      <form action="processcontents.jsp" method="post">
        <table>
          <tr>
            <td><label for="accidentalCover">
            Accidental damage cover (tick box)</label></td>
            <td><input type="checkbox" name="accidentalCover"
            id="accidentalCover" /></td>
          </tr>
          <tr>
           <td><label for="coverAmount">
           Amount of cover required:</label></td>
           <td>
            <select name="coverAmount" id="coverAmount" size="1">
```

```
          <option value="10000">10,000</option>
          <option value="20000">20,000</option>
          <option value="30000">30,000</option>
          <option value="50000">50,000</option>
          <option value="100000">100,000</option>
        </select>
        </td>
      </tr>
      <tr>
        <td>Policy excess / deductible required</td>
        <td>
         <input type="radio" name="deductibleAmount" id="none"
          value="0" checked="checked" />
         <label for="none">none</label>
        </td>
      </tr>
      <tr>
        <td></td>
        <td>
           <input type="radio" name="deductibleAmount" id="fivehundred"
            value="500" />
           <label for="fivehundred">500</label>
        </td>
      </tr>
      <tr>
        <td></td>
        <td>
           <input type="radio" name="deductibleAmount"
            id="thousand"value="1000" />
           <label for="thousand">1,000</label>
        </td>
      </tr>
      <tr>
        <td></td>
        <td>
           <input type="submit" value="Submit" />
        </td>
      </tr>
    </table>
   </form>
  </body>
</html>
```

Figure 10.16 shows what the 'contents.jsp' page looks like when it is displayed in Internet Explorer 7.

The 'processcontents.jsp' page which the form submits to is quite simple, since at this stage of the webflow it does not need to make any decisions about page routing. All it needs to do is to populate the 'ContentsDetails' JavaBean from the request, then include the quote process before forwarding on to display the quote.

FIGURE 10.16   The 'contents.jsp' page

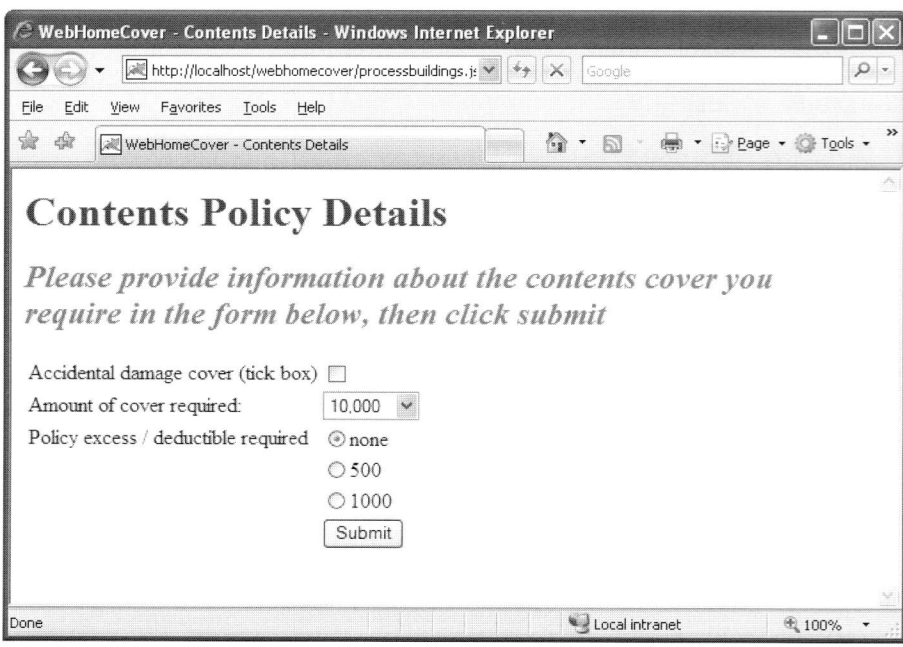

```
<jsp:useBean id="contents"
class="com.webhomecover.beans.ContentsDetails" scope="session" />
<jsp:setProperty name="contents" property="*" />
<jsp:include page="processquote.jsp" />
<jsp:forward page="displayquote.jsp" />
```

The 'ContentsDetails' bean has much in common with the 'BuildingsDetails' bean, It has properties that match the form submitted from the browser, along with a field and associated methods to store the insurance quote that will be calculated later:

```
package com.webhomecover.beans;
import java.text.NumberFormat;
import java.io. Serializable;

public class ContentsDetails implements Serializable
{
   private int coverAmount;
   private boolean accidentalCover;
   private int deductibleAmount;
   private double insuranceQuote;

   public ContentsDetails()
   { super(); }

   public int getCoverAmount()
   { return coverAmount; }
```

```java
   public int getDeductibleAmount()
   { return deductibleAmount; }

   public boolean getAccidentalCover()
   { return accidentalCover; }

   public double getInsuranceQuote()
   { return insuranceQuote; }

   public String getFormattedInsuranceQuote()
   {
     NumberFormat currencyFormat =
        NumberFormat.getCurrencyInstance();
     return currencyFormat.format(getInsuranceQuote());
   }

   public void setInsuranceQuote(double quote)
   { insuranceQuote = quote; }

   public void setCoverAmount(int newCoverAmount)
   { coverAmount = newCoverAmount; }

   public void setAccidentalCover(boolean newAccidentalCover)
   { accidentalCover = newAccidentalCover; }

   public void setDeductibleAmount(int newDeductibleAmount)
   { deductibleAmount = newDeductibleAmount; }
}
```

10.11 Process beans and the underlying model

So far all the pages of our web application just gather information from the user and store it in the session in JavaBeans. We do not yet invoke any business processes using this data, though of course this is in fact the key part of any web-based system. In this case, the main business process that we need is one that calculates an insurance quote based on the information that the user has provided. The question we need to address next is where does this business process reside?

We could write Java code to calculate an insurance quote in several places, for example, we could write a scriptlet in a JSP to do it or add the necessary code to our QuoteData bean. However the important thing to remember is that we should separate out as much as possible the different concerns of a web application. Controller JSPs handle the client's request but should not also execute business processes. View JSPs are intended for building the presentation of dynamic content, but not for the processes that provide that content. The JavaBeans we have introduced so far are Java objects, but have a specific role of being *Data Transfer Objects* (DTOs), whose role is to encapsulate data to enable it to be passed between different components, a role that does not include business processes (though, as we have seen, it might include data validation or formatting).

What is missing in our current architecture is any representation of the underlying model, the representation in code of the business domain to which our web application is intended to provide access. This model could be built using any number of Java technologies, from ordinary JavaBeans to Enterprise JavaBeans or the Java Messaging Service. However, our first step in providing an underlying model is to create a single class that acts as a *process bean*. A process bean is a Java object that encapsulates one or more related business processes. In our case, we need a process bean that can calculate a quotation for home insurance. Its interface might look something like the UML diagram of the 'com.webhome-cover.model.InsuranceQuoter' class in Figure 10.17.

Figure 10.17 shows a process bean called 'InsuranceQuoter' in a package called 'com.webhomecover.model' with methods to calculate buildings or contents insurance quotes. Since these methods simply take JavaBean objects as parameters, process them and return a result, without storing any local data, there is no need to actually create an instance of InsuranceQuoter. We can simply make the methods static and call them using the class directly, e.g.:

```
double premium=InsuranceQuoter.getBuildingsQuote(buildings);
```

The obvious place to call this method in our current set of components is in the 'processquote.jsp' page, since this is the point in the workflow where we have access to all the client data and are ready to process this data. We will need a page import directive for the 'InsuranceQuoter' class in the 'com.webhomecover.model' package:

```
<%@page import="com.webhomecover.model.InsuranceQuoter" %>
```

What then, is the implementation of the InsuranceQuoter class and its methods? Since this is a fictional web site, we can make up any algorithms we like to calculate the insurance, such as this one here for buildings insurance:

- Calculations begin with a base premium which is 0.2% of the market value.
- The base premium is then adjusted by property type. For a terraced building this is unchanged. However the premium for an apartment is 95% of the base, for a semi-detached building 105% and a detached building 110%.
- An additional 1% is then added to the premium for each bedroom.

FIGURE 10.17 UML diagram of the com.webhomecover.model. InsuranceQuoter class

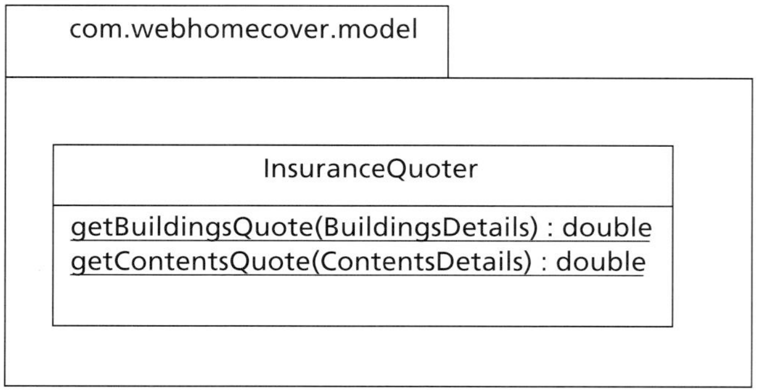

- Depending on which of the four age ranges the building falls into, we add 1%, 2%, 3% or 4% to the premium (the older the property the higher the premium).
- Finally, we add 10% for a timber building (more likely to burn down).

Here is a fictional formula for calculating contents insurance:

- The base premium is 0.04% of the required cover.
- If accidental damage cover is required, we add 25% to the premium.
- If the deductible amount on claims is more than 500, then we reduce the premium by 10%; if it is more than 1000, we reduce the premium by 20%.

Here is the implementation of the 'InsuranceQuoter' bean, with its two static methods, 'getBuildingsQuote' and 'getContentsQuote'.

```java
package com.webhomecover.model;

import com.webhomecover.beans.BuildingsDetails;
import com.webhomecover.beans.ContentsDetails;

public class InsuranceQuoter
{
    public static final int DETACHED = 1;
    public static final int SEMIDETACHED = 2;
    public static final int APARTMENT = 4;
    public static final int TERRACED = 3;

  public static double getBuildingsQuote
    (BuildingsDetails buildingsDetails)
  {
    System.out.println("in InsuranceQuoteBean::getBuildingsQuote");
    double premium = 0.0;
    double basicQuote = buildingsDetails.getMarketValue() * .002;
    int building = 0;
    String propertyType = buildingsDetails.getPropertyType();
    if (propertyType.equals("apartment"))
    {
     building = APARTMENT;
    }
    if(propertyType.equals("semi"))
    {
     building = SEMIDETACHED;
    }
    if(propertyType.equals("terraced"))
    {
     building = TERRACED;
    }
    if(propertyType.equals("detached"))
    {
     building = DETACHED;
    }
    switch (building)
```

```
    {
     case DETACHED :
      premium = basicQuote * 1.1;
      break;
     case SEMIDETACHED :
      premium = basicQuote * 1.05;
      break;
     case TERRACED :
      premium = basicQuote * 1;
      break;
     case APARTMENT :
      premium = basicQuote * 0.95;
    }
    premium = premium + (buildingsDetails.getBedroomCount() *
        (premium / 100));
    String yearString =
     buildingsDetails.getConstructionDate().substring(2, 4);
    int year = Integer.parseInt(yearString);
    switch(year)
    {
     case 00 :
      premium += premium * .04;
      break;
     case 01 :
      premium += premium * .03;
      break;
     case 51 :
      premium += premium * .02;
      break;
     case 71 :
      premium += premium * .01;
    }
    if(buildingsDetails.getConstructionType().equals("timber"))
    {
     premium += (premium * 0.1);
    }
    return premium;
  }

  public static double getContentsQuote
    (ContentsDetails contentsDetails)
  {
   System.out.println("in InsuranceQuoteBean::getContentsQuote");
   boolean accidentalCover = contentsDetails.getAccidentalCover();
   int cover = contentsDetails.getCoverAmount();
   int deductible = contentsDetails.getDeductibleAmount();

// calculate the initial premium
   double premium = cover * 0.004;
   if (accidentalCover)
   {
```

```
      premium *= 1.25;
    }
    if(deductible >= 1000)
    {
      premium -= (premium * 0.2);
    }
    else
    {
      if(deductible >= 500)
      {
        premium -= (premium * 0.1);
      }
    }
    return premium;
  }
}
```

Here is the 'processquote.jsp' page that interacts with the various beans in the application. It retrieves all three DTO beans from the session, so that it can pass them to the process bean and generate the necessary insurance quotes.

```
<%@ page import="com.webhomecover.model.InsuranceQuoter" %>
<jsp:useBean id="choice" class="com.webhomecover.beans.QuoteChoice"
scope="session" />
<jsp:useBean id="buildings" class="com.webhomecover.beans.BuildingsDetails"
scope="session" />
<jsp:useBean id="contents" class="com.webhomecover.beans.ContentsDetails"
scope="session" />

<%
// get the quote for a buildings policy (if required)
if(choice.getBuildings())
{
   double buildingsQuote =
       InsuranceQuoter.getBuildingsQuote(buildings);
// update the buildings details with the quote
   buildings.setInsuranceQuote(buildingsQuote);
// put the buildings details back in the session (for replicated servers)
   session.setAttribute("buildings", buildings);
}

// get the quote for a contents policy (if required)
if(choice.getContents())
{
   double contentsQuote = InsuranceQuoter.getContentsQuote(contents);
//update the contents details with the quote
   contents.setInsuranceQuote(contentsQuote);
// put the contents details back in the session
// (for replicated servers)
   session.setAttribute("contents", contents);
}
%>
```

NOTE

The comment in the code about setting the attribute back in the session for replicated servers is subtle but important. If you get a reference to an object in a session and make changes to it, the object in that session will be changed. However in systems that replicate the same application across multiple servers, there is usually a copy of each client session on another machine or in a file for failover purposes (i.e. if the current machine fails then the copy of the session can be used on another server instead). Explicitly re-setting the attribute in the session acts as a trigger to the server that the object in the session has been changed, so it will also update the copy of the session.

Finally, either the 'processbuildings.jsp' or 'processcontents.jsp' page will forward to the last page in the webflow, 'displayquote.jsp'. This JSP is not a controller component but a view component. It retrieves the JavaBeans from the session and uses them to display the insurance quote(s) on the page using 'jsp:getProperty' tags. At the end, it invalidates the user session (it's no longer needed and we should free up server-side resources when we have finished with them).

```
<jsp:useBean id="choice" class="com.webhomecover.beans.QuoteChoice"
scope="session" />
<jsp:useBean id="contents"
class="com.webhomecover.beans.ContentsDetails" scope="session" />
<jsp:useBean id="buildings"
class="com.webhomecover.beans.BuildingsDetails" scope="session" />

<?xml version="1.0"?>
<!DOCTYPE html PUBLIC
   "-//W3C//DTD XHTML 1.1//EN"
   "http://www.w3.org/TR/xhtml11/DTD/xhtml11.dtd">
<html xmlns="http://www.w3.org/1999/xhtml" xml:lang="en">
   <head>
      <link href="webhomecover.css" rel="stylesheet" type="text/css" />
      <title>WebHomeCover Insurance Quote</title>
   </head>
   <body>
      <h1>Here is your insurance quote from WebHomeCover</h1>
      <%
      if(choice.getBuildings())
      {
      %>
      <h2>Your Buildings Quote:</h2>
      <p>
       <jsp:getProperty name="buildings"
       property="formattedInsuranceQuote"/>
      </p>
      <%
      }
```

```
      if(choice.getContents() )
       {
    %>
      <h2>Your Contents Quote:</h2>
      <p>
        <jsp:getProperty name="contents"
         property="formattedInsuranceQuote"/>
      </p>
      <%
       }
       session.invalidate();
    %>
      <form action="welcome.jsp" method="get">
      <p>
       <input type="submit" value=
       "Thanks for the quote, now take me back to the home page" />
      </p>
      </form>
    </body>
  </html>
```

Figure 10.18 shows what the final page looks like if the data shown in Figures 10.15 and 10.16 has been chosen, requesting both contents and buildings quotes.

FIGURE 10.18 The 'displayquote.jsp' page showing one of the many possible results of the webflow that implements the 'get insurance quote' use case

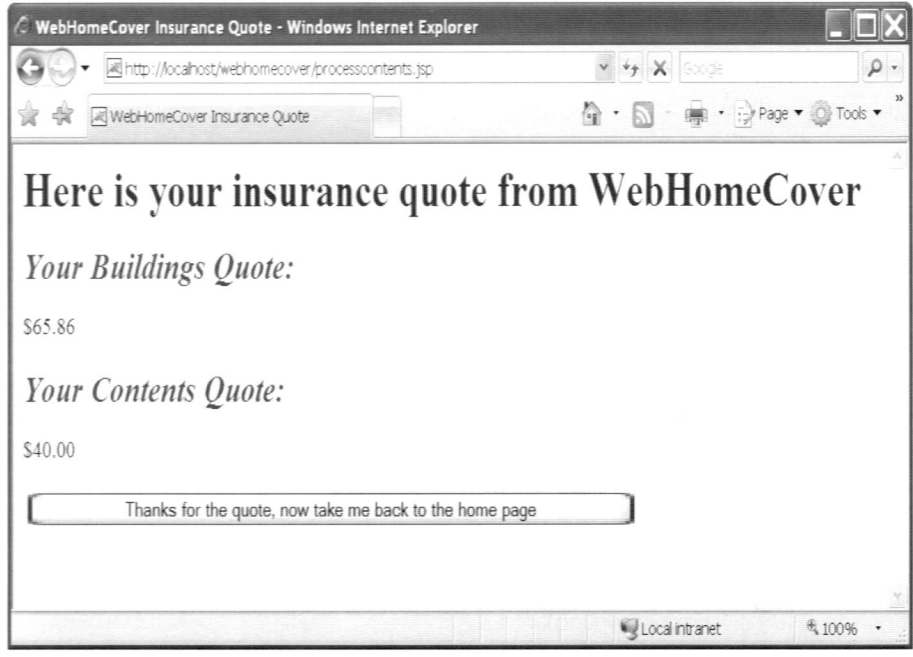

10.12 The JSP Standard Tag Library

In the JSPs we have written so far, we have had to use scriptlets containing Java code on several occasions to add control structures (specifically selections) to the pages. This has led to a somewhat complex mix of tags and code, having to be interwoven at various points. This part of 'processchoice.jsp' is a case in point:

```
<%
if(choice.getBuildings() )
{
%>
<jsp:forward page="buildings.jsp"/>
<%
}
else
{
    if(choice.getContents() )
    {
%>
<jsp:forward page="contents.jsp"/>
<%
    }
}
%>
```

Fortunately there is a simple solution to this problem: the JSP Standard Tag Library (JSTL). There are many tag libraries available for use with Java web applications, but many of these are specific to particular products or frameworks. In contrast, the JSTL provides us with a standard set of tags that can be used with any Java application server. These tags are distributed among four libraries:

- Core
- Internationalization and formatting
- Database access
- XML processing

In this chapter, we introduce some aspects of the core library. In the next chapter, we use some of the tags from the XML processing library to integrate XML documents into our Java web applications. There is an open-source implementation of the JSTL available from the Jakarta project, which we will use in these examples (Jakarta Project 2004).

 NOTE We use the Jakarta implementation of JSTL version 1.1. There is also a version 1.2 specification implemented as part of some Java EE 1.5 application servers, but this is not available as a separate project (at the time of writing).

Along with the JSTL, there is also an Expression Language (EL) that began as part of the JSTL and has now developed into a standard component of both JSP implementations and the JavaServer Faces framework. The intention of the expression language was to make it easier for web developers to manage application data without having to know the underlying implementation language. The result is that we can, for example, interact with JavaBeans by using JSTL tags rather than Java scriptlets.

Using the JSTL

The first step to using the JSTL in a web application is to add the necessary Java Archive (JAR) files to the application's classpath. Additional JAR files can be added to a web application by using a special folder called 'lib' which is a subfolder of the 'WEB-INF' directory. Any JAR file put into the folder is automatically included in the web application's classpath and is available to other Java components in the same application. The two JAR files that need to be added are 'jstl.jar', which contains the API of the JSTL, and 'standard.jar', which contains the implementation classes for the library. There are some other supporting JAR files required for the XML library that may or may not already be available in a Java application server, but we will look at these in the next chapter.

Figure 10.19 shows the various folders required by the Web application and the location of the two JSTL JAR files within the 'WEB-INF/lib' folder.

Once the JSTL JAR files have been included in the application, JSPs can reference the libraries by using a *tag library directive*. Each of the four libraries has a separate URI and prefix. For the core library, the directive looks like this:

```
<%@ taglib uri="http://java.sun.com/jsp/jstl/core" prefix="c" %>
```

NOTE	Be careful to use the correct URI in the directive for version 1.1. There are different directives for version 1.0 that are very similar but do not include the 'jsp' folder. Do not use this older library or you will find that some of the examples will not work.

FIGURE 10.19 The JSTL 'jar' files in the 'WEB-INF/lib' folder of the web application

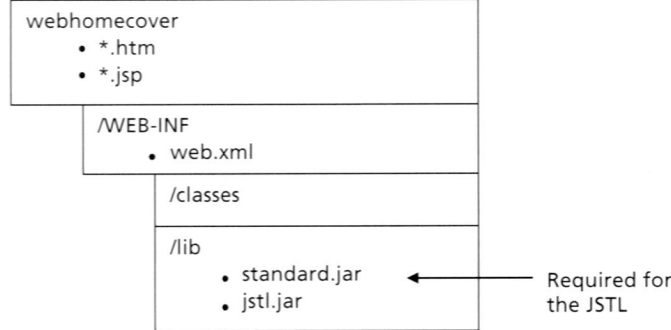

The 'c' prefix is the normal convention for this library. The core library contains a number of tags that have much in common with some XSLT tags. For example, the equivalent structure to the Java 'if … else' construct used in the current version of 'processchoice.jsp' is 'choose … when … otherwise', with a syntax you will find familiar from some of our XSLT examples.

```
<c:choose>
   <c:when test="condition">
      . . .
   </c:when>
   <c:otherwise>
      . . .
   </c:otherwise>
</c:choose>
```

Similarly there is an 'if' tag, which can be used where there is no alternative action:

```
<c:if test="condition">
. . .
</c:if>
```

For iterations, there is a 'forEach' tag:

```
<c:forEach var="varname" items="itemlist">
. . .
</c:forEach>
```

We will work through some examples that use these tags, but first we need to introduce the JSP Expression Language (EL).

Using the Expression Language

In order to use constructs such as the 'if' and 'choose' elements, we need to be able to express conditions which relate to the state of objects in our web application. To support this, the JSTL includes the Expression Language (EL), which includes the ability to use JavaBeans and their properties in conditional expressions. An expression is preceded by a dollar sign and surrounded by braces (like property values in an Ant build script):

```
${expression}
```

The role of an expression is to evaluate some kind of result, which may be the value of a variable or the result of a relational or arithmetic expression. Here is a simple example. One of the elements in the core library is 'set', which sets the value of a variable. Here, we declare a variable called 'localname'. The 'scope' attribute is set to 'request' (i.e. this variable will have request scope) and the optional 'value' attribute sets a default value for the variable.

```
<c:set var="localname" scope="request" value="no value" />
```

Here is an example of how we can use the expression language. The 'out' element writes the value of an expression to the current JSP response. We use the expression language to get the value of the 'localname' variable:

```
<c:out value="${localname}" />
```

We can also use the built-in JSP objects within EL expressions and some special EL operators. Here, for example, is an expression that uses the 'param' object to access a request parameter, and uses the 'empty' operator to check that the parameter is not empty or null. For this example, we assume there is a parameter called 'name'.

```
${!empty param.name}
```

In this code fragment, we combine together the 'set', 'out' and 'if' elements from the core library, and use expressions to set the value of a variable from the request, if the named request parameter is not empty or null. Otherwise the variable will retain its default value ('no value').

```
<c:set var="localname" scope="request" value="no value" />
<c:if test="${!empty param.name}">
  <c:set var="localname" value="${param.name}" />
</c:if>
<c:out value="${localname}" />
```

One important thing to be aware of is that a server may be ignoring your EL expressions, because servers can be configured not to process them. To make sure that your expressions are processed, you should include the following page directive in any JSPs that use the expression language:

```
<%@page isELIgnored="false" %>
```

Otherwise you may find that your web application behaves very oddly, with none of your conditional or iteration statements working. To make things worse, you will not get any error messages from the server if it is ignoring your expressions!

Using JavaBeans in expressions

Within an expression we can use the names of JavaBeans and access their properties using the dot operator:

```
${beanname.propertyname}
```

For example, if we wanted to access the 'bedroomCount' property (i.e. the 'getBedroomCount' method) of the 'buildings' bean, the expression would look like this:

```
${buildings.bedroomCount}
```

Here is a modified version of 'processchoice.jsp' using the JSTL core library. Note how the page now consists only of tags. Since there are no longer any scriptlets there is no Java code at all. The expression syntax is used for the conditions in the 'when' and 'if' tags, accessing the Boolean 'buildings' and 'contents' properties of the 'choice' bean. These properties are, of course, based on the 'getBuildings' and 'getContents' methods of the bean.

```
<%@ taglib uri="http://java.sun.com/jsp/jstl/core" prefix="c" %>

<jsp:useBean id="choice" class="com.webhomecover.beans.QuoteChoice"
scope="session" />
<jsp:setProperty name="choice" property="buildings" value="false" />
<jsp:setProperty name="choice" property="contents" value="false" />
<jsp:setProperty name="choice" property="*" />
```

```
<!-- select which page to go to depending on the check box selected -->
<c:choose>
   <c:when test="${choice.buildings}">
      <jsp:forward page="buildings.jsp"/>
   </c:when>
   <c:otherwise>
      <c:if test="${choice.contents}">
         <jsp:forward page="contents.jsp"/>
      </c:if>
   </c:otherwise>
</c:choose>
```

JSTL iterations and indexed JavaBean properties

Where a bean contains a property that is implemented as some kind of collection, it is called an 'indexed property'. Here is a very simple example of a JavaBean that has an indexed property called 'strings' (i.e. it has 'getStrings' and 'setStrings' methods that access an array). Since array elements can be accessed by an index number, 'strings' is an indexed property.

```
package com.webhomecover.beans;

public class StringBean
{
   private String[] strings =
      {"String 0","String 1","String 2","String 3","String 4"};

   public String[] getStrings()
   {
    return strings;
   }
   public void setStrings(String[] s)
   {
    strings = s;
   }
}
```

Standard JSP actions provide limited support for indexed properties. The 'jsp:setProperty' tag can be passed an indexed property, but the parameter type must be an array of Strings, and the 'getProperty' tag does not support the output of indexed properties, so they have to be accessed by scriptlets. In contrast, the JSTL core library provides support for indexed properties, and the type of the indexed property can be either an array or a Java Collection object.

We can use the JSTL core library to iterate over the elements of an indexed property using the 'forEach' tag. In this short code example, we create an instance of the StringBean class (using the 'jsp:useBean' tag) and then use the 'foreach' tag to iterate over its 'strings' property. The 'items' attribute of the 'forEach' tag contains an expression that identifies the indexed property ('stringBean.strings') while the 'var' attribute is the name of the local variable that will be used to contain the currently indexed value inside the loop. In this example, the 'out' tag is used to write that value to the page.

```
<%@ taglib uri="http://java.sun.com/jsp/jstl/core" prefix="c" %>

<?xml version="1.0"?>
<!DOCTYPE html PUBLIC
    "-//W3C//DTD XHTML 1.1//EN"
    "http://www.w3.org/TR/xhtml11/DTD/xhtml11.dtd">
<html xmlns="http://www.w3.org/1999/xhtml" xml:lang="en">
    <head>
        <link href="webhomecover.css" rel="stylesheet" type="text/css" />
        <title>WebHomeCover</title>
    </head>
    <body>
        <!-- File: indexedproperty.jsp -->
        <jsp:useBean id="stringBean"
    class="com.webhomecover.beans.StringBean" />
        <div>
            <c:forEach var="string" items="${stringBean.strings}">
                <c:out value="${string}"/>
                <br />
            </c:forEach>
        </div>
    </body>
</html>
```

To conclude this section, we see a simple example of how a bean with indexed properties might be useful in a web application. Most HTML form components send a single value to the server, accessible from the request object, but one exception to this is the 'select' component, which can be configured to allow multiple items from the select list to be chosen. This means that when the value of the select list is sent to the server, it may have multiple values. Here is a simple XHTML page that contains a list that enables multiple selections. We can do this by setting the value of the 'multiple' attribute to 'multiple'.

```
<?xml version="1.0"?>
<!DOCTYPE html PUBLIC "-//W3C//DTD XHTML 1.1//EN"
    "http://www.w3.org/TR/xhtml11/DTD/xhtml11.dtd">
<html xmlns="http://www.w3.org/1999/xhtml" xml:lang="en">
    <head>
        <title>Insurance Claim Form</title>
    </head>
    <body>
    <!-- File: interests.htm -->
        <form action="processinterests.jsp" method="post">
            <table>
                <tr>
            <td><label for="list">Please select all the services you would like
    information about:</label></td>
                </tr>
                <tr>
                    <td>
                        <select name="interests" id="list" size="4"
                        multiple="multiple">
```

```
                         <option id="quote">Getting home insurance quotes</option>
                         <option id="claim">Making a claim</option>
                         <option id="buy">Buying insurance</option>
                         <option id="change">Making a change to your policy</option>
                       </select>
                   </td>
               </tr>
               <tr>
                   <td><input type="submit" value="Submit" /></td>
               </tr>
           </table>
       </form>
   </body>
</html>
```

Figure 10.20 shows the form displayed in Internet Explorer 7. Users can select multiple lines from the list by holding down the CTRL or Shift keys while clicking on items in the list.

Here is a simple JavaBean ('InterestBean') that contains a single indexed property ('interests'):

```
package com.webhomecover.beans;

public class InterestBean
{
    private String[] interests;

    public String[] getInterests()
    {
        return interests;
    }
```

FIGURE 10.20 An HTML form with two items selected from a multiple select list

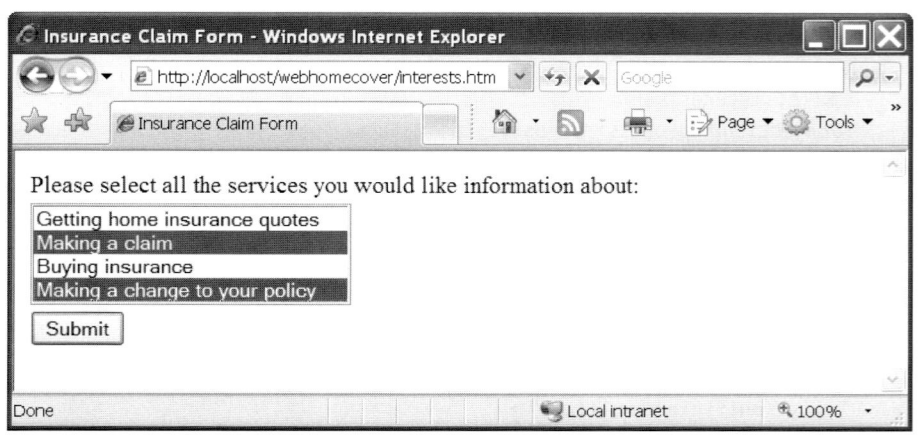

```
    public void setInterests(String[] arr)
    {
        interests=arr;
    }
}
```

This JSP populates an instance of the InterestBean from the request using the 'jsp:setProperty' tag, which does at least provide us with the ability to set an indexed property from the request. It then uses the 'forEach' tag from the core library to write the selected values in the indexed property to the response.

```
<%@ taglib uri="http://java.sun.com/jsp/jstl/core" prefix="c" %>
<?xml version="1.0"?>
<!DOCTYPE html PUBLIC
    "-//W3C//DTD XHTML 1.1//EN"
    "http://www.w3.org/TR/xhtml11/DTD/xhtml11.dtd">
<html xmlns="http://www.w3.org/1999/xhtml" xml:lang="en">
    <head>
        <link href="webhomecover.css" rel="stylesheet" type="text/css" />
        <title>WebHomeCover</title>
    </head>
    <body>
        <!-- File: processinterests.jsp -->
        <h1>Your interests</h1>
    <jsp:useBean id="interestBean"
        class = "com.webhomecover.beans.InterestBean" />
    <jsp:setProperty name="interestBean" property="interests"
        param="interests" />
    <div>
        <c:forEach var="selected" items="${interestBean.interests}">
            <c:out value="${selected}" />
            <br />
        </c:forEach>
    </div>
    </body>
</html>
```

Figure 10.21 shows the generated page if the user chooses the two options selected in Figure 10.20.

There is a lot more to the JSTL and the EL than we have introduced here, but we will revisit the JSTL in Section 11.5.

10.13 XML JavaServer Pages

So far in this chapter we have been generating valid XHTML pages from JSPs that have not themselves been XML pages. Using some of the non-XML JSP tags that we have introduced, such as the scriptlet and expression tags, means that some of our JSP documents cannot be well-formed XML. This is not necessarily a problem, since our view pages are

FIGURE 10.21 The generated page showing the values in the indexed property of the InterestBean

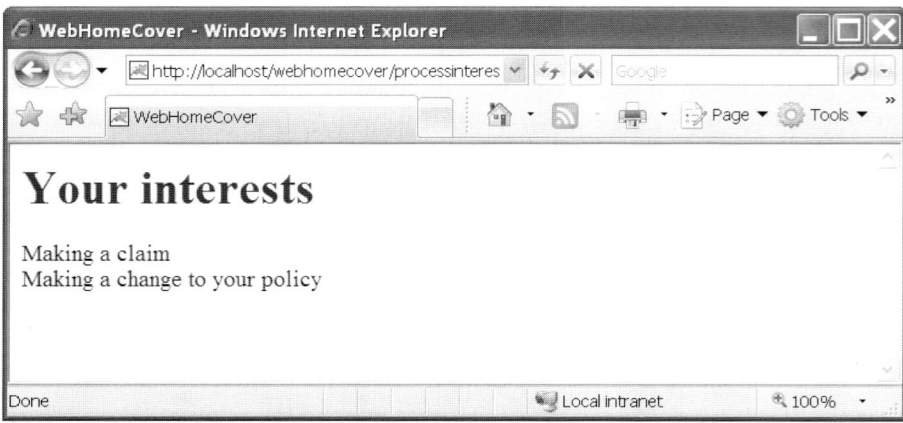

generating valid XHTML. However, if we write our JSP pages using only tags that are in valid XML format, then we can potentially benefit from this by, for example, being able to edit our JSPs in an XML editor, or transform JSP pages using XSLT. JSP pages that use the XML syntax are often given a '.jspx' file extension. To make it possible to write JSP pages as well-formed XML, the JSP tags that use the non-XML style also have an XML equivalent (Table 10.1).

Towards the end of the 'displayquote.jsp' page there is a scriptlet that invalidates the session:

```
<%
    session.invalidate();
%>
```

We can replace this with an XML-compliant version:

```
<jsp:scriptlet>
    session.invalidate();
</jsp:scriptlet>
```

TABLE 10.1 JSP and JSPX tags

JSP tag	Type	JSPX tag
<% %>	scriptlet	<jsp:scriptlet> </jsp:scriptlet>
<% = %>	expression	<jsp:expression> </jsp:expression>
<%@page ... %>	page directive	<jsp:directive.page ... />

Similarly, 'processquote.jsp' has the following page import directive:

```
<%@ page import="com.webhomecover.model.InsuranceQuoter" %>
```

The XML version of the tag would be:

```
<jsp:directive.page import="com.webhomecover.model.InsuranceQuoter" />
```

and the page directive to make sure the Expression Language is not being ignored would look like this:

```
<jsp:directive.page isELIgnored="false" />
```

Unfortunately, however, not all conversions to XML-style elements are simple. If we are using the JSTL, then our pages will include a taglib directive like this:

```
<%@ taglib uri="http://java.sun.com/jsp/jstl/core" prefix="c" %>
```

Unlike the page directive, there is no direct equivalent provided as an XML element. Instead, we have to define the namespace and URL of any tag libraries as attributes of the root element. There is no particular root element name defined for JSP pages, but there is an optional 'jsp:root' element that we can use as a kind of generic root element, and the taglib URIs can be added to this. For example, this 'jsp:root' element includes an attribute for the URI of the JSTL core library, along with the standard URI for the 'jsp' prefixed tags:

```
<jsp:root
    xmlns:jsp="http://java.sun.com/JSP/Page"
    xmlns:c="http://java.sun.com/jsp/jstl/core"
    version="2.1">
```

NOTE — If you choose to use the 'jsp:root' element, the JSP 'version' attribute is compulsory. Valid values for JSP versions are "1.2", "2.0", or "2.1". You may need to change this value depending on which versions your server supports.

As an example of the various aspects of converting a JSP page to a JSPX page, we will look at 'displayquote.jsp' which (as we showed earlier in this chapter) includes several scriptlets and a DOCTYPE declaration for the generated XHTML file. Both of these will have to be changed to make this page well-formed XML. Of course the scriptlet that contains the conditional 'if' statement can be replaced by the 'if' tag from the JSTL, and the remaining scriptlet that invalidates the session can be put in a 'jsp:scriptlet' tag. If we are going to use the JSTL then we will need to include its URI in a 'jsp:root' element, as already described. Dealing with the doctype is a little more complex. We will need to use a 'jsp:output' tag (which is used to configure the output document) to specify the 'html' root element and DTD in XML format. The 'omit-xml-declaration' attribute is set to 'false' here, to make the page begin with '<?xml version="1.0"?>'

```
<jsp:output omit-xml-declaration="false"
doctype-root-element="html"
```

```
doctype-public="-//W3C//DTD XHTML 1.1//EN"
doctype-system="http://www.w3.org/TR/xhtml11/DTD/xhtml11.dtd" />
```

Another issue with XHTML documents is to make sure that they are handled correctly by the browser in terms of their content type. A page directive element is handy here:

```
<jsp:directive.page contentType="text/html"/>
```

Bringing all of these aspects together here is a revised version of 'displayquote.jsp' renamed 'displayquote.jspx' which is comprised entirely of well-formed XML.

```
<?xml version="1.0"?>
<jsp:root xmlns:jsp="http://java.sun.com/JSP/Page"
    xmlns:c="http://java.sun.com/jsp/jstl/core"
    version="2.1">
  <jsp:directive.page contentType="text/html"/>
  <jsp:output omit-xml-declaration="false"
    doctype-root-element="html"
    doctype-public="-//W3C//DTD XHTML 1.1//EN"
    doctype-system="http://www.w3.org/TR/xhtml11/DTD/xhtml11.dtd" />

  <jsp:useBean id="choice" class="com.webhomecover.beans.QuoteChoice"
    scope="session" />
  <jsp:useBean id="contents" class="com.webhomecover.beans.ContentsDetails"
    scope="session" />
  <jsp:useBean id="buildings" class="com.webhomecover.beans.BuildingsDetails"
    scope="session" />
<html xmlns="http://www.w3.org/1999/xhtml" xml:lang="en">

  <head>
    <link href="webhomecover.css" rel="stylesheet" type="text/css" />
    <title>WebHomeCover Insurance Quote</title>
  </head>
 <body>
  <h1>Here is your insurance quote from WebHomeCover</h1>

  <c:if test="${choice.buildings}">
    <h2>Your Buildings Quote:</h2>
    <p>
     <jsp:getProperty name="buildings"
         property="formattedInsuranceQuote"/>
    </p>
  </c:if>

  <c:if test="${choice.contents}">
    <h2>Your Contents Quote:</h2>
    <p>
     <jsp:getProperty name="contents"
         property="formattedInsuranceQuote"/>
    </p>
  </c:if>

  <jsp:scriptlet>
```

```
      session.invalidate();
  </jsp:scriptlet>

    <form action="welcome.jsp" method="get">
        <div>
          <input type="submit"
            value="Thanks for the quote, now take me back to the home page"
            />
        </div>
      </form>
    </body>
  </html>
</jsp:root>
```

10.14 Integrating the three-region layout

Finally in this chapter, we integrate the pages we have created for the 'Get Insurance Quote' use case into the three-region layout we developed in Chapter 4 using Cascading Style Sheets. When we first introduced this layout, it was in the context of static HTML pages, as opposed to dynamic XHTML being generated by JSPs, so our approach here will be a little different. One feature of JSPs is that they provide an 'include' directive that can be used to integrate static XHTML fragments into a generated page:

```
<jsp:directive.include file="filename" />
```

This directive should not be confused with the 'jsp:include' action that is used to integrate dynamic content. The include directive is only for including static content.

To integrate the components of the three-region layout into our JSPs, we break the current HTML version down into two components, one that contains the header and sidebar information and another that contains the footer. Here is an XHTML fragment ('header.htm') that contains the mark-up for the header and side navigation bars. Note that this is not a complete XHTML document, only some mark-up that can be used inside a larger document.

```
<div id="navigationbar">
  <a href="welcome.jsp">
    <img src="webhomecoverlogo.gif" alt="WebHomeCover logo" />
  </a>
  <span class="topnavigationlink">
    <a href="quote.htm">Get a quote</a>
  </span>
  <span class="topnavigationlink">
    <a href="claim.htm">Make a claim</a>
  </span>
  <span class="topnavigationlink">
    <a href="policies.htm">See my policies</a>
  </span>
</div>
<div id="sidenavigation">
```

```
    <div class="sidenavigationlink">
      <a href="build.htm">buildings cover</a>
    </div>
    <div class="sidenavigationlink">
      <a href="content.htm">contents cover</a>
    </div>
    <div class="sidenavigationlink">
      <a href="deal.htm">special deals</a>
    </div>
    <div class="sidenavigationlink">
      <a href="more.htm">more info</a>
    </div>
  </div>
```

Similarly, here is the footer mark-up ('footer.htm').

```
<div id="pagefooter">
  <hr />
  <p id="footer"> &copy;WebHomeCover.com 2000–2008 </p>
</div>
```

To integrate these into our pages, we insert the appropriate JSP include directives into the page. We also need to apply the necessary style to the body of the main page. Here is the 'threeregion.css' style sheet that we first introduced in Chapter 4. We need to apply the 'content' style to the main body of each page so that its left margin matches the width of the side navigation bar.

```
a:link{color: white}
a:visited{color: red}
a:hover{font-weight: bold}
a:active{font-style:italic}
#navigationbar {color: white; background-color: rgb(0,0,150)}
#sidenavigation {float: left; height: 400px; color: white;
background-color: rgb(0,0,150)}
#content {margin-left: 10em}
#pagefooter {clear: left}
.topnavigationlink {clear: left; margin-left: 1em; font-size: 1.1em}
.sidenavigationlink {font-size: 1em}
```

Here is a modified version of the 'welcome.jsp' page, with the necessary tags to integrate the three-region layout. The two JSP include directives bring in the header ('header.htm') and the footer ('footer.htm') while the main body of the page has been put inside a 'div' with the id of 'content', so the correct style is applied. We also need to add the 'link' element to apply the three-region layout style sheet.

```
<!DOCTYPE html PUBLIC "-//W3C//DTD XHTML 1.1//EN"
  "http://www.w3.org/TR/xhtml11/DTD/xhtml11.dtd">
<html xmlns="http://www.w3.org/1999/xhtml" xml:lang="en">
  <head>
    <title>Welcome to WebHomeCover</title>
      <link href="threeregion.css" rel="stylesheet" type="text/css" />
      <link href="webhomecover.css" rel="stylesheet" type="text/css" />
```

```
    </head>
    <body>
        <jsp:directive.include file="header.htm" />
        <div id="content">
            <h1><em>Welcome to </em>
                <span class="companyname">WebHomeCover.com</span>
            </h1>
            <h2>
                Your home and possessions are important.
                <br/>
                We give you the very best insurance cover at the lowest prices.
            </h2>
            <p>
                <a href="choosequote.jsp">Get an insurance quote</a>
            </p>
        </div>
        <jsp:directive.include file="footer.htm" />
    </body>
</html>
```

Figure 10.22 shows what the welcome page looks like with the three-region layout applied.

FIGURE 10.22 The three-region layout integrated into a JSP-based webflow

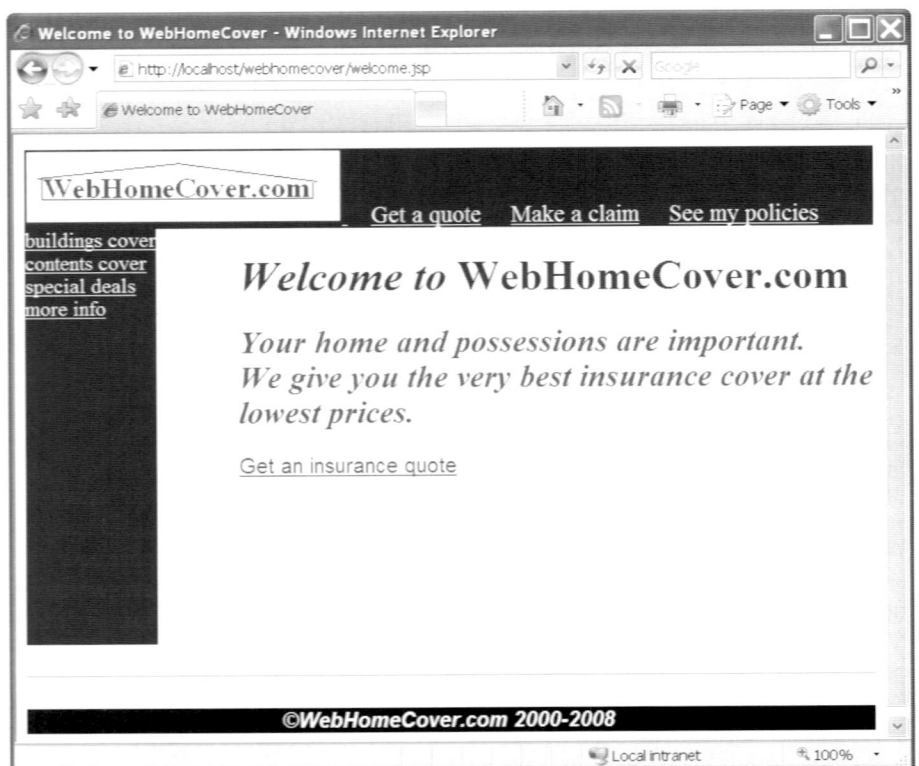

Exercises

10.1 Our example servlet accessed the 'User-Agent' field of the HTTP header. Another field of this header contains the client's language preferences, as set in their particular browser, represented by the 'Accept-Language' header. In this line of servlet code, we call the 'getHeader' method to access this field, which returns a string containing the language options in the browser's list.

```
String languages = request.getHeader("Accept-Language");
```

Create a new servlet called AcceptLanguageServlet that gets the user language preferences from the browser and displays these in the page. Remember that you must register your servlet in 'web.xml' and use the URL that your specify in the 'servlet-mapping' element to access the servlet via the browser. Try changing the language settings in your browser to make the servlet display different content for different preferences ('Tools … Options … General' tab in Firefox, 'Tools … Internet Options' in Internet Explorer. You have to close and reopen the browser for changes in Language preferences to take effect). Be aware that if the browser has more than one preference then they are all sent as part of the same string, so if your browser lists English, French and German in that order as its preferred languages, then the string will contain the elements 'en', 'fr' and 'de'. Depending on your browser there may be other characters too. We will be (indirectly) using the language information when we look at building multi-language web applications later in this book.

10.2 Write a JSP that is able to display the information about the browser sent with the request as the 'User-Agent' header (i.e. performs the same task as the UserAgentServlet). Compare the two implementations (servlet and JSP) and consider the strengths and weaknesses of the two approaches.

10.3 Convert the controller server pages from the insurance application example so that all the conditional statements that are currently written using scriptlets are replaced by tags from the JSTL.

10.4 Ensure that all of the pages of the insurance application are written using well-formed XML by replacing any remaining old-style JSP tags with the XML versions.

10.5 Create a webflow for the questionnaire application that maintains a record of the user's responses in a JavaBean that is stored in the session. Display all the responses of the user in the final screen.

SUMMARY

We began this chapter by looking at some commonly used architectural patterns for web applications, Model 1, which is a simple architecture with a single component processing both the request and the response, and Model 2, which is based on the Model–View–Controller architecture. In Model 2, a 'front component or front controller' (that may be either a servlet or a JSP) processes the request and a 'view component' (usually JSP) processes the response. We introduced the syntax for both servlets and JSPs, and saw how JSPs can be used to embed dynamic content into XHTML pages by using special tags that are understood by a JSP compiler, which generates a servlet that is deployed on the server. We began the examples with a simple servlet implementation, followed by a single JSP that both processed the request and generated the response, and then built a simple Model 1 architecture, where the JSP used a JavaBean to interact with the underlying data model. We continued to refactor our design until we had a Model 2 architecture, with separate JSPs taking on the roles of controller and view. We followed this by building a more complex webflow from the home insurance domain, using multiple request–response cycles and management of user sessions. The following section introduced the JSP Standard Tag Library (JSTL) and the JSP Expression Language (EL), and showed how they can be used together as an alternative to writing many scriptlets in JSPs. Finally, we looked at how JSPs can be written as JSPX pages, using well-formed XML, and concluded the chapter by integrating the three-region layout style into our example application.

Table 10.2 shows the main JSP tags that were introduced in the chapter, in both original and XML forms (where applicable).

Table 10.3 shows the tags from the JSTL core library that were introduced in this chapter.

TABLE 10.2	JSP tags

JSP tag name	Purpose	Syntax
scriptlet	Embedding multiple lines of Java in a JSP	`<% %>` `<jsp:scriptlet> ... </jsp:scriptlet>`

expression	Embedding a single Java expression that returns a value in a JSP page	`<% = ... %>`
		`<jsp:expression> ...`
		`</jsp:expression>`

directive	Use as a directive to the compiler, for example for importing Java packages	`<%@ ... %>`
		`<jsp:directive.page ... />`
		`<jsp:directive.include`
		`file="filename" />`

Use bean action	To use a JavaBean in a JSP	`<jsp:useBean id="id" scope="scope"` `class="classname" />`
Get bean property action	To write the value of a JavaBean property to the JSP	`<jsp:getProperty name="id"` `property="property" />`

Set bean property action	To set the value of a JavaBean property	`<jsp:setProperty name="name"`
		`property="property"`
		`value="value"/>`

Include action	Include the process of one JSP in another	`<jsp:include page="pagename"/>`
Forward action	Pass control from one JSP to another	`<jsp:forward page="pagename"/>`

TABLE 10.3	Tags from the JSTL core library	

JSTL core tag name	Purpose	Syntax
c:forEach	Iteration	`<c:forEach var="usedinloop" items="itemlist">` `</c:forEach>`

c:if	A conditional code block with no alternative action	`<c:if test="condition">`
		`...`
		`</c:if>`

c:choose	A conditional code block containing an alternative action	`<c:choose>`
		`<c:when test="condition">`
		`...`
		`</c:when>`
		`<c:otherwise>`

c:when	Part of the 'choose' structure, executed if the 'choose' condition is true	`...`
		`</c:otherwise>`
		`</c:choose>`

c:otherwise	Part of the 'choose' structure, executed if the 'choose' condition is false	
c:out	Write to the page	`<c:out value="value" />`
c:set	Set the value of a variable	`<c:set var="name"` `scope="scope" value="value" />`

References and further reading

Flanagan, D. (2005) *Java In A Nutshell*, 5th Edition. O'Reilly.

Fowler, M. (1999) *Refactoring: Improving the Design of Existing Code*. Reading, Mass: Addison-Wesley.

Jakarta Project (2004) *Jakarta Taglibs* http://jakarta.apache.org/taglibs/doc/standard-doc/intro.html

Mahmoud, Q. (2003) *Servlets and JSP Pages: Best Practices*. http://java.sun.com/developer/technicalArticles/javaserverpages/servlets_jsp/

Seshadri, G. (1999) Understanding JavaServer Pages Model 2 architecture: Exploring the MVC design pattern. *JavaWorld*, December 1999. http://www.javaworld.com/javaworld/jw-12-1999/jw-12-ssj-jspmvc_p.html

CHAPTER 11

Using Java and XML Together

LEARNING OBJECTIVES

- To understand the various ways that Java and XML work together

- To be able to process XML documents using both DOM and SAX parsers

- To be able to generate XML documents from JavaBeans

- To understand how the Java Architecture for XML Binding (JAXB) assists the translation between XML documents and Java objects

- To be able to process XML documents using the JSTL XML library

INTRODUCTION

In the first part of this book, we spent some time looking at various aspects of XML, including XHTML, XPath and XSLT. In Chapter 10, we introduced Java-based web applications, and saw how XML is used to configure both web applications and application servers. We also saw that JSP pages can be written as XML documents, which means that they can be validated and processed using XML tools. In this chapter, we draw the two technologies of XML and Java even closer together, and see how Java can be used to process and generate XML documents. We introduce a number of Java-based tools and libraries that help us process and manipulate XML documents, and see how we can generate Java objects from XML documents and vice versa.

There are many ways that Java and XML can be used together. For example, Java programs can be used to parse XML documents and process the data inside them, special tools can be used to convert between Java objects and XML documents, and tag libraries can be used to process XML in JavaServer Pages. There are two types of XML parser available in Java: Document Object Model (DOM) parsers and Simple API for XML (SAX) parsers. DOM parsers build a document object model in memory representing the whole of the source XML document, which can then be accessed via the DOM API. In contrast, SAX parsers process an XML document as a serial data stream and handle the content of the document by triggering processes based on events. Both parsers are, however, part of what is known as the Java API for XML Processing (JAXP). As well as the JAXP parsers, there is also Java Architecture for XML Binding (JAXB), which is a standard part of the Java Software Development Kit from version 6 onwards. This provides a set of software

FIGURE 11.1   Some Java and XML technologies and their interactions

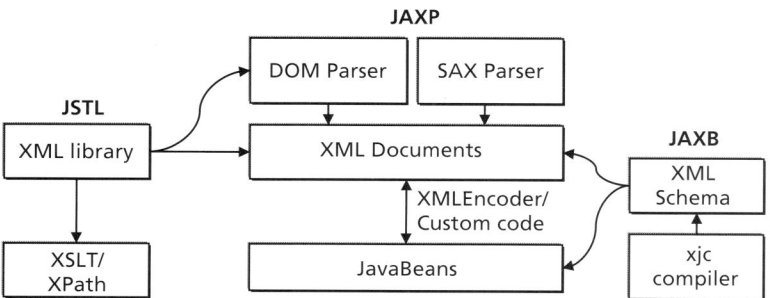

tools, including a special compiler ('xjc') for generating Java classes from XML Schemas, to integrate them with XML documents. Other types of software support for processing XML with Java includes the JSTL XML Library, which provides special JSP tags that can be used to apply XSL transformations to XML documents in JSP pages, or apply XPath expressions within a JSP.

Another aspect of XML and Java is generating XML from JavaBean methods. This is useful where we have a Java object model but want to generate XML documents within a web application. This can be done using one of a number of special tools (including JAXB) or can be done using custom code. Figure 11.1 shows some of the technologies that can be used to handle the interactions between Java and XML.

11.1 XML parsers

Parsers are software components that are able to process data using some methodical approach that both parses the input data and provides the means to process that data. In terms of XML documents, there are two general types of parser: Document Object Model (DOM) parsers and Simple API for XML (SAX) parsers. These have very different approaches, but each of them can have their own benefits depending on the programming context.

DOM parsers

DOM parsers are based on building an in-memory representation of the Document Object Model. The parser builds a document tree in memory that represents the entire document, and then a Java application can be written that navigates through the DOM to process its contents. DOM parsers are based on the W3C recommendation for the DOM that defines standard interfaces to access the document tree. The DOM is independent of platform and language (for example, we have already used the DOM with JavaScript), but of course Java parsers provide access to the model using Java interfaces, classes and methods.

SAX parsers

SAX parsers are very different from DOM parsers because they do not read the entire document into memory to build a tree of nodes that can be navigated. Instead, the application registers event handlers that 'listen' for particular features of the document as it is read sequentially by the parser. The parser tells the event handler what it reads, and the application can respond (or not) to each different type of event. Unlike DOM parsers, which are based on the Document Object Model standards published by the W3C, SAX parsers are not based on existing W3C standards. Instead, they are a development of the open-source community, growing out of the XML-DEV open forum and software released via SourceForge (2007). Originally developed for Java, there are also versions of SAX parsers available for other languages.

Comparing SAX and DOM parsers

If SAX and DOM parsers have very different approaches, why might we choose to use one over the other? Perhaps the most important aspect to consider is that the DOM approach builds an in-memory representation of the entire XML document. This may take up a lot of memory if the document is very large, and it may take some time to parse the document. Using a SAX parser can be much faster and more efficient, because the parser does not build an in-memory representation of the document for subsequent processing but both parses and processes it sequentially (Franklin 2001). Therefore if we wanted to process one small part of a large document, then using a SAX parser would probably be the best option. However, on the other hand, having a Document Object Model can be very useful if we need to apply a number of different processes to the same document, perhaps a series of queries that access different parts of the document. Using the DOM gives us the ability to randomly access the document, meaning that unlike a SAX parser, which has to process the elements sequentially as they are parsed, the processes of a DOM parser are not constrained by the document order.

Processing an XML document using a DOM parser

In this section, we explore some of the basic syntax of DOM parsing in Java. The example program that is used here simply demonstrates some of the features of the parser, rather than performing a particular business process.

For most of the examples in this chapter, we use the following XML document ('policies.xml') as the source XML for parsing and transformations.

```
<?xml version="1.0"?>
<policies>
  <company-domain>http://www.webhomecover.com</company-domain>
  <contents-image>contents.gif</contents-image>
  <buildings-image>buildings.gif</buildings-image>
  <policy type="contents">
    <policy-holder>A. Liu</policy-holder>
    <claims>
      <claim>
        <year>2002</year>
        <details>Stolen TV</details>
      </claim>
    </claims>
  </policy>
  <policy type="contents">
```

```
              <policy-holder>B. Singh</policy-holder>
          </policy>
          <policy type="buildings">
              <policy-holder>C. Jones</policy-holder>
              <claims>
                <claim>
                    <year>2004</year>
                    <details>Fire damage to Kitchen</details>
                </claim>
              </claims>
          </policy>
          <policy type="contents">
          <policy-holder>D. Umaga</policy-holder>
              <claims>
                <claim>
                    <year>1998</year>
                    <details>Stolen bicycle</details>
                </claim>
                <claim>
                    <year>2004</year>
                    <details>Dropped Ming Vase</details>
                </claim>
              </claims>
          </policy>
          <policy type="buildings">
          <policy-holder>E. Tolstoy</policy-holder>
          </policy>
      </policies>
```

To use the DOM parsing APIs, quite a few imports are required. Classes that relate to the components of the DOM ('Document', 'Element', etc.) are in the 'org.w3c.dom' package, while the 'javax.xml.parsers' package contains utility classes that let us access, create and parse XML documents. Although we are using a DOM parser in this example, we also need to import 'org.xml.sax.SaxException', which may be thrown by the underlying implementation of the parser. All of these packages are part of the standard version of Java, so no additional enterprise edition libraries are required. This means we can test the DOM parsers with a standard Java desktop application. Here is the set of imports that are required for our first example program, which is a simple DOM-parsing test class in the 'com.webhomecover.test' package.

```
package com.webhomecover.test;

import org.w3c.dom.Document;
import org.w3c.dom.Element;
import org.w3c.dom.NodeList;
import org.w3c.dom.Node;

import javax.xml.parsers.DocumentBuilderFactory;
import javax.xml.parsers.DocumentBuilder;
import javax.xml.parsers.ParserConfigurationException;

import org.xml.sax.SAXException;
```

```
import java.io.IOException;
import java.io.File;
```

At the beginning of the 'main' method of the test class, the first step is to parse an XML document, building a Document Object Model representation of the document in memory so that it can be accessed using the DOM API. The 'parse' method of the DocumentBuilder takes a File object and returns a Document object. (The DocumentBuilder is acquired from a DocumentBuilderFactory which is itself acquired by using the 'newInstance' factory method.) The document being parsed here is the 'policies.xml' file introduced earlier. The parsing phase can throw a number of exceptions, which may be caught here. The reference to the Document object is declared before the 'try' block since it will need to be used during the processing phase after parsing is complete.

```java
public class DOMParsing
{
   public static void main(String[] args)
   {
      // declare references
      Document doc = null;
      String xmlDocument = "policies.xml";

      // parse the input document
      try
      {
         DocumentBuilderFactory dbf = DocumentBuilderFactory.newInstance();
         DocumentBuilder db = dbf.newDocumentBuilder();
         doc = db.parse(new File(xmlDocument));
      }
      // catch lots of exceptions!
      catch(ParserConfigurationException e)
      {
         e.printStackTrace();
      }
      catch(SAXException e)
      {
         e.printStackTrace();
      }
      catch(IOException e)
      {
         e.printStackTrace();
      }
```

At this point in the program, the document has been parsed and is accessible via the DOM. In the rest of the code, we demonstrate some features of the DOM API. The following segment uses the 'getDocumentElement' method (of the Document class) to get the Element object that represents the root. It then retrieves the name of the element (using the 'getTagName' method) and writes it to standard output.

```java
// retrieve the root element and show its name
Element root = doc.getDocumentElement();
String rootTagName = root.getTagName();
System.out.println("The root element tag is <" + rootTagName + ">");
```

From previous examples we saw in the context of JavaScript, you should be familiar with the 'getElementsByTagName' method, which returns all the elements from the document that have a specific tag name. The Java version is very similar except that it returns a NodeList (JavaScript of course is not strongly typed so does not specify the return type of the method). In this part of the code, we use the 'getLength' method of the NodeList class to see how many tags are in the list. In this example, this will tell us how many 'policy' elements are in the document.

```java
// display the number of policies in the document
NodeList l = root.getElementsByTagName("policy");
int n = l.getLength();
System.out.println("There are " + n + " policies");
```

Other DOM operations that will be familiar to you from JavaScript are 'getFirstChild' (which returns the first child node of the current context node) and getting the value of the current node (using the 'getNodeValue' method). In this section, we retrieve the 'company-domain' element (again using the 'getElementsByTagName' method). This gives us a NodeList that contains a single node (since there is only one 'company-domain' element). Using the 'item' method of a NodeList, which takes an index value as a parameter, gives us access to a specific node within the list. The index numbers start at zero, so to access the first (and only) element we use zero as the parameter value in this example. To get to the text node inside the 'company-domain' element, we access its first child ('getFirstChild') and retrieve the value of the text node.

```java
// find the company-domain node
NodeList domainNodes = root.getElementsByTagName("company-domain");
Node domainNode = domainNodes.item(0);
// print its content (the text node is the child of the element)
System.out.println("Domain: " +
domainNode.getFirstChild().getNodeValue());
```

In this final section of the program, we use the 'getChildNodes' method, which returns a list of all the immediate children of the current node. We then iterate through them with a 'for' loop, using the index number to access each node in turn. We ignore all the text nodes (which have the name '#text') and simply write all the other node names to standard output.

```java
// list the child elements of the root node
System.out.println("The child elements for the root are:");
NodeList nodes = root.getChildNodes();
for(int i=0; i <nodes.getLength(); i++)
{
   Node node = nodes.item(i);
   String nodeName = node.getNodeName();
   // any spaces or line feeds between tags will be '#text' nodes
   if(!nodeName.equals("#text"))
   {
      System.out.println(nodeName);
   }
}
}
}
```

FIGURE 11.2 The output from the DOM-parsing example program

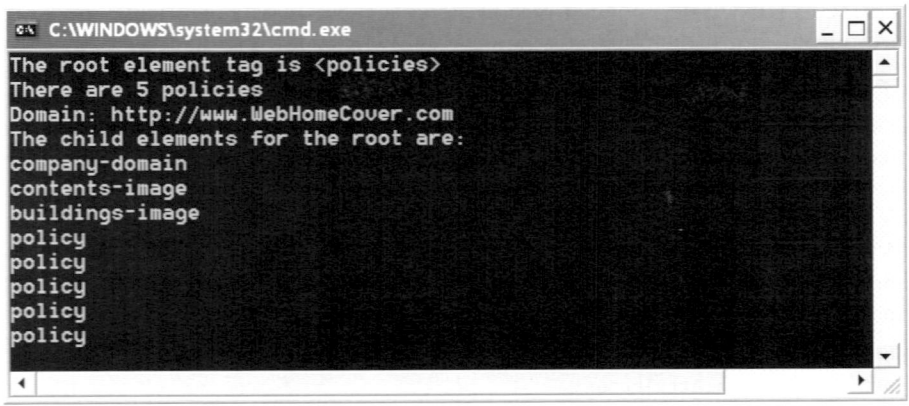

Figure 11.2 shows the output from the program in standard output. We see the name of the root element, the number of 'policy' elements (a count of 'policy' tags), the content of the 'company-domain' element and all the non-text child nodes of the root element.

Processing an XML document using a SAX parser

SAX parsers provide us with an approach which can be more efficient than DOM parsers in terms of processing speed and memory usage because the XML document is simply processed sequentially by the parser. Of course, the disadvantage is that it does not create a document object model to enable random access; we have to process the nodes as they are read. In the next example, we show how a simple SAX-parsing program can be written that responds to SAX events. There are many events that may be fired by a SAX parser as it reads an XML document, each of which triggers a particular method in response. These event-handling methods include the following:

- `startDocument()` **Receive notification of the beginning of the document**.
- `startElement(String uri, String localName, String qualifiedName, Attributes attributes)` **Receive notification of the start of an element.**
- `characters(char[] ch, int start, int length)` **Receive notification of character data inside an element.**
- `processingInstruction (String target, String data)` **Receive notification of a processing instruction.**
- `endElement(String uri, String localName, String qualifiedName)` **Receive notification of the end of an element.**
- `endDocument()` **Receive notification of the end of the document.**

The difference between the 'localName' and 'qualifiedName' parameters in the 'startElement' and 'endElement' methods is that the local name is only available if the XML parser is configured to use namespaces. Otherwise, the qualified name will be available. This example assumes the parser is not aware of namespaces, so we are using the qualified name.

In this section, we describe an example program that uses a SAX parser to respond to some of the events triggered while reading the XML document previously introduced. It is not a very practical example, since it simply rewrites much of the original document to standard output, but it demonstrates how we can write code that handles SAX events.

As with the DOM example, we need to import several classes. The SAX parser classes are in the 'javax.xml.parser' package, while other SAX classes are in the 'org.xml.sax' package. A subpackage, 'org.xml.sax.helpers', contains the DefaultHandler class, which can be used as a superclass to make SAX parsing relatively simple.

```java
package com.webhomecover.test;

import java.io.File;
import java.io.IOException;

import org.xml.sax.SAXException;
import org.xml.sax.Attributes;
import org.xml.sax.helpers.DefaultHandler;

import javax.xml.parsers.SAXParserFactory;
import javax.xml.parsers.ParserConfigurationException;
import javax.xml.parsers.SAXParser;
```

In the first part of this example, we create a SAX event handler and get a SAXParser object from the SAXParserFactory. The 'parse' method of the SAXParser takes two arguments, the first is the XML document to be parsed and the second is a suitable *handler* object that can respond to SAX events. Because our example class extends DefaultHandler we can use an instance of it as the handler object.

```java
public class SAXParsing extends DefaultHandler
{
  public static void main(String args[])
  {
   String xmlDocument = "policies.xml";
  // Use an instance of ourselves as the SAX event handler
   DefaultHandler handler = new SAXParsing();
  // Use the default (non-validating) parser
   SAXParserFactory factory = SAXParserFactory.newInstance();
   try
   {
     // parse the document
     SAXParser saxParser = factory.newSAXParser();
     saxParser.parse(new File(xmlDocument), handler);
   }
   catch(ParserConfigurationException e) {
     e.printStackTrace();
   }
   catch(SAXException e) {
     e.printStackTrace();
   }
   catch(IOException e) {
     e.printStackTrace();
   }
  }
}
```

While the SAXParser is processing the XML document, it fires events as it reads through the various nodes in the document. It is the responsibility of the 'handler' object to implement methods that respond to these events. Two simple events are those that relate to the opening and closing tags of elements, 'startElement' and 'endElement', which we implement next. They have different parameter lists because a start tag may contain attributes. If present, these are passed to the method inside an object that implements the 'org.xml.sax.Attributes' interface.

```java
public void startElement(String uri, String simpleName, String qualifiedName,
Attributes a)
{
  System.out.print("<"+ qualifiedName);

  for(int i = 0; i < a.getLength(); i++)
  {
    System.out.print(" " + a.getQName(i) + "=\"" + a.getValue(i) + "\"");
  }
  System.out.print(">");
}
```

11

In the 'startElement' method, we write the qualified name to standard output, followed by any attributes using a 'for' loop. If the length of the 'Attributes' parameter is greater than zero, then each attribute is written out in turn. Note that the names and values of the individual attributes can be accessed using an index number, starting at zero for the first attribute. As with elements, attributes may have a local or a qualified name (accessed by the 'getQName' method). The value is accessible via the 'getValue' method.

The 'endElement' method is a little simpler because there are no attributes in the closing tag. Here, we simply write the qualified name of the element to standard output:

```java
public void endElement(String uri, String simpleName, String qualifiedName)
{
  System.out.println("</"+ qualifiedName + ">");
}
```

Our example program contains one more event handler, the 'characters' method, which responds to text node events. Each time this is called, it is passed a character array of data, with the start position and length of the text node that is currently being processed. Here, we create a String from the character array and then use the other two values to extract the substring that is the current text node.

```java
public void characters(char[] ch, int start, int length)
{
  String claimString = new String(ch);
  System.out.print(claimString.substring(start, start + length));
}
```

Figure 11.3 shows the output from the SAX-parsing example. The code could contain more line feeds, spaces, etc. for a better layout, if required.

FIGURE 11.3   The output from the SAX-parsing example program

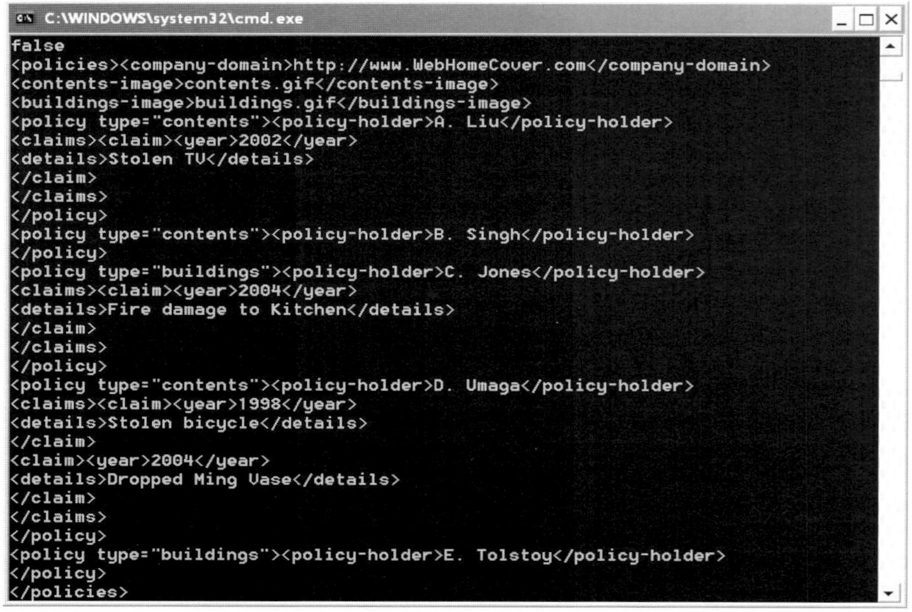

```
C:\WINDOWS\system32\cmd.exe                                    _ □ ×
false
<policies><company-domain>http://www.WebHomeCover.com</company-domain>
<contents-image>contents.gif</contents-image>
<buildings-image>buildings.gif</buildings-image>
<policy type="contents"><policy-holder>A. Liu</policy-holder>
<claims><claim><year>2002</year>
<details>Stolen TV</details>
</claim>
</claims>
</policy>
<policy type="contents"><policy-holder>B. Singh</policy-holder>
</policy>
<policy type="buildings"><policy-holder>C. Jones</policy-holder>
<claims><claim><year>2004</year>
<details>Fire damage to Kitchen</details>
</claim>
</claims>
</policy>
<policy type="contents"><policy-holder>D. Umaga</policy-holder>
<claims><claim><year>1998</year>
<details>Stolen bicycle</details>
</claim>
<claim><year>2004</year>
<details>Dropped Ming Vase</details>
</claim>
</claims>
</policy>
<policy type="buildings"><policy-holder>E. Tolstoy</policy-holder>
</policy>
</policies>
```

11.2   Generating XML from JavaBeans

Parsers are used to take an XML document and process it within a Java program. This is a very important aspect of XML processing, and one that we will be using in our example web application by using a tag library. However there is also an equally important process, which is the generation of XML documents from Java components. A simple example, which we will take as our starting point, is the XMLEncoder class from the 'java.beans' package that is a part of standard Java. This class enables JavaBeans (including graphs of related objects) to be sent to an output stream as an XML document. The intention of this class is very similar to standard object serialization, but writing beans in XML format is more resilient because they are not affected by changes in the internal implementation of the class, as serialized objects would be. Objects in this XML format can be read back into a Java representation using the XMLDecoder class. The reason for introducing the XMLEncoder here, however, is to introduce the concept of generating an XML document from a JavaBean, an approach we will build on with our own examples.

Model layer beans

There is a difference between the JavaBeans that we use to retrieve the data from HTML forms, which are part of the view–controller layer, and the beans that reside in the model layer. The beans that gather data from forms are *form beans* or *Data Transfer Objects* (DTOs), while the beans in the model layer are *system state* and *business logic* or *process* beans. System state beans represent things such as shopping carts, user profiles, catalogs and customers. Some of these represent persistent data and some represent a transitory state that is not stored long term. For example a 'customer' object is probably persistent but a 'shopping cart' probably isn't. The beans that we use to gather data from client pages can be used as Data Transfer Objects for these state beans. Business logic beans encapsulate

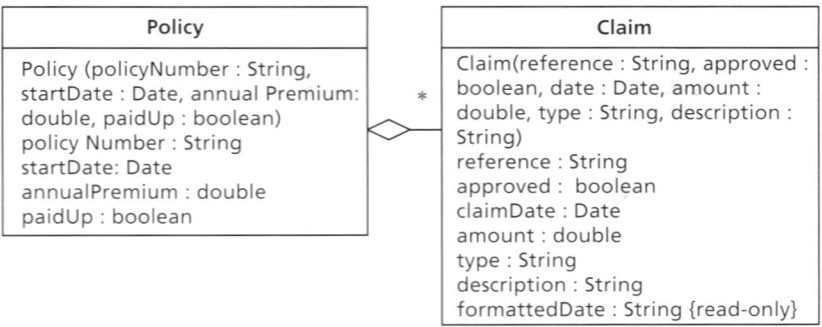

FIGURE 11.4 The Policy and Claim JavaBeans

Policy	Claim
Policy (policyNumber : String, startDate : Date, annual Premium: double, paidUp : boolean)	Claim(reference : String, approved : boolean, date : Date, amount : double, type : String, description : String)
policy Number : String	reference : String
startDate: Date	approved : boolean
annualPremium : double	claimDate : Date
paidUp : boolean	amount : double
	type : String
	description : String
	formattedDate : String {read-only}

the business processes (though these processes may also be part of state beans). We introduced a process bean in Chapter 10, where we used the 'InsuranceQuoter' class. It is important that these beans are not 'aware' of the web environment, because the state and logic of the model should be independent of the web layer. The example beans we will be using in this section are Claim and Policy beans (Figure 11.4). These classes are not just form beans, but part of the underlying model. One aspect of this is that they implement a bi-directional association. A Policy maintains a collection of Claims, and a Claim contains a reference to its owning Policy. They also have parameterized constructors that allow instances to be created and populated in one operation. The 'formattedDate' property of the Claim class is given a 'read-only' constraint on the diagram because there is a 'getFormattedDate' method, but no matching 'set' method (the formatted date is generated from the claim date).

The Claim class, below, is similar in some respects to the ClaimBean used to gather form data, but only contains claim-related data, so does not have a 'policyNumber' field. It also differs in that it contains fields that are relevant to a claim but not entered into the form page, namely 'reference', 'approved' and 'claimDate'. The values of these attributes are generated by the system, not entered by the user. In addition, it has a reference of type Policy that maintains the association with a policy object and a method to generate a formatted date.

```
package com.webhomecover.model;

import java.util.Date;
import java.text.*;

public class Claim implements java.io.Serializable
{
   private Policy policy;
   private String reference;
   private boolean approved;
   private Date claimDate;
   private double claimValue;
   private String claimType;
   private String description;

   public Claim()
   {
      super();
   }
```

```
public Claim(String reference, boolean approved, Date date, double value, String
type, String description)
  {
    super();
    setReference(reference);
    setApproved(approved);
    setClaimDate(date);
    setAmount(value);
    setType(type);
    setDescription(description);
  }

  public void setPolicy(Policy policy)
  { this.policy = policy; }

  public void setReference(String reference)
  { this.reference = reference; }

  public void setType(String type)
  { claimType = type; }

  public void setAmount(double amount)
  { claimValue = amount; }

  public void setDescription(String description)
  { this.description = description; }

  public void setApproved(boolean approved)
  { this.approved = approved; }

  public void setClaimDate(Date date)
  { claimDate = date; }

  public Policy getPolicy()
  { return policy; }

  public String getReference()
  { return reference; }

  public String getType()
  { return claimType; }

  public double getAmount()
  { return claimValue; }

  public String getDescription()
  { return description; }

  public boolean getApproved()
  { return approved; }

  public Date getClaimDate()
  { return claimDate; }

  public String getFormattedDate()
  {
    DateFormat dateFormat = new SimpleDateFormat("yyyy-MM-dd");
    return dateFormat.format(getClaimDate());
  }
}
```

The source code for the Policy class includes an ArrayList of Claim objects to implement the one-to-many association. When a Claim is added to a Policy, the association is set in both directions in the 'addClaim' method.

NOTE	The code relating to the collection of Claims uses generics to specify the type of collection:
	
	`Collection<Claim> claims;`
	
	`. . .`
	
	`claims = new ArrayList<Claim>();`
	
	Generics can only be used with Java version 5.0 or above.

```java
package com.webhomecover.model;

import java.util.Date;
import java.util.Collection;
import java.util.ArrayList;
import java.util.Iterator;
import java.text.DateFormat;
import java.text.SimpleDateFormat;

public class Policy
{
   private String policyNumber;
   private Date startDate;
   private double annualPremium;
   private boolean paidUp;
   private Collection<Claim> claims;

   public Policy()
   {
    super();
    claims = new ArrayList<Claim>();
   }

   public Claim(String reference, boolean approved, Date date, double value,
    String type, String description)
   {
    super();
    setReference(reference);
    setApproved(approved);
    setClaimDate(date);
    setAmount(value);
    setType(type);
    setDescription(description);
   }

   public void setPolicyNumber(String policynumber)
   { policyNumber = policynumber; }

   public void setStartDate(Date startDate)
   { this.startDate = startDate; }
```

```
public void setAnnualPremium(double premium)
{ annualPremium = premium; }

public void setPaidUp(boolean paidUp)
{ this.paidUp = paidUp; }

public void setClaims(Collection<Claim> claims)
{ this.claims = claims; }

public String getPolicyNumber()
{ return policyNumber; }

public Date getStartDate()
{ return startDate;}

public double getAnnualPremium()
{ return annualPremium; }

public boolean getPaidUp()
{ return paidUp; }

public Collection<Claim> getClaims()
{ return claims; }

public void addClaim(Claim claim)
{
  claims.add (claim);
  claim.setPolicy (this);
}

public String getFormattedDate()
{
  DateFormat dateFormat = new SimpleDateFormat("yyyy-MM-dd");
  return dateFormat.format(getStartDate());
}
}
```

The 'XMLEncoder' class

Using the 'java.beans.XMLEncoder' class is very simple. The constructor takes an output stream as a parameter:

```
XMLEncoder encoder = new XMLEncoder(OutputStream out)
```

Then objects can be written to the output stream as an XML string, using the 'writeObject' method:

```
encoder.writeObject(object);
```

Here is a simple test class written using standard Java. It creates an instance of Claim and an instance of Policy, and adds the claim to the policy. Then the policy and its associated claim are written to a file stream as an XML document.

```
package com.webhomecover.test;

import com.webhomecover.model.*;
import java.util.Date;
import java.util.Calendar;
import java.beans.XMLEncoder;
import java.io.*;

public class XMLEncoderTest
{
   public static void main(String args[])
   {
      Calendar cal = Calendar.getInstance();
      cal.set(2007,12,21);
      Claim claim = new Claim
         ("C2007-08-16-1",false,cal.getTime(),627.00,"Contents",
          "Flood damage");
      Policy policy = new Policy("8374635",new Date(),863.00,true);
      policy.addClaim(claim);
      try
      {
         XMLEncoder encoder = new XMLEncoder(new BufferedOutputStream
            (new FileOutputStream("policy.xml")));
         encoder.writeObject(policy);
         encoder.close();
      }
      catch(IOException e)
      {
         e.printStackTrace();
      }
   }
}
```

Here are the contents of 'policy.xml' after the XMLEncoderTest has been run. Note how the Claim object is nested inside the Policy object. Also note that there is no reference to the 'approved' property. This is because its value has not been altered from the default so there is no data that needs to be written to the XML representation. The XMLEncoder never writes default field values to the XML since these are already known to the class. When the XMLDecoder is used these values will be set to their defaults in the newly created object.

```
<?xml version="1.0" encoding="UTF-8"?>
<java version="1.6.0" class="java.beans.XMLDecoder">
  <object class="com.webhomecover.model.Policy">
     <void property="annualPremium">
        <double>863.0</double>
     </void>
     <void property="claims">
        <void method="add">
           <object class="com.webhomecover.model.Claim">
              <void property="amount">
                 <double>627.0</double>
```

```
      </void>
      <void property="claimDate">
        <object class="java.util.Date">
          <long>1200902465577</long>
        </object>
      </void>
      <void property="description">
        <string>Flood damage</string>
      </void>
      <void property="reference">
        <string>C2007-08-16-1</string>
      </void>
      <void property="type">
        <string>Contents</string>
      </void>
    </object>
  </void>
</void>
<void property="paidUp">
  <boolean>true</boolean>
</void>
<void property="policyNumber">
  <string>8374635</string>
</void>
<void property="startDate">
  <object class="java.util.Date">
    <long>1187254865577</long>
  </object>
</void>
  </object>
</java>
```

Generating XML from JavaBean methods

The XMLEncoder writes an XML representation of the structure of the Java objects themselves, with their classes, property names, types and values. It provides a graphic example of how the same set of properties can be represented by both XML documents and Java objects. Building on this idea, we can also represent the application concepts within a domain model as both Java objects and XML documents. However, instead of the XML documents representing information related to Java classes, we need to generate documents that contain the property names and values of business objects such as 'Claim' and 'Policy'. In addition, as well as being able to write XML to an output stream, we also want to generate in-memory XML strings that can then be processed by parsers. A simple approach to this requirement is to add methods to the classes that are able to generate XML, a technique described by Geary (2001). For example, here is a very simple method of the Claim class that can generate an XML element based on its properties:

```java
public String getXmlElement()
{
  StringBuffer element = new StringBuffer();
  element.append("<claim>");
```

```
element.append("<reference>" + getReference() + "</reference>");
element.append("<type>" + getType() + "</type>");
element.append("<description>" + getDescription() + "</description>");
element.append("<amount>" + getAmount() + "</amount>");
element.append("<approved>" + getApproved() + "</approved>");
element.append("<date>" + getFormattedDate() + "</date>");
element.append("</claim>");
return element.toString();
}
```

Why just an element rather than a document? The reason is that we may want a Claim object to generate part of a larger document, for example a document containing policies and their claims. In such a situation, the 'getXmlElement' method would be called by other methods to contribute to the overall document. To enable a 'Claim' object to create a String representing a separate document, we could add a second method that adds the necessary XML declaration and then calls the 'getXmlElement' method. We could, of course, also add a DTD or Schema declaration here, or other parts of the prolog such as processing instructions.

```
public String getXmlDocument()
{
   StringBuffer document = new StringBuffer();
   document.append("<?xml version=\"1.0\"?>");
   document.append(getXmlElement() );
   return document.toString();
}
```

Here is a simple test class that creates a Claim object and then invokes its 'getXmlDocument' method.

```
package com.webhomecover.test;

import com.webhomecover.model.Claim;
import java.util.Date;
import java.util.Calendar;

import java.io.*;

public class XMLClaimTest
{
public static void main(String args[])
{
   Claim claim = new Claim("C2007-08-16-1",false,
      new Date(),627.00,"Contents","Flood damage");
   String xmlClaimString = claim.getXmlDocument();
   System.out.println(xmlClaimString);
   }
}
```

Here is the resulting XML string. Line feeds have been added here for readability, but in fact the original XML string does not contain line feeds since these are unnecessary for processing the document and would be regarded as text nodes by a SAX parser.

```
<?xml version="1.0"?>
  <claim>
     <reference>C2007-08-16-1</reference>
     <type>Contents</type>
     <description>Flood damage</description>
     <amount>627.0</amount>
     <approved>false</approved>
  <date>2007-08-16</date>
</claim>
```

Generating XML from a Claim is relatively straightforward, because a Claim has no aggregated objects inside it, so does not require us to generate a document from a graph of objects. The Policy class is somewhat different, since it may be an aggregate of one or more claims. Depending on the type of XML documents we want to generate, we may or may not want to create a policy document that includes claims. To control this, we could write parameterized methods in the Policy class to specify whether or not the generated XML document should include aggregated objects. Here is an example 'getXmlElement' from the Policy class that takes a boolean parameter ('graph'). Inside the implementation of the method, this parameter is used to decide whether or not to call the 'getXMLElement' methods of the aggregated Claim objects (in the 'claims' collection).

```
public String getXmlElement(boolean graph)
{
StringBuffer element = new StringBuffer();
element.append("<policy policy-number=\"" + getPolicyNumber() + "\">");
element.append("<start-date>" + getStartDate() + "</start-date>");
element.append("<annual-premium>" + getAnnualPremium() + "</annual-premium>");
element.append("<number-of-claims>" + claims.size() + "</number-of-claims>");
element.append("<paid-up>" + getPaidUp() + "</paid-up>");
if(graph)
  {
    element.append("<claims>");
    Iterator<Claim>claimIter = claims.iterator();
    while(claimIter.hasNext())
    {
      Claim claim = claimIter.next();
      element.append(claim.getXmlElement());
    }
    element.append("</claims>");
  }
  element.append("</policy>");
  return element.toString();
}
```

As with the Claim class, there is a 'getXMLDocument' method that adds the XML declaration. Once again, we use the 'graph' parameter to specify whether or not to build a document that includes elements from nested objects.

```
public String getXmlDocument(boolean graph)
  {
    StringBuffer document = new StringBuffer();
    document.append("<?xml version=\"1.0\"?>");
```

```
      document.append(getXmlElement(graph) );
      return document.toString();
   }
```

Here is a test class that creates a claim and a policy, adds the claim to the policy and then calls the 'getXmlDocument' method on the Policy object, passing 'true' as the value of the 'graph' parameter.

```
package com.webhomecover.test;

import com.webhomecover.model.*;
import java.util.Date;
import java.util.Calendar;
import java.io.*;

public class XMLPolicyTest
{
   public static void main(String args[])
   {
      Calendar policyDate = Calendar.getInstance();
      policyDate.set(2006,06,23);
      Calendar claimDate = Calendar.getInstance();
      claimDate.set(2007,10,01);
      Claim claim = new Claim("C2007-08-16-1",false,claimDate.getTime(),
         627.00,"Contents","Flood damage");
      Policy policy = new Policy("8374635",policyDate.getTime(),863.00,true);
      policy.addClaim(claim);
      String xmlPolicyString = policy.getXmlDocument(true);
      System.out.println(xmlPolicyString);
   }
}
```

Here is the generated XML string, written to standard output (the actual string contains no line feeds or spaces; they have been added here for readability):

```
<?xml version="1.0"?>
<policy policy-number="8374635">
   <start-date>2006-07-23</start-date>
   <annual-premium>863.0</annual-premium>
   <number-of-claims>1</number-of-claims>
   <paid-up>true</paid-up>
   <claims>
      <claim>
         <reference>C2007-08-16-1</reference>
         <type>Contents</type>
         <description>Flood damage</description>
         <amount>627.0</amount>
         <approved>false</approved>
         <date>2007-11-01</date>
      </claim>
   </claims>
</policy>
```

11.3 Java Architecture for XML Binding

In Section 11.2, we looked at a simple approach to generating XML from JavaBeans, but this may not be sufficient for all the types of Java XML processing required by a web application because it works in one direction only, writing XML from Java objects, and also requires a lot of manual coding that can make a system hard to maintain. In some cases (for example, when consuming XML documents from external web services), we may also need to convert XML documents to Java objects, similar to the way that the XMLDecoder can create a Java object from an XML representation written using the XMLEncoder. Of course we could do this using SAX or DOM parsers, but this, like our XML-generating JavaBean methods, would also require quite a lot of custom-written code. An alternative approach to converting XML documents to and from Java objects is the Java Architecture for XML Binding (JAXB), which has been included in the standard Java development kit since version 6. In this section, we provide a brief introduction to the basics of JAXB.

Generating classes from XML schemas

The starting point for JAXB is to have XML Schemas for the XML documents in your system. These schemas are used to generate Java classes that can then be used to unmarshall and marshall XML documents. Unmarshalling is the conversion from an XML document to a Java object, while marshalling is creating an XML document from a Java object.

 NOTE The ability to create XML from Java objects was introduced into JAXB from version 2.0 onwards. Version 1.0 only converted from XML to Java.

The following XML Schema can be used to validate documents like the one we used at the beginning of this chapter in the DOM and SAX parser examples. It consists of a complex type ('policies') with one or more nested 'policy' complex types inside it. Each policy has a 'policy-holder' followed by an optional 'claims' element that may have multiple 'claim' elements nested inside it. Policy elements have a 'type' attribute and there are also 'company-domain', 'contents-image' and 'buildings-image' elements. To keep the examples to a manageable scale, a number of attributes of the Policy and Claim classes we have used in our previous examples have been excluded from this schema.

```xml
<?xml version="1.0"?>
<xsd:schema xmlns:xsd="http://www.w3.org/2001/XMLSchema">
  <xsd:element name="policies">
   <xsd:complexType>
    <xsd:sequence>
       <xsd:element name="company-domain" type="xsd:string"/>
       <xsd:element name="contents-image" type="xsd:string"/>
       <xsd:element name="buildings-image" type="xsd:string"/>
       <xsd:element name="policy" maxOccurs="unbounded">
          <xsd:complexType>
            <xsd:sequence>
              <xsd:element name="policy-holder" type="xsd:string"/>
              <xsd:element name="claims" minOccurs="0" maxOccurs="1">
```

```
            <xsd:complexType>
               <xsd:sequence>
                  <xsd:element name="claim" maxOccurs="unbounded">
                     <xsd:complexType>
                        <xsd:sequence>
                           <xsd:element name="year" type="xsd:integer"/>
                           <xsd:element name="details" type="xsd:string"/>
                        </xsd:sequence>
                     </xsd:complexType>
                  </xsd:element>
               </xsd:sequence>
            </xsd:complexType>
         </xsd:element>
      </xsd:sequence>
      <xsd:attribute name="type" type="xsd:string"/>
   </xsd:complexType>
</xsd:element>
</xsd:sequence>
</xsd:complexType>
</xsd:element>
</xsd:schema>
```

To generate a class from this schema using JAXB, we use the special schema binding compiler 'xjc'. This can be run from the command line or included in an Ant script.

 NOTE The JAXB compiler was not included in the standard Java SDK prior to version 6. Therefore these examples will not work with older versions.

To generate classes from our schema, we use the following command. Note that if you just use the default options of the 'xjc' compiler, the class is put into a package called 'generated'. Here, we use the '-p' option to specify the package into which the generated classes will be put ('com.webhomecover.xml'):

```
xjc -p com.webhomecover.xml policies.xsd
```

You should see the following messages from the compiler:

```
parsing a schema. . .
compiling a schema. . .
com\webhomecover\xml\ObjectFactory.java
com\webhomecover\xml\Policies.java
```

You can see that the compiler generates two classes, a Policies class, which is derived from the root element of the schema, and an ObjectFactory class, which can be used to create instances of the generated classes. The generated Policies class contains a static inner class that represents the complex type element nested inside the root element. In our example there is one nested complex type, 'policy'. Since the generated Policy class for this type is a static inner class of Policies, the name we use to refer to it in client code will be

FIGURE 11.5 The classes and properties generated by JAXB from 'policies.xsd' schema.

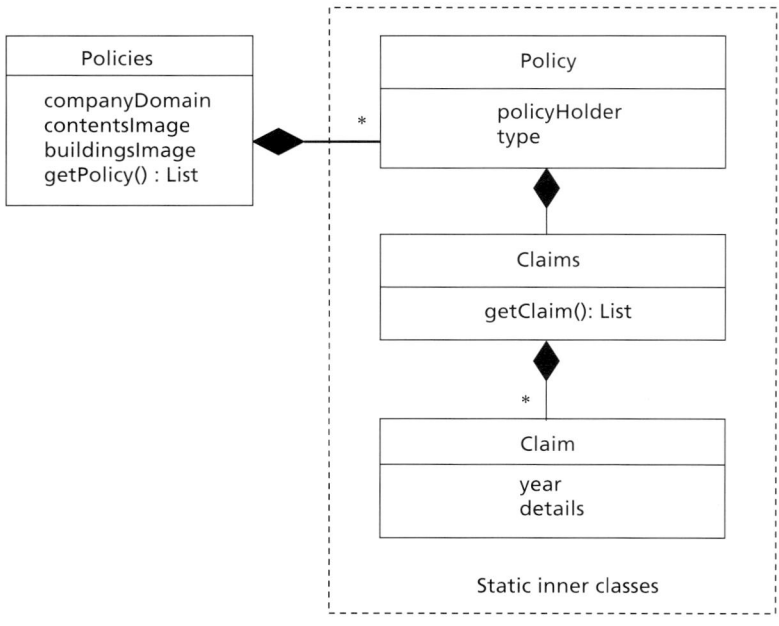

'Policies.Policy'. Similarly, 'policy' elements in the schema contain a nested 'claims' element, which is also a complex type, implemented by the Claims class. Finally, 'claim' elements are also complex types, so a Claim class is generated. JAXB only generates inner classes for complex types in the Schema; attributes and simple elements are both treated as properties in the generated classes. Figure 11.5 shows the classes generated by JAXB from the 'policies.xsd' schema, along with their properties. Where classes have a one-to-many relationship (e.g. Policies to Policy and Claims to Claim), the association is implemented as a List.

If you look at the generated code for the Policies class you will see that there are Java *annotations* (preceded by the '@' symbol) used to specify the relationships between the Java code and XML documents. Annotations were introduced into Java in version 5.0. They are basically a form of metadata that enables tools to generate code. For example, in this small fragment of the code there are annotations to specify that 'policies' is the root element, and that the subsequent elements are all required in a valid 'policies' document. The JAXB libraries use these annotations to generate the code that handles the transformations between XML and Java.

```
@XmlRootElement(name = "policies")
public class Policies {

    @XmlElement(name = "company-domain", required = true)
    protected String companyDomain;
    @XmlElement(name = "contents-image", required = true)
    protected String contentsImage;
    @XmlElement(name = "buildings-image", required = true)
    protected String buildingsImage;
    @XmlElement(required = true)
```

Since attributes and simple elements are both treated as properties in the generated classes, they are given different annotations for correct processing by JAXB. Here, for example, is the declaration of the elements and an attribute of the Policy class. 'policyHolder' and 'claims' are both elements, but 'type' is an attribute, though they are both declared the same way in the Java code.

```
@XmlElement(name = "policy-holder", required = true)
   protected String policyHolder;
   protected Policies.Policy.Claims claims;
@XmlAttribute
   protected String type;
```

Each annotation relates to a class that contains the implementation for generating code. For example, the '@XmlElement' annotation relates to the 'javax.xml.bind.annotation. XmlElement' class, which does the actual binding.

The other generated class, the ObjectFactory, contains factory methods that let us create instances of the classes declared in the class generated from the root element of the schema. In this case, there are methods to create objects of type 'Policies', 'Policy', 'Claims' and Claim'. Each method name begins with 'create' followed by the name of the class being created (Figure 11.6).

Generating XML documents from Java objects

Once we have generated code from the XML Schema, we can convert to and from Java objects and XML documents using these classes. For our first example, we generate an XML document from a Policies object and its inner classes. We need a number of imports from the 'javax.xml.binding' package, which contains JAXB classes, and also classes from the 'java.io' package so we can write the XML document to a file.

```
package com.webhomecover.xml;

import java.io.File;
import java.io.OutputStream;
import java.io.FileOutputStream;

import javax.xml.bind.JAXBContext;
import javax.xml.bind.JAXBException;
import javax.xml.bind.Unmarshaller;
import javax.xml.bind.Marshaller;
```

FIGURE 11.6 The methods of the generated ObjectFactory class

ObjectFactory
createPolicies() : Policies
createPoliciesPolicy() : Policies.Policy
createPoliciesPolicyClaims() : Policies.Policy.Claims
createPoliciesPolicyClaimsClaim() : Policies.Policy.Claims.Claim

11

The class includes a 'main' method that simply calls a static method (called 'createXMLFromJava' and catches any JAXBExceptions that may be thrown:

```
public class JAXBJavatoXMLTest
{
    public static void main(String[] args)
    {
        try
        {
            createXMLFromJava();
        }
        catch(JAXBException e)
        {
            e.printStackTrace();
        }
    }
}
```

The 'createXMLFromJava' method does the actual object creation and XML generation. In the first part of the method, we create an instance of the ObjectFactory and then use its 'createPolicies' method to return a new Policies object. We then create a series of objects to represent the various nested elements of the document to be created. In this particular example, we are going to create two Policies.Policy objects, each of which will contain a Claims object, and a Claim object inside that. The 'create' methods of the ObjectFactory are used to create the required objects. This particular example uses rather unsophisticated code in order to keep things reasonably clear, creating separate references for each object. For a more realistic implementation we could use collections to handle the object references.

```
public static void createXMLFromJava() throws JAXBException
{
ObjectFactory policiesFactory = new ObjectFactory();

// create objects that can be used to create each type of complex element
    Policies policies = policiesFactory.createPolicies();
    Policies.Policy policy1 = policiesFactory.createPoliciesPolicy();
    Policies.Policy.Claims claims1 =
        policiesFactory.createPoliciesPolicyClaims();
    Policies.Policy.Claims.Claim claim1 =
        policiesFactory.createPoliciesPolicyClaimsClaim();
    Policies.Policy policy2 = policiesFactory.createPoliciesPolicy();
    Policies.Policy.Claims claims2 =
        policiesFactory.createPoliciesPolicyClaims();
    Policies.Policy.Claims.Claim claim2 =
        policiesFactory.createPoliciesPolicyClaimsClaim();
```

Having created all the necessary objects, we set their properties.

```
// set the simple sub-elements of the 'policies' element
    policies.setCompanyDomain("www.webhomecover.com");
    policies.setContentsImage("contents.gif");
    policies.setBuildingsImage("buildings.gif");

// here is the first policy.
```

```
// set the attribute and the simple element
  policy1.setType("contents");
  policy1.setPolicyHolder("D. Parsons");

// now create a claim
  claim1.setYear(new java.math.BigInteger("2007"));
  claim1.setDetails("Van Gogh fell in the tumble drier");
```

Having created the various objects, we add them to their 'owning' objects.

```
// add the first claim to the first 'claims' List
  claims1.getClaim().add(claim1);

// now add the first 'claims' element to the first 'policy'
  policy1.setClaims(claims1);

// add the first 'policy' element to the 'policies' list
  policies.getPolicy().add(policy1);

// now add the other policy. . .
  policy2.setType("buildings");
  policy2.setPolicyHolder("S. Stobart");
  claim2.setYear(new java.math.BigInteger("2006"));
  claim2.setDetails("Roof blown off by tornado");
  claims2.getClaim().add(claim2);
  policy2.setClaims(claims2);
  policies.getPolicy().add(policy2);
```

Finally, we need a JAXBContext created to handle an instance of the Policies class. The JAXBContext is the entry point to the JAXB API, providing the necessary methods for marshalling and unmarshalling between Java objects and XML documents. In this example, we are marshalling from Java to XML, so we use the JAXBContext to create a Marshaller to write an XML representation of the Java objects to an output stream. Here we write the XML document to both standard output ('System.out') and a FileOutputStream, creating the document 'newpolicies.xml'. Setting the value of the 'JAXB_FORMATTED_OUTPUT' property specifies whether or not the output is written with line feeds and indentation.

```
// use the JAXB classes to write the XML document
  JAXBContext ctx = JAXBContext.newInstance(Policies.class);
  Marshaller m = ctx.createMarshaller();
  m.setProperty(Marshaller.JAXB_FORMATTED_OUTPUT, Boolean.TRUE);
  m.marshal(policies, System.out);
  try
  {
    OutputStream os = new FileOutputStream(new File("newpolicies.xml"));
    m.marshal(policies, os);
  }
  catch(Exception e)
  {
    e.printStackTrace();
  }
 }
}
```

Here is what the generated XML document looks like:

```xml
<?xml version="1.0" encoding="UTF-8" standalone="yes"?>
<policies>
    <company-domain>www.webhomecover.com</company-domain>
    <contents-image>contents.gif</contents-image>
    <buildings-image>buildings.gif</buildings-image>
    <policy type="contents">
        <policy-holder>D. Parsons</policy-holder>
        <claims>
            <claim>
                <year>2007</year>
                <details>Van Gogh fell in the tumble drier</details>
            </claim>
        </claims>
    </policy>
    <policy type="buildings">
        <policy-holder>S. Stobart</policy-holder>
        <claims>
            <claim>
                <year>2006</year>
                <details>Roof blown off by tornado</details>
            </claim>
        </claims>
    </policy>
</policies>
```

Generating Java objects from XML documents

So far we have seen XML being generated from a Java class, a process that we have already seen implemented in a different way by our custom coded 'getXmlElement' and 'getXml Document' methods. However, JAXB also enables us to easily generate Java objects from XML documents, as we see in the next example. Once again we use the 'policies.xml' document.

In the following program, we 'unmarshall' the XML document into a set of Java objects that represent its complex type elements. The import list is similar to the last example, with the notable difference that this time we need the javax.xml.bind.Unmarshaller class:

```java
package com.webhomecover.xml;

import java.io.File;
import java.util.Iterator;
import java.util.List;

import javax.xml.bind.JAXBContext;
import javax.xml.bind.JAXBException;
import javax.xml.bind.Unmarshaller;
```

The 'main' method is similar to the previous example, calling a method and catching the JAXBException:

```java
public class JAXBXMLtoJavaTest
{
```

```
public static void main(String[] args)
{
  try
  {
    createJavaFromXML();
  }
  catch(JAXBException e)
  {
    e.printStackTrace();
  }
}
```

The method begins by getting a JAXBContext, as we did before, then we create an Unmarshaller from the JAXBContext. The 'unmarshal' method of the Unmarshaller takes an XML document and converts it to an object that represents the root element of the document, in this case a Policies object.

```
public static void createJavaFromXML() throws JAXBException
{
  JAXBContext ctx = JAXBContext.newInstance(Policies.class);
  Unmarshaller unmarshaller = ctx.createUnmarshaller();
  Policies policies =
    (Policies) unmarshaller.unmarshal(new File("policies.xml"));
```

At this point, we have already created the Java Policies object from the XML document. The rest of this code simply demonstrates that this is the case by displaying the various properties of the object. We begin this section of the code by iterating through the list of Policy objects inside the Policies object, printing out their properties.

```
List<Policies.Policy>list = policies.getPolicy();
System.out.println ("Company Domain: " + policies.getCompanyDomain());
Iterator <Policies.Policy>iter = list.iterator();
Policies.Policy policy = null;
while (iter.hasNext())
{
  System.out.println("Policy Details:");
  policy = iter.next();
  System.out.println("\tPolicy Type: " + policy.getType());
  System.out.println("\tPolicy Holder: " + policy.getPolicyHolder());
  try
  {
    List<Policies.Policy.Claims.Claim> claimlist =
      policy.getClaims().getClaim();
    Iterator <Policies.Policy.Claims.Claim>claimiter =
      claimlist.iterator();
    System.out.println("\tDetails of past claims:");
    while(claimiter.hasNext())
    {
      Policies.Policy.Claims.Claim claim = claimiter.next();
      System.out.println("\t\tYear: " + claim.getYear());
      System.out.println("\t\tDetails: " + claim.getDetails());
    }
  }
```

```
            catch(NullPointerException e)
            {
                // OK - no claims for this policy. . .
            }
        }
    }
}
```

This is the output from the program, showing the properties and claims of the Policy objects that have been created by the Unmarshaller.

```
Company Domain: http://www.webhomecover.com
Policy Details:
        Policy Type: contents
        Policy Holder: A. Liu
        Details of past claims:
                Year: 2002
                Details: Stolen TV
Policy Details:
        Policy Type: contents
        Policy Holder: B. Singh
Policy Details:
        Policy Type: buildings
        Policy Holder: C. Jones
        Details of past claims:
                Year: 2004
                Details: Fire damage to Kitchen
Policy Details:
        Policy Type: contents
        Policy Holder: D. Umaga
        Details of past claims:
                Year: 1998
                Details: Stolen bicycle
                Year: 2004
                Details: Dropped Ming Vase
Policy Details:
        Policy Type: buildings
        Policy Holder: E. Tolstoy
```

In this section, we have covered the very basics of JAXB. There is a lot more to this architecture than the simple transformations we have shown in our code examples but, even with these limited examples, we can see how using JAXB can be very helpful in web applications that need to convert between XML documents and JavaBeans. In Section 11.4, we introduce the XML library of the JSTL and see how the various JavaBean components that process XML can be used with these tags to generate dynamic content.

11.4 XML processing with the JSP Standard Tag Library

We saw in Chapter 10 that the JSTL is a standard tag library for JSPs. It provides tags in four libraries: core, internationalization and formatting, database access and XML processing. In Chapter 10, we looked at some aspects of the core library. In this chapter, we look at XML processing tags, though some tags from the core library are also needed. As before, we use examples from version 1.1 of the JSTL (other versions have some differences).

In Chapter 10, we saw that the two JSTL library JAR files, 'jstl.jar' and 'standard.jar', had to be put into a 'lib' folder under the WEB-INF folder of the web application. Unfortunately these two standard jar files are not sufficient to use the XML library because we need several additional jars to support XML processing. Also, the contents of a particular jar file may vary depending on its source. The required jar files are a Java API for XML Processing (JAXP) implementation (the 'Xerces' parser and other supporting files, including those in 'serializer.jar', which contains classes that serialize SAX events into streams) and 'Xalan', which provides a Java implementation for XSL Transformations. Depending on the server you are using, these may or may not already be available in your server's library directory. For example JBoss includes them but Tomcat does not. To ensure that you have these available, regardless of which server you are using, these files have been included in the example source files with the JSTL libraries.

 NOTE Xerces is named after an extinct Californian butterfly. Xalan appears to be named after nothing at all, though it is similar to 'Xalam', which is a musical instrument.

Figure 11.7 shows the additional jar files required by the JSTL XML library, added to the existing JSTL jar files within the 'WEB-INF/lib' folder.

Using library namespaces

To use tag libraries in a JSP, we must add appropriate references to the tag libraries' URIs to the page. For our examples, we need to add both the core tag library and the XML tag library with different namespaces and prefixes. As we saw in Chapter 10, the 'c' prefix is

FIGURE 11.7 The additional JAR files needed to support the JSTL XML library

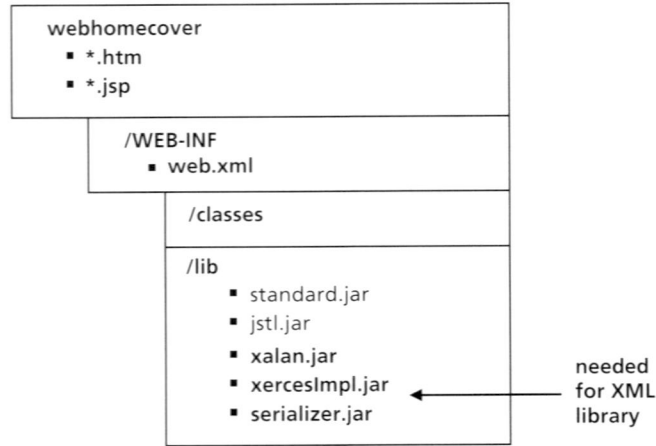

conventionally used for the core library. The conventional prefix for the XML library is 'x'. Using the older-style JSP 'taglib' directive, we would include the following lines at the top of the JSP:

```
<%@ taglib uri="http://java.sun.com/jstl/core" prefix="c" %>
<%@ taglib uri="http://java.sun.com/jstl/xml" prefix="x" %>
```

However for JSPX pages we should use the XML format introduced towards the end of Chapter 10, where we can use a 'jsp:root' element to include the tag library namespaces:

```
<jsp:root xmlns:jsp="http://java.sun.com/JSP/Page"
    xmlns:c="http://java.sun.com/jsp/jstl/core"
    xmlns:x="http://java.sun.com/jsp/jstl/xml"
    version="2.1">
```

In both cases, of course, the URIs are identical.

JSTL tags for XML processing

The XML library provides a number of tags for XML processing, some of which are very similar to tags in the core library and others that are specific to XML processing. One of the more familiar tags is 'out' which enables output to the server page response using the expression language. What, then, is the difference between the 'out' tag in the XML library and the 'out' tag in the core library? The key distinction between them is that the way the Expression Language is used with the XML library is a little different from what we have seen in the core library. An expression used in the context of the core library normally appears within braces and is preceded by a dollar sign, using this syntax:

```
${expression}
```

However, the XML library also includes a complementary syntax that does not include braces, for use in XPath expressions, like this:

```
$XPathexpression
```

The XML library provides versions of the 'if', 'choose', 'when', 'otherwise' and 'forEach' tags that support this XPath version of the Expression Language.

The tags that are unique to the XML library, include the 'parse' tag, which invokes a DOM parser on an XML document, and the 'transform' tag, which applies an XSL transformation to an XML document.

XSL transformations with the JSTL library

We can use the 'transform' tag to execute XSL transformations on the server, rather than the client. This means we are not dependent on the client being able to process style sheets, and we can also dynamically apply different style sheets to the same documents, perhaps to cater for different types of client (PC, PDA, mobile phone, etc.) or to generate different views of the same content. When the XSL transformation is to be done by the client, we send an XML document to the browser, along with an XSL style sheet. We did this in Chapter 9, setting up some simple static content on the web server that included

11

an XML document and an associated XSL transformation. However, when the transformation is to be done on the server, we do not want to send XML and XSLT documents to the client, since not all clients can process an XSL transformation. Rather, we process the transformation on the server to generate a document in XHTML (or some other mark-up appropriate for the client).

Importing XML files

To process files, such as XML documents, we need to import them into the page using the 'import' tag from the core library. This has two attributes: 'url', which is the URL of the document, and 'var', which is a variable name that will be applied to the document that has been imported. This variable name can then be used to refer to the document in subsequent EL expressions. The URL can be the full URL of a document elsewhere on the web or a local filename from the same web application. Note that because the 'import' tag is from the core library, not the XML library, it has the 'c' prefix.

```
<c:import url="fileurl" var="variablename" />
```

In the next example, we use the JSTL XML library to apply an XSL Transformation to an XML document by using the 'transform' tag. There are different ways of using this tag, but in the first example the result of the transformation is written directly to the generated client page. In the 'transform' tag, the expression language is used to refer to an XML document and an XSL transformation that have previously been imported.

```
<x:transform doc="${xmldocument}" xslt="${stylesheet}"/>
```

 NOTE In JSTL version 1.1, the 'doc' attribute replaced the previous (deprecated) 'xml' attribute.

Here is a complete JSP ('transformtest.jsp') that performs an XSL transformation. In this example, we import two files: an XML document ('policies.xml') and an XSL transformation ('policies.xsl'), both from the root of the same web application. The 'policies.xml' file and its associated transformation are the ones introduced at the end of Chapter 6. Note that in this example, the generation of the XHTML page is done entirely by the transformation, so the JSP does not write anything else to the generated page. However it does need to set the content type to 'text/html' so that the browser can correctly render the page that it receives.

```
<?xml version="1.0"?>
<!-- File: transformtest.jsp -->

<jsp:root xmlns:jsp="http://java.sun.com/JSP/Page"
    xmlns:c="http://java.sun.com/jsp/jstl/core"
    xmlns:x="http://java.sun.com/jsp/jstl/xml"
    version="2.0">

  <jsp:directive.page contentType="text/html"/>
  <jsp:directive.page isELIgnored="false" />
  <jsp:output omit-xml-declaration="true" />
  <c:import url=".\policies.xml" var="xmldocument" />
  <c:import url=".\policies.xsl" var="stylesheet" />
```

```
<x:transform doc="${xmldocument}" xslt="${stylesheet}"/>
</jsp:root>
```

Figure 11.8 shows the page generated by the server-side transformation.

Using XPath expressions with XML tags

Instead of using a complete transformation, which is somewhat inflexible, we can apply XPath expressions to an XML document using JSTL XML tags. This can be a very useful approach because it enables us to integrate the 'template view' approach of server pages and tags with the 'transform view' of XML transformations. First, we have to parse the XML document using the 'parse' tag from the XML library (assuming the document has been imported into a variable using the core library 'import' tag). The parsing process converts the input text document into an in-memory DOM document that can then be navigated using XPath expressions. The variable referencing the parsed document in this example is 'xml':

```
<x:parse doc="${xmldocument}" var="xml"/>
```

If the 'var' attribute is used, the DOM document type is implementation-dependent. An alternative is to use the 'varDom' attribute, which means the parsed document is an instance of 'org.w3c.dom.Document'.

```
<x:parse doc="${xmldocument}" varDom="xml"/>
```

FIGURE 11.8   A page generated by an XSL Transformation using JTSL tags

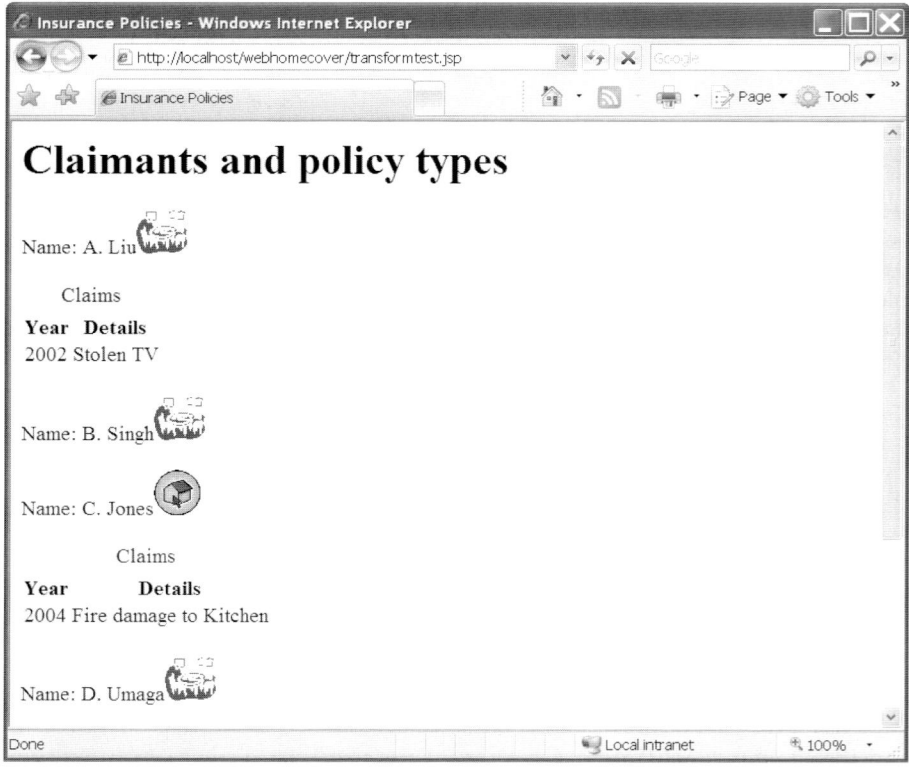

Once the original document has been parsed into a DOM representation, we can apply XPath expressions to it using the Expression Language. The results of these XPath expressions can be written to the client page using the 'out' element. This element has a 'select' attribute that can contain an EL version of an XPath expression. Here, for example, we navigate to the first 'policy-holder' element (note the syntax of the EL here, which does not include braces around the variable name at the root of the XPath expression).

```
<x:out select="$xml/policies/policy/policy-holder"/>
```

Here is a complete JSP that includes an 'out' tag that uses an XPath expressions to write a single policy-holder to the client page (the JSTL tags are highlighted).

```
<?xml version="1.0"?>
<!-- File: xpathtest.jsp -->
<jsp:root xmlns:jsp="http://java.sun.com/JSP/Page"
    xmlns:c="http://java.sun.com/jsp/jstl/core"
    xmlns:x="http://java.sun.com/jsp/jstl/xml"
    version="2.0">
  <jsp:directive.page contentType="text/html"/>
  <jsp:directive.page isELIgnored="false" />
  <jsp:output omit-xml-declaration="false"
    doctype-root-element="html"
    doctype-public="-//W3C//DTD XHTML 1.1//EN"
    doctype-system="http://www.w3.org/TR/xhtml11/DTD/xhtml11.dtd" />

  <html xmlns="http://www.w3.org/1999/xhtml" xml:lang="en">
    <head>
      <link href="webhomecover.css" rel="stylesheet" type="text/css" />
      <title>WebHomeCover Insurance Policies</title>
    </head>
    <body>
      <div>
        <c:import url="./policies.xml" var="xmldocument"/>
        <x:parse xml="${xmldocument}" var="xml"/>
        <x:out select="$xml/policies/policy/policy-holder"/>
      </div>
    </body>
  </html>
</jsp:root>
```

XML flow control

Similar flow controls ('if', 'choose', etc.) can be used in the XML library as in the core library. The difference is that we can use XPath expressions within these controls. As an example of flow control with tags, we use the 'forEach' tag for iteration. The XML library version of the 'forEach' tag has a 'var' attribute that is used inside the loop to represent the results of an XPath expression identified by the 'select' attribute. This identifies the element being used for the iteration. In the following example, the 'select' attribute contains an XPath expression that specifies a 'policy' node. The 'forEach' tag therefore iterates through all the policy nodes. Inside the loop, the 'policies' variable is used as the root of another XPath expression that navigates to the child element's 'policy-holder', which is then written to the response using the 'out' tag.

```xml
<?xml version="1.0"?>
<!-- File: foreachtest.jsp -->
<jsp:root xmlns:jsp="http://java.sun.com/JSP/Page"
    xmlns:c="http://java.sun.com/jsp/jstl/core"
    xmlns:x="http://java.sun.com/jsp/jstl/xml"
    version="2.1">
  <jsp:directive.page contentType="text/html"/>
  <jsp:directive.page isELIgnored="false" />
  <jsp:output omit-xml-declaration="false"
    doctype-root-element="html"
    doctype-public="-//W3C//DTD XHTML 1.1//EN"
    doctype-system="http://www.w3.org/TR/xhtml11/DTD/xhtml11.dtd" />


  <html xmlns="http://www.w3.org/1999/xhtml" xml:lang="en">
    <head>
      <link href="webhomecover.css" rel="stylesheet" type="text/css" />
      <title>WebHomeCover Insurance Policies</title>
    </head>
    <body>
      <div>
        <c:import url="./policies.xml" var="xmldocument"/>
        <x:parse xml="${xmldocument}" var="xml"/>
        <table>
        <tr><th>Policy Holder</th><th>Policy Type</th></tr>
        <x:forEach var="nextpolicy" select="$xml/policies/policy">
        <tr>
          <td><x:out select="$nextpolicy/policy-holder"/></td>
          <td><x:out select="$nextpolicy/@type"/></td>
        </tr>
        </x:forEach>
        </table>
      </div>
    </body>
  </html>
</jsp:root>
```

Figure 11.9 shows the list of policy holders that are written to the generated page.

11.5 Using beans that generate XML in JSPs

Earlier in this chapter we saw that one simple approach to generating XML from JavaBeans is to add a method that generates an XML String:

```
public String getXmlDocument()
```

FIGURE 11.9 Policy holders and policy types selected from an XML document by XPath expressions used within JSTL tags

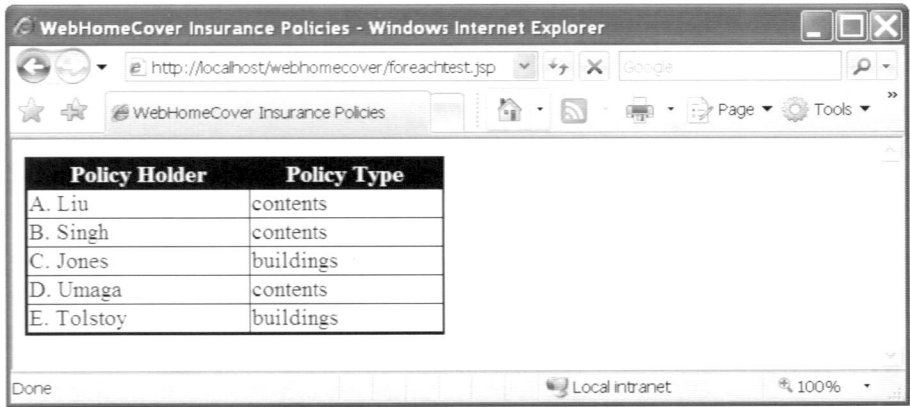

This type of method can then be used in JSP pages that perform XML transformations by accessing the 'xmlDocument' as a property. In this example, we use the 'transform' tag and access the bean property using the Expression Language:

```
<x:transform doc="${myBean.xmlDocument}" xslt="${stylesheet}"/>
```

Of course, before the bean can be used to generate an XML document, it must first be created and populated with data. In this section we describe a set of components that populate a controller-layer bean from HTTP request data, use that data to set the properties of a bean from the model layer, and use that model-layer bean to generate an XML document to be processed by a JSP.

Model layer façades

Earlier in this chapter we introduced the 'Claim' and 'Policy' classes as model-layer components rather than form beans because they had responsibilities related to the underlying processes of the application rather than just gathering data from forms. However in a web application, these objects may still need to be populated with data that originates from HTTP requests. Therefore in the controller layer we need to be able to translate between form bean and model-layer objects. We also need to consider where these transformations take place. One useful design pattern we can apply is the 'Façade' (Gamma *et al.* 1995). A façade is a class that acts as a central point of contact with an underlying subsystem. We can use a façade in a web application to separate the view–controller layer components from the underlying model, and the façade object can take responsibility for converting between form beans and model-layer objects, and vice versa. Figure 11.10 shows a façade object between the form bean and model-layer object that both relate to insurance claims.

Jakarta Commons bean utilities

One simple way of implementing the Façade's methods to transfer data between form beans and model layer objects is to use Apache Commons bean utilities (Apache Commons 2007). The Apache Commons project provides open-source utilities for various aspects of

FIGURE 11.10 A façade used to separate the view–controller layer from the model layer and transform between form beans and model objects

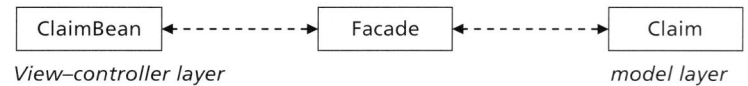

View–controller layer   *model layer*

reusable Java components. One of these is the bean utilities library ('BeanUtils') that provides simple wrappers around the Java reflection and introspection APIs.

 NOTE Application servers often include some Apache Commons components, as do web application frameworks such as Struts. However you will probably need to add the 'commons beanutils' JAR file to your web application's 'lib' folder to ensure it is available. (It can be downloaded from the Apache Commons web site and is also provided with the code examples for this chapter.)

To transfer data between beans from the view–controller and model-layers with the BeanUtils library, we can use the PropertyUtils class and its static 'copyProperties' method. This method takes two parameters, both of which must be Java Objects that follow the JavaBean conventions for specifying properties (i.e. having 'getXxx' and 'setXxx' methods). The readable properties of the second parameter bean are used to populate the writeable properties of the first parameter bean.

```
PropertyUtils.copyProperties(copyToBean, copyFromBean);
```

For example, if we had a form bean called 'claimBean' and a model-layer bean called 'claim', the following call to the method would populate the 'claim' from the 'claimBean'.

```
PropertyUtils.copyProperties(claim, claimBean);
```

Only matching properties are copied, of course. Therefore it is important that any property names of the two bean classes that need to be copied match exactly. Figure 11.11 shows the properties of the 'ClaimBean' and 'Claim' classes (the Claim class is slightly extended from Figure 11.4, including the XML-related methods we have subsequently added). In this case, there are three properties that can be copied between objects of these classes: 'amount', 'type' and 'description'.

Using the beans in an XML web application

In the next example, we use the ClaimBean and Claim classes in a simple web interaction that uses the now-familiar claim-form page that gathers some data about an insurance claim. However in this example the form action will be to a different controller JSP; the request sent from 'claimform.htm' is handled by 'processclaim.jsp', which forwards on to a second view JSP ('xmlbeanserverpage.jsp') that uses the XML-generating methods of the Claim. Figure 11.12 shows the main relationships between components in this interaction. The controller JSP creates and populates an instance of ClaimBean, and then uses a façade

FIGURE 11.11
The properties of the ClaimBean and Claim classes

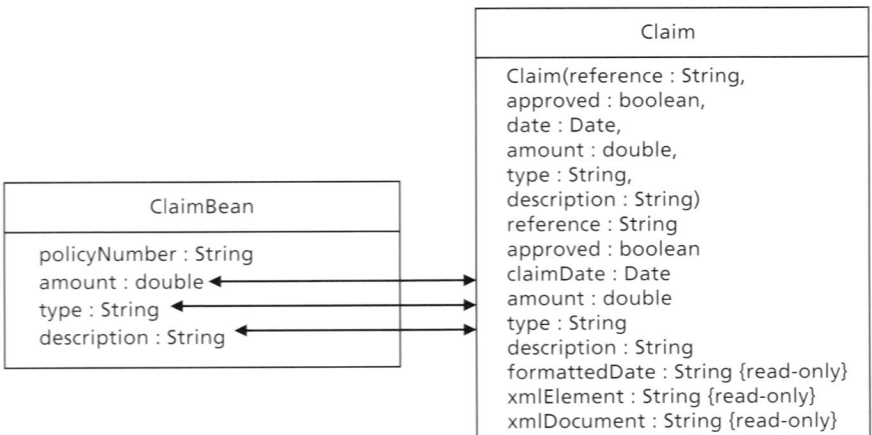

FIGURE 11.12
The components that transform an XML document generated from a JavaBean

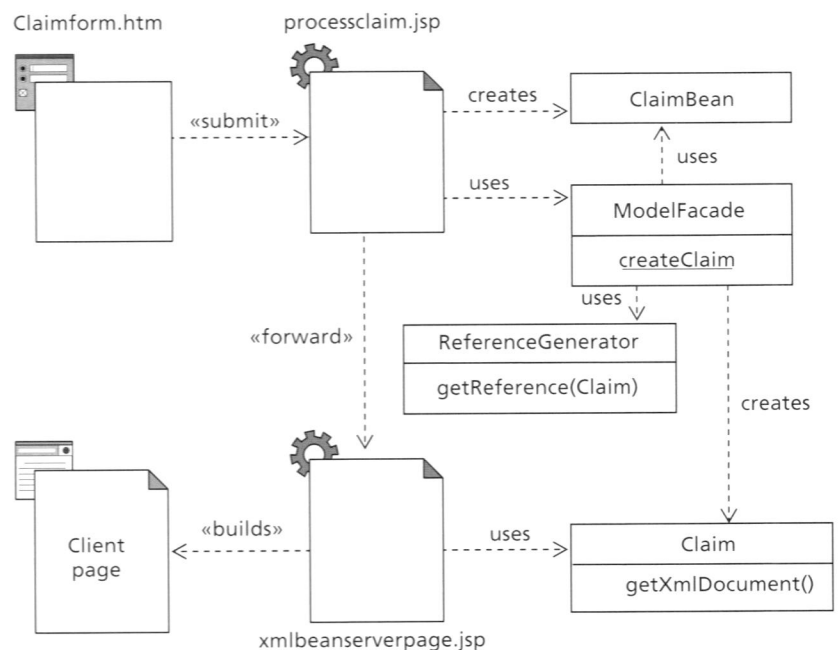

class called 'ModelFacade' to create a Claim object from the ClaimBean. The façade contains a static method to do this (since the façade holds no attributes, there is no need for non-static methods). In order to fully populate the Claim, we need some way of creating a reference number for it. We pass this responsibility to a ReferenceGenerator class (described next). The view JSP retrieves the Claim object from the request and uses it to render the view by transforming an XML document generated by the 'getXmlDocument' method of the Claim object.

The first component we look at is the ReferenceGenerator. Each Claim needs a reference number so that it can be uniquely identified. In the previous examples of Claim objects used in this chapter, we have used reference numbers similar to this one:

```
C2007-08-16-1
```

The basic structure of these references is that they begin with a letter based on the type of claim ('B' for buildings or 'C' for contents), followed by the (formatted) date of the claim, followed by a number. The following implementation takes a Claim object as a parameter, gets the claim type and the formatted date from it, then generates the final number using a random number generator. The components of the reference are appended to a StringBuffer, and finally a String is returned from the method. This is not a very robust implementation, since the same number may be generated more than once. A more realistic approach would be to use a database to generate sequence numbers, but this will serve for our examples.

```java
package com.webhomecover.util;

import com.webhomecover.model.Claim;

public class ReferenceGenerator
{
    public static String getReference(Claim claim)
    {
        StringBuffer reference = new StringBuffer();
        String type = claim.getType();
        if(type.startsWith("c") || type.startsWith("C"))
        {
            reference.append('C');
        }
        else
        {
            reference.append('B');
        }
        String date = claim.getFormattedDate().toString();
        reference.append(date);
        int rand = (int)Math.floor(Math.random()*999);
        reference.append(rand);
        return reference.toString();
    }
}
```

Next, we look at the ModelFacade and its static 'createClaim' method, which copies the properties of the ClaimBean into the Claim using the 'copyProperties' method of the PropertyUtils class. (PropertyUtils can be found in the 'org.apache.commons.beanutils' package, so the appropriate import is used here.) Once the relevant properties have been copied, the values of the 'claimDate' and 'approved' properties are set manually, since they do not come from the ClaimBean. Finally, we set the reference number using the ReferenceGenerator and return the claim.

```java
package com.webhomecover.model;
```

```
import com.webhomecover.util.ReferenceGenerator;
import com.webhomecover.beans.ClaimBean;
import org.apache.commons.beanutils.PropertyUtils;
import java.util.Date;

public class ModelFacade
{
   public static Claim createClaim(ClaimBean bean)
   {
     Claim claim = new Claim();

     try
     {
         PropertyUtils.copyProperties(claim, bean);
     }
     catch(IllegalAccessException e)
     {
      e.printStackTrace();
     }
     catch(java.lang.reflect.InvocationTargetException e)
     {
      e.printStackTrace();
     }
     catch(NoSuchMethodException e)
     {
      e.printStackTrace();
     }
     claim.setClaimDate(new Date());
     claim.setApproved(false);
     String reference = ReferenceGenerator.getReference(claim);
     claim.setReference(reference);
     return claim;
   }
}
```

The following JSP ('processclaim.jsp') handles the claim form when it is submitted. It creates and populates a ClaimBean from the request and then uses a scriptlet to invoke the ModelFacade's 'createClaim' method, which returns a Claim object. This object is then put into 'request' scope within the scriptlet (using the lookup name 'claim') and the page then forwards on to the view server page, 'xmlbeanserverpage.jsp'.

```
<?xml version="1.0"?>
<!-- File: processclaim.jsp -->
<jsp:root xmlns:jsp="http://java.sun.com/JSP/Page"
   xmlns:c="http://java.sun.com/jsp/jstl/core"
   version="2.0">
   <jsp:directive.page import="com.webhomecover.model.ModelFacade"/>
   <jsp:directive.page import="com.webhomecover.model.Claim"/>
   <jsp:useBean id="claimBean" class="com.webhomecover.beans.ClaimBean"
         scope="request"/>
   <jsp:setProperty name="claimBean" property="*" />
```

```
<jsp:scriptlet>
  Claim claim = ModelFacade.createClaim(claimBean);
  request.setAttribute("claim",claim);
</jsp:scriptlet>
<jsp:forward page="xmlbeanserverpage.jsp" />
</jsp:root>
```

The JSP that generates the view uses a JSTL expression, which accesses the 'xmlDocument' property of the ClaimBean, to generate the XML document that is used in an XSL transformation.

```
<?xml version="1.0"?>
<!-- File: xmlbeanserverpage.jsp -->
<jsp:root xmlns:jsp="http://java.sun.com/JSP/Page"
    xmlns:c="http://java.sun.com/jsp/jstl/core"
    xmlns:x="http://java.sun.com/jsp/jstl/xml"
    version="2.0">
  <jsp:directive.page contentType="text/html"/>
  <jsp:directive.page isELIgnored="false" />
  <jsp:output omit-xml-declaration="true" />
  <c:import url="claims.xsl" var="stylesheet" />
  <x:transform doc="${claim.xmlDocument}" xslt="${stylesheet}"/>
</jsp:root>
```

The style sheet used for the transformation is 'claims.xsl', which is similar to the style sheets we have used for previous XSL transformations. It generates a page that displays the details of the insurance claim and applies different images for contents or buildings claims.

```
<?xml version="1.0"?>
<xsl:stylesheet version="1.0"
xmlns:xsl="http://www.w3.org/1999/XSL/Transform" >
  <xsl:output method="xml"
    doctype-public="-//W3C//DTD XHTML 1.1//EN"
    doctype-system="http://www.w3.org/TR/xhtml11/DTD/xhtml11.dtd"/>
  <xsl:template match="/claim">
    <html xml:lang="en">
      <head>
        <title>Insurance Claim</title>
      </head>
      <body>
        <h1>Here are the details of your claim</h1>
        <p class="{type}">
          <xsl:choose>
            <xsl:when test="type='contents' ">
              <img src="contents.gif" alt="contents image"/>
            </xsl:when>
            <xsl:otherwise>
              <img src="buildings.gif" alt="buildings image"/>
            </xsl:otherwise>
          </xsl:choose>
        </p>
```

```
        <p>Reference: <xsl:value-of select="reference"/></p>
        <p>Description: <xsl:value-of select="description"/></p>
        <p>Amount: <xsl:value-of select="amount"/></p>
        <p>Claim Approved? <xsl:value-of select="approved"/></p>
        <p>Date of Claim: <xsl:value-of select="date"/></p>
        </body>
      </html>
    </xsl:template>
  </xsl:stylesheet>
```

When the web application is run, the output varies depending on the data entered into the claim form. In Figure 11.13, a claim has been made against a buildings policy.

Figure 11.14 shows that the generated view is based on the data input in Figure 11.13. In this particular example, we have not actually used the policy number (we address this in Chapter 12), so only the amount claimed, the description and the insurance type (represented by an image) from the original form appear in the page. However the reference, approval status and claim date, which are properties of the resulting Claim, are shown on the page.

FIGURE 11.13   Example data being entered into the claim form

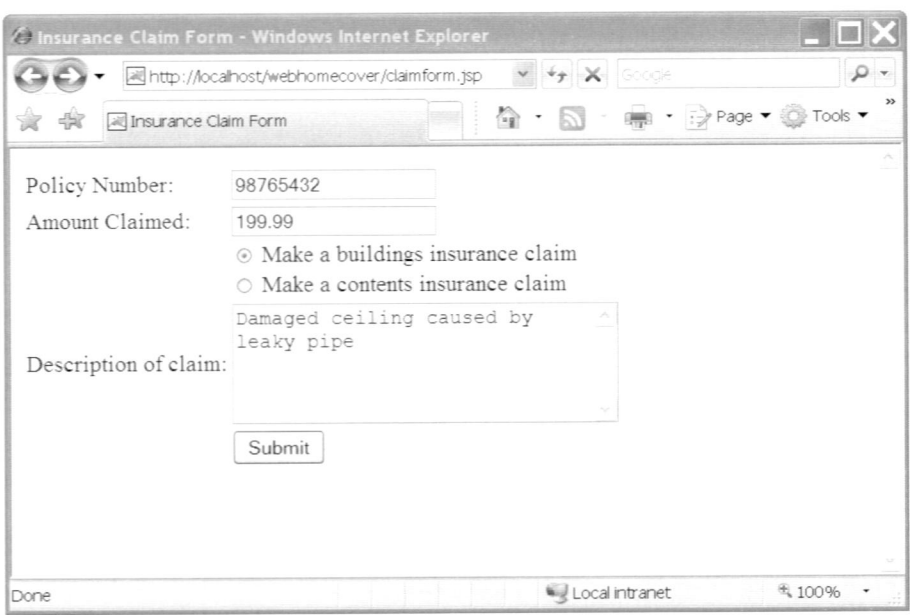

FIGURE 11.14 The resulting page generated from the claim data in Figure 11.13

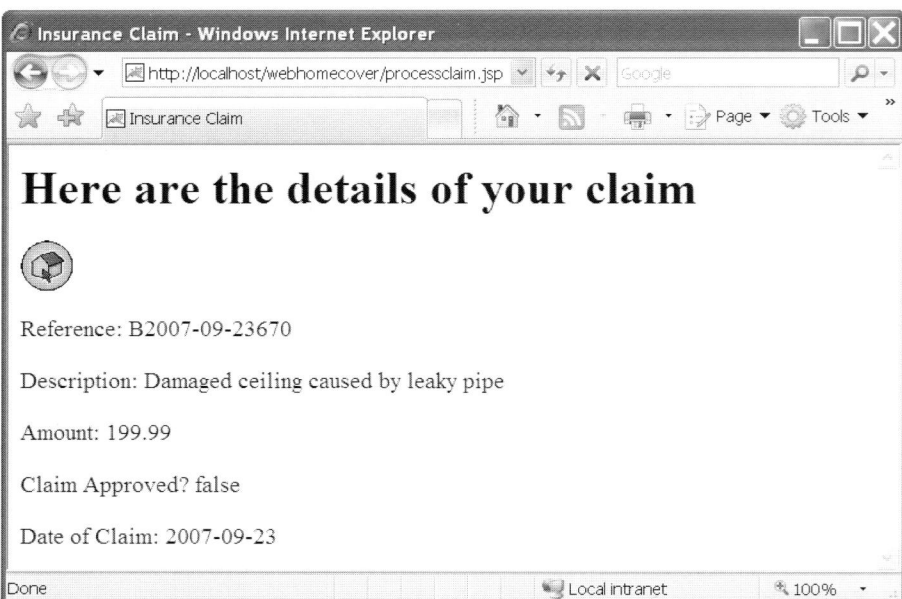

Exercises

11.1 Using either a DOM or a SAX parser, write a Java Standard Edition program that writes the number of 'claim' elements in 'policies.xml' to standard output.

11.2 In Chapter 10 we introduced a 'BuildingsDetails' class that encapsulated the details of a building that were used for generating an insurance quote. Create a class called 'Building' that has the same properties but is in the model-layer package. Add implementations of 'getXmlElement' and 'getXmlDocument' methods, and write a Java Standard Edition program to test these methods.

11.3 Here is a very simple XML Schema ('contents.xsd') that represents home contents details, based on the 'ContentsDetails' class we introduced in Chapter 10.

```
<?xml version="1.0"?>
<xs:schema xmlns:xs="http://www.w3.org/2001/XMLSchema">
  <xs:element name="contents">
    <xs:complexType>
      <xs:sequence>
        <xs:element name="cover-amount" type="xs:integer"/>
        <xs:element name="accidental-cover" type="xs:boolean"/>
        <xs:element name="deductible-amount" type="xs:integer"/>
        <xs:element name="insurance-quote" type="xs:decimal"/>
        <xs:element name="paid-up" type="xs:boolean"/>
      </xs:sequence>
    </xs:complexType>
  </xs:element>
</xs:schema>
```

Using JAXB, generate Java classes from this Schema:

xjc -p com.webhomecover.xml contents.xsd

This will create the 'Contents' and 'ObjectFactory' classes.

Here is an XML document ('contents.xml') that is valid against the Schema:

```
<?xml version="1.0" encoding="UTF-8"?>
<contents xmlns:xsi="http://www.w3.org/2001/XMLSchema-instance"
xsi:noNamespaceSchemaLocation="contents.xsd">
  <cover-amount>250</cover-amount>
  <accidental-cover>false</accidental-cover>
  <deductible-amount>50</deductible-amount>
  <insurance-quote>127.50</insurance-quote>
  <paid-up>true</paid-up>
</contents>
```

Write a Java Standard Edition class that creates an instance of the Contents class from 'contents.xml' and writes the values of its properties to standard output. Since this is a simpler document than the one used with JAXB earlier in this chapter, with no nested elements, there are no inner classes and you do not need a 'while' loop. Simply retrieve the single Contents object from the Unmarshaller and display its properties.

11.4 Write a JSP that creates an instance of your Building class, populates it with some test data and then uses the JSTL to perform an XSL Transformation to create a client page. You will need to create a suitable XSLT style sheet.

11.5 Write a JSP that creates an instance of your Building class, populates it with some test data and then uses the JSTL to parse the result of the 'getXmlDocument' method into a variable. Using this variable and the Expression Language, generate a page that displays data from the XML document using XPath expressions.

11.6 The last example in this chapter showed how an XML document generated from a JavaBean could be used within an XSL transformation. However it did not use JAXB. In this exercise, we integrate JAXB with the web application.

Copy the generated 'Policies' and 'ObjectFactory' source files to the 'java' folder of the web application.

Add a method with the following signature to the 'ModelFacade' class:

```
public static String getTestPolicyXML()
```

The role of this method is to provide a String representing an XML document that has been generated from a Policies object using JAXB. In the body of the method, create a Policies object from the ObjectFactory and populate it with data (as we did in the earlier JAXB example). This time, however, we use the Marshaller to send it out to a StringWriter and then return the XML String from the StringWriter:

```
java.io.StringWriter stringWriter = new java.io.StringWriter();
m.marshal(policies, stringWriter);
return stringWriter.toString();
```

When you are populating the policy object with data, an issue to be aware of with JAXB is that the data types used for the object's properties are not always those that we are familiar with. For example, to set a Date field in a JAXB object we must use the XMLGregorianCalendar class from the 'javax.xml.datatype' package. An instance of this class can be acquired from a javax.xml.datatype. DatatypeFactory, using the newXMLGregorianCalendar method. Some exception handling is required when creating the factory object, as in this example.

```
try
{
  javax.xml.datatype.DatatypeFactory datatypeFactory = null;
  try
  {
   datatypeFactory = javax.xml.datatype.DatatypeFactory.newInstance();
  }
  catch(javax.xml.datatype.DatatypeConfigurationException e)
  {
   e.printStackTrace();
  }
  javax.xml.datatype.XMLGregorianCalendar calendar =
  datatypeFactory.newXMLGregorianCalendar();
  //…etc.
```

The calendar's values can then be set using simple methods.

```
calendar.setYear(2007);
calendar.setMonth(10);
calendar.setDay(23);
```

Similarly, numeric properties of JAXB objects contain not primitive values but object of numeric types such as BigInteger and BigDecimal, for example:

```
policy.setNumberOfClaims(new java.math.BigInteger("1"));
policy.setAnnualPremium(new java.math.BigDecimal("123.4"));
```

Deploy the following JSP page ('jaxb.jsp') to the web application.

```
<?xml version="1.0"?>
<!-- File: jaxb.jsp -->
<jsp:root xmlns:jsp="http://java.sun.com/JSP/Page"
    xmlns:c="http://java.sun.com/jsp/jstl/core"
    xmlns:x="http://java.sun.com/jsp/jstl/xml"
    version="2.0">
  <jsp:directive.page contentType="text/html"/>
  <jsp:directive.page isELIgnored="false" />
  <jsp:directive.page import="com.webhomecover.xml.*"/>
  <jsp:directive.page import="com.webhomecover.model.*"/>
  <jsp:output omit-xml-declaration="true" />
  <c:import url="policies.xsl" var="stylesheet" />
  <jsp:scriptlet>
    String s = ModelFacade.getTestPolicyXML();
    request.setAttribute("xmlstring",s);
  </jsp:scriptlet>
  <x:transform doc="${xmlstring}" xslt="${stylesheet}"/>
</jsp:root>
```

When you load 'jaxb.jsp' into the browser, the example XML generated by the 'Policies' object should be transformed and a client page displayed.

SUMMARY

In this chapter we looked at a number of ways of integrating XML and Java, including DOM and SAX parsers, generating XML from Java objects and generating Java objects from XML documents. We introduced the Java API for XML Binding (JAXB), which provides us with a set of tools within Java SE for transforming XML documents into Java objects and vice versa. We saw how DOM parsers handle XML documents by building a Document Object Model in memory, whereas SAX parsers read an XML document sequentially and fire events based on its contents. We considered why one might choose a particular type of parser, based on requirements such as performance, document size and whether random access is required. We explored a number of ways that we can transform between XML documents and Java objects, including the XMLEncoder/ XMLDecoder, custom written methods and the JAXB framework. Towards the end of the chapter, we saw how some of these approaches could be integrated into web applications by using the JSTL XML tag library. Using this library, it is possible to integrate the template-view approach of JavaServer Pages with the transform-view approach of XSL transformations.

References and further reading

Apache Commons Project (2007) *Apache Commons*. http://commons.apache.org/

Franklin, S. (2001) *XML Parsers: DOM and SAX Put to the Test*. DevX.com, http://www.devx.com/xml/Article/16922

Gamma, E., Helm, R., Johnson, R. and Vlissides, J. (1995) *Design Patterns: Elements of Reusable Object-Oriented Software*. Reading, Mass: Addison-Wesley.

Geary, D. (2001) *Advanced JavaServer Pages*. Upper Saddle River, NJ: Prentice-Hall

SourceForge (2007) *SAX*. http://sax.sourceforge.net/

11

CHAPTER 12

Web Applications and Databases

LEARNING OBJECTIVES

- **To be able to create a database that reflects an entity–relationship diagram**

- **To be able to use JDBC to connect from Java code to the database**

- **To be able to utilize enterprise-level database connections via an application server**

- **To be able to implement the Data Access Object pattern**

- **To be able to present persistent data in a JSP**

- **To understand the main issues in object-relational mapping**

INTRODUCTION

Back in Chapter 2, when we looked at some design patterns for web applications, one of the patterns we looked at was 'store content in the database'. The dynamic content in our web applications needs to come from somewhere. It may come from external web services or other systems, and it may be generated by a programming component, but in most cases it will probably come from a database. Therefore we need to know how to get data in and out of a database so we can use it in our web applications. Although there are several different types of database available, including hierarchal, object-oriented and XML, most databases are relational. The focus of this chapter is how to bridge between the table schemas of a relational database and Java objects, a process known as *object-relational mapping*. We will see how we can use JDBC to connect Java programs to databases, both directly and via an application server, and introduce the Data Access Object pattern to encapsulate the persistence layer of our web applications. We also consider some of the issues involved in building a true object-relational mapping layer.

This chapter assumes that you have a basic understanding of relational databases and the Structured Query Language (SQL). However if you need an introduction to these topics, or a refresher, then the fundamentals are covered in Appendix A to this book. Also included in this appendix is an introduction MySQL, which is the relational database used for the examples in this chapter.

12.1 Object-relational mapping

One of the key challenges facing the Java developer is the integration of object-oriented systems with data in relational databases.

To succeed using objects and relational databases together you need to understand both paradigms, and their differences, and then make intelligent tradeoffs based on that knowledge. (Ambler 2006).

Relational databases are the most common storage technology used today, and are frequently a part of legacy systems with which new applications have to integrate. They are well understood and their underlying table model, which uses repeated data keys to relate normalized tables to each other, is based on sound mathematical foundations. Of course not all types of application with persistent data should necessarily use a relational database. Applications such as Computer Aided Design (CAD) tools, Computer Aided Software Engineering (CASE) tools or other check-in and check-out types of applications, where transactions are very long and there are no collisions, will probably use other forms of storage (Keller 1997) but, in general, relational databases are an effective solution to storage requirements and object-oriented developers frequently have to deal with them. In joining together an object model with a database schema, there are three basic scenarios:

- *Deriving the database schema from the object model*

  This is possible where no legacy database exists or the existing schema can be changed. Although this is the ideal scenario from an object-oriented perspective, it is not very common.

- *Deriving the object model from the database schema*

  This can be done where a complete database schema is already in place for the system to be developed, but is unlikely to translate directly into an ideal object model. At the very least, we might expect a level of denormalization to take place between the relational schema and the object design.

- *'Meet in the middle' mapping*

  This is where both a database schema and an object model exist and they need to be mapped to one another. This is the most likely scenario in practice and the one that is most likely to result in both an acceptable database schema and an acceptable object model (though there may well have to be some compromise in either or both of these).

Developers need techniques and tools to join together two very different models, the object-oriented design and the relational schema. Since the beginnings of object-oriented programming, this has been a recurrent problem in making objects persistent, since relational database schemas do not map easily to an object-oriented view of a business model. Trying to bridge this gap without either understanding the issues or using appropriate tools can lead to unsatisfactory design and poor performance. In this chapter, we look at some basic techniques for moving data between an object model and a relational database using JDBC (Java Database Connectivity). At the end of the chapter we discuss some further issues in object-relational mapping and consider some alternative tools and APIs that may be used for object persistence in Java.

12.2 The example database

In this chapter, we work with a simple database that will represent three entities from the home insurance domain, 'claim', 'policy' and 'policyholder'. Each policy holder may have multiple policies, while each policy belongs to one policy holder. Each claim is made against a single policy, but one policy may have many claims made against it. Figure 12.1 shows an entity-relationship diagram (ERD) of these entities and their relationships using Chen's notation (Chen 1976) where entities are rectangles and relationships are diamonds, with 'n' used to signify a 'many' relationship.

This database is incomplete in terms of the domain model of the home insurance application, but it provides enough detail for the examples in the rest of this chapter.

 NOTE In many real-life situations, a direct mapping between a domain model, an object model and a database schema is not possible, because the database schema may already exist, and our application may be only one of many that use the same database. In situations such as this, the object model and the database schema may be quite different, leading to some complex *object-relational mapping*.

Figure 12.2 shows the three tables with their column names and foreign key relationships.

FIGURE 12.1 An entity–relationship diagram from the home insurance domain

FIGURE 12.2 The columns in the three database tables with foreign key relationships

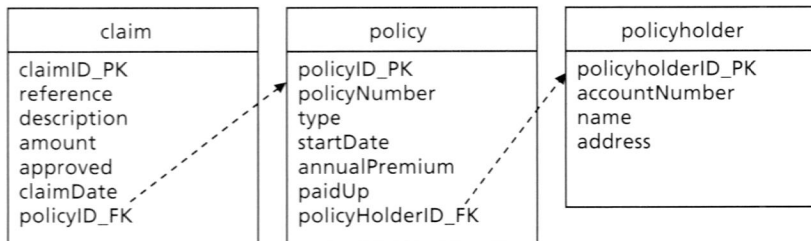

When using artificial keys as primary keys in the database, we need some way of generating unique key values. There are various strategies for this, but a simple approach is to let the database generate primary keys for us. In MySQL this is very simple; we just add 'AUTO_INCREMENT' to the configuration of the primary keys, for example:

```
CREATE TABLE claim (
   claimID_PK INTEGER NOT NULL PRIMARY KEY AUTO_INCREMENT,
etc...
```

This does not prevent us from providing a primary key value if we want to, but if we do not then MySQL will generate a new integer key every time a new record is inserted.

 NOTE Different databases have different ways of generating keys, so the AUTO_INCREMENT syntax used with MySQL is not portable to other databases. An alternative approach is to manage key generation with our own database-independent implementation. An example of this strategy can be found in (Reese 2003).

Here is a DDL file to create all three tables from Figure 12.2. All the tables have artificial primary keys that are auto incremented, but the original set of data inserted into the tables explicitly defines the primary keys.

```
USE webhomecoverdb;

DROP TABLE claim;
CREATE TABLE claim (
   claimID_PK INTEGER NOT NULL PRIMARY KEY AUTO_INCREMENT,
   reference VARCHAR(15),
   description VARCHAR(100),
   amount FLOAT,
   approved BOOLEAN,
   claimDate DATE,
   policyID_FK INTEGER
);

DROP TABLE policy;
CREATE TABLE policy (
   policyID_PK INTEGER NOT NULL PRIMARY KEY AUTO_INCREMENT,
   policyNumber INTEGER,
   type VARCHAR(20),
   startDate DATE,
   annualPremium FLOAT,
   paidUp BOOLEAN,
   policyHolderID_FK INTEGER
);

DROP TABLE policyholder;
CREATE TABLE policyholder (
   policyholderID_PK INTEGER NOT NULL PRIMARY KEY AUTO_INCREMENT,
   accountNumber INTEGER,
```

```
    name VARCHAR(30),
    address VARCHAR(50)
);

INSERT INTO claim
    VALUES (1,'B2007–11–051','Broken window',150.00,true,'2007–05–11',1);
INSERT INTO claim
    VALUES (2,'C2007–04–131','Stained carpet',1000.00,false,'2007–04–13',2);
INSERT INTO claim
    VALUES (3,'C2007–22–011','Stolen camera',650.00,true,'2007–01–22',2);
INSERT INTO claim
    VALUES (4,'B2007–04–011','House burned down',350000.00,true,'2007–01–04',3);

INSERT INTO policy VALUES
    (1,233142,'buildings','2007–02–12',45.60,true,1);
INSERT INTO policy VALUES
    (2,384475,'contents','2006–11–21',37.00,true,1);
INSERT INTO policy VALUES
    (3,332574,'buildings','2005–06–03',120.50,false,2);
INSERT INTO policy VALUES
    (4,928376,'buildings','2008–12–30',120.50,true,3);
INSERT INTO policy VALUES
    (5,885746,'contents','2007–10–13',120.50,true,3);

INSERT INTO policyholder VALUES(1,1625344,'Mr. Charles Babbage','55, Old Road,
London, United Kingdom');
INSERT INTO policyholder VALUES(2,5424882,'Dr. Bjarne Stroustrup','4, Wellington
Road, Auckland, New Zealand');
INSERT INTO policyholder VALUES(3,2314253,'Ms. Grace Hopper','1,Forest Heights,
San Francisco, United States');
```

12.3 Java and the database

Having set up a database to work with, the next step is to see how we can access data stored in a relational database from Java code so that it can be used to provide persistent and shareable data for the home insurance system. We will begin by seeing how Java code can be used to execute SQL statements, so that we can interact with the database using Java programs.

Java database access with JDBC

Java DataBase Connectivity (JDBC) is based on the concepts previously demonstrated by Open DataBase Connectivity (ODBC), a Microsoft technology based on a standard approach known as the *call-level interface* (CLI) defined by the SQL Access group in the early 1990s. The basic idea of ODBC was that any application could interact with any relational database that used SQL provided that they were both ODBC-compliant, meaning that they could both use an intermediate ODBC layer to communicate. The intermediate level consists of a core library, that the application uses, and a supporting database driver, that links the standard library to specific databases (Figure 12.3).

JDBC takes a very similar approach, with the difference being that the core library is written in Java and the driver layer consists of a JDBC driver rather than an ODBC driver.

FIGURE 12.3   The architecture of ODBC

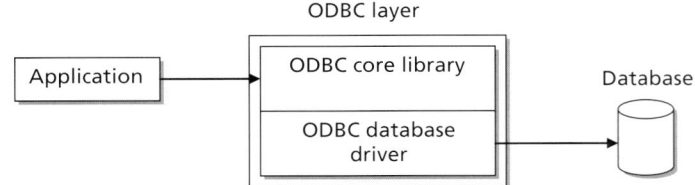

ODBC layer

Application → ODBC core library / ODBC database driver → Database

The job of JDBC is to provide the ability for a Java application to connect to a relational database in order to store the state of any objects that need to be persistent outside of the run time of the application. The advantage of using the services of a relational database is that we can store our object data reliably and efficiently using data-storage tools that are well developed and widely used. The disadvantage is that using a relational database with an object-oriented program requires some object-relational mapping, where we have to convert our data between object-oriented and relational structures.

JDBC drivers

The JDBC API, which is similar to the core library in ODBC, is a 'thin' API which lets us use SQL commands within our Java objects. JDBC specifies mostly interfaces, with only a few classes. This is because much of the implementation is done at the JDBC-driver level. The implementing classes for different JDBC drivers are supplied by different vendors. These vendors may be database suppliers (such as Oracle, Microsoft IBM, etc.), application server vendors, third-party suppliers or open-source projects. The main job of the JDBC driver is to enable communication between a Java program and a particular database, and to convert between Java types (such as 'String') and SQL types (such as 'VARCHAR').

There are four different types of JDBC driver with different characteristics. Sometimes there is no choice about which driver you can use with a particular database, but common databases often have many possible drivers available. Sun Microsystems maintains a web site of currently available JDBC drivers that includes a searchable database that will list all the drivers for a given database or other requirement (Sun Microsystems 2007).

 NOTE   At the time of writing, the Sun JDBC driver web site listed ten drivers for MySQL.

Which driver you use will depend on various factors such as which types are available for your database, how much you are willing to pay for one and how well a specific driver performs in practice. Not all drivers provide exactly the same support and different versions of JDBC may not all be supported by a particular driver. The four types of driver are shown in Figure 12.4. Type 1 drivers are only appropriate if you are already using an ODBC connection and want to reuse it from a Java application. Otherwise, they are not a good choice because the multiple levels of translation from JDBC to ODBC to the database are inefficient. Type 3 drivers are used to connect from a database client to a remote server, which will need another type of driver to connect to the database. In most cases, we will be choosing between a type 2 driver and type 4 driver. Since a type 4 driver has no levels of translation between Java and another API, we would expect a type 4 driver to be the best option. However this may not be the case in practice so in a real project it is best to test all the available drivers and see which one is best at meeting requirements such as performance, features and cost.

Using the JDBC API

The basic steps in using JDBC in a Java program are quite simple. However they will be different depending on whether you are making a simple two-tier connection (i.e. your application is connecting directly to the database) or whether you are connecting through an application server. We begin by looking briefly at how two-tier connections work and showing how we can integrate SQL code into Java using the JDBC APIs. Later, we see how to configure the server to enable us to make database connections in a web application. Server-side components that service many clients should not make direct connections to the database because they would not be able to scale up to cope with a large number of users. To manage large numbers of connections efficiently we have to use *connection pools* which are accessed through *data sources* and the Java Naming and Directory Interface (JNDI). We will look at these technologies in Section 12.4.

A two tier connection does not include an application server. The two tiers are a Java program (Java Standard Edition, not Enterprise Edition) and a database, connected via a JDBC Driver. The first step for a Java program using JDBC is to load the JDBC driver class, then use the driver to make a connection to the database. The connection can then be used to send SQL commands to the database, using the methods of Java classes and interfaces. For two-tier connections, all of these classes and interfaces are located in the 'java.sql' package.

FIGURE 12.4 The four types of JDBC driver

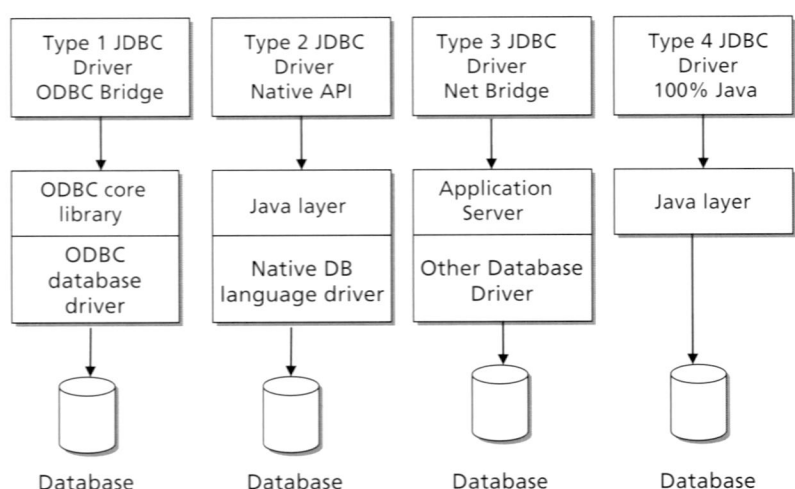

The first step in the code is to load the JDBC driver. This is usually done using a useful feature of Java known as *dynamic loading*. The 'Class' class has a static method called 'forName', which will load the named class into memory. The syntax for doing this is:

```
Class.forName("drivername");
```

The name of the driver class will of course be different for each type of database. For example, to load the driver to connect to the MySQL database, the class name is 'Driver', in the 'com.mysql.jdbc' package (note that it requires the fully qualified class name, including the package name):

```
Class.forName("com.mysql.jdbc.Driver");
```

NOTE	The 'com.mysql.jdbc.Driver' is the type 4 driver supplied with the MySQL Connector/J download. However there are other drivers from various sources that can be used with MySQL.

There are a couple of other things that are important for this to work. First, you must have the driver available on the classpath. The driver will probably be supplied in a Java Archive (JAR) file, so it is this JAR file that will need to be added to the classpath. For all our previous examples, the classpath has been set in the Ant script. For this example, which is not part of a web application, we need to set the classpath manually. You can set the classpath in various ways, depending on your development environment. For example, we could set this on the command line, e.g.

```
set classpath=%CLASSPATH%;path/databaselibrary.jar;.
```

Or we might add the library to an IDE, or even set the classpath using an environment variable. MySQL provides a JAR file containing the driver called 'mysql-connector-java-5.0.4bin.jar' (or something similar depending on the version). This JAR file comes as part of the 'Connector/J' download, which is separate from the MySQL database download.

NOTE	In the example classpath setting, %CLASSPATH% refers to the current classpath, and the period refers to the current directory. More information about the classpath can be found in (Harold 2006a and 2006b).

The other thing to be aware of is that the 'forName' method may throw a 'ClassNotFoundException' if it is unable to load the class, either due to a classpath problem or perhaps a misspelling of the class name. Therefore this line needs a 'try ... catch' block around it.

```
try
{
    Class.forName("com.mysql.jdbc.Driver");
}
catch(ClassNotFoundException e)
```

```
  {
    e.printStackTrace();
    System.exit(1);
  }
```

SQL exceptions

As well as being aware of the need to catch the 'ClassNotFoundException' when using dynamic loading, most of the methods in the 'java.sql' classes can throw 'java.sql.SQLException'. Since this is a checked exception, we must use 'try ... catch' blocks around our database access code or it will not compile, e.g.

```
try
{
  // JDBC code
}
catch(SQLException e)
{
  //. . .handle exception
}
```

Once we have loaded the database driver, we can make a connection to the database. To do this we need to know the database URL, and may also need to know the username and password that will authenticate our program to the database. MySQL database URLs have the following format:

```
jdbc:mysql://hostname:portnumber/databasename
```

The default port is 3306 and, if we are connecting to a database on the same machine, then the host can be 'localhost'.

Database connections are made using the static 'getConnection' method of the 'DriverManager' class (from the 'java.sql' package). This method returns a 'Connection' object. In this code fragment we connect to a database called 'webhomecoverdb' running on 'localhost', assuming the default port.

```
Connection connection = DriverManager.getConnection
  ("jdbc:mysql://localhost/webhomecoverdb");
```

Creating an authorized MySQL user

The connection code above will only be able to access the database if MySQL has been configured with an anonymous user (no username and password required). Since this is not necessarily the case, and indeed having an anonymous user for the database would clearly be a security risk in any real-world system, we will make sure that we can connect from our Java code to MySQL by creating a user with the necessary access privileges to the database. To do this we need to log onto MySQL as the root user and grant access privileges to a user identified by a username and a password. The following command provides a general set of privileges, including creating, updating and deleting records, across all databases. The username here is 'javaclient' and the password is 'webhomecover'. The URL of the database server is 'localhost'.

```
GRANT ALL PRIVILEGES ON *.* TO 'javaclient'@'localhost' IDENTIFIED BY 'webhomecover';
```

Now our connection code will use this username and password to connect the database, passing them as additional parameters to the 'getConnection' method:

```
Connection connection = DriverManager.getConnection
   ("jdbc:mysql://localhost/webhomecoverdb","javaclient","webhomecover");
```

 NOTE Connecting to the database as an authorized user with a username and password is required within a web application.

Creating statements

Once we have successfully connected to the database, we can create 'Statement' objects, using the 'createStatement' method of the connection:

```
Statement statement = connection.createStatement();
```

At this point we are ready to start executing SQL commands, such as SELECT, INSERT, UPDATE and DELETE, against the database, wrapped in Java code.

We can read data from the database by using the 'executeQuery' method of the statement. This is passed an SQL query as a parameter and returns a ResultSet object that contains the result of the query. Here, for example, we execute a single SELECT statement to retrieve all the rows from the 'claim' table.

```
ResultSet results = statement.executeQuery("SELECT * FROM claim");
```

Processing ResultSets

We can get the data from a ResultSet by iterating over it with a 'while' loop. Each iteration gives us the next row from the database query.

```
while (results.next() )
{
   // process the next row returned by the query
}
```

ResultSets have a number of different methods to retrieve different types of data. They each begin with 'get', followed by a data type, for example 'getString', which is used to retrieve data from character columns such as VARCHAR, and 'getInt', which is used where the column is of type INTEGER. The parameter to these 'get' methods may be either the column number or the column name. Here, for example, we use the column number to retrieve the second column from the result of the query against the 'claim' table, which is the 'description' column (of type VARCHAR). Unlike, for example, array indexes, Result-Set index numbers start at one rather than zero.

```
String description = results.getString(2);
```

However it is not good practice to access columns by number, since this may be unreliable if the database schema is changed. It is much better to retrieve data by column name. We would therefore use the name 'description' instead of the number '2':

```
String description – results.getString("description");
```

ResultSets, Statements and Connections should all be closed when they are finished with. You need to close these objects in the reverse order that they were opened: ResultSet first, then Statement, then Connection.

```
results.close();
statement.close();
connection.close();
```

Closure of these resources is automatic, but explicit closure can free database resources more quickly.

Here is a complete Java program that makes a connection to the 'webhomecoverdb' database using the MySQL JDBC driver, executes a SELECT query on the 'claim' table and then prints the contents of the ResultSet to standard output (note that the 'reference' column is not displayed, to reduce the width of the output, though it is available in the ResultSet).

```
package com.webhomecover.jdbc;

import java.sql.*;

public class DatabaseAccess
{
  public static void main(String[] args)
  {
    try
      {
        Class.forName("com.mysql.jdbc.Driver");
      }
    catch(ClassNotFoundException e)
      {
        e.printStackTrace();
        System.exit(1);
      }
    try
      {
        Connection connection = DriverManager.getConnection
          ("jdbc:mysql://localhost/webhomecoverdb",
           "javaclient","webhomecover") ;
        Statement statement = connection.createStatement();
        ResultSet results = statement.executeQuery("SELECT * FROM claim");
        int id = 0;
        String description = null;
        double amount = 0.0;
        boolean approved = false;
        java.sql.Date claimDate = null;
        System.out.println("id\tdescription\tamount\tapproved\tclaimDate");
```

12

```
    while(results.next())
    {
      id = results.getInt("claimID_PK");
      description = results.getString("description");
      amount = results.getDouble("amount");
      approved = results.getBoolean("approved");
      claimDate = results.getDate("claimDate");
      System.out.println(id + "\t" + description + "\t" + amount +
      "\t" + approved + "\t" + claimDate);
    }
    results.close();
    statement.close();
    connection.close();
    }
  catch(SQLException e)
  {
    e.printStackTrace();
  }
 }
}
```

This is the output from the program. Note that the rather clumsy use of tab characters will not guarantee a good column layout, since this depends on the length of the data in the 'description' field.

id	description	amount	approved	claimDate
1	Broken window	150.0	true	2007–05–11
2	Stained carpet	1000.0	false	2007–04–13
3	Stolen camera	650.0	true	2007–01–22
4	House burned down	350000.0	true	2007–01–04

Updating records

Update statements, which change the data by inserting, updating or deleting records, are supported by the 'executeUpdate' method of the 'Statement' class. Since updates are not queries, they do not return a result set. They do, however, return an integer value that indicates the number of rows affected by the update. Here for example, is an update that inserts a new record into the 'claim' table, and returns the number of rows updated into a variable. We assume here that 'rowsUpdated' has already been declared as an 'int' variable:

```
rowsUpdated = statement.executeUpdate("INSERT INTO Claim VALUES
(6, 'B2008–06–211', 'Water damage',2300.00,false,'2008–06–21',NULL)");
```

Here are examples of updating and deleting, again using the 'executeUpdate' method:

```
rowsUpdated = statement.executeUpdate
  ("UPDATE claim SET approved=true WHERE claimID_PK=6");

rowsUpdated = statement.executeUpdate
  ("DELETE FROM claim WHERE description='Water damage' ");
```

Using prepared statements

Prepared statements are useful where similar SQL commands are to be executed with different data. For example, it will be a common update to change the state of the 'approved' field from 'false' to 'true' when a claim has been approved. By using a prepared statement we can reuse the same piece of code to update different records. The SQL string used as the parameter to the 'prepareStatement' method (of the 'Connection' class) has one or more placeholders where data can be provided. These are indicated by question marks, for example:

```
PreparedStatement prepstatement = connection.prepareStatement
    ("UPDATE claim SET approved = ? WHERE claimID_PK = ?");
```

To use a prepared statement, each placeholder is populated using 'set' methods based on the data type of the column. These are very similar to the 'get' methods used with a result set. The placeholders are numbered from left to right, starting at '1'. In our example there are two placeholders so the first is numbered '1' and the second is numbered '2'. Here we set the values of the two placeholders, then execute the update:

```
prepstatement.setBoolean(1, true);
prepstatement.setInt(2, 2);
prepstatement.executeUpdate();
```

Because a prepared statement has already been configured with an SQL statement, we do not need to pass any parameters to the 'executeUpdate' method.

The point of doing this is that the same prepared statement can be used multiple times, for example (assuming a much larger database than we currently have!):

```
prepstatement.setBoolean(1, false);
prepstatement.setInt(2, 1723);
prepstatement.executeUpdate();
```

This reuse not only makes our Java code more elegant, it actually makes it much more efficient, because the underlying SQL code that a prepared statement uses only needs to be generated once, rather than each time as it would be for individual Statement objects (Byron and Thomson 2002).

12.4 Integrating persistence into a web application

In the previous section we saw how to use JDBC to make a direct (two-tier) connection from a Java program to a database. However this approach does not work well in a web application environment. Server-side Java components that need to connect to a database should not make direct connections to the database but rather should connect via a *data source*. A data source is an interface that provides connections to the database. Depending on the implementation, the data source may provide a standard connection, just like the DriverManager class or a *connection pool*, that supports pooling of distributed transactions which span more than one database. The idea of a connection pool is that it takes responsibility for the creation and management of multiple database connections, and enables them to be reused by different application components over time without the unnecessary

FIGURE 12.5 A data source acts as an interface to a connection pool, which manages multiple connections to the physical database

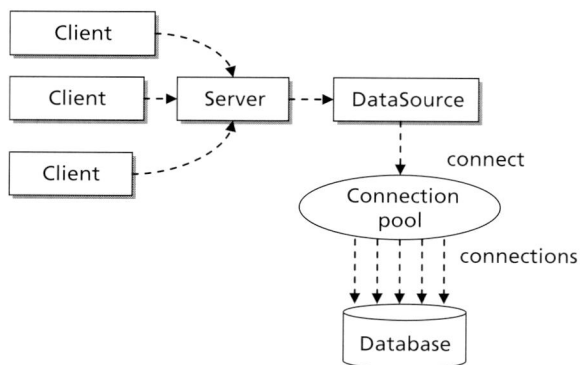

opening and closing of individual connections for each database access (Figure 12.5). Connection pooling is managed transparently for us if we connect to a database using a data source that supports it, rather than making a direct connection to the database using a DriverManager.

So far we have been using JDBC-related classes from the 'java.sql' package. For enterprise-level database connections, required for web applications, we also need some classes from the 'javax.sql' package, which includes the DataSource class that we use to get access to a connection pool. In addition, the data source needs to be configured and made available via the application server. Tomcat data source configuration is done using XML files, and the configured data sources need to be made available to client code using the Java Naming and Directory Interface (JNDI). Finally, we need to configure the web application descriptor ('web.xml') to make resources deployed into JNDI available to our Java components.

Java Naming and Directory Interface

The Java Naming and Directory Interface (JNDI) is a standardized API for accessing naming and directory services, which are a way of making application resources available through a central point of access. It provides a consistent interface for Java applications to access these services, regardless of the actual implementation that is being used. In this sense it is quite similar to JDBC, in that it has an API that is used by application programmers, regardless of which underlying implementation (e.g. a JDBC driver) is actually being used. JNDI provides enterprise Java applications with a global point of access for services, providing access using a hierarchical namespace (a tree structure) that can be used to access a whole range of services, including the data sources that give access to database connections. Many different implementations of JNDI are possible, but application servers usually provide an implementation that you can use without needing to install a separate product.

Data sources in the JNDI tree structure

The JNDI tree is made up of a number of *contexts* that can be nested inside each other, not unlike the elements of an XML document. Within each context, objects that contain various types of application resource can be *bound*. At the root of the tree is a special context called the *initial context*, which is from where we can navigate to find other sub-contexts. Within the JNDI tree is a special context called 'java:comp/env' (Java component environment) which is used for looking up Java programming resources. Within this context it is conventional to use some standard sub-context names for different types of resource. For example, we normally put data sources into a context called 'jdbc'. Figure 12.6 shows part of a JNDI tree, with the initial context, sub-contexts, and the special 'java:comp/env' context. Within this is the 'jdbc' context containing a data source called 'webhomecoverds'.

Configuring the server for data source access

Having introduced some of the main aspects of database access within web applications, we now work through each stage of making a connection to a data source. The necessary steps are:

1. Configure the server to be able to create the data source and bind it into the JNDI tree.
2. Configure the web application so that its Java components can look up the data source in the JNDI tree.
3. Write code in Data Access Objects within the web application that looks up the data source and uses it to make connections to the database.

The first step is to configure the server so that it can create a data source that connects to the database using the username and password we have specified. Tomcat Data Base Connection Pools (DBCP) use the Jakarta-Commons Database Connection Pool, which relies on a number of Jakarta-Commons components that are already available in the JAR files in the server's library folder. However, the JAR file for your JDBC driver (the MySQL connector JAR file) is not part of the server's default installation, therefore you will have to copy the JAR file containing the driver to the 'lib' folder of your server. For standalone Tomcat this will be:

```
Tomcat_home\lib
```

FIGURE 12.6 Part of a JNDI tree with a data source bound into the 'java:comp/env/jdbc' context

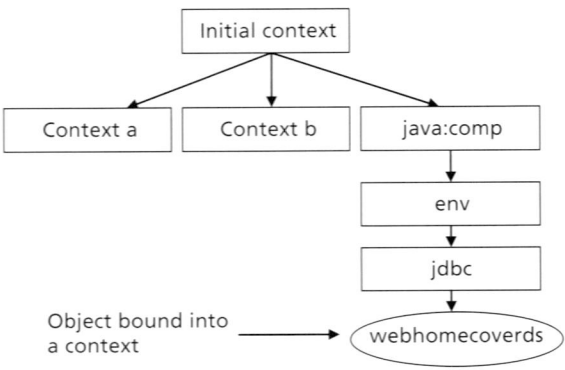

while for Tomcat running as part of JBoss it will be:

JBoss_home\server\default\lib

You will find the necessary JAR file in the root folder of the MySQL Connector/J download.

 NOTE The server cannot use this JAR file until it has been restarted.

Depending on whether you are using Tomcat standalone, or as part of JBoss, the configuration is different. We will look at Tomcat standalone configuration first and then at Tomcat running within JBoss.

To create a data source in Tomcat, we have to use attributes of the 'Context' (note the upper case 'C') element in the server's configuration files. It is possible to do this by directly editing the 'server.xml' file (in the 'conf' folder of the Tomcat home directory), but this is not a very flexible approach. A better option is to put the configuration in a separate XML file, called 'context.xml', in the web application, so that it is deployed with the application. The 'context.xml' file needs to be in a special folder of the web application root called META-INF. The attributes used with the 'Context' element include the name of the database driver and the database URL, the same kind of information we used when making a two-tier connection. We also need to provide the username and password for the server to authenticate itself to the database. Of the other attributes, 'maxActive' defines the maximum number of connections in the pool (a value of zero means no limit), 'maxIdle' is the maximum number of idle connections to be kept in the pool (a value of <minus>1 means no limit) and 'maxWait' is the maximum time in milliseconds to wait for a connection to become available (a value of <minus>1 means wait indefinitely). Adding an 'autoReconnect=true' argument to the end of the database URL ensures that the driver will automatically reconnect if MySQL closes the connection because it has been idle for a long time.

```
<Context path="/webhomecover" docBase="webhomecover">
  <Resource
    name="jdbc/webhomecoverds"
    auth="Container"
    type="javax.sql.DataSource"
    maxActive="100"
    maxIdle="30"
    maxWait="10000"
    username="javaclient"
    password="webhomecover"
    driverClassName="com.mysql.jdbc.Driver"
    url="jdbc:mysql://localhost:3306/webhomecoverdb?autoReconnect=true"
  />
</Context>
```

When you deploy your web application, Tomcat creates a file called 'webhomecover.xml' in the 'conf\Catalina\localhost' folder, containing the contents of your 'context.xml' file.

When using Tomcat within JBoss, there is a different approach. You create an XML file called 'mysql-ds.xml' that contains a 'datasources' root element, within which you can

specify one or more data sources. This file is then put into the 'JBoss_home\server\default\
deploy' folder. Here are the contents of this file. Once again we need the database URL,
the driver class name, the username and the password:

```
<?xml version="1.0" encoding="UTF-8"?>
<datasources>
  <local-tx-datasource>
    <jndi-name>jdbc/webhomecoverds</jndi-name>
    <connection-url>
     jdbc:mysql://localhost:3306/webhomecoverdb
    </connection-url>
    <driver-class>com.mysql.jdbc.Driver</driver-class>
    <user-name>javaclient</user-name>
    <password>webhomecover</password>
  </local-tx-datasource>
</datasources>
```

Once the server has been configured to make a data source available via JNDI, we have to
modify the 'web.xml' deployment descriptor by adding a *resource reference*. A resource
reference provides a look-up name that can be used by Java components in the web
application to refer to resources bound into JNDI. Resource references are added to the
end of the 'web.xml' file

```
<?xml version="1.0" ?>
<web-app xmlns="http://java.sun.com/xml/ns/javaee"
  xmlns:xsi="http://www.w3.org/2001/XMLSchema-instance"
  xsi:schemaLocation="http://java.sun.com/xml/ns/javaee
http://java.sun.com/xml/ns/javaee/web-app_2_5.xsd"
  version="2.5">

  <welcome-file-list>
   <welcome-file>/welcome.jsp</welcome-file>
  </welcome-file-list>

  <resource-ref>
   <description>DB Connection</description>
   <res-ref-name>jdbc/webhomecoverds</res-ref-name>
   <res-type>javax.sql.DataSource</res-type>
   <res-auth>Container</res-auth>
  </resource-ref>

</web-app>
```

For JBoss only, there is an additional step. An extra configuration file called 'jboss-web.xml'
has to be added to the WEB-INF folder. The role of this file is to provide a mapping
between the resource reference name used in 'web.xml' ('jdbc/webhomecoverds') and the
actual JNDI name that is used by JBoss. Note that JBoss uses a slightly different JNDI
name to the conventional one, preceding it with 'java:jdbc' rather than 'java:comp/env/
jdbc'. The contents of the file should look like this:

```
<?xml version="1.0" encoding="UTF-8"?>
<!DOCTYPE jboss-web PUBLIC
  "-//JBoss//DTD Web Application 2.4//EN"
```

```
            "http://www.jboss.org/j2ee/dtd/jboss-web_4_0.dtd">
<jboss-web>
  <resource-ref>
    <res-ref-name>jdbc/webhomecoverds</res-ref-name>
    <jndi-name>java:jdbc/webhomecoverds</jndi-name>
  </resource-ref>
</jboss-web>
```

Figure 12.7 summarizes the various files required to support web application database access when using either Tomcat or JBoss, and the interactions between the client, the server, JNDI and the data source.

12.5 Building a persistence layer using data access objects

Now we have introduced the basic syntax of JDBC, and looked at how to configure an application server to give us access to a data source, we need to integrate these aspects into the design of our object model so that we can begin to make the objects within a web application persistent. JDBC on its own is not a mechanism for making objects persistent. It is just a way of using Java to execute SQL statements. Therefore we have to provide some kind of mapping between the objects in our application and the database, using JDBC as the link between them. Linking object-oriented code to a relational database is known as object-relational mapping, and is quite a challenging aspect of software development.

FIGURE 12.7 The files and interactions required for database access from Java web applications deployed in Tomcat and JBoss

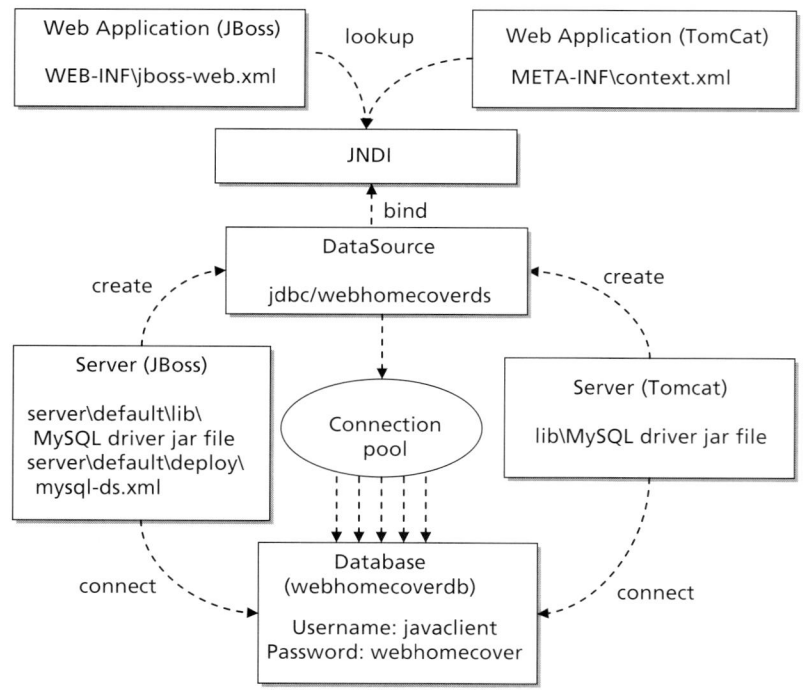

To get true object persistence, we need to consider how we can store objects in relational tables, when the two approaches to modeling data are quite different. There are many different approaches to this problem, but here we apply a simple design pattern known as the Data Access Object (DAO) (Figure 12.8) which is one of the core Java EE patterns (Alur *et al.* 2003).

The basic idea of the Data Access Object is that it encapsulates the create, read, update and delete (CRUD) processes necessary for passing objects to and from the database. Data is passed to and from the DAO by a Data Transfer Object (DTO) which is a model-layer JavaBean that does not contain any database access code, but contains the data that is going to or from the database. Business objects can pass DTOs to and from the DAO. The advantage of this pattern is that only the DAO needs to know about the persistence mechanism being used, so that the database layer could be changed without affecting any other objects.

For our next example we are going to create a 'ClaimDAO' object, which will use a Claim object as its DTO. Figure 12.9 shows the methods of the ClaimDAO and the properties of

FIGURE 12.8 The Data Access Object pattern (from Alur *et al.* 2003)

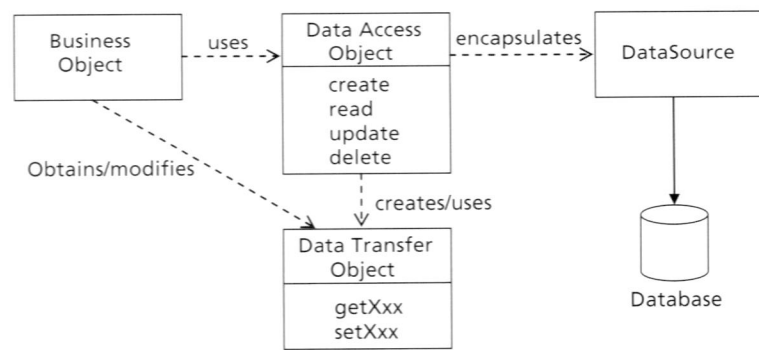

FIGURE 12.9 The methods of the ClaimDAO and the properties of the Claim that relate to persistent data

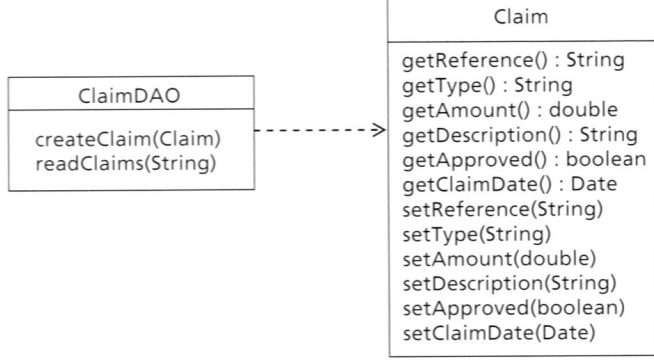

the Claim that relate directly to database columns. To simplify this example, the DAO only has methods to create and read Claims. A complete DAO would also have methods to update and delete claims in the database.

Writing a DAO for data source access

To implement the Data Access Object, we need to be able to connect to a server-side data source via JNDI. The JDBC connection code we used earlier for two-tier connections cannot be used within a web application, because it connected directly to the database using the 'DriverManager'. For server-side data access, we need to connect to JNDI and get the initial context object. With some JNDI implementations, you need to configure your connection to the JNDI service with a set of properties. However, if you are using the server's default JNDI implementation, these properties are typically stored somewhere in the server's configuration files, such as in a 'jndi.properties' file located somewhere on the classpath. In this situation, there is no need to pass any information to the 'InitialContext' constructor. Tomcat has a default JNDI configuration, so getting the initial context is simple.

The JNDI classes and interfaces are in the 'javax.naming' package, so we will need to import these:

```
import javax.naming.*;
```

Then we need to get hold of the InitialContext. Since the InitialContext class implements the 'Context' interface, we can use a Context reference when we call the constructor.

```
Context initial = new InitialContext();
```

To look up a resource in JNDI, we use the 'lookup' method with a parameter of the path through the JDNI tree to the resource we want (here represented by a static final field called 'DATASOURCE_NAME' which is set to 'java:comp/env/jdbc/webhomecoverds'). Since 'lookup' returns an Object, we need to cast this object to the appropriate type, which in this case will be a DataSource. After that point, we can get a Connection object from the DataSource and begin to use it in the same manner as we did for the two-tier connection. The only other new aspect to the code is that the JNDI methods can throw a 'NamingException', so we need to add a 'catch' block for this exception type. Here is the complete 'getConnection' method:

```
private void getConnection()
{
  if(connection == null)
  {
   try
   {
    Context initialContext = new InitialContext();
    DataSource ds = (DataSource)initialContext.lookup(DATASOURCE_NAME);
    connection = ds.getConnection();
   }
   catch(NamingException e)
   { e.printStackTrace(); }
   catch(SQLException e)
```

```
      { e.printStackTrace(); }
    }
```

A couple of other aspects of the class are worth highlighting. The 'readClaims' method has been given a String parameter to make it possible to add a 'where' clause to the query. If the parameter value is an empty string then all claims will be returned. Each claim record is used to create a Claim object, and a collection of Claims is returned by the method.

The 'createClaim' method is passed a Claim as a parameter, and uses a prepared statement to insert the data into the table. The fixed part of the prepared statement String is declared as a static final field:

```
private static final String INSERT_STATEMENT = "INSERT INTO Claim
(reference, description, amount, approved, claimDate) VALUES (?,?,?,?,?)";
```

There is a 'cleanup' method in the class, called by the 'finally' blocks of the methods that access the database. The role of this method is to attempt to close any resources that may have been left open by exceptions being thrown.

Here is the complete 'ClaimDAO' class:

```
package com.webhomecover.dao;

import com.webhomecover.beans.*;
import java.sql.*;
import java.util.*;
import javax.naming.*;
import javax.sql.*;

public class ClaimDAO
{
   private Connection connection = null;
    private Statement statement = null;
    private PreparedStatement prepStatement = null;
    private ResultSet results = null;
    private static final String DATASOURCE_NAME =
       "java:comp/env/jdbc/webhomecoverds";
    private static final String INSERT_STATEMENT =
     "INSERT INTO Claim (reference, description, amount, approved,
     claimDate) VALUES (?,?,?,?,?)";

    private void getConnection()
    {
    if(connection == null)
    {
      try
      {
       Context initialContext = new InitialContext();
       DataSource ds = (DataSource)initialContext.lookup(DATASOURCE_NAME);
       connection = ds.getConnection();
      }
      catch(NamingException e)
      {
       e.printStackTrace();
      }
```

```
        catch(SQLException e)
        {
          e.printStackTrace();
        }
    }
}

public void createClaim(ClaimBean claim)
  {
    try
    {
      getConnection();
      prepStatement = connection.prepareStatement(INSERT_STATEMENT);
      prepStatement.setString(1, claim.getReference());
      prepStatement.setString(2, claim.getDescription());
      prepStatement.setDouble(3, claim.getAmount());
      prepStatement.setBoolean(4, claim.getApproved());
    //convert from java.util.Date to java.sql.Date
      long time = claim.getClaimDate().getTime();
      java.sql.Date date = new java.sql.Date(time);
      prepStatement.setDate(5, date);
      prepStatement.executeUpdate();
      prepStatement.close();
      prepStatement = null;
      connection.close();
      connection = null;
    }
    catch(SQLException e)
    {
      e.printStackTrace();
    }
    finally
    {
      cleanUp();
    }
  }

public Collection<ClaimBean>readClaims(String whereClause)
{
  Collection<ClaimBean>claims = new ArrayList<ClaimBean>();
  try
  {
    getConnection();
    Statement statement = connection.createStatement();
    ResultSet results = statement.executeQuery
        ("SELECT * FROM claim " + whereClause);
    int id = 0;
    String reference = null;
    String description = null;
    double amount = 0.0;
    boolean approved = false;
    java.sql.Date claimDate = null;
```

```
      ClaimBean claim = null;
      while(results.next())
      {
         id = results.getInt("claimID_PK");
         reference = results.getString("reference");
         description = results.getString("description");
         amount = results.getDouble("amount");
         approved = results.getBoolean("approved");
         claimDate = results.getDate("claimDate");
         claim = new ClaimBean();
         claim.setId(id);
         claim.setReference(reference);
         claim.setDescription(description);
         claim.setAmount(amount);
         claim.setApproved(approved);
         claim.setClaimDate(claimDate);
         claims.add(claim);
      }
      results.close();
      results = null;
      statement.close();
      statement = null;
      connection.close();
      connection = null;
      }
      catch(SQLException e)
      {
        e.printStackTrace();
      }
      finally
      {
        cleanUp();
      }
      return claims;
    }
private void cleanUp()
{
// always make sure resources are closed,
   if(results != null) {
      try
      { results.close(); }
      catch(SQLException e)
      { e.printStackTrace(); }
      results = null;
   }
   if(statement != null) {
      try
      { statement.close(); }
      catch(SQLException e)
      { e.printStackTrace(); }
      statement = null;
```

```
        }
        if(prepStatement != null) {
          try
          { prepStatement.close(); }
          catch(SQLException e)
          { e.printStackTrace(); }
          prepStatement = null;
        }
        if(connection != null) {
          try
          { connection.close(); }
          catch(SQLException e)
          { e.printStackTrace(); }
          connection = null;
          }
        }
    }
```

In Chapter 11, we introduced the ModelFacade class, to provide a common entry point to the model layer for components in the view–controller layer. In order to enable the JSPs in the view–controller layer to access the components returned from the DAO, we need to add a method to the façade. The following 'getClaims' method uses the DAO to create a collection of Claim objects that it returns to the caller:

```
public static Collection<Claim>getClaims(String whereClause)
{
   // if no 'where' clause string is passed in, create an empty string
   if(whereClause == null)
   {
      whereClause = new String();
   }
   ClaimDAO cdao = new ClaimDAO();
   Collection<Claim>claimCollection = cdao.readClaims(whereClause);
   return claimCollection;
}
```

When the façade returns a collection of Claims to the view component, we need a way of handling that collection in the view JSP. Writing a scriptlet is one option, but a better one is to create a class with an indexed property that can be accessed by the JSP using tag libraries. Here is a simple JavaBean called 'ClaimCollection' that serves this purpose. Its 'getClaims' method reads the collection of Claim objects from the ModelFacade, making it available to the JSP. The 'getClaims' method provides an indexed property that populates an ArrayList of Claims from the ModelFacade, which in turn reads Claim objects from the database using the ClaimDAO. The String parameter to the 'whereClause' method can be used to add a 'where' clause to the query.

```
package com.webhomecover.beans;

import java.util.*;
import com.webhomecover.model.ModelFacade;
import com.webhomecover.model.Claim;
```

```
public class ClaimCollection
{
   private String whereClause = new String();

   public String getWhereClause()
   {
      return whereClause;
   }

   public void setWhereClause(String whereClause)
   {
      this.whereClause = whereClause;
   }

   public Collection<Claim> getClaims()
   {
      Collection<Claim> claims = ModelFacade.getClaims(whereClause);
      return claims;
   }
}
```

Reading from the database in a web application

Having set up all the necessary components to connect to a database within a web application, our next example is a JSP that uses the data-access layer of the system to read persistent objects from the database and display them on a web page. The JSP builds a dynamic page based around reading records from the 'claim' table. We use the DAO to connect to the database and read a collection of Claim objects from it. Figure 12.10 shows the classes and methods that we will use in this process. The server page (listclaims.jsp) uses the ClaimCollection JavaBean with its indexed 'claims' property to make a collection of Claim objects available within the page. We can then use the JSTL to iterate over the indexed property and retrieve the properties of the Claims.

FIGURE 12.10 The components used to read claims from the database and display them in a server page

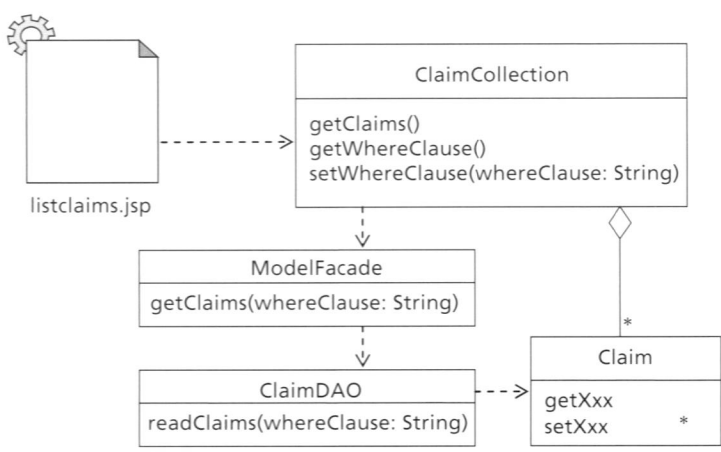

The server page uses JSP action tags to create a 'ClaimCollection' object. The 'forEach' method of the core library is used to iterate over the collection and the expression language is used to retrieve the properties of the bean for writing out to the page. In this case, the 'where' clause is left empty, but any valid SQL 'where' clause could be used here.

NOTE	When creating SQL queries in web applications, you should be aware of security risks. If any SQL can be entered or made visible at the view–controller layer then a web application may be open to 'SQL injection attacks' in which malicious SQL statements may be constructed. In production systems, any SQL code should be kept in the data-access layer. Our simplistic example, which enables an entire 'where' clause to be provided as a string, would not be best practice in a production system.

```xml
<?xml version="1.0"?>
<!-- File: listclaims.jsp -->

<jsp:root xmlns:jsp="http://java.sun.com/JSP/Page"
   xmlns:c="http://java.sun.com/jsp/jstl/core"
   version="2.0">
<jsp:directive.page isELIgnored="false" />
<jsp:directive.page contentType="text/html"/>
<jsp:output omit-xml-declaration="false"
   doctype-root-element="html"
   doctype-public="-//W3C//DTD XHTML 1.1//EN"
   doctype-system="http://www.w3.org/TR/xhtml11/DTD/xhtml11.dtd" />

<html xmlns="http://www.w3.org/1999/xhtml" xml:lang="en">
<head>
   <link href="webhomecover.css" rel="stylesheet" type="text/css" />
   <title>Insurance Claims</title>
</head>
   <body>
      <p>Here is a list of claims</p>
      <table>
        <tr>

<th>reference</th><th>description</th><th>amount</th><th>approved</th>
<th>claimDate</th>
        </tr>

        <jsp:useBean id="claimCollection"
         class="com.webhomecover.beans.ClaimCollection" />
        <c:forEach var="claim" items="${claimCollection.claims}">
         <tr>
           <td><c:out value="${claim.reference}" /></td>
           <td><c:out value="${claim.description}" /></td>
           <td><c:out value="${claim.amount}" /></td>
           <td><c:out value="${claim.approved}" /></td>
        <td><c:out value="${claim.claimDate}" /></td>
         </tr>
```

```
        </c:forEach>
      </table>
    </body>
  </html>
</jsp:root>
```

Figure 12.11 shows what the page looks like in Internet Explorer 7 when there are four records in the 'claim' table, read into Claim objects and written to a JSP using tags from the JSTL core library.

12.6 Integrating persistent objects

In our previous example, we saw how data stored in the database can be used to create Java objects, and these Java objects can then be used in a web application, both as objects in their own right and also as a means to generate XML documents. Our approach was from the perspective of reading data from the database, but we also need to be able to handle the translation of objects into their database representation and vice versa. Reading objects for rendering in a view component is an important aspect of web applications, but, we also need to be able to translate parts of the object model to and from the database, maintaining both object and entity relationships in the process. This is a little more complex, particularly when we need to manage foreign key relationships. Figure 12.12 shows this aspect of object-relational mapping. Not only do we need to read and write Java object data to and from the entities in the database, but we also need to write associations and read foreign-key relationships, and translate from one to the other.

To illustrate some of these issues, we return in the next example to the insurance claim use case that we first implemented in Chapter 10. However this time, rather than simply echoing the input data back to the user when the claim form is submitted, we write the claim to the database, link it with its matching policy (both in the database and in the object model) and provide the user with suitable feedback. Since each claim in the database

FIGURE 12.11 Data from 'ClaimBean' objects read from a database and displayed by a JSP

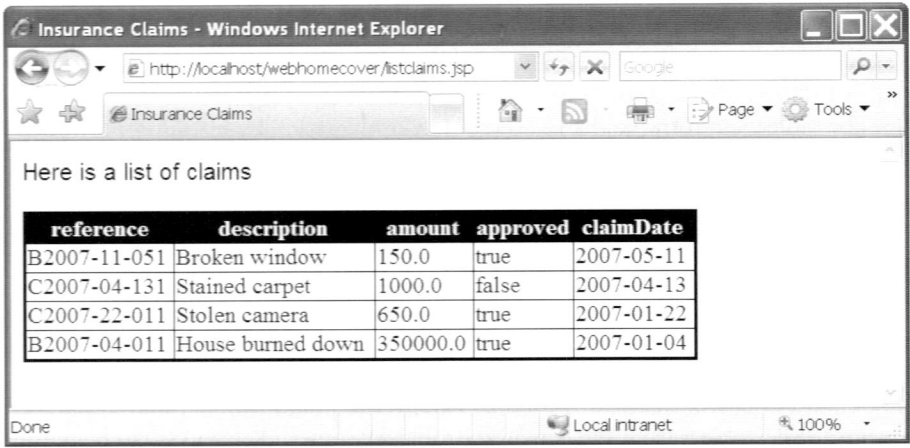

FIGURE 12.12 Mapping Java objects in memory to entities in the database

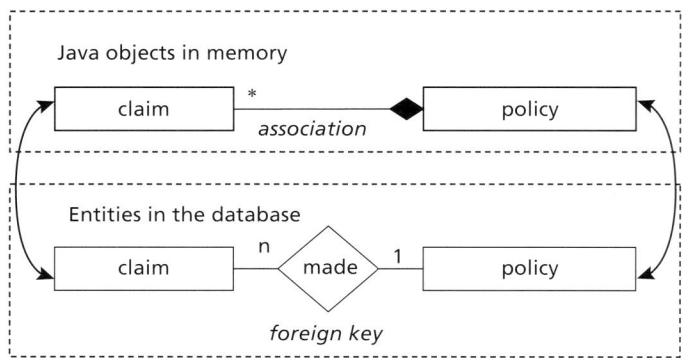

FIGURE 12.13 A flowchart showing how the web application processes an insurance claim

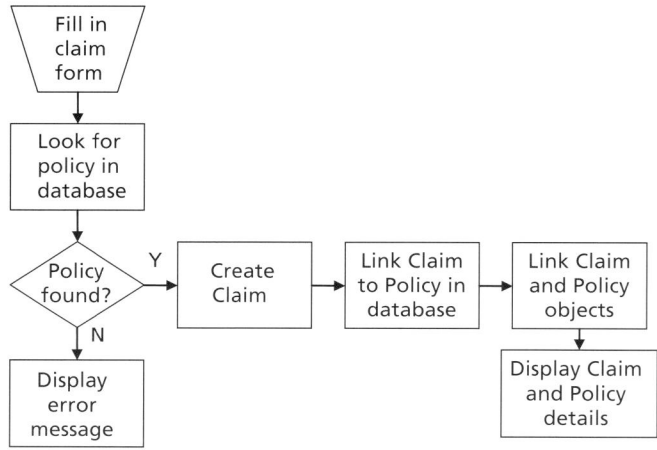

should be associated with a specific insurance policy, we will check that the policy number supplied by the user is valid. If the policy number exists in the policy table then we write the claim to the database (setting up the foreign-key relationship with the matching row in the policy table) and retrieve the related policy information by instantiating a Java Policy object. Then both the Claim and Policy objects can be used in the web application. If, however, the policy number does not exist then we display an error page to the user and no changes are made to the database. Figure 12.13 shows a simple flowchart that outlines the processes involved.

To implement the steps of the process, the application needs to do several things:

1. Get the policy number from the ClaimBean.
2. Look for a policy in the database that matches the policy number and, if one is found, create a Policy object from the data in the table. We need a PolicyDAO to help us do this.

3. If it finds a matching policy, it must populate the remaining properties of the claim bean ('approved', 'claimDate', 'reference') before writing the claim to the database via the ClaimDAO. It also needs to look up the correct primary key value from the policy and use that value in the foreign-key column of the claim.

4. The Property and Claim objects need to be associated and made available to the view JSP.

Figure 12.14 shows the Policy class, (which we introduced in Chapter 11) and its related DAO. Policy and Claim objects are associated in a one-to-many relationship (i.e. a single Policy can have many Claims, but a Claim is made against a single Policy).

The PolicyDAO has a similar implementation to the ClaimDAO, except that it processes Policy objects. Here is part of the class. (The 'getConnection' and 'cleanup' methods are the same as in the ClaimDAO – is there an opportunity for some refactoring here?)

```java
package com.webhomecover.dao;

import com.webhomecover.model.Policy;
import java.sql.Connection;
import java.sql.Statement;
import java.sql.PreparedStatement;
import java.sql.ResultSet;
import java.sql.SQLException;
import java.util.Collection;
import java.util.ArrayList;
import java.util.Date;
import javax.naming.Context;
import javax.naming.InitialContext;
import javax.naming.NamingException;
import javax.sql.DataSource;

public class PolicyDAO
{
    private Connection connection = null;
    private Statement statement = null;
```

FIGURE 12.14   The Policy and PolicyDAO objects

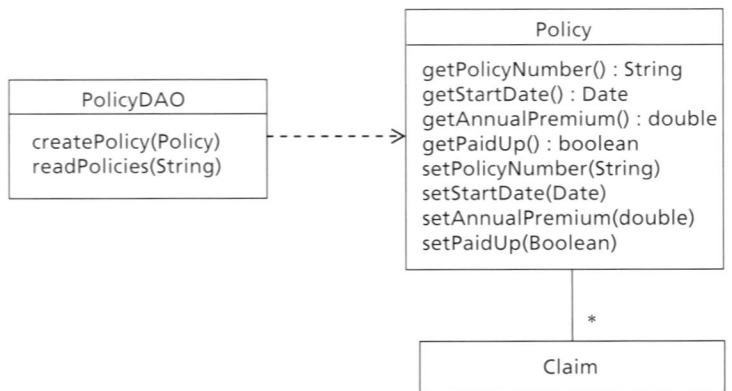

```
    private PreparedStatement prepStatement = null;
    private ResultSet results = null;
    private static final String DATASOURCE_NAME =
        "java:comp/env/jdbc/webhomecoverds";
    private static final String INSERT_STATEMENT = "INSERT INTO policy
      (policyNumber,startDate,annualPremium,paidUp) VALUES (?,?,?,?)";

    public void createPolicy(Policy policy)
    {
     try
     {
      getConnection();
      prepStatement = connection.prepareStatement(INSERT_STATEMENT);
      prepStatement.setString(1, policy.getPolicyNumber());

      java.sql.Date sqlDate = new
        java.sql.Date(policy.getStartDate().getTime());
      prepStatement.setDate(2, sqlDate);
      prepStatement.setDouble(3, policy.getAnnualPremium());
      prepStatement.setBoolean(4, policy.getPaidUp());
      prepStatement.executeUpdate();
      prepStatement.close();
      prepStatement = null;
      connection.close();
      connection = null;
     }
     catch(SQLException e)
     {
      e.printStackTrace();
     }
     finally
     {
      cleanUp();
     }
    }


    public Collection<Policy>readPolicies(String whereClause)
    {
     Collection<Policy>policies = new ArrayList<Policy>();
     try
    {
     getConnection();
     Statement statement = connection.createStatement();
     ResultSet results = statement.executeQuery("SELECT * FROM policy "
       + whereClause);
     int id = 0;
     String policyNumber = null;
     Date startDate = null;
     double annualPremium = 0.0;
     boolean paidUp = false;
     Policy policy = null;
```

```
    while(results.next())
    {
     id = results.getInt("policyID_PK");
       policyNumber = results.getString("policyNumber");
       startDate = results.getDate("startDate");
       annualPremium = results.getDouble("annualPremium");
       paidUp = results.getBoolean("paidUp");
       policy = new Policy();
       policy.setPolicyNumber(policyNumber);
       policy.setStartDate(startDate);
       policy.setAnnualPremium(annualPremium);
       policy.setPaidUp(paidUp);
       policies.add(policy);
       System.out.println("Read policy number" + policyNumber);
    }
    results.close();
    results = null;
    statement.close();
    statement = null;
    connection.close();
    connection = null;
    }
    catch(SQLException e)
    {
     e.printStackTrace();
    }
    finally
    {
     cleanUp();
    }
    return policies;
  }
}
```

The ClaimDAO needs to be able to do a little more than just write a claim to the database.
We also need to be able to link the new row in the 'claim' table to an existing row in the
'policy' table. Here is an additional method to be added to the ClaimDAO class called
'linkToPolicy', which takes a Claim and a Policy as parameters and joins them together in
the database. Basically it reads from the database to find a policy with the correct (natural)
key. If one is located then it uses an UPDATE statement to change the foreign key in the
claim table to contain the (artificial) primary key of the policy that has been located.

```
public void linkToPolicy(Claim claim, Policy policy)
{
   String reference = claim.getReference();
   String policyNumber = policy.getPolicyNumber();
   try
   {
      getConnection();
      Statement statement = connection.createStatement();
      ResultSet results = statement.executeQuery
```

```
        ("SELECT policyID_PK FROM policy WHERE policyNumber=\' " +
            policyNumber + "\' ");
        int key = 0;
        while (results.next())
        {
          key = results.getInt ("policyID_PK");
        }
        results.close();
        results = null;
        statement.close();
        statement = null;
        statement = connection.createStatement();
        statement.executeUpdate("UPDATE claim SET claim.policyID_FK = " + key
            + " WHERE claim.reference=\' " + reference + "\' ");
        statement.close();
        statement = null;
        connection.close();
        connection = null;
      }
      catch(SQLException e)
      {
        e.printStackTrace();
      }
      finally
      {
        cleanUp();
      }
    }
```

The ClaimBean, which is used to gather claim data from a client form page, contains
policy number data from the HTML claim form that relates not to the 'claim' table but to
the 'policy' table. We can use this information to set up the foreign-key relationship
between the 'policy' and 'claim' tables. The ModelFacade, which in Chapter 11 simply
copied the properties of a ClaimBean object into those of a Claim, and set a couple of other
values of the Claim, needs to do more in this version of the application. This time, it must
use the PolicyDAO to check the policy number against the database. If the policy is found
(and created), then the claim is also created, the two rows are linked in the database, the
two objects are associated and the claim reference is returned back to the view component.
Here is the class with the modified 'createClaim' method ('getClaims' is unaffected, so is
not repeated here):

```
package com.webhomecover.model;

import com.webhomecover.util.ReferenceGenerator;
import com.webhomecover.beans.ClaimBean;
import com.webhomecover.dao.ClaimDAO;
import com.webhomecover.dao.PolicyDAO;
import java.util.Collection;
import java.util.Iterator;
import org.apache.commons.beanutils.PropertyUtils;
import java.util.Date;
```

```java
public class ModelFacade
{
   public static Claim createClaim(ClaimBean claimBean)
   {
    Claim claim = null;

// get the policy number and look for a matching policy in the database
    String policyNumber = claimBean.getPolicyNumber();
    PolicyDAO policyDAO = new PolicyDAO();
    Collection<Policy>c = policyDAO.readPolicies
       ("WHERE policyNumber=\' " + policyNumber + "\' ");
    Iterator<Policy>iter = c.iterator();
// if we find a match, create a Claim and link it to the policy
   if(iter.hasNext())
   {
    claim = new Claim();
    try
    {
     PropertyUtils.copyProperties(claim, claimBean);
    }
    catch(IllegalAccessException e)
    {
     e.printStackTrace();
     return null;
    }
    catch(java.lang.reflect.InvocationTargetException e)
    {
     e.printStackTrace();
     return null;
    }
    catch(NoSuchMethodException e)
    {
     e.printStackTrace();
     return null;
    }
// finish populating the bean
    claim.setApproved(false);
    claim.setClaimDate(new java.sql.Date(new \
       java.util.Date().getTime()));
    String reference = ReferenceGenerator.getReference(claim);
    claim.setReference(reference);

// get the policy
    Policy policy = iter.next();

// write the claim to the database
   ClaimDAO claimDAO = new ClaimDAO();
   claimDAO.createClaim(claim);
// set up the foreign key in the database
   claimDAO.linkToPolicy(claim, policy);
// link the two objects
```

```
      claim.setPolicy(policy);
    }
// return the claim, associated with the policy
    return claim;
  }
}
```

The page that receives the HTTP request, 'processclaim.jsp' still interacts with the ModelFacade as it did in Chapter 11. However this time there are two possible results; the 'claim' that is returned from the façade may be a fully populated Claim object, but it may also be a null reference (if the policy number was not found). Therefore we need some conditional code to route the webflow accordingly. Here is a modified version of the JSP. It uses the JSTL core library to check if the 'claim' reference is null. If it is, then the page forwards to 'notfound.jsp'. If the claim is not null, then the page forwards to 'displayclaim.jsp':

```
<?xml version="1.0"?>
<!-- File: processclaim.jsp -->

<jsp:root xmlns:jsp="http://java.sun.com/JSP/Page"
  xmlns:c="http://java.sun.com/jsp/jstl/core"
  version="2.0">

  <jsp:useBean id="claimBean" class="com.webhomecover.beans.ClaimBean"
scope="request"/>
  <jsp:setProperty name="claimBean" property="*" />
  <jsp:scriptlet>
    com.webhomecover.model.Claim claim =
    com.webhomecover.model.ModelFacade.createClaim(claimBean);
    request.setAttribute("claim", claim);
  </jsp:scriptlet>
  <c:choose>
    <c:when test="${claim==null}">
      <jsp:forward page="notfound.jsp"/>
    </c:when>
    <c:otherwise>
      <jsp:forward page="displayclaim.jsp"/>
    </c:otherwise>
  </c:choose>
</jsp:root>
```

If the policy number is matched and we forward to 'displayclaim.jsp', it displays all the details of the claim and also the details of the policy.

In the updated version of 'displayclaim.jsp', not only do we display the data from a claim, as we did in Chapter 11, but we also display the details of the related policy. This requires a little use of the expression language. Since the object returned from the ModelFacade is a claim, we can use the normal 'useBean' tag to access it in the page:

```
<jsp:useBean id="claim" class="com.webhomecover.model.Claim"
scope="request"/>
```

In addition, the claim holds a reference to its associated policy. We can use the JSTL core library and expression language to navigate through the claim to the policy (using its 'getPolicy' method) and put a reference to the policy into the 'policy' variable within the page:

```
<c:set var="policy" value="${claim.policy}" />
```

Now the page can access the properties of both the claim and the policy.

```
<?xml version="1.0"?>
  <!-- File: displayclaim.jsp -->

<jsp:root xmlns:jsp="http://java.sun.com/JSP/Page"
    xmlns:c="http://java.sun.com/jsp/jstl/core"
    version="2.0">
<jsp:directive.page isELIgnored="false" />
<jsp:directive.page contentType="text/html"/>
<jsp:output omit-xml-declaration="false"
 doctype-root-element="html"
 doctype-public="-//W3C//DTD XHTML 1.1//EN"
 doctype-system="http://www.w3.org/TR/xhtml11/DTD/xhtml11.dtd" />

<jsp:useBean id="claim" class="com.webhomecover.model.Claim"
scope="request"/>
<c:set var="policy" value="${claim.policy}" />

<html xmlns="http://www.w3.org/1999/xhtml" xml:lang="en">
  <head><title>Insurance Claim Details</title></head>
  <body>
   <p>Thank you for making your insurance claim</p>
   <p>Here are the claim and policy details</p>
   <div>Policy Number: <strong>
       <jsp:getProperty name="policy" property="policyNumber"/>
       </strong></div>
       <div>Policy Taken out on: <strong>
       <jsp:getProperty name="policy" property="startDate"/>
       </strong></div>
       <div>Annual Premium: <strong>
       <jsp:getProperty name="policy" property="annualPremium"/>
       </strong></div>
       <div>Is policy paid up?: <strong>
       <jsp:getProperty name="policy" property="paidUp"/>
       </strong></div>
       <div>Reference: <strong>
       <jsp:getProperty name="claim" property="reference"/>
       </strong></div>
       <div>Date of claim: <strong>
       <jsp:getProperty name="claim" property="claimDate"/>
       </strong></div>
       <div>Amount of claim: <strong>
       <jsp:getProperty name="claim" property="amount"/>
       </strong></div>
```

12

```
      <div>Type of policy: <strong>
      <jsp:getProperty name="claim" property="type"/>
      </strong></div>
      <div>Description of claim" <strong>
      <jsp:getProperty name="claim" property="description"/>
      </strong></div>
   </body>
</html>
</jsp:root>
```

Here is 'notfound.jsp', which displays an error message and the policy number from the claim form, using the original claimBean, which is still in the request object.

```
<?xml version="1.0"?>
<!-- File: notfound.jsp -->

<jsp:root xmlns:jsp="http://java.sun.com/JSP/Page"
      version="2.0">
<jsp:directive.page contentType="text/html"/>
<jsp:output omit-xml-declaration="false"
   doctype-root-element="html"
   doctype-public="-//W3C//DTD XHTML 1.1//EN"
   doctype-system="http://www.w3.org/TR/xhtml11/DTD/xhtml11.dtd" />

<jsp:useBean id="claimBean" class="com.webhomecover.beans.ClaimBean"
scope="request"/>

<html>
   <head>
     <title>Policy not found</title>
   </head>
   <body>
     <div>policy number
     <jsp:getProperty name="claimBean" property="policyNumber" />
     not found
   </div>
   <hr />
   <a href="claimform.htm">Return to form page</a>
   </body>
</html>
</jsp:root>
```

There is another issue that we should perhaps address in this use case, which is that if we are writing data to the database we should have some error checking for other fields as well as the policy number, otherwise we may be writing null or invalid data to the database. In Chapter 8 we introduced the idea of client-side form validation using JavaScript. Although this is not foolproof (some browsers may not support JavaScript, or it may have been disabled) in combination with server-side validation it is very useful. In this chapter, we add some client-side validation to the form page and we look at server-side validation in the following chapters. Here is a JavaScript file that contains a function called 'validateClaimForm' that takes a claim form as a parameter and validates its fields. For the policy number, claim and description fields, it simply checks that they are not empty. If the claim field is not empty, a second-level check uses a 'for' loop to compare each character entered with a string of valid characters (the numerals and the decimal point). It also ensures that one of the radio buttons has been checked. If any of these validation checks fail, then the form is not submitted.

```javascript
// validateclaimform.js
function validateClaimForm(claimForm)
{
   var strPolicyNumber = claimForm.policyNumber.value;
   var fltAmount = claimForm.claim.value;
   var strDescription = claimForm.description.value;
   var booContents = claimForm.contents.checked;
   var booBuildings = claimForm.buildings.checked;
   var booValid = true;
   var strErrorMessage = "";
   if(strPolicyNumber == "")
   {
    strErrorMessage += "Please provide a policy number\n";
    booValid = false;
   }
   if(fltAmount == "")
   {
    strErrorMessage += "Please provide a claim amount\n";
    booValid = false;
   }
   else
   {
    var strValidChars = "0123456789.";
    var chrCurrentChar;
    for (i = 0; i < fltAmount.length && booValid; i++)
    {
     chrCurrentChar = fltAmount.charAt(i);
     if(strValidChars.indexOf(chrCurrentChar) == -1)
     {
      booValid = false;
     }
    }
    if(!booValid)
    {
     strErrorMessage += "Please provide a numeric claim amount\n";
    }
   }
   if(!booBuildings && !booContents)
   {
    strErrorMessage += "Please select either buildings or contents
insurance\n";
    booValid = false;
   }
   if(strDescription == "")
   {
```

```
    strErrorMessage += "Please provide a description\n";
    booValid = false;
  }
  if(!booValid)
  {
    alert(strErrorMessage);
  }
  return booValid;
}
```

Some changes need to be made to the claim form JSP to use this function. First, we need to add a script element to the header to use the JavaScript file that contains the function:

```
<script type="text/javascript" src="validateclaimform.js">
</script>
```

Then the form's action needs an 'onsubmit' attribute that invokes the 'validateClaimForm' function and passes the form to it as a parameter.

```
<form action="processclaim.jsp" method="post" onsubmit="return
validateClaimForm(this)">
```

We also need to ensure that all the form components, including both radio buttons, have unique 'id' attributes so they can be accessed by the JavaScript function:

```
<input type="radio" name="type" value="buildings" id="buildings" />

<input type="radio" name="type" value="contents" id="contents" />
```

Otherwise the form page is the same as before. Figure 12.15 shows an example of the JavaScript alert in action. In this case, the description is missing and the claim amount contains non-numeric characters, so there are two error messages in the alert.

FIGURE 12.15 The JavaScript alert displayed if the form fails client-side validation

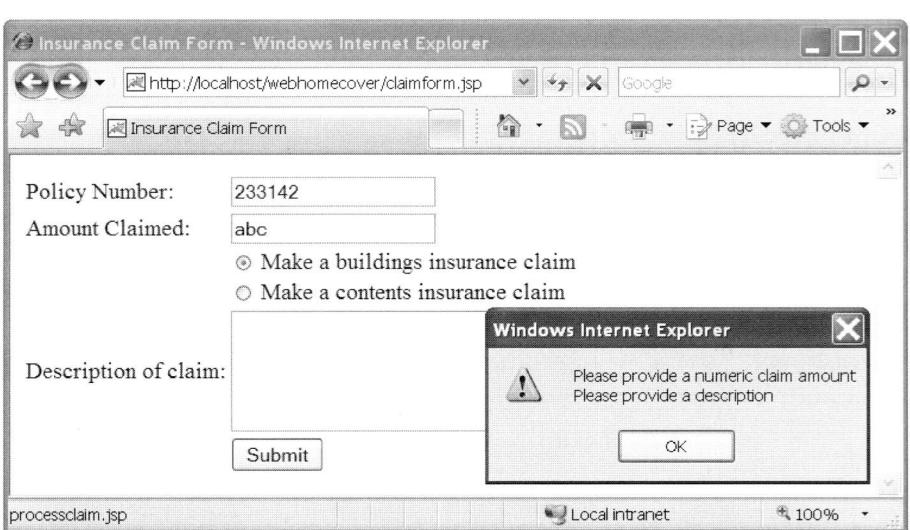

Once the form data passes validation, the form is submitted to the server. The client-side JavaScript function cannot validate whether the policy number exists in the database, so there are still two possible outcomes, a successful claim entry or an unsuccessful one.

Figure 12.16 shows an example of what the display page might look like if given a valid policy number, while Figure 12.17 shows the 'notfound.jsp' page that appears if the policy number is not in the database.

FIGURE 12.16 The display page showing details of a claim and its related policy

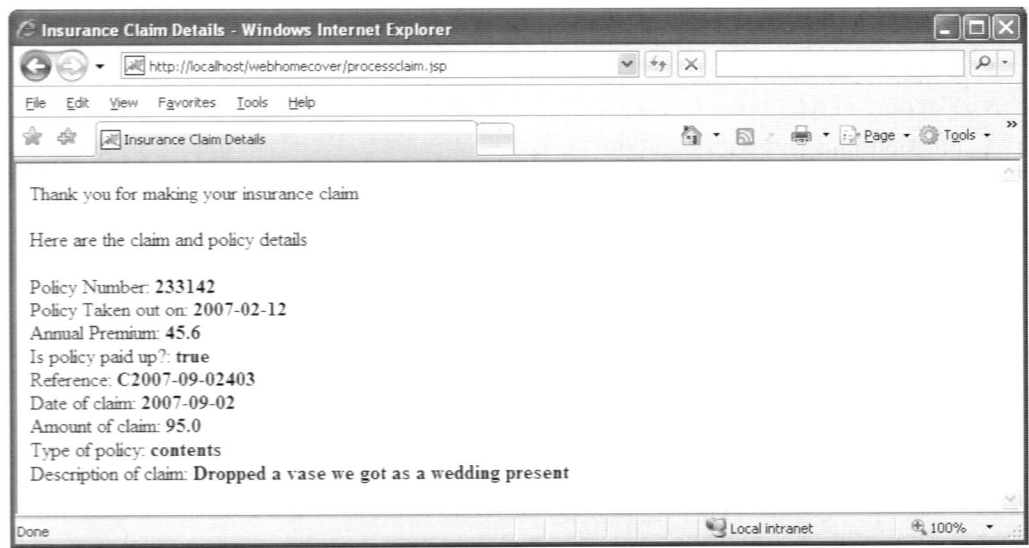

FIGURE 12.17 The error page that appears if the policy number entered for a claim cannot be found in the database

12.7 The object-relational impedance mismatch

At first glance there seems to be a simple relationship between objects and rows in a database table, which we have taken advantage of in the relatively simple examples used in this chapter. An object is defined by a class, which defines (among other things) the structure of its internal data. Similarly, a database table has a schema that defines its columns. An instance of a class (an object) contains data in the same way that a row (or tuple) contains data (Figure 12.18).

However, although there are some apparent similarities between an object-oriented model and a database schema, there are many areas where there is not a particularly good fit between the two technologies. This is often known as the *impedance mismatch*. This mismatch covers a number of problem areas:

- Unique object and table identifiers
- Mapping of data types
- Relationships and normalization
- Inheritance
- Operations

Unique Object and Table Identifiers

Java objects in memory are identified by references that, in effect, represent the memory space that the object occupies at a particular time. Two objects can have identical state but differ in their memory location. Data in a database, however, must have unique key data. Therefore any attempt to persist objects in a database requires that they have unique object identifiers, effectively key fields, and a suitable mechanism for generating these unique keys, typically integer-based but in some cases including type identification. It should be noted that these keys should not have any relationship to the actual business data in the objects or tables, and need to be generated in such way that an appropriate level of

FIGURE 12.18 The relationship between classes and tables, objects and columns, fields and rows

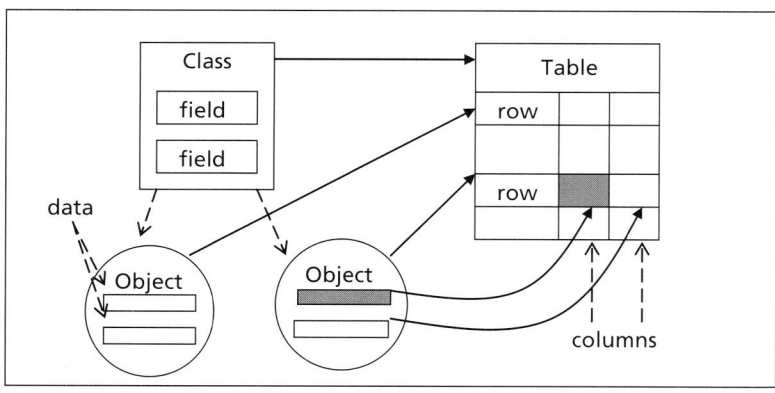

uniqueness is achieved without excessive locks on the database (Ambler 2006). Using database features to generate keys is an effective solution, but is not standard across different database products. Therefore, more portable strategies are sometimes needed that do not rely on a particular database (Marinescu 2002; Reese 2003).

Mapping of data types

Although simple data types have straightforward conversion mappings between Java and SQL data types (e.g. String to VARCHAR and vice versa), more complex types do not have a natural mapping. For example, Boolean types in Java often have to be mapped to character or number fields, and serialized Java objects are frequently stored as BLOBS (binary large objects) or other binary representations, which means that the data in these objects cannot be accessed directly while they are in the database. It is also sometimes necessary to use finer-grained components in the database than those in the object model, so that one field of an object may have to be mapped to more than one column of a database table.

Relationships and normalization

Objects that might be regarded as a single instance in an object model might be seen very differently in a normalized database schema. Whereas an object might maintain relationships using collections of objects, a database will need to use many tables and keys. What appears as a simple many-to-many relationship in an object model requires complex foreign key management in the database. There are different strategies to consider too, for example modeling one-to-many relationships can be done using either back pointers or a separate table. Alternatively a one-to-many relationship represented in an object model by a collection of references may simply be written to a single field as a serialized object. In all of these scenarios, the implementation of the object model must take account of the actual data representation in the database and handle type conversions and table navigation appropriately.

Inheritance

Relational databases do not directly support inheritance, so we have to find some workaround. There are a number of strategies to do this, each with their own advantages and disadvantages, but a common solution is to join multiple tables with common keys to represent the classes in the hierarchy. Although a reasonable design choice, this can lead to poor performance, requiring other more pragmatic solutions (Brown and Whitenack 1996).

Operations

Objects encapsulate both processes and data, with operations (methods) that relate specifically to the data in the object. In contrast, database operations such as stored procedures are not tied to particular object representations, so only the data from an object can be directly stored in a database, not its other characteristics. This usually means that objects can be aware of their data representation in the database but not vice versa: the object-relational metadata is not in the database but is implicit in the code or explicitly in code-related descriptors, such as XML files. This means that forward-engineering a database schema from an object model is likely to be more successful than reverse-engineering an object model from a database schema, since the reverse engineering provides no information about what operations objects should have.

12.8 Technologies for object-relational mapping

There are a number of technologies that can support object-relational mapping in Java, which are more or less transparent depending on the level of tool support. We can categorize these into two approaches: custom-written persistence using JDBC (which we have used in this chapter) or transparent persistence using some mapping tool that links client code and the persistence layer. Transparent persistence is any technology that hides the database access behind a higher-level API, and Java provides some standard APIs for this. There are many technologies that can implement a transparent-persistence layer and provide a range of services. The most important of these services are (Kruszelnicki 2002):

- Create, read, update and delete operations on objects
- Support for transactions (start, commit, rollback)
- Management of object identity
- Caching
- Creating and executing queries

The main benefits of transparent persistence tools are a reduction in the amount of code required to manage the persistent objects (Barry and Stanienda 1998), and in many cases an improvement in performance due to features such as caching. Transparent persistence mechanisms come in three general forms:

- Custom-written persistence layers built by developers within an organization for their own use
- Proprietary persistence tools such as Hibernate and TopLink
- Standard Java APIs such as the Entity Enterprise JavaBean specification and the related Java Persistence API.

These vary in a number of ways, for example in how easy they are to use, how much additional code is needed and what other services are provided, such as transaction support.

Writing a persistence layer is a challenging task, though the JDBC API does provide the necessary support for queries, result sets, stored procedures and transactions. In addition, the JDBC 2.0 APIs introduced support for enterprise-level database access including connection pools and data sources for scaleable distributed access. Custom written persistence layers can result in much greater reuse of persistence code across applications within an organization, and are preferable to the constant rewriting of JDBC code for standard actions. The difficulties tend to arise where there is a great deal of write and update behavior that requires complex transaction management, and in maintaining performance for high-demand systems. Transactions must be handled at the code level, and there is no intrinsic caching behavior in the JDBC APIs. For areas that go beyond basic JDBC, such as distributed transactions, the persistence layer will have to call out to other services. Depending on the nature of the system, Keller and Coldeway (1997) estimate a required development effort of between 0.5 and 35 person years for a relational database access layer. Because of the complexity of an enterprise persistence layer, and the fact that any such effort is to a large extent reinventing the wheel, it is not an ideal strategy, and many developers have looked elsewhere for persistence tools that can increase productivity, reliability and performance.

Java persistence standards

There have been a number of attempts over the years to provide transparent persistence as a standard feature of the Java APIs. One of the earliest of these to see widespread use was the Enterprise JavaBeans (EJB) specification (version 1.0 of the specification was published in 1997), which provided persistence of objects within Java EE. This specification has gone through some radical changes through its various major versions. Another approach, which was intended to work across all three editions of Java, was Java Data Objects (JDO), which was based partly on the Object Data Management Group's (ODMG) Java data-binding specification, which is part of a wider multi-language specification that has been in development since 1993. JDO APIs were designed to make object persistence as non-intrusive as possible, so that the code of the objects themselves does not have to contain any persistence-related syntax. More recently, there has been an effort to unify these approaches in the Java persistence API, which is used as part of the EJB specification version 3.0 (DeMichiel and Keith, 2006) but is also available in the standard edition of Java. One of the main intentions of this API is to simplify the code required to make Java object-persistent, using what are sometimes know as POJOs (Plain Old Java Objects) rather than special types of Java class with a lot of persistence-related code in them. There is no standard implementation of the persistence API provided with the Java Software Development Kit. Instead, various vendors provide implementations of the API, for example the TopLink Essentials (Oracle 2007).

Selecting persistence strategies

The various options for object persistence each have their own advantages and disadvantages, and which strategy to choose depends on the context of a given project. For small-scale systems where the database schema is very stable, custom-written JDBC code such as that described in this chapter may be appropriate. It is lightweight in that it does not require any third-party infrastructure and does not involve the purchase of extra tools, since the JDBC APIs are part of the standard Java SDK. Where database schemas are subject to change, or a system requires more complex mappings than simple types, some kind of higher-level persistence tool will pay off in terms of development time, robustness and maintainability. In particular, systems that extract the mapping into metadata that is manipulated using graphical tools are much easier to maintain and modify than hand-written JDBC code.

Exercises

12.1 Create the 'webhomecoverdb' database in MySQL and connect to it. Populate the database using the 'webhomecoverdb.ddl' file supplied. Now execute the following queries using the MySQL command-line client:

- Select all the records where the amount is less than 1,000. Display all the columns.
- Select all the records where the date is after 1 April 2007. Display the 'amount' and 'claimDate' columns.
- Select all the records where the date is before 1 May 2007 and the claims have not been approved. Display the 'description', 'approved' and 'claimDate' columns.

12.2 Write a Java class with a 'main' method that connects to your 'webhomecoverdb' database. Execute a query to read all the rows in the 'policyholder' table into a ResultSet. Iterate through the ResultSet and write the data to standard output. You will need the JAR file containing the MySQL database driver on the classpath.

12.3 Modify your code to use a prepared statement to query individual policies based on their policy number.

12.4 Configure a data source in your server and test it with the 'listclaims.jsp' page. Add the following 'setProperty' tag in the JSP (after the 'useBean' tag) to set the 'WHERE' clause, and provide a suitable SQL string for the value.

```
<jsp:setProperty name="claimCollection" property="claimsFromDAO"
value="" />
```

For example we could search for claims that are less than 1,000:

```
<jsp:setProperty name="claimCollection" property="claimsFromDAO"
value="WHERE amount <1000" />
```

Try some different values for the 'WHERE' clause.

12.5 Refactor the ClaimDAO and PolicyDAO classes so that they inherit from a common superclass. The superclass can contain the methods that are currently repeated in each DAO class. In addition, you may consider renaming the other methods so that they have a consistent name, enabling some polymorphism to be used. However if you do this, you will need to make some changes to the ModelFacade where it uses the existing methods.

12.6 Create a 'PolicyHolderDAO' class (as a subclass of your DAO superclass from Exercise 5) that has a suitable method to read PolicyHolder objects from the database. Add a method to the ModelFacade to use this DOA to return a collection of PolicyHolders, using a bean with indexed properties (you will also need to create this class). Using the 'listclaims.jsp' page as an example, create a 'listpolicyholders.jsp' page that uses the 'PolicyHolderDAO' to read the records from the 'policyholder' table and write them to a web page.

12.7 Add a 'getXmlDocument' method to the 'ClaimCollection' that returns an XML document based on the 'getXmlElement' methods of the claim objects it contains.

Write a JSP that renders the claims using the JSTL XML library to perform an XSL transformation of the generated XML document. You will need to create a suitable XSLT document to use in the transformation.

SUMMARY

In this chapter we saw how to use SQL statements embedded in JDBC code to interact with a relational database management system (RDBMS). We also saw how a JDBC driver enables Java code to interact with a relational database using a standard API. Examples in this chapter showed both simple two-tier connections between a Java program and the database, and connections made through a DataSource bound into JNDI that could be used within a web application. Our discussions included some coverage of issues in object-relational mapping, and considered alterative approaches to persisting Java objects, including the Java Persistence API.

Earlier in the chapter, we discussed how one of the jobs of a JDBC driver is to translate between SQL and Java types. It is important to understand these translations when mapping between Java classes and relational table schemas. Table 12.1 shows the standard mappings between SQL types and Java types. Similarly Table 12.2 shows the reverse mappings from Java types to SQL types. The mapping for Strings is normally VARCHAR but is LONGVARCHAR instead if a VARCHAR is not large enough. The situation is similar for byte arrays, which can map to two different binary types depending on the required size.

12

TABLE 12.1 Mapping from SQL to Java data types

SQL type	Java Type
CHAR	String
VARCHAR	String
LONGVARCHAR	String
NUMERIC	java.math.BigDecimal
DECIMAL	java.math.BigDecimal
BIT	boolean
TINYINT	byte
SMALLINT	short
INTEGER	int
BIGINT	long
REAL	float
FLOAT	double
DOUBLE	double
BINARY	byte[]
VARBINARY	byte[]
LONGVARBINARY	byte[]
DATE	java.sql.Date
TIME	java.sql.Time
TIMESTAMP	java.sql.Timestamp

TABLE 12.2	Mapping from Java to SQL data types

Java Type	SQL type
String	VARCHAR or LONGVARCHAR
java.math.BigDecimal	NUMERIC
boolean	BIT
byte	TINYINT
short	SMALLINT
int	INTEGER
long	BIGINT
float	REAL
double	DOUBLE
byte[]	VARBINARY or LONGVARBINARY
java.sql.Date	DATE
java.sql.Time	TIME
java.sql.Timestamp	TIMESTAMP

References and further reading

Alur, D., Crupi, J. and Malks, D. (2003) *Core J2EE Patterns: Best Practices and Design Strategies*, 2nd edition. Upper Saddle River, NJ: Prentice Hall.

Ambler, S. (2006) *The Object-Relational Impedance Mismatch*. http://www.agiledata.org/essays/impedanceMismatch.html.

Barry, D. and Stanienda, T. (1998) Solving the Java Object Storage Problem. *IEEE Computer*, 31(11).

Brown, K. and Whitenack, B. (1996) Crossing Chasms: A Pattern Language for Object-RDBMS Integration. In Vlissides, J., Coplien, J. and Kerth, N. (eds), *Pattern Languages of Program Design 2*. Addison-Wesley.

Byron, B. and Thomson, T. (2002) Overpower the PreparedStatement. *JavaWorld*, January 2002. http://www.javaworld.com/javaworld/jw-01–2002/jw-0125-overpower.html.

Chen, P. (1976) The Entity–Relationship Model: Toward a Unified View of Data. *ACM Transactions on Database Systems*, 1(1):9–36.

Codd, E. (1970) A Relational Model of Data for Large Shared Data Banks. *Communications of the ACM*, 13(6):377–87.

DeMichiel, L. and Keith, M. (2006) *JSR 220: Enterprise JavaBeans Version 3.0*, Java Persistence API. http://jcp.org/aboutJava/communityprocess/final/jsr220/index.html.

Harold, E. (2006a) *Managing the Java classpath (Windows)*. http://www-128.ibm.com/developerworks/java/library/j-classpath-windows/.

Harold, E. (2006b) *Managing the Java classpath (UNIX and Mac OS X)*. http://www.ibm.com/developerworks/java/library/j-classpath-unix/.

Keller, W. (1997) Mapping Objects to Tables: A Pattern Language. *Proceedings of EuroPLoP 1997*. http://www.riehle.org/europlop-1997/.

Keller, W. and Coldeway, J. (1997) Relational Database Access Layers: A Pattern Language. In Martin, R., Riehle, D. and Buschmann, F. (eds) *Pattern Languages of Program Design 3*. Addison-Wesley.

Kruszelnicki, J. (2002) Persist data with Java Data Object, Parts 1 and 2. *JavaWorld*, March and April 2002.

Marinescu, F. (2002) *EJB Design Patterns: Advanced Patterns, Processes and Idioms*. Wiley.

Oracle Corporation (2007) *TopLink JPA*. http://www.oracle.com/technology/products/ias/toplink/jpa/index.html.

Reese, G. (2003) *Java Database Best Practices*. Sebastopol, CA: O'Reilly.

Sun Microsystems (2007) *JDBC Access API*. http://developers.sun.com/product/jdbc/drivers.

CHAPTER 13

Mobile Web Applications

LEARNING OBJECTIVES

- To understand how mark-up languages for mobile devices have evolved

- To understand the relationships between XHTML, XHTML-Basic and XHTML-Mobile Profile

- To understand how the client browser identifies itself to a server-side application

- To be able to use the Wireless Universal Resource File and the Wireless Abstraction Library to build mobile web applications in Java

INTRODUCTION

In the first few years of the worldwide web, we saw an evolution from static to dynamic content, but a more recent evolution has been from single-format content to adaptive content. One of the most important aspects of an adaptive web application is the ability for the content delivery to be adapted to the capabilities of the client device, so that the same content can be delivered to a range of devices including desktop computers, PDAs, mobile phones, set-top boxes, games consoles, etc. It is becoming increasingly necessary to adapt presentation to these different device types, particularly as the penetration of mobile phones that are capable of web browsing has become widespread. The issue to address of course is that different devices have different presentation capabilities, for example you cannot run Ajax on every mobile device, because not all phones support JavaScript-enabled web browsers, and mobile browsers do not all support the same mark-up languages. Another aspect of the limitations of mobile browsers is that many of them are not able to process XSL transformations, so are unable to render XML documents. Style sheets are also problematical, because although many mobile browsers support style sheets they are not the same as the CSS used in desktop browsers. Despite these difficulties, it is possible to develop web applications that can adapt to different mobile device browsers by using appropriate tools. In this chapter, we look at the evolution and characteristics of the various types of mark-up that are supported by mobile browsers and introduce the Wireless Universal Resource File (WURFL) and the Wireless Abstraction Library (WALL) that make it simple to write device-adaptive web applications in Java.

13.1 Evolution of mobile mark-up languages

We saw in Chapter 3 that HTML has evolved through several versions, eventually being superseded by XHTML. However these mark-up languages have been primarily oriented towards the desktop PC browser. In parallel with the evolution of desktop browser mark-up, there have been a number of different types of mark-up specifically designed for mobile devices. Early examples of this type of mark-up included Compact HTML (cHTML) for iMODE phones, used primarily in Japan but also in some parts of Europe, and Handheld Device Mark-up Language (HDML), which was designed as a more generic mark-up language by Unwired Planet. There was also a W3C note about HTML 4.0 guidelines for mobile access (Kamada *et al.* 1999). The approach of these mark-up languages was to provide a simplified subset of desktop browser mark-up more suited to the restrictions (display, processing power, memory, etc.) of mobile devices.

Wireless Access Protocol (WAP) and Wireless Mark-up Language (WML)

In 1997, Nokia, Ericsson, Motorola and Unwired Planet cooperated to launch the Wireless Application Protocol (WAP) and provide an industry-standard platform for mobile web access. The group became the WAP Forum in 1998, and expanded to include members from across the mobile communications industry. The forum had 500 members by 2001. In 2003, the WAP Forum become the Open Mobile Alliance (OMA), supporting more general standardization efforts within the mobile communications industry.

Part of the WAP platform was the Wireless Mark-up Language (WML). cHTML and WML had rather different approaches to supporting the mobile web. cHTML was designed as a subset of HTML, compatible with all its major versions (2.0, 3.2 and 4.0). In order to make sure that pages could be rendered on the simplified browsers available in iMODE phones, style sheets, tables, background colors and multiple fonts were excluded from the specification. One advantage of cHTML was that its pages could also be rendered on a standard desktop browser. A note to the W3C provided a suggested DOCTYPE for cHTML:

```
<!DOCTYPE HTML PUBLIC "-//W3C//DTD Compact HTML 1.0 Draft//EN">
```

However, cHTML documents do not have to be well-formed and the DOCTYPE has not been used in practice.

WML had a very different approach, with many of its concepts based on HDML, and was much more ambitious. It included many features that were intended to leverage the specific characteristics of the mobile-phone platform, such as a 'deck of cards' architecture, which meant a single page could be downloaded that included multiple 'cards'. Each card provided a different view in the browser. Effectively this meant that a single download provided multiple web pages. WML also included its own scripting language and style sheets. Unlike cHTML, WML was not a subset of HTML and had its own mark-up syntax, though this syntax was XML-compliant, meaning that it was well-formed, and valid against the following DTD (for version 1.1):

```
<!DOCTYPE wml PUBLIC "-//WAPFORUM//DTD WML 1.1//EN"
    "http://www.wapforum.org/DTD/wml_1.1.xml">
```

The system doctype can also be directed to:

```
http://www.openmobilealliance.org/tech/DTD/wml_1_1.dtd
```

Note that while some of the following WML mark-up is compatible with XHTML, other tags are not, in particular the 'wml' root element and the 'card' element, which identifies one of the cards in the current deck.

```
<?xml version="1.0"?>
<!DOCTYPE wml PUBLIC "-//WAPFORUM//DTD WML 1.1//EN"
    "http://www.wapforum.org/DTD/wml_1.1.xml">
<wml>
  <template>
    <do type="prev" label="Back"><prev/></do>
  </template>
  <card id="w" title="Insurance Claim Details">
  <p>Policy Number:
    <input type="text" name="policyNumber" value="" size ="10"/>
    <br/>Amount claimed:
    <input type="text" name="amount" value="" size="10"/><br/>
    <select name="type">
      <option value="buildings">Buildings</option>
      <option value="contents">Contents</option>
    </select>
    <br/>Description of claim:<br/>
    <input type="text" name="description" value="" size="30"/><br/>
. . .
  </card>
</wml>
```

While cHTML was successful in the Japanese market, WAP did not find major market success in the early years. Slow mobile connections made it difficult to access the mobile web, and the restrictions of the mobile phone form factor also discouraged users. It was only with the introduction of the first WAP portal, Vodafone Live! in 2001, which was supported by customized handsets that could automatically access the portal to make access easier, that WAP began to become more popular.

XHTML-Basic and XHTML-Mobile Profile

The experience of both cHTML and WML led to standardization efforts across the mobile communications industry, to provide a global mark-up for all mobile devices. The outcome of this was XHTML-Basic, a subset of XHTML that is 'designed for Web clients that do not support the full set of XHTML features; for example, Web clients such as mobile phones, PDAs, pagers, and set top boxes.' (McCarron *et al.* 2007)

The first version (1.0) was defined in 2000 and version 1.1 in 2006. Like previous mobile mark-up, XHTML-Basic provides a simple set of tags that do not place undue burdens on the mobile device's display, processor or memory. Table 13.1 summarizes the elements that comprise XHTML-Basic.

TABLE 13.1   Elements in XHTML-Basic by type

Module	Element
Structure	`body, head, html, title`
Text	`dfn, div, em, h1, h2, h3, h4, h5, h6, kbd, p,` `pre, q, samp, span, strong, var`
Hypertext	`a`
List	`dl, dt, dd, ol, ul, li`
Basic forms	`form, input, label, select, option,` `textarea`
Basic tables	`caption, table, td, th, tr`
Image	`img`
Object	`object, param`
Meta information	`meta`
Link	`link`
Base	`base`

There are a few elements in XHTML-Basic that we have not introduced in previous chapters, so we will briefly cover them here. Most of them are text formatting elements that in practice render the text either in italics or in a monospaced font. The 'object' element is more complex, and of course the types of object that might be embedded into the page would be constrained by the capabilities of a given mobile device. Table 13.2 lists these elements and briefly describes their meanings.

XHTML-Basic is a generic approach to providing a subset of XHTML for a range of limited devices, but does not specify a particular type of device. In contrast, the mobile phone industry required a mark-up language that was intended specifically for mobile phones and did not need a language that was totally generic. Therefore the industry developed the specification for XHTML Mobile Profile (XHTML-MP), to produce a 'richer authoring language' than XHTML-Basic (OMA 2006). The OMA have adopted XHTML-MP as the migration path for WML, providing an updated version of WML (WML-2) for backward compatibility, which is otherwise superseded by XHTML-MP as the mark-up language used in WAP 2.0.

XHTML-MP is a superset of XHTML-Basic, which includes some additional elements and attributes from the full version of XHTML (Table 13.3). This table shows the additional elements and attributes in XHTML-MP version 1.2 (earlier versions supported only some of these).

One important aspect of XHTML-MP is its support for the 'style' element and attribute, enabling style sheets to be applied. These are not, however, intended for use with standard CSS but enable the use of WAP CSS (WCSS), a special type of style sheet definition that is defined in the WAP 2.0 specification. XHTML-MP also provides support for scripting using ECMA Script Mobile Profile, another initiative of the OMA. However it should be noted that an XHTML-MP browser may not provide support for all aspects of the specification. In addition, there are many other aspects to designing for the mobile phone format than simply using a particular mark-up (Passani 2007a).

TABLE 13.2   Elements from XHTML-Basic not previously introduced

Element	Meaning
dfn	Definition: surrounds the definition of a term
kbd	Keyboard: describes characters to be typed in at the keyboard
pre	Preformatted: maintains existing line feeds and spaces in the text
q	Quotation: adds quotation marks
samp	Example: describes text which is an example of something
var	Variable: describes text that is being used as a variable
object	A multimedia element that enables objects, such as applets, images, plugins and other documents, to be embedded in the page
param	Parameter: a parameter value used with the object element to define parameters to the embedded object
base	Base URL: enables a different URL to be used for relative references than the one the page actually came from

TABLE 13.3   Elements and attributes in XHTML-MP not present in XHTML-Basic

Module	Element/Attributes
Forms	fieldset, optgroup
Lists	start attribute in ordered lists value attribute in list items
Presentation	b, big, hr, i, small
Style sheet	style element
Style attribute	style attribute

In XHTML-MP there are elements that we have not previously introduced. These are 'fieldset' and 'optgroup'. The 'fieldset' element can be used to visually group together some of the elements in a form, for example by drawing a box around them. 'optgroup' is used with a 'select' tag. It is useful where a select list has a large number of entries that can be grouped in some way to make them easier to navigate.

The following example shows some XHTML-MP mark-up. Of course, much of an XHTML-MP document looks exactly like a standard XHTML document. The main differences, however, are the DOCTYPE (this example is for XHTML-MP version 1.2) and, in this case, the use of a 'style' attribute that refers to a WAP CSS style.

```
<?xml version="1.0"?>
<!DOCTYPE html PUBLIC "-//OMA//DTD XHTML Mobile 1.2//EN" "http://www.open
mobilealliance.org/tech/DTD/xhtml-mobile12.dtd">
<html xmlns="http://www.w3.org/1999/xhtml" xml:lang="en">
<head>
<title>Welcome to WebHomeCover</title>
</head>
<body>
```

```
<p>
<div style="display: -wap-marquee">Welcome to the claims department at
WebHomeCover.com</div>
<br/>click 
<a href="claimdetails.jsp">here</a>
 to enter your claim
</p>
</body>
</html>
```

Figure 13.1 summarizes the relationships between the various mark-up languages that we have looked at so far in this chapter. It can be seen from this diagram that any future development of applications using mobile mark-up should be using XHTML-MP rather than any earlier standards, particularly as it has been given very strong support by the OMA.

The .mobi top-level domain

With the move towards XHTML-MP as a standard mark-up for mobile device browsers, there has been an effort on behalf of part of the mobile communications industry to enable mobile web users to more easily identify web sites that can be browsed using mobile devices. Thirteen mobile and Internet organizations formed the mTLD (.mobi top-level domain) group to promote the adoption of a new top-level Internet domain with a '.mobi' extension. Any web application that uses this extension is expected to provide pages specifically for mobile devices, so that users of the mobile web know which sites are likely to work effectively on their mobile browsers. The mechanism for this is simply to encourage developers to create mobile mark-up using XHTML-MP. The guide document for .mobi developers states that 'the response must be encoded in XHTML-MP unless the device accessing it is known to support an alternative choice of markup'. (Cremin and Rabin 2006)

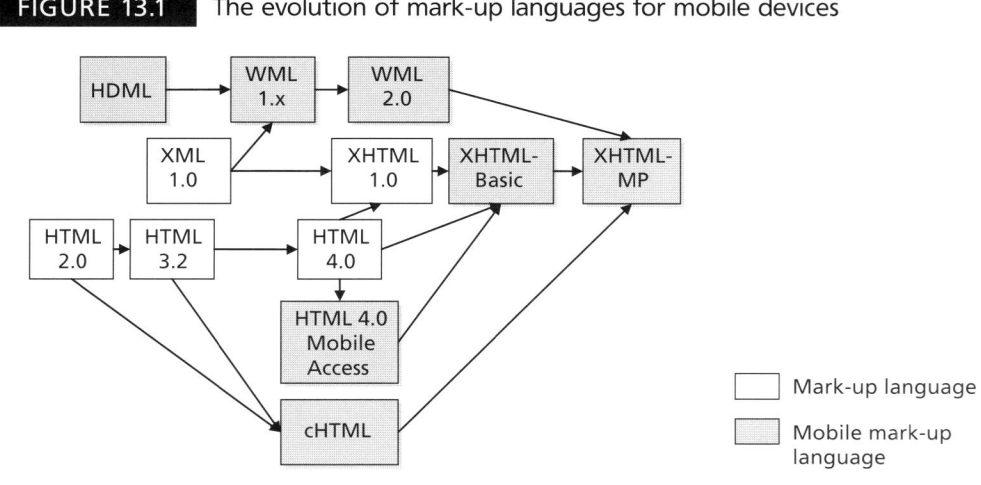

FIGURE 13.1   The evolution of mark-up languages for mobile devices

However there are some that object to the approach of having a specific domain name extension for mobile web applications, in particular Tim Berners-Lee, who objected strongly to the original proposals, and wrote:

> The Web must operate independently of the hardware, software or network used to access it, of the perceived quality or appropriateness of the information on it, and of the culture, and language, and physical capabilities of those who access it. (Berners-Lee 2004)

Nevertheless, the '.mobi' top-level domain was approved by ICANN in 2006 and seems to have found some popularity, at least according to the mTLD web site (http://pc.mtld.mobi/).

13.2 The WURFL/WALL Java framework for device adaptivity

So far in this chapter we have seen that mark-up used with mobile devices has developed through various different syntaxes, some that were subsets of HTML and some XML syntaxes. In addition, there are many different types of mobile device and new models are being introduced to the market all the time. These devices vary in physical form factors such as screen size and resolution, colors supported, layout of control buttons etc., as well as varying in the types of mobile browser that they support. This makes it difficult for the developer of a web application who wants to be able to support a wide range of mobile clients. Ideally, we would like to be able to provide customized versions of our web applications for each and every device capability, but this would be too time-consuming and difficult to maintain. Although there has been a gradual move towards XHTML-MP as the standard mark-up language for mobile browsers, there is still a wide range of mobile-device browsers in use, supporting many of the mark-up languages we have introduced. This means that in order to support all types of mobile browser, we need to write web applications that can generate dynamic content in a range of different mark-up languages. Doing this manually would be very arduous, but fortunately there is an open-source library that can make this task very simple, the Wireless Universal Resource File (WURFL) and the Wireless Abstraction Library (WALL) (Passani 2007b).

The Wireless Universal Resource File (WURFL) is a large (and continually updated) XML database of device capabilities. The structure of the WURFL is very simple; it is simply a list of devices. Within each device definition there is a list of capabilities for that device, grouped by types of capability, such as what type of mark-up they support:

```
<wurfl>
  <devices>
    <device. . .>
      <group. . .>
        <capability name=". . ." value=". . .">
        . . .
      </group>
      . . .
    </device>
    . . .
  </devices>
</wurfl>
```

There is a Java API for WURFL that enables you to write code that uses the capability database. However, on its own, WURFL leaves you to actually develop the adaptive code for the different devices. It becomes much more powerful when it is used in conjunction with the Wireless Abstraction Library (WALL).

WALL provides a set of tag libraries that enable you to write server pages that generate different mark-up for different devices, using WML, cHTML XHTML or XHTML-MP, depending on the device.

WALL is built on top of the WURFL device capability database. It provides a set of tags that abstract out the differences between different types of mark-up, so that a single server page can generate the client pages for a wide range of devices. The WURFL is able to match the 'User-Agent' header, which is passed as part of an HTTP request, to the specific device that sent the request. WALL provides us with a JSP tag library that uses the WURFL and generates device specific mark-up. This means that we can write JSPs that can generate code for different types of mobile client using a single set of source code. Figure 13.2 shows the components and interactions of a web application that uses WURFL and WALL. The view component JSP contains WALL tags that utilize the WURFL to identify the client device from the 'User-Agent' header. The structure of the document is controlled by the JSP using WALL tags but the actual mark-up is generated specifically for that user agent by the WALL library, using the WURFL database of device capability.

One of the key features of WURFL and WALL is that is we can use them to adapt to different device capabilities rather than limiting ourselves to the lowest common denominator. This means that the pages generated from a single WALL JSP will vary depending on the client device. Figure 13.3 shows some examples (from the WALL documentation) of how a single page could appear using different types of client. These clients vary not only in the mark-up languages they support (cHTML, WML or XHTML-MP) but also in some of their other capabilities, for example whether they support Java. A WALL JSP can include conditional statements to adapt its generated mark-up to such variations by making calls to the WURFL to identify the capabilities of the device.

FIGURE 13.2   Web application components and interactions using the Wireless Abstraction Library (WALL)

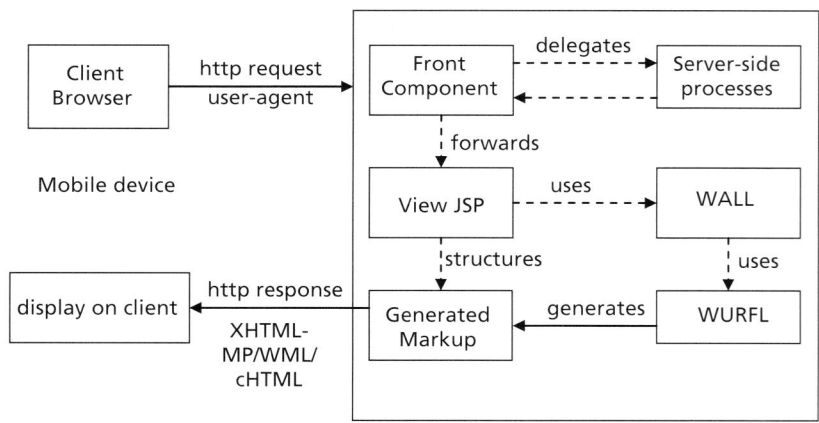

FIGURE 13.3 WALL-generated mobile web pages (from Passani 2007b)

Nokia 7110
WML 1.1
GSM EU

Nokia 7210
WML 1.2
GSM EU/US

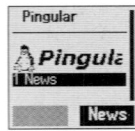

Siemens SL45
WML 1.1
GSM EU

Siemens SL45i
WML 1.1 GSM EU,
software upgrade of SL45
which enables J2ME

Sharp GX10
XHTML MP
Vodafone

Nec 341i
CHTML
IMode GSM EU

SonyEricsson
T616/T610
XHTML MP
GSM EU/US

LG LX-5350
XHTML MP
CDMA US

FIGURE 13.4 WALL mark-up generating pages for both mobile and desktop browsers

XHTML-MP
mobile browser
(Image courtesy
Openwave
Systems Inc.)*

WML Mobile
WAP browser
(Image courtesy
Yospace Smartphone
Emulator)

Desktop browser
(Internet Explorer 7)

WALL is flexible enough to generate pages for standard desktop browsers as well as mobile browsers. Figure 13.4 shows the same WALL source page with three different clients: an XHTML-MP browser, a WAP browser and a standard desktop browser (Internet Explorer 7).

The following example shows some WALL mark-up. The values being used in the EL expressions are derived from the WURFL.

*Openwave and the Openwave logo are registered trademarks and/or trademarks of Openwave Systems Inc. in various jurisdictions. All rights reserved.

```
<wall:load_capabilities />
<wall:head>
    <wall:title>WALL Demos</wall:title>
</wall:head>
<wall:body>
  <wall:menu autonumber="true">
    <wall:a href="body.jsp">body</wall:a>
    . . .
  </wall:menu>
  <wall:block>
    UA = <%= request.getHeader("User-Agent") %>
    <wall:br/>
    Wurfl ID = <wall:b>${device_id}</wall:b>
    <wall:br/>
    <wall:b>Capabilities</wall:b>:
    <wall:br/>
    Mark-up = <wall:b>${capabilities.wall_markup}</wall:b><wall:br/>
    preferred_markup = <wall:b>${capabilities.preferred_markup}
</wall:b>
<wall:br/>
```

Installing and configuring WURFL and WALL

The WALL library and the supporting WURFL can be downloaded from the SourceForge web site (http://sourceforge.net/project/showfiles.php?group_id=55408). The JAR files included in the download are the two JARs from the JSTL ('standard.jar' and 'jstl.jar'), along with the main WURFL/WALL tag library ('wurfltags.jar') and 'xom-1.0.jar', which contains an implementation of XOM, an open source XML processing API that is used by WALL. 'wurfltags.jar' and 'xom-1.0.jar' need to be copied to the 'lib' folder of your web application (the JSTL jars should already be there or in your server's 'lib' folder). The WURFL XML document included in the WALL download is not necessarily the most recent version, so you should also download the latest version of the WURFL from SourceForge. This download contains a single XML file ('wurfl.xml') which you need to copy to the 'WEB-INF' folder of your web application. In addition, there is a WURFL 'patch' file available that contains other updates to the WURFL file. This patch can be downloaded from the SourceForge WURFL patch page (http://wurfl.sourceforge.net/patchfile.php). The patch file needs to be called 'wurfl_patch.xml' and should also be put into the 'WEB-INF' folder.

In order for WURFL to successfully initialize in a web application, you need to register the WURFL servlet in the 'web-xml' deployment descriptor. The following 'servlet' entry should be added (the 'servlet-name' entry is arbitrary):

```
<servlet>
  <servlet-name>wurfl</servlet-name>
  <servlet-class>
    net.sourceforge.wurfl.wurflapi.WurflServletInit
  </servlet-class>
  <load-on-startup>2</load-on-startup>
</servlet>
```

Because the WURFL servlet is not used by any external clients, only the internal implementation, it has no external URI and therefore does not require a 'servlet-mapping' element (the 'load-on-startup' element should specify a different number from other servlets). Its role is to initialize the configuration of the WURFL. When the application server loads the servlet on startup, its 'init' (initialization) method will automatically be called. This method configures WURFL from the XML configuration files on the server.

Another aspect of the web application configuration is that the tag library descriptor (TLD) for WALL is not included in the 'wurfltags.jar' file, only as a separate file in the WALL download. Therefore the TLD needs to be copied to the web application. In our example, we assume that it is in a 'tld' folder under the 'WEB-INF' folder. WALL JSP pages can then refer to the TLD using the path '/WEB-INF/tld/wall.tld'.

Figure 13.5 shows the locations of the files necessary to support WALL in a web application.

Using the WALL tag library

To use WALL in a JSP we need to include a taglib directive in the page. Because of some subtle issues with WAP browsers, the documentation specifies certain aspects of how the tags should be used. Since this documentation only addresses the older style of JSP tags, we will use this format in our WALL examples. The following (older style) taglib directive is therefore required in any JSP that uses WALL ('wall' is the conventional prefix for the tag library).

```
<%@ taglib uri="/WEB-INF/tld/wall.tld" prefix="wall" %>
```

The content of a WALL page should be included inside a 'wall:document' element. This is essential if you want to support the generation of WML. In fact this tag needs to appear on the same line as the taglib declaration if you want to avoid the wrong MIME type being sent to WML devices:

```
<%@ taglib uri="/WEB-INF/tld/wall.tld" prefix="wall" %><wall:document>
```

FIGURE 13.5 Files required to configure WURFL and WALL within a web application

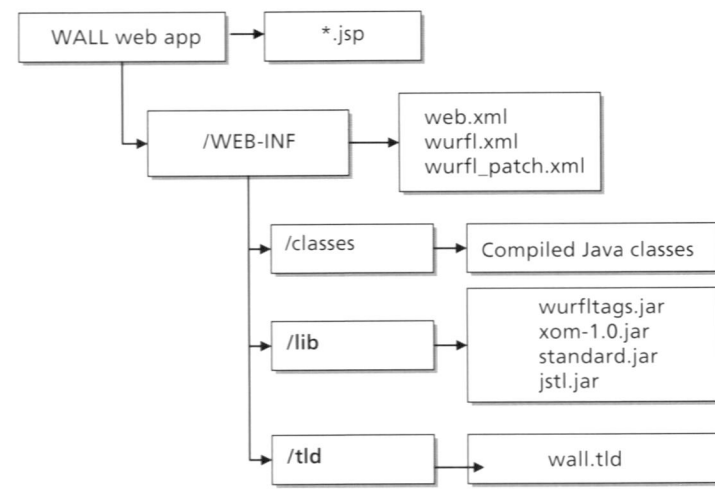

This should be followed by the XML Processing Instruction and DTD element, 'wall:xmlpidtd', i.e.

```
<%@ taglib uri="/WEB-INF/tld/wall.tld" prefix="wall"
%><wall:document><wall:xmlpidtd />
```

Again, this should appear on the same line. The WALL documentation states that;

> The wall:document tag needs to be on the very same top line immediately after the tag-lib declaration, if you intend to support WML too. The reason for this is that you don't want to give your application server a chance to produce the default MIME-Type (usually "text/html"). This would cause an error on WML devices. You may find that the xmlpidtd tag needs to be on the first line as well. This ensures that the XML processing instruction starts on the very first line as mandated by the XML spec (while this is insignificant in most cases, some old WAP gateways will break on this). (Passani 2007b)

After that we can build the main WALL document. Many wall tags are very similar to their XHTML equivalents, as we can see from Table 13.4, which lists some of the more common WALL tags.

In addition to the tags that are very similar to XHTML, there are also a number of elements that are specially targeted at the characteristics of mobile mark-up. These include the 'marquee' element, which displays content that scrolls horizontally across the screen:

```
<wall:marqee>. . .</wall:marquee>
```

The 'menu' element builds a mobile-phone-style menu. These are very important in mobile device interfaces because they are one of the few navigation tools we have on a basic mobile phone. The 'colorize' attribute uses colors to differentiate between different menu items, while the 'autonumber' attribute enables the menu items to be numbered:

```
<wall:menu colorize="true" autonumber="true">. . .</wall:menu>
```

TABLE 13.4 Common WALL tags and their XHTML equivalents

XHTML tag	WALL tag
`<head>...</head>`	`<wall:head>...</wall:head>`
`<title>...</title>`	`<wall:title>...</wall:title>`
`<body>...</body>`	`<wall:body>...</wall:body>`
`<form>...`	`<wall:form>...`
`<input type=... />...`	`<wall:input type=.../>...`
`</form>`	`</wall:form>`
`<a href=" ...">...</a>`	`<wall:a href=" ...">...</wall:href>`
`<b>...</b>`	`<wall:b>...</wall:b>`
`<i>...</i>`	`<wall:i>...</wall:i>`
` `	`<wall:br/>`

Following the good practice we have introduced in previous chapters, WALL supports the use of style sheets to separate presentation from content and structure. The following empty tag applies a style sheet:

```
<wall:menu_css />
```

Like a standard HTML style sheet tag, it is included in the head element, e.g.

```
<wall:head>
  <wall:title>Options</wall:title>
  <wall:menu_css />
</wall:head>
```

The style sheet implementation tries to apply a general style by reading the available colors from the device, so the colors in a 'colorized' menu will vary from platform to platform. You can try to set these colors explicitly using 'bgcolor' attributes:

```
<wall:menu_css bgcolor1="blue" bgcolor2="pink">
```

However you have to bear in mind that the device receiving the page may not be able to support the specific colors you have chosen.

A WALL page within the body of a WALL document needs to be structured into a series of blocks, menus and forms. In other words, anything that is not part of a menu or a form should be part of a block. A block is similar in concept to the 'div' element in HTML. The following example shows a very simple WALL page that just contains some text. Here, we use the block element inside the document body.

```
<%@ taglib uri="/WEB-INF/tld/wall.tld" prefix="wall"
%><wall:document><wall:xmlpidtd />
  <wall:head>
    <wall:title>WebHomeCover</wall:title>
  </wall:head>
  <wall:body>
    <wall:block>
      Welcome to <wall:b>WebHomeCover</wall:b>insurance
    <wall:block>
  </wall:body>
</wall:document>
```

There are some restrictions on forms in WALL, depending on how generic you want your presentation to be. If you do not need to support WAP, you can include radio buttons and check boxes on a form. However, if you want to be able to support WML clients, then the only form components you can use are text fields, hidden fields, passwords and select elements, with no radio buttons or check boxes.

13.3 Integrating WALL with a web application

In this section, we show how the WALL libraries can be integrated with a web application, so we can support multiple client types with the same content. For the example, we extend the existing web application that supports the use case for making an insurance claim.

Once the various files and resources have been set up for deployment, we need some way of integrating WALL mark-up into our existing web applications. Although it is possible to write an application entirely using WALL tags, this is rather limiting, because it means that desktop browsers will produce a very basic set of view components. If we want to maintain our support for the richness of desktop browsers in a web application, along with support for mobile devices, we have to support two streams of web-page generation, one for powerful, full-size browsers, supported by the dynamic page generation we already have in place, and another for other types of browser that we will support using the WALL library.

Determining the browser type

We can cater for different types of client by analyzing the 'User-Agent' header information sent within the browser's HTTP request. In fact this is exactly what WALL does in order to identify different types of mobile device, but all we need to do is filter out the main desktop browsers. Table 13.5 shows the 'User-Agent' header sent to the server by five of the major web browsers: Internet Explorer, Mozilla Firefox, Safari (Windows version), Netscape Navigator and Opera (some aspects of these will vary from machine to machine).

We can see from Table 13.5 that four of the major browsers' user agent strings contain the word 'Mozilla'. Therefore it is quite easy to identify these browsers. The Opera user agent string includes the word 'Opera', but because there are different versions of Opera for different types of client (i.e. there are Opera Mini and Opera Mobile browsers for mobile devices, and a version for the Nintendo games console) just identifying the 'Opera' string is not enough to specify an Opera desktop browser. Therefore we also need to check for the 'Windows' string to ensure that we can differentiate the different versions of Opera.

| **TABLE 13.5** | The 'User-Agent' header information sent to the server by five web browsers |

Browser	Version	'User-Agent' header
Internet Explorer	7	Mozilla/4.0 (compatible; MSIE 7.0; Windows NT 5.1; (R1 1.5); .NET CLR 1.1.4322; .NET CLR 2.0.50727)
Mozilla Firefox	2	Mozilla/5.0 (Windows; U; Windows NT 5.1; en-US; rv:1.8.1.4) Gecko/20070515 Firefox/2.0.0.4
Safari	3	Mozilla/5.0 (Windows; U; Windows NT 5.1; en) AppleWebKit/522.13.1 (KHTML, like Gecko) Version/3.0.2 Safari/522.13.1
Netscape Navigator	9	Mozilla/5.0 (Windows; U; Windows NT 5.1; en-US; rv:1.8.1.5pre) Gecko/20070604 Firefox/2.0.0.4 Navigator/9.0b1
Opera	9	Opera/9.21 (Windows NT 5.1; U; en)

The following 'if' statement can be used in server-side code to filter out the five major desktop browsers. Using just these substrings ('Mozilla', or 'Opera' and 'Windows') means that the code should be resilient against changes in details such as version numbers:

```
if(userAgent.startsWith("Mozilla") || (userAgent.contains("Opera") &&
userAgent.contains("Windows")))
```

Browsers that match these criteria can be sent pages generated using standard XHTML. In contrast, the 'User-Agent' header for other browsers will be very different, for example the OpenWave simulator Version 7 sends the header string:

```
OPWV-SDK UP.Browser/7.0.2.3.119 (GUI) MMP/2.0 Push/PO
```

Browsers such as this can be handled separately and pages can be generated using the WALL library. Of course any desktop browser that is not picked up by the 'if' statement will be sent pages generated by the WALL library. However they will still work. An associated problem is that some mobile devices will send user-agent headers that include the word 'Mozilla', For example the Nokia 6630 cell phone will send the following header:

```
Mozilla/4.0 (compatible; MSIE 5.0; Series60/2.8 Nokia6630/4.06.0
Profile/MIDP-2.0 Configuration/CLDC-1.1)
```

One way of dealing with this is to look for the 'Windows' string with Mozilla browsers, but this will exclude non-Windows desktop browsers, such as Safari running on the Mac. Alternatively we could exclude user agents that contain 'Nokia', though this would not deal with other mobile browsers that might include the 'Mozilla' string but are not Nokia phones. In the end, one or two browsers will probably slip through the cracks, but we will cater correctly for the vast majority of clients.

In order to integrate WALL with our existing pages and processes, we need to provide two paths through the web application, one that uses the existing XHTML page generation and one that uses the WALL libraries. Figure 13.6 shows the two paths, starting from a common default start page ('start.jsp') which forwards to the appropriate home page. In the rest of this section, we concentrate on the WALL JSPs. The others remain the same as in the previous version of the web application.

Our starting point for providing these separate paths is to create a default start page that can differentiate between different browser types, and then forward on to the appropriate page type for the response. Here is the default start page ('start.jsp'), configured as the welcome file in web.xml, which contains the code to check the 'User-Agent' header.

```
<?xml version="1.0"?>
<!-- File: start.jsp -->
<jsp:root xmlns:jsp="http://java.sun.com/JSP/Page"
  xmlns:c="http://java.sun.com/jsp/jstl/core"
  version="2.0">
  <jsp:directive.page isELIgnored="false" />
  <jsp:scriptlet>
    String useragent=(String)request.getHeader("User-Agent");
    System.out.println("User-Agent " + useragent);
    boolean useWALL=true;
    if(useragent.startsWith("Mozilla") || (useragent.contains("Opera")
      &amp;&amp; useragent.contains("Windows")))
```

```
    {
      useWALL=false;
    }
    request.setAttribute("useWALL", useWALL);
  </jsp:scriptlet>
  <c:choose>
    <c:when test="${useWALL}">
      <jsp:forward page="wallclaimhome.jsp"/>
    </c:when>
    <c:otherwise>
      <jsp:forward page="claimhome.jsp"/>
    </c:otherwise>
  </c:choose>
</jsp:root>
```

The JSP includes a scriptlet that gets the 'User-Agent' string from the request (using the 'getHeader' method) and then sets the value of a Boolean variable called 'useWALL' to either true or false, depending on the value of the user agent header. This variable is then put into 'request' scope so it can be retrieved by the EL expression that follows the scriptlet. (Note the code in the scriptlet includes '&&' instead of '&&' so that the document remains valid XML and can be correctly parsed by the server.) Then the 'choose' tag from the JSTL core library is used to forward to either 'wallclaimhome.jsp' or 'claimhome.jsp', depending on whether the browser is a mobile browser or a desktop browser.

FIGURE 13.6   The two paths through the use case

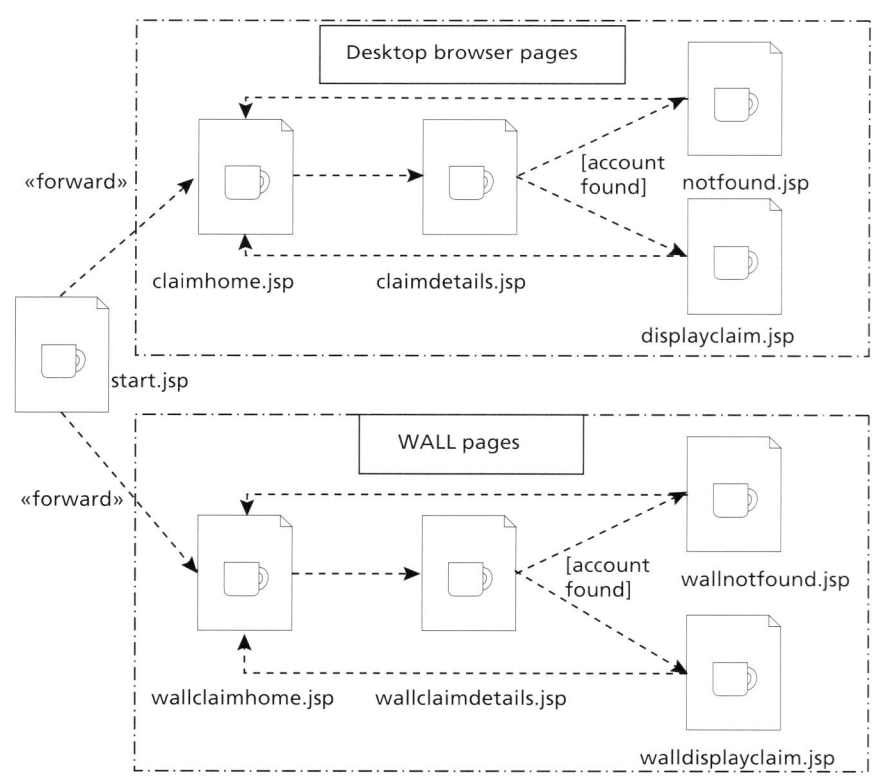

Here is 'wallclaimhome.jsp', which of course uses WALL markup ('claimhome.jsp' is the same as in the previous example):

```
<!-- File: wallclaimhome.jsp -->
<%@ taglib uri="/WEB-INF/tld/wall.tld" prefix="wall"
%><wall:document><wall:xmlpidtd />
 <wall:head>
  <wall:title enforce_title="true">
     Welcome to WebHomeCover
  </wall:title>
 </wall:head>
 <wall:body>
    <wall:block>
     <wall:marquee>
      Welcome to the claims department at WebHomeCover.com
     </wall:marquee>
     <wall:br/>
     click <wall:a href="wallclaimform.jsp">here </wall:a>
     to enter your claim
    </wall:block>
 </wall:body>
</wall:document>
```

Figure 13.7 shows what (part of) the 'wallclaimhome.jsp' page looks like when rendered in the Openwave simulator. This simulator, which was used to create all the mobile browser screen images in this section, can be downloaded from the Openwave Developer Network (http://developer.openwave.com/dvl/tools_and_sdk/phone_simulator/).

The Openwave simulator also includes a console that shows the contents of the HTTP requests and responses. This is part of the HTTP request made by the simulator, showing the 'User-Agent' string and also the 'X-Wap-Profile'. This is a reference to a *UAProf* (User

FIGURE 13.7   The home page displayed in the Openwave simulator (Openwave Systems Inc.)

Agent Profile), an XML document that contains detailed information about the mobile device's features and capabilities.

```
User-Agent: OPWV-SDK UP.Browser/7.0.2.3.119 (GUI) MMP/2.0 Push/PO
X-Wap-Profile: "http://devgate2.openwave.com/uaprof/OPWVSDK70.xml"
```

Here is part of the HTTP response, including the generated mark-up, as shown in the simulator console. Note that the response is sent to the simulator as an XHTML-MP document. Note also that the server sends a 'JSESSIONID' value to the 'Set-Cookie' header. This is used to maintain client session identity.

```
HTTP/1.1 200 OK
Server: Apache-Coyote/1.1
Set-Cookie: JSESSIONID=2DBEEECEBFCEC3BB7DD916F710CCE1E7;
Path=/webhomecover Content-Type: text/html
<!-- File: wallclaimhome.jsp -->
<?xml version="1.0"?>
<!DOCTYPE html PUBLIC "-//WAPFORUM//DTD XHTML Mobile 1.0//EN"
"http://www.wapforum.org/DTD/xhtml-mobile10.dtd">
<html xmlns="http://www.w3.org/1999/xhtml" xml:lang="en">
  <head>
    <title>
    Welcome to WebHomeCover
    </title>
  </head>
  <body>
    <p>
      <div style="display: -wap-marquee">
      Welcome to the claims department at WebHomeCover.com
      </div>
      <br/>
      click <a href="wallclaimform.jsp">here </a>to enter your claim
    </p>
  </body>
</html>
```

Server-Side Validation

From the 'wallclaimhome.jsp' page, the hyperlink takes us to 'wallclaimform.jsp', where the user will enter the details of their claim. In Chapter 12 we introduced some client-side validation that would ensure that, in the event of a valid policy number being entered, the other data in the form would also be valid when written to the database. The application of client-side validation depends, of course, on the client browser supporting JavaScript. Since many mobile-phone browsers do not support JavaScript, we need some other approach to validation, which is to perform the validation checks on the server. There are a number of strategies that we could apply to do this, but our approach is to perform validation in the ClaimBean. There are some additions to the ClaimBean class that we need to make to achieve this. First, we need a field of the bean that can contain a set of error messages. Here, we use a Collection reference to an ArrayList of Strings:

```
private Collection<String>errors = new ArrayList<String>();
```

This will need to be accessible via a readable property, so we also need a suitable 'get' method:

```java
public Collection<String> getErrors()
{
  return errors;
}
```

The main change to the bean is that we need a method to perform validation. Here is such a method, 'validate', which clears the error message collection of any previous errors, then checks the bean properties for invalid values. Each time an error is found another message is added to the 'errors' Collection.

```java
public void validate()
{
  errors.clear();
  if(getPolicyNumber().isEmpty())
  {
    errors.add("Please provide a policy number");
  }
  if(getAmount()== 0)
  {
    errors.add("Please provide a valid claim amount");
  }
  if(getType() == null)
  {
    errors.add("Please select either buildings or contents insurance");
  }
  if(getDescription().isEmpty())
  {
    errors.add("Please provide a description");
  }
}
```

Where should we trigger this validation process? The most sensible place is in the controller JSP that receives the request, 'wallprocessclaim.jsp'. This JSP populates the ClaimBean from the request then, using a scriptlet, calls the 'validate' method of the bean. If there are any errors in the error collection, then the JSP forwards back to the claim form page again (note the use of the 'return' statement – there should be no code executed in a JSP after a 'forward' element). If there are no errors, we pass the ClaimBean to the façade for processing, as we have done in previous examples.

```xml
<?xml version="1.0"?>
<!-- File: wallprocessclaim.jsp -->
<jsp:root xmlns:jsp="http://java.sun.com/JSP/Page"
  xmlns:c="http://java.sun.com/jsp/jstl/core"
  version="2.0">

  <jsp:directive.page isELIgnored="false" />
  <jsp:useBean id="claimBean" class="com.webhomecover.beans.ClaimBean"
      scope="request"/>
  <jsp:setProperty name="claimBean" property="*" />
```

13

```
<jsp:scriptlet>
  claimBean.validate();
  java.util.Collection errors=claimBean.getErrors();
  if(!errors.isEmpty())
  {
</jsp:scriptlet>
  <jsp:forward page="wallclaimform.jsp"/>
<jsp:scriptlet>
  return;
  }
  com.webhomecover.model.Claim claim=
    com.webhomecover.model.ModelFacade.createClaim(claimBean);
  request.setAttribute("claim", claim);
</jsp:scriptlet>
<c:choose>
  <c:when test="${claim == null}">
    <jsp:forward page="wallnotfound.jsp"/>
  </c:when>
  <c:otherwise>
    <jsp:forward page="walldisplayclaim.jsp"/>
  </c:otherwise>
</c:choose>
</jsp:root>
```

The final aspect of the validation process is to provide some feedback to the user if the form data has failed validation. The bean's 'errors' property can be used to display error messages in the form page. The claim form page first needs to access the bean:

```
<jsp:useBean id="claimBean" class="com.webhomecover.beans.ClaimBean"
scope="request"/>
```

Then we can iterate over the error collection:

```
<c:forEach var="error" items="${claimBean.errors}">
  <c:out value="${error}" /><br />
</c:forEach>
```

There is one more important aspect to this type of validation, which is that the user will not want to fill in the entire form again just because one of the fields was invalid. This means we would ideally want to be able to keep all the existing data in the form and simply enable the user to correct the errors. Fortunately this is quite simple. We already have the ClaimBean in scope in the page. To redisplay any data already entered, all we need to do is use the 'getProperty' tag to set the 'value' attributes of the form components from the bean.

Here is the complete WALL form page, which is written to be WML-compatible. Therefore there are no radio buttons (as there are in the desktop browser version of the form page). Instead, the choice of insurance type is made using a select list. The ClaimBean is used both to display error messages and to populate the form components with any previously entered values:

```
<!-- File: wallclaimform.jsp -->
<%@ taglib uri="http://java.sun.com/jsp/jstl/core" prefix="c" %>
<%@ taglib uri="/WEB-INF/tld/wall.tld" prefix="wall"
```

```
%><wall:document><wall:xmlpidtd />
<jsp:useBean id="claimBean" class="com.webhomecover.beans.ClaimBean"
scope="request"/>
<wall:head>
   <wall:title enforce_title="true">
    Insurance Claim Details
   </wall:title>
</wall:head>
<wall:body>
   <wall:block>
      <c:forEach var="error" items="${claimBean.errors}">
       <c:out value="${error}" /><br />
      </c:forEach>
   </wall:block>
    <wall:form action="wallprocessclaim.jsp" method="post">
      <wall:br/>Policy Number:
      <wall:input type="text" name="policyNumber" size="10"
       value="${claimBean.policyNumber}" />
      <wall:br/>Amount claimed:
      <wall:input type="text" name="amount" size="10"
        value="${claimBean.amount}"/>
      <wall:br/>
      <wall:select name="type">
       <wall:option value="buildings" selected="selected" >
        Buildings
       </wall:option>
       <wall:option value="contents">Contents</wall:option>
      </wall:select>
      <wall:br/>
      Description of claim:
      <wall:br/>
      <wall:input type="text" name="description" size="30"
       value="${claimBean.description}"/>
      <wall:br/>
      <wall:input type="submit" value="submit" />
    </wall:form>
    <wall:br/>
   </wall:body>
</wall:document>
```

Figure 13.8 shows how part of the form looks in the Openwave simulator.

There are three possibilities when we submit the form. First there may be validation errors, in which case the form is redisplayed with error messages. Second, the data may pass validation but the policy number may not be found, in which case the page routing leads to 'wallnotfound.jsp'. Third, if the policy number is matched in the database then the claim details are displayed. The 'wallnotfound.jsp' page is quite simple:

```
<!-- File: wallnotfound.jsp -->
<%@ taglib uri="/WEB-INF/tld/wall.tld" prefix="wall"
%><wall:document><wall:xmlpidtd />
```

FIGURE 13.8 The insurance claim form rendered by the Openwave mobile phone
simulator (Openwave Systems Inc.)

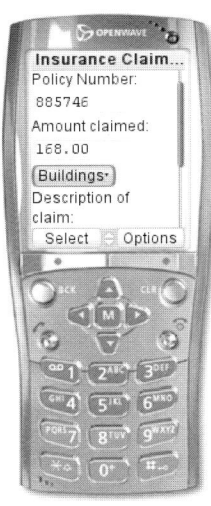

```
<jsp:useBean id="claimBean" class="com.webhomecover.beans.ClaimBean"
scope="request" />
  <wall:head>
    <wall:title enforce_title="true">
        Insurance Claim Details
    </wall:title>
  </wall:head>
  <wall:body>
    <wall:block>
      policyNumber <jsp:getProperty name="claimBean"
      property="policyNumber"/>not found
    </wall:block>
    <wall:hr />
    <wall:a href="wallclaimhome.jsp">Home Page</wall:a>
  </wall:body>
</wall:document>
```

'walldisplay.jsp' is also quite straightforward, displaying the properties of the claim and
the policy.

```
<!--File: walldisplayclaim.jsp -->
<%@ taglib uri="http://java.sun.com/jsp/jstl/core" prefix="c" %>
<%@ taglib uri="/WEB-INF/tld/wall.tld" prefix="wall"
%><wall:document><wall:xmlpidtd />
<%@ page isELIgnored="false" %>
<jsp:useBean id="claim" class="com.webhomecover.model.Claim" scope="request" />
<c:set var="policy" value="${claim.policy}" />

  <wall:head>
    <wall:title enforce_title="true">
    Insurance Claim Details
```

```
                </wall:title>
            </wall:head>
        <wall:body>
            <wall:block>
                Thank you for making your insurance claim
                <wall:br/>Here are the claim and policy details
                <wall:br/>Policy Number: 
                <wall:b><jsp:getProperty name="policy" property="policyNumber"/>
                </wall:b>
                <wall:br/>Policy Taken out on: 
                <wall:b><jsp:getProperty name="policy" property="startDate"/>
                </wall:b>
                <wall:br/>Annual Premium: 
                <wall:b><jsp:getProperty name="policy" property="annualPremium"/>
                </wall:b>
                <wall:br/>Is policy paid up?: 
                <wall:b><jsp:getProperty name="policy" property="paidUp"/>
                </wall:b>
                <wall:br/>Claim reference: 
                <wall:b><jsp:getProperty name="claim" property="reference"/>
                </wall:b>
                <wall:br/>Date of claim: 
                <wall:b><jsp:getProperty name="claim" property="claimDate"/>
                </wall:b>
                <wall:br/>Value of claim: 
                <wall:b><jsp:getProperty name="claim" property="amount"/></wall:b>
                <wall:br/>Type of insurance policy: 
                <wall:b><jsp:getProperty name="claim" property="type"/></wall:b>
                <wall:br/>Description of claim: 
                <wall:b><jsp:getProperty name="claim" property="description"/>
                </wall:b>
                <wall:br/>
                <wall:a href="wallclaimhome.jsp">Home Page</wall:a>
            </wall:block>
        </wall:body>
    </wall:document>
```

Figure 13.9 shows the three possible pages displayed when the form is submitted; an error page, a 'policy not found' page, or details of a successfully lodged claim.

13.4 Alternative approaches to adaptivity

In this chapter, we have taken a particular approach to adaptivity, namely utilizing an open-source tag library to generate different mark-up for different client devices. There are a number of other approaches we could take to adaptivity, including the use of XSL transformations, and simply relying on the mobile browser.

Why, then, did we do not simply use an XSL Transformation, based on the type of client, and then generate a suitable page? The problem with this is that if a JSP contains an XSL

FIGURE 13.9 WALL-generated mobile web pages showing a) validation error messages, b) a failed claim due to an invalid policy number and c) a successful claim registration (Openwave Systems Inc.)

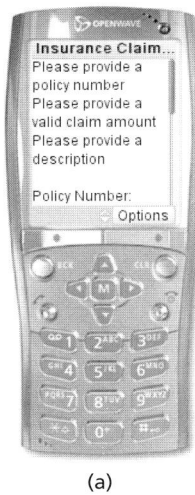

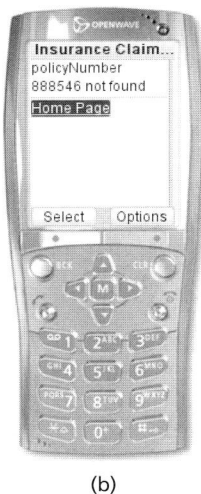

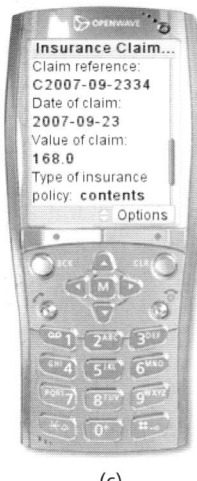

(a)   (b)   (c)

transformation, then that transformation will be processed when the page is generated. If the generated page contains WALL tags, then that page needs to be processed again by the JSP engine. This would mean that each page would be processed twice, first for the transformation and then again to process the generated WALL tags. This would be highly inefficient. On the other hand, if we did not use the WALL tags then we would have to write our own device-specific transformations, though we could still use the WURFL to assist us in this approach.

Another option to adaptivity would be simply to rely on the mobile browser to transform standard web content for the mobile device. This is increasingly possible with the continuing development of the Opera Mini and Opera Mobile Browsers. Both of these browsers are based on Java Micro Edition technology. Opera Mini is a generic Java-based mobile browser that is able to render standard web pages on a small screen by converting the original pages. Opera Mobile is a more powerful browser, which is targeted to the specific mobile device on which it is installed, so there are different versions of the browser available for a range of mobile phones. Opera Mobile is a more fully featured mobile browser than Opera Mini, and includes support for JavaScript, making it possible to develop mobile Ajax applications.

Exercises

13.1 Take the XHTML contents details form from the 'get insurance quote' use case and rewrite it using the WALL library. First, create a page that includes radio buttons and check boxes. Test the page renders correctly by using a suitable mobile phone simulator.

13.2 Write another version of the contents details form but this time make it WML-compatible by replacing the check box and radio buttons with select lists.

13.3 Write a WML-compatible version of the buildings details form from the 'get insurance quote' use case.

13.4 Implement a set of WALL pages that enable a mobile user to enter an account number and view the related policy-holder details.

SUMMARY

In this chapter, we reviewed the evolution of mark-up languages designed for mobile devices, and described the move towards a common mobile mark-up. In the context of '.mobi' domains, we saw how XHTML-MP is increasingly being used as a standard mark-up language for mobile phones. In order to generate web pages that are adaptive to different types of mobile device, we introduced the WURFL and WALL libraries, which enable us to write JSPs using tags from the WALL library that generate device adaptive mark-up. We also saw how to use the 'User-Agent' header in the HTTP request to differentiate between desktop browsers and other types of browser.

Table 13.6 shows the available tags in the WALL library. These come directly from the WALL tag library descriptor.

TABLE 13.6 Tags in the WALL library

element	body	description	Attributes
document	JSP	Container tag	disable_wml_extensions disable_xhtml_extensions disable_cache disable_content_type_gen eration
xmlpidtd		Generate appropriate XML Processing Instruction and DTD	Encoding
head	JSP	Multiserve head description	title enforce_title

▶

element	body	description	Attributes
title	JSP	Multiserve title attribute	enforce_title
body	JSP	Multiserve body tag	bgcolor text wml_back_button_label disable_wml_template newcontext
block	JSP	Multiserve p tag	Align
br		Multiserve br tag to fix trailing slash	
hr		Multiserve horizontal-rule	Color
h1		Header level 1	
h2		Header level 2	
h3		Header level 3	
h4		Header level 4	
h5		Header level 5	
h6		Header level 6	
menu_css		Serve some CSS to 'good' XHTML browsers to embellish menus	bgcolor1 bgcolor2
menu	JSP	Multiserve menu	colorize autonumber
cool_menu	JSP	Cool graphical menu	colnum tabularize
cool_menu_css		Serve CSS to optimize cool menus for XHTML devices	colnum tabularize
Cell	JSP	Cool menu cell	
a	JSP	Multiserve link and menu item	href accesskey title opwv_icon
form	JSP	Multiserve forms	enable_wml action method
input		Multiserve input element	accesskey format checked disabled emptyok maxlength name

element	body	description	Attributes
			size
			type
			title
			value
select		Multiserve select element	name
			disabled
			size
			title
			multiple
option		Option element	value
			selected
img		image element	src
			alt
alternate_img		Alternate image element	test
			src
			nopicture
			opwv_icon
			eu_imode_icon
			ja_imode_icon
b		Bold element for WML compatibility	
i		Italics element for WML compatibility	
font		Font tag	color
			size
			face
marquee		Scrolling horizontally	direction
			behavior
			loop
			bgcolor
caller		Making WAP/Imode phone calls	tel
			cti
			alt
			opwv_icon
			accesskey
load_capabilities		Create the hash map that integrates with JSTL	
wurfl_device_id		Print out the WURFL ID found for this device (debugging utility)	Ua

References and further reading

Berners-Lee, T. (2004) *New Top Level Domains .mobi and .xxx Considered Harmful.* http://www.w3.org/DesignIssues/TLD.

Cremin, R. and Rabin, J. (2006) *dotMobi Switch On! Web Developer Guide.* http://dev.mobi/files/dotmobi_Switch_On_Web_Developer_Guide_1.0_External_Draft.html.

Kamada, T., Asada, T., Ishikawa, M. and Matsui, S. (1999) *HTML 4.0 Guidelines for Mobile Access.* http://www.w3.org/TR/NOTE-html40-mobile.

McCarron, S., Ishikawa, M., Baker, M., Matsui, S., Stark, P., Wugofski, T. and Yamakami, T. (2007) *XHTML™ Basic 1.1 W3C Working Draft.* http://www.w3.org/TR/xhtml-basic.

OMA (2006) *XHTML Mobile Profile Approved Version 1.1.* http://www.openmobilealliance.org/release_program/docs/browsing/v2_2–20061020-a/oma-wap-xhtmlmp-v1_1–20061020-a.pdf.

Passani, L. (2007a) *Global Authoring Practices for the Mobile Web.* http://www.passani.it/gap/.

Passani, L. (2007b) *Introducing WALL: a Library to Multiserve Applications on the Wireless Web.* http://wurfl.sourceforge.net/java/tutorial.php.

13

CHAPTER 14

XML Messaging: Web Services and Server-Side Ajax

LEARNING OBJECTIVES

- **To understand the role of web services in web applications**

- **To be able to build a simple web service using Java Enterprise Edition tools**

- **To be able to develop a web service client within a Java web application**

- **To be able to implement server-side Ajax components**

INTRODUCTION

In this chapter, we look at two different aspects of sending XML messages from web applications: web services and Ajax. Web services are based on sending XML messages over an HTTP connection, regardless of the type of server, the type of client, or the programming languages that either the client or the server are written in. However, in the context of this book we look at how to implement web services and clients within Java web applications. Because developing both services and clients can be quite complex, we use the NetBeans 5.5 IDE to generate some of the necessary code and configuration files.

In terms of Ajax, we have already seen in Chapter 8 how to implement an Ajax client using JavaScript in the browser, but in previous examples we were using existing services (RSS feeds) from external sources. In this chapter, we see how to implement an end-to-end Ajax system by developing both the client and the server. While Ajax applications do not have to use XML messaging (the server may just send a non-XML character string), it is a very common approach and one that is supported by the XMLHttpRequest object. Building on the work we have done so far, we see how to integrate Ajax components into a Struts-based web application.

We begin the chapter by exploring web services and conclude by developing an Ajax version of the 'make insurance claim' use case.

14.1 Web services

There is no single concrete definition for what constitutes a *web service*, since the term is used to describe a range of XML message-based systems that work over the web. In essence, a web service is a technology that enables distributed applications to provide data and services to other applications, based on common web protocols and data formats. Using these common protocols supports interoperability between different applications regardless of their platform, language or location. Web services are good for niche applications that do not require high levels of interaction, such as weather services, stock quotes, mortgage interest rates and credit-card validation. They are not, however, limited to providing content for parts of a web application; they can also be used as a way for different organizations to communicate with one another in business-to-business (B2B) systems, and inside an organization to integrate internal systems that do not run on the same technology platform. Although the concept of a web service is generic, the set of technologies that are commonly used to implement web services are governed by standards published by the W3C and the Web Services Interoperability Organization (WS-I), an industry consortium, provides a set of test tools that measure a given service against a set of *profiles* that mandate certain technologies and behaviors. Therefore the common use of the term 'web service' tends to refer to a specific technology stack that includes Simple Object Access Protocol (SOAP), Web Services Description Language (WSDL) and Universal Description, Discovery and Integration (UDDI).

Technologies that enable distributed computer systems to communicate with one another have been around for a long time, but web services are easier to implement than many other approaches because they are based on commonly used existing standards, in particular HTTP and XML. The benefits of the common communication mechanism provided by sending XML documents over HTTP connections are that we can have loosely coupled systems, using different underlying implementations, running on different platforms, working together. A particular advantage of using HTTP connections is that the HTTP ports (80, and 443 for HTTPS) are generally enabled by Internet firewalls, while different ports that might be used by other communication channels may be blocked for security reasons.

14.2 Web service technologies

Web services support a service-oriented architecture (SOA) on the web. In this type of architecture, different providers can make a range of XML services available to any clients that have an HTTP connection. For a service-oriented architecture to work, there are three basic requirements. First, you need some way of finding out which web services are available for use. You then need to know where these services are located, and finally you need to know how to interact with a particular service in terms of how to invoke it and then how to interpret the reply. For this interaction to be successful there has to be an agreed messaging format and a standard way of publishing and looking up web services. Figure 14.1 shows the main standards that are used to support these requirements. A common messaging format for web services is the Simple Object Access Protocol (SOAP), which is used to send XML messages over an HTTP connection. Web service providers can publish their available services to potential clients using Universal Description, Discovery and Integration (UDDI). The details of an individual service are then described using the Web Services Description Language (WSDL). In addition, WS-Inspection can be used to provide a list of services that are available at a particular web service provider location.

FIGURE 14.1 The standards, components and relationships that may be used in a web service implementation

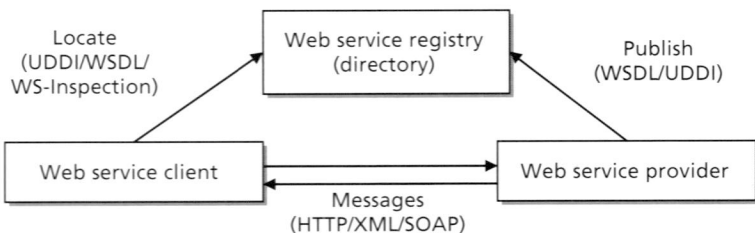

Simple Object Access Protocol (SOAP)

The Simple Object Access Protocol (SOAP) is a web service message format using XML. It consists of an envelope that describes a message and how to process it, data encoding rules for describing data types (based on XML Schema) and a set of rules for how to make remote calls and get responses. Those calls and responses can be either remote procedure calls (RPC) or messages. The difference is that a remote procedure call is very much like making a standard HTTP request to a web application, where the client makes a call to the service and then waits for the response. In contrast, messaging is asynchronous. A message is sent but the client does not wait for the response (similar to the asynchronous XMLHttpRequest in Ajax systems, which we introduced in Chapter 8).

SOAP is designed to be simple and independent of other protocols and languages, emphasizing interoperability between different systems. A SOAP 'envelope' contains two main parts, the message itself (the data) and a header (the metadata) that provides information about the message. The actual contents of the header are not specified by the SOAP standard, but the basic idea is that the header may be made available to *SOAP intermediaries* that may process the message as it goes from the sender to the receiver, as well as being available to the actual receiver. Both the header and the body contain application-specific XML content. This is the basic element structure of a SOAP message:

```
<?xml version='1.0'?>
<env:Envelope xmlns:env="http://www.w3.org/2003/05/soap-envelope">
<env:Header>
 . . .
</env:Header>
<env:Body>
 . . .
</env:Body>
</env:Envelope>
```

SOAP messages can be carried within the body of an HTTP 'post' request. Figure 14.2 shows an HTTP request containing the HTTP header and also a SOAP envelope, which in turn contains a SOAP header and body.

Web Services Description Language (WSDL)

The Web Services Description Language (WSDL) uses XML to describe web services.

FIGURE 14.2 SOAP messages can be sent as part of an HTTP request

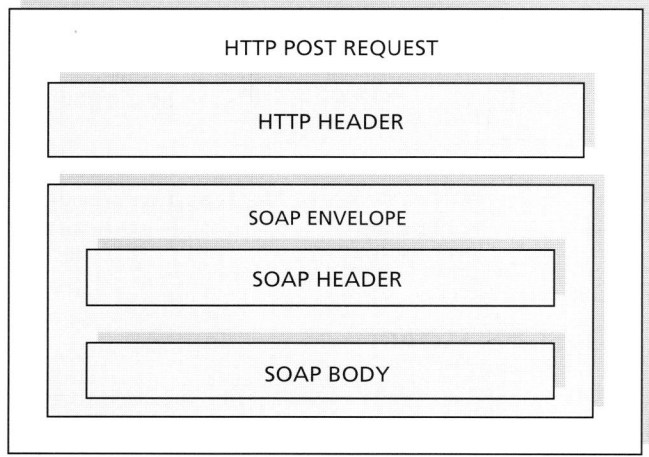

FIGURE 14.3 WSDL Components

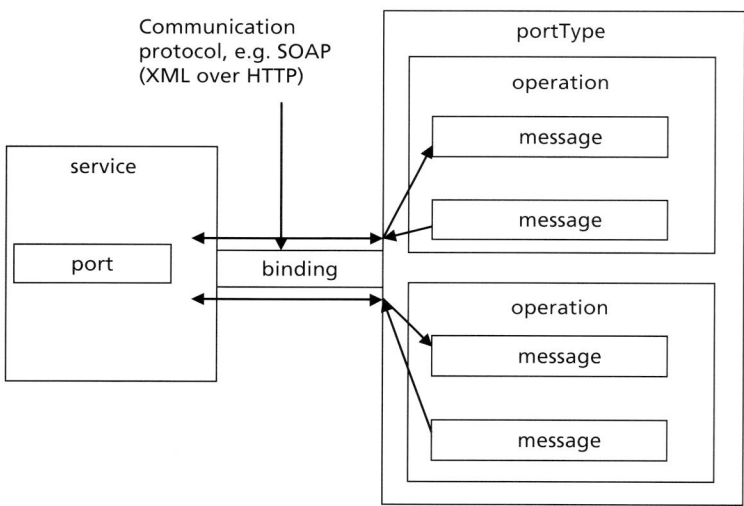

A WSDL document describes the operations available from the web service, the input and output data for these operations and the mechanism for contacting the web service. Each of these operations exchanges messages: an incoming message and an outgoing message, which will either be the response from the successful operation or an error message. Each XML message structure is defined by an XML Schema. Figure 14.3 shows the main components described by the elements of a WSDL document. A WSDL 'portType' describes all the operations of a service, and the input and output 'message' components used for each operation. The 'binding' describes the supported protocols of the service and the transport mechanism used, while the 'service' provides the URI of the service (the 'port').

WSDL provides the XML-based contract for a web service, but we also need to provide the actual implementation of the service so that messages can be processed. This implementation can easily be generated using tools (coding web services by hand is rather complex and tedious). In general, the tools that help us to generate the web service implementation also generate the WSDL file.

Searching for a WSDL File: UDDI and WS-Inspection

To invoke a service, you need its description, which is defined in a WSDL document, but how can you find a WSDL description? If you do not already know its URI, then there are two approaches that can be used: the Universal Description, Discovery and Integration (UDDI) service and WS-Inspection. UDDI allows web services to be published to clients on a web-wide basis and acts as a general directory for web services. It has two APIs, the publishers API and the inquiry API. Web services are described in different ways using three types of directory, yellow, green and white pages. White pages directories are based on addresses, contacts and other identifiers. In the white pages directory, each element has attributes such as name, description, address, and a unique universal identifier (UUID) which is generated by the system. The yellow pages directory is based on service types, with elements classified by hierarchical categories such as the North American Industry Classification System (NAICS), the United Nations/Standard Products and Services Codes (UN/SPSC) and ISO 3166 geographical region codes. A single element can belong to more than one of these categories. Finally, the green pages directory contains technical information about services, such as the industry-specific XML specifications that they implement. Examples of these include RosettaNet (introduced briefly in Chapter 5) and ebXML (Electronic Business using eXtensible Markup Language). The main features of the UDDI API are the ability to manage the publication of services (creating, updating and deleting) and to search for published services. Using the search API, any type of element can be searched for and the search criteria may be based on all three directory types.

WS-Inspection is different from UDDI in that it is not used to provide a global directory space. Rather, it is used as a directory to a single service provider. WS-Inspection allows you to search a provider's site for available web services. It provides a 'natural-language' description of the services and the URI of the WSDL service description. WS-Inspection provides an intermediate solution between the global approach of UDDI and a solution where you already know the service and WSDL. To locate WS-Inspection files, an 'inspection.wsil' file is located at a common location. A single organization may provide numerous web services with a large number of associated descriptions. WS-Inspection can help manage this by referencing other files, so that a WS-Inspection document may reference other WS-Inspection documents.

14.3 Implementing web services

Although web services provide generic interoperability between different systems using common web protocols, a *provider* or *agent* is required to actually implement the underlying service on a specific technology platform. While XML web service standards that relate to how services are exposed to clients such as SOAP and WSDL are common across the web, the underlying implementations of different web services will vary widely. Whichever platform is chosen, it must provide support for publishing, consuming and locating web services, so there are a number of different aspects to each web service implementation platform. Depending on the technology you are using on your server, there are a range of possible things that can be exposed as a web service. These include enterprise components, objects, server pages, database stored procedures, or indeed any other process that a particular tool is able to expose as a web service. To get an idea of the range of things that can be made available as web services, it is interesting to have a look at http://www.xmethods.com, a web site that gathers together a large number of example services. As well as the more usual types of services, such as weather and currency exchange rates, you will find examples such as the Icelandic phone book, Urdu to English translations, German bank codes, verses from the Quran and a whole raft of other fascinating possibilities. In many cases the implementation platform of the service is given as well as the available clients that have been implemented for that service.

In our examples, we use Java to build web services, and the components that implement these services are Java classes. The Java platform for web service development has changed quite considerably over recent years. For example, the Java APIs for XML based on RPC (JAX-RPC) have been superseded by the Java API for XML Web Services (JAX-WS). JAXB, which we introduced in Chapter 11, is also part of the Java web service technology stack. There is a raft of other implementations and projects in the Java web services arena too, but this chapter will focus only on the basics of implementing Java web services using JAX-WS.

In the following section, we use a simple example to show how a Java web service can be implemented and integrated into a Java web application. Our example relates to a fictional pet insurance company, WebPetCover, which sells pet insurance online. One potential use of web services is for organizations with complementary products or services to provide these to each others' customers. In this context, WebHomeCover and WebPetCover might decide to partner online, to sell their respective insurance services through the other's web site. Figure 14.4 shows the web service interaction from the perspective of WebHomeCover using a web service from WebPetCover. Clients of WebHomeCover's web application are able to access some services from WebPetCover that are made available via the WebHomeCover web pages but are supported by services provided

FIGURE 14.4   A pet insurance web service in a home insurance web application

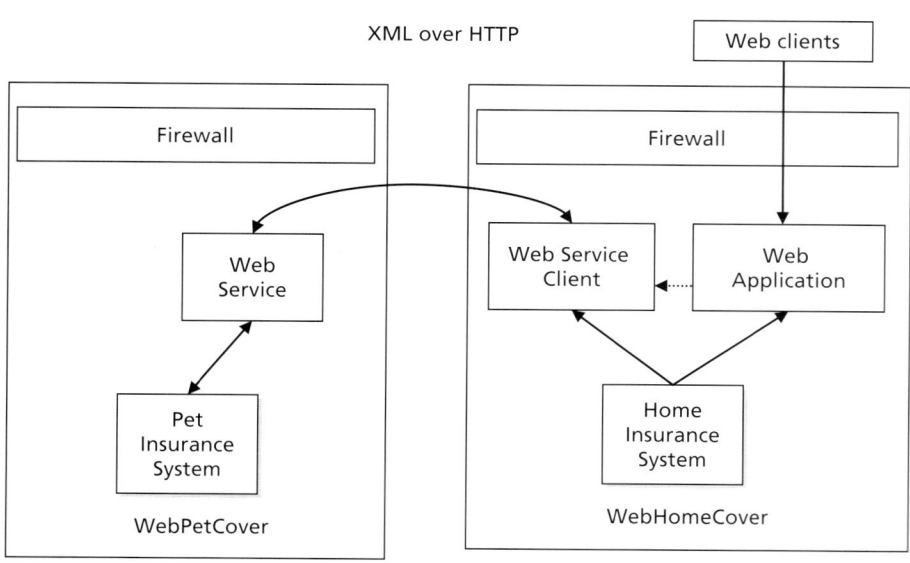

by WebPetCover. Communication between WebHomeCover's web application and WebPetCover's web service is done using XML over HTTP so the message can pass through each company's firewall.

14.4 Creating a web service with Java 6.0

Since Java version 6.0, it has been possible to create and deploy a test web service just using the standard JDK. It is quite a simple process. First of all we need to write a class that will provide the basic functionality of the web service. In this example, we build a service that can provide quotes for pet insurance. The following class ('PetInsuranceWebService') has a single method called 'getPetInsuranceQuote' that takes an animal's type and age as parameters and uses some trivial algorithms to generate quotes for different pets. There are two particular aspects to this class that are special to web service classes. The first is the import of the 'WebService' and 'WebMethod' classes from the 'javax.jws' package, and the use of the two annotations based on these classes '@WebService' and '@WebMethod'. The 'WebService' annotation on the class means that 'PetInsuranceWebService' is made into a web service, and the 'WebMethod' annotation means that 'getPetInsuranceQuote' is used as a web service operation, with input and output messages. It is not essential to use the 'WebMethod' annotation because, by default, all methods declared in a web service class are web service methods. However, in this example this would mean that 'main' was also processed as a web method, which it is not intended to be. Using the explicit annotation means that only the annotated method is processed as a web service operation. The second important feature is the implementation of the 'main' method, which publishes the class as a web service. This uses the 'publish' method of the 'Endpoint' class in the 'jaxa.xml.ws' package and specifies the URI of the service (the port number must be 8080 for the test server).

```
package com.webpetcover.ws;

import javax.jws.WebService;
import javax.jws.WebMethod;
import javax.xml.ws.Endpoint;

@WebService
public class PetInsuranceWebService
{
   @WebMethod
public double getPetInsuranceQuote(String animalType, int age)
{
   if(animalType.equalsIgnoreCase("cat"))
   {
     return 20 * (age / 10.0);
   }
   if(animalType.equalsIgnoreCase("dog"))
   {
     return 30 * (age / 10.0);
   }
   if(animalType.equalsIgnoreCase("rabbit"))
   {
     return 10 * (age / 10.0);
```

14

```
        }
        if(animalType.equalsIgnoreCase("crocodile"))
        {
            return 50 * (age / 10.0);
        }
        return -1.0;
    }

    public static void main(String[] args)
    {
        Endpoint.publish("http://localhost:8080/webservice/petinsurance",
          new PetInsuranceWebService());
    }
}
```

Once the code is written, it can be compiled as a normal Java class (make sure you use the '-d' option to generate the package folders):

```
javac -d . PetInsuranceWeService.java
```

If compilation is successful, the next step is to run the web service generator tool, 'wsgen', which is part of Java 6.0. The '-cp' option is used here to set the classpath to the current folder.

```
wsgen -cp . com.webpetcover.ws.PetInsuranceWebService
```

This tool generates Java code in the folder 'com\webpetcover\ws\jaxws', in other words it creates a subfolder of the existing package folders called 'jaxws' for the generated classes. If you look in this folder you should see that the classes 'GetPetInsurance Quote' (for the input message) and 'GetPetInsuranceQuoteResponse' (for the output message) have been created. If you look at the source code you will find that they contain little Java, but include many annotations that are used for binding them to the input and output XML messages. 'GetPetInsuranceQuote' has properties ('arg0' and 'arg1') to represent the two parameters passed into the web service, while 'GetPetInsuranceQuoteResponse' has a single property representing the value returned from the service.

When you run the Java class, it publishes the web service to the test server that is provided with Java 6.0, and should automatically start the server running on port 8080 (i.e. the same port number on which Tomcat runs by default). You can check that the service is indeed running by opening a browser and going to the following URI, which will display the WSDL of the web service:

```
http://localhost:8080/webservice/petinsurance?wsdl
```

Figure 14.5 shows the first part of the WSDL generated by the web service displayed in a browser.

Of course creating and deploying a web service is only part of the story. We also need to have some way of creating a client application that can communicate with the service and some way of integrating both the web service and its client into separate web applications. In the next section, we deploy a web service as part of a web application and also create a JSP that acts as a web service client.

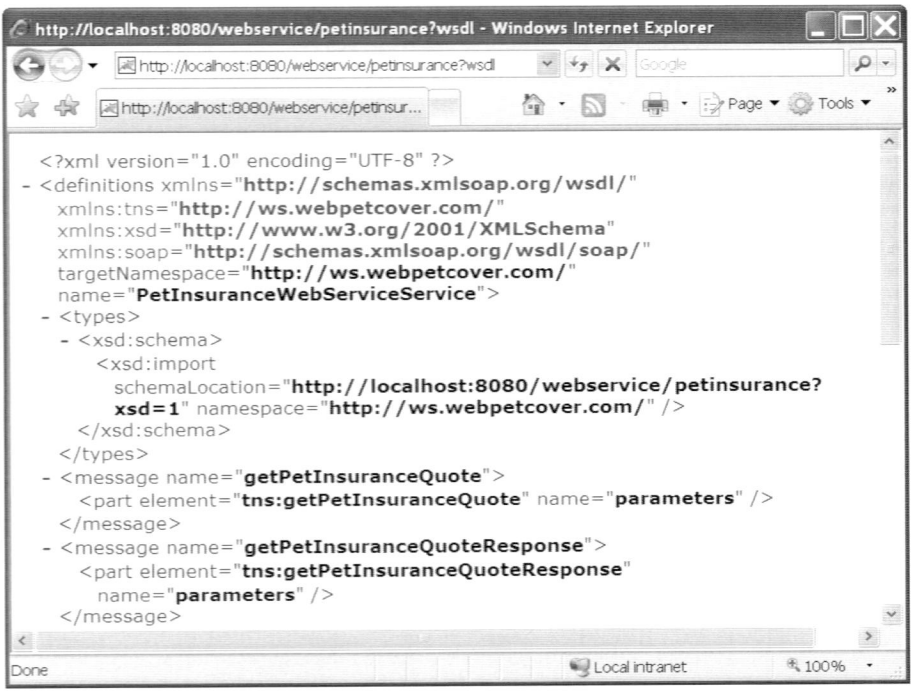

14.5 Integrating web services with web applications

So far in this book we have been describing how to build web applications completely independently of a particular Integrated Development Environment (IDE). In the previous section, we saw that it was fairly straightforward to develop a web service and deploy it on a test server using just the facilities included with Java 6.0. Unfortunately, when we come to integrating web services with web applications, generating the necessary Java code and hand coding all the configuration files is complex and tedious. Therefore for this example we use the NetBeans 5.5 Integrated Development Environment to build both a web service and a web service client using separate web applications that can be deployed to Tomcat.

The first step is to create a new NetBeans web Application project (select 'New Project ...' from the 'File' menu). In the dialog that appears, select the 'Web' folder in the left hand 'Categories' pane and 'Web Application' in the right hand 'Projects' pane (Figure 14.6).

After clicking the 'Next >' button, the 'Name and Location' stage of the dialog appear (Figure 14.7). Here, we give the project a name ('webpetcover') and a location. NetBeans will create a subfolder for the project beneath the location that you specify. Select 'Bundled Tomcat (5.5.1.7)' as the application server, and make sure the 'Set Source Level to 1.4' check box is NOT checked (we need the source level to be 1.5), then click the 'Finish' button. This will create the 'webpetcover' web application in the NetBeans environment.

FIGURE 14.6   Creating a new web Application in NetBeans 5.5

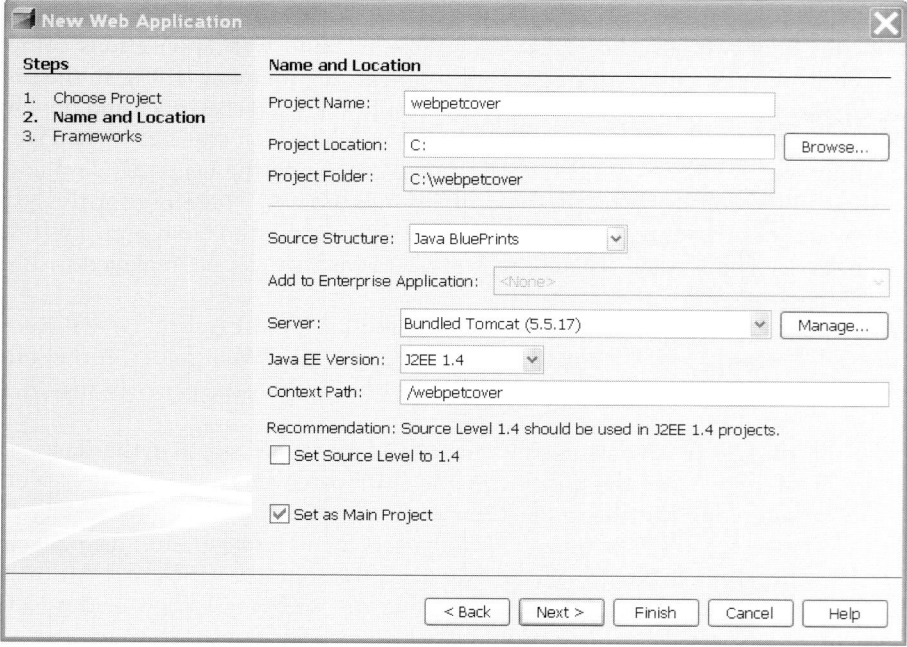

FIGURE 14.7   Setting the project name, location, server and source level in the 'Name and Location' section of the 'New Web Application' dialog

| NOTE | The project name is used as the default name of the context root of the web application. This can be edited in the 'Context Path' text field. However for this example we use a lower case project name to generate a lower case web application context. |

The next step is to create a web service within this web application. To do this, right click on the project name in the 'Projects' tab, then select 'New. . .Web Service' from the pop-up menu. You will see a dialog like the one in Figure 14.8. Enter 'petinsurance' for the 'Web Service Name', and 'com.webpetcover.ws' for the 'Package'. Then click the 'Finish' button.

| NOTE | The web service name should use Pascal case (upper case first letter and upper case for the first letter of any embedded words) because this name is used for a generated Java class. |

NetBeans will create the basic template for the implementation of your web service, which will look something like this.

```
/*
 * PetInsurance.java
*/

package com.pethomecover.ws;

import javax.jws.WebService;

/**
 * @author
 */

@WebService()
public class PetInsurance {
}
```

FIGURE 14.8 Creating the PetInsurance web service

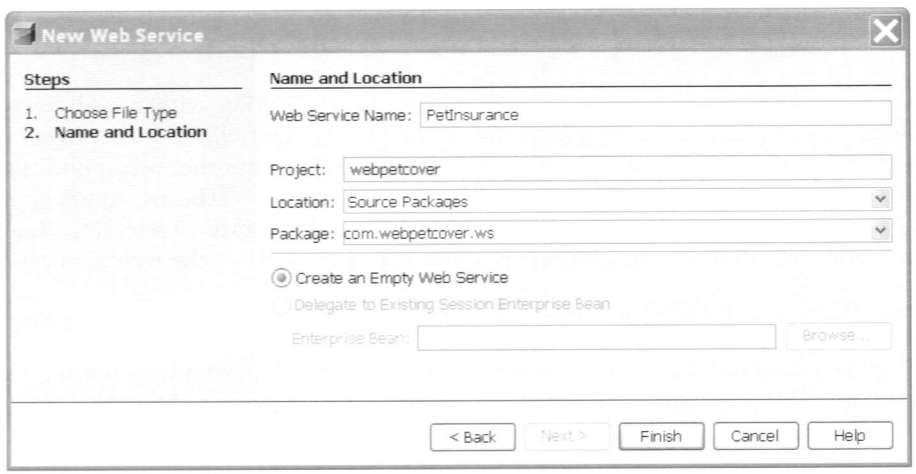

The 'PetInsurance.java' source file that has been created contains a class called 'PetInsurance', with no methods. Note however that the class has the annotation '@WebService()', which indicates that this class will be used to implement a web service (the extraneous parentheses can be removed).

The next step is to implement the service by providing one or more methods. For this example, we use exactly the same code as we did in the Java 6.0 web service example: a method that calculates pet insurance based on the type of animal and its age.

```java
@WebService
public class PetInsurance
{
    @WebMethod
    public double getPetInsuranceQuote(String animalType, int age)
    {
        if(animalType.equalsIgnoreCase("cat"))
        {
            return 20 * (age / 10.0);
        }
        if(animalType.equalsIgnoreCase("dog"))
        {
            return 30 * (age / 10.0);
        }
        if(animalType.equalsIgnoreCase("rabbit"))
        {
            return 10 * (age / 10.0);
        }
        if(animalType.equalsIgnoreCase("crocodile"))
        {
            return 50 * (age / 10.0);
        }
        return -1.0;
    }
}
```

Remember that if you add the 'WebMethod' annotation before the operation, you also need to add the import for the related class:

```java
import javax.jws.WebMethod;
```

That is pretty much all there is to building a web application with a web service in NetBeans. All you have to do now is deploy it. To do this, right click on the project in the 'Projects' tab and select 'Deploy Project'. This builds and deploys the web application and its web service to the version of Tomcat that is bundled with NetBeans, running on port 8084. You can test that your web application has deployed properly by selecting 'Run Main Project' from the 'Run' menu. This opens a browser at the URI of the web application:

```
http://localhost:8084/webpetcover/
```

However, this does not access the web service that has been deployed with the application, only a simple JSP page. To test that your web service has deployed, direct the browser to the following URI:

```
http://localhost:8084/webpetcover/PetInsurance
```

FIGURE 14.9 The window that appears at the web service URI

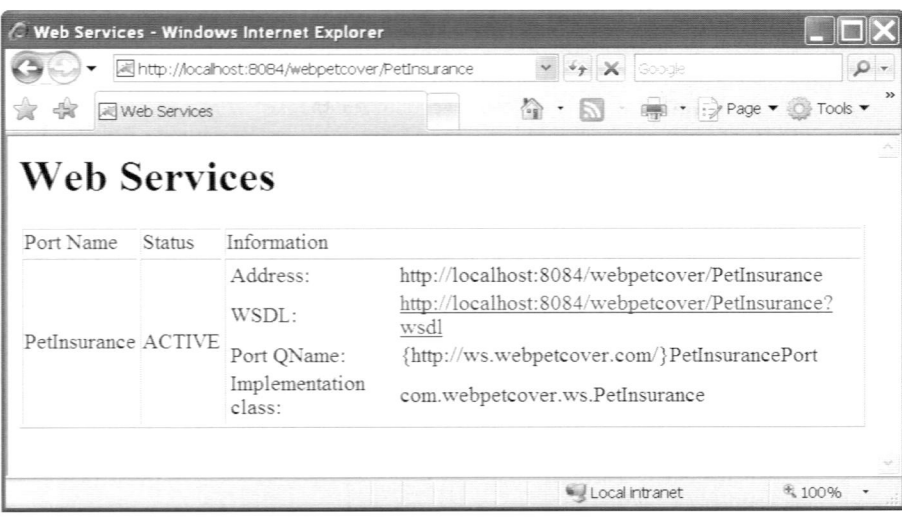

The browser window should display a web page that shows the web service is active, including a hyperlink to the generated WSDL file (Figure 14.9).

The link to the WSDL file is

```
http://localhost:8084/webpetcover/PetInsurance?wsdl
```

Here is the complete WSDL file that appears if you click on this link. This WSDL is generated by the web service implementation classes; it is not a static file. As we see later, its contents vary depending on where the service is deployed. Here, for example, it shows the port number as being 8084, because that is the port number currently used by the server. This contrasts with our earlier WSDL example using the test server provided with Java 6.0, which was running on port 8080.

```
<?xml version="1.0" encoding="UTF-8" ?>
<definitions xmlns:tns="http://ws.webpetcover.com/"
  xmlns:xsd="http://www.w3.org/2001/XMLSchema"
  xmlns:soap="http://schemas.xmlsoap.org/wsdl/soap/"
  xmlns="http://schemas.xmlsoap.org/wsdl/"
  targetNamespace="http://ws.webpetcover.com/"
  name="PetInsuranceService">
<types>
  <xsd:schema>
    <xsd:import namespace="http://ws.webpetcover.com/"
schemaLocation="http://localhost:8084/webpetcover/PetInsurance?xsd=1" />
  </xsd:schema>
</types>
  <message name="getPetInsuranceQuote">
    <part element="tns:getPetInsuranceQuote" name="parameters" />
  </message>
  <message name="getPetInsuranceQuoteResponse">
```

```
          <part element="tns:getPetInsuranceQuoteResponse" name="parameters" />
        </message>
        <portType name="PetInsurance">
          <operation name="getPetInsuranceQuote">
          <input message="tns:getPetInsuranceQuote" />
          <output message="tns:getPetInsuranceQuoteResponse" />
          </operation>
        </portType>
        <binding type="tns:PetInsurance" name="PetInsurancePortBinding">
        <soap:binding style="document"
            transport="http://schemas.xmlsoap.org/soap/http" />
        <operation name="getPetInsuranceQuote">
          <soap:operation soapAction="" />
          <input>
            <soap:body use="literal" />
          </input>
          <output>
            <soap:body use="literal" />
          </output>
        </operation>
        </binding>
        <service name="PetInsuranceService">
          <port binding="tns:PetInsurancePortBinding" name="PetInsurancePort">
            <soap:address
              location="http://localhost:8084/webpetcover/PetInsurance" />
          </port>
        </service>
      </definitions>
```

If you look at the WSDL, you can see that it also defines the location of the XML Schema used by the web service:

```
http://localhost:8084/webpetcover/PetInsurance?xsd=1
```

This is what the XML Schema contains. It basically specifies the names and types of the input and output message bodies.

```
<?xml version="1.0" encoding="UTF-8" ?>
<xs:schema xmlns:xs="http://www.w3.org/2001/XMLSchema"
    targetNamespace="http://ws.webpetcover.com/" version="1.0">
  <xs:element xmlns:ns1="http://ws.webpetcover.com/"
    name="getPetInsuranceQuote" type="ns1:getPetInsuranceQuote" />
  <xs:complexType name="getPetInsuranceQuote">
    <xs:sequence>
      <xs:element name="arg0" type="xs:string" minOccurs="0" />
      <xs:element name="arg1" type="xs:int" />
    </xs:sequence>
    </xs:complexType>
  <xs:element xmlns:ns2="http://ws.webpetcover.com/"
    name="getPetInsuranceQuoteResponse"
    type="ns2:getPetInsuranceQuoteResponse" />
  <xs:complexType
```

14

```
            name="getPetInsuranceQuoteResponse">
        <xs:sequence>
          <xs:element name="return" type="xs:double" />
        </xs:sequence>
    </xs:complexType>
  </xs:schema>
```

You may wonder what files NetBeans has generated in order to make a deployable web service. In fact, there is not that much to it really. If you look in the 'dist' folder of the 'WebPetCover' project folder, you will find the deployable WAR file containing the web application. Figure 14.10 shows the files in this WAR file:

There is a default welcome page called 'index.jsp', which is irrelevant to the web service but is useful to check if the web application is deployed. There is a largely empty 'context.xml' file for Tomcat in the 'META-INF' folder, and a lot of JAR files in the 'WEB-INF\lib' folder that support the JAX-WS implementation. In fact, it is the code in these JAR files that does most of the work. In the 'classes' folder are the compiled class files for the same two Java classes that we saw when we created the web service with Java 6.0, 'getPetInsurance Quote' and 'getPetInsuranceQuoteResponse'. (The generated source files are elsewhere in the NetBeans folder structure.) The only other components of the web application are 'web-xml' and another configuration file called 'sun-jaxws.xml'. This is the contents of the 'web.xml' file, the main part of which relates to the registration of a JAX-WS servlet called 'WSServlet', which is deployed using the URL 'PetInsurance'. There is also a reference to a 'listener' class. A listener is a class that can be triggered by certain events. A servlet context listener, like the one referred to in the file, is a class that responds to the main servlet lifecycle events of initialization and destruction, which are managed by the server.

```
<?xml version="1.0" encoding="UTF-8"?>
<?xml version="1.0" encoding="UTF-8"?>
<web-app version="2.4" xmlns="http://java.sun.com/xml/ns/j2ee"
    xmlns:xsi="http://www.w3.org/2001/XMLSchema-instance"
    xsi:schemaLocation="http://java.sun.com/xml/ns/j2ee
    http://java.sun.com/xml/ns/j2ee/web-app_2_4.xsd">
```

FIGURE 14.10   The files in the WebPetCover.war file

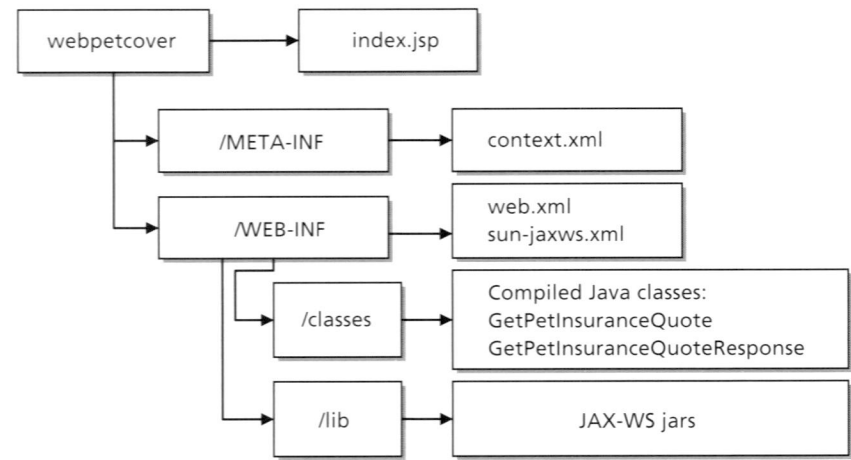

```
<listener>
  <listener-class>
    com.sun.xml.ws.transport.http.servlet.WSServletContextListener
  </listener-class>
</listener>

<servlet>
  <servlet-name>PetInsurance</servlet-name>
  <servlet-class>
    com.sun.xml.ws.transport.http.servlet.WSServlet
  </servlet-class>
  <load-on-startup>1</load-on-startup>
</servlet>

<servlet-mapping>
  <servlet-name>PetInsurance</servlet-name>
  <url-pattern>/PetInsurance</url-pattern>
</servlet-mapping>

<session-config>
  <session-timeout>
    30
  </session-timeout>
</session-config>

<welcome-file-list>
  <welcome-file>
    index.jsp
  </welcome-file>
 </welcome-file-list>
</web-app>
```

This is the 'sun-jaxws.xml' file, which maps the implementation class 'com.webpetcover.ws.
PetInsurance' to the 'PetInsurance' URL pattern:

```
<?xml version="1.0" encoding="UTF-8"?>
<endpoints version="2.0"
  xmlns="http://java.sun.com/xml/ns/jax-ws/ri/runtime">
  <endpoint implementation="com.webpetcover.ws.PetInsurance"
    name="PetInsurance"
    url-pattern="/PetInsurance"/>
</endpoints>
```

At the moment, the web service is running on the version of Tomcat bundled with
NetBeans running on port 8084. However, it is very easy to deploy the web application
to a standalone Tomcat server, simply by copying the WAR file from the 'dist' folder of
your NetBeans project to the 'webapps' folder of your Tomcat installation (or the
'deploy' folder if using Tomcat with JBoss). If you start Tomcat and direct the browser
to the web service (this time running on the default port number, port 80, which we
configured Tomcat to use in Chapter 9) then the WSDL is also generated using port 80
(Figure 14.11).

FIGURE 14.11 The web page that displays details of the PetInsurance web service, including a link to the WSDL, deployed on a server using port 80.

14.6 Developing a web service client

Because web services provide interoperability between different types of system using XML messaging, a web service client may be developed using any of a number of different technologies. However, for our particular example we need to be able to integrate the web service from WebPetCover into the Java web application used by WebHomeCover. Therefore we need to be able to create a web service client running in a Java web application. Again, NetBeans provides us with the tools to do this. First, we need to create another project to represent the client web application. The first steps are exactly the same as before. Select 'New Project . . . ' from the 'File' menu. In the dialog that appears, select the 'Web' folder in the left hand 'Categories' pane and 'Web Application' in the right hand 'Projects' pane. This time, we call the project 'petinsuranceclient' (Figure 14.12).

Click the 'Finish' button, and NetBeans creates the web application. Now we need to add web service client code to the application. Before doing this, you need to make sure that the web service is running on port 80 of your Tomcat server. Then, right click on the project name in the 'Projects' tab, and from the pop-up menu select 'New' and then 'Web Service Client . . . ' In the dialog that appears (Figure 14.13), select the 'WSDL URL' radio button and then put the URL of the WSDL into the text box.

```
http://localhost/webpetcover/PetInsurance?wsdl
```

You can copy this from the browser window when the WSDL is being displayed.

You also need to enter the package name of the client code. For this example we will use 'com.webhomecover.wsclient'. Remember that the client application will be run on the WebHomeCover site, using a web service from the WebPetCover application.

After you click 'Finish', the necessary code will have been generated for the web service client within the web application, but we now need to add some code to actually invoke the web service. NetBeans makes this extremely simple. The 'index.jsp' page of your web

FIGURE 14.12 Creating the web service client web application

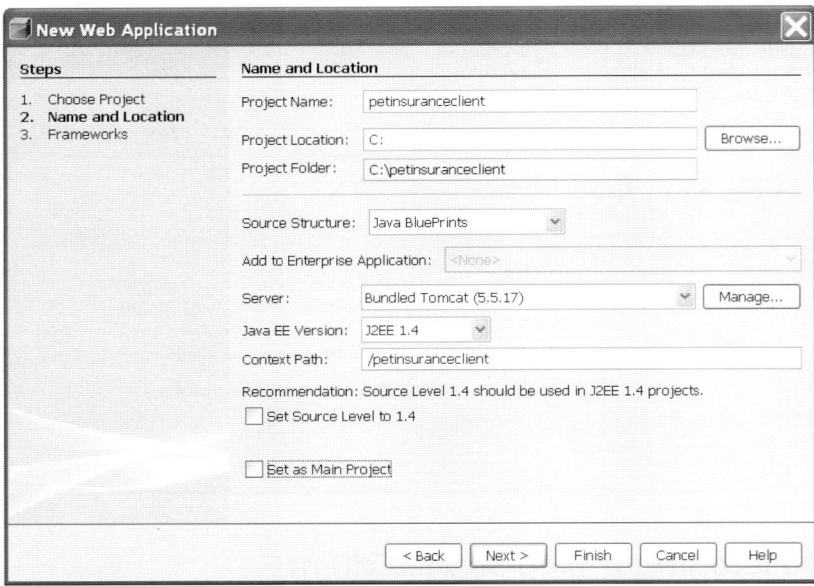

service client application should be open in NetBeans (if not, you'll find it listed under the 'Web Pages' folder). With the source to this JSP open, right click in the source code window and select 'Web Service Client Resource', then 'Call Web Service Operation'. A dialog appears showing the available web services (Figure 14.14).

You need to drill down the tree to select the name of the method, 'getPetInsuranceQuote', then press the 'OK' button. The following scriptlet is automatically inserted into the JSP.

```
<%-- start web service invocation --%><hr/>
<%
   try
   {
     com.webhomecover.wsclient.PetInsuranceService service =
       new com.webhomecover.wsclient.PetInsuranceService();
     com.webhomecover.wsclient.PetInsurance port =
       service.getPetInsurancePort();
   // TODO initialize WS operation arguments here
     java.lang.String arg0 = "";
     int arg1 = 0;
   // TODO process result here
     double result = port.getPetInsuranceQuote(arg0, arg1);
     out.println("Result = " + result);
   }
   catch(Exception ex)
   {
     // TODO handle custom exceptions here
   }
%>
<%-- end web service invocation --%><hr/>
```

FIGURE 14.13 Generating a web service client from the WSDL available from a
running Tomcat server

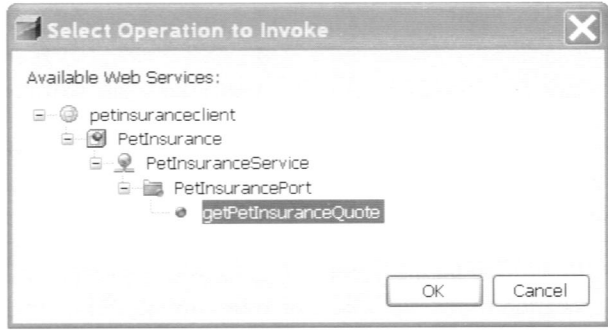

FIGURE 14.14 Selecting an available web service

The final step is to edit this scriptlet to provide actual values for the two arguments to the
'getPetInsuranceQuote' method. Here, the animal type is set to 'cat' and the age to '4'

```
java.lang.String arg0 = "cat";
int arg1 = 4;
```

If you make these changes, then build, deploy and run the project, you should see a JSP
page displayed in the browser that shows the value of the pet insurance quote (Figure 14.15).

Once again we can extract the generated WAR file from the project's 'dist' folder and
deploy it to a server running outside NetBeans. In a real system, of course, the web service
and the client would be running on different servers, but for this example we are running
the service and the client on the same server in separate web applications.

If you look at the contents of the deployed WAR file, you will see that there is no
'sun-jaxws.xml' file on the client, but there are several generated class files that implement
the web services client code used by the JSP, including an 'ObjectFactory', which you may

FIGURE 14.15 The web service client JSP running in Internet Explorer

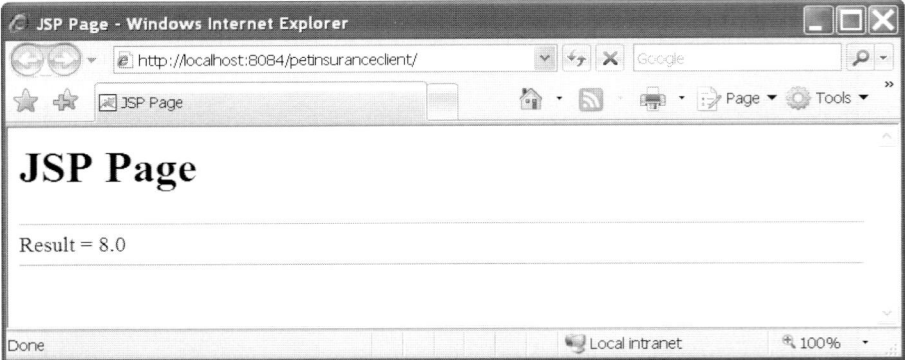

recall from our JAXB examples in Chapter 11. This time, the classes that can be created from the ObjectFactory are 'GetPetInsuranceQuote' (a class that represents the request to the web service) and 'GetPetInsuranceQuoteResponse' (a class that represents the response).

14.7 Integrating the web service into the WebHomeCover application

In the example so far, we have deployed two web applications: one that provides a web service from WebPetCover and another that consumes it. However what we want to do in our example scenario is to integrate the WebPetCover service into the WebHomeCover application. To do this, we simply need to add the appropriate page to interact with the web service, and copy the required library and class files across from the current web service client to our WebHomeCover application. You will need to extract all the files from the 'petinsurance-client.war' file into a temporary folder. Then all you need to do is copy the files from the 'lib' folder of the web application to the 'lib' folder of your current WebHomeCover build folders. Equally importantly, you also need to copy all the generated Java files to the 'java' folder so they can be compiled by your build process. You will find these in the following folder (Figure 14.16):

```
build\generated\wsimport\client\com\webhomecover\wsclient
```

We also need a new form page to select details of a pet. In addition, we need to create a new form bean class and a new front component on the server to process the new form's request. Finally, we need to add a JSP to call the web service and display the results.

Here is a JSP form page ('petdetails.jsp') with two select lists that enable the user to choose the animal type and age. There is no validation used here because in this simple example there is no possibility of invalid input. The select lists will always submit valid values to the web service.

```
<?xml version="1.0"?>
<!-- File: petdetails.jsp -->

<jsp:root xmlns:jsp="http://java.sun.com/JSP/Page"
  version="2.0">
<jsp:directive.page contentType="text/html"/>
<jsp:output omit-xml-declaration="false"
```

FIGURE 14.16 The folder location of the Java source files generated by
NetBeans for the web service client

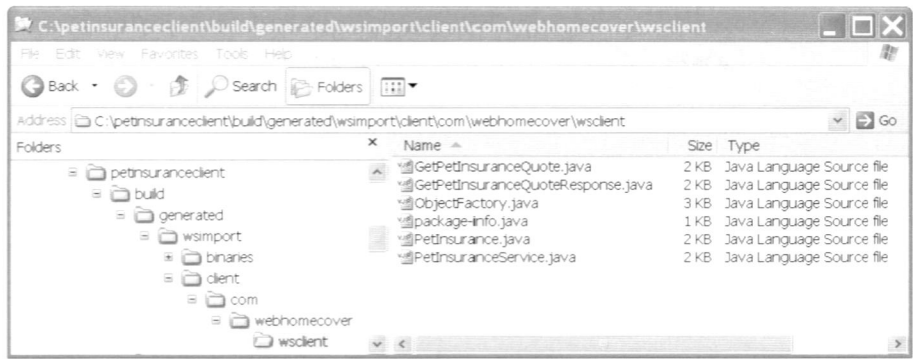

```
doctype-root-element="html"
doctype-public="-//W3C//DTD XHTML 1.1//EN"
doctype-system="http://www.w3.org/TR/xhtml11/DTD/xhtml11.dtd" />
<html xmlns="http://www.w3.org/1999/xhtml" xml:lang="en">
    <head>
        <link href="webhomecover.css" rel="stylesheet" type="text/css" />
        <title>Pet Insurance from WebPetCover</title>
    </head>
    <body>
        <h1>Pet Insurance from WebPetCover</h1>
        <h2>Our partner organization can give you a quote for pet insurance!</h2>
        <form action="petwebservice.jsp" method="post">
          <table>
            <tr>
              <td>Select the type of animal</td><td>
              <select name="animalType" size="1">
                <option value="cat">Cat</option>
                <option value="dog">Dog</option>
                <option value="rabbit">Rabbit</option>
                <option value="crocodile">Crocodile</option>
              </select>
              </td>
              </tr>
              <tr>
              <td>Select the age of the animal</td><td>
              <select name="age" size="1">
                <option value="1">1</option>
                <option value="2">2</option>
                <option value="3">3</option>
                <option value="4">4</option>
                <option value="5">5</option>
                <option value="6">6</option>
                <option value="7">7</option>
                <option value="8">8</option>
                <option value="9">9</option>
```

14

```
                    <option value="10">10</option>
                    <option value="11">11</option>
                    <option value="12">12</option>
                  </select>
                  </td>
              </tr>
              <tr>
            <td></td>
            <td><input type="submit" value="Submit" /></td>
          </tr>
        </table>
        </form>
        </body>
      </html>
    </jsp:root>
```

Figure 14.17 shows this form page displayed in Internet Explorer 7.

The associated form bean is a simple JavaBean with only two properties, 'animalType' and 'age'.

```
package com.webhomecover.beans;

import java.io.Serializable;

public class PetBean implements Serializable
{
   private String animalType;
   private int age;

   public void setAnimalType(String animalType)
   {
      this.animalType = animalType;
   }
```

FIGURE 14.17   The pet details form page

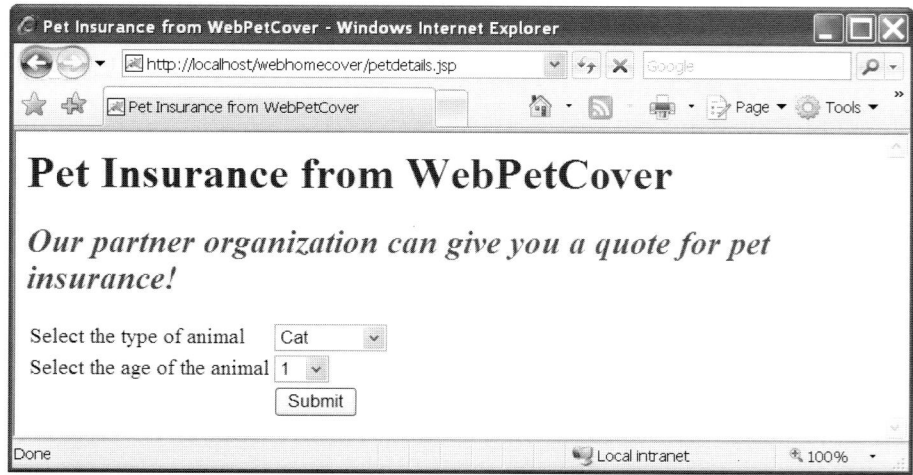

```
   public void setAge(int age)
   {
      this.age = age;
   }

   public String getAnimalType()
   {
      return animalType;
   }

   public int getAge()
   {
      return age;
   }
}
```

For this particular interaction we do not need a front component. In fact this client–server interaction works simply as a Model 1 architecture with a simple JSP ('petwebservice.jsp') that receives the request, invokes the web service and generates the response. The scriptlet here is a tidied up version of the generated code used in our earlier example and uses the request parameters to pass the form data to the web service (the service invocation is high-lighted in bold).

```
<?xml version="1.0"?>
<!-- File: petwebservice.jsp -->

<jsp:root xmlns:jsp="http://java.sun.com/JSP/Page"
      version="2.0">
  <jsp:directive.page contentType="text/html"/>
  <jsp:directive.page import="com.webhomecover.wsclient.*"/>

  <jsp:output omit-xml-declaration="false"
    doctype-root-element="html"
    doctype-public="-//W3C//DTD XHTML 1.1//EN"
    doctype-system="http://www.w3.org/TR/xhtml11/DTD/xhtml11.dtd" />

  <html xmlns="http://www.w3.org/1999/xhtml" xml:lang="en">
    <head>
       <link href="webhomecover.css" rel="stylesheet" type="text/css" />
       <title>Pet Insurance from WebPetCover</title>
    </head>
    <body>
       <h1>Pet Insurance from WebPetCover</h1>
       <!-- start web service invocation -->
       <hr/>
       <jsp:scriptlet>
        try
        {
           PetInsuranceWebServiceService service = new
             PetInsuranceWebServiceService();
           PetInsuranceWebService port =
```

```
            service.getPetInsuranceWebServiceort();
        String animalType = request.getParameter("animalType");
        int age = Integer.parseInt(request.getParameter("age"));
        double result = port.getPetInsuranceQuote(animalType, age);
        out.println("The insurance quote for your " + age + "-year-old " +
            animalType + " is $" + result);
    }
    catch(Exception ex)
    {
        out.println(ex);
    }
    </jsp:scriptlet>
    <!-- end web service invocation -->
    <hr/>
    </body>
    </html>
    </jsp:root>
```

Figure 14.18 shows the result of calling the web service for a 1-year-old cat.

14.8 Server-side Ajax

In Chapter 8, we saw how JavaScript can be used on the client to implement Ajax code that can make asynchronous requests to the server and process the response without requiring the current page to be reloaded. In the second part of this chapter, we look at the server side of an Ajax implementation, and see how we can refactor our 'make insurance claim' use case to use Ajax.

There are two main advantages to an Ajax implementation: a more interactive user experience (due to the ability to make asynchronous calls to the server and rebuild the current page using DHTML) and a reduction in network traffic (because we do not need

FIGURE 14.18   The resulting web page when calling the web service for a pet insurance quote

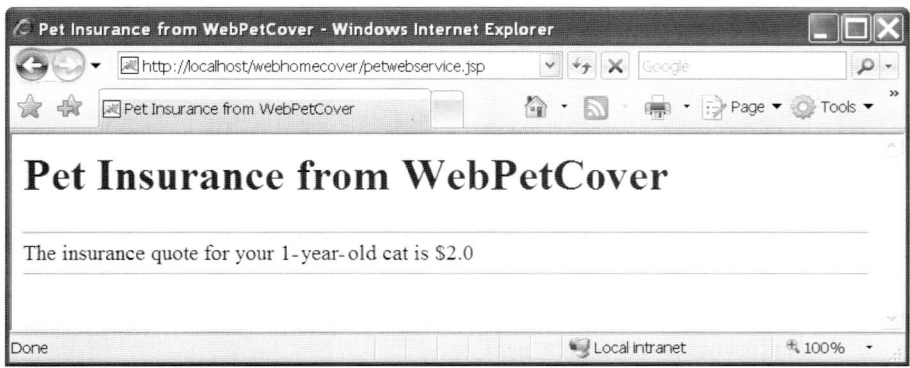

to download the entire page content for every update). Our current use case takes the course illustrated in Figure 14.19, where the claim form page submits to the web application via the 'processclaim.jsp', which then forwards to the appropriate view JSP to build the response, either 'displayclaim.jsp' or 'notfound.jsp'. If validation fails, however, the 'claimform.jsp' page is rebuilt with error messages. This process involves the building of several different client pages. Where the claim form fails validation, the whole page must be rebuilt to display, in some cases, a single error message.

In contrast, the Ajax webflow is based around a single page that calls an Ajax function to update its content. It sends an XMLHttpRequest to a server-side front component, which could be either a servlet or a JSP. This component does not forward to a new view component. Instead, it generates an XML document and sends it back directly as a response (Figure 14.20). In this architecture, the Ajax JSP ('ajaxclaimform.jsp') sends

FIGURE 14.19 The view–controller layer components and dependencies of the current use case implementation for making an insurance claim

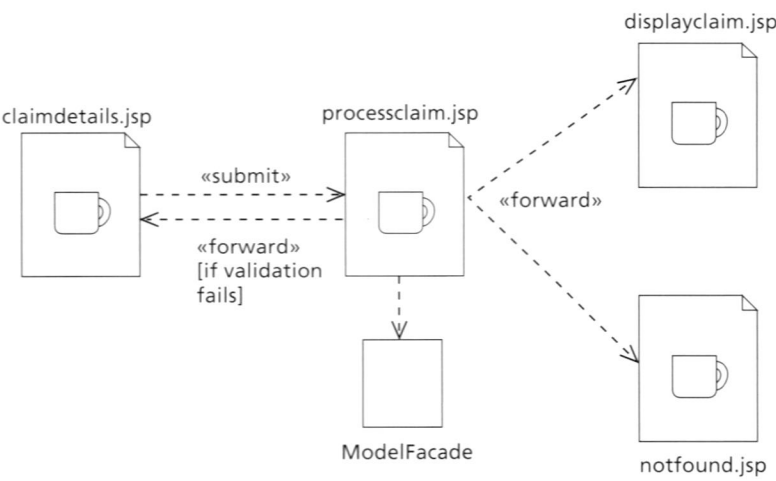

FIGURE 14.20 The view–controller layer components and dependencies of the Ajax-based implementation for the 'make insurance claim' use case

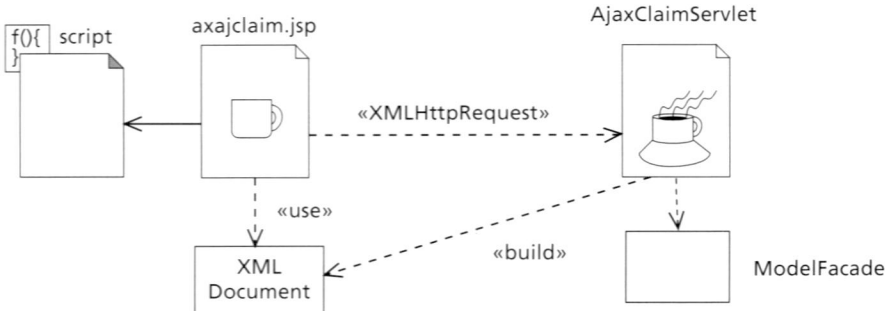

an XMLHttpRequest to a servlet. The servlet class receives this request, and responds with an XML document that is used by the script associated with the Ajax JSP to rebuild the current page. The XML document is generated via the underlying model, using the façade. The script component (containing JavaScript functions) provides the client-side Ajax implementation and local validation using DHTML.

Here is the 'ajaxclaim.jsp' server page that integrates some Ajax functionality. Much of the page is similar to previous versions of the claim form, but there are some important differences. These have been highlighted in bold text (and we will examine each of them in turn).

```
<?xml version="1.0"?>
<!-- File: ajaxclaimform.jsp -->

<!DOCTYPE html PUBLIC "-//W3C//DTD XHTML 1.1//EN"
   "http://www.w3.org/TR/xhtml11/DTD/xhtml11.dtd">
<html xmlns="http://www.w3.org/1999/xhtml" xml:lang="en">
   <head>
      <title>Insurance Claim Form</title>
      <link href="webhomecover.css" rel="stylesheet" type="text/css" />
      <script type="text/javascript" src="getxmlhttprequest.js">
      </script>
      <script type="text/javascript" src="ajaxclaim.js">
      </script>
   </head>
   <body>
      <h1>Please enter the details of your claim</h1>
      <h2>Please provide information about your claim in the form below,
          then click submit</h2>
     <table>
      <tr>
       <td><label for="policyNumber">Policy Number:</label></td>
       <td>
         <input type="text" id="policyNumber" name="policyNumber" />
       </td><td id="policymessage" class="errormessage"></td>
      </tr>
      <tr>
       <td><label for="claim">Amount Claimed:</label></td>
       <td><input type="text" id="claim" name="claim" /></td>
       <td id="claimmessage" class="errormessage"></td>
      </tr>
      <tr>
      <td></td><td>
       <input type="radio" name="type" value="buildings" id="buildings" />
       Make a buildings insurance claim
      </td><td id="typemessage" class="errormessage"></td>
      </tr>
      <tr>
      <td></td><td>
         <input type="radio" name="type" value="contents" id="contents" />
         Make a contents insurance claim
         </td>
```

```
        </tr>
        <tr>
          <td><label for="description">Description of claim:</label></td>
          <td>
            <textarea id="description" name="description" rows="5" cols="30">
            </textarea>
          </td><td id="descriptionmessage" class="errormessage"></td>
        </tr>
        <tr>
          <td></td>
          <td>
            <input type="button" onclick="ajaxClaim();" value="Submit" />
          </td>
        </tr>
      </table>
    <div id="returnmessage"></div>
  </body>
</html>
```

Within the head element of the document we have two 'script' elements. One of these refers to the 'getxmlhttprequest.js' file that we introduced in Chapter 8. The other script file ('ajaxclaim.js') contains the implementation code for the Ajax interaction used in the example.

Inside the form itself, there are four table data ('td') elements (one for each part of the form data) that belong to the 'errormessage' class and are given unique 'id' attributes. These are used to display validation error messages using DHTML. Here is one of these elements, for the policy number error message:

```
<td id="policymessage" class="errormessage">
```

The 'errormessage' class relates to the CSS style sheet, so that we can style error messages in a particular way, for example with red text:

```
.errormessage {color: red}
```

You may have noticed that the page does not contain form elements, that the button is not of the 'submit' type. With an Ajax interaction, instead of supplying a form to the server, we send data using JavaScript and the XMLHttpRequest. The button component on the page, when clicked, invokes a JavaScript function called 'ajaxClaim', which is defined in the 'ajaxclaim.js' file.

```
<input type="button" onclick="ajaxClaim();" value="Submit" />
```

The final change from the previous version of the page is the empty 'div' element with the id 'returnmessage'. This is used by the JavaScript Ajax function to write response data to the page.

```
<div id="returnmessage"></div>
```

Most of the client-side work, of course, will be done by the Ajax function contained in 'ajaxclaim.js'. This file defines two functions, 'ajaxClaim', which includes some DHTML

14

form validation, and sends an asynchronous XMLHttpRequest call to the server, and 'processMessage', which processes the XML document that is returned by the response to the XMLHttpRequest. We begin by looking at the function that sends the XMLHttpRequest to the server, then look at the server-side code, then finally come back and look at the second JavaScript function.

Here is the first part of the code for the first JavaScript function, 'ajaxClaim', which uses the DOM to set the values of a set of variables from the components on the form. Note that the first variable ('strPolicyNumber') is global (it is not preceded with 'var'). This is so it can also be visible to the other function. Unlike the validation function we looked at in Chapter 8, there is no form passed to this function as a parameter, since there is no form used on the page. Therefore we need to navigate to the page components via the 'document' object.

```
function ajaxClaim()
{
    // make this a global variable – also used in the processMessage function
    strPolicyNumber = document.getElementById("policyNumber").value;
    var fltAmount = document.getElementById("claim").value;
    var strDescription = document.getElementById("description").value;
    var booContents = document.getElementById("contents").checked;
    var booBuildings = document.getElementById("buildings").checked;
    var booValid = true;
```

This is followed by some code that simply initializes all of the error messages and returns message elements used by this function, by setting their 'innerHTML' properties to empty strings. This is necessary so that each time the function is called, any existing messages are cleared from the page.

```
document.getElementById("policymessage").innerHTML="";
document.getElementById("claimmessage").innerHTML="";
document.getElementById("typemessage").innerHTML="";
document.getElementById("descriptionmessage").innerHTML="";
document.getElementById("returnmessage").innerHTML="";
```

The next part of the function does some DHTML form validation. The validation processes are the same as those we have used before, but instead of using a JavaScript alert, we write the error messages to the page using the elements of the page with unique ids. This is DHTML rather than Ajax, because we are not sending anything to the server using the XMLHttpRequest if there are validation errors in the form. Instead, we check the data on the client and write error messages to the page using the 'innerHTML' property of the error message 'td' elements. Using this example perhaps helps to illustrate the main difference between DHTML and Ajax; it is only Ajax if it uses the XMLHttpRequest. At the end of the validation process, if the Boolean variable 'booValid' has been set to 'false, then the function simply returns, without going on to send a request to the server.

```
// validation error checks
    if(strPolicyNumber == "")
    {
        document.getElementById("policymessage").innerHTML=
            "Please provide a policy number";
        booValid = false;
    }
```

```
    if(fltAmount == "")
    {
      document.getElementById("claimmessage").innerHTML=
        "Please provide a claim amount";
      booValid = false;
    }
    else
    {
      var strValidChars = "0123456789.";
      var chrCurrentChar;
      for (i = 0; i < fltAmount.length && booValid; i++)
    {
      chrCurrentChar = fltAmount.charAt(i);
      if(strValidChars.indexOf(chrCurrentChar) == -1)
      {
        document.getElementById("claimmessage").innerHTML=
          "Please provide a numeric claim amount";
        booValid = false;
      }
    }
  }
}

if(!booBuildings && !booContents)
{
  document.getElementById("typemessage").innerHTML=
    "Please select either buildings or contents insurance";
  booValid = false;
}
if(strDescription == "")
{
  document.getElementById("descriptionmessage").innerHTML=
    "Please provide a description";
  booValid = false;
}

if(!booValid)
{
  return;
}
```

This part of the function is necessary in order to build the parameter string that is to be sent to the server. We need to be able to provide a value to the 'type' attribute, based on the state of the radio buttons.

```
var strType="type";
  if(booContents)
  {
    strType="contents";
  }
  else
  {
    strType="buildings";
  }
```

The next part of the function creates a URL string that includes a parameter list to be sent to the server.

```
var url="processajaxclaim?policyNumber=" + strPolicyNumber + "&claim=" +
fltAmount + "&type=" + strType + "&description=" + strDescription;
```

Finally, we use an XMLHttpRequest object to send the request to the server. This code is very similar to the code we saw in Chapter 8, except for the name of the function that is called by the 'onreadystatechange' event. Note that we are sending a 'post' request. This is important because we have to make sure our server-side front component can process 'post' requests.

```
xhrequest = null;
  try
  {
    xhrequest = getXMLHttpRequest();
  }
  catch(error)
  {
    document.write("Cannot run Ajax code using this browser");
  }
  if(xhrequest != null)
  {
    xhrequest.onreadystatechange = processMessage;
    xhrequest.open("post", url, true);
    xhrequest.send(null);
  }
}
```

So much for sending the XMLHttpRequest, but what happens when it is sent to the server? We need to implement a server-side front component that can receive the request and send back an XML document. We could use either a servlet or a JSP for this, since it will not be a view component. We use a servlet in this example. The disadvantage is that, without JSP tags, we must manually create an instance of the ClaimBean and populate its properties. On the other hand, the method is very simple Java, and probably easier to read and write than the equivalent JSP. Because the Ajax JavaScript function sends a 'post' request, we must implement the 'doPost' method in the servlet. The process that takes place inside this method (shown in the following code listing) is similar to the one we have used before, where we populate a claimBean from the request, pass the claimBean to the ModelFacade and get back either a populated Claim object or a null reference. However, instead of forwarding to a view component, the servlet needs to write an XML document to the response. If the Claim reference is not null, the servlet writes the XML document to the response by calling the object's 'getXmlDocument' method. On the other hand, if the Claim object reference is null (this will happen if the account number is not found) then a very short XML document is written to the response, containing an empty element named 'policynotfound'.

```
package com.webhomecover.servlet;

import javax.servlet.ServletException;
import javax.servlet.http.HttpServlet;
```

```
import javax.servlet.http.HttpServletRequest;
import javax.servlet.http.HttpServletResponse;
import java.io.IOException;
import java.io.PrintWriter;

import com.webhomecover.beans.ClaimBean;
import com.webhomecover.model.Claim;
import com.webhomecover.model.ModelFacade;

public class AjaxClaimServlet extends HttpServlet
{

   public void doPost(HttpServletRequest request, HttpServletResponse response)
   throws ServletException, IOException
   {
// get a PrintWriter from the response object
   PrintWriter out = response.getWriter();

   ClaimBean claimBean = new ClaimBean();
   claimBean.setPolicyNumber(request.getParameter("policyNumber"));
   claimBean.setClaim(request.getParameter("claim"));
   claimBean.setType(request.getParameter("type"));
   claimBean.setDescription(request.getParameter("description"));

// write out the response
   Claim claim = ModelFacade.createClaim(claimBean);
   if(claim != null)
   {
      out.print(claim.getXmlDocument());
// close the output stream
      out.close();
   }
   else
   {
      out.println
         ("<?xml version=\"1.0\"?><policynotfound></policynotfound>");
// close the output stream
      out.close();
   }
  }
}
```

We need to register this servlet in the 'web.xml' file, giving it the URL used in the JavaScript function, namely 'processajaxclaim', so that when the JavaScript function sends its request it is routed to the servlet:

```
<servlet>
   <servlet-name>AjaxClaimServlet</servlet-name>
   <servlet-class>
     com.webhomecover.servlet.AjaxClaimServlet
   </servlet-class>
</servlet>
```

```
<servlet-mapping>
    <servlet-name>AjaxClaimServlet</servlet-name>
    <url-pattern>/processajaxclaim</url-pattern>
</servlet-mapping>
```

Back on the client, which receives the XML response, the second function, 'processMessage', is triggered by the 'onreadystatechange' event of the XMLHttpRequest. Most of the function is taken up with using the DOM to retrieve the data from the XML document, followed by using the innerHTML property to write the content to the page. If the root element of the returned XML document is 'policynotfound', then an error message is written to the page, using the global 'policyNumber' variable. Otherwise, we process the XML document that contains the claim details. The DOM processing looks a little clumsy because we are using the 'getElementsByTagName' method, which means we then have to access the first element of each of the resulting sets of elements (though in fact there will be only one in each case). However this is a reliable approach across different browsers.

```
function processMessage()
{
    if(xhrequest.readyState == 4) // Complete
    {
        if(xhrequest.status == 200) // OK response
        {
            var root = xhrequest.responseXML.documentElement.nodeName;
            if(root=="policynotfound")
            {
                document.getElementById("returnmessage").innerHTML=
                    "<h3>Cannot find policy number " + strPolicyNumber + "</h3>";
            }
            else
            {
                var claimTypes = xhrequest.responseXML.getElementsByTagName('type');
                var firstClaimType = claimTypes[0];
                var references =
                    xhrequest.responseXML.getElementsByTagName('reference');
                var firstReference = references[0];
                var dates = xhrequest.responseXML.getElementsByTagName('date');
                var firstDate = dates[0];
                var amounts = xhrequest.responseXML.getElementsByTagName('amount');
                var firstAmount = amounts[0];
                var approveds =
                    xhrequest.responseXML.getElementsByTagName('approved');
                var firstApproved = approveds[0];
                var descriptions =
                    xhrequest.responseXML.getElementsByTagName('description');
                var firstDescription = descriptions[0];
                document.getElementById("returnmessage").innerHTML=
                    "<h3>Thank you, your claim has been registered, with the following
                        details</h3>" +
                    "<strong>Policy Number: </strong>" + strPolicyNumber +
                    "<br /><strong>Policy Type: </strong>" +
```

```
        firstClaimType.firstChild.nodeValue +
      "<br /><strong>Claim Date: </strong>" + firstDate.firstChild. nodeValue
      +"<br /><strong>Amount of Claim</strong> " +
      firstAmount.firstChild.nodeValue +
      "<h3> Please quote the reference number " +
      firstReference.firstChild.nodeValue +" in all correspondence</h3>";
    }
  }
 }
}
```

The following series of screen shots show the behavior of the Ajax application. Figure 14.21 shows the DHTML form validation in action. In this example, none of the required values has been provided, so four error messages are written to the body of the page. This is the same form page, rather than a regenerated one, as would be the case when using server-side validation. Unlike using the form validation in Chapter 8, we are not using JavaScript alerts. Of course this client-side validation would not work on browsers that do not support JavaScript, but then those browsers cannot support Ajax either!

Figure 14.22 shows what happens if an invalid account number is entered into the form. The XMLHttpRequest is sent to the server but, if the policy number is not found in the database, an error message is written to the current form page.

Finally, Figure 14.23 shows the page after a successful XMLHttpRequest to the server, using a valid set of data. The details of the claim are written to the page using the 'innerHTML' property. Some of these details are in the original form, but others (such as the claim date and the reference number) have been returned from the server-side process.

FIGURE 14.21   Writing error messages to a form page using DHTML

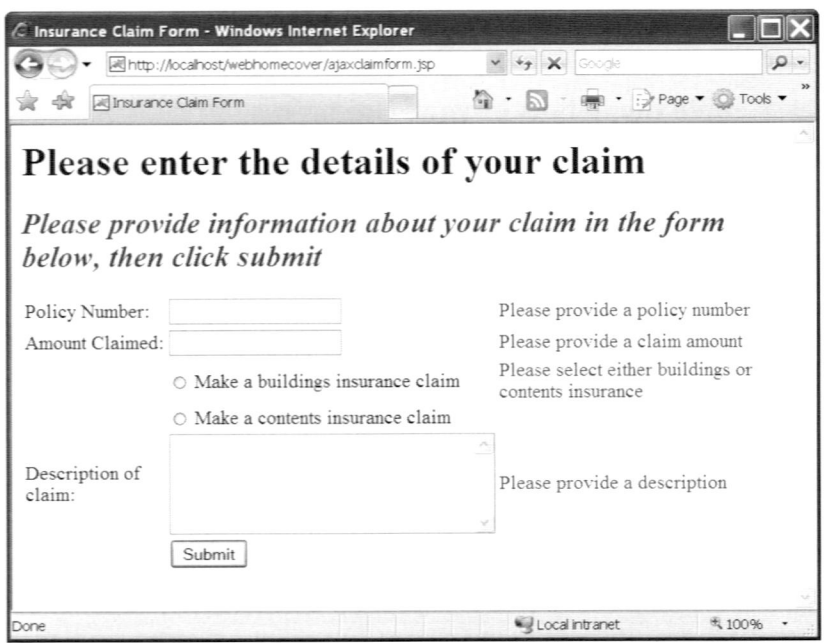

FIGURE 14.22 Ajax being used for server-side validation of the policy number

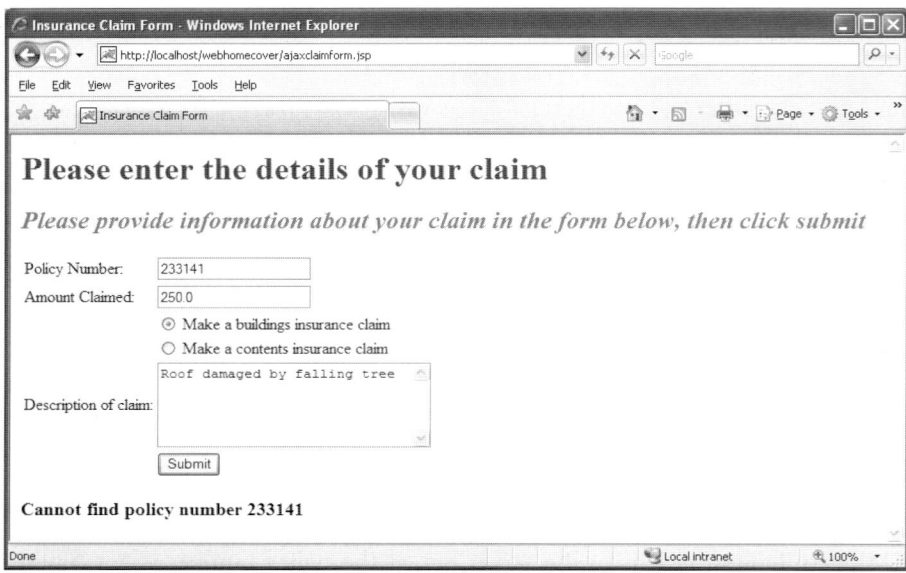

FIGURE 14.23 The Ajax form page showing the results of a successful lodging of an insurance claim

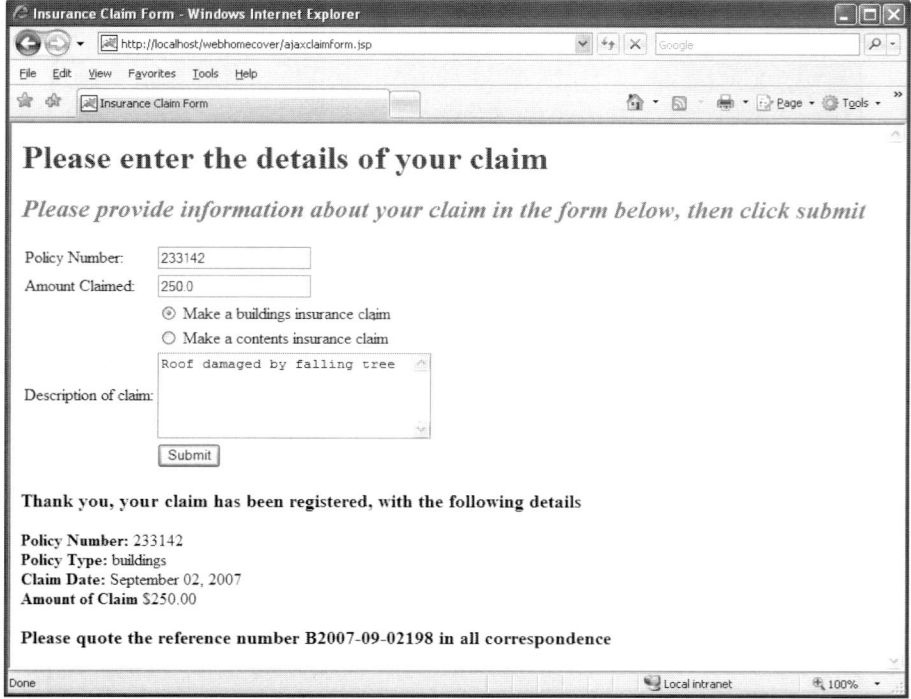

Exercises

In our earlier examples we created a web service for a pet insurance system. We also described how the pet insurance company might integrate home insurance quotes into their own web application. The first four exercises are based on that concept.

14.1 Using Java 6.0, create a web service that provides contents insurance quotes. Use the same parameter values that are already used in WebHomeCover's web application, namely whether accidental damage cover is required, the amount of the cover, and the deductible. You can use the existing 'getContentsQuote' method of the 'InsuranceQuoter' class as the basis for your implementation, though in this case a bean will not be passed as a parameter, but separate values. Once you have compiled your web service class and processed it with 'wsgen', check that you can access the generated WSDL using a browser directed to the 'localhost' server running on port 8080.

14.2 Using NetBeans, generate a web application that incorporates your web service class. Deploy the application to the NetBeans test server (running on port 8084) to check that it is running correctly. Then deploy the generated web application WAR file to your Tomcat server running on port 80. Check that the WSDL can be accessed on this server.

14.3 Using NetBeans, generate a web application client for your web service. Make sure that the server is running and generate the client based on the WSDL available from the server running on port 80.

14.4 Create part of a web application for WebPetCover that includes an HTML form to submit data to the web service (you can simply adapt the 'contents.jsp' page that we used in the 'WebHomeCover' application). Create a second JSP, invoked by the form page, which calls the web service and displays the result on the page.

Back in Chapter 8 we saw how to write a JavaScript client that used some Ajax techniques to connect to an RSS feed. In the following exercises, we develop both the client- and server-sides of an Ajax system that processes an RSS document. For this example, we use an RSS version 0.91 document because the elements are simpler and easier to process than later versions. Here is the example document:

```
<rss version="0.91">
  <channel>
    <title>The 'Lord of the Web' Trilogy</title>
    <link>http://www.thomsonlearning.co.uk</link>
    <description>Books on dynamic web application development from
Thomson Learning</description>
    <language>en</language>
    <item>
      <title>Dynamic Web Application Development with PHP and
      MySQL</title>
      <link>http://www.thomsonlearning.co.uk/stobart</link>
      <description>The first book in the trilogy is written by Simon
Stobart and David Parsons and focuses on the PHP language</description>
    </item>
    <item>
```

```
    <title>Dynamic Web Application Development with XML and Java</title>
    <link>http://www.thomsonlearning.co.uk/parsons</link>
    <description>The second book is by David Parsons, and provides more in-
depth coverage of XML, and uses Java as the implementation language</description>
   </item>
   <item>
    <title>Dynamic Web Application Development with .NET</title>
    <link>http://www.thomsonlearning.co.uk/gravell</link>
    <description>In the final book of the series, Andrew Gravell and
David Parsons cover the important aspects of developing web applications
using the Microsoft .NET framework</description>
   </item>
  </channel>
</rss>
```

You will need to work through the following steps to implement the Ajax RSS exercise.

14.5 Create a JSP page that contains a button or a JavaScript hyperlink to invoke a JavaScript function called 'ajaxGetRSS' (this is shown later). Include a 'div' element on the page (with an id) that you can write to using the innerHTML property when you implement the JavaScript function triggered by the XMLHttpRequest.

14.6 Write an Ajax function called 'processRSSFeed' that is able to process an RSS document and display all the 'title', 'link' and 'description' elements. In Chapter 8, we saw a simple implementation that was able to process an RSS document but only accessed the first description. In this example, you should use a 'for' loop to iterate through all of the titles, links and descriptions. Your 'processRSSFeed' function needs to be called by the 'onreadystatechange' event of the XMLHttpRequest. The following function ('ajaxGetRSS') does this, and connects to a server URL ('http://localhost/webhomecover/rssfeed'). It reuses the 'getXMLHttpRequest' function that we used in Chapter 8 (in the 'getxmlhttprequest.js' file).

```
function ajaxGetRSS()
{
  // no 'var', so this is a global variable!
  xhrequest = null;
  try
  {
    xhrequest = getXMLHttpRequest();
  }
  catch(error)
  {
    document.write("Cannot run Ajax code using this browser");
  }
  if(xhrequest != null)
  {
    xhrequest.onreadystatechange = processRSSFeed;
    xhrequest.open("post", "http://localhost/webhomecover/rssfeed", true);
    xhrequest.send(null);
  }
}
```

14.7 Create a servlet class called 'AjaxRSSServlet' with a 'doPost' method that reads the content of the XML file and streams it back to the client. Here is a suitable body for the 'doPost' method, which assumes the XML file is on the root of the 'C:' drive (you can change this path).

```
PrintWriter out = null;
try
{
    response.setContentType("text/xml");
    out = response.getWriter();
    File xmlfile = new File("c:/bookrss.xml");
    StringBuffer sb = new StringBuffer();
    BufferedReader br = new BufferedReader(new FileReader(xmlfile));
    String s = br.readLine();
    while (s != null)
    {
        sb.append(s.trim());
        s = br.readLine();
    }
    System.out.println(sb);
    out.print(sb);
}
catch(IOException e)
{
    e.printStackTrace();
    return null;
}
return null;
```

You should now be able to test your RSS reader JSP. You are recommended to test it using Mozilla Firefox because of its superior error console. Keep the error console open when attempting to run the application, then you will be able to see if any JavaScript errors occur.

14.8 If you feel ambitious, you might try to change the servlet class so that instead of streaming a local file it connects to an eternal RSS feed (check the version number is compatible with your code) and then streams that back to the client.

SUMMARY

In this chapter we covered two aspects of XML messaging between server and client. In the first part of the chapter we introduced web services, which enable XML messages over HTTP to be used as a common communication mechanism between different systems. We saw how common web service protocols such as WSDL and SOAP can be used with Java web applications to integrate third-party services into web applications. In the second part of the chapter we built on our previous Ajax examples running on the client to create a complete Ajax application with the server sending XML documents to the client for processing.

CHAPTER 15

Apache Struts Web Application Framework

LEARNING OBJECTIVES

- To understand how Struts can be used as a framework for building Java web applications

- To understand the design patterns that underlie the Struts architecture

- To be able to build and configure web applications using Struts

- To be able to use the Struts HTML and bean tag libraries

- To be able to create internationalized web applications

- To be able to use the JavaScript Struts validator

INTRODUCTION

Apache Struts is an open-source framework based on the model–view–controller architecture that supports the development of Java web applications. The name 'Struts' is not an acronym, it is simply meant to suggest the 'invisible underpinnings' of an integrated Java web architecture. Although there are now a very large number of frameworks available for developing Java web applications, Struts was the first of these frameworks. The original Apache Struts project was been launched in May 2000 by Craig McClanahan, with version 1.0 being released in July 2001. Since that time, many other Java web frameworks have been developed, and some of these have become widely used, including JavaServer Faces, Shale, Spring, Velocity, Tapestry and Cocoon (among many others). Some of these frameworks are complementary to Struts, and can be integrated with it, while others, such as Shale, actually began as subprojects of Struts. At the time of writing there are two development strands on the Struts project, one of which (Struts 2.0) is actually developed from another framework called WebWork, while Struts 1.x continues to be developed from the original framework. It remains to be seen how it will evolve, but in this book we concentrate on the original, mature framework.

Whether to choose Struts over other frameworks is a difficult decision in technical terms, since all of the popular frameworks have their own strengths (and weaknesses). The Struts documentation claims that:

> While some people characterize the space of Java web application framework as being "fragmented", the truth is that more web developers use Struts than all other alternatives combined (Apache Software Foundation 2007)

Regardless, you will also find that whichever framework you learn first, you will find many similarities between them, so learning one can help you to learn any of the others.

We already have the beginnings of a working web application using JSP Model 2 architecture, so why would we want to use a framework like Struts? Like any framework, the purpose of Struts is to save development effort by factoring out common code. Most web applications need the same basic set of components: some sort of controller that can handle client requests; a set of server-side components that can respond to these requests and process them accordingly; JavaBeans acting as Data Transfer Objects that can encapsulate the data entered into client form pages; tag libraries to assist in writing JSPs; and support for issues such as data validation, formatting and internationalization. Using a framework like Struts means that the overall architecture of these components is already in place, so you do not have to write it yourself. In addition, these components have been developed and tested by many people over many years, so the chances are that you will end up with a more robust application, as well developing it more quickly than you would if you built everything yourself from scratch.

15.1 Struts command and control patterns

Struts is based on implementing web applications using the model–view–controller (MVC) architecture. Within that architecture there are some fundamental design patterns that we introduce in this section. The web application we have worked with so far has also been based on MVC, using JSP Model 2, but without a supporting framework. The general pattern of interaction in our current Model 2 application is that each form page that submits to the server sends its data to a dedicated server page that processes the request. This is an example of the *page controller* pattern, which works on the basis that each page has its own controller (Fowler 2003). Therefore there is a server page for each form page, in a one-to-one relationship. Figure 15.1 shows how the page controller pattern results in many controllers being deployed into the web application, each one responsible for handling requests from a specific page, managing one small part of the overall webflow, and delegating processes to other server-side components (JavaBeans and view layer JSPs). The current implementation of the 'Get Insurance Quote' use case clearly follows this page controller pattern.

The page controller pattern is perfectly workable, and can be used to develop web applications without any major problems, However, it has the drawback that a web application built this way will have a proliferation of controllers, each one with its own processes. With this model it is difficult to identify much in the way of reusable components, because each controller is tailored to a particular page's request. In addition, the control of the overall webflow is spread amongst multiple components, making the page routing difficult to trace. One consequence of this is that it is difficult to build a reusable framework using the page controller pattern. An alternative approach, and the one that is used by Struts, is the *front controller* pattern.

FIGURE 15.1 The 'page controller' pattern

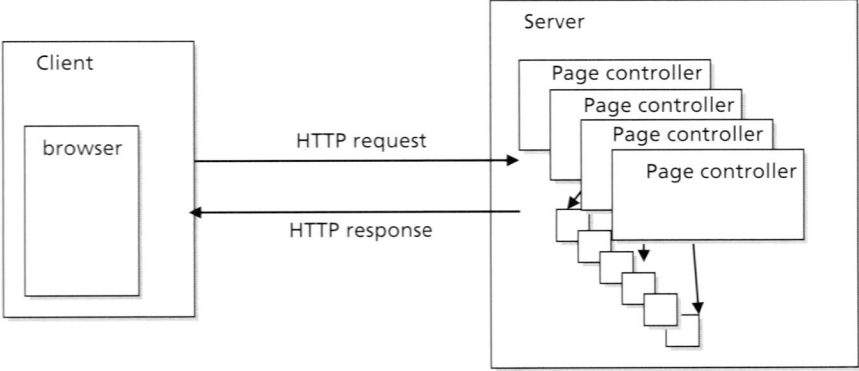

Front Controller Pattern

In this pattern, instead of each page submitting its HTTP request to a specialized controller, there is a single component that receives all client requests. This component is known as the 'front controller' because it acts as the front door of the web application and controls all access (Fowler 2003). It acts like a receptionist (or possibly a bouncer), directing all client requests to the appropriate server-side processes that implement the required use cases. In high-level design terms, some kind of server page acts as the front controller. In the Struts implementation (and in most other frameworks), the front controller is a servlet. Since JSPs are translated into servlets by the JSP engine, the front controller could be implemented as a JSP. However, it is a little simpler and more efficient in a framework to use a servlet, since using a JSP for a component that never needs to be changed or recompiled, or provide any part of the view layer, has no real benefits.

Of course having a front controller alone is not enough, since there is still page-specific processing that needs to take place on the server, such as conditional code that manages the webflow. In our existing design, these processes are encapsulated in server pages. In Struts, these processes are encapsulated into separate *command* objects. The front controller receives client requests and delegates the server-side processing to the specific command object that relates to a particular page (Figure 15.2).

Command Pattern

In our description of the Front Controller pattern, we referred to the use of 'command' objects. The basic idea of the *command pattern* (Gamma *et al*. 1995) is that it encapsulates the execution of a particular process into an object. Each object that represents a process implements a polymorphic method that executes that process, typically called something like 'process' or 'execute'. Figure 15.3 shows how the command pattern is integrated into the front controller (Fowler 2003). The handler (the front controller servlet) receives the HTTP request (typically 'get' or 'post') and delegates to the appropriate command object for that particular request. Each command inherits from some common abstract superclass and implements the abstract 'execute' method.

15

FIGURE 15.2 The Front Controller pattern

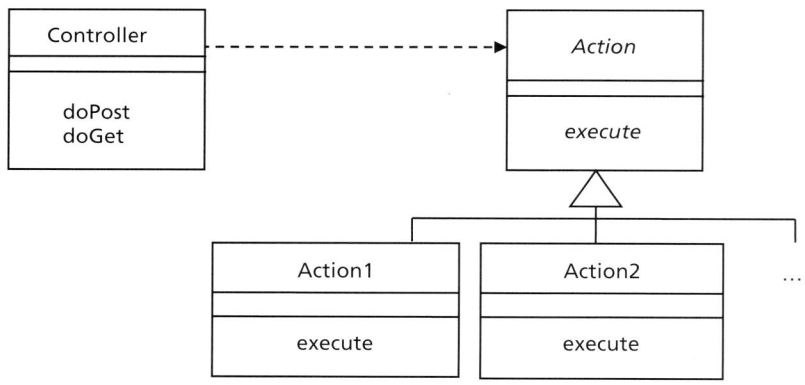

FIGURE 15.3 The Command Pattern as part of the Front Controller pattern

 NOTE In Struts, the command objects are called 'Actions', so we have used 'Action' rather than 'Command' in Figure 15.3.

15.2 Struts components

The controller servlet that is provided as part of the Struts framework is the 'org.apache.struts.action.ActionServlet', with other technologies providing the model and view. In our examples, the view is implemented as JSPs that may include XML transformations. The model continues to be implemented as JavaBeans and other Java objects. The command objects in Struts are known as 'Actions'. The controller invokes these Actions, based on the requests that it receives. The Data Transfer Objects in Struts are known as 'ActionForms' and they transfer data between components in the view and controller layers. Since the Action objects are part of the view–controller layer, they need to interact with the underlying model. As we have seen in our previous examples, using the simple 'Facade' pattern (Gamma *et al.* 1995) can be useful here, using a single component to act as the access point to the underlying model (Figure 15.4).

FIGURE 15.4   Struts components in the view–controller layer

```
┌──────────┐   ┌──────────┐   ┌──────────┐   ┌──────────┐   ┌──────────┐
│ JSP View │◄─►│  Struts  │◄─►│  Action  │◄─►│  Model   │◄─►│ JavaBean │
│          │   │Controller│   │          │   │  Facade  │   │  Model   │
└──────────┘   └──────────┘   └──────────┘   └──────────┘   └──────────┘
      │                            ▲
      │        ┌────────────┐      │
      └───────►│ ActionForm │──────┘
               └────────────┘
```

15.3 Configuring Struts

To start using Struts as our web application framework, there are a number of configuration steps. First, we need to add the Struts libraries to the library folder of either the web application or the server to which we are deploying. The Struts library JAR files can be found in the 'lib' folder of the Struts download. The main Struts JAR file is called 'struts-core-1.3.8.jar' (or something similar, depending on the version of Struts). There are, however, a number of other JAR files in the library folder. You may not need all of these for a given web application, since it depends which aspects of Struts you intend to use. However the simplest option is to include them all. You should, however, replace the two JAR files for the JSTL, which come from version 1.0, with the version 1.1 jars that we have previously used.

 NOTE	If you put the Struts JAR files in the 'lib' folder of the web application, Tomcat cannot dynamically reload the application. Therefore to maintain the ability to dynamically deploy to Tomcat without restarting the server, put the Struts JAR files in the server's 'lib' folder, not the web application's 'lib' folder. For actual deployment, the JAR files should be put into the web application's 'lib' folder. This is not an issue for Tomcat when running under JBoss, so the JAR files can always be put into the web application's 'lib' folder.

Once the JAR files are in place, we need to register the Struts 'ActionServlet' in the 'web.xml' deployment descriptor and create an XML configuration file for Struts itself. Later, we also need to provide some *message resource* files to support some of the Struts tag libraries, added to the WEB-INF\classes folder of the web application.

Configuring the Struts servlet in 'web.xml'

Servlets need to be configured in the 'web.xml' deployment descriptor, using the 'servlet' and 'servlet-mapping' elements, which appear immediately below the opening 'web-app' tag. We saw how to do this servlet registration in Chapter 10, but that was for servlets that we had written ourselves. In this case, the servlet class files are not in the 'classes' folder of the web application but in the Struts JAR file. Also, we have not previously introduced the 'init-param' and 'load-on-startup' elements.

```
<servlet>
  <servlet-name>name</servlet-name>
  <servlet-class>Fully-qualified class name</servlet-class>
    <init-param>
      <param-name>parameter name</param-name>
      <param-value>parameter value</param-value>
    </init-param>
    <load-on-startup>integer value</load-on-startup>
  </servlet>

<servlet-mapping>
  <servlet-name>name</servlet-name>
  <url-pattern>url</url-pattern>
</servlet-mapping>
```

The 'init-param' element can appear zero or more times. It is used to provide initialization parameters to the servlet, each parameter having a name and a value. The 'load-on-startup' element is useful when there are multiple servlets in an application. This element can be used to define in which order the servlets are loaded. Here is an example 'servlet' element to configure the Struts 'ActionServlet':

```
<servlet>
  <servlet-name>action</servlet-name>
  <servlet-class>org.apache.struts.action.ActionServlet</servlet-class>
  <init-param>
    <param-name>config</param-name>
    <param-value>/WEB-INF/struts-config.xml</param-value>
  </init-param>
  <load-on-startup>1</load-on-startup>
</servlet>
```

The example above includes a servlet initialization parameter called 'config'. This is just one example of several initialization parameters that can be used with the Struts servlet. The 'config' parameter value is the context-relative path to the XML configuration file, though in fact the default is '/WEB-INF/struts-config.xml', so the entry in the example could have been left out. Other possible parameter names include:

- 'validating' – use a validating XML parser to process the configuration file (the default value is 'true')
- 'convertNull' – if this parameter is set to 'true', bean properties that have numeric Java wrapper class types (such as java.lang.Integer) default to null (rather than 0) if a bean is populated from a form where a value has not been provided when the form is submitted. This can be useful in some aspects of validation, as we see later. The default value of the 'convertNull' parameter is 'false'.

In the 'servlet-mapping' element we specify which request URIs are mapped to this servlet. Since the servlet is a front controller, we want to route multiple requests through this one component. To do this, we can use a wildcard ('*') for the file name and apply a generic filename extension pattern. One of the commonly used extensions for the Struts 'url-pattern' is '*.do', which means that all requests that have a '.do' extension will be routed through the Struts ActionServlet. Here is the servlet mapping entry in 'web.xml'. Note that the 'servlet-name' value must match the one used in the 'servlet' element.

```
<servlet-mapping>
   <servlet-name>action</servlet-name>
   <url-pattern>*.do</url-pattern>
</servlet-mapping>
```

 NOTE If an application has more than one servlet, all the 'servlet' elements appear first in 'web.xml', followed by all the 'servlet-mapping' elements.

Struts configuration file

Struts is configured using an XML file, which has the default name of 'struts-config.xml' and is usually deployed in the WEB-INF folder of the web application. The root element name is 'struts-config'. In this file, we declare the JavaBeans that are used to gather data from form pages (the 'form-beans' element), manage the page routing in the webflow ('action-mappings') and specify the name of the properties file that is used for messages and internationalization ('message-resources'). In the version of Struts being used for this book (version 1.3), DTDs rather than XML Schemas are used for validation. Here is the basic outline of a 'struts-config.xml' file.

```
<?xml version="1.0"?>
<!DOCTYPE struts-config PUBLIC
   "-//Apache Software Foundation//DTD Struts Configuration 1.3//EN"
   "http://struts.apache.org/dtds/struts-config_1_3.dtd">
<struts-config>
   <form-beans>
   . . .
   </form-beans>
   <action-mappings>
   . . .
   </action-mappings>
   <message-resources . . . />
</struts-config>
```

In the next section, we will see how to use this configuration file to manage the webflow. Figure 15.5 shows the various files that we have introduced so far and where they fit into the web application folder structure.

15.4 Managing the webflow

We introduce each major aspect of Struts by starting with a very simple application that only uses Struts for page routing. Routing is done via the ActionServlet and the Struts

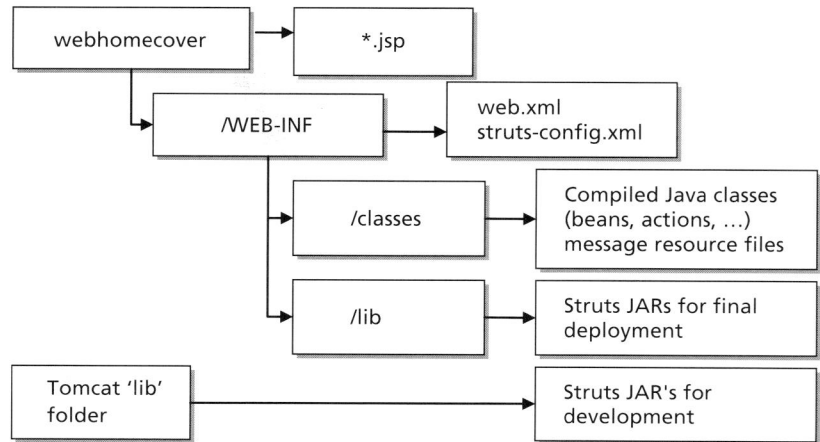

FIGURE 15.5 The web application folder structure used for Struts applications

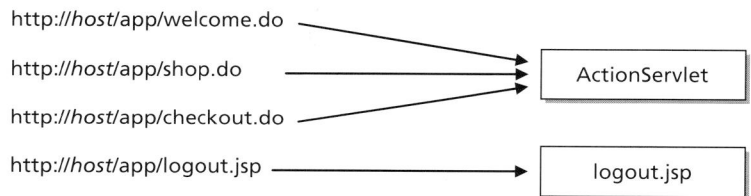

FIGURE 15.6 Request URIs with a .do extension are routed via the ActionServlet

configuration file. In the 'web.xml' file, we specified the file extension '.do' to be mapped to the Struts ActionServlet. This means that all request URIs with a '.do' extension will automatically route via the ActionServlet. Any other request URIs are handled normally. Figure 15.6 shows an example of four URIs, three of them have a '.do' extension, so they are routed to the ActionServlet, whereas the fourth does not and is handled normally, not being processed by the Struts framework.

To use Struts only for simple page routing, with no intermediate processes, only the ActionServlet and the configuration file are required. To go via the Struts framework, each page can use an anchor with a '.do' extension, using standard HTML tags (as we see later, we can also use Struts tags). Figure 15.7 shows the pages we will use in our first Struts example. There are four JSP pages, each of which contains an anchor that has a '.do' extension to submit their requests to the ActionServlet. Note that the URIs do not specify what the next page should be, they simply specify where the request has come from so that, for example, 'page1.jsp' uses a URI of 'frompage1.do'. This URI is used in the 'struts-config.xml' file.

Each JSP page is extremely simple. Apart from the URI in the anchor, the title and the heading text, the other pages are identical to 'page1.jsp'.

```
<?xml version="1.0"?>
<!DOCTYPE html PUBLIC "-//W3C//DTD XHTML 1.1//EN"
    "http://www.w3.org/TR/xhtml11/DTD/xhtml11.dtd">
<html xmlns="http://www.w3.org/1999/xhtml" xml:lang="en">
```

FIGURE 15.7 The pages and anchors in the first Struts example

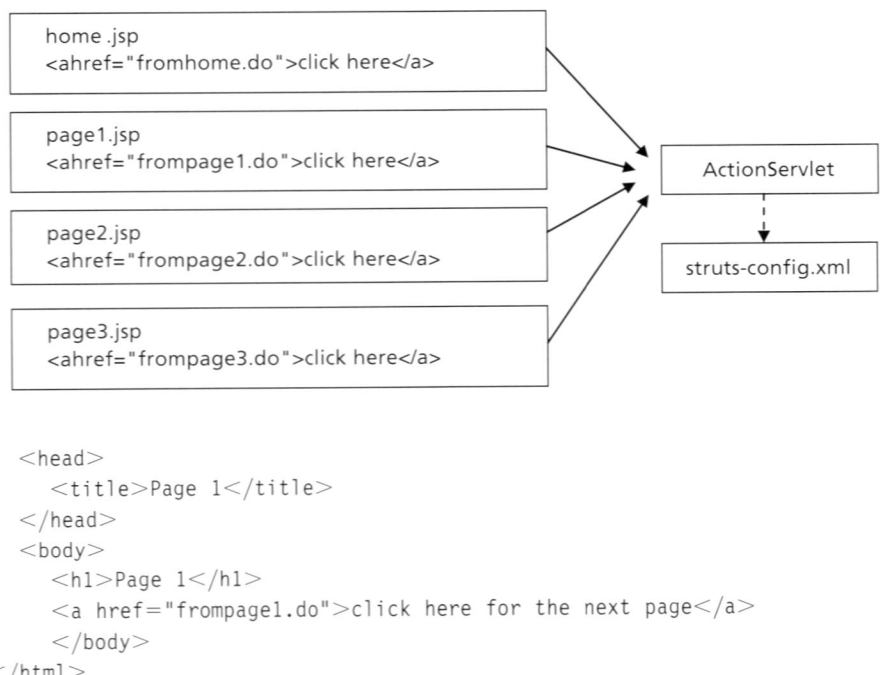

```
<head>
   <title>Page 1</title>
</head>
<body>
   <h1>Page 1</h1>
   <a href="frompage1.do">click here for the next page</a>
   </body>
</html>
```

Changes to the Ant build file

To build and deploy the Struts application we need to use a slightly different Ant build script. The Struts core JAR file needs to be added to the classpath so that when we start to write Struts Java components they can be compiled. We also create a different web application from the previous chapters, so that we do not replace the existing 'webhome-cover' application at this stage. For the examples that follow, we assume the web application is called 'strutswebapp'. Here are the differences between the current 'build.xml' file and the one we use for the Struts application:

- A different project name (not essential, but needed if Ant is being run inside an Integrated Development Environment such as Eclipse, for example):

  ```
  <project name="strutswebapp" default="copy-war" basedir=".">
  ```

- A different folder name for the build:

  ```
  <property name="web-root" value="${root}\strutswebapp" />
  ```

- A different name for the web archive:

  ```
  <property name="war-file" value="${root}\strutswebapp.war" />
  ```

- A different web application name for the property used by the Tomcat 'manager' application:

  ```
  <property name="webapp-name" value="strutswebapp" />
  ```

15

- An addition to the project classpath to include the path to the Struts core jar file. However if it has been copied to the server's 'lib' folder, then it is on the existing classpath, so no changes are necessary.

```
<path id="project-classpath">
  <fileset dir="${tomcat-home}/lib">
    <include name="*.jar/" />
  </fileset>
  <fileset dir="${tomcat-home}/bin">
    <include name="*.jar/" />
  </fileset>
  <pathelement path="path/struts-core-1.3.8.jar" />
</path>
```

Configuring action mappings

The Struts configuration file contains an 'action-mappings' element that includes an individual 'action' element for each page routing action in the application. For simple page routing, each of these elements need only contain two attributes:

- A 'path' attribute that specifies the request URI that was used in the page that submitted the request. Note that within the configuration file the '.do' extension is not used, just the first part of the URI.
- A 'forward' attribute that contains the path to another page in the application.

The following Struts configuration file shows the mappings for the four URIs in our pages. These action mappings define a simple page routing without any intermediate processes taking place on the server, i.e. there are no Java Actions used between these pages. All that happens is that the Action servlet routes from the home page to page1, from page 1 to page 2, from page 2 to page 3 and from page 3 back to page 1 again.

```
<?xml version="1.0"?>
<!DOCTYPE struts-config PUBLIC
    "-//Apache Software Foundation//DTD Struts Configuration 1.3//EN"
    "http://struts.apache.org/dtds/struts-config_1_3.dtd">

<struts-config>
  <action-mappings>
    <action path="/fromhome" forward="/page1.jsp" />
    <action path="/frompage1" forward="/page2.jsp" />
    <action path="/frompage2" forward="/page3.jsp" />
    <action path="/frompage3" forward="/page1.jsp" />
  </action-mappings>
</struts-config>
```

Now everything is in place you should be able to build and deploy your web application and invoke it as:

```
http://localhost/strutswebapp/home.jsp
```

The starting point would be 'home.jsp', not 'home.do' since that URI does not exist in the configuration file. Only when we submit the request from the home page anchor do

FIGURE 15.8   The Struts webflow between the four pages

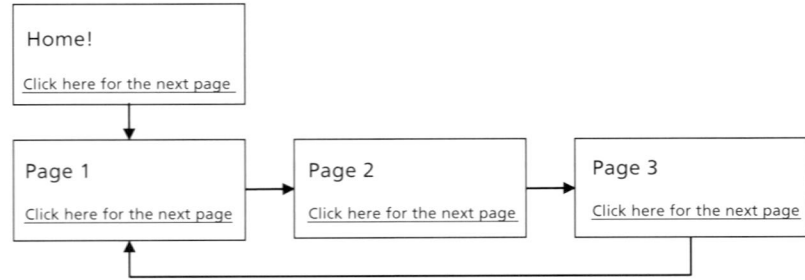

we start going via the Struts ActionServlet. You may also want to set up the welcome file for the Struts web application in 'web.xml':

```
<welcome-file-list>
   <welcome-file>/home.jsp</welcome-file>
</welcome-file-list>
```

Figure 15.8 shows the resulting webflow between the pages.

15.5 Action objects

In the previous example, we used Struts to route between pages but did not perform any server-side Java processes outside of the ActionServlet. To integrate server-side components into a Struts web application we use 'Action' objects. These objects act as the link between the controller layer and the underlying object model, and are integrated into Struts by including them in action mappings in the 'struts-config.xml' file. Using the configuration file, the ActionServlet can delegate to a specific Action object. As well as performing any relevant server-side processing, it is the Action's responsibility to contribute to the webflow page routing by returning a string (inside an 'ActionForward' object) that represents the result of the process. This string is mapped to an actual URL in the 'struts-config.xml' file. In many cases, this string is as simple as 'success', or some other string that indicates that we can move on to the next page in the webflow. Figure 15.9 shows an ActionServlet delegating to different Actions, and each time receiving the 'success' string.

Writing action classes

To write your own action classes you subclass 'org.apache.struts.action.Action'. This class only has one public method, 'execute', which you must override in your Action subclass to provide application-specific behavior (Figure 15.10.)

The 'execute' method receives four parameters: an ActionMapping (which is used to pass the string that determines the page routing back to the Struts framework), an ActionForm (a bean that has been populated from a form, if one is present) and the HTTP request and response objects. The main roles of an action are to validate the user's state in terms of

15

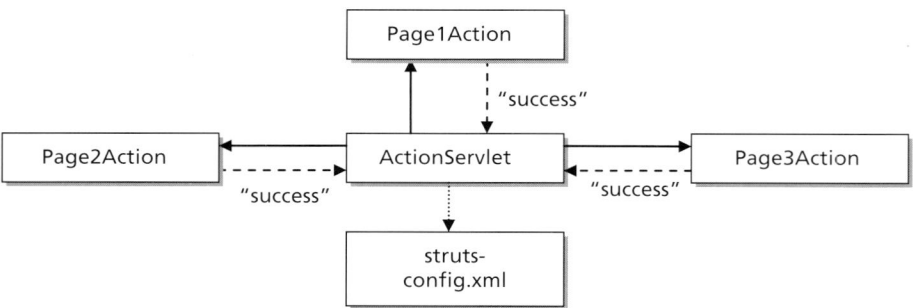

FIGURE 15.9 The ActionServlet delegating to Action objects

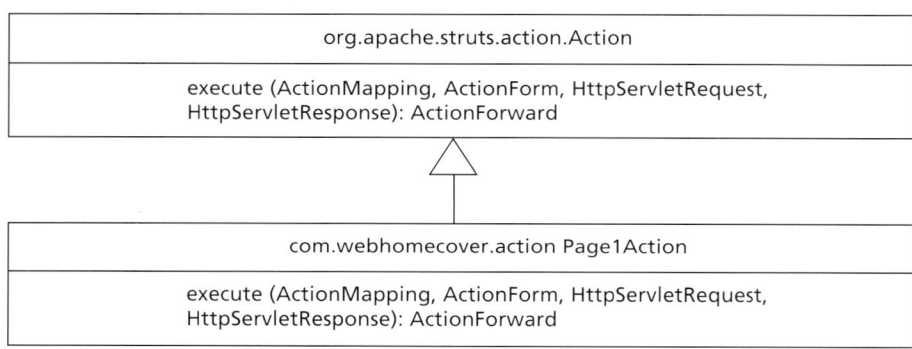

FIGURE 15.10 Action classes are subclasses of 'org.apache.struts.action.Action'

the workflow, delegate server-side processes to the model layer and most importantly return the ActionForward so that the next page can be sent to the response. An ActionForward object is returned from the 'findForward' method of the ActionMapping object that is passed to this method as a parameter, so we do not need to explicitly create one.

 NOTE In earlier versions of Struts, the Action's method was called 'perform'. This method name no longer works within the framework.

Here is a very simple action class that does nothing other than return the ActionForward object. The only parameter we actually use is the ActionMapping, in order to call its 'findForward' method and pass it the String that will be used by the ActionServlet to route the webflow.

```
package com.webhomecover.action;
import org.apache.struts.action.* ;
import javax.servlet.http.*;

public class Page1Action extends Action
{
```

```
    public ActionForward execute(ActionMapping mapping, ActionForm form,
      HttpServletRequest request, HttpServletResponse response)
    {
      return mapping.findForward("success");
    }
}
```

Configuring actions in the Struts configuration file

To configure the integration of Action objects into the webflow, the 'action' element needs to be set up a little differently. Instead of being an empty element with a 'forward' *attribute*, it needs to have a body with one or more nested 'forward' *elements*. This is to make it possible for action objects to provide different possible routing options depending on the state of the webflow or the users' choices.

The 'action' elements may specify several attributes, not all of which are required for every action:

- 'path' – the URL that was mapped to this action (without a '.do' extension)
- 'type' – the fully qualified Java class name of the Action that handles this request
- 'input' – the name of the JSP page that sent the request
- 'name' – the name of a JavaBean that is used in this action
- 'unknown' – can be set to 'true' to indicate that this action should be configured as the single default for this application
- 'validate' – set to true if the JavaBean is to be used to validate the contents of a form

The nested 'forward' elements have two attributes:

- 'name' – a string that may be returned from the Action object
- 'path' – the actual page to be used for the response

It is possible for an action to return one of several different ActionForward strings, each one specifying a different state for the webflow. Each of these strings would have a matching 'forward' element in the 'action'. Here is a simple 'action' element that passes the request to an Action called 'com.webhomecover.action.Page1Action'. The original URI that invoked this action was 'frompage1', and the name of the original page was 'page1.jsp'. The 'forward' element says that if the action object returns 'success', then the next page to be sent to the response is 'page2.jsp'.

```
<action-mappings>

    <action path="/frompage1"
        type="com.webhomecover.action.Page1Action"
        input="/page1.jsp" >
      <forward name="success" path="/page2.jsp" />
    </action>

    . . . other mappings

</action-mappings>
```

Later we look at a more complex webflow where the Action may return different strings depending on the state of the webflow.

Using Logging in Actions

When we are using components such as Actions that execute without any visible output, we may find things difficult to debug. It is sometimes helpful to add logging to our server-side components so that we can trace what is going on. An easy way to do this is to use *Jakarta commons logging*, which is a thin wrapper around other logging implementations. If the 'Log4J' logging framework is available on the system, it uses that, but if not it uses standard JDK logging, assuming that the JDK being used is version 1.4 or above. If an older JDK is being used that does not support logging, then the 'SimpleLog' class is used; it is included in the commons logging JAR file. Struts uses commons logging automatically for its own components, but you can also use it with your own code. To do this you will need to have the commons logging JAR file and other supporting commons JAR files on the classpath when you compile (if they are already copied to the server's library directory, they are already on the classpath of your Ant build script) and include the following imports in any classes that use logging:

```
import org.apache.commons.logging.Log;
import org.apache.commons.logging.LogFactory;
```

You then need to declare a 'Log' object in your class, using the 'getLog' method of the 'LogFactory'. Passing the class object as the parameter means that the log uses the fully qualified class name in its output.

```
public class MyClass
{
   private static Log log = LogFactory.getLog(MyClass.class);
   //. . .
```

You can then use the 'log' object inside your methods, as in this 'execute' method of an Action class:

```
package com.webhomecover.action;

import org.apache.struts.action.* ;
import org.apache.commons.logging.Log;
import org.apache.commons.logging.LogFactory;
import javax.servlet.http.*;

public class Page1Action extends Action
{
   private static Log log = LogFactory.getLog(Page1Action.class);

   public ActionForward execute(ActionMapping mapping, ActionForm form,
      HttpServletRequest request, HttpServletResponse response)
   {
      if(log.isInfoEnabled())
      {
         log.info("In Page1Action");
```

```
        }
        return mapping.findForward("success");
    }
}
```

By default, Tomcat should already be logging at the 'info' level, so any logging output you include in your Actions should appear in the server log. Figure 15.11 shows some logging output in Tomcat (some of the 'INFO' messages are from Struts, others from the code in the Action objects).

We eventually need to do more with our Action objects than just returning a single string, so there are a couple of simple guidelines to bear in mind. First, actions are multi-threaded, so they should not contain any attributes, only local variables, since any attribute would be accessed by all threads. Second, we should not use actions for business processes. Rather, we should keep them short and simple and delegate to the model. However, Actions are a good place to deal with application exceptions, since these usually affect the state of the application and therefore the webflow, which is the responsibility of the action layer.

Global forwards

Global forwards are useful where a number of actions all direct to the same resource. For example, there may be many actions in the application that take the user back t o the home page. Global forwards are defined in 'struts-config.xml' using a 'global-forwards' element, which has an attribute to specify the class used for forwarding, usually the 'ActionForward'. This element can contain multiple 'forward' elements, one for each global forward, and each of these has the following attributes:

- 'name' – the logical name for this forward. This is the string put into the ActionForward by the Action's 'execute' method, for example 'home'.
- 'path' – the context-relative path to the resource, for example: '/home.jsp'
- 'redirect' – 'true' or 'false'. If set to 'true', the ActionServlet redirects to the resource (i.e. sends a response to the browser to redirect a new request) instead of forwarding. The default is 'false'.

FIGURE 15.11 Output from Action objects using commons logging

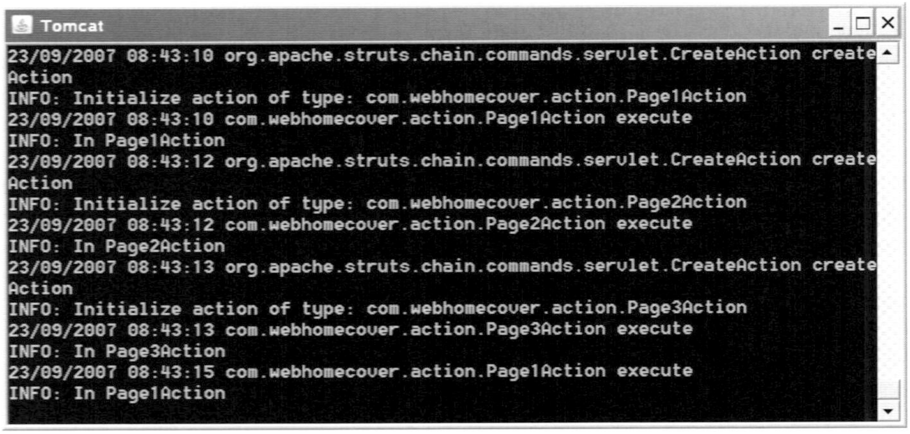

This example of a global forward means that any Actions that return the 'home' string will forward to the 'home.jsp' page. (The 'global-forwards' element comes before the 'action-mappings' element in the Struts configuration file.)

```
<global-forwards type="org.apache.struts.action.ActionForward">
  <forward name="home" path="/home.jsp" redirect="false" />
</global-forwards>
```

15.6 Struts tag libraries

So far we have been concentrating on page routing using the configuration files and actions. However we now need to turn our attention to integrating JavaBeans and form pages into our webflow. To do this we can take advantage of the Struts tag libraries, specifically the 'html' and 'bean' libraries. In each JSP page that uses the Struts custom tags, we need a suitable tag library directive or namespace entry in the 'jsp:root' element. Using a traditional tag library directive, we would use the following tags:

```
<%@ taglib uri="http://struts.apache.org/tags-bean" prefix="bean" %>
<%@ taglib uri="http://struts.apache.org/tags-html" prefix="html" %>
```

However for JSPX pages we would use the 'jsp:root' element and add the namespaces like this:

```
<jsp:root xmlns:jsp="http://java.sun.com/JSP/Page"
   xmlns:bean="http://struts.apache.org/tags-bean"
   xmlns:html="http://struts.apache.org/tags-html"
   version="2.0">
```

 NOTE There are two other Struts tag libraries, 'logic' and 'nested', along with another tag library for Struts Tiles which supports page layout templates. However we do not cover these libraries in this chapter.

Here is a simple page using just the Struts HTML tag library. The most important tag being used here is 'html:html', which replaces the standard 'html' tag. Setting the 'xhtml' attribute to 'true' means the client page is generated with an XHTML style 'html' opening tag and can be validated as an XHTML document. There are many other Struts HTML tags that can be used instead of standard HTML tags. Here for example we also use the 'html:link' element, which is the equivalent of an HTML anchor. When we use this tag, we no longer need to add the '.do' extension to URIs, since the Struts tag automatically routes the request through the ActionServlet. It has another advantage too, in that it supports automatic 'URL rewriting'. This is a technique that supports session management even if browser cookies (the default technique for supporting sessions) are disabled.

```
<?xml version="1.0"?>
<!-- File: claimhome.jsp -->
<jsp:root xmlns:jsp="http://java.sun.com/JSP/Page"
    xmlns:html="http://struts.apache.org/tags-html"
    version="2.0">
```

```
<jsp:directive.page contentType="text/html"/>
<jsp:output omit-xml-declaration="false"
 doctype-root-element="html"
 doctype-public="-//W3C//DTD XHTML 1.1//EN"
 doctype-system="http://www.w3.org/TR/xhtml11/DTD/xhtml11.dtd" />

<html:html xhtml="true">
  <head>
    <title>Welcome to WebHomeCover</title>
  </head>
  <body>
    <h2>Welcome to the claims department at WebHomeCover.com</h2>
    <div>
      click <html:link action="claimform">here</html:link>
      to enter your claim
    </div>
    </body>
  </html:html>
</jsp:root>
```

Using Struts HTML tags to populate JavaBeans

The HTML tags have some uses on their own, but become much more powerful when used in conjunction with forms and JavaBeans, because they make it easy to match form data to bean properties. In the simple example that follows, we build a Struts version of the insurance claim form process that we have been developing for the past few chapters. Here is a modified version of the 'claimform.jsp' page, this time with a Struts 'form' element including a number of tags that have a 'property' attribute: 'form', 'text', 'radio' and 'textarea'. Note that these are simple replacements for the standard HTML elements for form components.

```
<?xml version="1.0"?>
<!-- File: claimform.jsp -->
<jsp:root xmlns:jsp="http://java.sun.com/JSP/Page"
      xmlns:html="http://struts.apache.org/tags-html"
      version="2.0">
<jsp:directive.page contentType="text/html"/>
<jsp:output omit-xml-declaration="false"
 doctype-root-element="html"
 doctype-public="-//W3C//DTD XHTML 1.1//EN"
 doctype-system="http://www.w3.org/TR/xhtml11/DTD/xhtml11.dtd" />
<html:html xhtml="true">
  <head>
    <title>WebHomeCover.com - claim details form</title>
  </head>
  <body>
    <h1>Please enter the details of your claim</h1>
    <h2>Please provide information about your claim in the form below, then click
    submit</h2>
    <html:form action="/processclaim" >
      <table>
```

```
    <tr>
      <td>Policy Number:</td>
      <td><html:text property="policyNumber" size="10" />
    </td>
    </tr>
    <tr>
      <td>Amount Claimed:</td>
      <td><html:text property="amount" size="10" /></td>
    </tr>
    <tr>
      <td></td>
      <td>
        <html:radio property="type" value="buildings"/>
        Make a buildings insurance claim
      </td>
    </tr>
    <tr>
      <td></td>
      <td>
        <html:radio property="type" value="contents"/>
        Make a contents insurance claim
      </td>
    </tr>
    <tr>
      <td>Description of claim:</td>
      <td><html:textarea property="description" rows="5" cols="30" />
    </td>
    </tr>
    <tr>
      <td></td>
      <td><html:submit>Submit</html:submit></td>
    </tr>
    </table>
    </html:form>
    </body>
    </html:html>
  </jsp:root>
```

The property attributes can be matched to the properties of a JavaBean, using the same principles as in previous examples, e.g. the name of a form component can be used to auto-populate the property of a JavaBean from the HTTP request. Although it is not necessary to use the HTML tag library to do this, these tags are often simpler than the standard HTML tags, and are more explicit, since the 'property' attribute relates to the property of a JavaBean (as opposed to the 'name' attribute that would be used with a standard HTML element).

ActionForm JavaBeans

The JavaBeans used with the Struts framework to gather data from client form pages are subclasses of 'org.apache.struts.action.ActionForm'. The advantage of using ActionForms rather than ordinary JavaBeans is that they can be configured from the 'struts-config.xml' file to associate them with form pages and specify their scope, and we can also use them for validation. As we see later, ActionForms can be used with the Struts bean tag library.

Figure 15.12 shows the general pattern of a Struts webflow using the various Struts components that we have introduced so far. JSP pages containing forms that use Struts library tags submit requests to the ActionServlet front controller. The ActionServlet populates the ActionForm bean with request parameter data from the form, and invokes its validation method (if present). If validation fails, the original form page is regenerated and the user must resubmit the page. Assuming validation is either successful, or not applied, the ActionServlet then forwards to an Action object that may process the bean's data and

FIGURE 15.12 The general pattern of a Struts webflow

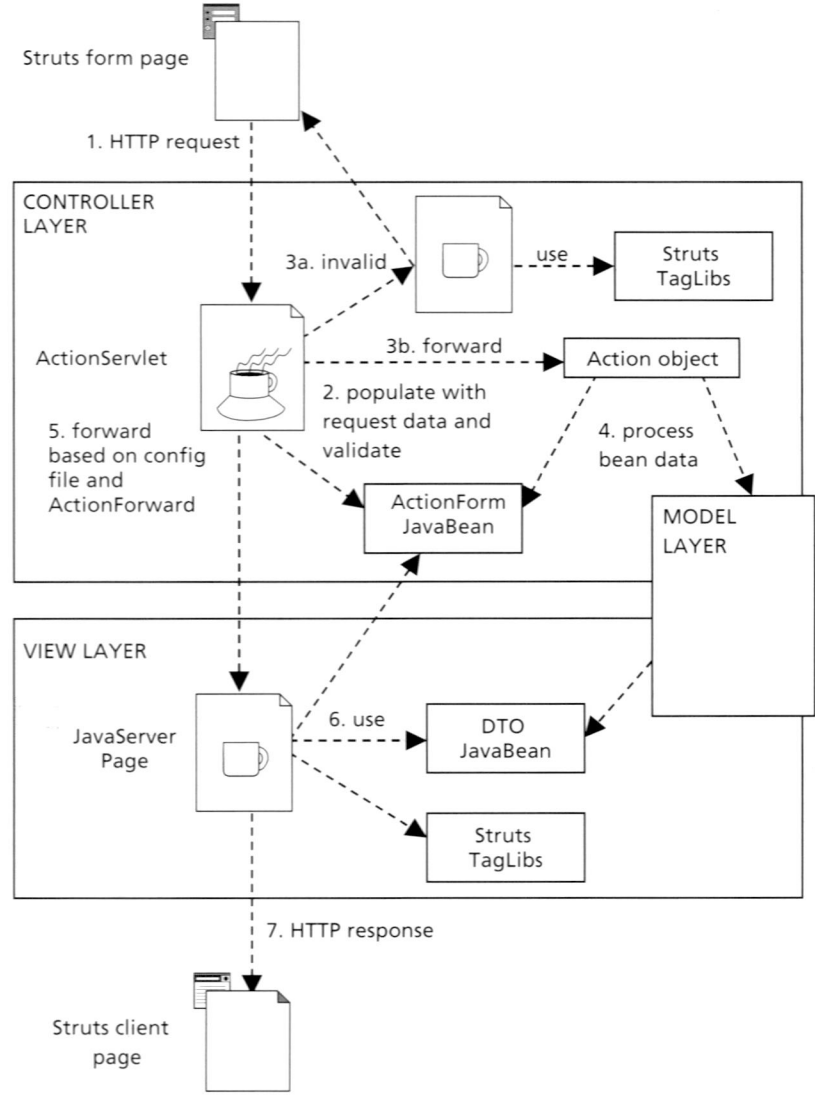

interact with the underlying model. The ActionServlet then forwards to a JSP, based on the string in the ActionForward returned by the Action object. The JSP creates the next client page using Struts tag libraries and information from ActionForms or other JavaBeans that may have come from the model.

To convert our existing ClaimBean into a Struts ActionForm, all we need to do is add 'extends ActionForm' to the class declaration (having added the necessary 'import' statement). The rest of the class is the same as it was before except that we remove the manual validation process introduced in Chapter 14, because Struts provides its own validation support.

```
package com.webhomecover.beans;

import org.apache.struts.action.ActionForm;
import java.text.NumberFormat;
import java.io.Serializable;

public class ClaimBean extends ActionForm implements Serializable
{
// 'get' and 'set' methods as before, but no 'validate' method
}
```

The configuration file includes the declaration of ActionForms inside a 'form-beans' element, immediately after the opening 'struts-config' tag. The body of the 'form-beams' element consists of one or more nested 'form-bean' elements that define the name (used locally within the configuration file and also with Struts tags) and the type (fully qualified class name) of the ActionForm. Here we use an instance of the ClaimBean class and give it the local name 'claimBean':

```
<form-beans>
  <form-bean name="claimBean" type="com.webhomecover.beans.ClaimBean" />
</form-beans>
```

Down in the 'action-mappings' element, we define an action that includes attributes related to the use of the ActionForm, namely 'name', 'scope' and 'validate'. The 'name' is the name of a bean declared in a 'form-bean' element ('claimBean' in this example), the 'scope' is the scope into which the bean will be put ('request' in this example) and if 'validate' is set to 'true' then the bean's 'validate' method is called after it has been populated from the request parameters. Here is the complete 'action' entry to integrate the ClaimBean into the webflow (without validation, at this stage). There are two possible outcomes from this action, 'found' and 'notfound', which route to different pages.

```
<action path="/processclaim"
  type="com.webhomecover.action.ClaimAction"
  validate="false"
  name="claimBean"
  scope="request"
  input="/claimform.jsp" >
  <forward name="found" path="/displayclaim.jsp" />
  <forward name="notfound" path="/notfound.jsp" />
</action>
```

Using this information in 'struts-config.xml', the ActionServlet can perform the following tasks:

- Look for a bean of the appropriate type in the specified scope.
- Create a new bean and add it to the specified scope if it is not already there.
- Populate bean properties from the request.
- Pass the bean to the 'execute' method of the appropriate Action class.

The Action class in this example is called 'claimAction'. It performs a similar role to the 'processclaim.jsp' server page in previous examples, except that it is written using mostly standard Java, not JSP tags. Since the form bean is passed, ready populated to the Action as the 'form' parameter, all we need to do is cast it to the appropriate type and use it.

```java
package com.webhomecover.action;

import org.apache.struts.action.Action;
import org.apache.struts.action.ActionForward;
import org.apache.struts.action.ActionMapping;
import org.apache.struts.action.ActionForm;

import javax.servlet.http.HttpServletRequest;
import javax.servlet.http.HttpServletResponse;

import com.webhomecover.beans.ClaimBean;
import com.webhomecover.model.Claim;
import com.webhomecover.model.Policy;
import com.webhomecover.model.ModelFacade;

import org.apache.commons.logging.Log;
import org.apache.commons.logging.LogFactory;

public class ClaimAction extends Action
{
   private static Log log = LogFactory.getLog(ClaimAction.class);

   public ActionForward execute(ActionMapping mapping, ActionForm form,
      HttpServletRequest request, HttpServletResponse response)
   {
     if (log.isInfoEnabled())
     {
       log.info("In ClaimAction");
     }
     ClaimBean claimBean = (ClaimBean)form;
     Claim claim = ModelFacade.createClaim(claimBean);
     request.setAttribute("claim", claim);
     if (claim == null)
     {
       return mapping.findForward("notfound");
     }
     else
     {
```

15

```
        Policy policy = claim.getPolicy();
        request.setAttribute("policy", policy);
        return mapping.findForward("found");
    }
  }
}
```

NOTE	In this code, the claim is being written to the database using the Façade and DAO we introduced earlier. Previous versions of Struts supported a 'Struts DataSource' for making database connections from Actions. However, use of this component has been deprecated, because it brings database access too close to the controller layer. The DAO pattern is now the preferred approach.

The 'displayclaim' page is very similar to previous versions, with the exception of a couple of Struts HTML tags. Note that the standard 'useBean' tag retrieves the Claim and Policy beans from the request, where they have been put by the Action class:

```
<?xml version="1.0"?>
<!-- File: displayclaim.jsp -->
<jsp:root xmlns:jsp="http://java.sun.com/JSP/Page"
  xmlns:c="http://java.sun.com/jsp/jstl/core"
  xmlns:html="http://struts.apache.org/tags-html"
  version="2.0">
<jsp:directive.page contentType="text/html"/>
<jsp:output omit-xml-declaration="false"
  doctype-root-element="html"
  doctype-public="-//W3C//DTD XHTML 1.1//EN"
  doctype-system="http://www.w3.org/TR/xhtml11/DTD/xhtml11.dtd" />
  <jsp:useBean id="claim" class="com.webhomecover.model.Claim"
scope="request" />
  <jsp:useBean id="policy" class="com.webhomecover.model.Policy"
scope="request" />
  <html:html xhtml="true">
    <head>
      <title>Insurance Claim</title>
    </head>
    <body>
      <h2>Thank you for making your insurance claim</h2>
      <p>Please take a note of the reference number below</p>
      Policy Number: <strong><jsp:getProperty name="policy"
        property="policyNumber"/></strong><br />
      Reference:<strong><jsp:getProperty name="claim"
        property="reference"/></strong><br />
      Date of claim: <strong><jsp:getProperty name="claim"
        property="claimDate"/></strong><br />
      Policy start date: <strong><jsp:getProperty name="policy"
```

```
                property="startDate"/></strong><br />
          Is policy paid up?: <strong><jsp:getProperty name="policy"
              property="paidUp"/></strong><br />
          Annual premium: <strong><jsp:getProperty name="policy"
              property="annualPremium"/></strong><br />
          Amount of claim: <strong><jsp:getProperty name="claim"
              property="amount"/></strong><br />
          Type of policy: <strong><jsp:getProperty name="claim"
              property="type"/></strong><br />
          Description: <strong><jsp:getProperty name="claim"
              property="description"/></strong>
          <hr />
          <html:link action="claimhome">Home page</html:link>
      </body>
    </html:html>
</jsp:root>
```

Likewise, the 'notfound' page has much in common with previous versions, apart from some Struts HTML tags:

```
    <?xml version="1.0"?>
  <!-- File: notfound.jsp -->

  <jsp:root xmlns:jsp="http://java.sun.com/JSP/Page"
    xmlns:html="http://struts.apache.org/tags-html"
    version="2.0">
  <jsp:directive.page contentType="text/html"/>
  <jsp:output omit-xml-declaration="false"
   doctype-root-element="html"
   doctype-public="-//W3C//DTD XHTML 1.1//EN"
   doctype-system="http://www.w3.org/TR/xhtml11/DTD/xhtml11.dtd" />
  <jsp:useBean id="claimBean" class="com.webhomecover.beans.ClaimBean"
  scope="request" />
  <html:html xhtml="true">
    <head>
      <title>Policy not found</title>
    </head>
    <body>
      Policy number
      <jsp:getProperty name="claimBean" property="policyNumber" />
      not found
    <hr />
    <html:link action="home">Home page</html:link>
    </body>
  </html:html>
</jsp:root>
```

At the moment, the application behaves much as it did before, but it is missing any validation support, so entering invalid data may cause problems with the application. In the next section, we integrate Struts server-side validation into the ActionForm bean.

15

15.7 Validation with message resources

We can configure ActionForms to validate the contents of their associated form pages. To do this effectively, we need to take several steps:

- Create a resource file that contains error messages
- Create a CSS file that can manage the presentation of error messages
- Register the message resource file in the Struts configuration file
- Add 'html:errors' elements to the form page to display error messages
- Implement a 'validate' method in the ActionForm that checks the state of the bean properties and reads the error messages from the resource file
- Ensure that the value of the 'validate' attribute of the relevant 'action' element in the Struts configuration file has been set to 'true'.

If we only implement the 'validate' method and set validate to 'true' in the 'struts-config.xml' file, then validation takes place. If there are any errors, the form page is redisplayed. However this is not very helpful on its own, since the user will not know what errors are in the page. The other steps enable error messages to be shown on the form page.

Creating an error message resource file

The file that contains the error message text is knows as a *message resources* file, based on the Java 'PropertyResourceBundle' class. The Struts class 'org.apache.struts.util. MessageResources' lets you treat a set of resource bundles like a database. Each resource bundle takes the form of a *properties file*, which consists of a set of key–value pairs. The keys can contain periods, which means we can use the first part of the key to identity the type of property, and the second part to identify the property name. For example our error messages might all be prefixed with 'error', as in this example of an error message related to the policy number. The value (after the '=' sign) is the text that is used as the error message.

```
error.policyNumber=You must enter your policy number
```

As well as the text of the error messages, there are also special 'errors.header' and 'errors.footer' entries that you can use to top and tail each error message. These are useful for managing the presentation of the error messages. Here, we wrap the error messages in 'span' elements that are given a class related to error messages.

```
errors.header=<span class="errormessage">
errors.footer=</span>
```

In a linked CSS file, we can apply a suitable format. In this example, we set the text color of members of the 'errormessage' class to red:

```
.errormessage{color: red}
```

Here is the complete properties file, containing the header and footer for errors, and error messages for the four input components on the claim form: policy number, claim amount, policy type and claim description:

```
errors.header=<span class="errormessage">
errors.footer=</span>
```

```
error.policyNumber=You must enter your policy number
error.amount=Please enter a monetary value
error.type=You must select either "buildings" or "contents"
error.description=You must enter a description of your claim
```

For Struts to use a message resources file, it has to be registered in the 'struts-config.xml' file, using the 'message-resources' element that appears just before the closing 'struts-config' tag and identifies the name of the file. In this example, the name of the file is 'ApplicationResources.properties'. The name of the resource file is declared in 'struts-config.xml' without the 'properties' extension.

```
<message-resources parameter="ApplicationResources" />
```

Message resource files need to be on the classpath of the web application, so the easiest option is to put the 'ApplicationResources.properties' file into the 'WEB-INF/classes' folder.

Implementing the 'validate' method of an ActionForm

To enable input validation, the ActionForm class includes a 'validate' method that can optionally be overridden in subclasses to provide for application-specific validation processing. This method returns an 'ActionErrors' object that is used in conjunction with the Struts HTML tag library (Figure 15.13).

The ActionErrors object returned by the 'validate' method needs to be created inside it.

```
ActionErrors errors = new ActionErrors();
```

This creates an empty ActionErrors object. If this object remains empty when it is returned from the method, then the ActionServlet regards the bean as valid; by adding error messages to this object, we flag that the form data is invalid.

In the rest of the method we perform any required validation steps, checking each input component for errors such as empty fields, numeric fields with inappropriate values, unselected radio buttons, etc. If an error is found, an ActionMessage object is created that

FIGURE 15.13 ActionForm subclasses can optionally override the 'validate' method

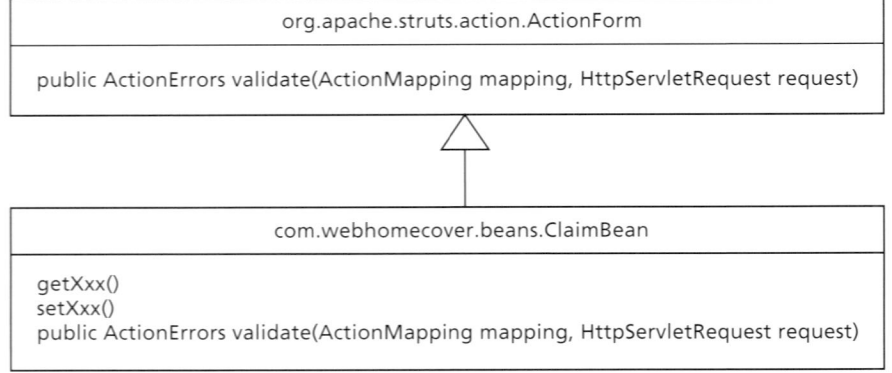

relates to an error message key in the message resources file. The ActionMessage constructor takes a string parameter that contains a key from the message resources file. The associated error message value can then be accessed by the ActionErrors object, associated with the name of a bean property. Here for example, we add an ActionMessage about the policyNumber, (using the error message key 'error.policyNumber') linked to the 'policyNumber' property.

```
errors.add("policyNumber", new ActionMessage("error.policyNumber"));
```

Here is a complete 'validate' method for the ClaimBean, checking the four input components for empty, null or invalid values.

```
public ActionErrors validate(ActionMapping mapping, HttpServletRequest request)
{
    ActionErrors errors=new ActionErrors();
    if(policyNumber == null || policyNumber.equals(""))
    {
        errors.add("policyNumber", new ActionMessage("error.policyNumber"));
    }
    if(claimValue == 0.0)
    {
        errors.add("amount", new ActionMessage("error.amount"));
    }
    if(claimType== null)
    {
        errors.add("type", new ActionMessage("error.type"));
    }
    if(description == null || description.equals(""))
    {
        errors.add("description", new ActionMessage("error.description"));
    }
    return errors;
}
```

To ensure that the ActionForm's 'validate' method is invoked by the ActionServlet when the form is submitted, the 'validate' attribute must be set to 'true' in the action configuration.

```
<action path="/processclaim"
    type="com.webhomecover.action.ClaimAction"
    validate="true"
    name="claimBean"
    scope="request"
    input="/claimform.jsp" >
    <forward name="found" path="/displayclaim.jsp" />
    <forward name="notfound" path="/notfound.jsp" />
</action>
```

When validation is enabled, the ActionServlet uses the 'input' attribute to regenerate the original input form page if validation fails, rather than forwarding to the Action. Once all of these features are in place, we can use the Struts 'html:errors' tag to show the messages at appropriate places on the page. The tag is quite simple, having a 'property' attribute that refs to the property that is being validated, as in this example that refers to the 'description' property:

```
<html:errors property="description" />
```

Here is a modified version of 'claimdetails.jsp' with 'html:errors' tags added. Note that there is also a 'link' element to apply the style sheet that formats the error messages.

```xml
<?xml version="1.0"?>
<!-- File: claimform.jsp -->
<jsp:root xmlns:jsp="http://java.sun.com/JSP/Page"
 xmlns:html="http://struts.apache.org/tags-html" version="2.0">
<jsp:directive.page contentType="text/html"/>
<jsp:output omit-xml-declaration="false"
 doctype-root-element="html"
 doctype-public="-//W3C//DTD XHTML 1.1//EN"
 doctype-system="http://www.w3.org/TR/xhtml11/DTD/xhtml11.dtd" />
<html:html xhtml="true">
  <head>
    <link href="struts.css" rel="stylesheet" type="text/css" />
    <title>WebHomeCover.com - claim details form</title>
  </head>
  <body>
    <h1>Please enter the details of your claim</h1>
    <h2>Please provide information about your claim in the form below,
     then click submit</h2>
    <html:form action="/processclaim" >
      <table>
        <tr>
          <td>Policy Number:</td>
          <td><html:text property="policyNumber" size="10" /></td>
          <td><html:errors property="policyNumber" /></td>
        </tr>
        <tr><td>Amount Claimed:</td>
          <td><html:text property="amount" size="10" /></td>
          <td><html:errors property="amount" /></td>
        </tr>
        <tr><td></td>
          <td><html:radio property="type" value="buildings"/>
           Make a buildings insurance claim</td></tr>
        <tr><td></td>
          <td><html:radio property="type" value="contents"/>
           Make a contents insurance claim</td></tr>
        <tr><td></td>
          <td><html:errors property="type" /></td>
        </tr>
        <tr><td>Description of claim:</td><td>
        <html:textarea property="description" rows="5" cols="30" />
        </td>
        <td><html:errors property="description" /></td>
        </tr>
```

```
<tr><td></td>
    <td><html:submit>Submit</html:submit></td>
  </tr>
  </table>
  </html:form>
  </body>
  </html:html>
</jsp:root>
```

Figure 15.14 shows the effect of pressing the 'submit' button with the input components at their default values. All four are invalid, so there are four error messages. If the bean fails validation when the form is submitted, the generated page is populated from the current bean properties, this means that the data that was entered into the form when it was submitted is still there. The user does not have to re-enter all the data each time, only correct the errors.

15.8 Using the Struts bean tag library

So far we have only used the Struts HTML tag library, but the bean tag library also has some very useful features. One of these is the 'bean:message' tag that enables us to substitute literal text in a JSP with text read from the properties file. This makes it possible to change the text that appears on a generated client page without changing the JSP itself. It also means we can reuse the same text labels on multiple pages, and support internationalization, by providing multiple versions of each message, one for each language.

FIGURE 15.14   Error messages being displayed using the 'html:errors' tag when the ClaimBean ActionForm fails validation

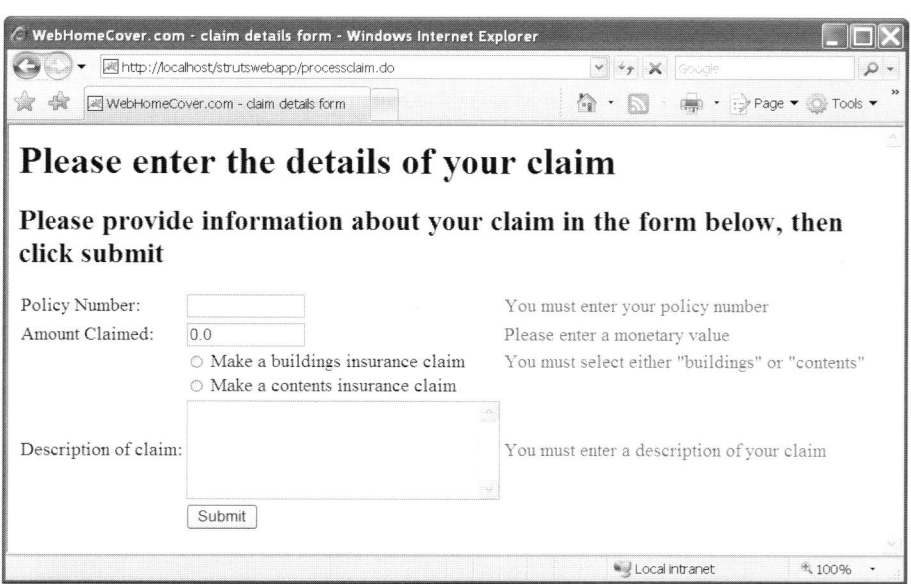

Here are a set of message keys and values that represent all the text displayed on the four pages in our web application (they are added to the same properties file that currently contains the error messages). To aid readability, each message key consists of a prefix that identifies the context in which the text is used. Some relate to specific pages ('home', 'claim', 'display') while the 'label' messages are more generic, so might be reusable across more than one page.

```
home.title=Welcome to WebHomeCover
home.heading=Welcome to the claims department at WebHomeCover.com
home.messagepart1=click 
home.messagepart2=here
home.messagepart3= to enter your claim
claim.title=WebHomeCover.com – claim details form
claim.heading=Please enter the details of your claim
claim.subheading=Please provide information about your claim in the form below,
then click submit
claim.buildingsradioprompt=Make a buildings insurance claim
claim.contentsradioprompt=Make a contents insurance claim
display.title=Insurance Claim Details
display.heading=Thank you for making your insurance claim
display.message=Here are the details you entered
display.link=Home Page
label.policynumber=Policy Number: 
label.amount=Amount claimed: 
label.type=Type of insurance policy: 
label.description=Description of claim: 
label.reference=Claim reference: 
label.date=Date of claim: 
label.startdate=Policy started on: 
label.premium=Annual premium: 
label.paidup=Is policy paid up?: 
label.submit=Submit
notfound.title=Policy Number Error!
notfound.message= not found
```

Each of these messages can be (re)used by 'bean:message' tags in JSP pages. The 'bean:message' tag has an attribute called 'key', which contains a key string from the properties file. For example, this one refers to the title of the claim form page:

```
<bean:message key="claim.title" />
```

To use the bean tags, our pages have to include the namespace of the bean tag library as well as the HTML tag library:

```
<jsp:root xmlns:jsp="http://java.sun.com/JSP/Page"
    xmlns:html="http://struts.apache.org/tags-html"
    xmlns:bean="http://struts.apache.org/tags-bean"
    version="2.0">
```

Here is the modified home page using five of the message keys from the properties file:

```
<?xml version="1.0"?>
<!-- File: claimhome.jsp -->
```

```
<jsp:root xmlns:jsp="http://java.sun.com/JSP/Page"
    xmlns:html="http://struts.apache.org/tags-html"
    xmlns:bean="http://struts.apache.org/tags-bean" version="2.0">
<jsp:directive.page contentType="text/html"/>
<jsp:output omit-xml-declaration="false"
  doctype-root-element="html"
  doctype-public="-//W3C//DTD XHTML 1.1//EN"
  doctype-system="http://www.w3.org/TR/xhtml11/DTD/xhtml11.dtd" />
  <html:html xhtml="true">
    <head>
      <title><bean:message key="home.title" /> </title>
    </head>
    <body>
      <h2><bean:message key="home.heading" /> </h2>
      <div>
        <bean:message key="home.messagepart1" />
        <html:link action="claimform">
          <bean:message key="home.messagepart2" />
        </html:link>
        <bean:message key="home.messagepart3" />
      </div>
    </body>
  </html:html>
</jsp:root>
```

Note that there is now no literal text on the page, only tags. The other messages are used on the claim form and display pages.

As well as the 'message' tag, the bean library includes a 'write' tag that is similar to <jsp:getProperty>.

```
<bean:write name="claimBean" property="policyType" />
```

With this tag, there is no need to use the 'jsp:useBean' and 'jsp:getProperty' tags. Struts looks up the bean name in all four possible scopes until it finds a match, in order of visibility: page, request, session and application. In our current example, it finds 'claimBean' in the request scope. Here is a modified version of the 'display.jsp' page that uses both bean messages and the 'bean:write' tag:

```
<?xml version="1.0"?>
<!-- File: displayclaim.jsp -->

<jsp:root xmlns:jsp="http://java.sun.com/JSP/Page"
 xmlns:c="http://java.sun.com/jsp/jstl/core"
 xmlns:html="http://struts.apache.org/tags-html"
 xmlns:bean="http://struts.apache.org/tags-bean"
 version="2.0">
<jsp:directive.page contentType="text/html"/>
<jsp:output omit-xml-declaration="false"
 doctype-root-element="html"
 doctype-public="-//W3C//DTD XHTML 1.1//EN"
 doctype-system="http://www.w3.org/TR/xhtml11/DTD/xhtml11.dtd" />
```

```
<html:html xhtml="true">
    <head>
        <title><bean:message key="display.title" /></title>
    </head>
    <body>
        <h2><bean:message key="display.heading" /></h2>
        <p><bean:message key="display.message" /></p>
        <bean:message key="label.policynumber" /><strong>
        <bean:write name="policy" property="policyNumber"/>
        </strong><br />
        <bean:message key="label.reference" /><strong>
        <bean:write name="claim" property="reference"/></strong><br />
        <bean:message key="label.date" /><strong>
        <bean:write name="claim" property="claimDate"/></strong><br />
        <bean:message key="label.startdate" /><strong>
        <bean:write name="policy" property="startDate"/></strong><br />
        <bean:message key="label.paidup" /><strong>
        <bean:write name="policy" property="paidUp"/></strong><br />
        <bean:message key="label.premium" /><strong>
        <bean:write name="policy" property="annualPremium"/></strong><br />
        <bean:message key="label.amount" /><strong>
        <bean:write name="claim" property="amount"/></strong><br />
        <bean:message key="label.type" /><strong>
        <bean:write name="claim" property="type"/></strong><br />
        <bean:message key="label.description" /><strong>
        <bean:write name="claim" property="description"/></strong>
        <hr />
        <html:link action="claimhome">
        <bean:message key="display.link" /></html:link>
    </body>
</html:html>
</jsp:root>
```

None of our pages change their appearance as a result of using these bean tags, but they make it possible for us to separate the text content of a page from its structure. One of the big advantages of this is that it provides the foundation for internationalizing our web applications, which we look at in Section 15.9.

Figure 15.15 shows an example of what the display page might look like if given a valid policy number, and Figure 15.16 shows the 'notfound.jsp' page that appears if the policy number does not appear in the database.

15.9 Internationalization

Internationalization is providing a web application in different languages. 'i18n' is a commonly used shorthand for 'internationalization' because there are 18 letters between the 'i' and the 'n'. Struts makes it relatively easy to provide dynamic web pages in different languages because you don't need to replicate all the pages in different languages. Instead, message resources are provided for each locale and used by Struts based on the language

FIGURE 15.15 The display page showing details of a claim and its related policy

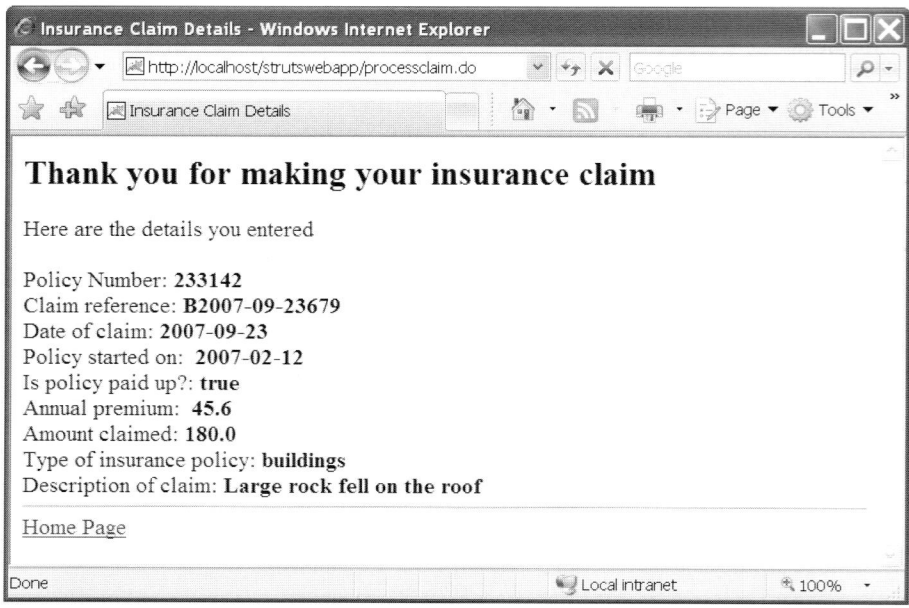

FIGURE 15.16 The error page that appears if the policy number entered for a claim cannot be found in the database

preferences of the requesting browser. The implementation of internationalization in Java is based on using the 'java.util.Locale' class, which is able to recognize different language and data formats. The Struts 'MessageResources' class allows you to request a particular message string for a particular locale.

Internationalized message resources

We have already seen that bean messages can be provided using a properties file. Here, for example, are all the error and text messages that relate specifically to the claim form page.

```
error.policyNumber=You must enter your policy number
error.amount=Please enter a monetary value
error.type=You must select either "buildings" or "contents"
```

```
error.description=You must enter a description of your claim
claim.title=WebHomeCover.com – claim details form
claim.heading=Please enter the details of your claim
claim.subheading=Please provide information about your claim in the form below,
then click submit
claim.buildingsradioprompt=Make a buildings insurance claim
claim.contentsradioprompt=Make a contents insurance claim
```

To internationalize this page, we simply define another resource file with the ISO Language Code appended to the file name, preceded by an underscore. For example we might want to provide the web application in French as well as our default language, which is English. The name of the second resource file would be:

```
ApplicationResources_fr.properties
```

 NOTE You do not need to supply the complete language codes. 'fr', for example, matches all the locales that begin with 'fr' (France, Canada, Belgium, etc.).

The content of the file would be the same set of keys but with values written in the chosen language. Here is the part of the file relating to the claim form, with French message values:

```
error.policyNumber=Vous devez écrire votre nombre de politique
error.amount=Veuillez écrire une valeur monétaire
error.type=Vous devez choisir les "bâtiments" ou le "contenu"
error.description=Vous devez écrire une description de votre réclamation
claim.title=WebHomeCover.com – la réclamation détaille la forme
claim.heading=Veuillez écrire les détails de votre réclamation
claim.subheading=Veuillez fournir les informations au sujet de votre réclamation
sous la forme ci-dessous
claim.buildingsradioprompt=Vous devez choisir un des types de politique
claim.contentsradioprompt=Vous devez choisir un des types de politique
```

We have just shown the 'claim' messages here, but you have to make sure that every key appears in every properties file, since if any of the keys cannot be found the JSP page cannot be rendered.

Internationalization tags

Once we have multiple message resources files to support multiple languages, we can use HTML and bean tags to enable internationalization. To get the ActionServlet to use the internationalized resources, we set the 'lang' attribute to 'true' in the 'html:html' tag of every JSP.

```
<html:html xhtml="true" lang="true">
```

This causes the ActionServlet to get the locale from the browser that sent the request and look for a resource file that uses a matching country code. If it does not find one then it reverts to the default (the file that has no country code extension).

NOTE In earlier versions of Struts, there was a 'locale' attribute that had to be set to 'true', but this attribute is no longer recognized by the Struts HTML tag library.

Setting up the Browser to test internationalized pages

To test whether your internationalized resources are working, you have to change the language preferences in your browser. In Internet Explorer, you select 'Tools' from the menu bar, then 'Internet Options'. In the resulting dialog, you press the 'Languages' button, which shows you the dialog in Figure 15.17. In this dialog, you can add new languages (with the 'Add' button) and change their order of preference. In Figure 15.17, we have added French and moved it to the top of our list of preferences. The browser now includes French as its preferred language when it sends HTTP requests.

 NOTE You have to restart the browser for changes in language settings to take effect.

Setting up the language preferences in Mozilla Firefox 2 is very similar. Again we choose 'Tools' from the menu bar, then select 'Options' and press the 'Choose' button next to the 'Languages' label on the dialog. Figure 15.18 shows the Firefox language dialog. In Opera, select 'Tools', then 'Preferences', then press the 'Details' button next to the 'Language' drop-down list.

If we change the language settings and connect to our internationalized Struts web application, then we see the page text and error messages appear in French (Figure 15.19).

FIGURE 15.17 The language preferences dialog in Internet Explorer 7

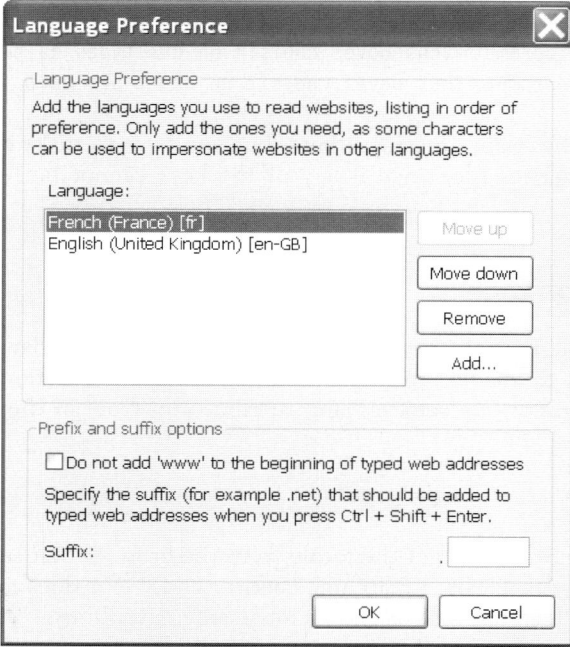

FIGURE 15.18
The language preferences dialog in Mozilla Firefox 2

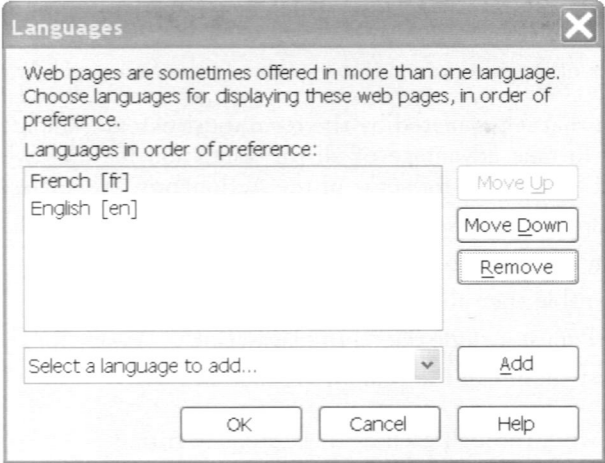

FIGURE 15.19
An internationalized Struts web application with the browser language preference set to French

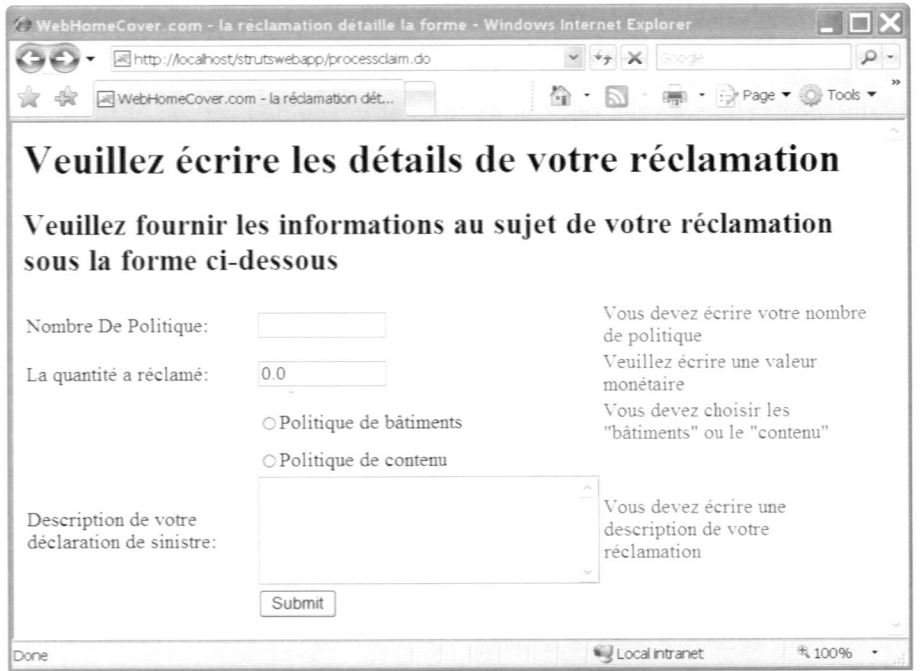

15.10 The Struts validator

In Chapter 8, we introduced the concept of client-side validation using JavaScript and we used some client-side validation in Chapters 12 and 14. Although we should not rely only on this type of input validation, because some browsers will not be running JavaScript, it can be used in combination with server validation to reduce the load on the server. It can also reduce the time users have to wait for feedback and prevent multiple submission of the same data. Struts enables automatic client-side form validation via the Struts validator, (based on the Jakarta commons validator) which generates JavaScript in client form pages.

There are a number of steps required in order to use the Struts validator:

- The JavaBean that is populated by the form must extend ValidatorForm rather than ActionForm. To take advantage of all the validation features we may also have to reconsider the types used for some of the ActionForm properties.
- A set of standard error message keys need to be included in the application resources file.
- The validation rules have to be specified in an XML file.
- You need to enable the validator plugin in 'struts-config.xml'.
- The form's JSP must include the <html:javascript . . ./>tag for client-side validation.
- The form must submit to the validation function.

In this section, we work through each of these steps in turn.

Extending ValidatorForm

A standard Struts form bean extends ActionForm, but one that is used with the Struts Validator must extend 'org.apache.struts.validator.ValidatorForm' instead. Another thing that may be worth thinking about is not using Java primitive number types for properties, since they will default to zero, which of course is a valid number. To force a user to actually enter a numeric value we can change the property types to use wrapper classes such as Integer and Float. Here are the relevant sections of a modified version of the ClaimBean that extends ValidatorForm and uses the 'Double' wrapper type for the 'amount' property.

```
package com.webhomecover.beans;

//we need to import the ValidatorForm class
import org.apache.struts.validator.ValidatorForm;

//other imports. . .

public class ClaimBean extends ValidatorForm implements java.io.Serializable
{
// make the claim attribute a Double (object)
// rather than a double (primitive)
    private Double claimValue;

// other attributes. . .

//'get' and 'set' methods for the 'amount' property use the Double type
    public void setAmount(Double amount)
    {
        claimValue = amount;
    }

    public Double getAmount()
    {
        return claimValue;
    }
```

15

```
// The getClaim method that formats the amount as a String
// needs to use the 'doubleValue' method to get the primitive
// from the wrapper
   public String getClaim()
   {
      NumberFormat currencyFormat = NumberFormat.getCurrencyInstance();
      String valueOfClaimFormatted =
        currencyFormat.format(claimValue.doubleValue());
      return valueOfClaimFormatted;
   }


// other methods. . .
   public ActionErrors validate(ActionMapping mapping, HttpServletRequest request)
   {
// when we validate the amount we have to check if the object is
// null before attempting to get the double value
   if (claimValue == null || claimValue.doubleValue() == 0.0)
   {
      errors.add("amount", new ActionMessage("error.amount"));
   }
   // other error checks. . .
}
```

Standard Message Keys

You have to add a set of standard message keys for the JavaScript validator to your message
resource files. These messages take advantage of the 'java.text.MessageFormat' class, which
allows you to replace portions of a message string with arguments specified at run time. Each
part of the string that can contain a run-time argument is numbered from 0 and surrounded
by braces. Most of the messages have a single placeholder ('{0}') which is replaced by a single argument. However the range checks have three runtime arguments. The 'arg' positions
are used in the XML validation file, which defines which messages are used for which errors.

 NOTE A line preceded by a '#' in a properties file is treated as a comment.

These are the standard keys and the messages suggested by the Struts documentation. Of
course the messages can be changed but they must make sense in the context of the data
in the placeholders.

```
# Struts Validator Error Messages
errors.required={0} is required.
errors.minlength={0} can not be less than {1} characters.
errors.maxlength={0} can not be greater than {1} characters.
errors.invalid={0} is invalid.

errors.byte={0} must be a byte.
errors.short={0} must be a short.
```

```
errors.integer={0} must be an integer.
errors.long={0} must be a long.
errors.float={0} must be a float.
errors.double={0} must be a double.

errors.date={0} is not a date.
errors.range={0} is not in the range {1} through {2}.
errors.creditcard={0} is an invalid credit card number.
errors.email={0} is an invalid e-mail address.
```

To make use of these error messages we need to provide values that make sense in terms of the placeholders. Here are some error messages designed to work within the validator's message placeholders for the four properties that we validate in the claim form. They have been preceded with 'v' to make it clear that these messages are used with the validator.

```
error.vpolicyNumber=A policy number
error.vamount=The amount of the claim
error.vtype=Select either "buildings" or "contents"
error.vdescription=A description of your claim
```

Of course these keys also have to be included in all the different language resource files, with suitable values.

XML validation file

The XML validation file has a root element of 'form-validation', with nested 'formset' and 'form' elements. Each 'form' element defines the name of the ValidatorForm bean and the fields to be validated.

```
<form-validation>
  <formset>
    <form name="ValidatorFormName">
      <field>elements  . . .

    </form>
  </formset>
</form-validation>
```

A 'field' element has 'property' and 'depends' attributes, and includes nested elements for each message argument:

```
<field property="propertyName" depends="validationtype">
  <arg position="n" key="messageKey"/>
</field>
```

The 'property' attribute must be a property of the ValidatorForm bean named in the 'form' element. The 'depends' attribute is the type of validation. This can contain a comma-separated list of different validations. Using a list of validations is often necessary, since the 'required' validation is needed before we can perform more specific types of validation. For example, we may want to check that the amount of a claim is a floating point number within a certain range, but first we have to check that there is something present to check, and then check that the value is a floating-point number before we can check its range, so we

15

must use a sequence of validations: 'required, float, floatRange'. The nested 'arg' elements each define a placeholder position and a message key, relating to where the error text is inserted into the error messages from the resources file.

As well as checking for required fields, our example here includes an example of a range check. The 'amount' property is checked to see if it is a floating-point number in the range 25 to 1,000,000. There are three nested 'arg' elements for this field because the error message has three placeholders. Only the first is populated from the resource file. The second and third are populated from local variables declared within the XML element. The '${var:*varname*}' expression is used to refer to variables that are declared within the 'field' element. Each variable ('min' and 'max' in this example) is declared inside a 'var' element that defines the name and value of the variable. Because these two argument values do not come from the resource file, we set the value of the 'resource' attribute for these elements to 'false'. Here is the complete validation file, which should be placed in the WEB-INF folder of the web application.

```xml
<?xml version="1.0"?>
<!DOCTYPE form-validation PUBLIC
   "-//Apache Software Foundation//DTD Commons Validator Rules
Configuration 1.3.0//EN"
   "http://jakarta.apache.org/commons/dtds/validator_1_3_0.dtd">

<form-validation>
   <formset>
      <form name="claimData">

         <field property="policyNumber" depends="required">
            <arg position="0" key="error.vpolicyNumber"/>
         </field>

         <field property="amount" depends="required, float, floatRange">
            <arg position="0" key="error.vamount"/>
            <arg position="1" name="floatRange" key="${var:min}"
               resource="false"/>
            <arg position="2" name="floatRange" key="${var:max}"
               resource="false"/>
            <var><var-name>min</var-name><var-value>25.0</var-value></var>
            <var><var-name>max</var-name><var-value>1000000.0</var-value></var>
         </field>

         <field property="type" depends="required">
            <arg position="0" key="error.vtype"/>
         </field>

         <field property="description" depends="required">
            <arg position="0" key="error.vdescription"/>
         </field>

      </form>
   </formset>
</form-validation>
```

15

Enabling the validator plugin

To get Struts to use the validator, you must enable the ValidatorPlugin in the 'struts-config.xml' file, just before the closing 'struts-config' element. The 'value' property refers first to the 'validator-rules.xml' file, which is in the Struts core JAR file, and then to the name and location of your own validation file. In this case, we assume that the file is called 'validation.xml' and is in the application's 'WEB-INF' folder.

```
<plug-in className="org.apache.struts.validator.ValidatorPlugIn">
  <set-property property="pathnames"
    value="/org/apache/struts/validator/validator-rules.xml,
      /WEB-INF/validation.xml"/>
</plug-in>
```

If your required form property is one of the Java object representations of primitive types (e.g. 'java.lang.Double'), you should set the ActionServlet's 'convertNull' initialization parameter in the 'web.xml' deployment descriptor to 'true'.

```
<init-param>
  <param-name>convertNull</param-name>
  <param-value>true</param-value>
</init-param>
```

Failure to do this results in numeric validation checks not being performed on empty fields that use numeric wrapper class objects because their values default to 0 instead of null.

Enabling JavaScript validation

To enable the JavaScript validator in a JSP you need to include the 'html:javascript' tag in the body of the 'html:html' element. For the 'formName' attribute, use the name of the ValidatorForm bean defined for that page in the Struts configuration file.

```
<html:javascript formName="claimData" />
```

You also need to add an 'onsubmit' attribute to the form element so that it calls the JavaScript validation function. The name of the function is based on the 'validate*ValidatorFormName*' format, and a reference to the form is passed as a parameter to the function. Here, we validate the 'claimData' bean:

```
<html:form action="/processclaim" onsubmit="return
validateClaimData(this);">
```

The JavaScript validator uses JavaScript alerts to provide error messages. Figure 15.20 shows the alert that is displayed if none of the required fields have data in them, and the alert that is displayed if all the required fields have data but the amount of the claim does not fit within the required range.

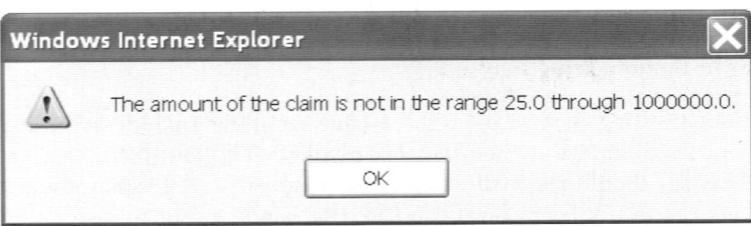

Exercises

15.1 Change the page routing of the first Struts example (the JSP pages only) so that instead of cycling 1–>2–>–3 after starting at the home page, the pages cycle 3 –>2 –>1. Add an extra page to the application and include it in the page cycle.

15.2 Consider the design for a webflow that involves two data entry forms and a final page that displays a confirmation message that the data entered has been processed. The first page should ask for entry of a username based on an email address and a password, while the second page should be credit card details. Sketch the required ActionForm and Action classes and the JSP pages required. What validation could be done in the ActionForm?

15.3 Implement the first part of your three-page webflow. Include some logging in your Action classes to indicate when they are invoked. The first form page (email address and password) should route directly to the display page. Display the input onto the page using the ActionForm JavaBean (no, this is not meant to be a how secure logon actually works!). You will need to use the Struts HTML library. Do not include validation at this stage.

15.4 Add the second form page (credit card details) to your web application and change the routing as necessary. You will need a second ActionForm bean for the second form; put both your beans into session scope. Display all the data from both forms on the final page. Do not add any validation yet.

15.5 Add some validation to both form pages using the 'validate' methods of the two ActionForms. You will need to create a message resources file for the error messages.

15.6 Introduce the Struts bean library to your pages. Use bean messages for the page text (you will need to add these to the message resources file) and use the 'bean:write' tag in your display page.

15.7 Internationalize your web application using a language of your choice.

15.8 Use the Struts Validator to validate your input forms. In particular, you can use the email and credit card number validations.

SUMMARY

In this chapter, we have covered the key features of the Struts web application framework. We have used the framework to handle page routing, validation and internationalization, and implemented some core features of one of the home insurance application use cases (making an insurance claim). There are many features of Struts that we have not covered in this chapter, and many other similar Java frameworks that we have not covered at all. However, now you have an awareness of the role of web application frameworks in enabling the reuse of standard components, you should have an idea of how such frameworks can increase productivity for the Java web application developer. Table 15.1 shows some of the elements in the Struts HTML tag library and Table 15.2 shows the various validation types that can be used with the Struts validator.

TABLE 15.1   Some elements from the Struts HTML tag library

Tag Name	Description
html:checkbox	Render a Checkbox Input Field
html:form	Define an Input Form
html:html	Render an HTML <html> Element
html:link	Render an HTML anchor or hyperlink
html:option	Render a Select Option
html:password	Render a Password Input Field
html:radio	Render a Radio Button Input Field
html:reset	Render a Reset Button Input Field
html:select	Render a Select Element
html:submit	Render a Submit Button
html:text	Render an Input Field of Type text
html:textarea	Render a Textarea

TABLE 15.2   The validations that can be performed using the Struts validator

'depends' attribute value	Validates
required	Mandatory fields; has no variables
validwhen	One field against another
minlength	If input data is not less than a specified minimum length; requires a 'minlength' variable
maxlength	That input data doesn't exceed a specified maximum length
mask	Field format according to a regular expression; requires a mask variable to specify the regular expression
byte, short, integer, long, float and double	Values against the required data types; these validators depend on the 'required' validator
date	That a field can be converted to a Date; this validator uses 'java.text.SimpleDateFormat' to parse the date
intRange, longRange, floatRange, doubleRange	That a numeric field is within a specified range; requires 'min' and 'max' variables to specify the range; this validator depends on the appropriate numeric type validator, which must also be in the field's 'depends' attribute (e.g. 'intRange' depends on 'integer')
creditCard	Credit card number format based on the Luhn checksum (http://www.speech.cs.cmu.edu/~sburke/pub/luhn_lib.html)
email	Email address format; checks for a number of character patterns, including the presence of the '@' character
url	URL format

References and further reading

Apache Software Foundation (2007) *Struts Kickstart FAQ*. http://struts.apache.org/1.3.8/faqs/kickstart.html

Fowler, M. (2003) *Patterns of Enterprise Application Architecture*. Boston: Addison-Wesley.

Gamma, E., Helm, R., Johnson, R. and Vlissides, J. (1995) *Design Patterns: Elements of Reusable Object-Oriented Software*. Reading, Mass: Addison-Wesley.

Relational Databases, SQL and MySQL

A.1 What is a database?

A database is a way of storing data persistently, outside of computer memory, so that it exists beyond the run time of a single program, and can be accessed by multiple programs that need to share the same data. In the early days of computing, external storage used serial access technologies such as magnetic tape. To access data on a tape you have to start at the beginning and read along it until you find what you want. Data was stored in 'flat files' which is where the data is organized in a fixed, physical sequence. To assist in navigating between records, *indexed sequential* files were used, where each data record had a unique index to help identify it. With the development of random-access storage devices such as hard disks, it became possible to store data in more sophisticated ways, to support complex relationships between different parts of the data and access them directly without having to read sequentially through the records. At this point, the concept of the database began to emerge, to manage all the data in a system using direct-access storage.

Back in Chapter 1, we mentioned the four main things that we do with a database, represented by the acronym 'CRUD': Create, Read, Update and Delete. In this appendix, we look at how we can perform these four actions using database tools.

A.2 Relational databases

At the time of writing, the most common database technology is the relational database. There are many relational database products available, including Oracle, IBM DB2, Microsoft SQL Server and MySQL, among many others. Relational database theory was originally developed by Edgar Codd (1970), though most relational databases do not follow his theoretical basis very strictly. A relational database can be regarded simply as a collection of *tables* consisting of *rows* and *columns*, filled with data. There is a relation between the table's *metadata*, which is what specifies the valid type and range of data in each column, and the data itself. Each row in the table, also known as a *tuple*, represents a data record and each record in a table has the same structure, defined by the column headings. Each item of data (where a row and column meet) is known as a *field* (Figure A.1).

Both the rows and columns in a relational table are sets, which means that they are unique and occur in no particular order, making it impossible to retrieve the 'first row' or the 'last

FIGURE A.1 The structure of a relational database table

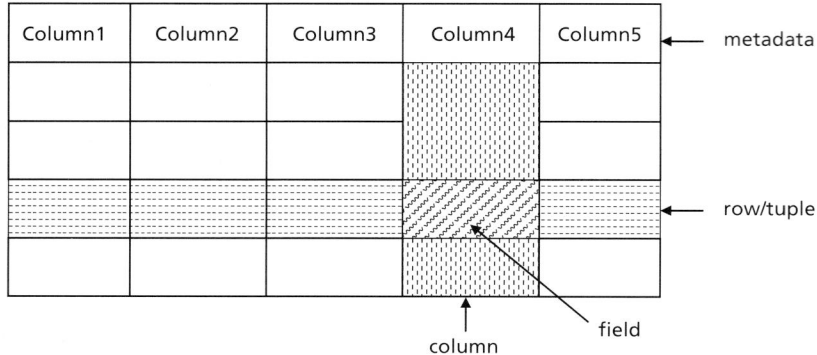

row' in a relational table. It is only possible to retrieve rows by specifying their content, e.g. 'row with account number 1023041' or 'all rows with date of birth field before January 1st 1998'. That, at least, is the theory. In practice, actual implementations of relational databases have a physical order of columns and rows, but we should not make assumptions about this order or try to use it in our interactions with the database. Since relational databases need to have tools associated with them to enable users to manage them and the data they store, the combination of the database and its tools is known as a relational database management system (RDBMS).

Table schemas

The way that a table is organized in terms of the names, types and constraints of its columns is known as its *schema*, and the *database schema* is the collection of schemas of all its tables. A table schema defines the name of each column, the data type stored in that column and the *primary key*. The types of data used in relational databases are known as Structured Query Language (SQL) types. These are reasonably consistent between different databases but there can be some differences. Common SQL data types include VARCHAR (a variable length character field), INTEGER and BOOLEAN. Each table needs a primary key column, which will contain data that is guaranteed to be unique. Since the rows in a table comprise a set, there cannot be any duplicates in the primary key column. The primary key is usually defined in a single column but it can also be a *compound key*, made up of the data from more than one field. The primary key can be a *natural key*, which means that it is part of the actual data in the record, for example a reference number. However there are two potential problems with using natural keys. One is that there is no guarantee that something about the data might not change over time (we might need to change the way reference numbers are structured, for example) and the other is that natural keys, particularly compound ones, can be inefficient when searching for records in the database. Therefore a better strategy is to use an *artificial key*, which is just an arbitrary value used as a key that is not part of the actual data in the record. Artificial key values can be generated for us by the database.

In addition to the types and names of the columns, the table schema might define additional information such as default values for columns or a constraint on what is acceptable data for a given column.

In the following example we create a simple table schema for a 'claim' table that contains data about insurance claims. The schema includes an artificial primary key called 'claimID_PK', which is an integer value; a reference, which is a natural key for the data using the VARCHAR data type; a textual description (also a VARCHAR); a floating-point value for the amount of the claim; a Boolean value to show whether or not the claim has been approved; and the date the claim was made. There is also a column containing some key data that enables us to refer to the policy against which the claim was made. This is an example of a *foreign key*, which we discuss shortly. Figure A.2 describes the schema of the 'claim' table.

You might wonder about the naming conventions for tables, columns and primary keys. Unfortunately there aren't any, or, rather, there are so many different conventions that there is no standard that everyone agrees upon. For our purposes, we adopt a naming convention that is reasonably compatible with the naming conventions we have used in our Java code. For example, we name our tables with singular nouns rather than plural, so our table here is called 'claim' rather than 'claims', using the same naming approach that we would for a Java class. Since MySQL (the database we will use for our examples) displays all table names in lower case, regardless of how they are entered, we use lower case for our table names. However MySQL does maintain the case of column names, so the columns are named in a similar way to Java fields, using *camel case* (i.e. a lower case first letter but upper case first letters for any embedded words). We also adopt a couple of common database-naming conventions. First, we add a suffix to all identifying columns of 'ID'; in this example, we have claimID (identifies a claim) and policyID (identifies a policy). In addition, the primary key of a table has a further '_PK' suffix. Similarly, any foreign keys have an '_FK' suffix. The data types are written in upper case, to distinguish them from Java data types which are written either in lower case, for primitive types, or Pascal case (like camel case but with an upper case first letter) for class names. It should be noted, however, that SQL is not case sensitive, so our use of upper and lower case here is just a convention and makes no difference to how our SQL statements work.

Foreign keys

A foreign key references a primary key from another row, which is often in another table. For example, we have a foreign key in the 'claim' table called 'policyID_FK', which is a foreign key that matches a primary key in another table, which we assume in this example is a 'policy' table (Figure A.3). Using foreign keys enables us to build relationships between different tables.

Foreign keys can be set up in the database with special constraints so that, for example, *cascade deletes* can be built into the tables. This means that we can set up the database so that if we delete a policy, for example, then all its related claims are automatically deleted too.

One-to-many relationships

A single foreign key references a single primary key. In the case of a one–to-many relationship between tables, there may be many different foreign keys referencing a single primary key

FIGURE A.2 The schema for the 'claim' table

claimID_PK (INTEGER, Primary Key)	reference (VARCHAR)	description (VARCHAR)	amount (FLOAT)	approved (BOOLEAN)	claimDate (DATE)	policyID_FK (INTEGER)

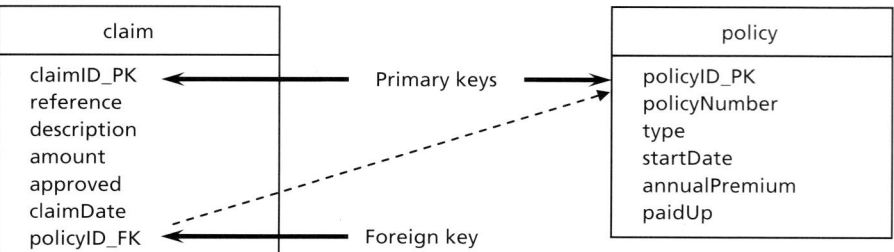

FIGURE A.3 The 'claim' and 'policy' tables related by foreign keys

FIGURE A.4 A one-to-many relationship between one policy and many claims, implemented with foreign keys in the 'claim' table

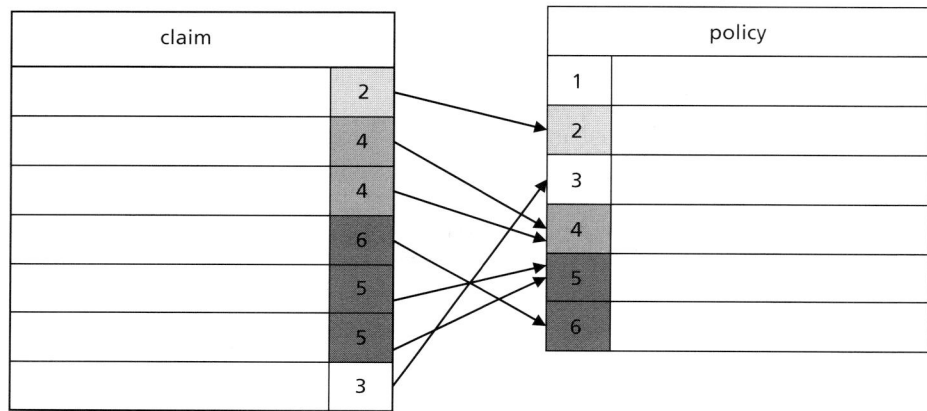

in another table. For example, there may be many claims made against a single policy. To implement this relationship, there can be multiple rows in the 'claim' table that have the same foreign key, all referencing the same row in the 'policy' table (Figure A.4).

A.3 Using MySQL

Before looking any further into database tables and their relationships, we introduce the MySQL relational database, which will enable you to work through the examples and exercises in the remainder of this Appendix.

MySQL is one of the more popular open-source database systems. It is a fully featured relational database management system (RDBMS), with a number of tools to help with configuration and management. If you are running Windows, MySQL can be run as a Windows service so it does not necessarily have to be started manually.

 NOTE This section refers to MySQL installed under Windows, but there are versions of MySQL for many different operating systems.

When MySQL is installed, it includes a configuration wizard which can be used to reconfigure the database after installation if required. This can be accessed in Windows using:

```
Start -> Programs -> MySQL -> MySQL Server -> MySQL Server Instance Config Wizard
```

One of the configuration options is to enable the command-line client. We describe how to use this client application to set up our database, so you need to ensure that the command-line client is enabled in the configuration wizard. If the client is enabled, you should be able to start it in Windows using:

```
Start -> Programs -> MySQL -> MySQL Server -> MySQL Command Line Client
```

When you start the command-line client, it asks you for the password which you selected when MySQL was installed. If you log in successfully, you see a 'mysql' prompt (Figure A.5).

 NOTE When you want to exit the command-line client, simply type 'exit' or 'quit' at the 'mysql' prompt.

Creating a new database

To create a new MySQL database, use the 'create database' command:

```
create database databasename;
```

For example, to create a new database called 'webhomecoverdb', we would enter the following command (note the semicolon required at the end of the command):

```
create database webhomecoverdb;
```

Once a database has been created, we can connect to it with 'use *databasename*'. To connect to the 'webhomecoverdb' database, we would enter the following command:

```
use webhomecoverdb;
```

This should result in the 'Database changed' message coming back from MySQL. At this point, however, the database has no schema, so there is not much to connect to. The next step is to set up the schemas of the tables in the database using Structured Query Language (SQL).

FIGURE A.5   The MySQL command-line client

```
MySQL Command Line Client

Enter password: ****
Welcome to the MySQL monitor.  Commands end with ; or \g.
Your MySQL connection id is 1 to server version: 5.0.15-nt

Type 'help;' or '\h' for help. Type '\c' to clear the buffer.

mysql>
```

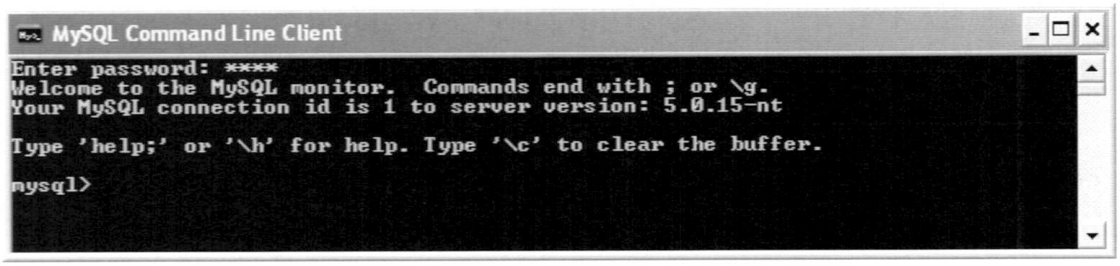

When using the command-line client, all commands need to be terminated by a semicolon. If you type a line that does not end in a semicolon and press the 'Enter' key, MySQL keeps giving you a prompt, waiting for more lines of the command or a semicolon to be entered. This facility means that you can enter a single command over a series of lines, and the command is only executed when you add the semicolon at the end (Figure A.6).

Creating a database schema with SQL

SQL is the standard language for accessing relational databases. It allows you to:

- Create tables (CREATE statements)
- Insert data rows into tables (INSERT statements)
- Update (change) data in tables (UPDATE statements)
- Retrieve data from tables according to various criteria, i.e. execute queries (SELECT statements)
- Remove rows from tables (DELETE statements)
- Perform other operations connected with data and table management, such as dropping tables from the database (DROP statements).

 NOTE In all the examples that follow, we use upper case for SQL keywords; since SQL is not case sensitive, this is not a requirement.

The SQL syntax for creating a table is CREATE TABLE, followed by the name of the table and, in parentheses, the description of each of the columns in the table. For each description, the name of the column is followed by its type. For the VARCHAR type, which is a variable-length character field, we need to specify the maximum allowed size of the data in characters. There may be some other information, such as whether a field is a primary key or whether it is allowed to have a 'NULL' value (i.e. does not have to have any data in it). The column descriptions are separated by commas (the line feeds here are just to aid

FIGURE A.6 Multi-line input in the command-line client

```
MySQL Command Line Client                                        - □ ×
Enter password: ****
Welcome to the MySQL monitor.  Commands end with ; or \g.
Your MySQL connection id is 3 to server version: 5.0.15-nt

Type 'help;' or '\h' for help. Type '\c' to clear the buffer.

mysql> create
    -> database
    -> webhomecoverdb
    -> ;
Query OK, 1 row affected (0.00 sec)

mysql> _
```

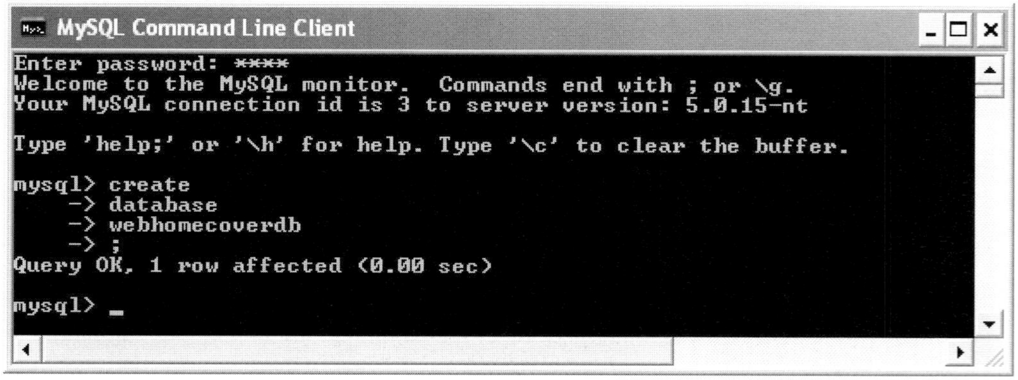

readability). Here is the SQL to create a table called 'claim' with the columns that were described in Figure A.2.

```
CREATE TABLE claim (
    claimID_PK INTEGER NOT NULL PRIMARY KEY,
    reference VARCHAR(15);
    description VARCHAR(100),
    amount FLOAT,
    approved BOOLEAN,
    claimDate DATE,
    policyID_FK INTEGER
);
```

A long command like this can be entered over multiple lines in MySQL, with the final semicolon ending the command:

```
mysql> create table claim(
    -> claimID_PK INTEGER NOT NULL PRIMARY KEY,
    -> reference VARCHAR(15),
    -> description VARCHAR(100),
    -> amount FLOAT,
    -> approved BOOLEAN,
    -> claimDate DATE,
    -> policyID_FK INTEGER
     -> );
```

Viewing table schema

In MySQL, the 'show tables' command lists all the tables in the database to which you are connected. In our case there is only one table, so the result of the 'show tables' command would look like this:

```
+- - - - - - - - - - - - +
| Tables_in_webhomecoverdb   |
+- - - - - - - - - - - - +
| claim                      |
+- - - - - - - - - - - - +
```

To see the schema of the 'claim' table, we can use the 'describe' command, which shows the schema of the named table:

```
describe claim;
```

This is the table schema that MySQL displays:

```
+- - - - - - -+- - - - - - - + - - - + - - -+- - - - -+- - - +
| Field       | Type         | Null  | Key | Default | Extra |
+- - - - - - -+- - - - - - - + - - - + - - -+- - - - -+- - - +
| claimID_PK  | int(11)      | NO    | PRI |         |       |
| reference   | varchar(15)  | YES   |     | NULL    |       |
| description | varchar(100) | YES   |     | NULL    |       |
| amount      | float        | YES   |     | NULL    |       |
```

approved	tinyint(1)	YES		NULL		
claimDate	date	YES		NULL		
policyID_FK	int(11)	YES		NULL		
+- - - - - - -+- - - - - - - - +- - - +- - -+- - - - -+- - - +

A.4 Adding data to tables

Having set up the schema of a single table in the database, we can add data to it using SQL INSERT statements. The structure of an INSERT statement looks like this:

```
INSERT INTO tablename VALUES (comma-separated list of values, one for each column);
```

Here is an INSERT statement that adds a row to the table, providing data for each of the columns. If there is a column where we do not yet have data to enter, we can use a NULL value, which effectively means that this column is empty. This can only be done with columns that do not have the 'NOT NULL' constraint in the schema, so we cannot do this with the primary key column ('claimID_PK'). Here, since we have not yet created a policy table, the foreign key to the policy is given a NULL value.

```
INSERT INTO Claim VALUES
   (1,'B200705111','Broken window',150.00,TRUE,'2007-05-11',NULL);
```

This SQL syntax only works if you are providing data for every single column in the table. If, on the other hand, you are using an INSERT statement where you are not providing data for all of the columns, you have to specify which columns you are populating, followed by the values that are being inserted, using this syntax:

```
INSERT INTO tablename (column1, column2, etc.) VALUES (value1, value2, etc.);
```

For example, instead of specifically entering NULL into the foreign key column, we could choose to let the database do this for us by default. However, we then need to specify the column names and values for which we are providing data, as in this example:

```
INSERT INTO Claim
   (claimID_PK, reference, description, amount, approved, claimDate)
   VALUES (2,'B200705111','Stained carpet',1000.00,FALSE,'2007-04-13');
```

Manually entering SQL to set up and populate tables can be a tedious and error-prone process. A much better option is to write all the SQL statements into a Data Definition Language (DDL) file that can be executed in one go by MySQL. A DDL file simply combines a series of SQL statements. This one combines the schema creation and table population into a single file, which writes four data records to the 'claim' table:

```
USE webhomecoverdb;

DROP TABLE claim;
CREATE TABLE claim (
   claimID_PK INTEGER NOT NULL PRIMARY KEY,
   reference VARCHAR(15),
   description VARCHAR(100),
   amount FLOAT,
   approved BOOLEAN,
```

```
    claimDate DATE,
    policyID_FK INTEGER
);

INSERT INTO claim VALUES
    (1,'B200711051','Broken window',150.00,true,'2007-05-11',1);
INSERT INTO claim VALUES
    (2,'C200704131','Stained carpet',1000.00,false,'2007-04-13',2);
INSERT INTO claim VALUES
    (3,'C200722011','Stolen camera',650.00,true,'2007-01-22',2);
INSERT INTO claim VALUES
    (4,'B200704011','House burned down',350000.00,true,'2007-01-04',3);
```

The CREATE statement is preceded by a DROP statement, which removes the named table from the database. This is useful where we are recreating the 'claim' table with a new schema, since before this can be done we need to drop the existing table. The first time the DROP statement is executed, MySQL may display an error message that the 'claim' table is unknown, if it has not been created previously. However this does not prevent the CREATE statement from being executed.

To execute a DDL file in MySQL you use the 'source' command, followed by the path and filename. You have to be careful here, because the separator character between subfolders in the path must be a forward slash, not a back slash. In this example, we assume that the DDL file is called 'webhomecoverdb.ddl' and resides in a folder called 'ddlfiles' on the C: drive:

```
source C:/ddlfiles/webhomecoverdb.ddl;
```

A.5 Querying the database

Once you have created your schema and populated the table, you can read data from it by executing SQL queries against the database, using SELECT statements. The simplest type of SELECT statement, which displays columns from tables without any kind of query filter, is:

```
SELECT columnname, columnname, columname...FROM tablename;
```

This selects all the rows from the table but only includes data from the selected columns. If the names of the columns to be selected are replaced by the '*' wildcard, then all the columns are selected. This query therefore selects all the columns and rows from the 'claim' table:

```
SELECT * FROM claim;
```

This is the data that is returned by the query (the column names have been removed to fit within the page width).

```
+- -+- - - - - -+- - - - - - - - - +- - - - - - - +- - - - - +- -+
| 1 | B200711051 |Broken window    |    150 | 1 | 2007-05-11 | 1 |
| 2 | C200704131 |Stained carpet   |   1000 | 0 | 2007-04-13 | 2 |
| 3 | C200722011 |Stolen camera    |    650 | 1 | 2007-01-22 | 2 |
| 4 | B200704011 |House burned down | 350000 | 1 | 2007-01-04 | 3 |
+- -+- - - - - -+- - - - - - - - - -+- - - - - - - +- - - - - +- -+
```

In contrast, this next query selects only some of the columns. The names of the columns in the query must be separated by commas:

```
SELECT description, amount, claimDate FROM claim;
```

This is the data that is selected by the query:

```
+- - - - - - - - - -+- - - - +- - - - - - +
| description       | amount | claimDate  |
+- - - - - - - - - -+- - - - +- - - - - - +
| Broken window     |    150 | 2007-05-11 |
| Stained carpet    |   1000 | 2007-04-13 |
| Stolen camera     |    650 | 2007-01-22 |
| House burned down | 350000 | 2007-01-04 |
+- - - - - - - - - -+- - - - +- - - - - - +
```

Using SELECT to specify query conditions

So far we have seen SELECT statements that specify the columns returned by the query, but each time all the rows have been selected. To apply queries to the actual data in the rows, we add a WHERE clause to the SELECT statement, following this structure:

```
SELECT columnname(s) FROM tablename WHERE condition;
```

The 'where' condition relates to the data that is stored in the table, and selects rows from the table based on that condition. For example, we might select only those rows from the table where the amount of the claim is less than 750. SQL supports the usual set of relational operators. Some of these use the same symbols that we use in Java and JavaScript, for example '>' means 'greater than' and '<' means 'less than'. You should note, however that there are also some differences. For example '<>' is the symbol for 'not equal', which of course differs from Java and JavaScript, where the 'not equal' symbol is '!= '. The 'equal to' operator in SQL is ' =', which of course again differs from Java and JavaScript where ' = ' is the assignment operator and the equality operator is ' == '.

In this example we use the 'less than' operator ('<') in the WHERE condition:

```
SELECT description, amount FROM claim WHERE amount < 750;
```

Here is the data returned by the SELECT query:

```
+- - - - - - - -+- - - - +
| description   | amount |
+- - - - - - - -+- - - - +
| Broken window |    150 |
| Stolen camera |    650 |
+- - - - - - - -+- - - - +
```

Querying on columns that contain text (such as VARCHAR columns) requires the search string to be in apostrophes or speech marks. For example, if we wanted to search for the text 'House burned down' in the 'description' column, our query would look like this:

```
SELECT description, amount, claimDate FROM claim WHERE description = 'House
burned down';
```

Here is the single row that would be returned by this query:

```
+- - - - - - - - - -+- - - - +- - - - - - +
| description      | amount | claimDate |
+- - - - - - - - - -+- - - - +- - - - - - +
| House burned down | 350000 | 2007-01-04 |
+- - - - - - - - - -+- - - - +- - - - - - +
```

Querying on NULL values

As we have seen from the 'policyID_FK' column, if a value is unknown or not applicable it can be represented by a NULL value. Here is an INSERT statement that only puts data into three columns: the primary key, the description and the claim date:

```
INSERT INTO claim (claimID_PK, description, claimDate) VALUES (5, 'Meteor damage',
'2007-05-20');
```

This leads to NULL values being inserted into the remaining columns, as we can see here (the primary and foreign key names have been truncated to fit within the page width).

```
+--+- - - - - -+- - - - - - - - -+- - - - +- - - - - +- - - - - -+- - +
|PK | reference | description    | amount | approved | claimDate |FK  |
+--+- - - - - -+- - - - - - - - -+- - - - +- - - - - +- - - - - -+- - +
|5  | NULL      | Meteor damage  | NULL   | NULL     | 2007-05-20 |NULL |
+--+- - - - - -+- - - - - - - - -+- - - - +- - - - - +- - - - - -+- - +
```

NULL values can be used in queries in the same way that data values can. When querying on these values, however, the WHERE clause of a query that refers to a NULL value uses the terms 'IS' and 'IS NOT' rather than the equality operator, for example:

```
SELECT description, approved FROM claim WHERE approved IS NULL;
```

This returns the following result.

```
+- - - - - - - -+- - - - - +
| description   |  approved|
+- - - - - - - -+- - - - - +
| Meteor damage |     NULL|
+- - - - - - - -+- - - - - +
```

We can also query for values that are NOT NULL, for example:

```
SELECT description, amount FROM claim WHERE amount IS NOT NULL;
```

In this case, we get the four rows that do not have a null value in the 'amount' column:

```
+- - - - - - - - - -+- - - - +
| description      | amount |
+- - - - - - - - - -+- - - - +
| Broken window    |    150|
| Stained carpet   |   1000|
```

```
| Stolen camera      |     650|
| House burned down  |  350000|
+- - - - - - - - - -+- - - - +
```

Combining conditions

Multiple conditions can be combined into a single query by using the Boolean AND and OR operators. We can apply multiple criteria to a single column or apply conditions to multiple columns. In this example, we look for approved claims that are worth more than 500:

```
SELECT amount, claimDate FROM claim WHERE amount > 500 AND approved=true;
```

Here is the data selected by the query:

```
+- - - - +- - - - - - +
|   amount| claimDate  |
+- - - - +- - - - - - +
|     650| 2007-01-22 |
|   350000| 2007-01-04 |
+- - - - +- - - - - - +
```

In contrast to the last query, which used an 'and' condition, this one uses an 'or' condition, selecting those records where claims have not been approved or the claim was prior to February 2007.

```
SELECT description, amount, claimDate, approved FROM claim WHERE claimDate
<'2007-02-01' OR approved <>true;
```

```
+- - - - - - - - - -+- - - - +- - - - - - +- - - - - +
| description       | amount | claimDate  | approved |
+- - - - - - - - - -+- - - - +- - - - - - +- - - - - +
| Stained carpet    |   1000| 2007-04-13 |        0|
| Stolen camera     |    650| 2007-01-22 |        1|
| House burned down |  350000| 2007-01-04 |        1|
+- - - - - - - - - -+- - - - +- - - - - - +- - - - - +
```

Note that queries on date fields require the date to be treated like a character string, enclosed in apostrophes or speech marks.

A.6 Updating the database

So far all our interactions with the database, apart from the initial creation, have been queries that read data. However we also need to be able to make changes to the database by updating or deleting records. To make a change to an existing record, we use the UPDATE ... SET statement. Here, for example, we update a row by changing the 'approved' column value to 'false' in the row with the id of '4':

```
UPDATE claim SET approved = false WHERE claimID_PK = 4;
```

After this update has been executed, MySQL should return the following message:

```
Rows matched: 1 Changed: 1 Warnings: 0
```

We can also check the update was successful by executing a query on the row we updated:

```
SELECT claimID_PK, approved FROM claim WHERE claimID_PK = 4;
```

The resulting data shows that the value in the 'approved' column is now 0 (false):

```
+ - - - - - + - - - - - +
| claimID_PK | approved |
+ - - - - - + - - - - - +
|        4 |       0 |
+ - - - - - + - - - - - +
```

Records can be deleted from tables using the DELETE FROM statement. In this example we delete the 'Stained carpet' record:

```
DELETE FROM claim WHERE description='Stained carpet'
```

Remember that to delete an entire table we use the DROP command, as we did in the DDL script e.g.

```
DROP TABLE claim;
```

A.7 Adding more tables to the database

So far all our examples have been based on a single table. However a database that consists of one table is not very useful. The overall database schema needs to reflect the data model of our application, which consists of many different *entities*. Each entity represents a complex data type in the system domain, in a very similar way to the concepts of the domain model that we looked at in Chapter 2. The most important difference between domain model concepts and entities is that entities are things that are stored persistently in the database, whereas the concepts in a domain model include many things that are not represented by persistent data.

To describe the structure of the simple database we use in this chapter, we draw an entity–relationship diagram (ERD). Entity–relationship diagrams are a way of describing a database schema. There are, however a number of different notations for these diagrams. In this book we use Chen's original notation (Chen 1976) where entities are rectangles and relationships are diamonds, with 'n' used to signify a 'many' relationship (Figure A.7). In our example, we are going to base our database schema on some of the main concepts in our domain model, which also provides the basis for our object model. This means that it is easy to map between the object model running in our web application and the structure of the data stored in the database. Figure A.7 shows an ERD of the simplified database we create and use for the rest of the examples and exercises in this chapter. It consists of three entities, 'policyholder', 'policy' and 'claim'. Each policy holder may have multiple policies, while each policy belongs to one policy holder. Each claim is made against a single policy, but one policy may have many claims made against it.

This database is incomplete in terms of the domain model of the home insurance application, but it provides enough detail for the examples in the rest of this appendix.

An entity–relationship diagram of entities from the home insurance domain

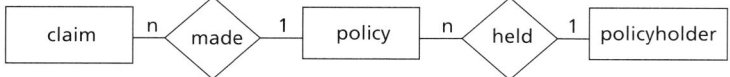

NOTE	In many real-life situations, a direct mapping between a domain model, an object model and a database schema is not possible, because the database schema may already exist and our application may be only one of many that use the same database. In situations such as this, the object model and the database schema may be quite different, leading to some complex *object-relational mapping*.

Figure A.8 shows the three tables with their column names and foreign key relationships.

Generating primary keys

In the DDL file that we used to create and populate the 'claim' table, the primary keys are provided as part of the set of values that are inserted into the record. This is relatively straightforward when creating the initial database, but it means that any further inserts into any of the tables rely on us knowing how to provide a value for the artificial primary keys. There are various strategies for this, but a simple approach is to let the database generate primary keys for us. In MySQL, this is very simple; we just add 'AUTO_INCREMENT' to the configuration of the primary keys, for example:

```
CREATE TABLE claim (
    claimID_PK INTEGER NOT NULL PRIMARY KEY AUTO_INCREMENT,
. . .
```

This does not prevent us from providing a primary key value if we want to, but if we do not then MySQL generates a new integer key every time a new record is inserted.

NOTE	Different databases have different ways of generating keys, so the AUTO_INCREMENT syntax used with MySQL is not portable to other databases. An alternative approach is to manage key generation with our own database-independent implementation. An example of this strategy can be found in (Reese 2003).

Here is a DDL file to create all three tables from Figure A.8. All the tables have artificial primary keys that are auto-incremented, but the original set of data inserted into the tables explicitly defines the primary keys.

The columns in the three database tables with foreign key relationships

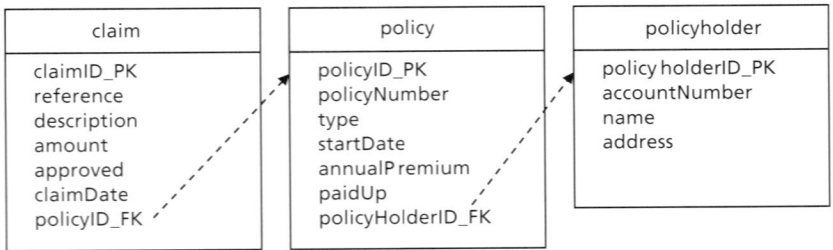

```
USE webhomecoverdb;

DROP TABLE claim;
CREATE TABLE claim (
   claimID_PK INTEGER NOT NULL PRIMARY KEY AUTO_INCREMENT,
   reference VARCHAR(15),
   description VARCHAR(100),
   amount FLOAT,
   approved BOOLEAN,
   claimDate DATE,
   policyID_FK INTEGER
);

DROP TABLE policy;
CREATE TABLE policy (
   policyID_PK INTEGER NOT NULL PRIMARY KEY AUTO_INCREMENT,
   policyNumber INTEGER,
   type VARCHAR(20),
   startDate DATE,
   annualPremium FLOAT,
   paidUp BOOLEAN,
   policyHolderID_FK INTEGER
);

DROP TABLE policyholder;
CREATE TABLE policyholder (
   policyholderID_PK INTEGER NOT NULL PRIMARY KEY AUTO_INCREMENT,
   accountNumber INTEGER,
   name VARCHAR(30),
   address VARCHAR(50)
);

INSERT INTO claim
   VALUES (1,'B2007-11-051','Broken window',150.00,true,'2007-05-11',1);
INSERT INTO claim
   VALUES (2,'C2007-04-131','Stained carpet',1000.00,false,'2007-04-13',2);
INSERT INTO claim
   VALUES (3,'C2007-22-011','Stolen camera',650.00,true,'2007-01-22',2);
```

```
INSERT INTO claim
    VALUES (4,'B2007-04-011','House burned down',350000.00,true,'2007-01-04',3);

INSERT INTO policy VALUES
    (1,233142,'buildings','2007-02-12',45.60,true,1);
INSERT INTO policy VALUES
    (2,384475,'contents','2006-11-21',37.00,true,1);
INSERT INTO policy VALUES
    (3,332574,'buildings','2005-06-03',120.50,false,2);
INSERT INTO policy VALUES
    (4,928376,'buildings','2008-12-30',120.50,true,3);
INSERT INTO policy VALUES
    (5,885746,'contents','2007-10-13',120.50,true,3);

INSERT INTO policyholder VALUES(1,1625344,'Mr. Charles Babbage','55, Old Road,
London, United Kingdom');
INSERT INTO policyholder VALUES(2,5424882,'Dr. Bjarne Stroustrup','4, Wellington
Road, Auckland, New Zealand');
INSERT INTO policyholder VALUES(3,2314253,'Ms. Grace Hopper','1,Forest Heights,
San Francisco, United States');
```

Joining multiple tables

The simple SQL queries we have looked at so far have retrieved data from a single table, but it is also possible to retrieve data from more than one table, based on some common values, using a *join*. For example, our database includes the 'claim' table, which contains data such as the description and amount of the claim along with a foreign key of rows in a policy table. It also includes the 'policy' table, which contains data including the policy type and the start date. Joining the two tables by these key values matches the description and amount of a claim against the date and type of policy, for example. When we create a query that joins tables, we have to specify which columns belong to which table, using the following syntax:

```
tablename.columnname
```

To refer to the description column in the claim table for example, we would use:

```
claim.description
```

Here is an example SELECT statement that joins the claim and policy tables using a foreign key. We look for the policy with policy number '384475', and then select records from the 'claim' table where the foreign key matches the selected policy's primary key.

```
SELECT policy.policyNumber, claim.description, claim.amount, claim.claimDate
FROM claim, policy WHERE policy.policyNumber=384475 AND claim.policyID_FK=
policy.policyID_PK;
```

The resulting data from the query is a combination of results from the two tables, showing us details of the claims related to that policy.

```
+- - - - - - - +- - - - - - - - +- - - - +- - - - - - +
| policyNumber | description    | amount|   claimDate |
+- - - - - - - +- - - - - - - - +- - - - +- - - - - - +
| 384475       | Stained carpet |   1000|  2007-04-13 |
| 384475       | Stolen camera  |    650|  2007-01-22 |
+- - - - - - - +- - - - - - - - +- - - - +- - - - - - +
```

 NOTE | The example here is an *implicit join*. An alternative approach is to use the 'JOIN' keyword in SQL to create an *explicit join*.

Although joins are very important when programming just at the database level, they are not necessarily going to be of assistance when linking an object model to the database. We are more likely to manage relationships between objects within the application itself.

Table A.1 summarizes the MySQL commands we introduced when using the MySQL command-line client.

TABLE A.1   MySQL commands

MySQL Command	Meaning
create database *dbname*	Create a new database
use *dbname*	Connect to an existing database
show databases	Show the names of all databases
exit *or* quit	Exit from MySQL
source *path/filename*	Execute a SQL script file
describe *tablename*	Show the schema of a table

Using XMLSpy

INTRODUCTION

XMLSpy is an XML editor from Altova® GmbH that provides tools for modeling, editing, transforming and debugging XML technologies. Among its many features, it provides support for XML validation, XPath evaluation and XSL transformation.

This appendix refers to the Altova® XMLSpy 2007 Enterprise Edition which is supplied with this book. The current version, along with an evaluation licence key, can be downloaded from http://www.altova.com/download. Altova are also able to provide special site licences for educational partners and extended evaluation licences for students enrolled on recognized courses. Enquiries by academic staff should be made to the Altova Partner program (partners@altova.com).

B.1 Why do we need XMLSpy?

Browsers such as Internet Explorer can check if XML and DTD documents are well formed. Figure B.1 shows Internet Explorer 7 displaying an error message about an XML document that is not well formed.

Most browsers do not, however, validate XML documents without special tools being added. In addition, browsers offer little editing support for XML documents. Therefore it can be much more productive to edit and process XML documents using a dedicated tool like XMLSpy, which can, among other things:

- Check if XML documents are well-formed
- Validate XML documents against DTD
- Validate XML documents against an XML Schema
- Perform XSLT transformations
- Display HTML / XHTML

Internet Explorer 7 displaying an error message because an XML document is not well formed

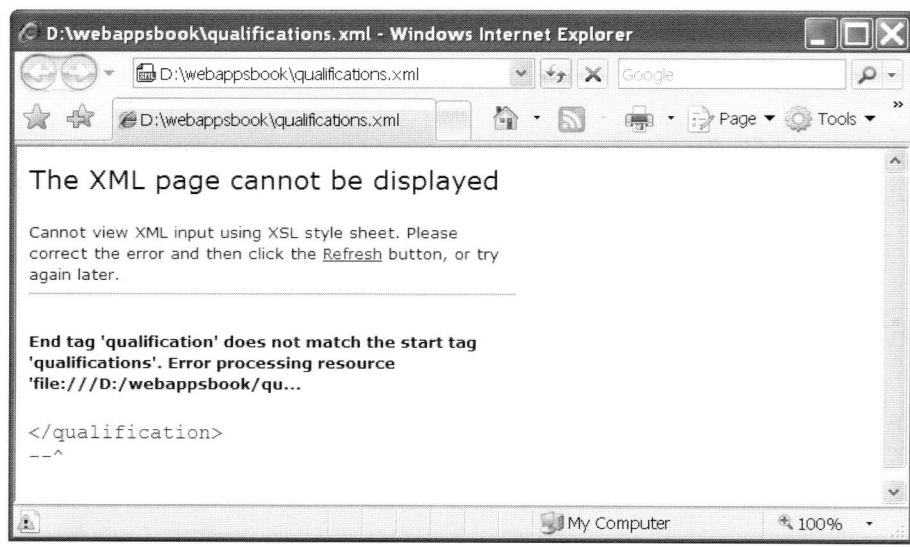

The XMLSpy windows and helpers

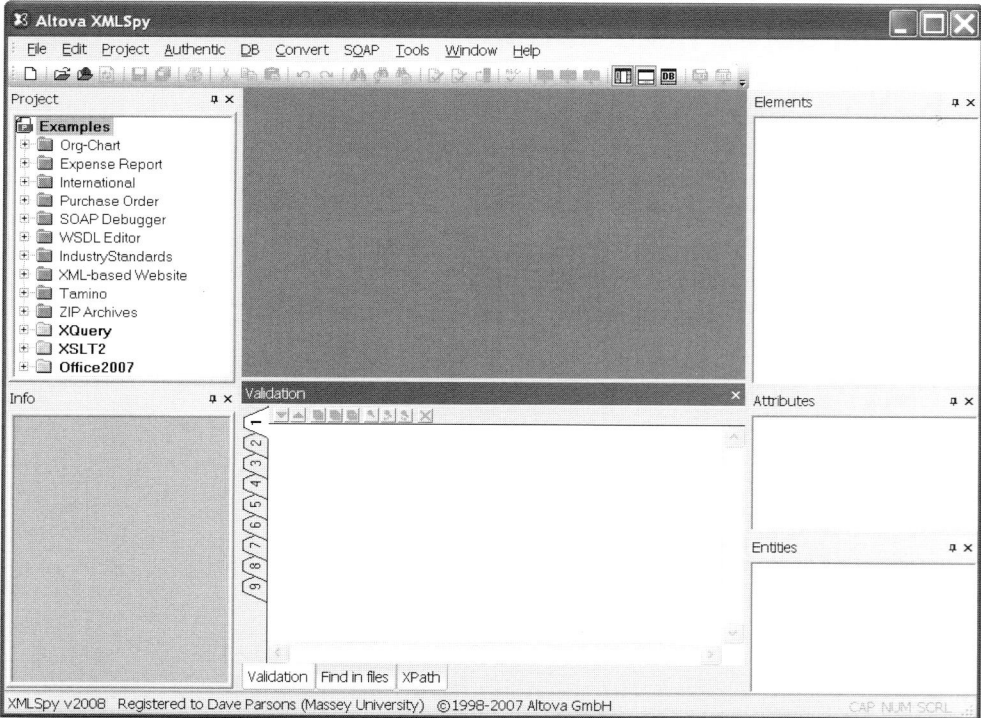

B.2 Using XMLSpy

To install XMLSpy, you will need to run the installation file, which is available both on the CD supplied with this book and from the Altova web site. Once the program has been installed, you will need to run it for the first time in order to enter your license details. These can be copied from the email that will be received from Altova once you have applied for an evaluation licence.

The XMLSpy environment comprises a number of windows and 'helpers' (Figure B.2), which can be toggled on and off using the 'Window' menu item. The left hand view is the 'Project' window, but you do not have to use a project in XMLSpy. Documents can be created and manipulated independently of a project file. However a project is useful if you want to group multiple documents together for loading and saving as a unit, for example an XML file and its associated DTD.

Creating a New File

To create a new file, click on the 'File' menu and then select 'New'. A dialog box will appear similar to that shown in Figure B.3. From here, you can choose the type of file you want to create, for example a new XML document.

If you choose to create a new XML document, another dialog will appear that asks you to choose either a DTD or an XML Schema to validate the document (Figure B.4). If you do not yet have one of these, you can simply click the 'Cancel' button. Otherwise another dialog will appear that lets you browse for a DTD or an XML Schema to apply to the document.

FIGURE B.3 The 'Create new document' dialog in XMLSpy

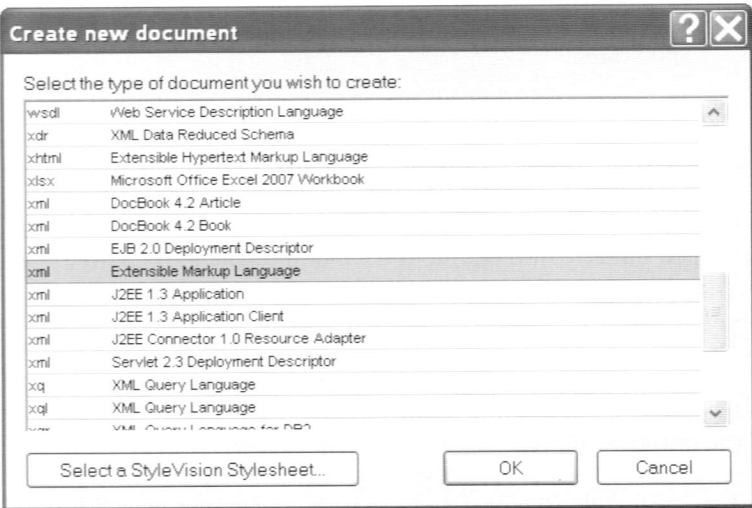

FIGURE B.4 The Dialog that enables a DTD or XML Schema to be assigned to a new XML document

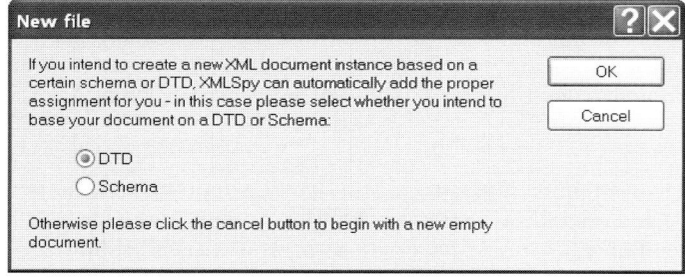

FIGURE B.5a XMLSpy indicating that an XML document is not well-formed

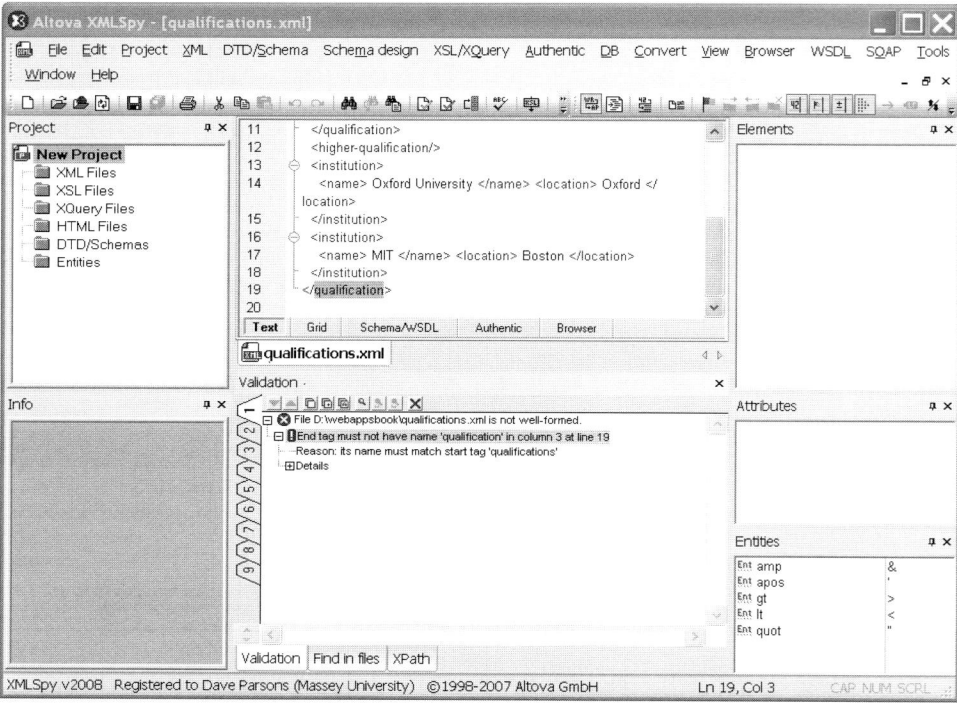

Testing if XML Documents are Well-Formed and Valid

You can use XMLSpy to test if XML documents are both well-formed and valid. The XML source can be typed directly into editing the window, copied and pasted from an external editor or loaded from an external file (XMLSpy also provides a number of different editing views that make it easy to create and edit a document). To test if the XML document is well formed, select 'XML' from the main menu and then select 'Check well-formedness'. The result will appear in the output window at the bottom of the screen. Figure B.5a shows an XML document that is not well formed, with an error message displayed in the output window.

Figure B.5b shows the 'tick' icon that appears if the document is well formed.

XMLSpy indicating well-formed XML document

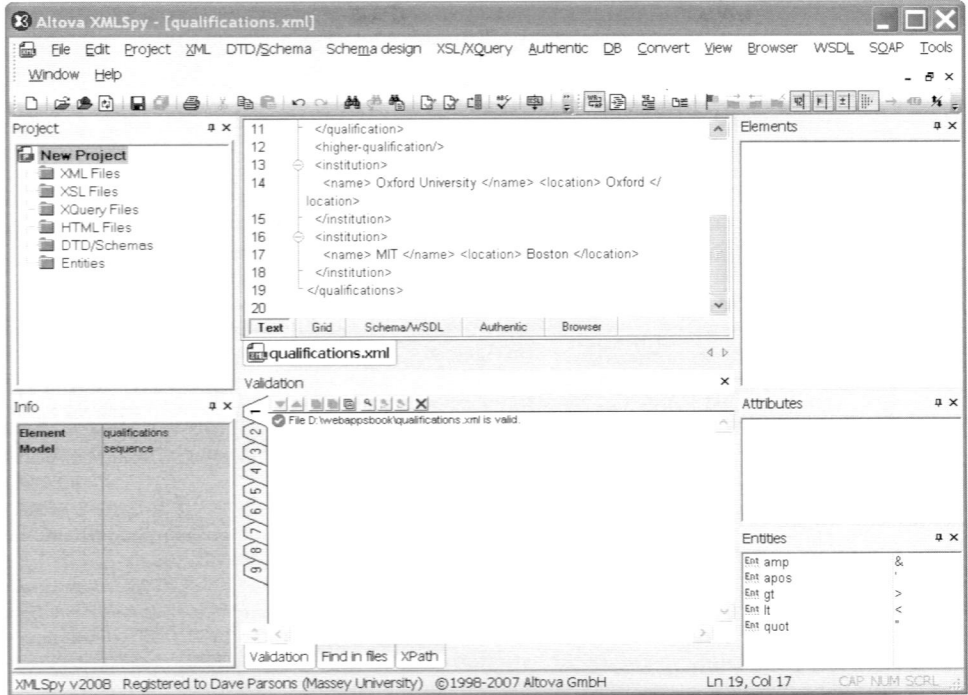

FIGURE B.6   The dialog that enables you to browse for a validating document

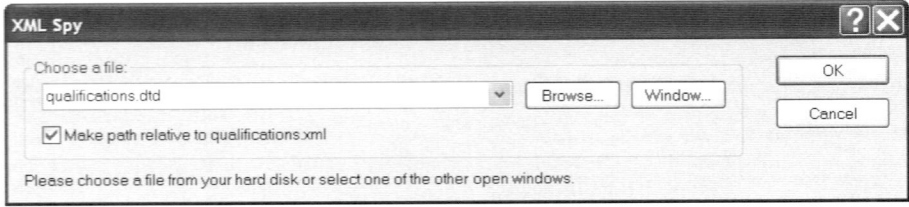

Validating XML

To validate an XML document you can assign either a DTD or an XML Schema. This assignment can either be done manually or by browsing for the validating document via the 'DTD/Schema' menu item. To assign a DTD, for example, select 'Assign DTD' from the 'DTD/Schema' menu and find the document in the file system (Figure B.6).

Once a DTD has been assigned to an XML document, you can check if it is valid by selecting 'XML' from the top level menu and then selecting 'validate' from the menu. Figure B.7 shows an error message being displayed by XMLSpy because an XML document has failed validation.

Figure B.8 shows a valid document being checked by XMLSpy.

FIGURE B.7 XMLSpy indicating that an XML document has failed validation

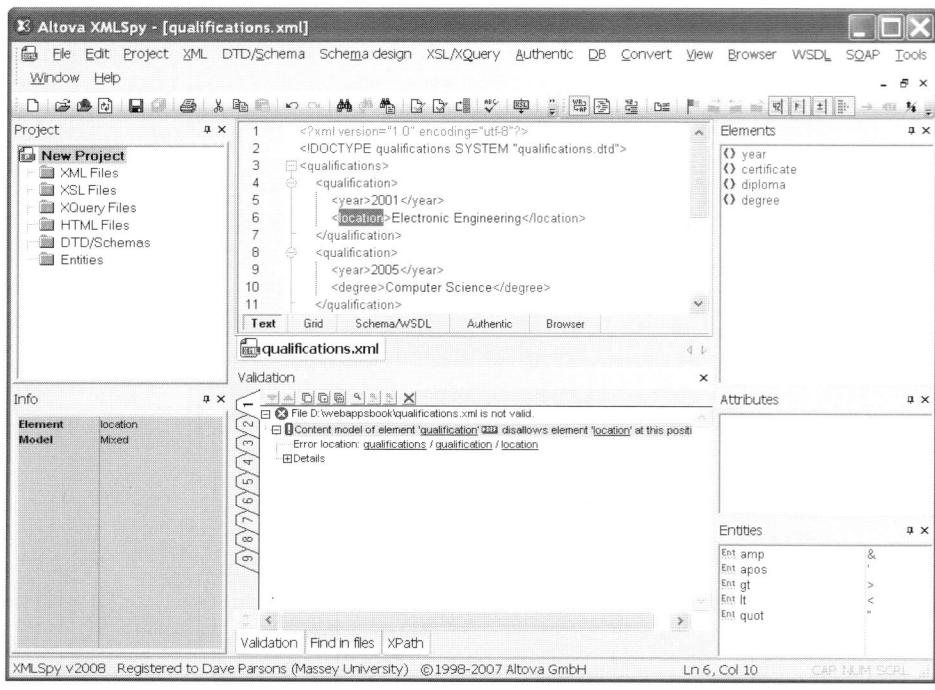

FIGURE B.8 An XML document passing validation in XMLSpy

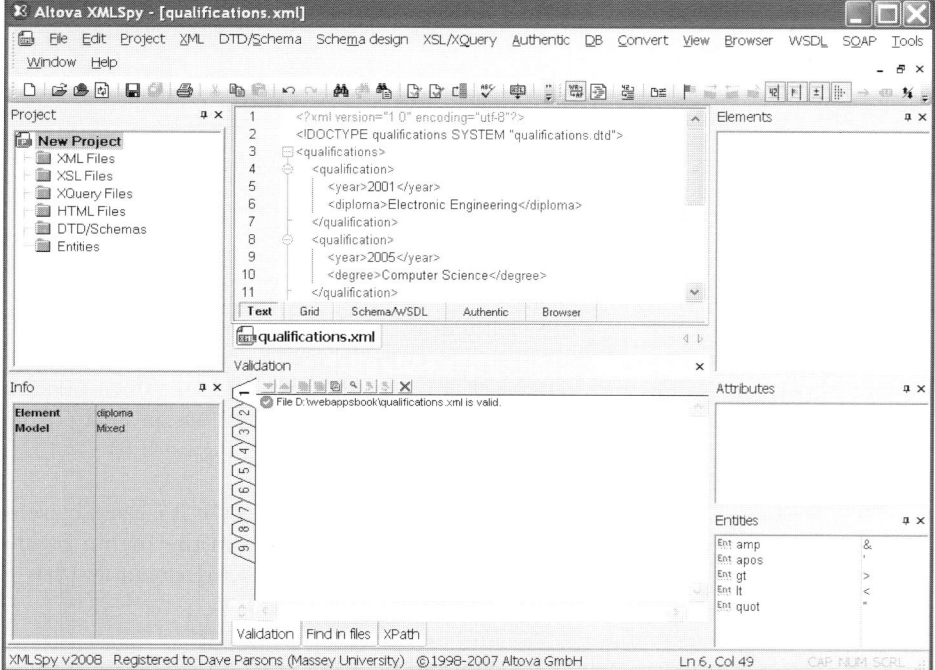

Evaluating XPath

XMLSpy includes a special output window to evaluate Path expressions. The output windows are tabbed, so to bring the XPath window to the front, simply click on the 'XPath' tab in the output window area. Figure B.9 shows the result of an XPath expression being evaluated against the 'policy-claims.xml' document that was used for the examples in Chapter 6.

There are a number of buttons on the toolbar that can be used to manage XPath evaluations. One of these is the 'Show complete result' button, which looks like this:

<. . .>

This button toggles between showing just the content of selected elements and the elements themselves. Figure B.10 shows the output when this button has been toggled on.

FIGURE B.9   Evaluating an XPath Expression in XMLSpy

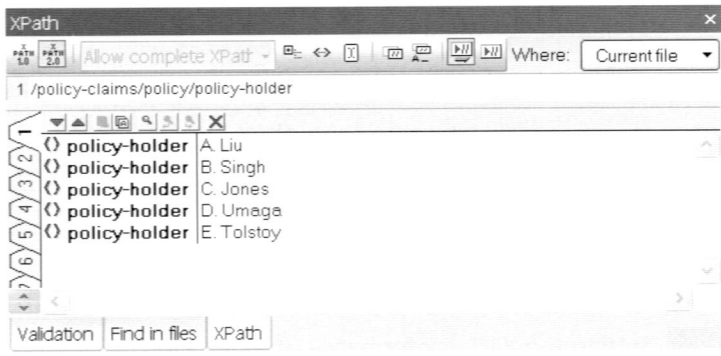

FIGURE B.10   Evaluating an XPath Expression in XMLSpy with the complete result displayed

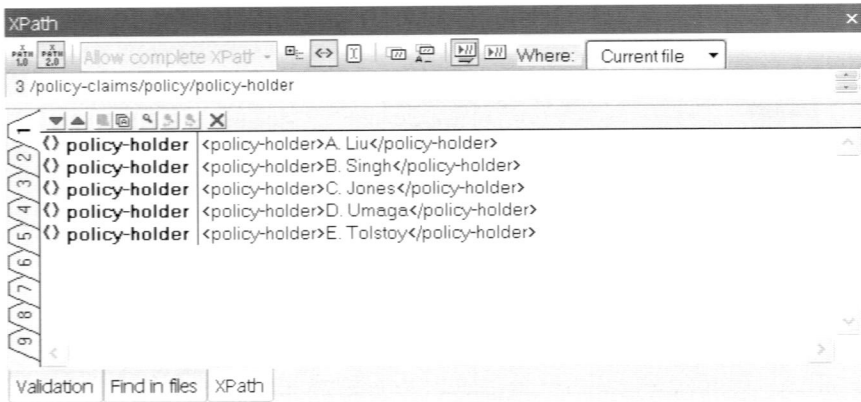

There is also a 'toggle' button that is used to specify if the XPath expression is to be evaluated as it is typed. This is shown in Figure B.11. If this button is off, then the button to its right, which has a similar symbol on it, can be used to evaluate a complete XPath expression after it has been typed in.

XML Transformations

Transforming an XML document using XSLT is simple in XMLSpy. However in some of our examples we have transformed XML into HTML documents that are not valid XHTML. In order to avoid problems with transforming these documents, it may be necessary to change the settings in XMLSpy that specify how files with '.htm' and '.html' extensions are validated. To check this setting, select the 'Tools' menu, then select 'Options'. In the Dialog box that appears, select the 'File types' tab. If the 'XML conformant' radio button is selected, then you will need to select the 'Other format' radio button (Figure B.12).

FIGURE B.11 The toggle button that specifies whether XPath expressions are to be evaluated on typing

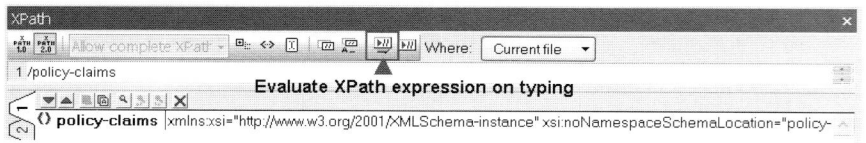

FIGURE B.12 Setting the XML conformance of HTML files

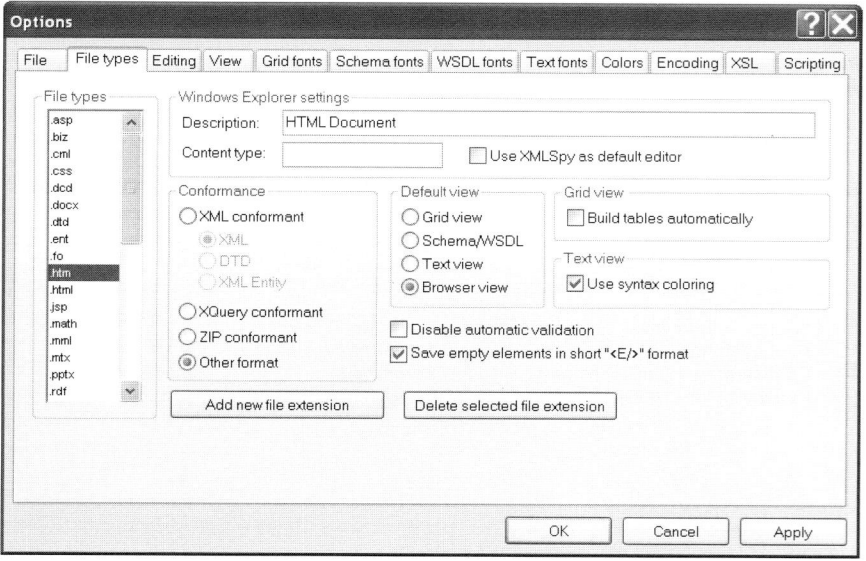

This will prevent XHTML validation errors from appearing when HTML output files are generated by XMLSpy.

If an XML document contains an 'xml-stylesheet' processing instruction that assigns an XSL Transformation to the document, then performing an XSL transformation is very simple. All that you need to do is to open the relevant XML document and then select 'XSL/XQuery' from the menu bar. This will perform the transformation and open an output document called 'XML Output.xml'. If the XML document does not already have a transformation processing instruction, XMLSpy can apply a transformation dynamically. If you select 'XSL/XQuery' from the menu bar for a document with no XSLT stylesheet, then a dialog will appear (Figure B.13) that allows you to browse for an XSL transformation document.

After an XSL transformation has been processed, XMLSpy provides two tabbed views of the generated document; a browser view and a text view. Figure B.14a shows the text view, which shows the generated HTML mark-up. Figure B.14b shows the browser view, which shows the resulting page as it would appear in a web browser.

FIGURE B.13   The dialog that is used to dynamically apply an XSL transformation

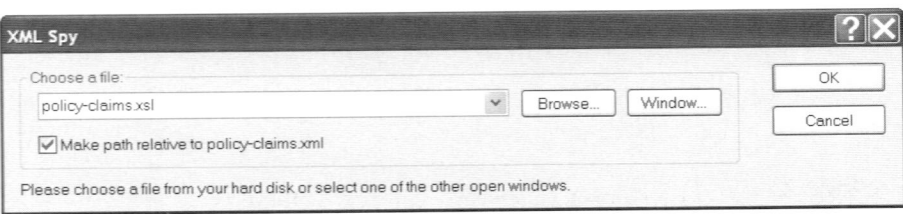

FIGURE B.14a   The text view of the output from an XSL transformation

```
1      <HTML>
2        <HEAD>
3          <meta http-equiv="Content-Type" content="text/html; charset=UTF-8">
4          <TITLE>Insurance Claims</TITLE>
5        </HEAD>
6        <BODY>
7          <H1>Claimants</H1>
8          <H2>A. Liu</H2>
9        </BODY>
10     </HTML>
```

Text   Browser

policy-claims.xml   XSL Output.html

Further information

For further information about XMLSpy, refer to the Altova web site (http://www.altova.com) or the 'Help' facility within XMLSpy itself (accessible from the main menu bar).

Web Application Security

C.1 Authentication and authorization

Some parts of a web application need to be secured against inappropriate access. Java web applications support declarative, role based security, which means we can use the server's configuration to declare certain roles that may be given access to specific resources. In fact we already saw how this works in Chapter 9, when we enabled the Tomcat manager application by adding a user to the 'tomcat-users.xml' file and giving them the role of 'manager'. Once this role had been added to the user, it became possible to log in to the manager application with a valid user name and password for that user. In this appendix we see how to incorporate our own secure pages into a web application.

Web application security covers two main aspects, authentication and authorization. Authentication is about identifying who a particular user is in terms of their role, while authorization is about specifying which resources that user role has access to. For example, Figure C.1 shows some of the home insurance system use cases from Chapter 2, where actors are used to represent roles. Users of the system would have to be authenticated as being in a particular role. In this role they would be authorized in different ways, for example a policy holder should be able to access only their own policy details, but call centre staff and insurance underwriters should have access to all policies or applications. In this way, we can consider which access permissions are appropriate for particular use cases.

We use the term *security principal* to refer to either a user or a group of users, and *security realm* to refer to the set of principals that are applied to a particular system. The actual implementation of the security realm can be very simple, as it is in the XML file based system used by default with Tomcat, or it can be a much more sophisticated security database. Clearly, for systems with many users that change regularly, a simple XML file would be totally inadequate, but is useful to demonstrate the basic principles of security.

C.2 Adding security roles

To apply some security to a page in our web application, the first thing we will do is add a new role to the 'tomcat-users.xml' file that would be appropriate to specifying rights to access parts of the insurance application. We will call this role 'insuranceadmin'. We will

FIGURE C.1   Some of the roles in the insurance system and use cases that relate to access permissions

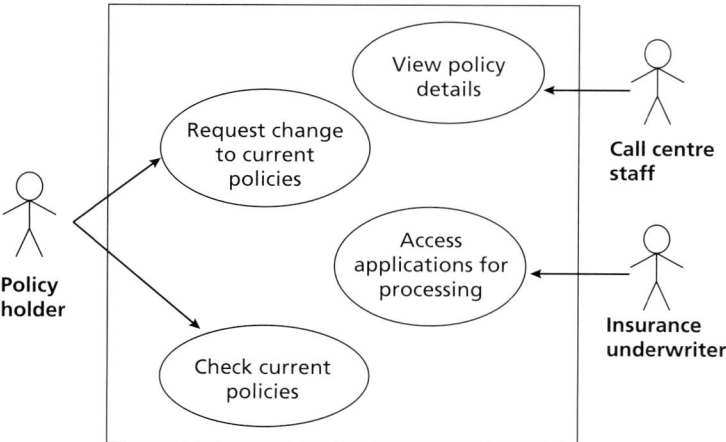

then add this new role to the user we added in Chapter 9, 'webhomecover'. Here is the updated 'tomcat-users.xml' file (with changes indicated in bold)

```
<?xml version='1.0' encoding='utf-8'?>
<tomcat-users>
   <role rolename="manager"/>
   <role rolename="insuranceadmin"/>
   <user username="webhomecover" password="webhomecover"
     roles="manager,insuranceadmin"/>
</tomcat-users>
```

To link this security role with a specific web application, we can add a 'security-role' element to the 'web.xml' file. Here, we add the 'insuranceadmin' role to our web application.

```
<security-role>
   <description>Insurance administrator</description>
   <role-name>insuranceadmin</role-name>
</security-role>
```

It is now possible to refer to this security role in other parts of 'web.xml' that will specify which secure resources this principal can access.

C.3 Securing a web page

In order to secure web based resources so they can only be accessed by certain security principals we need to add a 'security-constraint' element to 'web.xml'. This can be used to specify particular parts of the web application (the 'web-resource-collection') and the roles that are allowed to access those resources (the 'auth-constraint' element).

In this example, we specify that the 'insuranceadmin' role is able to access the 'listclaims.jsp' page (which we introduced in Chapter 12). Since this page lists multiple claims, it should not be generally accessible by all clients. Therefore we are restricting access only to those users who are in the role of 'insuranceadmin'.

```
<security-constraint>
 <web-resource-collection>
  <web-resource-name>Claims</web-resource-name>
  <url-pattern>/listclaims.jsp</url-pattern>
 </web-resource-collection>
 <auth-constraint>
  <role-name>insuranceadmin</role-name>
 </auth-constraint>
</security-constraint>
```

NOTE	The 'url-pattern' does not have to refer to a single file, and can include wildcards to refer to multiple files. For example, this pattern means all the files in the 'secure' folder `<url-pattern>/secure/*</url-pattern>` There can also be multiple 'url-pattern' elements to specify different resources.

By default, a security constraint applies to all HTTP method types. However it is possible to specify which HTTP method types are affected by the constraint, by adding 'http-method' elements after the 'url-pattern' element. For example, this constraint only applies to 'GET' and 'POST' requests:

```
<web-resource-collection>
 <web-resource-name.Claims</web-resource-name>
 <url-pattern</listclaims.jsp</url-pattern>
 <http-method>GET</http-method>
 <http-method>POST</http-method>
</web-resource-collection>
```

Now that the 'listclaims'jsp' page is secured, clients will only be able to access it if they log on to the system using an appropriate username and password for the 'insuranceadmin' role. The way that they log on can also be configured in 'web.xml' using the 'login-config' element. In this element the 'auth-method' element can be set to BASIC, DIGEST, FORM or CLIENT-CERT. In this example, the method is set to BASIC, which means that basic HTTP security is used, where a dialog asks the user for a username and password to log in but the data is not encrypted in any way.

```
<login-config>
 <auth-method>BASIC</auth-method>
 <realm-name>WebHomeCover</realm-name>
</login-config>
```

Figure C.2 shows the dialog that appears in Internet Explorer 7 if a page is accessed that uses BASIC authentication. Note that the 'realm-name' element is simply used by the dialog when it displays its message.

When DIGEST authentication is used, the data is encrypted by the browser, as reported in the dialog box that appears (Figure C.3). However this encryption is not particularly secure as the algorithm used is well known and easily broken.

FIGURE C.2   The dialog box used to log in using BASIC authentication

FIGURE C.3   The dialog box used to log in using DIGEST authentication

The third type of authorization, FORM, is similar to BASIC authentication in that it is unencrypted, but uses a custom form rather than the browser's dialog box. To use this type of authorization you need to create a special form page, and also an optional error page (which is displayed if the login fails), and register the names of these files in the 'login-config' element. In this example, we use 'FORM' authentication, specifying the custom login page as 'loginform.jsp' and the error page as 'loginerror.jsp'.

```
<login-config>
 <auth-method>FORM</auth-method>
 <form-login-config>
  <form-login-page>/loginform.jsp</form-login-page>
  <form-error-page>/loginerror.jsp</form-error-page>
 </form-login-config>
</login-config>
```

For this to work, you have to create the form using special field names and a specific value for the 'action' attribute of the form. There needs to be a text entry field called 'j_username' and a password entry field named 'j_password'. The form must submit to the 'j_security_check' action. Here is a simple implementation of 'loginform.jsp' that meets these criteria:

```
<?xml version="1.0"?>
<!DOCTYPE html PUBLIC "-//W3C//DTD XHTML 1.1//EN"
  "http://www.w3.org/TR/xhtml11/DTD/xhtml11.dtd">
<html xmlns="http://www.w3.org/1999/xhtml" xml:lang="en">
 <head>
  <title>Login Form</title>
 </head>
 <body>
 <form action="j_security_check" method="post">
  <label for="username">Username:</label>
  <input type="text" name="j_username" id="username" />
  <br />
  <label for="new">Password:</label>
  <input type="password" name="j_password" id="password" />
  <br />
  <input type="submit" value="Submit" />
 </form>
 </body>
</html>
```

Now when a client tries to access 'listclaims.jsp', the custom login form will appear (Figure C.4).

FIGURE C.4 The custom login form

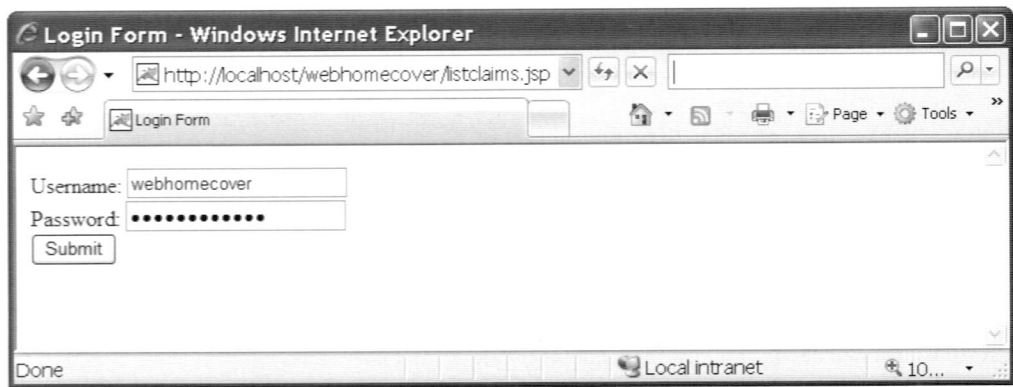

The final type of authentication., CLIENT-CERT, is beyond the scope of this appendix but relies on the client having its own security certificate. In the next section we look at data encryption using server side certificates, which is a more common requirement.

C.4 Secure communication

Although the configuration we have looked at so far manages authentication and authorization, we have seen only a minor aspect of secure communication, with the somewhat limited 'DIGEST' method of encrypting the user's login details. To make our application more secure, we also need to ensure that certain parts of the system are encrypted so they cannot be intercepted and read whilst being transferred between client and server. This is very important when communicating sensitive information, such as credit card numbers or other confidential information. To do this we need to use the Secure Sockets Layer (SSL) which underlies the HTTPS protocol, and requires a server certificate to be installed. Normally, these certificates must be purchased from a trusted *Certificate Authority*, but for testing purposes we can generate our own certificates using the 'keytool' program that is provided as part of the Java SDK. The following example shows how to use 'keytool' from the command line.

```
C:\>keytool -genkey -alias tomcat -keyalg RSA -keystore "C:/Documents and Settings/
user"/.keystore -validity 365
```

Note that by default, when using Windows, a Tomcat server that has an HTTPS connection will look for a '.keystore' file in the current user folder under 'Documents and Settings', so we specify this path as the '-keystore' option. You will need to modify the 'user' part of the path to be the appropriate user name for your system (don't forget to put speech marks around the path because of the spaces in the 'Documents and Settings' folder name). The 'alias' option is the name used for the key store, 'keyalg' is the algorithm used for generating keys and the 'validity' option is the number of days the certificate is valid. All three of these options have default values so do not have to be included.

You will need to respond to a series of questions from the tool. The default password is 'changeit'. You should get something like the following interaction:

```
Enter keystore password: (enter changeit)
Re-enter new password: (enter changeit)
What is your first and last name?
  [Unknown]: (enter www.webhomecover.com)
What is the name of your organizational unit?
  [Unknown]: (can leave blank)
What is the name of your organization?
  [Unknown]: (can leave blank)
What is the name of your City or Locality?
  [Unknown]: (can leave blank)
What is the name of your State or Province?
  [Unknown]: (can leave blank)
What is the two-letter country code for this unit?
  [Unknown]: (can leave blank)
Is CN=localhost, OU=Unknown, O=Unknown, L=Unknown, ST=Unknown,
C=Unknown correct
?
```

```
    [no]: (enter y)
  Enter key password for <tomcat>
      (RETURN if same as keystore password): (press return)
```

At this point, you should find that the '.keystore' file has been created in your user directory.

Configuring the server

Back in Chapter 9, we saw how Tomcat can be configured by editing the 'server.xml' file. To enable HTTPS connections we need to edit this file again. You should find the following entry in 'server-xml', but by default it will be commented out.

```
<!--
<Connector port="8443" protocol="HTTP/1.1" SSLEnabled="true"
 maxThreads="150" scheme="https" secure="true"
 clientAuth="false" sslProtocol="TLS" />
-->
```

Remove the XML comment that surrounds this element, and change the port number from 8443 to 443, (the standard HTTPS port number) then restart Tomcat. You should see in the server's console output that a connection has been started on port 443. If the server is unable to find the keystore file, it will fail on startup and will not open the port, so check the console output carefully for errors.

Using HTTPS in a web application

Once the server is able to provide an HTTPS connection with a supporting certificate, it is possible to secure web pages using this mechanism. To do this, we add a further element to the 'security-constraint' element in 'web.xml'. This is the 'user-data-constraint' element, which contains a 'transport-guarantee'. If we set the value of this element to CONFIDENTIAL, it will use HTTPS encryption for the web resources to which it is applied. In this example, we apply it to the 'listclaims.jsp' page

```
<security-constraint>
 <web-resource-collection>
  <web-resource-name>Claims</web-resource-name>
  <url-pattern>/listclaims.jsp</url-pattern>
 </web-resource-collection>
 <auth-constraint>
  <role-name>insuranceadmin</role-name>
 </auth-constraint>
  <user-data-constraint>
  <transport-guarantee>CONFIDENTIAL</transport-guarantee>
  </user-data-constraint>
 </security-constraint>
```

Now when you try to access 'listclaims.jsp' you must access it using a URL that uses the HTTPS protocol:

```
https://localhost/webhomecover/listclaims.jsp
```

FIGURE C.5 The warning page displayed by Internet Explorer 7 when it encounters an untrusted certificate

FIGURE C.6 Internet Explorer 7 using the secure HTTPS protocol despite issuing a warning about the certificate

When you do so, the browser will warn you that the certificate is not trusted. Figure C.5 shows the page displayed by Internet Explorer 7.

However you can just choose to continue by clicking on the 'Continue to this webpage' link and the page will be displayed after you log on as an 'insuranceadmin' user. The browser will continue to warn you about the certificate error but will connect using the secure HTTPS protocol (Figure C.6).

abbreviated XPath operator
    syntax 173
action object 44–5
Active Server Pages *see* ASPs
ActiveX objects 266–8
activity diagrams 22
adaptivity 491–2
Advanced Research Projects Agency
    see ARPA
agility 20
Ajax 13–14, 16, 264–75
    Ajax code with JavaScript 265–70
    architecture 264
    asynchronous communication 26
    definition 265
    one-page web application 264
    RSS 270–1
    security issues with
        XMLHttpRequest 271–2
    server connection with
        XMLHttpRequest 272–3
    XML data reading with
        XMLHttpRequest 273–5
    XMLHttpRequest 264–5
    XMLHttpRequest object
        methods 270
    XMLHttpRequest object
        properties 270
Ajax code with JavaScript 265–70
    XMLHttpRequest 265–70
alert dialog 256
alternate flows 39
Amazon 1
American National Standard Institute
    see ANSI
analysis tools 30–8
    domain models 30–3
    storyboards 36–8
    system sequence diagrams 36
    use case diagrams 33–6
anchors
    active 117
    hover 117
    link 117
    visited 117
Another Neat Tool *see* Ant
ANSI 54, 88

Ant 297–301
    build file 297–8
    installation and configuration 297
    jar task 299
    properties 298
    Tomcat Web Application Manager
        305–6
    WAR file deployment 299–301
Ant build file 297–8
    properties 297
    targets 297
Apache Commons bean utilities
    411–12
Apache Struts *see* Struts
Apache Tomcat *see* Tomcat
APIs 13, 16, 265, 310, 428–9
apostrophe 55
Application Programming Interface
    see API
application servers 279–80
architectural design 42
arithmetic on numeric variables 219
ARPA 4, 16
ARPAnet 4
Arrays 212, 225–7
ASPs 280
association lines 31
asterisk 31–2
asynchronous communication,
    Ajax 26
Asynchronous JavaScript and
    XML *see* Ajax
attribute declarations, in XML
    Schemas 160
attribute declarations in DTDs
    148–51
    attributes non-CDATA 150–1
    CDATA attribute type 149
    CDATA keywords 149
    name type value 149
attributes 160
    names 58
    nodes 170
    non-CDATA 150–1
    vs elements in XML 136–8
    writing to output document 192–7
    in XPath queries 175–6

attributes in HTML 69–73
    email links 72–3
    images 70
    links 70–2
attributes in tags 55–6
    apostrophe 55
    quotation mark 55
    XMLSpy 55

B2B 10, 16, 130, 498
    XML 130
BEA Weblogic 294
beans generating XML in
    JSPs 410–18
    beans in XML web application
        412–18
    Jakarta Commons bean utilities
        411–12
    model layer façades 411
Berners-Lee, Tim 4, 57
    HTML 57
    mobile web applications 475
block and inline elements 108–11
blog 2, 16
Booch, Grady 22
breadcrumbs pattern 45, 47
browser type 482–6
browser-related objects 212
business logic beans 386–7
business objectives 26–7
Business to Business *see* B2B
button events response 249–51
button gravity 38

C# 211, 280
CAD 424
candidate concepts 31–3
cardinality 30–1
Cascading Style Sheets *see* CSS
CASE 424
case-order attribute 190
CDATA
    attribute type 149
    keywords 149
    sections 138
CERN 4, 16, 57, 92
CGI 5, 16, 280

character codes 197–9
child nodes 210, 242
citations and block quotes 64–5
class
    attribute 105–6
    model 32
client data in view layer 327–8
client page 37–8
client-side form validation 255–63
    form component validation 260–3
    functions processing forms 255–6
    pop-up dialogs 256–7
    surface validation 255
    validation routine dialogs 257–60
CLR 280
coding 37
command object 340
comment nodes 170
comment syntax 60
comments in JavaScript source code
    213–14
commitment 3
Common Gateway Interface see CGI
Common Language Runtime see CLR
communication diagrams 22
complex types and elements 158
Computer Aided Design see CAD
Computer Aided Software Engineering
    see CASE
Computer Languages for the
    Processing of Text
    committee 54
concurrency 2
confirm dialog 256–7
connection pools 429, 435–6
Conseil Européen pour la Recherche
    Nucléair see CERN
construction phase 24–5
content, structure and validation
    125–68
    HTML limitations 125–7
    Schema choice 165
    semi-structured data 127–9
    XHTML 151–5
    XML 129–31
    XML components 131–8
    XML document validation
        139–51
    XML Schema 155–8
    XML Schema document
        application 164–5
    XML Schema tags 158–64
content types 59, 70
    media types 59
    MIME 59
context 172–3, 283
    root 283
controls 80
cookie 43
cost-benefit analysis 28

Create, Read, Update, Delete see
    CRUD
CRUD 12, 16, 441, 579
CSS 50, 52–3, 58, 91–123
    block and inline elements 108–11
    class and id attributes 105–8
    Häkon Lie 92
    inline styles 93–5
    level 1 92
    level 2 92
    level 3 92
    lists and tables 111–14
    page layout 116–20
    properties 122
    separating out presentation 91–3
    style sheet cascades 114–16
    style sheets 96–104
    syntax 93–5
    three-region layout pattern 116–17
CSS for page layout 116–20
    CSS with anchors 117
    layout styles application 118–20

DAO 423, 441–3
    data source access 442–7
data
    addition to tables 586–7
    sources 429, 435
Data Access Object see DAO
Data Transfer Object see DTO
data types 19, 159
    XML Schema 159
data-type attribute 190
databases 579
    example 425–7
    indexed sequential files 579
    query 587–90
    relational 579–82
    schema 580
    tables addition 591–5
    updating 590–1
Date objects 212, 225–6
debugging JavaScript 217–18
declaring and using variables, rules 218
default scripting language for web
    page 211
    intrinsic events 211
denial of service 80
deployment descriptor 283
deployment diagrams 22
deployment to Tomcat 288–93
design 41–2
    architectural design 42
    guidelines 50
    patterns 14
    static and dynamic content 42
    transition from analysis to
        design 41–2
destination anchors 70–2
DHCP 6, 16

DHTML 242–5, 264
    DOM navigation 242–3
    interaction with nodes 243–4
    value changes in DOM 24
disciplines 23
DNS 6–7, 16
document 212
    order 129, 172
document object model see DOM
document type definitions see DTDs
DOM 126–7, 210
    child nodes 210
    displaying node types, names,
        values 244
    element nodes 210
    leaf nodes 210
    level 0 210
    level 1 210
    level 2 210
    level 3 210
    navigation 242–3
    node hierarchy 210
    parsers 377–88
    text nodes 210
    value changes 245
domain models 30–3
    arrow heads 31–2
    association lines 31
    asterisk 31–2
    candidate concepts 31–3
    cardinality 30–1
    class model 32
    key concepts 30
    many to many association 32
Domain Name System see DNS
domain names 6–7
    DNS 6–7
    email addresses 7
    IANA 6
    ICANN 6
    resolver programs 6
    root domain 6
    zones 6
dot coms 4
DreamWeaver 61
DTD operator symbols 146–7
DTDs 28, 61, 139–45
    data-typing problems 156–7
    elements definition 140–1
    prolog addition 141–2
    separation from XML
        document 143
    system or public doctype 143–5
    validation with XMLSpy 143
DTOs 329, 353, 357, 386,
    441, 553
dynamic client pages 43–4
    action object 44
dynamic content 42, 279
    using Java 309–76

Dynamic Host Configuration Protocol
    see DHCP
Dynamic HTML *see* DHTML
dynamic style sheets 252–4
dynamic webflow 44–5
    action object 45
    sequence diagram 45
    server page 45

e-business 5
e-commerce 279
ECMAScript 210–11
EL 361–3
elaboration phase 24–5
    executable architecture 24
    walking skeleton 24
element declarations in DTDs 145–8
    DTD operator symbols 146–7
    empty elements 147–8
element multiplicity 160–1
element names 58
element nodes 170, 210
elements 55
    DTDs 140–1
    nested 55
    XML 136–8
email addresses 7
email links 72–3
    anchors 72–3
empty elements 63, 147–8, 152–3
enterprise application deployment
        294–6
    enterprise application folder
            structure 295–6
    enterprise archive (EAR) 294–6
Enterprise JavaBeans 294, 465
entities 151
entity characters 197
enumerated types and restrictions
        161–4
Eriksson 22
European Computer Manufacturers'
        Association *see* ECMAScript
event handlers 212
executable architecture 24
Expression Language *see* EL
eXtensible HyperText Markup
        Language *see* XHTML
eXtensible Markup Language *see* XML
eXtensible Stylesheet Language
        Transformations *see* XSLT
external style sheets 102–4
extranets 10
    B2B 10

façades 411–12
factory method 327
family tree vocabulary 172
feedback loop 21–2
File Transfer Protocol *see* FTP

filtering 175
focus groups 27
font
    families 97–8
    size 101–2
for loops 231–2
form beans 386
form component validation 260–3
form data in controller layer 326–7
Formal Public Identifier *see* FPI
forms 78–84
    controls 80
    denial of service 80
    elements 79–80
    get request 79–80
    input types 80–4
    method attribute 79
    post request 79–80
    select lists 85–6
    text areas 84–5
    see also client-side form
            validation
FPI 144
FrontPage 61
FTP 5, 16, 215
functional requirements 27
functions processing forms 255–6
    onsubmit event 255–6

General Electric 22
get request 79–80
GIF 70
GML 54, 88
goals 34
Goldfarb, Mosher, Lorie *see* GML
Google 1
    Ajax API 265
    Suggest 264
graphical user interfaces *see* GUIs
Graphics Interchange Format
        see GIF
grouping styles 97
GUIs 310

HL7, XML 130
home page pattern 45, 48
horizontal rules 63
HotJava 5
HTML 7–9, 16, 42–3, 50, 53,
        56–7, 470
    elements 88
    hyperlinks 57
    mark-up 8
    tags 8
    Tim Berners-Lee 57
    version 2.0 57
    version 3.2 57
    version 4.0 57, 151
    version 4.01 57, 152
    web browser 9

XHTML version 1.0 57
XSLT and CSS 176
HTML document structural
        elements 57–60
    angle brackets 57
    attribute names 58
    content types 59
    CSS 58
    element names 58
    HTML document creation 58–9
    structural elements 58
    tags 57
    text elements 59–60
HTML document type 61–3
    DTDs 61
    META 62
    type definition 61
    UTF-8 62
    web-based validation 61–3
HTML limitations 125–7
    poorly formed documents 126–7
HTTP 7–8, 16
    codes 8
    HTTPS 8
    PKI encryption 8
    port 296–7
    request 53
    request parameters 324–5
    request-response cycle 7–8, 43
    security 8
    server 279
    SSL 8
HTTP request data 322–9
    client data in view layer 327–8
    form data in controller layer 326–7
    HTTP request parameters 324–5
    JSP scriptlets 325–6
    posting data from HTML form
            328–9
HTTPS 8
hyperlinks 50, 70
HyperText Markup Language *see* HTML
hypertext reference 71
HyperText Transfer Protocol *see* HTTP

IANA 6, 16
IBM Websphere 294
ICANN 6, 16, 475
id element attributes 108, 242, 245
IDE, web service integration 505
idiomatic (phrase) elements 65
IETF 57
if/else statements 228
images 50, 70
    content type 70
    GIF 70
    IMG empty element 70
    JPEG 70
    PNG 70
    src 70

IMG empty element 70
impedance mismatch 462–3
inception phase 24–6
   spikes 24
increment and decrement operators
   219–20
innerHTML and DOM 248–9
input driven (push) transformation
   199–205
Integrated Development Environment
   see IDE, web service integration
interaction with nodes 243–4
internal style sheets 96–7
International Standards Organisation
   see ISO
Internet Assigned Numbers Authority
   see IANA
Internet Corporation for Assigned
   Names and Numbers *see*
   ICANN
Internet Engineering Task Force *see*
   IETF
Internet Explorer 4, 125, 482
   ActiveX object 266
   DOM level 0 210
   innerHTML 248
   XMLHttpRequest 264–6
   XSL Transformation 180, 293
Internet Service Provider *see* ISP
Internet technologies 5–7
   domain names 6–7
   IP addresses 5–6
   TCP/IP 5
Internet and WWW 4–5
intranets 10
intrinsic events 211
IP addresses 5–6
ISO 54, 88, 132, 199, 501, 567
ISP 5–6, 16
iteration 25
   length 25
   over multiple elements 184–5
iterative methods 21–2
   feedback loop 21–2

Jacobson, Ivar 22–3
   Objectory 22
Jakarta Commons bean utilities
   411–12
jar task 299
Java 210–11
   applets 264
   archive (JAR file) 284
Java API for XML Processing *see* JAXP
Java Architecture for XML Binding *see*
   JAXB
Java compiler in Ant script 316–19
Java and database 427–35
   creating statements 432
   Java database access with JDBC
      427–8

JDBC API 429–31
JDBC drivers 428–9
   MySQL authorized user
      creation 431–2
   prepared statements 435
   ResultSets processing 432–4
   SQL exceptions 431
   update records 434
Java Database Connectivity *see* JDBC
Java for dynamic content 309–76
   HTTP request data 322–9
   Java on server 310–11
   JavaBeans in JSPs 329–35
   JavaServer Page 319–22
   JSP Model 1 architecture 313–19
   JSP Model 2 architecture 335–8
   JSP tags 375
   JSTL 360–7
   MVC architecture 311–13
   process beans 353–9
   refactoring 335
   session management 340–53
   tags from JSTL core library 376
   three-region layout integration
      371–3
   webflow management 338–40
   XML JavaServer Pages 367–71
Java EE 280, 294, 310
   JNDI 311
   web components 311
Java EE packaging 284
   JAR file 284
Java Enterprise Edition *see* Java EE
Java ME 310
Java Micro Edition *see* Java ME
Java Naming and Directory Interface
   see JNDI
Java SE 310, 429
   APIs 310
   GUIs 310
   Java JDK 310
   Java SDK 310
Java on server 310–11
   APIs 310
   Java EE 310
   Java EE web components 311
   Java ME 310
   Java SE 310
   javac 310
   javadoc 310
Java Standard Edition *see* Java SE
Java web application deployment 284
   Java archive (JAR file) 284
Java and XML 377–422
   beans generating XML in JSPs
      410–18
   JAXB 396–404
   XML from JavaBeans 386–95
   XML parsers 378–86
   XML processing with JSTL
      404–10

JavaBeans
   in expressions 363–4
   and sessions 342
   webflow 343–53
JavaBeans in JSPs 329–35
   DTO 329
   JSP Tags for JavaBeans 333–4
   properties 330–1
   writing bean properties to response
      334–5
JavaScript 5, 14, 209–39
   characteristics 211–12
   control structures 227–32
   debugging 217–18
   development 210
   DOM 127, 210
   keywords, types, objects 239
   mouse events 210
   object use and creation 222–7
   objects 212–17
   purpose 209–10
   purposes 210
   types and variables 218–22
   URLs 251–2
   writing functions 232–5
JavaScript characteristics 211–12
   default scripting language for web
      page 211
   prototype language 211
   scripts added to web pages 211–12
   window 211
JavaScript control structures 227–32
   if/else statements 228
   logical operators 229
   for loops 231–2
   relational operators 228–9
   selection simulating throwing coin
      229–30
   while loops 230–1
JavaScript events 245–52
   button events response 249–51
   innerHTML and DOM 248–9
   JavaScript URLs 251–2
   onload event 246–7
   timer events 247–8
JavaScript interaction 241–78
   Ajax 264–75
   client-side form validation 255–63
   DHTML 242–5
   dynamic style sheets 252–4
   JavaScript events 245–52
JavaScript object use and creation
   222–7
   Arrays 225–7
   Date objects 225–6
   strings 223–4
JavaScript objects 212–17
   Array 212
   browser-related objects 212
   comment syntax in source code
      213–14

Date 212
document 212
event handlers 212
location 212
Math 212
methods 212
navigator 212
object methods 215
object properties 212–13
objects as properties 214–15
properties 212
script positioning 215–17
String 212
window 212
JavaScript types and variables
218–22
arithmetic on numeric
variables 219
declaring and using variables
218–19
increment and decrement operators
219–20
order of precedence 221–2
prefix and postfix operators 220
shorthand expressions for
arithmetic operators 220–1
JavaScript writing functions 232–5
definition outside body element
233–4
external files 234–5
JavaServer Page see JSP
JAXB 377–8, 396–404
generating classes from XML
schemas 396–9
generating Java objects from XML
documents 402–4
generating XML documents from
Java objects 399–402
JAXP 377–8
JBoss application server 294, 301
JDBC 424, 427–8, 464
drivers 428–9
JDBC API 428–31
connection pools 429
data sources 429
JNDI 429
JNDI 311, 429, 436
JNDI tree data sources 436–7
bound objects 436
contexts 436
initial context 437
Joint Photographic Experts Group see
JPEG
joint requirements workshop 27–8
JPEG 70
JSP
compiler 280
directives 321–2
expressions 320–1
scriptlets 325–6
tags 319, 368, 375

webflow 343–53
welcome file 320
JSP Model 1 architecture 312–19
Java compiler in Ant
script 316–19
JavaBeans 329–40
servlet container 313
servlet creation 314–16
servlet deployment 316
servlet engine 313
JSP Model 2 architecture 312–13,
335–8
forward 336
page structure 336
request scope 337–8
JSP Standard Tag Library see JSTL
JSP Tags for JavaBeans 333–4
JSP writing 319–22
JSP directives 321–2
JSP expressions 320–1
JSP welcome file 320
JSPX tags 368
JSTL 309, 345, 360–7, 378
core 360
database access 360
EL 361–3
internationalization and
formatting 360
Jakarta 360
JAR files 361
JavaBeans in expressions 363–4
JSTL iterations and indexed
JavaBean properties 364–7
tag library directive 361
using JSTL 361–2
XML processing 360

LAMP 280
layers 11–12
word-processing 11
leaf nodes 210
line breaks and horizontal rules 63
empty elements 63
linking XSLT stylesheet 179–80
links 70–2
destination anchors 70–2
hyperlink 70
hypertext reference 71
IMG elements 72
site logo at top left pattern 72
source anchors 70–1
target anchors 71
web link 70
Linux, Apache, MySQL, PHP see
LAMP
lists 66–9
bulleted 67
definition 68–9
nesting ordered and unordered lists
67–8
ordered 67

style application 111–14
unordered 66–7
localhost URL and port number
282–3
location object 212, 214–15
location path 172–3
logical operators 229

many to many association 32
mapping
from SQL and Java types 467–8
XML nodes to document tree
structure 171
mark-up 8
mashups 13–14
Math 212
Math object 222–3
media types 59
META 62, 94
metadata 54
method wars 22
methods 212
Microsoft
JScript 210
.NET 280
MIME 59, 88, 479–80
minimization 59
XHTML 153
mission statement 26–7
mobile mark-up languages 470–5
mTLD 474–5
WAP and WML 470–1
XHTML-Basic 471–4
XHTML-Mobile 472–4
mobile web applications 469–96
adaptivity 491–2
mobile mark-up languages 470–5
tags in WALL library 493–5
WALL 469
WALL integration 481–91
WURFL 469
WURFL/WALL Java framework
475–81
model layer beans 386–90
business logic beans 386–7
DTOs 386
form beans 386
process beans 386–7
system state beans 386
model layer façades 411
model-view-controller see MVC
modeling requirements 26–30
business objectives 26
mission statement 26–7
prioritizing requirements 28–30
ROI 26
web application requirements
gathering 27–8
MoSCoW 29, 52
mouse events 210
Mozilla Firefox 4, 125, 482

mTLD 474–5
Multipurpose Internet Mail Extension *see* MIME
Must have, Should have, Could have, Want to have *see* MoSCoW
MVC architecture 311–13
MySQL 423, 428, 582–6
   authorized user creation 431–2
   commands 595
   database creation 583–4
   database schema with SQL 584–5
   viewing table schema 585–6

n-tier architecture 12
name type value 149
namespace nodes 170
namespaces 152
   XML 157–8
National Center for Supercomputing Applications *see* NCSA
navigation bar pattern 45–7
navigation flow 50
navigator 212
NCSA 4–5, 16
   Mosaic graphical browser 4
Netscape Navigator 4, 92, 482
   DOM level 0 210
   JavaScript 210
node
   hierarchy 210
   interaction 243–4
non-functional requirements 28
null 257
numeric codes 197–9

Object Management Group 22
Object Modeling Technique *see* OMT
object properties 212–13
object-relational impedance mismatch 462–3
   inheritance 462–3
   mapping data types 462–3
   operations 462–3
   relationships and normalization 462–3
   Unique Object and Table Identifiers 462–3
object-relational mapping 423–4
   CAD tools 424
   CASE tools 424
   JDBC 424
object-relational mapping technologies 464–5
   Java persistence standards 465
   persistence strategy selection 465
   transparent persistence layer 464
Objectory 22
OMT 22
on-line 5
one-form-per-page usability pattern 38
one-page web application 264

onload event 246–7
onsubmit event 255–6
Opera 4, 482
order attributes 190
order of precedence 221–2
Outlook Web Access 2000 264
output driven (pull) transformation 199–200
output types 179

parsers 378–86
PDF 42, 52
performance 3
Perl 280
persistence 3
persistence integration 435–40
   JNDI 436
   JNDI tree data sources 436–7
   server configuration 437–40
persistence layer using DAOs 440–9
   DAO for data source access 442–7
   read from database in web application 447–9
persistence objects integration 449–61
PHP 5, 16, 79, 280
PKI 8, 16
   encryption 8
PNG 70
pop-up dialogs 256–7
   alert dialog 256
   confirm dialog 256–7
   null 257
   prompt dialog 256–7
Portable Document Format *see* PDF
Portable Network Graphics *see* PNG
portals 10–11
   portlets 10
post request 79–80
posting data from HTML form 328–9
prefix and postfix operators 220
prepared statements 435
presentation layer structure and content 53–89
   attributes in HTML 69–73
   forms 78–84
   HTML 56–7
   HTML document structural elements 57–60
   HTML document type 61–3
   lists 66–9
   SGML 53–6
   tables 74–8
   text structure 63–6
prioritizing requirements 28–30
   could haves 29
   MoSCoW 29
   must haves 29
   should haves 29
   story cards 30
   want to haves 30
process beans 353–9, 386–7

processing 176–80
   instruction nodes 170
   XML document using DOM parser 379–83
   XML document using SAX parser 383–6
programmable web 13
prolog 131–3, 141–2, 393
prompt dialog 256–7
properties 212
prototype language 211
Public Key Infrastructure *see* PKI
Python 280

quotation mark 55

Rational Corporation 22
Rational Unified Process *see* RUP
RDF Site Summary *see* RSS
Really Simple Syndication *see* RSS
refactoring 335
relational databases 579–82
   foreign keys 581
   one-to-one relationships 581–2
   structure 579–80
   table schemas 580–1
relational operators 228–9
reliability 3
request-response cycle 7–8
resolver programs 6
ResultSets processing 432–4
Return on Investment *see* ROI
Rich Site Summary *see* RSS
ROI 26, 52
roles 34
root domain 6
root nodes 170
RosettaNet, XML 130, 501
routers 5
RSS 14, 16, 270–2
   Ajax 270–1
Rumbaugh, James 22
   OMT 22
RUP 22–3

Safari 4, 482
SAX parsers 377–9, 383–6
scalability 3
Schema choice 165
scripts 244
   added to web pages 211–12
   positioning 215–17
Secure Sockets Layer *see* SSL
security 2, 8, 607–14
   adding security roles 607–8
   authentication and authorization 607
   HTTPS 614–15
   secure communication 612–14
   securing web page 608–12
   server configuration 613
   XMLHttpRequest 271–2

select attribute 190
select lists 85–6
    options 85
selection elements 185–90
selection simulating throwing coin
    229–30
semi-structured data 127–9
    document order 129
    as a tree 129
    variations in structure 128–9
    and XML 127–9
sequence diagrams 22, 34, 45
sequences 158–9
server configuration for data source
    access 437–40
server connection with
    XMLHttpRequest 272–3
server page 42–3, 45
Server-side Ajax 520–30
Server-Side Validation 486–91
Service-Oriented Architecture see SOA
servlet
    container 313
    creation 314–16
    engine 280, 313
session management 340–53
    JavaBeans and sessions 342
    JSPs and JavaBeans creation for
      webflow 343–53
    stateless protocol 340
SGML 53–7, 88
    ANSI 54
    attributes in tags 55–6
    Computer Languages for the
      Processing of Text
      committee 54
    elements 55
    GML 54
    ISO 54
    metadata 54
    tags 54
    validation 54
    well-formed documents 56
    XML 54
shorthand expressions for arithmetic
    operators 220–1
Simple API for XML see SAX parsers
Simple Mail Transfer Protocol see SMTP
Simple Object Access Protocol see
    SOAP
site logo at top left pattern 45, 72
site map pattern 45, 48–9
SMTP 5, 16
SOA 13–14, 16, 498
    APIs 13
    mashups 13–14
    programmable web 13
    RSS 14
SOAP 498–9
software development lifecycles 20–2
    agility 20

iterative methods 21–2
    waterfall model 20–1
sorting output 190–2
    case-order attribute 190
    data-type attribute 190
    order attributes 190
    select attribute 190
source anchors 70–1
special characters 66
spikes 24, 26
SQL 423, 580
    exceptions 431
SSL 8, 16, 612
Standard Generalized Markup
    Language see SGML
state diagrams 22
stateless protocol 340
statement creation 432
static content 42, 279
    on HTTP server 283–4
stereotype labels 37
store content in database pattern 45,
    49–50, 423
story cards 30
storyboards 34, 36–8, 41
    button gravity 38
    client page 37–8
    coding 37
    form 37–8
    one-form-per-page usability
      pattern 38
    stereotype labels 37
    summary page 38
    web pages 36–8
    webflow 36–8
    wizard style 38
String 212
strings 223–4
structural elements 58
Structured Query Language
    see SQL
Struts 535–78
    bean tag library 562–5
    command and control patterns
      536–8
    Command Pattern 537–8
    components 538–9
    configuration 539–41
    Front Controller pattern 537–8
    HTML tag library 577
    page controller pattern 536
    validations 577
    webflow management 541–5
Struts Action objects 545–56
    action configuration 547–8
    commons logging 548–9
    global forwards 549–50
    writing action classes 546–7
Struts internationalization 565–9
    Browser to test internationalized
      pages 568–9

message resources 566–7
    tags 567–8
Struts tag libraries 550–7
    ActionForm JavaBeans 552–7
    Struts HTML tags and JavaBeans
      551–2
Struts validation with message
    resources 558–62
    ActionForm validate method
      559–62
    error message resource file 558–9
Struts validator 569–75, 577
    enable JavaScript validation 574–5
    enable ValidatorPlugin 574
    standard message keys 571–2
    ValidatorForm extension 570–1
    XML validation file 572–3
style application with class and id
    attributes 105–8
    class attribute 105–6
    id element attributes 108
    subset of elements 106–7
style sheet cascades 114–16
style sheets 96–104
    external 102–4
    font size 101–2
    grouping styles 97
    internal 96–7
    multiple styles with STYLE
      element 100–1
    text formatting styles 97–100
    and transforms 177–8
style sheets and XML 291–3
    JAR file 291
subscripts and superscripts 65–6
summary page 38
Sun Application Server 294
superscripts 65–6
surface validation 255
system or public doctype 143–5
system sequence diagrams 36–7, 40
    UML notation for boundary
      object 36
system state beans 386

table tags 74–5
    table cells 74
    table elements and rows 74
    table example 74–5
tables 74–8
    borders 77–8
    organization 76
    schemas 80–1
    spanning with attributes 76–8
    style application 111–14
    tags 74–5
tags 8, 54, 57
    attributes 5–6
    end 54
    JSTL core library 376
    start 54

tags (*continued*)
    tables 74–5
    WALL 493–5
target anchors 71
Tcl 211
TCP/IP 5, 16
    FTP 5
    SMTP 5
template matching 177–9
text
    areas 84–5
    formatting styles 97–100
    nodes 170, 210
text elements 59–60
    comment syntax 60
    minimization 59
    text management 59
text structure 63–6
    citations and block quotes 64–5
    idiomatic (phrase) elements 65
    line breaks and horizontal rules 63
    special characters 66
    subscripts and superscripts 65–6
three-region layout integration 371–3
three-region layout pattern 45, 47–8
    CSS 116–17
    no frames on public sites 47
tiers and distributed systems 12
    CRUD 12
    multiple tiers 12
    n-tier architecture 12
timer events 247–8
Tomcat 280–3, 294
    Catalina servlet engine 280–1,
        305, 319
    Coyote HTTP server 280–1, 319
    Jasper JSP compiler 280–1
    localhost URL and port number
        282–3
    starting Tomcat version 6 281–2
Tomcat deployment 288–93
    style sheets and XML 291–3
    web archive creation 289–90
    web archive deployment 290
Tomcat Web Application Manager 301–6
    enable 301–2
    remote connection 304
    running 302–4
    Tomcat Ant tasks 305–6
transactions 3
transformations using template
    matching 199–205
    input driven (push) transformation
        199–205
    output driven (pull) transformation
        199–200
transforming XML 169–207
    transformations using template
        matching 199–205
    transforming from XML to
        XML 199

XML special characters 197–9
XPath 169–76
XSLT 176–97
transition phase 25
Transmission Control Protocol/Internet
    Protocol *see* TCP/IP
transparent persistence 464
tree of nodes 129, 170–2, 242

UDDI 498–9, 501
UML 19, 22–3, 30, 34, 36–8,
    40, 42, 52
    activity diagrams 22
    communication diagrams 22
    deployment diagrams 22
    notation for boundary object 36
    Object Management Group 22
    sequence diagrams 22
    state diagrams 22
Unified Modeling Language *see* UML
Unified Process *see* UP
Uniform Resource Identifier *see* URI
Uniform Resource Locator *see* URL
Uniform Resource Name *see* URN
Universal Description Discovery and
    Integration *see* UDDI
UP 19, 23–5
    construction phase 24–5
    disciplines 23
    elaboration phase 24
    inception phase 24
    iteration 25
    transition phase 25
    whale diagram 23
update records 434
URI 7, 9, 16
URL 7, 9, 16
URN 7, 9, 16
use case descriptions 34–6
    actors 35
    start page 36
    use case name 35
use case diagrams 33–6, 38–40
    actor 33–4
    alternate flows 39
    goals 34
    roles 34
    storyboard 41
    system boundary 33–4
    system sequence diagram 40
    use case 33–4
    use case descriptions 34–6
    use case realization 34
use case realization 34
    sequence diagrams 34
    storyboards 34
    UML 34
    WAE 34
user and contributor
    communities 14
UTF-8 62

validation 54
    form component 260–3
    XHTML 153–5
    XML documents 139–51
    see also client-side form validation
validation routine dialogs 257–60
value changes in DOM 24
value selection from XML document
    180–3
    XSLT tags 180
VB.Net 280
VBScript 211
Vodafone Live! 10

W3C 5, 16, 57, 470
    Markup Validation Service 61–3,
        154–5
WAE 34, 42–5
    server page icon 43
walking skeleton 24
WALL 469
    tag library 479–81
    tags 493–5
WALL integration 481–91
    browser type 482–6
    Server-Side Validation 486–91
WAP and WML 470–1
WAR file deployment 299–301
waterfall model 20–1
Web 2.0 and Ajax 13–14
    Ajax 14
    service-oriented architectures
        13–14
    user and contributor
        communities 14
    web as software platform 13
web, as software platform 13
web application architectures 11–12
    layers 11–12
    tiers and distributed systems 12
web application developer 14
    design patterns 14
Web Application Extensions *see* WAE
web application folders and resources
    284–6
web application requirements 19–52
    analysis tools 30–8
    design 41–2
    inception phase 26
    modeling requirements 26–30
    software development
        lifecycles 20–2
    UML and UP 22–5
    use case 38–40
    web page design patterns 45–50
    webflow design 42–5
web application requirements
    gathering 27–8
    business objectives 27
    cost-benefit analysis 28
    focus groups 27

functional requirements 27
joint requirements workshop 27–8
non-functional requirements 28
web application server 2
web application structure and
        deployment 283–8
    context 283
    context root 283
    deployment descriptor 283
    Java EE 283
    Java EE packaging 284
    Java web application deployment
        284
    static content on HTTP server
        283–4
    web application folders and
        resources 284–6
    XML deployment descriptors
        286–8
web applications 1–17, 279
    blog 2
    commitment 3
    concurrency 2
    extranets 10
    features 3
    Internet technologies 5–7
    Internet and World Wide Web 4–5
    intranets 10
    performance 3
    persistence 3
    portals 10–11
    reliability 3
    scalability 3
    security 2
    transactions 3
    Web 2.0 and Ajax 13–14
    web application architectures 11–12
    web application developer 14
    web application server 1–4
    web pages 2
    web server 2
    wiki 2
    World Wide Web technologies 7–9
web applications and databases
        423–68
    example database 425–7
    Java and database 427–35
    mapping from SQL and Java types
        467–8
    object-relational impedance
        mismatch 462–3
    object-relational mapping 424
    object-relational mapping
        technologies 464–5
    persistence integration 435–40
    persistence layer using data access
        objects 440–9
    persistence objects integration
        449–61
web applications on default HTTP
        port 296–7

web archive creation 289–90
    JAR file 289
web archive deployment 290
web browser 4, 9
web link 70
web page design patterns 45–50
    breadcrumbs 45, 47
    design guidelines 50
    home page 45, 48
    navigation bar 45–7
    site logo at top left 45
    site map 45, 48–9
    store content in database 45,
        49–50
    three-region layout 45, 47–8
web pages 2, 36–8
web server 2, 279
web service client development
        513–16
web service implementation
        501–3
web service integration 516–20
    IDE 505
web service with Java 6.0 503–5
web service technologies 498–501
    SOA 498
    SOAP 498–9
    UDDI 498–9
    WSDL 498–501
    WSDL file search: UDDI and
        WS-Inspection 501
web services 498
Web Services Description Language see
        WSDL
web services and web applications
        505–13
web surfing 5
web-based validation 61–3
webflow 36–8
    JSPs and JavaBeans 343–53
webflow design 42–5
    cookie 43
    dynamic client pages 43–4
    dynamic webflow 44–5
    server page 42–3
    static content 42–3
webflow management 338–40
    command object 340
    user sessions 338
well-formed documents 56
    attribute values 6
    balanced tags 56
    HTML 56
    nested tags 5
    poorly formed document effects
        126–7
    root element 56
    XML 56
well-formed XML 135–6
whale diagram 23
while loops 230–1

Wiki 2–3, 14, 16
Wikipedia 2, 14
WikiWikiWeb see Wiki
window 211–12
Wireless Abstraction Library
        see WALL
Wireless Access Protocol see WAP
        and WML
Wireless Mark-up Language see WAP
        and WML
Wireless Universal Resource File see
        WURFL
wizard style 38, 40
World Wide Web see WWW
World Wide Web Consortium see
        W3C
writing attributes to output document
        192–7
WS-Inspection 501
WSDL 498–501
WSDL File search 501
    UDDI 501
    WS-Inspection 501
WURFL 49
WURFL/WALL Java framework
        475–81
    installation and configuration
        478–9
    WALL tag library 479–81
WWW 16
WWW technologies 7–9
    HTML 8–9
    HTTP 7–8
    URLs, URIs and URNs 9

XHTML 53, 57, 151–5, 470
    empty elements 152–3
    generation 183–4
    and minimization 153
    name space 152
    validation 153–5
    version 1.0 151
    version 1.1 152
    version 2.0 152
    XHTML-Basic 471–4
    XHTML-Mobile 472–4
XML 16, 53–4, 56, 127, 129–31
    data description language 130
    data reading with
        XMLHttpRequest 273–5
    declaration 132–3
    deployment descriptors 286–8
    design goals 130
    document validation 139–51
    generation from JavaBean methods
        392–5
    industry standardization 130
    metalanguage 129
    parsers 377
    processing 360
    and semi-structured data 127–9

XML components 131–8
  attributes vs elements 136–8
  CDATA sections 138
  elements and parsed character data
    133–5
  processing instructions 133
  prolog 131–2
  viewing XML pages 135
  well-formed XML 135–6
  XML declaration 132–3
XML document validation
  attribute declarations in DTDs
    148–51
  DTDs 139–45
  element declarations in DTDs
    145–8
  entities 151
XML from JavaBeans 386–95
  model layer beans 386–90
  XML generation from JavaBean
    methods 392–5
  XMLDecoder class 386, 390–2
  XMLEncoder class 386, 390–2
XML JavaServer Pages 367–71
  JSP and JSPX tags 368
XML messaging 497–533
  Server-side Ajax 520–30
  web service client development
    513–16
  web service implementation
    501–3
  web service integration 516–20
  web service with Java 6.0 503–5
  web service technologies 498–501
  web services 498
  web services and web applications
    505–13
XML parsers 378–86
  compare SAX and DOM
    parsers 379
  DOM parsers 378
  processing XML document using
    DOM parser 379–83
  processing XML document using
    SAX parser 383–6
  SAX parsers 378–9

XML Path see XPath
XML Pointer Language see XPointer
XML processing with JSTL 404–10
  import XML files 407–8
  JSTL tags for XML processing 406
  library namespaces 405–6
  XML flow control 409–10
  XPath expressions with XML tags
    408–9
  XSL transformations with JSTL
    library 406–7
XML Schema 139, 155–8, 286–8
  document application 164–5
  DTDs data-typing problems 156–7
  JAXB class generation 396–9
  XML namespaces 157–8
XML Schema tags 158–64
  attributes 160
  complex types and elements 158
  data types 159
  element multiplicity 160–1
  enumerated types and restrictions
    161–4
  sequences 158–9
XML special characters 197–9
  entity characters 197
  numeric codes 197–9
XML transfer to XML 199
XMLDecoder class 386, 390–2
XMLEncoder class 386, 390–2
XMLHttpRequest 264–5
  object methods 270
  object properties 270
  security issues 271–2
  server connection 272–3
  XML data reading 273–5
XMLSpy 55, 143, 597–606
  functions 597
  using XMLSpy 599–606
  XPath 170
XPath 169–77
  abbreviated operator syntax 173
  context 172–3
  examples 173–6
  location path 172–3
  XML trees 170–2

XMLSpy 170
  XSLT processing 176–7
XPath examples 173–6
  attributes in XPath
    queries 175–6
  filtering 175
XPath and XML trees 170–2
  attribute nodes 170
  comment nodes 170
  document order 172
  element nodes 170
  family tree vocabulary 172
  mapping XML nodes to document
    tree structure 171
  namespace nodes 170
  processing instruction nodes 170
  root nodes 170
  text nodes 170
  tree of nodes 170
XPointer 169–70
XSL transformations 180, 293
XSLT 176–97
  HTML and CSS 176
  iteration over multiple elements
    184–5
  processing 176–80
  selection elements 185–90
  sorting output 190–2
  value selection from XML
    document 180–3
  writing attributes to output
    document 192–7
  XHTML generation 183–4
XSLT processing 176–80
  linking XSLT stylesheet 179–80
  output types 179
  stylesheets and transforms 177–8
  template matching 177–9
  XPath 176–7
  XSL namespace 177
  XSL transformations in Internet
    Explorer 180

Yahoo 1

zones 6